Tartīb al-Madārik

Tartīb al-Madārik

wa taqrīb al-masālik li-maʿrifa aʿlām madhhab Mālik

Organising the faculties and facilitating the method for recognising the eminent scholars of the School of Mālik

Volume 1

Imām Mālik and his students

by Qāḍī ʿIyāḍ ibn Mūsā al-Yaḥṣubī

Translated by Aisha Abdurrahman Bewley

DIWAN PRESS

Tartīb al-Madārik

Published by: Diwan Press Ltd.
311 Allerton Road
Bradford
BD15 7HA
UK
Website: www.diwanpress.com
E-mail: info@diwanpress.com

Author: Qadi 'Iyad
Translation: Aisha Abdurrahman Bewley

A catalogue record of this book is available from the British Library.

ISBN-13: 978-1-914397-47-9 (Paperback)
978-1-914397-48-6 (Casebound)
978-1-914397-49-3 (ePub and Kindle)

Contents

Preface

The *Tartīb al-Madārik* (Organising the means and revealing the methods for discovering the eminent scholars of the School of Mālik) by Qāḍī 'Iyād al-Yaḥṣubī is a seminal biographical compendium of the scholars of the Mālikī school. It begins with an extensive biography dealing with Imām Mālik and records the chains of scholars from him, divided by region, listing over 1300 scholars in nine generationsin eight volumes. through nine generations to the time of the author.

Shaykh Abdalqadir as-Sufi regarded the *Tartīb al-Madārik* as the essential record of the intellectual lineage of the scholars who transmitted the school of Madina, and it is the foundational reference in his seminal work, *Root Islamic Education* because of how it highlights the knowledge and behaviour exemplified in the lives of the early scholars. He says:

> 'We can show you a line that goes from Madinah al-Munawwara at the time of the Messenger of Allah, may Allah bless him and give him peace, through to Imam Malik, and from Imam Malik continues for five hundred years–in the Middle East, to the gates of India and to the gates of Russia, right across North Africa, right into Europe. For five hundred years, you find that the leadership was in the hands of slaves who were *fuqahā'* and before whom amirs bowed their heads. And I say that is Islamic history, and not this other thing that has been invented by the orientalists which we have fallen for – of dynasties and epochs marked by changes in the style of jugs and arches.' (p.16)

You could say that the *Tartīb al-Madārik* provides the foundation and blueprint for the understanding conveyed by *Root Islamic*

Education. The work provides biographies of the scholars and their historical positions and how they dealt with the problems that arose in times of conflict because we see the interaction of scholars with the Abbasids, Aghlabids, Fatimids, Andalusian Umayyads, Murābitūn, and others. We see how they interacted with power, and the role and proper behaviour of the *qāḍī*. It also fleshes out the implementation of the *dīn*, providing a practical guide to education and action. It shows Islam embodied in real people and the action which that produces in society. It is a corrective to an abstract or idealised approach to Islam. It also provides us with a rich tapestry of the history in which the scholars lived, particularly North Africa and Andalusia, and a sort of historical map of Maliki scholars. It is, as Shaykh Abdalqadir says in *Root Islamic Education*:

> 'We would take the *Tartīb al-Madārik* of Qadi Iyad because it gives this record and will let them see an example on which they must be based, and on which they have no choice but to be based. The *Tartīb al-Madārik* is a record of human achievement, Islamically, that, I tell you, when you study it, you will say, "I did not know such men existed on the face of the earth!" And the *Tartib al-Madarik* is more electrifying than any of the books of the *Tadhkirat al-Awliya'* and so on–much more electrifying as a phenomenon of the human splendour of the people that this Islamic deen has produced. It is magnificent, in its raising up of the human being.' (p. 21)

Foreword

'If it had not been for 'Iyāḍ,
the Maghrib would not have been remembered.'

This encapsulates how the Maghribī community describes 'Iyāḍ's historical significance. It sums up the legacy of his full and exemplary life, his vast knowledge and his praiseworthy conduct which left a profound impression on the hearts of his compatriots. The people of knowledge in both the east and the west extol him fervently and praise his abiding achievements.

'Iyāḍ! He is renowned in the east and the west – in every land of Islam! It is appropriate that his renown should endure and his excellence should be extolled. It is fitting that gatherings of knowledge in every Muslim land should hold him in respect and esteem.

When Qāḍī 'Iyāḍ reported *ḥadīth*s – and he was always concerned with why he was asked for *ḥadīth* – from one of his shaykhs, he used to say, 'What is the matter with you? You take knowledge from us and learn from us and then you mention us without asking for mercy for us!' He valued the recognition of a man who possessed useful knowledge and gratitude for knowledge and knew that it was a debt which must be repaid by the later ones who benefit from it. It is the early generations who are known for truthfulness among the later ones.

Allah desired that people be faithful to 'Iyāḍ. Some people wrote about him and some recounted his biography.

Our goal in this work is not to exhaustively analyse the minutiae of the life of Qāḍī 'Iyāḍ. Even if we had intended to do that here, we could not have achieved it. His life – from whatever aspect you look at it – was full and rich. This is just one part of it, and its discussion is actually a discussion about one of the finest ages of the history of this land. That is the second aspect of our work.

Our aim is to record the highlights of his life, particularly what is connected to its reflective dimension, out of the desire to gain insights into factors which might have affected his methodology in investigation and writing, particularly his book, *Tartīb al-Madārik*, for which we have written this preface.

His Lineage

His son Muḥammad and Abū al-Qāsim ibn al-Maljūm both transmitted from Qāḍī 'Iyāḍ that his full name was 'Iyāḍ ibn Mūsā ibn 'Iyāḍ ibn 'Amrūn ibn Mūsā ibn 'Iyāḍ ibn Muḥammad ibn 'Abdullāh ibn Mūsā ibn 'Iyāḍ al-Yaḥṣubī.

It is a lineage which goes back – as we will see – to Yaḥṣub ibn Mālik ibn Zayd. Yaḥṣub was the brother of Dhū Aṣbaḥ al-Ḥārith ibn Mālik ibn Zayd from whom Imām Mālik ibn Anas al-Aṣbahī was descended.

Thus Qāḍī 'Iyāḍ is connected to Imām Mālik in two ways. First, there is the connection to the Mālikī School on which the inhabitants of the Maghrib base their *dīn* and to which they still adhere. 'Iyāḍ was one of the most prominent and renowned of the leaders of their school. Then there is also a connection of kinship and lineage to the tribe of Ḥimyar among the Arabs of Yemen, which enjoys great fame in Islamic history.

It is plausible – and we do not believe it is more than plausible – that this familial connection is an additional reason on top of the reasons mentioned by Qāḍī 'Iyāḍ in the introduction of the *Tartīb al-Madārik* and beyond affiliation to the school. This led Qāḍī 'Iyāḍ to become interested in the life of the Imām and to present it with respect and esteem and to persevere in removing from it anything that might tarnish its purity or diminish its splendour.

The abode of his forebears

The home of his forebears was located in the region of Baza which is about one kilometre northeast of Granada. From there they moved to Fes and subsequently to Ceuta.

His son Muḥammad mentioned that his ancestors resided in Kairouan although he did not know whether they dwelt there before or after they arrived in Andalusia.

We are unaware of any of his ancestors who were not prominent figures in the influential houses of Fez and Ceuta. His grandfather, ʻAmrūn, who moved from Fes to Ceuta around 373 AH, was among the best of people, a *ḥāfiẓ* of Qur'an. He went on *ḥajj* several times. He went on many expeditions with al-Manṣūr ibn Abī ʻĀmir.[1] He bought land in Ceuta with his money and made part of a *waqf* for the Muslims in which they could bury their dead. In part of it, a mosque was built along with some homes which were made a *waqf* of the mosque. He continued to worship in this mosque until he died in 397 AH.

These are all noble characteristics.

His birth

According to the Qāḍī himself and what his son Muḥammad transmitted from him, ʻIyāḍ was born in Ceuta in the middle of Shaʻbān in 476 AH.

Ceuta is one of the main hubs of the Maghrib. Its geographical position turned it into a meeting-place of the scholars, whether they came to it from the east or the west, intending to cross over to Andalusia or coming to it from Andalusia en route to Morocco for travel or residence. As a result of that, it became a meeting-place for many types of culture. The scholars who lived in Ceuta and those who came to it turned it into an important cultural centre.

The extant sources which deal with ʻIyāḍ's life agree that he possessed exceptional intellect, understanding, perspicacity, cleverness, alertness and an intense desire to seek knowledge. These are qualifications which elevate a person to high ranks in knowledge and excellence.

ʻIyāḍ began his quest for knowledge with these distinguished intellectual gifts in the scholarly environment which existed in his birthplace, Ceuta.

The books studied by a seeker of knowledge exert a profound

[1] The chancellor of Hisham II in Córdoba.He was the de facto ruler.

influence on the development of his character as do the shaykhs under whom he studies. 'Iyāḍ's God-given intellectual gifts coupled with the books on various different subjects which he studied in Ceuta indicate that his scholarly personality was complete before he departed from his homeland. His lasting fame was ensured because of his great effort.

In his native city, he memorised the Qur'an with the seven readings with the *riwāya*s of Nāfi', Ibn Kathīr, Abū 'Amr ibn al-'Alā' and Ibn 'Āmir. He learned these *riwāya*s with their various known paths from 'Abdullāh ibn Idrīs ibn Sahl ibn al-Muqrī' (d. 515 AH) and the *riwāya* of Ḥamza from Ḥabīb ibn az-Zayyāt from 'Abdullāh ibn Muḥammad an-Nifzī (d. 538 AH).

He studied Arabic in its both texts and literature using *Kitāb al-Faṣīḥ* by Abū al-'Abbās Tha'lab, *Kitāb al-Amālī* by Abū 'Alī al-Qāli, *al-Kāmil* by Abū al-'Abbās Muḥammad ibn Yazīd al-Mubarrad, and *Adab al-Kuttāb* by Abū Muḥammad ibn Qutayba.

He learned its grammatical rules from *Kitāb al-Juml* by az-Zajjājī, *al-Wāḍiḥ* by Abū Bakr az-Zubayrī, *al-Kāfī* by Ibn an-Naḥḥās, *al-Muqtaḍab* by al-Mubarrad, *al-Īḍāḥ* by Abū 'Alī al-Fārisī, and the commentary on *al-Jumal* by Ibn Faḍḍāl.

As for the fundamentals of *fiqh*, the fundamentals of the *dīn*, the science of *kalām* in the school of Abū al-Ḥasan al-Ash'arī, and debate and argument, he studied the fundamentals of the *dīn* with the Qāḍī of Ceuta, 'Abdullāh ibn Muḥammad ibn Ibrāhīm ibn Qāsim al-Lakhmī (d. 458), and he studied the *Risāla* of Ibn Abī Zayd al-Qayrawānī with Muḥammad ibn 'Īsā at-Tamīmī. He kept the company of Abū al-Ghālib ibn Yūsuf as-Sālimī (d. 516), an Ash'arī *mutakallim* in the school of the people of the *Sunna,* while he lived in Ceuta. He gave him many of his *Collections*. He studied his *Urjūza* with Yūsuf ibn Mūsā al-Kalbī, the Ash'arī *mutakallim*, which he had compiled on the creeds, and he also studied *Kitāb al-Minhāj* on debate and argument by Abū al-Walīd al-Bājī.

In the *Shifā'*, 'Iyāḍ frequently employs as proof the views of Abū al-Ḥasan al-Ash'arī, Qāḍī Abū Bakr al-Baqillānī, Abū Bakr ibn Fūrak, and Abū al-Ma'ālī and al-Juwaynī. All of that confirms his unwavering adherence to the Ash'arī school and their books and demonstrates the fact that he read their books on beliefs. He referred to al-Baqillānī and Abū Bakr ibn Fūrak as 'one of our Imāms' indicating that he followed the Ash'arī school.

His penetrating arguments against the opinions of the Mu'tazilites and the various sects of Islamic creeds, the philosophers, the Sufis and the Khārijites will show the student that 'Iyāḍ had carefully studied the schools of beliefs and the views of their people.

Qāḍī 'Iyāḍ's connection to the science of *kalām* and the debates and arguments subordinate to it, coupled with his knowledge of the fine points of the opinions of opponents of the people of the *Sunna* in it, leads us to the school which produced Qāḍī 'Iyāḍ and his shaykhs with whom he studied *kalām* and the fundamental principles of the *dīn*. Many of the scholars of Morocco were concerned with the science of *kalām* and were renowned for it. Their biographies are found in the *Tartīb al-Madārik*.

We say that this school possessed a comprehensive understanding of argument and debate, the fundamental principles of the *dīn*, and *kalām* according to the school of Abū al-Ḥasan al-Ash'arī, and that the books of the Ash'arīs about the science of *kalām* were known among its men who studied them in all the parts of the Maghrib.

This leads us to the lack of validity of the false claims made by the Muwaḥḥid Mahdī that scholars of the Maghrib in the time of the Murabitūn did not possess the science of debate and investigation, and thus were unable to counter him in his debates, that their creed was dominated by anthropomorphism. Then Ibn Tūmart brought the creed of *tawḥīd* and promulgated it, and his followers were called Muwaḥḥidūn (unifers) and presented his other claims.

That is a political ploy which Ibn Tumart and his supporters disseminated in order to consolidate their influence over the masses. Unfortunately, historians have been deceived by it. It is very odd that the usually discerning Ibn Khaldūn was one of its victims.

In Ceuta, 'Iyāḍ also studied the science of *Ḥadīth*, its texts, its *gharīb* (unusual) words, its men and its usages from its leaders and *ḥadīth* scholars.

He studied the *Muwaṭṭā'* of Imām Mālik, the *Musnad* of the *Muwaṭṭā'* by Abū al-Qāsim al-Jawharī, the *Ṣaḥīḥ al-Bukhārī* in the *riwāya* of al-Farabrī and an-Nasafī, the *Ṣaḥīḥ Muslim*, the *Sunan* of an-Nasā'ī, the commentary on *gharīb ḥadīth* by Abū 'Ubayd al-Qāsim ibn Salām, *The Correction of Error on Abū 'Ubayd* by Abū Muḥammad ibn Qutayba, *Gharīb Ḥadīth* by Abū Sulaymān al-Khaṭṭābī, *The Sciences of Ḥadīth* by al-Ḥākim, *Kitāb aṭ-Ṭabaqāt* by Muslim al-Ḥajjāj, the author of the *Ṣaḥīḥ*, *Kitāb aḍ-ḍu'afā wa-l-matrūkīn* by an-Nasā'ī and his *Kitāb aṭ-Ṭabaqāt*, *Kitāb at-Taqaṣṣī* by Ibn 'Abd al-Barr, *al-Mu'talif wa-l-mukhtalif* of ad-Dāraquṭnī, *al-Mu'tanif fī akmila al-mu'talif wa-l-mukhtalif* by al-Khaṭīb al-Baghdādī, *Mushkil al-ḥadīth* by Ibn Fūrak and *al-Ikmāl* by Ibn Mākūlā.

As for Mālikī *fiqh*, he studied the *Risāla* of Ibn Abī Zayd, the *Mudawwana* and a book on necessary belief by Qāḍī Abū Bakr ibn al-'Arabī al-Ma'āfirī. He studied it with him in Ceuta when he passed through there.

He studied the fundamental principles of *fiqh* with Muḥammad ibn Dāwūd ibn 'Aṭiyya al-Qal'ī.

HIS JOURNEY

Having obtained this impressive scholarly obtainment, 'Iyāḍ then travelled to Andalusia.

Historians have attempted to pinpoint the beginning of his journey and its duration. While this is a laudable concern which does possess certain merits, the beginning of his journey and its period is not of primary interest to us. It does not provide us with the benefit which we derive from learning what the Qāḍī did in the course of his journey and the impact that this journey had on his knowledge and thought.

A journey undertaken for the purpose of seeking knowledge, specifically in the realm of scholarly instruction and the refinement of Islamic thought, encompasses two essential components.

Firstly, it is imperative to ascertain the soundness and completeness of the path of transmission. That necessitates verification of the transmitted texts and investigation into their roots and connecting their *isnād*s to their narrators, and identifying the highest, straightest and soundest of those *isnād*s. If this transmitted material is not established in a sound form which is ascribed to its people, then it cannot be used as a basis for investigation and study, and consequently judgements cannot be based on it, whether these judgements pertain to the *dīn*, knowledge or *adab*.

The desire for a sound and complete path of transmission is evident in the efforts of Qāḍī 'Iyāḍ to extend his knowledge of *riwāya* and his reading. We find him reading new books which he had not read in his city and comparing his books with sound originals and investigating the written roots of the *isnād* scholars and determining the soundest and most excellent of its variants with its people, even if the paths and variants are numerous. It was the same with the texts which he compared or verified.

Secondly one must employ a sound method of thought and base it on firm rules. The sources of his biography state that his aim in his journey was to meet shaykhs. 'Iyāḍ's primary goal in his journey was not simply to see the faces of the shaykhs, but to compare their ideas and weigh them against the ideas which he had learned in his homeland, after having verified that the path of transmission was sound. It used to be said, 'If you want to know the true measure of your shaykh, then sit with someone else.'

Meeting the shaykhs allowed 'Iyāḍ to observe their methods of reflection at firsthand and to witness how they dealt with questions through study and investigation. They rejected what they deemed unacceptable and accepted what they deemed acceptable. He incorporated what he saw and understood into the fundamentals and methods he had already learned from the scholars of his homeland. He compared them and subsequently favoured one of them. After a critical evaluation and examination, he kept what he felt should remain and discarded that which could not stand up to criticism.

Through this method of examination and comparison, and repeated re-examination and interpolation, he refined the structure of his critical tools and perfected the principles of thinking on the basis of comparison and choice.

The people of knowledge attesting to him

His position was known among his shaykhs both while he was travelling and before he returned home. Reports have come from them which indicate their scrutiny and evaluation of him, and their recognition of his excellence and knowledge.

His teacher, Abū 'Abdullāh ibn Ḥamdīn, said to him while he was on his journey, 'Abū al-Faḍl, it is my duty to have left someone like you in the Maghrib.'

He wanted to travel to study with one his shaykhs in Andalusia. The minister Abū al-Ḥusayn ibn Sirāj said to him, 'He needs you more than you need him.'

Abū Muḥammad ibn Abī Ja'far stated, 'No one more noble than 'Iyāḍ has come to us from the Maghrib.'

The *wazīr*, poet and scribe, 'Abd al-Majīd ibn 'Abdūn (d. 527), met him in Ceuta. He swore to him that he only went to Ceuta to meet him.

In his journey, Abū 'Āmir Muḥammad ibn Aḥmad ibn Ismā'īl aṭ-Ṭulayṭilī wrote down some things that he had said.

When 'Iyāḍ returned from his journey, he was a radiant torch of light, a sweet spring overflowing with undiminished knowledge, a clarion voice calling to the truth, a right guide and man of judgement. His call was heard. He was a prodigious force in belief, affirmation and character.

There was a sensitivity in all of this. He was attentive to himself and his land, and the place which was prepared for him by what he inherited from his predecessors, and by what he learned by his striving and evaluation of the weighty questions which the customs of this place demanded of him in seeking guidance, direction, illumination, and protection since security in human honour and in sacred things are only preserved through vigilant guardianship.

His land was opened before him, and he loved and esteemed it and based his guidance on it. In all of that 'Iyāḍ was a trusty leader who did not reject his people.

His son related in the *Ta'rīf*, Ibn Ṣa'd in *an-Najm ath-Thāqib*, and al-Ifrānī in *Durar al-ḥijāl fī manāqib sab'at rijāl* in the second part of it that when Qāḍī 'Iyāḍ assumed the judgeship in his city, the elite and common people loved him greatly and held him in high esteem and respect. Rulers and governors held him in awe and respect which made them accept his words when he asked them to carry out one of the rights of the people while they had disputed that that right should be carried out and the obligation undertaken.

They mentioned the life of the Qāḍī among his people, and they said that he was firm in the truth and unaffected by anyone's criticism. He loved those who sought knowledge and encouraged them to seek it. He was very humble and devoted himself to the very poor and the paupers, and he asked them about their circumstances and gave them a lot of *ṣadaqa*. He dealt with people showing good character and leniency, and dealt with them according to what he found. He spent in that more money than he had inherited from his father. He sold his quarters and property in Ceuta to that end, and when he died, he was five hundred dinars in debt.

As for Qāḍī 'Iyāḍ's worship of his Lord, he remained firm in the *dīn* and exerted himself in that. He fasted often and prayed at night. He recited a *juz'* of the Book of Allah in the last part of the night and he did not omit that while he was able to recite it in any circumstances. He kept to the limits of the Sharī'a, and was a Sunnī in his creed and he held strongly to that with the greatest possible zeal.

His duties in the *dīn* and social obligations did not divert him from the obligation of sacred knowledge. He was constantly involved with knowledge and did not part from his books. He read and studied, investigated and wrote.

The way that events transpired compelled him to enter the fray. There are certain definite tenets of the Sunnī creed which cannot be disregarded. The people of the Maghrib believed in them. Scholars strove to preserve them using every means they had at their disposal.

The Sunnī creed comes at the head of these definite tenets. In it, it is confirmed that no individual possesses infallibility (*'isma*) except for the Prophets. Furthermore the issue of infallibility arose due to the emergence of Shi'ism.

There was a stance of caution or even hostility on which the Maghribi scholars agreed, or nearly so, regarding certain topics and positions in the book, *Iḥyā' al-'Ulūm* by al-Ghazālī.

These themes which the intellectual milieu of the Maghrib rejected can be categorised into two distinct areas:

1. The severe negative position which al-Ghazālī in the *Iḥyā'* and others took toward the pursuit of Islamic sciences other than Sufism.

2. What it contains of investigation into the 'sciences of unveiling' and the principles and rules underlying it.

'Iyāḍ believed in what the people of the *Sunna* in the Maghrib believed and was steadfast in his convictions. He studied under Muḥammad ibn 'Abd al-'Azīz at-Taghlibī (d. 508), reading his refutation of al-Ghazālī. It is most highly probable – and there is nothing to prevent it – that he had knowledge of the position of al-Māzirī, his shaykh, about the *Iḥyā' al-'Ulūm* of al-Ghazālī.

In all of this, 'Iyāḍ maintained his own opinion about the books and opinions of al-Ghazālī. It was similar to what his shaykhs and contemporaries thought. 'Iyāḍ thought that if al-Ghazālī had shortened the *Iḥyā'* and confined himself to pure knowledge in it – and this is an expression he uses – it would have been a useful book. What is other than pure knowledge in the *Kitāb al-Iḥyā'* is what concerned 'Iyāḍ, namely the science of unveiling.

Ibn al-'Imād al-Ḥanbalī and ash-Sha'rānī related that 'Iyāḍ used to think that the *Kitāb al-Iḥyā'* should be burned. The view that they related from him was not uncommon. In the *Kitāb ash-Shifā'*, 'Iyāḍ also gives a very harsh judgement on Abū Ḥāmid al-Ghazālī.

Then 'Iyāḍ also had his stance regarding the infallibility with which the Mahdī had described himself. The Muwaḥḥid Mahdī came and clashed with the people of the Maghrib about the purest thing they had: their Sunnī creed. He accused them of being anthropomorphists and unbelievers, and fought them as unbelievers are fought and restricted *tawḥīd* to his companions and followers.

The movement of the Muwaḥḥid Mahdī was underpinned by two fundamental principles:

1. The infallibility of the Imāms – and the Mahdī was the Imām.

2. His knowledge of unseen things which he derived from the *Kitāb al-Jafr* which contains the sciences of the People of the House.

The concept of the infallibility of the Imāms is found among the *Shi'a*, and Ibn Tūmart adopted it from them. It means that the Imām cannot commit even a small act of disobedience against Allah nor is he capable of any oversight in the *dīn.* He cannot forget any of the judgements. In their view, part of the special prerogative of the Imām is that he can discern the inner consciences of individuals and anticipate future events.

The position of the Sunnī creed about the infallibility of the Imāms is that infallibility is reserved exclusively for the Prophets. They also reject the idea that the Imāms know the unseen, what the minds of people conceal, or the future.

Al-Ghazālī takes up the sciences of unveiling, goes on at length about them and relies on them. That is one of the reasons which led Maghribī scholars to take up their well-known hostile position to the *Kitāb al-Ihyā'*. This is part of the reason for the position of 'Iyāḍ and his opinion about al-Ghazālī and his books.

After what I have shown you, it is easy for a student to grasp why the people of the Maghrib opposed the call of the Muwaḥḥidūn in every location. That is why Ceuta rebelled, and its rebellion recurred under the leadership of 'Iyāḍ against Muwaḥḥidūn rule.

This essay does not permit me to go into the details of this here, but I want to say that 'Iyāḍ never abandoned his Sunnī belief or shirked what he thought he should do. The Muwaḥḥidūn never forgave him. That is why they exiled him from his land, and he was deeply grieved about having to leave it. He said to his compatriots when he bade them farewell at Ceuta, 'Allah has made me your ransom,' and he wept. They disturbed the final years of his life until he met his Lord on 7 Jumādā al-Ākhira or in Ramaḍān, 544 AH.

Following his death, there were visions, dreams, stories and tales both for and against him. How many tales are fabricated about famous people after they have left the life of this world! How easy it is for people to say that they are mere superstitions that do not stand up to criticism, and they put them far from the subject matter of history. That is an erroneous omission where expertise mocks the mentalities of peoples and nations.

These multitudinous stories, which is what our forebears embraced, are in a pure linguistic style which transcends time and place using the established rules of formal *ḥadīth*s. It is the method which the masses choose to express their feelings about people whom they do not wish to forget and the manner in which they record their opinion of them.

They gave expression to their thoughts in their visions, dreams, stories, rhymed prose, and parables and their short passages that resemble parables and are straight to the point in all these forms, and their love or hatred for those who have been committed to the earth spills out. It is said, 'The tongues of people are the pens of the truth.'

There are two groups who buried 'Iyāḍ: the Muwaḥḥid judges and their masters, and the community of the Maghrib. The feelings of these two groups towards him are widely divergent.

As for the Muwaḥḥidūn, their stories relate that al-Ghazālī heard of 'Iyāḍ's opinion of his books and he cursed him, so 'Iyāḍ died suddenly in the bath-house on the day he cursed him. They also said that the Mahdī was the one who ordered that he be killed after the people of his land claimed that he was a Jew because he did not go out on Saturdays. So the Mahdī killed him because of al-Ghazālī's curse.

As for the Maghribī community, they directed their suspicions towards the Muwaḥḥidūn, saying, 'Ibn al-'Arabī was poisoned. Al-Yaḥṣubī was strangled.' They said, deeming him to be one of the martyrs: 'A Jew poisoned him.'

All their visions connected with 'Iyāḍ and that which is connected to his city where he grew up, developed, benefited and guided, and Algeciras where he eliminated the injustices of some of its governors, and Marrakesh where he put himself as ransom for his compatriots. These visions indicated that he was honoured and blessed in the Garden as a reward for the good actions which he did in the time when he was striving on his own. His community consistently refuted every criticism of him with their words: 'If it had not been for 'Iyad, the Maghrib would not have been remembered.'

His books

In the course of his full life, 'Iyāḍ was a renowned writer who wrote a lot and whose books were praised by scholars and were used by them.

There are approximately thirty books ascribed to him, but only a few of them have reached us. We will mention them all alphabetically, hoping that to convey what is known about them:

1. *Al-Ajwiba al-muhabbira 'ala-l-masā'il al-mutakhayyira* (*Answers to Selected Questions*). It is one of the books which Qāḍī 'Iyāḍ did not complete. His son mentioned it in *at-Ta'rīf*, pp. 134-135, stating that he found some of it and supplemented it with what he found in his father's papers or with his friends on the unusual meanings of various things about which he was asked. He collated all of that into one section. It is also mentioned in *al-Iḥāṭa*, 183A, *Azhār ar-Riyāḍ*, 2:239C, and *Kashf aẓ-Ẓunūn*, 1:11.
2. *Ajwiba 'ammā nazala fī ayyām quḍā'ihi min nawāzil al-aḥkām* (*Answers about what judgements occurred in his Judgeship*) It was also incomplete and sources disagree about the amount that remains of it. According to *al-Iḥāṭa*, 183A and *at-Ta'rīf*, 134, it was one section. *Azhār ar-Riyāḍ*, 2:239C, says that it is written in two sections.
3. *Ajwiba al-Qurṭubiyyīn* (*Answers to the People of Cordoba*). His son said, 'I saw this in his own handwriting, but I did not find a fair copy with him although I found it among his papers, so I collected it with the answers of others.' It is mentioned in the *Ta'rīf*, 134,*al-Iḥāṭa*, 183-A, and *Azhār ar-Riyāḍ*, 2:239c.
4. *Akhbār al-Qurṭubiyyīn* (*Reports about the People of Cordoba*) It is mentioned *Kashf aẓ-Ẓunūn*, 1:23, *Hidāyat al-'Ārifīn*, 1:805, and *Tārīkh al-Fikr al-Andalusī*, 283 where he said that he had a history about the scholars of Córdoba called *Akhbār al-Qurṭubiyyīn.* It is possible that this is *Ajwiba al-Qurṭubiyyīn* which was already mentioned.
5. *Ikhtiṣār sharaf Muṣṭafā (Summary of the Honour of Muṣṭafā) Sharaf Muṣṭafā* is the name of a book by Abū Sa'd 'Abd al-Malik ibn Muḥammad al-Wā'idh an-Naysābūrī al-Kharkūshī (d. 406) which consists of eight volumes. It is also called *Sharaf an-Nubuwwa.* Qāḍī 'Iyāḍ wrote a summary of it, and Ibn Khayr related it from him with an *ijāza* orally and with permission. He mentioned it in the Index of what he related from his shaykhs, 289, 487. It is also mentioned by the author of the *Kashf aẓ-Ẓunūn*, 2:1045. It appears that the Qāḍī was preparing to write his book, *ash-Shifā'*, and he found the *Kitāb Sharaf Muṣṭafā* too long, and summarised it to make it easier for reference and use.

6. *Al-I'lām bi-ḥudūd qawā'id al-Islām*[1] (*Signs of the Limits of the Rules of*

[1]The translation by Aisha Bewley is published as *The Foundations of Islam* by Diwan Press.

Islam). His son mentioned it in *at-Ta'rīf*, 133, and *al-Iḥāṭa*, 183-A, *Kashf az-Ẓunūn*, 1:127, and *Hidāyat al-'Ārifīn*, 1:805. The Department of Islamic Affairs published it.

7. *Ikmāl al-Mu'allim bi fawā'id Muslim* (*The Completion of Instruction on the Benefits of Muslim*). It is a commentary on the *Ṣaḥīḥ* of Imām Muslim ibn al-Ḥajjāj. In it, he completed the Summary of Abū 'Abdullāh Muḥammad ibn 'Alī al-Māzirī, called *al-Mu'allim bi fawā'id Muslim*.

8. *Al-Ilmā' fī ḍabṭ ar-riwāya wa taqyīd as-samā'* (*Indication of the Accurate Determination of the Riwāya and the Recording of Oral Tradition*). His son mentioned it in *at-Ta'rīf*, 133, as did aḍ-Ḍabbī in *Bughya al-Multamis*, 425, *al-Iḥāṭa*, 183-A, *Kashf az-Ẓunūn*, 1:158, *Hidāyat al-'Ārifīn*, 1:805, and *Tārīkh al-Fikr al-Andalusī*, 397.

It is one of the books which *mutakallimūn* frequently relied on for the technical words of *ḥadīths*. It is located in the Escorial library, and the Aya Sofia has a copy of it.

9. *Bughyat ar-Rā'id limā taḍammanahu ḥadīth Umm Ẓar' min al-fawā'id* (*The Desire of the Guide in the Benefits in the ḥadīth of Umm Ẓar'*). It is the fullest and most comprehensive commentary on this *ḥadīth*. His son mentioned it in *at-Ta'rīf*, 133, adh-Dhahabī in *Tadhkira al-Ḥuffāẓ*, 4:97, Ibn Khayr in the Index of what he related from his shaykhs, and he related it from its author, 197, 478, Ibn Khallikān, 1:496, *Kashf az-Ẓunūn*, 1:248, and *Hidāyat al-'Ārifīn*, 1:805. It is in the Public Repository, and there is a copy of it in Berlin.

10. *Tārīkh al-Murābiṭīn* (*The History of the Murābiṭūn*). It went as far as 540 AH. Ibn Khātima mentioned it in *History of Almeria* and *Azhār ar-Riyāḍ*, 2:239c. *See the General History.*

11. Tartīb al-Madārik which will be discussed.

12. *At-Tanbīhāt al-Mustanbaṭa 'alā kutub al-Mudawwana wa-l-Mukhtaliṭa* (*Discovered Admonitions in the Mudawwana and the Mukhtaliṭa*). His son and *al-Iḥāṭa* reckoned that it consisted of ten sections.

It was relied on to unravel the expressions used in the *Mudawwana* and resolve its problems, determine its variants and name its *riwāyas*. The reason for that derives from the combination of the commentary of the meanings, their clarification and definition of the expressions. He mentioned those who related it among the shaykhs and the *ḥuffāẓ*. His son mentioned it in *at-Taʿrīf*, 132 and in *al-Wafiyāt*; 1:496 and from him adh-Dhahabī in the *Tadhkira al-Ḥuffāẓ*, 4:97, *al-Iḥāṭa*, 183-A; *Azhār ar-Riyāḍ*, 3:21; *Kashf aẓ-Ẓunūn*, 1493, 2:1644; and *Hidāyat al-ʿĀrifīn*, 1:805. There is a copy of it in the Public Repository.

13. *Al-Jāmiʿ fī at-Tārīkh* (*The General History*). Qāḍī ʿIyāḍ said in the biography of ʿAbdullāh ibn Yāsīn, the Murābiṭ leader, 'We gave details about him in the *Book of History*.' ʿIyāḍ's student, Muḥammad ibn Ḥammāda al-Burnusī as-Sibtī mentioned it, and adh-Dhahabī quoted it in the *Tadhkira al-Ḥuffāẓ*, 4:97, under the title *Jāmiʿ at-Tārīkh*, as does al-Maqarrī in *Azhār ar-Riyāḍ*, 2:239c, stating that it covers the history of the Murābiṭūn up to 540 AH. It is a book which surpasses all other books. It contains information about the kings of Andalusia and the Maghrib from the time of the arrival of Islam there, and it contains full reports about Ceuta, its inhabitants, its *fuqahā'* and all the events that transpired there. It provides full reports of the Ḥasanī dynasty. It is mentioned in *Kashf aẓ-Ẓunūn*, 1:538 under the title of *Jāmiʿ at-Tārīkh* and is also so mentioned in *Hidāyat al-ʿĀrifīn*, 1:805. They did not add anything more to this title.

14. The *Book of Khuṭba*s in a single volume. His son mentioned it in *at-Taʿrīf*, 133 and they mentioned in the Qāḍī's biography that he only gave *khuṭba*s that he himself had written.

15. *Sirr as-Sarā fī ādāb al-quḍā'* (*The Secret of the High-minded in the proper manners in the judgement*). His son said in *at-Taʿrīf*, 134, 'I also saw this subject in his handwriting while I did not find anything of this book or any mention of it.' It is mentioned in *al-Iḥāṭa*, 183-A and *Azhār ar-Riyāḍ*, 2:238. He said, 'Part of what he left in a fair copy was *Sirr as-Sarā*,' but that it is a statement which does not have any meaning after what his son already said.

16. *Kitāb su'ālāt wa tarsīl* (*The Book of Questions and Correct Reading*). *See Ghunya aṭ-Ṭālib.*

17. *As-Sayf al-Maslūl ʿalā man sabba aṣḥāb ar-Rasūl* (*The Unsheathed Sword against those who cursed the Companions of the Messenger*). It is mentioned in *Kashf aẓ-Ẓunūn*, 2:1018, and *Hidāyat al-ʿĀrifīn*, 1:805.

18. *Ash-Shifā' bi-taʿrīf ḥuqūq al-Muṣṭafā* (*Healing identifying the rights of*

Muṣṭāfā). Adh-Dhahabi called it *ash-Shifā' fī sharaf al-Muṣṭafā*. It is too famous to require mention. The Qāḍī taught it in his lifetime and gave *ijāza* for it. His son mentioned it, 132, as did *al-Iḥāṭa*, 183-A, and reckoned it to consist of six sections. It is mentioned in *Azhār ar-Riyāḍ*, 2:238, *Tadhkira al-Ḥuffāẓ*, 4:97, *Kashf aẓ-Ẓunūn*, 2:1052, 1055, and *Hidāyat al-'Ārifīn*, 1:805.

19. *Aṣ-Ṣafā bi-taḥrīr ash-Shifā'* (*Clarity in the formulation of the Shifā'*) by the Qāḍī which was already mentioned. This is in *Kashf aẓ-Ẓunūn*, 2:1079. It is a doubtful expression where Ismā'īl Pāshā al-Baghdādī understood that a*ṣ-Ṣafā bi-taḥrīr* a*sh-Shifā'* is the name of a book by 'Iyāḍ. He mentioned it as being written by him in his biography, 1:805. That is an incorrect understanding. *Aṣ-Ṣafā bi-taḥrīr* a*sh-Shifā'* is one of the books of Muḥammad ibn Muḥammad ibn al-Khayḍarī (d. 834) as is stated in *Kashf aẓ-Ẓunūn* in the discussion on the commentaries of the *Shifā'*.

20. *Al-'Uyūn as-Sitta fī akhbār Sabta* (*The Six Sources in the News of Ceuta*). That is how it is mentioned in *Kashf aẓ-Ẓunūn*, 2:1186, *Hidāyat al-'Ārifīn*, 1:805, and *Tārīkh al-Fikr al-Andalusī*, 283. See *al-Fanūn as-Sitta.*

21. *Gharīb ash-Shihāb* (*The Unusual Words of ash-Shihāb*). *Kashf aẓ-Ẓunūn* mentions it in 2:1027 as does *Hidāyat al-'Ārifīn*, 1:805.

22. *Ghunya fī asmā' shuyūkhihi* (*Wealth in the names of his Shaykhs*). It is mentioned and Ibn Khayr quotes it in the Index of what he related from his shaykhs, 437, 513, *al-Iḥāṭa*, 183-A, *at-Ta'rīf*, 133, *Kashf aẓ-Ẓunūn*, 2:1213, and *Hidāyat al-'Ārifīn*, 1:805.

23. *Ghunya al-Kātib wa-l-bughya aṭ-ṭālib fi aṣ-Ṣudūr wa-t-tarassul* (*The Wealth of the Writer and the Desire of the Seeker in the Beginning and Correct Reading*). That is how his son relates it in *at-Ta'rīf*, 133 as does al-Maqarrī in *Azhār ar-Riyāḍ*, 2:239. Sources vary in the presentation of this name. In the *Kashf*, it is *'ṣudūr ar-rasā'il'* and in *al-Iḥāṭa,* it is *'aṣ-ṣudūr wa-r-rasā'il'*. Ibn Khātima said, "The book dealing with some questions and correct reading and consists of four volumes. Al-Maqarrī said, "Look at what Ibn Khātima said and whether it is *Bughyat aṭ-ṭālib* that is mentioned or something else.

24. *Kitāb al-'Aqīda* (*The Book of the Creed*). Adh-Dhahabī mentioned it in the *Tadhkira al-Ḥuffāẓ*, 4:37, and in *Hidāyat al-'Ārifīn*, 1:805.

In the index of the old house of Egyptian books, 7:295, it is titled 'Commentary on the words of the one the excellent men on the creed of the majestic Imām, Qāḍī 'Iyāḍ'. I think that this creed is part of the book *al-I'lām bi-ḥudūd qawā'id al-Islām* which was already mentioned.

25. *al-Funūn as-Sitta fī akhbār Sabta* (*The Six Arts in the Reports of Ceuta*). That is how it is referred to in *al-Iḥāṭa*, 183-A, by his son in *at-Ta'rīf*, 133, and al-Maqarrī in *Azhār ar-Riyāḍ*, 2:239C, and it is one of the books which he did not complete. According to *al-Iḥāṭa*: 'It is part of what he left in a fair copy.' *See al-'Uyūn as-Sitta* and *al-Jāmi' fī Tārīkh.*

26. *Al-Qawā'id* (*Rules*). It is the same, without ascription. He mentioned it in*Hidāyat al-'Ārifīn*, and no other source mentions it. It is most likely *al-I'lām bi-ḥudūd qawā'id al-Islām.*

27. *Mas'ala al-ahl al-mushtarak baynahum at-tazāwur* (*The Question of the Family when exchanged visits is a precondition*). It is one of the books which the Qāḍī left in a fair copy. His son mentioned it in *at-Ta'rīf*, 133, and al-Maqarrī in *Azhār ar-Riyāḍ*, 2:239C.

28. *Mashāriq al-Anwār 'alā ṣiḥāḥ al-athār* (*The Rising Lights on Sound Traditions*). It is one of the most apposite works that the Qāḍī left. In it he studied the *Muwaṭṭā'*, *Ṣaḥīḥ al-Bukhārī,* and *Ṣaḥīḥ Muslim.* He dealt with the words in the texts, the names of places, and the men with their *kunya*s and titles and organised all of that alphabetically. Then he began his work, and made the texts exact and verified them with their roots. He noted their different variants and indicated the right course or the most likely of them, relying on comparison of the variants and the texts of the language, and the usage and the lessons of the early generations who preceded him. After all this, he relied on minute investigation and a great deal of research.

Then he devoted a section to the names of places and pinpointed them. He did the same with the names, titles, *kunya*s, and lines of lineage which have come in the *isnād*s of these three books. He applied himself to what occurred in each of these sections, meticulously correcting grammatical mistakes and distortions, and highlighting what is correct in it. He concluded this wonderful section with a brief commentary on the unusual words in the three books.

He left a fair copy of this book. The handwriting of the Qāḍī in it is described as being very unclear, compact and challenging, lacking diacritical marks. The *ḥadīth* scholar, Abū 'Abdullāh Muḥammad ibn Sa'īd al-Ghurāṭī, known at aṭ-Ṭarrār, compiled the complete roots and matrices from the books of rare words and dialects, and he used that to produce the text of this book from its rough copy.

His son mentioned it in *at-Ta'rīf*, 133 and *al-Iḥāṭa*, 183-A and so did al-Maqarrī in *Azhār ar-Riyāḍ*, 2:239C. They reckoned it to consist of six large sections. Also Ibn Khallikān, 1:496, *Kashf aẓ-Ẓunūn*, 2:1687, and *Hidāyat al-'Ārifīn*, 1:805. Sultan Moulay 'Abdu-l-Ḥafīẓ published it in Fes, 1328.

29. *Maṭāmiḥ al-afhām fī sharḥ al-aḥkām* (*Goals of Understanding in the commentary on judgements*) It is mentioned in the *Kashf aẓ-Ẓunūn*, 2:1718, and *Hidāyat al-'Ārifīn*, 1:805.

30. *Al-Mu'jam fī dhikr Abī 'Alī aṣ-Ṣadafī wa akhbārihi wa shuyūkhihi wa akhbārihim* (*Lexicon on Abū 'Alī aṣ-Ṣadafī and his reports and his shaykhs and their reports*). It contains about two hundred shaykhs. Qāḍī 'Iyāḍ himself mentioned it in *al-Ghunya*, 123, and his son in *at-Ta'rīf*, 133 and in *al-Iḥāṭa*, 183-A.

31. *Al-Maqāṣid al-ḥisān fīmā yalzamu-l-insān* (*The Excellent Goals which a person must have*). It is one of the books which he did not finish. Ibn Khātima said that it is in two volumes. His son mentioned it, 133 as do *al-Iḥāṭa*, 183-A, and *Azhār ar-Riyāḍ*, 2:283C. He also left a fair copy of it, which is in one section.

32. *Naẓm al-Burhān 'alā ṣiḥḥa jazm al-adhān* (*The Order of the Proof of Soundness of Shortening the adhān*). His son mentioned it, 133, and it is mentioned in *al-Iḥāṭa*, 183A, *Azhār ar-Riyāḍ*, 2:283C, *Kashf aẓ-Ẓunūn*, 1:1961, and *Hidāyat al-'Ārifīn*, 1:805.

As for *Tartīb al-Madārik wa taqrīb al-masālik fī ma'rifa a'lām madhhab Mālik*, (*Organising the faculties and facilitating the method for recognising the eminent scholars of the School of Mālik*), his son, Ibn al-Khaṭīb and al-Maqarrī after him reckoned it to be five volumes.

There are certain things which the reader sees in the handwritten texts of the book which require explanation. They can be summarised as follows:

1. The texts vary in the number of sections into which the book is divided. By this we mean the sections into which we think the author divided the book. They are sections whose existence is indicated by the fact that each section begins with the *basmala,* connection, and ends with a statement about the end of the section. The texts in our possession do not consistently demand a statement at the beginning of each section and its end in the form which we mentioned. I omitted more of it which I will mention.
2. Many of the differences in the texts and sentences reach a level which demands investigation. In certain cases, it reached a point where each text had a variant not common to another text.
3. The order of the biographies differs among the texts.
4. Biographies are repeated, and the biography of the same person comes in two places. These elements must have a logical explanation.

The various sources about the biography of 'Iyāḍ agree that he did not let anyone listen to his book, *Tartīb al-Madārik*, during his lifetime. We believe that this explains the differences between the various versions. In any case, it means that people did not study the book with its author, resulting in a lack of clarity and finality in its sections and a unified overall structure. The transcript heard from him would have been a single text and in a single order and the repeated biographies omitted from it.

The book was not read out, but it remained in the author's rough draft until the hands of the copyists passed it on, so they refined it from the rough draft through their efforts.

The handwriting of 'Iyāḍ in the discussion of *Mashāriq al-Anwār* is described. He said that it is 'very unclear, compact, difficult without any diacritical marks.'

Whatever the case, differences occurred and that had an impact on our work in publishing this book. In light of this, we were forced to rely on a significant number of texts to achieve a high level of confidence.

We had to choose from the differences whose proof of a sound meaning is confirmed, although we preferred to entrust all or most of the differences to the hands of the readers, allowing them to make a choice. We only exerted our efforts to select a text which we deemed be firm and believed to be the probable text. The text with the least amount of differences is the preferred text in most cases.

In revising this section, we relied on the following texts:

A. The text preserved at the Royal Treasury, which is a good copy. We had to number its pages, and the number in parentheses to the left or the right of the text indicates the handwritten pages of this text. It is the same with the numbers in the table of contents.

B. The text at the Public Repository under the number 2634-D.

C. A private text in our library.

D. Another private text in our library.

E. A text in the Public Repository under the number 2635-D.

F. A text in the Public Repository under the number 2633-D.

Qāḍī 'Iyāḍ's clarification in the preface of the *Tartīb al-Madārik* relieved us of the need to discuss his method of writing. He cites the confirmed bases of knowledge in his commitment and their application, providing the full sources with their critiques, so we do not need to discuss that. He has a more eloquent tongue than us when he deals with his own work.

'Iyāḍ and his books have enjoyed a special place with the Mālikī 'Alawī family for a long time. Sultan Moulay Muḥammad ibn 'Abdullāh exhibited a profound interest in 'Iyāḍ's books. He read them and was familiar with their finer points and criticised what did not please him in them. He commanded a group of scholars to write a commentary on *Mashāriq al-Anwār* by aṣ-Ṣāghānī. Shaykh at-Tāwudī ibn Sūda (Sidi Taoudi Ben Souda) wrote a commentary on the first third of it. It was left to Shaykh 'Abd al-Qādir Bū Kharīṣ – following the command of the Sultan – to write a commentary on the second third. Sultan Moulay Muḥammad ibn 'Abdullāh directed the shaykh to sources and references which included 'Iyāḍ's commentary on *Ṣaḥīḥ Muslim*.

He read the *Shifa'*, although he did not like its minute investigation of the details in the section on the judgement of the one who curses the Messenger of Allah ﷺ. Therefore he did a critique of 'Iyāḍ and sent his critique to the scholars of Egypt seeking their opinion. He received a reply from the scholars of al-Azhar, Shaykh Amīr and Shaykh 'Abd al-Mu'ṭī al-Ḥarīrī who supported the gist of his opinion.

Sultan Moulay 'Abd al-'Azīz initiated the daily reading of the *Shifā'* of Qāḍī 'Iyāḍ at the tomb of Idrīs in Fes at sunrise. He singled out a group of the distinguished scholars for that, and gave each of them a daily stipend to cover undertaking this task.

Sultan Moulay 'Abd al-Ḥafīẓ's interest in 'Iyāḍ is well-known. At his own expense, he published his book, *Mashāriq al-Anwār,* and he intended to publish the *Tartīb al-Madārik* in Cairo. He entrusted it to the Moroccan state agent at that time, Ḥājj Muḥammad ibn al-'Abbās ibn Shaqrūn. He was to publish it within the precious *Collection* of books which were published at his own expense there and in Morocco. He sent some handwritten copies to him to enable him to begin the work. However, various obstacles arose to prevent that.

In 1320 AH, Moulay 'Abd al-Ḥafīẓ began to publish the *Tartīb al-Madārik* in Fes at his own expense. He printed sixteen pages of it, but then an unforeseen event led to the discontinuation of the publication.

During the days of the festival when the *Ulfaya* was being recited at the Qarawiyyin University, one of the Qur'an reciters of the King, Muḥammad V, informed me that the King intended to publish the *Tartīb al-Madārik* and had commanded that its manuscripts be collected for this purpose. However, it was not decreed that this desire be realised at that moment.

Similarly, interest in the *Tartīb al-Madārik* was passed on through the succession of the kings of this noble 'Alawī family, one to another. They all desired to revive the glory of this community and to preserve its pure teachings.

However, the Divine Decree denied their noble aspirations, and there were numerous obstacles that hindered their efforts. Then the Decree decided that that goal be carried out, and it was achieved by King Moulay Ḥasan II. This glorious achievement of knowledge was connected to his reign, and this accepted good deed was inscribed in his pages.

The King commanded that the *Tartīb al-Madārik* be published and gave permission for the use of a copy of it which was in the Royal Treasury. The King took an interest in the work on it from beginning to end.

The work progressed in the light of his right guidance, and the merit, beginning and end, belongs to the King for the publication of this section of the *Tartīb al-Madārik*.

The Ministry of Awqaf and Islamic Affairs assisted in bringing out the second section from the treasures of Qāḍī 'Iyāḍ for the prince. Consequently, it is hoped that Allah will guide it and protect it so that it reaches the Community in a position which befits it and its glories, and that He will be pleased with the individual entrusted with this responsibility. Allah has charge of the granted answer.

The department responsible for writing, biography and publication within this Ministry felt compelled to express its immense gratitude to his excellency, minister Ḥājj Aḥmad ibn Barkāsh because of his unwavering encouragement and interest. May Allah repay him for his work in the best way.

As for myself, I have expended myself fully, and it is enough for me that I have expended whatever I could. If I was correct, that is by the success of my Lord. If it is otherwise, I still have the wage for my efforts. May Allah guide me to that which is the most straight.

Muḥammad ibn Tawīb aṭ-Ṭanjī
Ribat
17 Shawwāl 1384 / 19 February 1965

In the name of Allah, the Merciful, the Compassionate

May Allah bless Sayyidunā Muḥammad, the Chosen Noble Prophet, and his family and Companions and grant them abundant peace.

Author's Preface

The shaykh, *faqīh* and equitable *qāḍī*, the *ḥadīth* scholar and *ḥāfiẓ*, the righteous, intelligent and model scholar of several sciences, Abū al-Faḍl 'Iyāḍ ibn Mūsā ibn 'Iyāḍ al-Yaḥṣubī as-Sabtī, may Allah have mercy on him and be pleased with him and forgive him and give us the benefit of him by His favour!, said:

Praise be to Allah who poured out His favour on His slaves in blessings beyond measure and Who decreed by His justice who would obey and who would disobey. He singled out the people of the Garden from those of the Fire in the two separate handfuls of the Decree and He distinguished between the two parties of happiness and wretchedness while they were still in the loins of Ādam.

Then in order to complete His justice, He selected elite and pure friends from among them and He placed the Messengers and Prophets among them so that through them His path would be made clear for those He wanted to guide and so that His veil would remain over those who obstruct it and turn away from His Signs. They expended their effort for the sake of Allah and advised people as much as they could that Allah would choose for them what is with Him and give each of them what was written for him in period and term of life. May such blessings of Allah be bestowed upon them as cannot be quantified or counted.

Then Allah completed His overflowing favour to the believers and sealed His Prophets and Messengers with the one among them who had the strongest weight, the highest position, the noblest character, and most excellent lineage, and who was the most generous of them in virtues and the one with the most numerous community and followers: Abū al-Qāsim, the master of the children of Adam ﷺ as he is honoured and esteemed. He strove for the sake of Allah as one should strive and he resolved important difficult matters in the right guidance of His slaves until He set them straight on His path and leading them, willing or unwilling, by his eloquent proof, driving them to the Garden in chains, and they entered the *dīn* of Allah in droves through his call. Allah fulfilled His promise by him and Allah alone was worshipped. Allah bestowed on him the best Community that has come out to the people and they helped him establish his *Sharīʿa* during his lifetime and they continued to safeguard and protect it after his death. Elsewhere there are texts which deal with their excellence and the command to follow them and the threat against following other than their Way. Allah placed them in the abode of His revelation, the shelter of His *dīn*, the seat of His *Sharīʿa*, the place where the angels alighted and to which His Prophet ﷺ emigrated, where the Book was sent down, and the resting-place of the refuge of His Messengers and the gathering place of all good, the cave of belief and wisdom, the spring of the *Sharīʿa* and the *Sunna*, the lamp of guidance by whose light all parts of the east and west are illuminated, and the fountain of knowledge from which all rivers and ravines derive.

Then they were followed in each century by truthful and just followers, and successors who also possessed guidance and virtues. They were repositories of recognition and knowledge and lodes of good and forbearance. The Imāms of the Muslims were chosen from among them, and leaders from them were set up for this world and the *dīn*. They made clear to people what had been sent down to them, clarified for them what was difficult for them, and guided them to the *sunna*s which were firmly established for them. By their extraction and sound efforts, they looked into the judgement of matters which did not have a specific text. They formed an analogy based on what they understood from the *Sharīʿa* in relation to a judgement on something else. They adhered to the established customs of realisation, and did not deviate from the path nor impose misguiding opinions in the *dīn* and were not negligent like the heretics nor pig-headed and obstinate like aggressors. They followed in the tracks of those before them and they imitated them by adhering to their paths on the roads of the *Sharīʿa*. They were not harmed by the disputes of the parties who disagreed with them nor the turmoil of those who persisted in erroneous ideas and perished. The one who is given success is the one who follows their tracks and does not deviate, unlike the one who wanders off and whose followers follow suit. The one who is successful knows that the truth lies in this Path which is Allah's guidance, and he follows its guidance without turning to every dog that barks, even if it deludes the intellects by the tone of its voice.

May Allah makes us among those who follow and are safe and who pursue what the immense masters travelled on by His favour!

Then my friends repeated their request – may Allah encompass us and them in His happiness! – that I write down what I intended to do and make a fair copy of what I wanted to write in a book which would contain the names of the notable men and leaders of the Mālikīs, clarify their ranks, times, virtues and reports, and disseminate their various biographies and reports. It should be comprehensive and inclusive. Its lessons are astonishing and its sources and springs are sweet. It is a subject on which no comprehensive book has been written nor has there been any impressive *Collection* which would bring the seeker to his goal and convey the one with desire to what he desires. This is in spite of the fact that this is a very strong prerequisite for those with *ijtihād* and those with *taqlīd*, as well as the compelling need for *faqīhs* and those who are studying *fiqh* to know what it contains. There is, however, what was compiled on that by ʿAbdullāh ibn Muḥammad ibn Abī Dulaym al-Qurṭubī and Muḥammad ibn Ḥārith al-Qaranī in their time. There is also what Shaykh Abū Isḥāq al-Fayrūzābī extracted about them in his *Mukhtaṣar*.

None of the books provided relief to the individual with a burning thirst, and they only contained a scant trace of the abundant substance. Even though Ibn Abī Dulaym was very extensive in what he mentioned about the people of the Maghrib among the transmitters of Mālik among the Egyptians and a group of those from Kairouan, he was content to simply mention their ranks and their names without any information about them or any clarification of their states. None of the people of the Hijaz or the east were mentioned despite the majesty of their position and the great number of their leaders.

The Qāḍī said: Since the time when I became eager to learn this subject and formed the intention of doing so, I have continued to investigate its paths of transmission and delve into its sources. I limited the time spent in examining its anomalies and used the time I spent investigating its indexes to compile some of that for myself after an extensive and intense investigation, total concentration and repeated reading. I did not find it adequate to meet my expectations, and so it increased my hope and intention of devoting myself to it.

I have not encountered anyone whose words are considered and whose opinion paid attention to who has had any involvement in this business or who has had some report about it except that they were anxious to see it completed and encouraged that end. It was, however, postponed, and I procrastinated, encountering obstacles and occupations one after another which diverted me from that until the present moment. Now my firm resolution is to complete the book and put its contents in order.

I asked Allah for the best in that and I sought His help in smoothing these roads. I gathered my papers and retrieved the manuscript out from where I had stored it. I reviewed my notes and understood their hidden secrets, and I consulted my archives which provided me with supportive quotes. So I corrected the prose, organised the fragments and arranged the back and front, and I brought it out as a single work with its contents, being extensive in abridgements of the forms of this field of knowledge.

In respect of achieving a goal, it is crucial to present the necessary premises which the circumstances require, and then the benefit is obtained through studying them. The text contains chapters concerning Madina and its excellence, the preferment of its scholars and opinion, the binding nature of the evidence provided by the consensus of its people, and preference for the school of its Imām,

Mālik ibn Anas. These chapters are investigated in a way which will sate the thirsty. I have taken great pains to look into the position which is just and accurate.

Then I followed the method of the imāms, the praise of scholars, and disseminated their virtues and biographies, along with all that is necessary in the knowledge of history and lineage, and acquaintance with some of the events of their daily lives and proper manners. I absorbed all of this while summarising its forms and being concise in its source, with a subject which could require has lengthy books and fill up many volumes since a group of the Imāms, the early generations, and later ones among the parties of this community have written on the virtues and excellent qualities of Mālik and his news.

Some of those who wrote at length about that are:

Qāḍī Abū 'Abdullāh at-Tustarī al-Mālikī in about three volumes.
The like of that by Abū al-Ḥasan ibn Fihr al-Miṣrī
Abū Muḥammad al-Ḥasan ibn Ismā'īl aḍ-Ḍarrāb
Qāḍī Abū Bakr Ja'far ibn Muḥammad al-Firyābī
Abū Bishr ad-Dūlabī
Abū al-'Arab at-Tamīmī
Qāḍī Abū al-Ḥasan ibn al-Muntāb
Abū 'Ilāqa Muḥammad ibn Abī Ghassān
Abū Isḥāq ibn Sha'bān
Az-Zubayr ibn Bakkār, Qāḍī az-Zubayrī
Abū Bakr Aḥmad ibn Muḥammad ibn al-Yaqṭīnī
Ḥāfiẓ Abū Naṣr ibn al-Ḥabbāb
Abū Bakr ibn Rāzawayh
Qāḍī Abū 'Abdullāh al-Barakānī
Abū Muḥammad ibn al-Jārūd
Al-Ḥasan ibn 'Abdullāh az-Zubayrī
Aḥmad ibn Marwān al-Mālikī
Qāḍī Abū al-Faḍl al-Qushayrī
Abū 'Umar al-Maghāmī
Aḥmad ibn Rishdīn
Abū Bakr Muḥammad ibn Ṣāliḥ al-Abharī
Abū Bakr ibn al-Labbād
Abū Muḥammad 'Abdullāh ibn Abī Zayd

Ḥāfiẓ Abū 'Umar ibn 'Abd al-Barr
Qāḍī Abū Muḥammad ibn Naṣr
Abū 'Abdullāh al-Ḥākim an-Naysābūrī
Abū Dharr al-Harawī
Abū 'Umar aṭ-Ṭalamankī
Ibn Imām at-Tuṭaylī
Ibn Ḥārith al-Qarawi
Ibn Ḥabīb
Qāḍī Abū al-Walīd al-Bājī
Abū Marwān ibn al-Aṣbagh al-Qurayshī an-Naqīb

I primarily relied on the books of at-Tustarī and aḍ-Ḍarrāb. I studied other books to ascertain any additional benefits they offered or to discover rare stories that were not included in either of these two sources. I omitted much of what they discussed at length in commentary, general statements and biographical information since that was not my goal. That has a place which is appropriate for it.

Then after that, I compiled a list of the names of the famous transmitters from Mālik and those who learned *fiqh* and knowledge from him, including specific details about them with a little of their history and news since we went on in detail in the reports of the *fuqahā'* among them later, and it was not our intention to mention others.

In these pages I did not intend to deal fully with all that is mentioned about the subject in transmission, assembly or questioning since we put that in another book dedicated to all the transmitters of Mālik. It contains more than 1300 transmitters which I investigated through the books written. A number of books have been written on that, like:

The book of Abū al-Ḥasan ad-Dāraqutnī
The book of Ismā'īl aḍ-Ḍarrāb al-Misrī
Abū Bakr Aḥmad ibn Thābit al-Khaṭīb al-Baghdādī
Abū Isḥāq ibn Sha'bān al-Qurṭubī
Abū al-Ḥasan ibn Abī 'Umar al-Balkhī
Abū 'Abdullāh ibn al-Ḥārith al-Qarawī
Abū Nu'aym al-Iṣbahānī

Some of them reached a thousand and some had less than that.

The Andalusians included Abū 'Abdullāh Muḥammad ibn Mufarrij and 'Abdullāh ibn Abī Dulaym, and the two of them had a fewer number [of men], and Abū Muḥammad 'Abd ar-Raḥmān ibn Muḥammad al-Bakrī. Each of these books contained what the others did not mention.

I pursued this assiduously and added to what had been separated from it and what had slipped away from it in what I read of the books of the People of *Ḥadīth* and others.

We condensed it to about a thousand of them in these pages whose names are known, whose transmission is sound and whose companionship is famous. We thought that we should not omit this number from this register in order to complete its benefits in this subject and to perfect its knowledge in this science.

Subsequently the objectives of the book progressed at a rapid pace, and I arranged the generations in chronological order. We began by writing about the *fuqahā'* among his companions and then their followers, generation by generation, and their successors, community by community, up to our shaykhs whom we met and contemporary Imāms whose imamate is famous, whose knowledge is recognised or whose books have appeared and whose words are transmitted and whose *fatwā*s and opinions are obeyed according to the precedence of their times and their historical succession.

We recorded their names and clearly stated their lineages and titles. We wrote down the missing diacritical marks so that there would not be any mistake in it. We removed the cause of their uncertainty so that the one who reads it will be safe from distortion. Abū Isḥāq Ibrāhīm ibn 'Abdullāh an-Najīramī said, 'The first thing is to be exact with the names of people because there is no analogy in it, nor anything before or after it which will indicate it.'

'Alī ibn al-Madīnī said, 'The greatest mistakes are those in the names of the men.'

Ibn Jurayj said, 'I looked for the name of Junda' ibn Ḍamra for eighty years until I learned it.'

Much of what I saw and heard in some of the mistakes is attributable to partisan bias, which is too repugnant to discuss further, and its imperfection is perceived by even those who are ignorant of it.

Generally the *fuqahā'* say Aḥmad ibn Muyassir with a *kasra*, while it is properly Muyassar with *fatḥa*. That is how 'Abd al-Ghanī and others recorded it. It is like that with Aḥmad ibn Mu'adhdhal. Many make it 'Mu'addal' while the correct form of that is with *dhāl*.

In his book, Shaykh Abū Isḥāq ash-Shīrāzī mentioned Ibrāhīm ibn Muḥammad ibn Dayyān among the transmitters of Saḥnūn among the people of Andalusia. However, that is not known among the Andalusians. The people of this field rejected that. It is most likely that it is Ibn Bāz. He was one of the group of that generation.

He made similar errors with many of their names and lineages. They are mentioned in other than their proper generations.

As for distinguishing the dubious among them, that is part of what is only known by the adept and only recognised by the intelligent person with insight into this subject.

Saḥnūn investigated Muḥammad ibn Razīn when he heard that he had related from 'Abdullah ibn Nāfi'. He asked him, 'Did you listen to Ibn Nāfi'?' He answered, 'May Allah put you right! That was az-Zubayrī. It was not aṣ-Ṣā'igh.' He said to him, 'Why did you swindle?' Saḥnūn added, 'What scorpions will emerge after me?'

Saḥnūn thought that it was necessary to make the two of them clear, even though they were both reliable Imāms so that their *riwāya* and words would not be mixed together. Aṣ-Ṣā'igh was greater, older and firmer in Mālik because of the length of his companionship with him. He is the one who succeeded him in his assembly after Ibn Kināna. He is the one from whom Saḥnūn and Yaḥyā ibn Yaḥyā related. They reported from him. Saḥnūn did not receive his narrations orally. He heard it from Ashhab as we will mention later. He died in 186 AH.

Az-Zubayrī was one of the companions of Mālik. He is Shaykh Ibn Ḥabīb and Sa'īd ibn Ḥassān. He died in 216 AH.

Their transmissions are frequently muddled together by the *fuqahā'* to the extent that most of them do not know that they are two men. A transmission from one of them might come that contradicts the transmission of the other, resulting in the assertion that there is disagreement in the *riwāya* of Ibn Nāfi' from Mālik. One of the great shaykhs of the people of Andalusia had a wrong idea about them after he had distinguished between them. He claimed that the one who received the narration orally was az-Zubayrī and that he is mentioned in *al-'Utibiyya.*

That is also the case with 'Alī ibn Ziyād at-Tūnisi and 'Alī ibn Ziyād al-Iskandarānī. Both were companions of Mālik and both were excellent and famous. The first was a *faqīh*, the shaykh of Saḥnūn and others. The other was a good man known as al-Muḥtasib.

Once Ibn Ziyād was mentioned in the presence of someone who understood this subject. He did not have any doubt that the famous *faqīh* was al-Iskandarānī. I said to him, 'They are two different men,' and I acquainted him with the one who said that.

This knowledge is necessary, especially when there is a great disparity in their knowledge and a difference in their justice and excellence.

Then we mentioned where they were born and died, and their shaykhs and transmitters. We sorted out their time and their generations as far as we know them, and verified its transmission so that their times will be known by that and their ranks will be made clear before and after, and the one who is connected will be distinguished from the one who is cut off in their transmissions.

The *fuqahā'* have made errors in this area. Sometimes they relate the *riwāya* and give its *isnād* as having the earlier transmitter transmit it from a later one when their generations are unclear to them and their times not distinct.

I saw an esteemed individual among them who mentioned a question from the *faqīh*, Ibn Ḥārith. He said, 'Ibn Ḥārith is in it. I saw that Aḥmad ibn Naṣr had given a *fatwā* on that.' It is probable that this shaykh was Ibn Naṣr ad-Dāwūdī whose generation came after the later Ibn Ḥārith. Ibn Ḥārith died in 362 AH and ad-Dāwūdī died in 402 AH. 'Ibn Ḥārith' meant the earlier Aḥmad ibn Aḥmad ibn Ziyād al-Harāwī, one of the companions of Saḥnūn and Ibn 'Abdūs, the scribe of Qāḍī Ḥimās, who died in 317 AH. If the shaykh had known that they were two men – and Allah knows best – and separated their generations, he would not have made this mistake.

It is due to their lack of knowledge in this that a group erred and they counted among the transmitters of Mālik and his companions those who could not have transmitted from him or ever met with him at any point in time. Allah knows best.

Shaykh Abū Isḥāq ash-Shīrāzī mentioned that Abū Yaḥyā al-Waqqār was one of those who listened orally to Mālik and he included him within the generation of his companions. None of those who compiled the transmitters of Mālik mentioned this. They counted him as one of the followers of his companions, and that is what is said, and Allah knows best. Similarly Abū Isḥāq mentioned among the followers of his companions those who are far from what others mention as being among his companions.

Abū Isḥāq ibn Sha'bān mentioned Ibrāhīm ibn Muḥammad ibn Baz al-Andalusī among the transmitters of Mālik while he was actually one of the companions of Saḥnūn, born some time after the death of Malik. He died in 274 AH.

Similarly, in spite of his precedence, Abū Bakr al-Khaṭīb mentioned and kept 'Abd al-Malik ibn Ḥabīb among the transmitters from Mālik, and included him in a *ḥadīth* transmitted from him. That is a significant error, especially from someone like him. 'Abd al-Malik ibn Ḥabīb travelled in 208 AH, about thirty years after Mālik's death. He was born two years after Mālik's death according to what you will see in his reports, Allah willing.

It is the same with what ash-Shīrāzī mentioned. He said that 'Abd al-Malik ibn Ḥabīb first studied *fiqh* with Yaḥyā and 'Īsā and Ḥusayn ibn 'Āṣim. He erred. They were equals, and he first studied *fiqh* with the shaykhs of those men in Andalusia: Ziyād, Ṣa'ṣa'a, al-Ghāzī ibn Qays and their likes.

Similarly, 'Abdullāh ibn Ghāfiq is mentioned as being in the generation of Saḥnūn. He claimed that he studied with 'Alī ibn Ziyād, but that is untrue. He was one of the companions of Saḥnūn, and he was not one of those of the same age as them. He was born more than twenty years after the death of 'Alī ibn Ziyād as will be mentioned.

Similarly, in his *Isti'āb*, ar-Rāzī and Aḥmad ibn 'Abd al-Barr mentioned that 'Īsā ibn Dīnār studied orally with Mālik and that he travelled with Ziyād and stayed with him. All of this wrong. We will clarify all of this in its proper place, Allah willing, with examples.

Then after this, we mentioned some of their virtues and good qualities, the praise bestowed upon the illustrious among them, the success of those who were declared honest among them, their ranks in intelligence and justice, their positions in knowledge and transmission, and those of them who spoke on the fewness of their number and were reckoned among them to be worthy of precedence and being an Imām as well as what the striving seeker needs to learn of his differences and consensus. Someone studying *fiqh* and the imitator both require this knowledge of those who are imams and their followers.

We disproved the forgery perpetrated against individuals among them through the prejudice of the fanatics or the embellishment of the people of doubt who ascribed to them the opposite of what is correct about them and well known as we will make clear, Allah willing, about them, since Allah freed the people of their *madhhab* from what the people of other schools *mudd*led with erroneous views. He safeguarded them from the cause of dissensions and inconsistency. By the praise of Allah, there is no one among the Imāms for whom innovation has been substantiated nor any for whom the people who ascertain integrity have agreed to abandon due to of lying or crime.

Abū Khaythama Zubayr ibn Ḥarb spoke about Abū Muṣ'ab az-Zuhrī, and Yaḥyā ibn Ma'īn spoke about Ismā'īl ibn Abī Uways and Yaḥyā ibn Bukayr, and that did not harm them. The just Imām and author of the *Ṣaḥīḥ*, Muḥammad ibn Ismā'īl al-Bukhārī related from them since he did not ascribe lying or doubt to them.

As-Sājī was arbitrary in what he related about the faults of 'Abd al-Malik ibn al-Mājishūn. The sound position from him is the opposite of that. He was famous in his school as we will make clear when each of them is mentioned in his proper place.

This is like what Yaḥyā did to 'Abdullāh ibn 'Abd al-Ḥakam. He is not followed in what he said, and Abū Hatim ar-Rāzī and others opposed him in that, saying it was like the statement of Qāḍi Abū al-Walīd that al-Qazwīnī was unknown. One does not pay any attention to it. The same is true in his remarks about aṣ-Ṣāliḥī.

If he had concerned himself with that subject, he would have known that aṣ-Ṣāliḥī was Abū Bakr Muḥammad ibn Ṣāliḥ al-Abharī, and he would not have said this about him. The state of Abū Sa'īd al-Qazwīnī and his importance and leadership in knowledge and his excellent books would have been clear to him. His *riwāya* is sound, and there is no doubt in his *riwāya* is sound and there is no doubt in his transmission.

Similarly, there is what he mentioned about Ibn Khuwayzimandād being unknown when he was so famous and wrote so many books that he must be recognised. He said, 'One of our Imāms in Baghdad did not mention him.' This was ash-Shīrāzī who did mention him in his book. That was Abū Muḥammad 'Abd al-Wahhab who related from him and said in it that 'Abū 'Abdullāh al-Baṣrī said:

'O equitable person! when you consider them along with others, will find them to be the soundest in certainty and firmest in the *dīn*. They have the most followers and purest company and followers so that their evil deeds are the good deeds of others. Others pay no attention to the criticisms they level at one another.'

This is why Saḥnūn said, 'Then al-Madanī was not like that,' meaning in the *dīn* and the firmest in authority, 'and there is none equal to him' or words to that effect.

Al-Ḥakam al-Mustanṣir (the Andalusian Umayyad) was one of those who had read books and thoroughly investigated the information about scholars in depth, to a level that many of the people of knowledge have not reached, and he wrote in a letter to the *faqīh* Abū Ibrāhīm: 'Whoever strays from the school of Mālik is someone whose heart has become rusty and whose evil actions have become appealing to him.'

We have thoroughly examined the information about the *fuqahā'* and read what was written down of their reports until now, and we did not see any school sounder than it. There were Jahmites, Rāfiḍites, Khārijites, Murji'ites and Shi'ites among them except for the school of Mālik, may Allah have mercy on him. We did not hear of anyone who followed his school who followed any of the innovations. Holding on to it is a source of salvation if Allah wills.

The people of Kairouan abandoned what they had heard from Ibn Abī Ḥassān and discarded it because of a single word that he spoke to the governor of Tunis which incited him against the rebels. It is not impossible that it is correct in certain cases, but something else is more fitting for someone like him because of his position as an Imām, his exceptional qualities, and his precedence.[1]

This is why they ceased to convey from Muḥammad ibn Rāshid who was a reliable man on the model of Saḥnūn who had travelled with him, because of some indulgence seen in him regard to behaviour and a tendency to compromise regarding an *'ina* (either selling on credit for future payment, and bring what one has sold for less than one what sold it) and adopting an opinion of someone who was not seen to have proper access. Therefore they abandoned him. When he died, Saḥnūn did not even look into what he left. He referred it to Ḥabīb, the agent in charge of complaints.

Qāḍi Abū al-Faḍl said:

> 'Then we collected some of their stories and reports, excerpts from the biographies of their judges and *qāḍīs*, and the rare *fatwās* of their *fuqahā'* and imāms which judges require and which the scholars cannot dispense with. We recorded some of the wisdoms of their judgements, the moving statements of their preachers, and the methods of their virtuous men and their ascetics whose *baraka* is to be hoped for and whose benefit will not fail, Allah willing.'

Sufyān ibn 'Uyayna said, 'Mercy descends when the righteous are mentioned.' Abū Ḥanīfa said, 'The stories of the scholars and their virtues are dearer to me than a lot of *fiqh* because they depict the manners of the people.' One of the shaykhs said, 'Stories are one of the armies of Allah by which He makes the hearts of His friends firm.' He added, 'Its testimony lies in His words, "*We have given you all this news about the Messengers so We can make your heart firm by means of it.*" (11:120)'

We mentioned some of the trials that they underwent, the afflictions which they endured which will give solace to those in tribulation, and proofs of the firmness of their position among the righteous. The Prophet ﷺ said, 'The people with the strongest affliction are the Prophets, then the virtuous, and the excellent and the less excellent.' (*Fayḍ al-Qadīr*, 1:519)

Man is tested according to the decree of his belief. If his belief is

[1] Mentioned in his entry in this book.

strong, the affliction is more intense for him until the person tested walks on the earth without any error remaining on him. The Prophet ﷺ said, 'When Allah loves someone, He tests him in order to hear his humble supplication.' (*Fayḍ al-Qadīr*, 1:254)

We mentioned some of their homelands and countries, those of them who travelled and those who remained in residence since the spring of the School of Madina overflowed and spread out from it. All of Madina was of that persuasion and it went out from it in the direction of the Hijaz and Yemen. It spread there through Qāḍi Abū Qurra, Muḥammad ibn Ṣadaqa al-Fadakī and those like them.

In the cities of Iraq, the School settled in Basra and dominated it through Ibn Mahdī, al-Qa'nabī and others, and then their followers from Ibn al-Mu'adhdhal, Ya'qūb ibn Shayba and the family of Ḥammād ibn Zayd, until some of the Shāfi'ites joined the school, and the two schools have coexisted there until our time. The last of the Mālikī imāms there in our time and with the rank of our shaykhs were Abū Ya'lā al-'Abdī, Abū Manṣūr ibn Bākhī and Abū 'Abdullāh ibn Ṣāliḥ. This school entered Baghdad and other Iraqi cities. It spread with other schools, but it was dominant and spread during the days when Ḥammād ibn Zayd was *qāḍī*. It was cut off in Baghdad and it did not have an *imām* there from about 450 AH when Abū al-Faḍl ibn 'Abdūs died. Then Ibn Ṣāliḥ lived there after 90. [490?]

As for Khurasan and what is beyond Iraq in the east, this School first entered this area with Yaḥyā ibn Yaḥyā at-Tamīmī, 'Abdullāh ibn al-Mubārak and Qutayba ibn Sa'īd. There were Imāms there over the course of time, and it spread at Qazwīn and Abhar and where it was followed in the lands of the mountains. Another who studied it in Nishapur was Abū Isḥāq ibn al-Qaṭṭān. The schools of Abū Ḥanīfa and ash-Shāfi'ī dominated that land.

One of the Imāms of this school also entered Persia: Qāḍi Abū 'Abdullāh al-Barkāni, who was appointed to the judgeship of Ahwaz, and this school subsequently spread under his influence. The School of Dāwūd dominated Persia.

As for Syria, some of Mālik's people were found there: al-Walīd ibn Muslim, Abū Mushir, Marwān ibn Muḥammad aṭ-Ṭāṭarī and others. It was at first dominated by the School of al-Awzā'ī and then the other schools entered Syria.

As for Egypt, it was the first land to which Mālik's School spread after Madina and it dominated it, and its people agreed to follow it until the arrival of ash-Shāfi'ī. He was one of them and was counted among them until the young men of Ibn Abī as-Samḥ from their *fuqahā'* ganged up against him, and then certain matters passed between the two of them which forced him to isolate himself with his companions as we will mention in its proper place. Then the school of ash-Shāfi'ī sprang up there and he had many companions and partisans, and it spread in all directions. Mālik's school in all of that remained evident there and it has dominated it until this time. The Imāms of the people of Abū Ḥanīfa have entered Egypt.

As for Tunis and the Maghrib beyond it, of old it was dominated by the School of the people of Kufa until 'Alī ibn Ziyād, Ibn Ashrash and al-Bahlūl ibn Rāshid entered it, and after them Asad ibn Furāt and others, with the School of Mālik. Many people adopted it, and it continued to spread until Saḥnūn came. It became dominant in his time. He broke up the circles of the opponents, and the school remained after him with his companions, and it has spread throughout those areas until this day.

In Kairouan there were a few people long ago who adopted the School of ash-Shāfi'ī, and something of Dāwūd's school entered it. However, at that time it was dominated by the Schools of Madina and Kufa. During the rule of the Banū 'Ubayd,[1] the School of the people of Kufa was in the ascendant because they agreed with them in the question of preference, and they held the leadership and judgment.

Some of them became Shi'ites, aiming for their pleasures and seeking this world. They directed their anger against the Madinans and afflictions befell the Mālikīs during that period. However, in spite of that, they remained numerous. The common people followed them. Its growth among them was evident. This lasted until the state of the Banū 'Ubayd grew weak on account of the rebellion of Abū Yazīd al-Khārijī. Then they triumphed and spread among them. They wrote sublime books and among them came sublime Imāms whose renown spread throughout all areas of the earth. Things continued like that until Kairouan and its people, its neighbouring

[1] The 'Ubaydites, also known as the Fatimids, the Shi'ite dynasty in North Africa.

areas and all of the Maghrib agreed on this school and embraced it. No others were known to reside among them.

As for the people of Andalusia, their position since the time it was conquered was that of al-Awzāʿī until Ziyād ibn ʿAbd ar-Raḥmān, Qaʿrūs ibn al-ʿAbbās, al-Ghāz ibn Qays and those after them travelled to Mālik. They brought back his knowledge and made his excellence clear to the people and the fact that the community followed him. His merit was recognised and his school was studied until the ruler of Andalusia at that time, Hishām ibn ʿAbd ar-Raḥmān ibn Muʿāwiya ibn Hishām ibn ʿAbd al-Malik ibn Marwān, made all the people hold to the school of Mālik, and had the judgements and *fatwās* issued according to it. That was in 170 AH during Mālik's lifetime. The shaykh of the *muftīs* at that time was Ṣaʿṣaʿa ibn Sallām, the Imām of the Awzāʿites and their *riwāya*. A number of the people of Mālik had joined with them. Then people adopted this school and defended it against all others with the sword. Some travellers and strangers brought into Andalusia some of the schools of ash-Shāfiʿī, Abū Ḥanīfa, Ibn Ḥanbal and Dāwūd. However, these schools failed to gain widespread acceptance and these schools died when they died in their various times, except for those who took on a personal *dīn* among those whose teachings did not gain traction. The rulers of Andalusia have continued to hold to this school until today.

We began each generation with the people of Madina, then those from the Arabian peninsula, then the people of the east, then back to the Egyptians and those after them the people of the Maghrib. We finished with the people of Andalusia except for those whose names we did not find among the people of those lands in that generation. Then we extended on to what was after that in the records.

In the course of that, we selected some rare anecdotes, exemplary manners and fine poetry which will stimulate the soul when it is lazy and remove its rust. ʿAlī said, 'Polish the selves for an hour. They grow rusty just as iron rusts.'

We mentioned what each of them claimed of knowledge as well as the qualities ascribed to them. We noted the main types of knowledge which they possessed, and we named the books they wrote and their dictations which cannot be dispensed with and what the one studying *fiqh* notes in seeking to learn it.

In what we compiled in that, we did not fail to clarify it, to summarise its sciences and to investigate in order to its sources and to shorten the paths and *isnāds*, and to integrate its separate parts and fragments.

We selected from the great books of the People of *Ḥadīth* and the matrices of the works of the historians like:

The book of Abū 'Abdullāh al-Bukhārī (*at-Tārīkh al-Kabīr*) (d. 256)
'Abd ar-Raḥmān ibn Abi Ḥātim (*al-Jarḥ wa at-Ta'dīl*) (d. 327)
Abū al-Ḥasan ad-Dāraquṭnī
Qāḍi az-Zubayr ibn Bakkār .
Qāḍi Abū Bakr ibn Ḥayyān Wakī' in *The History of the Qāḍis* (d. 306)
The books of Abū Ja'far aṭ-Ṭabarī (d. 310)
Aṣ-Ṣūlī (d. 335)
Ibn Kāmil (d. 256)
The books of Abū 'Umar al-Kindī
Aḥmad ibn Yūnus al-Miṣrī on the Egyptians (d. 302)
Some of the *History* of Ibn Abī 'Umar aṣ-Ṣadafī al-Qurṭubī
Some of the books of Abū 'Abdullāh ibn Ḥārith on the people of Kairouan and the Andalusians
Some of the book of Abū al-'Arab at-Tamīmī
Abū Isḥāq ibn ar-Rafīf al-Kātib
Abū 'Alī al-Baṣrī on the people of Kairouan
Some marginal notes which I found in the handwriting of Shaykh Abū 'Imrān al-Fāsī (d. 430) on that.
What I found in the *History* of Abū Bakr ibn Abī 'Abdullāh al-Mālikī on the people of Kairouan.
Some of the histories of the people of Andalusia like the book of Abū 'Abdullāh Mālik ibn 'Abd al-Barr, *Kitāb al-Intifāl* by Abū 'Umar ibn 'Afīf, *al-Intikhāb* by Abū al-Qāsim ibn Mufarrij, the book of Qāḍi Abū al-Walīd ibn al-Faraḍī, the histories of Abū Marwān ibn Ḥayyān, ar-Rāzī, the book of Aḥmad ibn 'Abd ar-Raḥmān ibn Muṭāhir of the Toledans and other books like the book of Ibn Abī Dulaym already mentioned.

Part of what I found was taken from the book of Abū Bakr al-Khaṭīb on the people of Baghdad and some pages gathered together by al-Ḥakam al-Mustanṣir billāh, which I found in his handwriting in a book of the Iraqis, and what I found of that in the book of Amīr Abū Naṣr, in the books of Shaykh Abū al-Isḥāq, and the book of Abū 'Umar ibn 'Abd al-Barr concerning the three Imāms and their *riwāyas* and other books which might contain a small trace of our goal, even what we snatched from the mouths of men and gleaned with great concern and attention.

I humbly entreat the One with Might and Majesty not to make my portion of this book be nothing but toil, continual sleeplessness and fatigue, and to make my intention in it good and to complete the favour by pardoning our errors.

Its reader should have a good opinion and not leap to the attack until he has had a thorough examination and verified what he dislikes. If he is certain of an error, he can then rectify it, or if he finds something obscure, he can clarify it. He should be grateful for the mental work we have spared him by compiling it and giving him freedom for research and investigation, and he should excuse whatever hidden or apparent errors he might come across. Generally speaking, man is negligent and the business which I have undertaken is weighty. A little is excused by a lot.

May Allah bless Sayyidunā Muḥammad, the bringer of good news, the warner, and his family and grant them peace.

Traditions regarding the excellence of Madina and the supplication of the Prophet ﷺ for it

Anas ibn Mālik related that the Prophet ﷺ said, 'O Allah, bless them in their measure and bless them in their *ṣā'* and *mudd*,' which means 'bless the people of Madina.' (*Muwaṭṭā'* 45.1.1)

Abū Hurayra reported that the Prophet ﷺ said, 'O Allah, bless us in our fruits and bless us in our city and bless us in our *ṣā'* and *mudd*! O Allah, Ibrāhīm is Your slave, Your close friend and Your Prophet. I am Your slave and Your Prophet. He prayed to You for Makka. I pray to You for Madina asking for the same that he prayed to You for Makka, and the like of it with it.' (*Muwaṭṭā'* 45:1.2)

'Umar ibn al-Khaṭṭāb asked 'Abdullāh ibn 'Ayyāsh, 'Do you say that Makka is better than Madina?' 'Abdullāh answered, 'I say that it is the Ḥaram of Allah and His sanctuary and His House is in it.' 'Umar said, 'I am not speaking at all about the Ḥaram of Allah nor about His House and sanctuary.' Then 'Umar asked the like of what he had said the first time, and 'Abdullāh answered him in the same way and 'Umar replied in the same way as he had done the first time. This happened three times. Then he left. That is the gist of the account.

Ibn 'Umar related that the Prophet ﷺ said, 'No one will be patient in enduring hunger and hardship in Madina without my being a witness or an intercessor for him on the Day of Rising.' One variant has 'and an intercessor'. (*Muwaṭṭā'*, 45.2.3)

Jābir ibn 'Abdullāh reported that the Messenger of Allah ﷺ said, 'Madina is like the blacksmith's furnace. It removes impurities and purifies the good.' (al-Bukhārī 3:21; *Muwaṭṭā'* 45.2.4)

We find in the *ḥadīth* of Abū Hurayra: 'It expels bad people like the blacksmith's furnace expels the impurities from the iron.' (al-Bukhārī 3:21; *Muwaṭṭā'* 45:2:5)

And we find in the *ḥadīth* of Zayd ibn Thābit: 'It expels men as the blacksmith's furnace expels the dross of silver.' (al-Bukhārī 3:23)

Sufyān ibn Abī Zuhayr related that the Messenger of Allah ﷺ said, 'Yemen will be conquered and people will be attracted to it, taking their families and whoever obeys them. Madina would have been better for them had they but known.' (al-Bukhārī 3:21; *Muwaṭṭā'* 45.2.7)

He mentioned something similar regarding the conquest of Iraq and Syria but I have shortened what he said.

Abū Hurayra transmits something similar in which the Prophet ﷺ said, 'By the One in whose hand my soul is, no one leaves it preferring to live elsewhere but that Allah replaces him in it with someone better than him.' (*Muwaṭṭā'* 45.2.6)

Abū Hurayra reported that the Prophet ﷺ said, 'There are angels at the gates of Madina. Neither the plague nor the Dajjāl will enter it.' (*Muwaṭṭā'* 45:4.16)

Mālik ibn Anas said, 'Madina is guarded by witnesses, and there are angels stationed on its roads who guard it. Neither the Dajjāl nor the plague will enter it. It is the abode of the Hijra and the *Sunna*. The best of people after the Messenger of Allah ﷺ were in it, and the Prophet ﷺ and his Companions made *hijra* to it. Allah chose it for him after his death and placed his grave in it; one of the meadows of the Garden in there as is the minbar of the Messenger of Allah ﷺ. That does not belong to any land except it.'

One version has: 'From it the nobles of this community will be followed on the Day of Rising.'

These are words which Mālik did not express without any foundation since that such a position cannot be taken based on mere analogy.

Ḥammād ibn Wāqid aṣ-Ṣaffār asked Mālik, 'Abū 'Abdullah, which do you prefer? To reside here or to reside in Makka?' He answered, 'Here. That is because Allah Almighty chose it for His Prophet ﷺ

from all of the places of the earth.' Then he mentioned the *ḥadīth* reported by Abū Hurayra regarding its excellence.

Ja'far ibn Muḥammad said, 'Someone remarked to Mālik, "You choose to remain in Madina and you have left the rural and fertile lands." He responded, "How could I not choose it when there is no road in Madina but that the Messenger of Allah ﷺ walked on it and Jibril, peace be upon him, came down to him from the Lord of the Worlds in less than an hour?"'

Abū Muṣ'ab az-Zuhrī said, 'Malik was asked, "Why do the people of Madina have soft hearts while the people of Makka are hard-hearted?" He replied, "Because the people of Makka drove out their Prophet ﷺ and the people of Madina gave him refuge."'

Muḥammad ibn Maslama said, 'I heard Mālik say, "I went to al-Mahdī and he said, 'Advise me.' I said, 'I advise you to have fear of Allah alone and to show kindness towards the people of the city of the Messenger of Allah ﷺ and his neighbours. We have heard that the Messenger of Allah ﷺ said, "Madina is the place to which I made *hijra*. I was sent from it and my grave will be in it and its people are my neighbours. It behooves my community to guard me in my neighbours. If someone guards them for me, I will be a witness or an intercessor for him on the Day of Rising. If someone disregards my instruction regarding my neighbours, Allah will make him drink from the foul pus of his skin in the Fire."'"'

Traditions singling out Madina for superior knowledge, belief, the *Sunna* and the Qur'an

'Ā'isha related that the Prophet ﷺ said, 'The cities were conquered with the swords, but Madina was conquered with the Qur'an.' (*Taḥqīq an-Naṣra*)

Abū Sa'īd al-Maqburī narrated from Abū Hurayra that the Messenger of Allah ﷺ said, 'Madina is the dome of Islam, the Abode of Faith, the land of Hijra and the starting point of the *ḥalāl* and the *ḥarām*.' (aṭ-Ṭabarānī)

Kathīr ibn 'Abdullāh related from his father from his grandfather that the Messenger of Allah ﷺ said, 'The *dīn* will seek shelter in Madina (one version has, 'in the Hijaz') as a snake seeks refuge in its hole. The *dīn* will take itself to the Hijaz like the refuge of the wild goats at the peak of the mountains. The *dīn* began as a stranger and it will return a stranger. Good fortune to the strangers who put right what people have corrupted of my *Sunna* after me!' (at-Tirmidhī)

'Ā'isha reported that the Prophet ﷺ said, 'Islam will retire to Madina as the flood sinks in the remains of the watering-trough.'

Abū Muṣ'ab az-Zuhrī said about this *ḥadīth*, 'By Allah, it only seeks refuge in its people who established it, promulgated its laws, recognised its interpretation and established its judgements.'

This praise from the Messenger of Allah ﷺ is not for mere land and houses, but praise for its people. This will remain among them and will disappear from others when knowledge is removed and people follow ignorant men as their leaders, and when they speak without knowledge when they are questioned, and when they are misguided and misguide others.

Ibn Abī Uways stated, 'I heard Mālik say in the same meaning as the *ḥadīth*, "Islam came as a stranger and will return as a stranger as it began," meaning it will return to Madina as it began from Madina.'

THE EXCELLENCE OF THE KNOWLEDGE OF THE PEOPLE OF MADINA AND ITS BEING PREFERRED OVER THE KNOWLEDGE OF OTHERS, AND THE *SALAF* FOLLOWING THEM

Zayd ibn Thābit said, 'When you see the people of Madina doing something, know that it is the *Sunna*.'

Ibn 'Umar said, 'When a sedition occurs, if people would only refer the business to the people of Madina, and when they agreed on something, do it, then the business would be put right. But when a dog barks, the people follow it.'

Mālik said, 'Ibn Mas'ūd was asked about something in Iraq and he spoke about it and then he went to Madina and asked and discovered that the matter was different from what he had stated. When he returned, he did not dismount nor enter his house until he had gone back to that man and informed him of that.'

He said, "Umar ibn 'Abd al-'Azīz wrote to the cities to instruct them in the *sunan* and *fiqh*. He wrote to Madina to ask them about what had passed and if it were based on some normative behaviour (*'amal*) which they had.

'He wrote to Abū Bakr ibn Ḥazm asking him to compile the *sunan* for him and to record them for him, but then 'Umar ibn 'Abd al-'Azīz died. Ibn Ḥazm had written some letters to him but had not sent them.'

Mālik said, 'By Allah, do not be averse to Sa'īd ibn al-Musayyab or any other of the people of Madina because of what any person says.

Had it not been that 'Umar ibn 'Abd al-'Azīz acquired this knowledge in Madina, many people would have doubted it.'

'Abdullāh ibn 'Umar ibn al-Khaṭṭāb said, "Abdullāh (i.e. Ibn az-Zubayr) and 'Abd al-Malik ibn Marwān both wrote to me and summoned me to a conference (*mashūra*). I wrote to them. "If you both desire counsel, then you must have the abode of the *Sunna* and the Hijra."'

A man sought advice from Abū Bakr ibn 'Amr ibn Ḥazm on some matter, saying, 'By Allah, I do not know what to do in this.' Abū Bakr said, 'Nephew, if you find that the people of this city agree on something, then do not doubt that it is the truth.'

Ash-Shāfi'ī said, 'When you find one of the people of Madina applying something, there should not be anything negative in your heart regarding it.'

Ash-Shāfi'ī also said, 'There are no legal tricks in the fundamental principles of the people of Madina because of their soundness.'

Ibn Nāfi' said, 'Mālik used to relate that when the people of the two Ḥarams (Makka and Madina) pledged their allegiance, that allegiance became binding on all the people of Islam.'

Mālik said, 'Ibn Sīrīn was the most like the people of Madina in one sphere of knowledge which he took.'

Abū Nu'aym said, 'I asked Mālik about something and he said to me, "If you want knowledge, then take up residence," meaning in Madina. "The Qur'an was not revealed on the Euphrates."'

Ash-Shāfi'ī said, 'I travelled to Madina and recorded their differences there.' He added in one version, 'about the [inheritance of a] grandfather.'

Mis'ar said, 'I asked Ḥabīb ibn Abī Thābit, "Who has the most knowledge of the *Sunna* or *fiqh*? The people of the Hijaz or the people of Iraq?" He replied, "The people of the Hijaz."'

Ash-Shāfi'ī said, 'Every *ḥadīth* which does not have a root in Madina and which is broken (*munqaṭi'*).has weakness in it.'

Mālik, may Allah be pleased with him, said after mentioning the *tashahhud* in the *Waṣiyya:* 'That is what I found the people of this city doing, so do not doubt that it is the truth.'

'Abdullāh ibn 'Umar said, "Umar ibn 'Abd al-'Azīz sent Nāfi' to Egypt to teach them the *sunan*.'

Mujāhid, 'Amr ibn Dīnār and other people of Makka said, 'Our business has remained ambiguous and in contention since 'Aṭā' ibn Abī Rabāḥ went to Madina. When he returned to us, his excellence became clear to us.'

THE LETTER OF MALIK TO AL-LAYTH IBN SA'D STATES ABOUT THIS:

'From Mālik ibn Anas to al-Layth ibn Sa'd. Peace be upon you. I praise Allah to you. There is no god but Him.

'May Allah hold us and you to His obedience, both in secretly and in public, and preserve us and you from every disliked thing! Know, may Allah have mercy on you, that I have been informed that you give people *fatwā*s which are contrary to what is done by our community and in our city. You are an *imām* and have importance and position with the people of your city, and they need you and rely on what they get from you. Therefore you ought to fear for yourself and follow that whose pursuit you hope will bring you salvation.

'Allah Almighty says in His Mighty Book, *'The outstrippers, the first of the Muhājirūn and the Anṣār.*' (9:100) Allah Almighty further says, *"So give good news to My slaves, those who listen well to what is said and then follow the best of it.'* (39:17-18) It is essential to follow the People of Madina. The Hijra was made to it, the Qur'an was sent down in it, and the *ḥalāl* was made *ḥalāl* and the *ḥarām* was made *ḥarām* there. The Messenger of Allah ﷺ was among them and they were present when the Revelation was revealed. He commanded them and they obeyed him. He set out the *Sunna* for them and they followed it until Allah caused him to die and chose for him what is with Him. May the blessings of Allah and His mercy and blessing be upon him.

'Then after his death, the Muslims followed those from among his community who were given authority after him. When something happened to them that they knew how to deal with, they carried it out. If they had no knowledge on the subject, they asked about it and then they followed the most appropriate course of action based on *ijtihād*. In this they were helped by their personal proximity (with the Prophet ﷺ). If someone opposed them or proposed an alternative view which was stronger and better than the ruling they had made, they left the former and acted upon the latter.

'Then the Tābi'ūn after them also travelled this Path and followed those *sunan*. If there is a practice which is clearly acted upon in Madina, I do not think that anyone may oppose it because of the inheritance they had received which no one is allowed to plagiarise or lay claim to. If the people of other cities were to say, "This is the practice in our city," and "This is what those before us used to do," that would not be permissible for them.

'Investigate for yourself, may Allah have mercy on you, what I have written to you. Know that I hope that what has impelled me to write this for you was solely good counsel for the sake of Allah alone. Investigation is up to you and your opinion is up to you. Treat my letter as such. If you do that, you will know that I have not neglected to offer you good counsel. May Allah give us and you success in obeying Him and obeying His Messenger in every matter and in every circumstance. Peace be upon you and the mercy and blessing of Allah.'

Written on Sunday, 9 Ṣafar. We have presented this letter in its own unique manner to highlight its benefits. It is sound and has been transmitted reliably.

Part of al-Layth's Reply to this Letter

'...It has come to your attention that I have issued *fatwās* that differ from those your community agrees on and that I must fear for myself because those near me rely on my *fatwās*, whereas people should follow the people of Madina to which the Hijra was made and where the Qur'an was revealed. You are correct in what you wrote about that, Allah willing, and it came to me in a way which I do not dislike. No one is more strongly inclined than I am to prefer the knowledge of the people of Madina who have passed away and no one acknowledges their *fatwās* more readily than I do. Praise be to Allah, the Lord of the worlds, who has no partner.

'As for what you mentioned about the Messenger of Allah ﷺ residing in Madina, the Qur'an being sent down to him among the Companions and what Allah taught them from him and that people became their followers, it is as you have stated.'

I have summarised this and I put some of it where it is required.

What is reported from the *Salaf* and scholars regarding the obligation to consult the action of the people of Madina and the fact that they consider it to be a proof, even if that is contrary to traditions (*Āthār*)

It is related that 'Umar ibn al-Khaṭṭāb said on the minbar, 'I forbid by Allah Almighty that a man relate a *ḥadīth* different from the normative practice (*'amal*).'

Ibn al-Qāsim and Ibn Wahb said, 'I saw that in Mālik's opinion, normative behaviour (*'amal*) was stronger than the *ḥadīth*.'

Malik said, 'The men of the people of knowledge among the Followers reported *ḥadīths* which had been conveyed to them from others and they said, "We are not ignorant of this, but the past normative action is other than it."'

Mālik said, 'I saw Muḥammad ibn Abī Bakr ibn 'Amr ibn Hazm who was a *qāḍī*. His brother was 'Abdullāh who had a lot of *ḥadīths* and was a truthful man. When Muḥammad gave a judgement when there was a *ḥadīth* which was contrary to the judgement, I heard 'Abdullāh criticise him, saying, "Has not this and this come in this *ḥadīth*?" He answered, "Yes." His brother said to him, "Then what is wrong with you? Why don't you give judgement based on it?" He responded, "Where are the people in respect to it?" meaning "What is the consensus of action on it in Madina?" He meant that the normative practice is stronger than the *ḥadīth* in it.'

Ibn al-Mu'adhdhal said, 'I heard a man ask Ibn al-Mājishūn, "Why did you relate the *ḥadīth* and then leave it?" He answered, "That is so that it will be known that we left it while having full knowledge of it."'

Ibn Mahdī said, 'The previous *sunna* of the people of Madina is better than the *ḥadīth*.' He also said, 'It may be that I have many *ḥadīth*s on a subject and then I find that the people of the courtyard have something different than that. Therefore it becomes weak in my estimation,' or words to that effect.

Rabī'a said, 'I prefer a thousand from a thousand over one from one because one from one can strip the *Sunna* out of your hands.'

Ibn Abī Ḥazm said, 'Abū ad-Dardā' was questioned and he gave some answers. He was told, "Such-and-such has reached us which is different from what is said." He said, "I have heard that, but I found the normative action different from that."'

Ibn Abī az-Zinād said that 'Umar ibn 'Abd al-'Azīz gathered the *fuqahā'* together and asked about the *sunan* and the judgements which were acted upon, and confirmed them. He threw out those among them were not acted on by the people, even if they came from a reliable source.

Mālik said, 'About so many thousand Companions came with the Messenger of Allah ﷺ from a certain expedition at such-and-such a time. Of these, about ten thousand died in Madina, and the rest split up in the cities. Which would you prefer to follow and whose words would you prefer to take? Those in whose presence the Prophet ﷺ died with his Companions I have mentioned, or the one who died with one or two of the Companions of the Prophet ﷺ?'

'Ubaydullāh ibn 'Abd al-Karīm ar-Rāzī said, 'The Messenger of Allah ﷺ died in the presence of twenty thousand living eyes.'

Clarification that proof is based on the consensus of the People of Madina, and the school of Mālik regarding that

Know that all the masters of the *madhhab*s among the *fuqahā'*, *mutakallimūn*, the people of tradition and theory who form a unified front against our companions on this matter, and attack us on the basis of their assertions, raising objections against us obliquely until some of them overstep the limits of fanatical partisanship and sectarianism and even attack Madina itself, enumerating its faults are not, in fact, addressing the subject under dispute. Some of them do not even formulate the question or investigate our school. Instead, they speak about it based on mere conjecture and surmise. Some of them begin to speak about it, taking their view from those who have not looked into us. Some of them make changes and then attribute to us things we did not say about it, as was done by aṣ-Ṣayrafī, al-Muḥāmilī and al-Ghazālī. They reported from us in the matter as saying what we did not say and they argued against us with whatever is needed by those who attack the consensus.

Here I will divide the discussion on it into distinct sections so that the unbiased reader will not find any way to deny it after careful consideration. I will clarify the positions of agreement and dispute on it, Allah willing.

Know that the consensus of the people of Madina comprises two distinct types: one type comes by way of transmission and the reports in which all relate from all and they act on that and it is not unknown.

The masses transmitted from the masses from the time of the Prophet ﷺ. This sort of consensus is divided into four categories:

Category One:

First is the transmission of the Sharīʿa from the Prophet ﷺ in word or action, like the *ṣāʿ* and *mudd*, and the fact that he used to take their *zakāt* and their *zakāt al-fiṭr* from them using that measure, the *adhān* and the *iqāma* and not saying, *'In the name of Allah, the All-Merciful, the Most Merciful'* aloud in the prayer, and the *waqf* and the *ḥabūs*. Their transmission of these matters in words and actions is like their transmission of the place of his grave, his mosque, his minbar, his city and other things that are incontrovertibly known about his states, his biography and the description of his prayer in the number of *rakʿats*, prostrations and the like of that.

There is also what is transmitted that the Prophet ﷺ affirmed when he saw them doing and his objection to that was not transmitted: like the transmission of a contract made by a slave and the like of that. There is also the transmission that he left certain matters and judgements without making them obligatory in spite of the fact that they were well-known and evident among them – for instance, he did not collect *zakāt* on vegetables although he knew that they were plentiful among them. This sort of consensus in these matters is a proof which must be accepted, and whatever is contrary to it in the form of a single tradition or analogy must be abandoned. This transmission is verified and what is known by it is undeniable and definite. It is not abandoned for the balance of probabilities. This is what Abū Yūsuf and other opponents who argued with Mālik and other people of Madina referred to in the question of the *awqāf* and the *mudd* and the *ṣāʿ* when they saw the transmission and verified it.

A just person should not deny the evidence of this. It is that about which Mālik spoke according to many of our shaykhs. There is no dispute regarding the validity of this method and that it constitutes a proof for intelligent people, and it transmits knowledge which is perceived by necessity. There is opposition on those questions from other than the people of Madina who have not received its transmission directly.

Qāḍī Abū Muḥammad 'Abd al-Wahhāb said, 'There is no disagreement among our companions regarding this.' Aṣ-Ṣayrafī and others among the adherents of ash-Shāfi'ī agreed with it. Al-Abhurī related it from him.

Some of the Shāfi'ites opposed that out of unwavering obstinacy. There is no rest for an opponent when he simply states, 'This is not its method.' They and others among the people of the provinces of Basra, Kufa and Makka are the same since they live in these lands where there is a group of the Companions from whom the *sunnas* were transmitted. 'Traditions reported by multiple transmission must be accepted in any aspect in which they come and knowledge arises from it, and so the proof comes from the transmission. Madina was not singled out by that and therefore that is the end of the matter.' This is the strongest of what they base themselves on.

We say to them: This is also what we say that this is also our stance if the question had been formulated in respect of others. However, an equivalent to this transmission is not found with others: the precondition of the transmission of multiple transmission is that the two ends and middle are the same. This exists with the people of Madina and their transmission of group from group from the Prophet ﷺ or the normative action in his time. The people of other cities transmit from their group when they refer to one or two of the Companions. So the question is being referred to the traditions of individuals.

To illustrate this point, consider the question of the action of the people of Makka in the *adhān*. There are multiple transmissions of the *adhān* in the presence of the Prophet ﷺ. This, however, is countered, by one of two ways in which the Messenger of Allah ﷺ had it done, and that which was in use when he died in Madina.

This is why Malik said to the one who argued with him on this matter, 'I do not know what is the *adhān* of a day or a night. This is the Mosque of the Messenger of Allah ﷺ and the *adhān* was given in it from his time, and it is not retained from anyone that he objected to what was given in the *adhān* in it.'

Category Two: Consensus on the normative practice achieved by *ijtihād* and deduction

This is a category about which our companions disagree. Most of them believe that it is not a proof nor is predominant. That is the position of the great men of Baghdad. Some of them were: Abū Bukayr, Abū Ya'qūb ar-Rāzī, Abū al-Ḥasan ibn al-Muntāb, Abū al-'Abbās aṭ-Ṭayyālisi, Qāḍī Abū al-Faraj, Abū Bakr al-Abhurī, Abū at-Tammām, and Abū al-Ḥasan ibn al-Qaṣṣār. They said, 'Because they are part of the community, but the proof is by all of it.' This is the most general and comprehensive statement of the opponents.

This was the position of Qāḍī Abū Bakr ibn aṭ-Ṭayyib and others. They denied that Mālik said this, and that it was his school or that of the Imāms among his people.

Some of them believed that it was not a proof, but it was preferred to the *ijtihād* of others.

That is the statement of a group of those who studied their *fiqh*. One of the Shāfi'ites took that view while Qāḍī Abū Bakr, our precise Imāms and others did not like it.

Some of the Mālikīs believe that this category is a proof like the first category. They related that from Mālik. Qāḍī ibn Naṣr said, 'It is indicated by the words of Aḥmad ibn al-Mu'adhdhal and Abū Muṣ'ab. Qāḍī Abū al-Ḥasan ibn Abī 'Umar among the people of Baghdad believed that as did a group of the Maghribīs among our companions. They thought that it takes precedence over the tradition of one person and analogy. The opponents agreed that it is the school of Mālik, although it is not authenticated from him at all.'

Qāḍī Abū al-Faḍl said, 'In respect of single reports, the normative action of the people of Madina must follow one of three positions:

> 'Either it agrees with them, so it is firmer in its soundness, if that is by way of transmission, or it is probable if it is by way of *ijtihād* without any dispute in this since it is only opposed here by the *ijtihād* of others and their analogy before the single tradition.
>
> 'If it agrees with a report contradicted by another report, their normative practice is preferred by their tradition. It is the strongest text which makes traditions probable when they are contradictory.

That is what was believed by the master Abū Isḥāq al-Isfarā'inī and those who followed him among the rigorous Mālikī legists (*uṣūlī*) and *fuqahā'* and others.

'If it is contrary to reports in general, and their consensus is by way of transmission, the report is abandoned for it without opposition among them and according to other rigorous people as was already stated. In verification, it is not necessary to formulate opposition in this nor to turn to it since the absolute and certain is not abandoned for probabilities as was clear to this fair opponent who retracted. This is the crux of the question – like the question of the *ṣā'* and the *mudd*, the *waqf*, *zakāt* on vegetables and other things.

'If their consensus is based on *itjihād*, then the report takes precedence over it according to most people. There is disagreement in it among our adherents as we already stated.

'If there is no action in opposition or agreement, then the question falls away and one must refer to the acceptance of the report of one individual, which can be from their transmission or from the transmission of others if it is sound and not opposed. If this report which they transmit is opposed by another report which other people of distant areas transmitted, what they transmitted is preferred according to the master Abū Isḥāq and other meticulous scholars because of their extra advantage of witnessing factual evidence and their sitting down to transmit the reports of the Messenger ﷺ and the fact that they consisted of a great number relating from a great number from him.

'Opponents have distorted a lot of what they transmit from Mālik regarding that – except for what we already stated. Abū Bakr as-Ṣayrafī and Abū Ḥāmid al-Ghazālī related that Mālik said, "One only considers the consensus of the people of Madina to the exclusion of others." This is not what Malik said nor was that stated by any of his companions. One of the legists among the opponents related that Mālik thought that the consensus of the seven *fuqahā'* at Madina constituted consensus, and said that according to him, they were the people of *ijtihād* in that moment to the exclusion of others. This is not what Mālik said and it is not related from him.

'One of them related about us that we do not accept reports unless they are accompanied by the action of the people of Madina. This is sheer ignorance or lies. They did not distinguish between our statement regarding the rejection of a report which is contrary to their actions. If they use as an argument against us in this area the fact that Mālik rejected the *ḥadīth* about the two sellers with the option to withdraw which he and the people of Madina related with their soundest *isnād*s and the statement of Malik about this *ḥadīth* and what he mentioned about it in his *Muwatta'*: "There is no specified limit nor any matter which is applied in this case according to us." This objection is the greatest of the bugbears and the ugliest of their calumnies. They said, "This is a refutal of the sound report since the action of the people of Madina did not embellish it so that the people of Madina blamed him for it." Ibn Abī Dhi'b said some famous harsh words about it.

'The answer is that this was misconstrued, leading to a misunderstanding. This statement of Mālik does not mean that he rejects the sale with the option of withdrawal. It means what he said in the rest of the *ḥadīth*. That is his words, "Except the sale with the option of withdrawal." He stated that the sale with the option of withdrawal does not have a limit in their opinion which can be exceeded except according to what is used for testing the commodity. That varies with different sales. In it, one refers to *ijtihād*, the custom of the land, the conditions of the sale and what he meant by it.

'This is how our meticulous Imāms, may Allah have mercy on them, explain his words. Acting by the *ḥadīth* without the interpretation of the distinction in it by word and the contract of sale is abandoned. They have the option of withdrawal as long as they are bargaining with one another. This is the meaning of what is understood from the two individuals who are interacting. They are legally competent in the business they are transacting. This indicates that the option is before its completion. That is supported by his words, "None of you should bid against the sale of his brother." This is also the case with two equals. It is called known as a sale before completion and conclusion.

'One of our companions said that the *ḥadīth* is abrogated by his words in another *ḥadīth*, "When two parties are in dispute about a business transaction, the seller's word is taken." If they had had the option of withdrawal, there would be no need for disagreement and argument. Mālik's statement is based on what is more likely by one of the two reports supported by the action of the people of Madina when it is in conflict, as was already stated. Many of our companions took the *ḥadīth* of the two sellers with the option of withdrawal and acted on it: Ibn Ḥabīb and others.

'Part of what the opponents quoted from Mālik is, "The believers whom Allah commanded to be followed are the people of Madina." Mālik did not say this. How could be say this when he related that consensus is a proof?

'One of the objections which opponents raised against us is that they say: we preserved the door of transmission which we mentioned, so what is the use of mentioning consensus and action? When the transmission is obtained from a group of them, then knowledge of their report is obtained and must be referred to, even if others oppose them. So what is the benefit of you mentioning consensus when there is agreement on this?

'The answer is that we say that the transmission of some does not exclude the rest: either opposition is related from them or it is not. If it is not related, that is what we meant. If opposition is known, and it is from a small group, one does not pay any attention to it. The opposition of a few does not detract from the transmitted consensus.

'There is disagreement about the opposition of a few in respect of a consensus based on *ijtihād* – according to what the masters of the fundamentals affirmed whose precondition in verification is that on which the *mujtahids* agree.

'As for what is transmitted, it must have a number which demands knowledge for us. When a few people dispute it, error and mistake are ascribed to them since that which is definite through multiple sound transmission invalidates any opposition to it.

'If the opposition is from another group and that second large group is one in which there is multiple transmission as well, Qāḍī

Abū Muḥammad ʿAbd al-Wahhāb said, "This contradictory transmission is not a proof. This is not our question."'

Qāḍī Abū al-Faḍl said:

'In my opinion, it is impossible to conceptualise this taking place since the multiple transmission must be known when it comes with its preconditions. It is not valid that the multiple transmission of another contradict it because that would demand that one of them be false, and that is impossible. The intellect rejects such reasoning.

'It is not valid that both of them be true nor can they both be false, so the question falls aside again, unless there is contradictory multiple transmissions on two distinct events or two different states or two different times. So one judges in that case by the judgement of the two sound contradictory proofs, and looks to see whether it is possible to combine them and confine each of them to its event and subject, or to refer to historical evidence, the judgement of abrogation and other aspects of judgement in contradiction and preference. The place of its explanation lies in the fundamental principles of *fiqh*.

'They said, "When what they explained is confirmed, the judgement refers to their transmission and the report with multiple paths and their knowledge and proof is derived from it. So what is the point of calling it consensus?"

'We replied, "It means that transmission and action is ascribed to all inasmuch as none of them transmitted nor acted contrary to it."

'If it is said: "You have switched the question and you have gone from consensus to agreement on transmission by word or action," the answer is that our words in this question demand the opposition of the Iraqis and others against us in the questions whose path is transmission and detailed action. In that, they rely on individual reports while our companions accept the transmission of the people of Madina and their action, which is agreed upon by multiple transmission as a proof to leave those reports as we already stated.

'If they said that Allah says, *"If you have a dispute about something, refer it back to Allah and the Messenger"* (4:59), and this is referring it to other than the Messenger as it is reference to the action of certain people of his Community, our reply is that we only refer to the Messenger since it is confirmed with us by multiple transmission that the normative action is the *Sunna* of the Messenger ﷺ and his action and acknowledgement.'

Qāḍī Abū al-Faḍl said:

'As for the statement of those of our companions who say that their consensus by way of *ijtihād* is a proof, their argument for that lies in what they possess of the excellent company, association, close relationship, questioning, and analysis of means and circumstances. All of this is excellence and merit in the strength of the *ijtihād*.

'Our companions and our opponents said, "The explanation of a Companion who relates to someone about what is probable in the report is better than the explanations of other people, and constitutes a proof. The explanation of someone who opposes him is abandoned since the Companion saw the Messenger and heard that *ḥadīth* from him and understood it from his state, the articulation of his words and the reason for his judgement. By that, he possessed some knowledge of what it means which others do not have. Therefore his explanation is preferred. Hence it is like that with the consensus of the people of Madina in the same way. Their striving precedes that of others among those who lived far away and only recited the simple report without its circumstances, and lacks the reason why it was spoken.

'That is why ash-Shāfi'ī preferred the *ḥadīth* of the shaykhs of the Companions over the *ḥadīth* of Usāma regarding homicides. He said that is because Ibn 'Umar, 'Ubāda and the shaykhs knew the Messenger of Allah ﷺ better than Usāma. That is why some of the legists and *fuqahā'* preferred the analogy of a Companion over the analogy of others. That is why many of them preferred the action of a Companion by a *ḥadīth* when he related over other *ḥadīths* whose transmitter did not act on them. Ash-Shāfi'ī once said, "I prefer the consensus of the people of Madina to analogy." This is a statement saying that their consensus is a proof in one aspect as opposed to the consensus of others where no one disagrees that it does not have an affect in the judgements unless it is related from one of the legists that the consensus of the people of Makka and Madina and the two cities are a proof as we have already stated. What the people of the legal principles prefer in the mutual opposition of reports is through the action of the people of Madina and Makka.'

This concludes the discussion on this subject and the core of minds and hearts. The correct objective of the question is seen to every unbiased person through verification and scrutiny.

Preference for the School of Mālik and the Proof of the Obligation to Imitate Him and Prefer Him over Other Imāms

Qāḍī Abū al-Faḍl said: Before delving into this, we deemed it necessary to provide a preface and set out the rule for the duty of *taqlīd* (imitation). Our intention is to base this discussion on it.

May Allah give us and you success! Know that the one who worships according the commands and prohibitions of Allah and enacts the *Sharīʿa* of the Prophet ﷺ seeks to learn that: so that he knows how he must worship, what he must do and what he must abandon, what is obligatory for him and what is unlawful, and what is allowed and what is encouraged by the Book of Allah and the *Sunna* of His Prophet ﷺ. They are the two roots without which the *Sharīʿa* cannot be known, and it is only by their knowledge that Allah can be worshipped. Then there is the consensus (*ijmāʿ*) of the Muslims which is based on and dependent on both of those two sources. It can only exist and be deduced from them, either by a text which they know whose transmission was abandoned, or from *ijtihād* based on both of them according to the statement about the validity of consensus by means of *ijtihād*.

All of this is only achieved by ascertaining that knowledge along with the means and the tools which lead to it: transmission, investigation, seeking it, gathering it, retaining it, knowing what is sound and famous of the *Sunna*, knowing how to understand, and that by which one can understand the literal meaning of expressions: knowledge of Arabic and its language, knowledge of its meanings and the meanings of what is meant and intended by the *Sharīʿa*, and the text of the words and their outward meaning, their import and all their forms. This is designated as 'the science of the fundamentals of *fiqh*'. Most of it is closely connected to the science of Arabic and the objectives of speech and direct address. Then analogy is used for what does not have a text based on what does have a text by noting its causality or its resemblance.

All of this requires time while worship is immediately obligatory.

Those who reach this path which is the path of *ijtihād* and judge by it in the *Sharīʿa* are few, and this number diminishes further after the first generation, the virtuous early generations, and the three praiseworthy first generations.

Since this is the case, there must be those who do not reach this position among the people who have the responsibility to learn that by which they can worship or that which they are obligated to perform of the duties of their *Sharīʿa* from those who transmit it to him and inform him of it, and he relies on them in his transmission, his knowledge and his judgement. That is imitation (*taqlīd*) and it is the degree of the common people. Indeed, most people are like this.

If this is the case, then he is obliged to follow a reliable man of knowledge in that. If there are many men of knowledge, then he follows the one with the most knowledge.

This is the portion of the one who imitates in respect of *ijtihād* in his *dīn*. The imitator does not abandon the one with the most knowledge and turn to another, even if he is occupied with knowledge. He then asks about what he does not know until he learns it as Allah says, *'Ask the people of the Reminder if you do not know.'* (16:43) The Prophet ﷺ commanded that the caliphs and his Companions after him be followed. The Prophet ﷺ sent his Companions to people so that they could acquaint them with the *dīn* and teach them what they were obliged to do. Allah urged all of that: *'If a party from each group of them were to go out so that they could increase their knowledge of the dīn, they would be able to notify their people when they returned to them.'* (9:122)

This, then, is necessary and obligatory, and those who ought to be followed by common ignorant people, worshipping believers, and seekers looking for guidance are the *fuqahā'* of the Companions of the Messenger of Allah ﷺ who acquired knowledge from him and knew the underlying reasons behind the revealing of the commands and the prohibitions, the duties of the *Sharī'a*, and the nuances of what the Prophet ﷺ said regarding that. They saw the circumstances and context. They mentioned most of that to the Prophet ﷺ and they asked him to explain it to them in spite of their vast knowledge, recognition of the meanings of words, illuminated hearts and expanded breasts. Without a doubt, they are the Imāms with the most knowledge, and those whom it is most appropriate to imitate. However, they only spoke a little on the events that occurred and secondary questions did not arise with them, and they only spoke on the *Sharī'a* regarding fundamentals and facts. They were mostly occupied in doing what they knew, defending the territory of the *dīn* and strengthening the Muslim *Sharī'a*.

Subsequently there were disagreements between them in some of what they said which leave the imitator perplexed and compel him to investigate and abstain. Secondary questions, deductions and detailed discussions occurred after them. The Tābi'ūn came and investigated their disagreements and built on their roots. Then came the scholars among the Followers of the Tābi'ūn. Events had proliferated leading to new occurrences, and *fatwās* on those matters developed. They compiled the statements of all, preserved their *fiqh*, and investigated their disagreements and agreements. They were cautious about disseminating the matter and about dispute which exceeds what is correct. They strove to gather the *sunan* and make their bases precise. They were questioned and they gave answers. They constructed the principles and organised the fundamentals. Events developed for them to deal with and they wrote books for people about that and arranged them into topics. Each of them acted according to what he perceived and what he was given success in. The knowledge of the fundamentals and branches, disagreement and agreement, reached them, and they employed analogy in what reached them from what indicated or resembled it. May Allah be pleased with all of them and give them the reward for their *ijtihād*!

It is a specific obligation for a common imitator and novice seeker of knowledge to refer in *taqlīd* to those people for the texts of events and to refer them regarding what is obscure because of their immersion in the knowledge of the *Sharī'a* and its role. They must examine with precision the schools of those before them and to safeguard that for those who came after them.

However, the *taqlīd* of all of them is not in agreement on many events and many questions due to their difference arising from the different roots on which they are based. It is not valid for the imitator to imitate the one he wishes among them based on appetite, choice or according to what he perceives as the practices of his country and family.

His portion of *ijtihād* here is to to ascertain who possesses the most knowledge among them so that the common man can rely on his *fatwās* in his actions and apply what he thinks in his devotions. The common man puts the one with the most knowledge from those who cling to the schools of these men in this position. It is not lawful for him to go seeking *fatwās* from someone who is not from his school. One of the shaykhs said, "For someone who clings to the imitation of his school, his Imām is like the Prophet ﷺ is with his community. It is not permitted for him to oppose him." This is sound in consideration, and through what we have explained and the preconditions we have given, its accuracy will be obvious to those with insight and perception.

Similarly, in the beginning this seeker of knowledge must study what the most knowledgeable of these men had of primary fundamental and secondary cases and he must learn what he wrote and compiled, and be guided by his investigation in that and incline where he inclines. The reason for this is that if the seeker had started in each question to seek to understand the truth in it by way of *ijtihād*, that would have been very difficult for him since he will only have success in it after he possessed all its qualities and his perfection is completed, and then when he is on this path, he would not need to imitate the masters of the schools and would himself be one of the *mujtahids*. So his path consists of imitating the one who will teach him that this is the truth until he obtains the knowledge which is destined for him and he acquires of it what Allah has allotted him and is successful and there is a place for investigation and *ijtihād* in it to which he moves and arrives at.

When this premise is affirmed, then we say that the consensus of the Muslims in all the areas of the earth has emerged about *taqlīd* of this sort, following them and studying their schools rather than those before them, while still acknowledging the excellence of those before them, and recognising that they came before them and had this extra knowledge. However it is due to the reasons which we have mentioned and the skill with which they selected from that as we have already stated.

Then opinions and aspirations vary in determining who to imitate among them according to what they believe about that person being the most knowledgeable and worthy to be followed, either by a belief which they hold, or because of his fame and praise which they have heard, or by taking it from some of his followers who rely on him and follow him, or from the *taqlīd* of their fathers or the people of their countries in which they grew up and with which they were familiar.

Those who are imitated and whose schools are emulated and who have followers in all lands and areas used to be numerous:

Mālik ibn Anas in Madina, Abū Ḥanīfa and ath-Thawrī in Kufa, al-Ḥasan al-Baṣrī in Basra, al-Awzā'ī in Syria, ash-Shāfi'ī in Egypt and Aḥmad ibn Ḥanbal after him in Baghdad. Abū Thawr also had followers there.

Then Abū Ja'far aṭ-Ṭabarī and Dāwūd al-Isbahānī appeared in Baghdad, and they wrote books, selecting teachings in the schools according to the opinion of the People of *Ḥadīth*. Dāwūd discarded analogy. Each of them had followers.

All of these schools spread in all directions. The school of Mālik dominated the Hijaz, Basra and Egypt, and neighbouring lands of Africa, Andalusia, Sicily and the Furthest Maghrib, extending to the lands of those who became Muslims among the blacks until this very day. It was strong in Baghdad and then grew weak there after 400 AH. It became weak in Basra after 500 AH. It went from the land of Khurasan to become dominant in the Caspian and Abhar. It appeared first in Nishapur and had leaders and teachers there and other places. We will mention some of them later in their generations to whom Allah gave inspiration. It existed in Persia, and it spread in the Yemen and many of the cities of Syria.

The school of Abū Ḥanīfa has been dominant in Kufa, Iraq and Transoxiana and much of Khurasan until this very day. It remained very strong in North Africa (Ifriqiya) until about 400 AH, and then it dwindled. In the past, it was found beyond that region in Andalusia and the city of Fes.

The school of al-Awzā'ī dominated Syria and Andalusia at first until the school of Mālik became dominant there after 200 AH. Then it disappeared there.

As for the schools of al-Ḥasan and ath-Thawrī, they did not have many followers and their imitation did not last long. Their schools soon disappeared.

As for the Shāfi'īs, they had many followers and the school ash-Shāfi'ī spread as the schools of Mālik and Abū Ḥanīfa before him had spread. It first made an appearance in Egypt, and he had many followers there alongside the Mālikīs. Then it spread to Iraq and Baghdad and became dominant there and in many of the lands of Khurasan, Syria and Yemen and continues until this present day. It entered Transoxiana and Persia. Some of it entered Africa and Andalusia after 300 AH.

As for the school of Aḥmad ibn Ḥanbal, it emerged in Baghdad, and then it spread in many of the cities of Syria and elsewhere. It is weak now.

As for the people of aṭ-Ṭabarī and Abū Thawr, they were not numerous and did not last long. The followers of Abū Thawr disappeared after 300 AH, and the followers of at-Tabari disappeared after 400 AH.

As for Dāwūd, he had many followers and his school spread in Baghdad and Persia. A few people advocated it in North Africa and Andalusia, but it is weak now.

Those are the scholars that the people agree can be imitated while there is some disagreement about their notable men. Scholars agree that they are to be followed, their schools emulated, their books studied and *fiqh* learned from their sources. One builds on their fundamentals and branches out from their roots rather than others who are earlier than them or contemporary with them for the reasons which we mentioned.

Today people in the lands of the world fall into five schools: the Mālikīs, the Ḥanafīs, the Shāfi'īs, the Ḥanbalīs and the Dāwūdīs. They are the ones who are known.

The seeker of knowledge and the one who desires to know what is correct and true must recognise who is the best of them to follow so that he can rely on his school and travel his path in learning *fiqh*.

Here we will make it clear that Mālik, may Allah have mercy on him, was that man since he possessed all of the tools of the Imamate and obtained the degree of *ijtihād*. He was the most knowledgeable of people, and, indeed, the people of his time agreed in their testimony that he possessed that and was advanced. He is the model and people then were the people and the time was the time. Then there is the report about 'the man of knowledge of Madina', and Madina was his home, and this description was applied to him on the tongues of the people in general. His circumstances tallied with those mentioned in the *ḥadīth* from him and the interpretation of the virtuous *Salaf* was that he was the one who was meant.

We will discuss two areas of that:

The first of them is that it is supported by transmission and tradition, and there are two things probable in that.

The course of the second is consideration and investigation and there are three things probable in that. We conclude by preferring his school, its immense worth in knowledge and its high position by five proofs, all of which we will expound on extensively to preclude any evasion. Some of it almost reaches the level of the categorical certainty.

SECTION ONE

Know that Mālik's school is preferred over others, its position is lofty in knowledge, and its worth is great based on the path of transmission and tradition. This is not rejected by anyone except by some obstinate person or someone who is uninformed when that has not reached him in spite of its fame in the books of the opponents and the helpers.

Here we will support that using two pieces of evidence. The first of them should be mentioned before the other: the famous sound tradition regarding that from the Messenger in a *ḥadīth* transmitted by reliable men. They included Sufyān ibn 'Uyayna from Ibn Jurayj from Abū az-Zubayr from Abū Ṣāliḥ from Abū Hurayra that the Messenger of Allah ﷺ said, 'The time is near when people will flog their camels in quest of knowledge.' One version has, 'They will seek for knowledge, and they will not find a man with more knowledge (in one version, 'more understanding (*fiqh*)') than the man of knowledge of Madina.' (at-Tirmidhī, Ibn Ḥanbal) One version has, 'than a man of knowledge at Madina.' One has they will beat 'the shoulders of the camels' instead of 'the livers of the camels'.

People besides Sufyan related a similar *ḥadīth* from Ibn Jurayj. They include al-Muḥāribī, from Abū Hurayra (*mawqūf*), and Muḥammad ibn 'Abdullāh al-Anṣārī with an *isnād*. He is a trustworthy reliable man.

This path of transmission is the most famous of its paths, and the men of this path are famous and reliable. Al-Bukhārī, Muslim and the people of the *Ṣaḥīḥ* reported it from all of them.

Al-Maqburī also related it from Abū Hurayra with different wording. Qāḍī Abū al-Bakhtarī also gave it as: Wahb ibn Wahb from 'Abd al-A'lā ibn 'Abdullāh from al-Maqburī from Abū Hurayra that the Prophet ﷺ said, 'The Hour will not come until the people flog their camels from every direction to the man of knowledge of Madina, seeking his knowledge.' However, in their opinion Abū al-Bakhtarī is weak. An-Nasā'ī also related it and put it in his book as being from 'Alī ibn Muḥammad from Muḥammad ibn Kathīr from Sufyān from Abū az-Zinād from Abū Ṣāliḥ from Abū Hurayra who said, 'The Prophet ﷺ said, "They will flog their camels seeking knowledge and they will not find a man with more knowledge than the man of knowledge of Madina."'

An-Nasā'ī said, 'This is an error and the correct version is Abū az-Zubayr from Abū Ṣāliḥ.'

Abū Mūsā al-Ash'arī also related it from the Prophet ﷺ in another expression which was related by Ma'n ibn 'Īsā from Ibn al-Mundhir at-Tamīmī, Zuhayr, from 'Abdullāh ibn 'Umar from Sa'īd ibn Abī

Hind from Abū Mūsā al-Ash'arī in which the Messenger of Allah ﷺ said, 'People will go out from the east and the west in search of knowledge. They will not find a man with more knowledge than the man of knowledge of Madina' or 'a man of knowledge at Madina.'

Ibn Ḥabīb mentioned a *ḥadīth* in which he gives an *isnād* from Abū Ṣāliḥ from Jābir ibn 'Abdullāh who said that the Messenger of Allah ﷺ said, 'This world will not end until there is a man of knowledge in Madina to reach whom camels are flogged, and there is no one on the face of the earth with more knowledge than him.'

Sufyān ibn 'Uyayna is related from more than one path as saying, 'We think that it is Mālik ibn Anas who is meant by the *ḥadīth*.' One version simply has, 'It is Mālik ibn Anas.'

The like of it is related from Ibn Jurayj (in *Tārīkh Baghdād*) and 'Abd ar-Razzāq that Sufyān said, 'I used to say that it was Ibn al-Musayyab until I said, "There were Sulaymān, Sālim and others in the time of Ibn al-Musayyab." Today I say that it is Mālik. That is because he lived until he had no equal in Madina.'

This is the sound version from Sufyān. Reliable men and Imāms related it from him: Ibn Mahdī, Yaḥyā ibn Ma'īn, 'Alī ibn al-Madinī, az-Zubayr ibn Bakkār, Isḥāq ibn Abī Isrā'īl, Dhu'ayb ibn 'Umāma as-Sahmī and others. All of them heard Sufyān say when he reported the *ḥadīth* to them that it was Malik, or that he thought it, or reckoned that it was him, or that it was his opinion or as they related it.

Ibn Mahdī said, 'When Sufyān said, "they related it," he meant the Followers.'

Qāḍī Abū 'Abdullāh at-Tustarī said, 'That is information from others like him or from one above him stating that his position among them was this position because of what they saw of his state which resembled what was mentioned in the *ḥadīth*.' He added, 'This *ḥadīth* has been reported with two forms of words. One of them is, "They will not find a man of knowledge with more knowledge than the man of knowledge of Madina." The other is "than a man of knowledge at Madina." Each of them has a sound meaning.'

As for his words, 'a man of knowledge at Madina', that indicates a particular man who is there and in no other place. None is found to whom the knowledge of the people of Madina reached and who lived there and did not leave it or reside elsewhere in the time of Mālik upon whom there is agreement except for Mālik. There was none of the scholars who gave *fatwā* at Madina and *ḥadīth* for some sixty years from whom the people of the east and west learned, and to whom they flogged their camels except for Mālik.

As for the version, 'the man of knowledge of Madina' or 'the people of Madina,' Abū al-Mughīra Muḥammad ibn Isḥāq al-Makhzūmī mentioned that the interpretation of that is that as long as the Muslims seek knowledge, they will not find anyone with more knowledge than the man of knowledge of Madina, be he present there or elsewhere. According to this, it was Sa'īd ibn al-Musayyab because he was the last in his time, and then after him it was someone else among those who were like him among the shaykhs of Mālik, and then after them, it was Mālik himself, and after him whoever established his knowledge and became the most knowledgeable of his companions or his school. And so it is like that as long as there is a seeker of knowledge and an Imām for the school of the people of Madina.

According to this interpretation, it is permitted to say that it was Ibn Shihāb in his time and his knowledge, al-'Umarī in his time and knowledge, and Mālik in his time and knowledge. Then if the two phrases are combined, it is Mālik in particular by his words, 'a man of knowledge at Madina.' All of the scholars of Madina are included under the other expression.

One of the Mālikīs said, 'When the great number of those who related from Malik among the scholars who preceded him, were contemporary with him or after him, are considered according to their different generations, lands and the frequency with which they travelled to him, and the reliance they placed on him in his time, that indicates without a doubt that he is the one who is meant by the *ḥadīth* since we do not find another among the scholars of Madina who preceded him or came after him among those who transmitted took except that it is part of what we found that he had.

'Those who transmitted from him have been compiled together by more than one person, and some of them went on to name a thousand transmitters in those who were known to transmit from him, let alone those he did not know. I have gathered from their *Collection* more than thirteen hundred transmitters. The great number who went to him indicates to him that he was the man with the most knowledge in his time. That is the state and the quality which the Prophet ﷺ announced. Similarly the early generations did not doubt that he was the one referred to in the *ḥadīth*. The *ḥadīth* is counted as one of the Prophet's miracles and signs in which he mentioned matters that occurred as he had foreseen.'

Qāḍī Abū Muḥammad 'Abd al-Wahhāb said that it means that none of the masters of the schools dispute this claim this since none of them have an Imām from the people of Madina. He says, 'What is meant by it is my Imām, and we claim that he is our companion by the testimony of the early generations for him. When he is designated by the people of knowledge, they say, "the man of knowledge of Madina and the Imām of the Abode of the *hijra*." They meant Mālik by that rather than any other of its scholars. Similarly, when they say "the Kufan", they meant Abū Ḥanīfa rather than the the other *fuqahā'* of Kufa.'

Qāḍī Abū al-Faḍl said that there are three aspects to the proof that this *ḥadīth* refers to Mālik.

The first aspect is imitating the early generations in the belief that he was the one meant by the *ḥadīth* according to what we have transmitted from them. They only said that by exact determination, and they did not state that by caprice. They were free of caprice as they were also free of the rivalry of generations and the natural tendency towards unfairness among peers. Therefore how can it be the opposite of this?

The second aspect is that if you consider what we have related and provided of the testimony of the virtuous *Salaf* that he was the most knowing of people, the Imām of the people, the man of knowledge of Madina, the Imām of the Abode of the *Hijra*, The *Amīr al-Mu'minīn* in *ḥadīth*, the most knowing of the men of knowledge of Madina, and they relied on him, followed him, agreed to advance him, and you have read the like of this in what we will bring of his reports about him, it will be evident that he is the one who is meant by the *ḥadīth* since these qualities have not been acquired by anyone else, nor do they agree on this testimony for anyone else.

The third aspect is what one of the shaykhs stated: that the seekers of knowledge did not flog their camels from the east and west of the earth to any man of knowledge nor ride their mounts to him from all directions except for Mālik because of the precedence which they believed he held over all the men of knowledge of his time. If they had believed that about someone else, they would have sought him out.

People are too astute to praise a man
without finding the marks of excellence on him.

The second probability in this section is by way of transmission.

Relying on it is pure *taqlīd* of the *Salaf* and the Imāms of the Muslims and their scholars in the question of admitting that Malik was the one with the most knowledge of his time and their Imāms and the most knowledgeable of people and the most knowing of the men of knowledge of Madina and other things like this which testify to that for him and their admission of it, their imitation of him and following him when many of them were firmly rooted in knowledge. They preferred his school to the school of others as we will bring in the two chapters later on their praise of him and their following him when we mention his qualities and virtue. It covers two extensive chapters.

We will mention some indications of that which will indicate what lies beyond it, Allah willing.

Part of that is that Ibn Hurmuz, his shaykh, said of him: 'He is the man of knowledge of the people.'

When Sufyān ibn 'Uyayna heard of his death, he remarked, 'His like is not left on the earth.' He said, 'Mālik is the Imām. Mālik is the lamp of the community. Where are we in relation in Mālik? We would follow the tracks of Mālik.'

Ash-Shāfi'ī said, 'Mālik is my master and I took knowledge from him and there was none more gracious to me than Mālik. I have put Mālik between me and Allah as a proof. When scholars are mentioned, Mālik is the piercing star. None has reached Mālik's level in knowledge by his retention, his proficiency, and his care.'

He said, 'Knowledge revolved around three men: Mālik, al-Layth and Sufyān ibn 'Uyayna.'

It is related that al-Awzā'ī said when Mālik was mentioned, 'The man of knowledge of the men of knowledge, the man of knowledge of the people of Madina, and the *muftī* of the Ḥarams of Makka and Madina.'

Baqiyya ibn al-Walīd said, 'There is no one on the face of the earth with more knowledge of the past or remaining *sunna* than you, Malik.'

Abū Yūsuf said, 'I have not seen anyone with more knowledge than three men.' He mentioned Mālik, Abū Ḥanīfa and Ibn Abī Laylā.

Ibn Mahdī said when he was asked about Mālik and Abū Ḥanīfa, 'Mālik has more knowledge than the master, Abū Ḥanīfa.'

Ibn Ḥanbal put him ahead ofal-Awzā'ī, ath-Thawrī, al-Layth, Ḥammād ibn Zayd and al-Ḥakam in knowledge. He said, 'He is the Imām in *ḥadīths* and *fiqh*.' He was asked about someone who wanted to write *ḥadīths* and study *fiqh*, 'Which *ḥadīths* should he write? Whose opinions should he look into?' He replied, 'The *ḥadīths* of Mālik and Mālik's opinion.'

Yaḥyā ibn Sa'īd al-Qaṭṭān said, 'Mālik is the Imām to be followed.'

Ibn Ma'īn said, 'Mālik is one of the proofs of Allah to His creation. He is one of the Imāms of the Muslims, one whose excellence is unanimously agreed upon.'

Ayyūb ibn Suwayd said, 'Mālik is the Imām of the Abode of the *Hijra*.'

Abū Ja'far al-Manṣūr (the Abbasid caliph) said to him, 'He is the most knowledgeable of the people of the earth.'

Sa'īd ibn al-Ḥaddād said, 'Mālik was one of those firmly rooted in Islam, firmer in knowledge than the unshakeable mountains.'

Ḥumayd ibn al-Aswad said, 'The Imām of the people with us after 'Umar was Zayd ibn Thābit, and after him it was 'Abdullāh ibn 'Umar.'

'Alī ibn al-Madīnī said, 'Among those who followed the opinion of Zayd, twenty-one took from him. Then the knowledge of those men went to three men: Ibn Shihāb, Bukayr ibn 'Abdullāh and Abū az-Zinād. The knowledge of all of those went to Mālik ibn Anas.'

Asad ibn al-Furāt said, 'If you desire Allah and the Next World, then you must have Mālik ibn Anas.'

Ḥammād ibn Zayd said, 'I entered Madina when a caller

announced, "Only Mālik ibn Anas gives people *fatwā* and *ḥadīths* in the mosque of the Messenger of Allah ﷺ.'"

We will present these testimonies and acknowledgements in full later.

Yaḥyā ibn Sa'īd, his shaykh, al-Awzā'ī, al-Layth, Ibn al-Mubārak and a group of similar individuals and those after them like al-Bukhārī, Muḥammad ibn 'Abd al-Ḥakam, Abū Zur'a ar-Rāzī and innumerable others recognised his knowledge and that he was an Imām.

Similarly we mentioned in another chapter that the early generations and the people of his age among the scholars and all people followed him. We will mention something of that here.

Sa'īd ibn Manṣūr said, 'I saw Mālik doing *ṭawāf* with Sufyān ath-Thawrī behind him. Whenever Mālik did something, Sufyān did it as well and followed him.'

Ibn Abī Uways said, 'All of the people used to start from the opinion of Mālik. The governor had a man accompanying him to question him. It was the same with the Qāḍī and the *Muḥtasib*.'

A man asked Ibn 'Uyayna about the sacrifice (*ḍaḥiya*, done at the time of *ḥajj*) when done at night. Sufyān said to him, 'There is no harm in that.' Ibn Wahb said to him, 'Mālik said, "Do not sacrifice at night." He recited, "*in known days.*" (22:28)' Sufyān called the man and said, 'This one has informed me that Mālik said, "Do not sacrifice at night."'

Ḥumayd ibn al-Aswad said, 'After Zayd ibn Thābit the people of Madina did not follow anyone as they followed the words of Mālik.'

'Atīq ibn Ya'qūb said, 'After the death of the Prophet ﷺ, no one at Madina agreed on anyone except for Abū Bakr and 'Umar. Mālik died and we do not know of any of the people of Madina who did not agree on him.'

You will read later in this chapter the rest of what is like what we mentioned, Allah willing.

The second section in its probability is by means of consideration and investigation. It has three points.

The first point is that we will make it clear that Mālik combined the degrees of *ijtihād* in the *dīn* and that he possessed the qualities of perfection in knowledge. In all of that he reached the position which none of those who are imitated had reached, pursuing the goal of the truth by that without relying on any partisanship, speaking truthfully, maintaining moderation in what he remembered, not deeming it permissible to harm the honour of any of the Imāms and the leaders of creation. This is where the battles of controversy and struggle and the impetus for bias and obstinacy originates.

I say, asking Allah for help, that it is evident to a fair-minded person that one cannot conceal the position of Mālik being the Imām in the sciences of the *Sharī'a* and the knowledge of the Book and the *Sunna*, and that he is the Imām of the Muslims and the one with the most knowledge among them in his time regarding the past and remaining *Sunna*, and the Amīr al-Mu'minīn in *ḥadīth* and the knowledge of disagreement and agreement. All of this is part of what neither the opponent nor the friend rejects unless his heart is stamped with fanaticism. That is strength in the *Sunna*. He was the first of those who wrote and he did so with proficiency. He organised books and chapters, and corrected the obscure and wrote in a manner which the writers after him have used as a model and a guide until this very day in all areas of the earth. This is in spite of the challenges associated with being the first to do something and the inherent confusion involved in invention. He was the first to speak on the rare words of *ḥadīths* and to explain much of that in his *Muwaṭṭā'*. Al-Aṣma'ī said, 'Mālik informed me that '*istinjār*' means to clean oneself with stones after going to the lavatory, and I only heard that from Mālik.'

He also spoke a lot on *tafsīr* of the Qur'an and it has been gathered, and his *tafsīr* has been related from him by some of his companions. Abū Muḥammad Makkī compiled a book in which he related from him *tafsīr*, discussion on the meanings and judgements of the Qur'an, its *tajwīd* and precise vowelisation of its letters. Abū 'Amr al-Muqri' mentioned it in his book on the generations of the reciters of the early men, and he mentioned that its *riwāya* is from Nāfi'.

Al-Bahlūl ibn Rāshid and others said, 'I have not seen anyone who used an *āyat* of the Book of Allah in refutation more than Mālik ibn Anas, utilising his knowledge of the sound and weak, what is acted upon in *ḥadīth* and what is abandoned, his distinguishing the men, the soundness of his memory and his immense powers of critical examination, and what was related from him in other areas of knowledge – like his letter to Ibn Wahb refuting the people of *Qadar* (predestination) and like his words, "I have sat with Ibn Hurmuz for thirteen years (and sixteen years is related) in a knowledge which I did not disseminate to any of the people."'

He said, 'He was one of the people with the most knowledge of refutation against the people of sects and that about which the people disagreed.'

Al-Mahdī said, 'One of the Mu'tazilite critics from Kairouan told me, "I went to Mālik ibn Anas, and I asked him in the presence of the people about a question dealing with predestination. He indicated that I should be silent. When the assembly was over, he said to me, 'Ask now.' He did not want to answer me in the presence of other people." The Mu'tazilite questioned him about every one of their positions and Mālik refuted them all and established the falseness of their school until he had gone through what the Mu'tazilite had and he left him.

He wrote about the times and the stars and his indications of the sources of *fiqh* and its roots which the people of fundamentals among his companions took as waymarks for guidance and rules which they used as a foundation. Others whom we mentioned did not have all of this nor reach this degree in spite of the *fiqh* and knowledge they possessed. '*But over everyone with knowledge is a Knower*' (12:76) with complete reliability, *taqwā* and intense investigation into *ḥadīth* and *fiqh*.

In this way, ash-Shāfi'ī refuted Muḥammad ibn al-Ḥasan [ash-Shaybānī], proving that the knowledge of Mālik was better than the knowledge of Abū Ḥanīfa when they argued about that. Ash-Shāfi'ī asked him, 'Do you want fairness or self-importance?' He replied, 'Fairness.'

Ash-Shāfi'ī said, 'I ask you by Allah, who is the one with the most knowledge of the Book of Allah and what abrogates and is abrogated?' Muḥammad ibn al-Ḥasan answered, 'O Allah, your man.'

Ash-Shāfi'ī said, 'I ask you by Allah, who has the most knowledge of the *Sunna* of the Messenger of Allah ﷺ?' He replied, 'O Allah, your man.'

Ash-Shāfiʿī asked, 'Who has the most knowledge of the words of the Companions of the Messenger of Allah ﷺ?' He responded, 'O Allah, your man.'

Ash-Shāfiʿī said, 'Only analogy remains.' Muḥammad said, 'Our man is better in analogy.'

Ash-Shāfiʿī said, 'Analogy is only through these things, so on what basis do you make your analogy?' Then ash-Shāfiʿī said, 'We claim for our man what you do not claim for yours.'

In one version, 'Analogy was not vague for our man, but he protected himself and made careful investigation.' He meant that he based himself on those before him.

May Allah have mercy on ash-Shāfiʿī and Muḥammad ibn al-Ḥasan! They were fair. That which ash-Shāfiʿī said was the absolute truth. *Ijtihād*, analogy and derivation are based on the fundamental roots. When someone has the most knowledge of the roots, his derivation is sounder and his analogy is truer. If this is not the case, and his knowledge of the fundamentals is deficient, he makes analogy based on delusion and builds on the edge of the precipice of an abyss.

Imām Abū Isḥāq ash-Shīrāzī employed this account as a proof against the people of Khurasan when they restricted their investigation to questions of analogy which they called '*ṭubūliyyāt*' due to the discussion resulting in it. The debate among its people went on at length. Subsequently there was agreement about what ash-Shāfiʿī said, and it is the statement of all the scholars: *ijtihād* and analogy are only valid for those who possess all the necessary tools: knowledge of the Book and the *Sunna* and deploy that as necessary. Then they add to that the tools of *ijtihād* and understanding phrases, meanings, conjugation and declination which cannot be dispensed with. Then they must know the areas of consensus and agreement, and the questions of the dispute. When any of that is lacking in a scholar, it diminishes his leadership and decreases his perfection, and so his *ijtihād* is not valid and he is not allowed to speculate in the *dīn* unless he possesses all of that. When these fundamentals are imperfect, neither *ijtihād* in the *dīn* nor issuing *fatwās* between the Muslims nor analogy is permitted him according to what he did not obtain.

It has been confirmed by both his friends and opponents that

Mālik possessed these fundamental principles. One does not pay any attention to a fanatical partisan bleating at the end of time attempting to detract from him in *ijtihād*. That only diminishes that critic. It is clearly stated that Mālik is the man with the most knowledge among the men of knowledge of Madina and the Amīr al-Mu'minīn in *Ḥadīth*. The statement that his Imām was ash-Shāfi'ī is a lie and patently absurd. The virtuous *Salaf*, the Imāms of guidance, and the notable men of the scholars whom we mentioned and those we will mention, Allah willing, disagreed with this assertion and testified that what the partisan critic said is absurd and is sheer ignorance.

Then we looked at the Imāms who are imitated in this time, and we did not find that any of them possessed what he had of that, nor were they proficient in these fundamentals to the level that he was.

As for Abū Ḥanīfa and ash-Shāfi'ī, they had excellent analysis as well as precision in investigation, analogy, excellent *fiqh* and were Imāms in it.. However, they were not Imāms in *ḥadīth* or knowledge of it. They did not master its science and they did not claim that nor was it claimed for them. The people of this science consider them weak in it. The people of the *Ṣaḥīḥ Collection*s did not relate a single letter from them nor are they mentioned at all in most *Collection*s.

Even though ash-Shafi'i pursued *ḥadīths* and investigated the *sunnas*, that was by *taqlīd* of someone else and relying on the opinion of someone else while acknowledging his own limitations in his knowledge of it. He used to say to Ibn Mahdī and Ibn Ḥanbal, 'You know more *ḥadīths* than I do. tell me what you consider sound and I will take it.' This is a degree which is less than the degree of high *ijtihād*. Where will a *mujtahid* in every age find an Imām in *Ḥadīth* if he himself has not delved deeply into it or in the knowledge of the Qur'an when he himself has not mastered it so that he can ask whether it pertains to an event in which a root is seen? There is no way at all to deny Mālik's imamate in *fiqh*.

In the establishment of the fundamentals, arrangement of the basic rules, organisation of the proofs and sources and the explanation of that, ash-Shāfi'ī possessed an expertise that none before him had. All of those who came after him relied on him in this regard, and he was a master in the science of the Arabic language, particularly in the areas of predicates and relative adjectives. Everyone finds what he was created for made easy.

As Ibn Ḥanbal and Dāwūd were among those knew *ḥadīths*, and the imamate of neither of them is denied in that field, but imamate in *fiqh* was not sound for them nor excellent investigation into its sources. They did not speak on the words of others about many events, and they inclined to what was understood from *ḥadīths*. In fact, Dāwūd follows the path of those who take the literal meaning and he rejects analogy. He opposed the early generations and the later ones as well as what proceeded of the behaviour of the Companions and those after them until one of the scholars stated, 'His school is an innovation which appeared after 200 AH.' Qāḍī Ismā'īl objected to that position of his in the strongest possible terms. Since he did not advocate the use of analogy, which is one of the pillars of *ijtihād* for those who practise it, then on what does he rely when no text exists? It is not appropriate to criticise an individual for their inferiority in a particular science when his rank falls below that of another. Each of them possessed virtues and excellence which would fill numerous pages, and the early generations and the later ones transmitted that. However, lacking one of the pillars of *ijtihād* detracts from him in any case, and Allah is the master of right guidance.

The second point is turning to the source of all in their *fiqh* and their manner of investigation in their knowledge since individual events and the ramifications of occurrences arise whose correctness is only perceived by those who are occupied with knowledge. It takes a long time to make it clear to others, and it is only perceived over a period of time in which lives end and the years pass. The beginner reckons that it will reveal itself to him through an allusion which the intelligent man understands and he will answer it with a correct probability. We have mentioned the qualities of *ijtihād*, and then its sources.

The sources are organised according to what logic demands and that to which the *Sharī'a* testifies:

The Book of Allah Almighty is put first in the order of the clarification of its proofs derived from its unequivocal texts, then its probable texts, and then what is understood from it.

It is the same with the *Sunna* of the Messenger of Allah ﷺ according to the order: multiple transmission, famous traditions, and single traditions.

Then its texts are put in order: unequivocal texts (*nuṣūṣ*), probable texts (*ẓawāhir*) and understood texts according to what preceded regarding the Book.

Then comes consensus in the absence of the Book and multiple transmissions.

After that, if these bases are lacking, then comes analogy based on them and deduction from them since the Book of Allah is absolute as is the case with what comes with multiple transmission from the *Sunna* of the Prophet ﷺ.

It is like that with unequivocal and explicit texts, and all of that must be placed first. Then come probable texts. Then comes what is understood from them when the meaning is probable.

Then individual reports must be acted on and referred to in the absence a text of the Book and multiple transmission. They are advanced before analogy by the consensus of the Companions in both cases. They would abandon their own speculation when a tradition of a reliable person reached them from the Prophet ﷺ. They obeyed what it necessitated without any opposition to that.

Then analogy is last since one resorts to it when these bases are lacking in the event and one derives from its proof and considers things like it according to what the Companions and the pleasing *Salaf* did after them and what is known from the schools of all of them.

When you examine the methods of these Imāms and the establishment of their sources in *fiqh* and *ijtihād* in the *Sharī'a*, you will find that Mālik pursued clear methods in these fundamentals and placed them in their proper ranks and degrees. He put the Book of Allah first, and then put the traditions with it. He placed them before analogy and consideration. He left of it what was not considered probable by reliable men known for what they took on themselves or for what he found that the masses and a great number of the people of Madina did contrary to it. He did not pay any attention to the one who interpreted it by his own supposition with a bad interpretation in this manner and attributed to it what it did not say. Indeed, he explicitly declared that it was false and baseless. Then he hesitated about obscure things and inquired into discussion about things which were difficult to explain as was the path of the righteous *Salaf*. He preferred following and disliked innovation and departure from the *sunan* of past men.

Then ash-Shāfi'ī embarked on his scholarly journey and expanded his sources in *fiqh* and the fundamentals. However, he differed from Mālik in certain things to which his *ijtihād* and keen intelligence had led him. His lack of competence in the science of *ḥadīth* and tradition did not stop him from reaching that conclusion in his recognition. Then there occurred what passed between him and some of the Mālikīs in Egypt and their attack on him so that he set himself apart from them after he had been counted among them and considered as one of their number. This separation resulted in his estrangement from his people and students. Then he clearly articulated the disagreement and refutation of the greatest of his masters as we will mention in his reports later, Allah willing, in his story with Fityān ibn Abī as-Samḥ and his ganging up against him and the later trial of Fityān and the development of mutual aversion between him and their group because of that.

Section

As for Abū Ḥanīfa, he advocated putting analogy and consideration before the *sunan* and traditions. He abandoned the texts of the roots and held to what was known by the intellect. He preferred opinion, analogy, and *istiḥsān*. Then he put *istiḥsān* before analogy, be that as probable as he wished. (*Istiḥsān* is roughly the application of one's own personal opinion and discretion in a decision).

One of them defined *istiḥsān* as 'inclination to the statement without a proof'. This is blameworthy personal inclination, appetite, innovation and invention in the *dīn* so that ash-Shāfi'ī said, 'Whoever uses *istiḥsān* has legislated in the *dīn*.' This is why his people, Muḥammad [ibn al-Ḥasan] and Abū Yūsuf, differed from him in about a third of his school when they found that the *sunan* contradicted them in what he had left by what we mentioned, either intentionally in order to convey analogy and to put it first, or what did not reach him and he did not know it since he was not one of those who were well-versed in its sciences. He was condemned for it, and the insolent rush to blame the innocent through the attack. Then those *sunan* to which he clung were not agreed upon and they are weak and abandoned *ḥadīths*.

As a result, the party of the People of *Ḥadīth* rallied against the People of Opinion, and they maligned them in speech and opinion. Aḥmad ibn Ḥanbal said, 'We continued to curse the People of Opinion and they cursed us until ash-Shāfi'ī came and joined us together.' He meant that he achieved this by holding to the sound traditions and using them. Then he showed them that opinion which was necessary and on which the rules of the Sharī'a are based, and that analogy is based on its roots and taken from them. He showed them how to derive it and the connection to its causes and its cautions. The People of *Ḥadīth* then recognised that sound opinion is a branch of the root, and the People of Opinion realised that there is no branch without the root. The *sunan* and sound traditions must be put first.

Similar to this in this area is the statement of Ibn Wahb, '*Ḥadīths* can misguide people other than the scholars. Had it nor been for Mālik and al-Layth, we would have been misguided.'

As for Ibn Ḥanbal and Dāwūd, they travelled the path of following the traditions and they swerved from the path of due consideration. However, Dāwūd went to excess in that and abandoned analogy all together, and he and his people spoke from the word by the literal meaning in a manner which was contrary to the Imāms of the community. Clinging to a fourth of the proofs of the Sharī'a deceived him and he turned away from what was given impetus from *ijtihād* and reflection. He called whatever he did not find a text for or a literal meaning *'afwu* (effacement) and he applied permissibility to some of it. The statements of his people clashed in that because of the narrowness of the path in it. Therefore his school fell apart and his viewpoint was deficient. The followers of the literal text made statements, many of which are rejected when they are heard and the intellect dislikes them.

Ibn Ḥanbal said, 'I consider the weak *ḥadīth* to be better than analogy,' and 'The intuition of the intellect rejects this. There is no good in building without a foundation.'

This is about the excellence of a noble person which will indicate to the unbiased person the one among them who travels the open road.

The third point requires profound reflection, an unbiased perspective and exact precision. It involves examining the principles of the Sharī'a and those things which are agreed upon in it, and understanding the wisdom intended in that by the Lawgiver.

We say that the judgements of the Sharī'a, or its commands and prohibitions, call for encouragement to perform good actions and those actions which bring one closer to Allah, restraint from detested things and shameless actions, and allowing what is good for this world and that which will foster its prosperity for humanity. The contents of *fiqh* and the topics of its books all deal with these words. We will point out indications of the entirety of these principles so that things will be clear to the investigator who pursues the intended meaning of the Sharī'a or what differs in it and diverges from the correct and deviates from the path of right guidance. In all of that Mālik was the most guided on the way, the most direct in speech and the soundest in roots and branches.

The first thing to discuss in its topics is purification which the Giver of the Shari'a explicitly stated is half of belief. (Muslim 1:80) Allah commands purification from minor impurity and impure things and stipulates that it should be done with water when He says, *'water to purify you with'* (8:11) and *'He sent down pure water from heaven.'* (25:48)

Abū Ḥanīfa is the one who thought that purification from minor impurity is permitted with *nabīdh* during a journey when water is unavailable, although most scholars judge that what reaches *nabīdh* is impure and *ḥarām*. In his opinion, it is permitted to purify oneself from the impure thing with any type of *nabīdh* or liquid, be it vinegar, bitter liquids, honey or milk. Both he and ash-Shāfi'ī, in one of two views, allow every water which has something added to it and which is changed by the addition, even if it is with tar or its like, as long as that does not predominate it.

Do you think the the two of them interpret the expressions 'purification' and 'cleansing' as having a specific quantity when a limb is further spoiled by that, or do they make a special ruling for water or a special meaning for purification?

Similarly, ash-Shāfiʿī and Ibn Ḥanbal stipulated the amount held by two jugs (216 litres) as a precondition for water into which the impure things falls (remaining pure), but their *ḥadīth* is not firm and their estimation is a guess and surmise which is not agreed upon nor is their statement regarding it confirmed. If a small jug lacks that amount, the impure thing affects it. When a small impurity falls into many small jugs, all of them are impure as long as they are separate. When they are together in the pond, they become pure. If he scoops up water the amount of the two jugs with an impure vessel, what is in the vessel is pure while the rest of the two jugs are impure. This leads to misgiving in this area. All of it is far from correct so that many of his people said, 'The precondition of the two jugs is the source of misgivings.'

It is the same with Dāwūd when he confined himself to the prohibition against urinating in standing water by taking only its literal meaning. That does not spoil it in his opinion. The prohibition only applies the one who urinates in it. So if someone urinates in a small jug and pours it into it or defecates in it or urinates near it and his urine flows into it – all of this is not included under the prohibition in his opinion and none of that spoils the water unless it changes it. Does he not know absolutely that this is contrary to what the Sharī'a meant and forbade?

Another example of misinterpretation is what they understood of the specification of some of the limbs for *wuḍū'* with the previous meaning of cleaning and betterment which is the meaning of *wuḍū'* since those limbs – the face, the hands, the head, and the feet – are the parts of human beings which are generally apparent and that which always needs to be cleaned and improved. As for the hands and feet, then one takes care with them from actions which are followed by dirt and filth and what they encounter of things which result in dirt and filth. Look at the one who does not concern himself with *wuḍū'* with water and purification among the people of the deserts and the boorish bedouins. The dirt is black on his finger joints and knuckles and the periodic filth piles up in black on his elbows and wrists.

Similarly, the face is the distinguishing feature of the descendant of Ādam and his countenance, his form and mien with which Allah has honoured him. It is the focal point for the assault of the heat of the midday sun and the recipient of the dust of feet and hooves. It contains the pores of the skin which discharge their filth there along with the motes of the eye, the snot of the nose and the spit of the mouth. All that needs to be cleaned. Allah prescribed washing and repetition for all of it. Since the head is generally covered, he prescribed wiping, being content to rub it with water to remove its unkemptness because washing it with every minor impurity is part of what would split and destroy it.

Was ash-Shāfi'ī faithful to this root when he was content with pouring water without rubbing and with wiping one or three hairs of the entire head? Or Abū Ḥanīfa when he was content with the forelock? Or ath-Thawrī with a single hair?

There is no objection to the easing in that when *tayammum* is a substitute for *wuḍū'* in the absence of water. There is no cleaning or amelioration in it. It is the opposite of that.

Know that this has a wondrous secret in the Sharī'a in the case of someone who lacks water for purification. It is repetitive and harsh on wounds. The prayer is done without it for as long as this state persists. The soul relies on it by its love for equanimity but it is feared that it will adapt that as a habit. Therefore the Sharī'a prescribed *tayammum* to warn that the prayer is only allowed in a state of purity and so that the self will continue to employ purity. He prescribed what is not lacking on the face of the earth and made its state easier for certain limbs. There is a ruling in all of that. Allah knows best and He gives success.

Similarly the Prophet ﷺ said, 'Actions are according to intentions.' (al-Bukhārī) Yet Abū Ḥanīfa and ath-Thawrī thought that the purification for the prayer is allowed without the intention while it begins the most glorious of acts of nearness. They make a distinction between it and *tayammum* without any proof at all except by illusions which lack validity. Al-Awzā'ī treated all actions the same and he did not make the intention obligatory.

Then we move to the most glorious acts which bring us near to Allah along with the words of the *shahāda*. That is the prayer and *zakāt*. Abū Ḥanīfa, in his opinion, deemed the prayer allowable by the most lenient criteria among the schools of thought. It is the discipline of the headstrong selves, the polishing of the rusty hearts, the times of humility and intimate conversation and the secret of pure slavedom.

He also thought that there can be legal stratagems which remove *zakāt* after it is obligatory at the beginning of the year by transferring it from the person's property outwardly by what someone else agrees to repay to him after the year. *Zakāt* is the purification of property and the proof of the soundness of belief as the Prophet ﷺ said, '*Ṣadaqa* [i.e. *zakāt*] is a proof' (Muslim) and meeting the neediness of the weak. The Sharī'a forbade legal stratagems of dispersal and conglomeration. It forbade duplicity and fraud.

Can the one who says this about these two pillars fulfil its covenant? Is his action consistent with the meaning given to it in th*e Sharī'a* and its judgement?

It is like that with the prohibition against drinking wine. The reason for that is that it results in and hate, and hinders remembrance of Allah and the prayer. The first Companions understood the meaning when the *āyat* was revealed, so they applied it universally. The Prophet ﷺ said, 'Every intoxicant is wine, and every wine is unlawful.' (an-Nasā'ī)

Any of the people of Kufa who make a distinction between raw grapes and cooked ones and all intoxicants allows them as long as the person does not reach the level of lack of discrimination has opposed the two basic principles, and thus has destroyed the basis of the Sharī'a in the two areas.

Then we look at the private parts, and it is absolutely certain that the wisdom of Allah lies in protecting them. This is why He made the greatest and ugliest of the *ḥadd* punishments apply to those who prefer fornication over what is permitted for them through marriage and ownership in the manners which the Sharī'a has permitted for the welfare of this creation and maintaining distinction and mutual recognition for these offspring.

If someone thinks that prostitution removes the *ḥadd* punishment prescribed for it and that someone who fornicates with someone he has employed does not have any *ḥadd* punishment inflicted on him because of the terms of employment, and similarly believes that sodomy between two men – which is the most atrocious of foul actions – does not entail any *ḥadd* punishment, but rather disciplinary punishment according to his position and that of the people of literal interpretation, he has violated what the Sharī'a has laid down and undermined the basis of this principle.

Similarly, Allah made lives and honour sacrosanct with the strongest possible prohibition and for those who violate them He obliged the infliction of the *ḥadd* punishment and a painful punishment. He protected property for its owners except for what it due from it, and He laid down the *ḥadd* punishment of amputation for those who steal and execution for those who commit violence to obtain it (meaning highway robbery).

So what of the statement about cancelling the *ḥadd* punishment for someone who steals any fresh sort of food to such an extent that if the thief puts a drop of honey or water in a gold cistern and then steals it, his hand is not cut off for it?

It is like that when he removes the *ḥadd* punishment for the theft of all whose root is permitted in the form of valuable jewels, the extracts of valuable minerals, and the precious things cast up by the sea, and removes the *hadd* punishment from those who steal the shrouds of the dead, those who open the locks protecting property and make it easy to come to attack much of it without any great fear of punishment, especially in his school and the school of Dāwūd who make the disciplinary punishment light and their being content with that being very light indeed.

It is like that when he said, 'Whoever takes a man's garment and spoils it, or his sheep and then slaughters and cooks it, that has become his property and his possession, and his liability is that he pays its price to its owner as he would desire if the capital existed, even if it does not exist so that he can obtain it.' This is without paying any attention whatsoever to the prohibitions of the Sharī'a about infractions. It perpetuates the usurpation of property and allows it to be taken from the hands of its owners without paying its price.

Then Allah appointed retaliation as life and an obstacle for aggressors. Abū Ḥanīfa said that the one who kills people without doing it by an iron implement, such as burning, drowning, strangling, poison and other type types of attack and injustice, is not subject to retaliation for it. He has nullified this root and made an opening for criminals to commit the most horrendous sorts of murder while remaining safe from retaliation for this action.

Similarly the domain of honour is guarded and its respect is protected by the *ḥadd* punishment inflicted on slanderers. Ash-Shāfi'ī is the one who did not think that there was a *ḥadd* punishment for implied and hidden slander. He thought that if a group of notorious corrupt people who were the number required for the witnesses to fornication and more were to come to the assemblies of the judges and clearly state the slander of the best of people, the *ḥadd* punishment would not be obliged against them because of this position.

Is every corrupt rash person able to destroy the honour of every innocent Muslim with various types of ugly slander or by offering testimony about clear abominations with his ilk at the front of the assembly as they are given the means, even if their testimony is unacceptable, and they are safe from the *ḥadd* punishment so that sound flesh is rent?

It is quite evident that the wisdom of Allah in establishing the judgement and the decision is to verify the truth and to invalidate the false by the principle of outward proofs and to put an end to dispute and argument between the litigants. Their judgement by that takes effect while inward affairs are left to Allah. Whoever attempts to deceive Allah has only deceived himself. The altering of the judgement of man inwardly is ceded to the judgement of Allah and His wisdom by the words of the Prophet ﷺ, 'The company of the Prophets judge by the outward, and Allah takes charge of the secrets.' It is related: 'Allah takes charge of the inward.' One version has, 'I am commanded to judge by the outward and Allah takes charge of the secrets.' The Prophet ﷺ said, 'Perhaps one of you is more eloquent in his argument than the other, and I will give judgement according to what I have heard from him. Whatever I decide for him which is part of the right of his brother, he must not take any of it, for I am granting him a portion of the Fire.' (*Muwaṭṭā'*, al-Bukhārī, etc.)

Abū Ḥanīfa held the opinion that a *qāḍī* should give judgement based on the testimony of false witnesses in the case of the marriage of a woman or the transfer of property which allows the one for whom they testify and who bribed them to do so, to have sexual intercourse with that person and to consume that property both secretly and openly, outwardly and inwardly, while he fully knows that that is forbidden and its ascription to him is false. Similarly, he said about the person who unlawfully appropriates a slave-girl and then later claims that she has died that the judgement is that he pays her price. Then that man reveals that she is alive and healthy, and she is lawful for him. It is like that in his opinion about when a woman uses a legal stratagem by two false witnesses who testify that her husband has divorced her. The *qāḍī* gives judgement based on that and makes her lawful for another man, even if he was one of the two witnesses.

May Allah give you success! Where is this in relation to what is desired by the *Sharī'a* and its goal to make the barrier and prohibition harsh in making the private parts lawful without right? Does this make it difficult for the corrupt person to attain his lust on whatever chaste women are prohibited him or does it forbid any appetite?

We ask Allah for success by His mercy. He protects and is not exhausted.

May Allah give you success! There are five probabilities, all of which demand certainty, and the clarification of the clear truth despite the partisans. It is enough for the one who looks into this last consideration to have good interpretation first and general interpretation last. We do not wish to give cause in it for the injury of any of the Imāms nor to harm the honour of the *Salaf* and the community. However, we recognise the Truth and its people. In spite of that, we do not deny the advancement and excellence of any of them. The fortunate one is the one whose mistakes are abandoned.

'Who is given perfection so that he is perfect?'

Then we will provide the reports about Mālik, his biography, and his general history and reports, chapter by chapter, as we have already promised, and we will begin with the presentation of the discussion of his lineage. Then we will present the generations of his companions, one after the other, and the notable men of his school, group by group. Allah gives help to realise what He allows to flow on our tongues of that. There is no god but Him.

The Lineage of Mālik ibn Anas al-Aṣbaḥī

The Qāḍī said: Ismā'īl ibn Abī Uways said in what Qāḍī az-Zubayr ibn Bakkār and others related from him that his name is Mālik ibn Anas ibn Mālik ibn Abī 'Āmir ibn 'Amr ibn al-Ḥārith ibn Ghaymān ibn Khuthayl ibn 'Amr ibn al-Ḥārith, who is Dhū Aṣbaḥ. Furthermore, the name is 'Ghayman'. That is how more than one person mentioned it. That is how Amīr Abū Naṣr ibn Makūlā recorded it and related it from Ismā'īl ibn Abī Uways. The name is 'Khuthayl'. This is sound, and that is how the Amīr Abū Naṣr ibn Makūlā recorded it and made it exact and precise. He related it from Muḥammad ibn Sa'd from Abū Bakr ibn Abī Uways.

Abū al-Ḥasan ad-Dāraquṭnī and others said, 'It is Juthayl,' and he related that from az-Zubayr. As for those who say, "Uthmān ibn Ḥisl' or 'Ibn Ḥanbal', that is a mistake.

As for Dhū Aṣbaḥ, there is great disagreement about his lineage. Az-Zubayr said that he was Dhū Aṣbaḥ ibn Suwayd ibn 'Amr ibn Sa'd ibn 'Awf ibn 'Adī ibn Mālik ibn Zayd ibn Sadad ibn Ḥimyar al-Aṣghar ibn Sabā' al-Aṣghar ibn Ka'b ibn Kahf aẓ-Ẓulm ibn Zayd ibn Sahl ibn 'Amr ibn Qays ibn Mu'āwiya ibn Jushum ibn 'Abd Shams ibn Wā'il ibn al-Ghayth ibn Qaṭn ibn Abyan ibn Zuhayr ibn al-Ghayth ibn Aymān ibn al-Hamaysa' ibn Ḥimyar ibn Sabā' al-Akbar who is 'Abd Shams (and he is called Sabā' because he was the first to take captives and raid the tribes) ibn Ya'rub ibn Yashjub ibn Qaḥṭān.

Another said that he is Dhū Aṣbaḥ al-Ḥārith ibn 'Awf ibn Mālik ibn Zayd ibn Shaddād ibn Zur'a, and he is Ḥimyar al-Aṣghar ibn Sabā' al-Aṣghar ibn Ḥimyar al-Akbar ibn Sabā' al-Akbar ibn Yashjub ibn Qaḥṭān.

It is said that he is Dhū Aṣbaḥ ibn Mālik ibn Zayd ibn 'Awf ibn Sa'īd ibn 'Ufayr ibn Mālik ibn Zayd ibn Sahl.

It is said that he is Ibn Mālik ibn Zayd ibn al-Ghayth ibn Sa'd ibn 'Awf ibn Nabt ibn Mālik ibn Zayd ibn Zayd ibn Sahl ibn 'Amr ibn Qays ibn Mu'āwiya ibn Jushum ibn 'Abd Shams.

It is said that he is ibn 'Awf ibn Mālik ibn Zayd ibn 'Amr ibn Rabī'a ibn Nabt ibn Mālik ibn Zayd ibn Kahlān ibn Yashjub.

It is said that Dhū Aṣbaḥ and Yashjub were the sons of Mālik ibn Zayd ibn Ḥimyar.

There are the disagreements mentioned in the lineage of Dhū Aṣbaḥ. There is no disagreement that he was from Qaḥṭān.

There is disagreement about the lineage of Qaḥṭān going further back, and whether he was descended from Ismā'īl or not. There was a lot of dispute which cannot be covered completely and it is not our intention here, so we will omit it.

Qāḍī Abū al-Faḍl said:

The scholars of biography, reports and lineages do not dispute this in the lineage of Mālik and that he is connected to Dhū Aṣbaḥ with the exception of what was mentioned from Ibn Isḥāq and others. He stated that he was a client of the Banū Taym. We will clarify the error of the one who said that and the cause which led them to that erroneous impression.

As for Abū 'Abdullāh Muḥammad ibn Ḥamduwayh al-Ḥākim, known as Ibn al-Bayyi', he quite evidently erred horribly, and no one before him or after him made that statement and he made a great mistake in this. He said: "Mālik ibn Anas, the Imām. He is Mālik ibn Anas ibn 'Āmir al-Ḥārith ibn Ghaymān ibn Khuthayl ibn 'Amr ibn al-Ḥārith ibn 'Abd ar-Raḥmān ibn 'Uthmān ibn 'Ubaydullāh from the tribe of Taym ibn Murra who met the Messenger of Allah ﷺ with Murra ibn Ka'b.»

I wonder where he could find this error and from where did it come to him? Then he said in another chapter, "He was from Khawlān." Where does he get this? Both are mistakes.

As for those who claim that he was a client of Taym, this erroneous impression arose when he found that he had connections with them and was considered one of them due to his alliance with them. His lineage from Dhū Aṣbaḥ is sound. More than one of the leaders of Quraysh and their men of lineage and the people of knowledge mentioned that, including Muḥammad ibn 'Imrān aṭ-Ṭalḥī, 'Abd al-Malik ibn Ṣāliḥ, Muṣ'ab ibn Thābit az-Zubayrī, 'Āmir ibn 'Abdullāh az-Zubayrī, Abū Bakr al-'Umarī and his son Ṭalḥa, Abū Muṣ'ab az-Zuhrī, Ibn Abī Khaythama, Aḥmad ibn Ṣāliḥ, Qāḍī az-Zubayr ibn Bakkār, and those after them among the *ḥuffāẓ* like ad-Dāraquṭnī, Qāḍī Abū 'Abdullāh at-Tustarī, Abū Muḥammad aḍ-Ḍarrāb, Abū al-Qāsim al-Jawharī, Abū al-Qāsim al-Lalāka'ī, Abū Naṣr ibn

Makūlā and those who are too many to count. All have their lineage mentioned.

None of those who came after him followed Ibn Isḥāq in his statement. They make the manner of his error quite clear.

'Āmir ibn 'Abdullāh az-Zubayrī mentioned the lineage of Mālik ibn Anas: 'They were from the Arabs of Yemen, with kinship to an-Naḍr ibn Yarīm.'

Ad-Darāwardī said, 'Abū Suhayl ibn Mālik said to me, "We are people from Dhū Aṣbaḥ. No one has given us a *walā'* (client relationship) or treaty."'

Abū Muṣ'ab said, 'Mālik was from the Arabs by blood and his alliance in Quraysh was with the Banū Taym ibn Murra.'

Muhammād ibn 'Imrān answered the one who asked him about him, 'He was a man from the Arabs from Ḥimyar themselves. There is no lineage between him and us except for the fact that his mother was a client of my uncle, 'Uthmān ibn 'Ubaydullāh.'

Abū Bakr al-'Umarī as-Sālimī said, 'Mālik was one of the Arabs, sound in lineage from themselves. He was not one of their clients.'

Muṣ'ab ibn 'Abdullāh az-Zubayrī said, 'The Banū aṣ-Ṣabbāḥ were kings, the tribe of the uncle of Mālik.'

Al-Firyābī said, 'I asked Mus'ab about Mālik. He stated, "A noble Arab, honoured in his place from Dhū Aṣbaḥ, a Yemeni sub-tribe from the kings of the Yemen, the Banū Abraha ibn aṣ-Ṣabbāḥ."'

Aḥmad ibn Ṣāliḥ said, 'Mālik had sound lineage from Dhū Aṣbaḥ.'

The daughter of Ṭalḥa said, 'We did not have any treaty or *walā'* with him,' i.e. the grandfather of Mālik.

When Ziyād ibn 'Ubaydullāh came to Madina, he asked, 'Are there any of the people of knowledge here?' They related Mālik's lineage to him. He stated, 'This is the house of Yemen.' And he was the first from whom he asked *fatwā*.

'Abd al-Malik ibn Ṣāliḥ al-Hāshimī said, 'Mālik ibn Anas was from Dhū Aṣbaḥ.'

Abū al-Muhājir went to 'Uthmān ibn 'Ubaydullāh at-Taymī or someone else, to complain about Abū 'Āmir, the grandfather of Mālik ibn Anas. Abū al-Muhājir was in charge of *ṣadaqa (zakāt)*. He asked at-Taymī, 'Do you absolve me from your client?' He replied, 'He is not my client. He is a man of the Arabs from the people of the Yemen.'

The reason for connecting Mālik and his people to Taym ibn Murra from Quraysh, and his mother's lineage

Abū 'Umar ibn 'Abd al-Barr said, 'I do not know of anyone who denies that Mālik and his descendants were allies of the Banū Taym ibn Murra from Quraysh nor is there is any dispute in it except what was mentioned from Ibn Isḥāq who claimed that he was one of their clients.' He stated, 'It is related that Ibn Shihāb said, "Nāfi' ibn Mālik, the client of Taym, informed me." We do not consider this sound from Ibn Shihāb.'

Imām Qāḍī Abū al-Faḍl said, 'The statement of Ibn Shihāb in this regard is found in the *Ṣaḥīḥ al-Bukhārī* at the beginning of the chapter on fasting. In Arabic, *mawlā* can be used to mean "ally, helper" as well as other things as is known. Perhaps that is what Ibn Shihāb meant. The same is true about what 'Abd al-Malik ibn Ṣāliḥ al-Hāshimī said, "Mālik is from Dhū Aṣbaḥ, the client of Quraysh."'

Az-Zubayr ibn Bakkār said, 'He is counted among the Banū Taym ibn Murra.'

It is related that when the statement of Ibn Shihāb reached him, Mālik said, 'I wish that he had not related anything from me.' [Ibn 'Abd al-Barqī, *al-Intiqā'*, p. 14)

Abū Suhayl, Mālik's uncle stated, 'We are people from Dhū Aṣbaḥ. Our grandfather came to Madina and married among the Taymīs. So he remained with with them and was ascribed to them.' This aligns with the statement of Qāḍī Ibn 'Imrān at-Taymī: 'There is no lineage between him and us except that his mother was a client of my uncle, 'Uthmān ibn 'Ubaydullāh.'

Ar-Rabī' ibn Mālik, the brother of Abū Suhayl, reported from his father: "Abd ar-Raḥmān ibn 'Uthmān ibn 'Ubaydullāh at-Taymī, the nephew of Ṭalḥa, said to me while we were travelling along the Makkan road, "Would you like to have that to which others call us so that we make it clear that our blood will be your blood and what angers us will anger you for as long as the foaming sea remains wet?" And I agreed to that with him.'

'Abdullāh ibn Muṣ'ab said, 'Mālik ibn Abī 'Āmir came to Madina complaining about one of the governors in Yemen. He was partial to one of the Banū Taym ibn Murra and made a treaty with them and joined them.'

It is related that Mālik ibn Abī 'Āmir did not agree to the alliance to which 'Abd ar-Raḥmān ibn 'Uthmān ibn 'Ubaydullāh invited him. He said, 'I have no need of it.' The first is sounder and more widely recognised.

It is mentioned that Abū 'Amir formed an alliance with 'Uthmān ibn 'Ubaydullāh in the *Jāhiliyya*, and that they came to Madina together. It is also said that Abū 'Āmir made an alliance with 'Abdullāh ibn Jud'ān in the *Jāhiliyya*.

Ibn Abī Uways said, 'We became the allies of the Banū Taym, so we prefer to be related to Quraysh than to the Yemen.'

For the reasons previously stated, they were joined to Taym either though an alliance, which is the most well-known and reliable, or by being in-laws. So they were related to Taym. Ibn Isḥāq and those who did not verify the business thought that they were their clients since they did not have any known lineage with them.

As for his mother, az-Zubayr said that she was al-'Āliyya bint Sharīk ibn 'Abd ar-Raḥmān ibn Sharīk al-Azadiyya.

Ibn 'Ā'isha said that his mother was Ṭulayḥa, a client of 'Ubaydullāh ibn Ma'mar, and the statement of Ibn 'Imrān was already mentioned.

Mālik's family, house and children

Qāḍī ibn al-'Alā' al-Qushayrī mentioned that Abā 'Āmir ibn 'Amr, the grandfather of Mālik's father, was one of the Companions of the Prophet ﷺ. He said, 'We went on all the expeditions with the Prophet ﷺ, except for Badr.'

His son Mālik was Mālik's grandfather, and his *kunya* was Abū Anas. He was one of the great Tābi'ūn. More than one narrator mentioned that he related from 'Umar, Ṭalḥa, 'Ā'isha, Abū Hurayra and Ḥassān ibn Thābit. He was one of the most excellent people and men of knowledge. He was one of the four men who carried 'Uthmān [ibn 'Affān] to his grave under the cover of night and washed and buried him. He was a close friend of Ṭalḥa. His sons, Anas, Abū Suhayl Nāfi' and ar-Rabī', related from him. He died in 112 AH.

Abū Muḥammad aḍ-Ḍarrāb mentioned that 'Uthmān sent him on an expedition to North Africa which was conquered.

Qāḍī Muḥammad ibn Aḥmad at-Tustarī related that he was one of those who wrote down the copies of the Qur'an when 'Uthmān compiled the Qur'an together. 'Umar ibn 'Abd al-'Azīz used to consult him. Mālik mentioned that in his *Collection* of *al-Muwaṭṭā'*.

Abū al-Qāsim al-Lālakā'ī said, 'Abū Anas Mālik ibn Abī 'Āmir had four sons. One of them was Anas, the father of Mālik the *faqīh*.' Another said that his *kunya* is by him and his son Mālik related from him.

Aḍ-Ḍarrāb said that Ibn Shihāb related from him. Ibn Abī Ḥātim said that he related from his father.

Abū Isḥāq ibn Sha'bān said, 'Mālik related the *ḥadīth* of *ghusl* and dressing from his father from his grandfather from 'Umar.'

Ibn Wahb said, 'Mālik was asked about his father and said, "My uncle Abū Suhayl was a reliable man."'

Abū Muṣ'ab said, 'Mālik's father was lame. He had a fortress at al-Jurf known as the Castle of the Lame (Muq'ad).

Another said that his livelihood came from making arrows.

Al-Lālakā'ī said, 'The second son was Nāfi', Abū Suhayl. Mālik also related from him as well as Ismā'īl and Muḥammad, the son of Ja'far ibn Abī Kathīr and ad-Darāwardī and others.'

Imām Abū al-Faḍl said, 'Ibn Shihāb also related from him.'

The third son was Uways. He was the grandfather of Abū Uways Ismā'īl and Abū Bakr. They will be mentioned. Someone else called him Aws the older, but that is wrong. He also related from his father. Aḍ-Ḍarrāb claimed that Ibn Shihāb also related from him.

The fourth son was ar-Rabī'. Ismā'īl said, 'I sat with him.' Abū Ḥātim said, 'He did not relate knowledge from him.' Abū al-Qāsim al-Jawharī said, 'Only Sulaymān ibn Bilāl related from him.' At-Tustarī mentioned a *riwāya* from Abū Bakr al-Uwaysī from him, and his son, Mālik ibn ar-Rabī', also mentioned it. There is some speculation about it.

All four of them related from their father, Mālik ibn Abī 'Āmir.

The people of the *Ṣaḥīḥ*, al-Bukhārī and Muslim, and those after them related a lot from Mālik ibn Abi 'Āmir and Abū Suhayl, his son.

Abū Isḥāq ibn Sha'bān said, 'Mālik had three uncles: Nāfi', an-Naḍr and Yasār.' Aḍ-Ḍarrāb said, 'Mālik had an uncle called an-Naḍr. Mālik was known by him first. He was called "Mālik, the nephew of an-Naḍr." But it was not long before people said, "An-Naḍr, the uncle of Mālik." Muḥammad ibn Ṭalḥa said that. The most widely accepted account is that an-Naḍr is the one by whom Mālik was first known, and then an-Naḍr began to be known as a brother of Mālik. That is what Aḥmad ibn Ṣāliḥ mentioned. What is soundest and most well-known is that he was the first and was one of the uncles of Mālik.'

Mālik said, 'I had a brother the same age as Ibn Shihāb. My father put a question to us one day and my brother was right and I was wrong. My father asked me, "Have the pigeons distracted you?"'

Mālik had two sons: Yaḥyā and Muḥammad, and a daughter called Fāṭima who was married to his nephew and cousin, Ismā'il ibn Abī Uways.

Ibn Sha'bān said, 'Yaḥyā ibn Mālik related a text from his father and he mentioned that he related the *Muwaṭṭā'* from him in Yemen.' Muḥammad ibn Maslama related from him.

His son Muḥammad went to Egypt and wrote from him. Al-Ḥārith ibn Miskīn and Zayd ibn Bishr reported *ḥadīths* from him.

Abū 'Umar ibn 'Abd al-Barr said that Mālik had four children: Yaḥyā, Muḥammad, Ḥammāda and Umm al-Bahā'. As for Yaḥyā and Umm al-Bahā', he did not give their guardianship to anyone. He gave the guardianship of the other two to Ibrāhīm ibn Ḥabīb, one of the people of Madina.

Ibn Sha'bān said, 'Ḥabīb is the family, and is known as Bābayn. His guardian was with Dāwūd ibn Abī Zanbar. Perhaps Ibrāhīm was the son of Ḥabīb, but Allah knows best.'

He mentioned him among those who transmitted from him and his *kunya* was Abū Isḥāq. He is also mentioned as Isḥāq ibn Ibrāhīm ibn Ḥabīb, known as Bābayn. He mentioned them as three men in Madina. Allah knows best, but I think the statement 'Isḥāq' is incorrect, and that it was Abū Isḥāq.

Qāsim ibn Aṣbagh said, 'Ibrāhīm ibn Ḥabīb was a reliable man among the companions of Mālik, and he was his trustee.'

Az-Zubayrī said, 'Mālik had a daughter who memorised his knowledge, i.e. the *Muwaṭṭā'*. She would stand behind the door and when the reader made an error, she knocked on the door. So Mālik would notice and repeat it to him. His son Muḥammad arrived while Mālik was recounting *ḥadīths,* carrying a sparrow-hawk and with red leather sandals in his hands, and his trousers hung loosely on him. Malik turned to his companions and said, "The *adab* is the *adab* of Allah. This is my son, and this is my daughter."'

Al-Farawī said, 'We used to sit with him and his son Yaḥyā would come in and then go out without sitting down. He turned to us and said, "Part of what makes it easy for me is the fact that this business is not inherited and that no one has followed his father in his assembly except for 'Abd ar-Raḥmān ibn al-Qāsim."'

His son Muḥammad had a son called Aḥmad who listened to his grandfather Mālik. Abū 'Abdullāh ibn Mufarrij al-Qurṭubī mentioned that among the transmitters of Mālik as did Abū 'Abdullāh al-Khwārazmī al-Barqānī in his book on the weak men who, according to his opinion and that of Abū Manṣūr ibn Ḥakam, with Abū al-Ḥasan, they agreed to abandon. This Aḥmad died in 256 AH.

The birth of Mālik, how long he was in the womb, the length of his life and when he died

Qāḍī Abū al-Faḍl said that there is significant disagreement about Mālik's birth. The most famous account is what is related about that in the statement of Yaḥyā ibn Bukayr that he was born in 93 AH during the caliphate of Sulaymān ibn 'Abd al-Malik ibn Marwān.

Muḥammad ibn 'Abd al-Ḥakam said, 'It was 94 AH.' Ismā'īl ibn Abī Uways said that. He said that it was in the caliphate of al-Walīd. Another said said that it was in Rabī' al-Awwal of that year.

It is related from Muḥammad ibn 'Abd al-Ḥakam that he was born in 93 or 94 AH. Abū Mushir said that it was was 90 AH. Other accounts say that it was 96 and it is said that it was 97. Abū Dāwūd as-Sijistānī said 93. Abū Isḥāq ash-Shīrazī said 95.

Muḥammad ibn Sa'īd, the client of Safīna, said that Mālik said, 'My uncle, Abū Sahl, brought me to 'Umar ibn 'Abd al-'Azīz who was the governor of Madina to make me responsible for the obligations. He asked, "Has he had a wet-dream?" He answered, "Ask his father. He knows him better than me."'

Muṣ'ab ibn 'Abdullāh said, 'This is incorrect. 'Umar was dismissed from Madina in 93 AH.'

As for his death, the sound version supported by most of his companions and those after them among the *ḥuffāẓ* and the scholars of the knowledge of tradition and innumerable others is that he died in 179 AH.

They disagree about what time of the year it was. Most say that it was in Rabī' al-Awwal. Ismā'īl ibn Abī Uways, Ibn Abī Zanbar, Ibn Bukayr, Abū Muṣ'ab az-Zuhrī and others said that.

They disagree on making that more precise. Ibn Abī Uways, al-Wāqidī, and Ibn Sa'd say that it was on the morning of the 14th of that month. Abū Muṣ'ab said, 'It was the 10th of it.' Abū 'Alī ibn al-Baṣrī related in the book, *al-Muqarrib*, that he died on Monday, the 3rd of that month.

Ibn Wahb said in the history of Ibn Saḥnūn, 'It was Monday, the 13th.' Abū 'Umar ibn 'Abd al-Barr related that it was the 10th. Ibn Saḥnūn said, 'It is said that it was on the 11th,' and it is also said, 'on the 12th of Rajab of that year.' Muṣ'ab az-Zubayrī and Ma'n ibn 'Īsā said that it was in Ṣafar.

Ḥabīb, his scribe, disagreed with all of that as did Muṭarrif in what is mentioned from him. They said that it was 180 AH.

Al-Farawī disagreed, and Ibn Saḥnūn and Abū al-'Arab at-Tamīmī related from him that Mālik died in 198. This is wrong. This first is correct.

They disagreed about the year. Ibn Nāfi', aṣ-Ṣā'igh, Ibn Abī Uways, Muḥammad ibn Sa'd and Ḥabīb say that he died in 185 AH. Saḥnūn said that.

Al-Wāqidī said that it was 190. Al-Firyābī and Abū Muṣ'ab said 186. It is mentioned from Ibn al-Qāsim that it was 187. Ibn Saḥnūn and Abū al-'Arab said that. Al-Qa'nabī says 186. Ayyūb ibn Ṣāliḥ said 192.

Abū Muḥammad aḍ-Ḍarrāb said, 'This is an error, and the correct statement is 186 AH. That is the most likely according to the statement of Ibn al-Qāsim about the soundest position about the dates of his birth and death.'

They disagree about the length of time his mother was pregnant with him. Ibn Nāfi', aṣ-Ṣā'igh, Ma'n and Muḥammad ibn aḍ-Ḍaḥḥāk said, 'His mother was pregnant with him for three years.' Bakkār ibn 'Abdullāh az-Zubayrī said the like of that. He said, 'She carried him longer than the natural term, by Allah!' He recited verses by aṭ-Ṭirrimāḥ):

> The wombs cling to carrying us until the terms of pregnant women carry us beyond the natural term.

Ibn al-Mundhir said, 'That is known.' It is also related from al-Wāqidī that his mother was pregnant with him for two years. 'Aṭṭāf ibn Khālid said that.

There is no disagreement that he died in Madina.

His description and physical form

Abū 'Āṣim said, 'I have not encountered a man of *Ḥadīth* with a handsomer face than Mālik.' 'Īsā ibn 'Umar al-Madanī said, 'I have not seen a white or red face at all handsomer than that of Mālik, not any whiter garment than his.'

More than one of his companions described him. They included Muṭarrif, Ismā'īl and ash-Shāfi'ī. Combining their accounts, we learn that Mālik was tall, corpulent, with a large head, white hair and beard which ranged from a very intense white to yellowness, and eyes of a pleasing shape. He was bald at the front of his head, and had a fine high nose and a full beard that reached his chest, both wide and long. He used to trim the bottom of his moustache, but he did not shave or remove it completely. He thought that shaving it was a sort of mutilation. He left two long moustaches. He justified that by the fact that 'Umar used to twist his moustaches when he was preoccupied with something.

Abū Ḥanīfa described him as having a ruddy complexion and blue eyes.

Qāḍī Abū al-'Abbās ibn Surayj said when his description was

mentioned to him, 'This is the description of a man of intellect' or 'Physiognomy indicates the one who has this description is a man of intellect.'

Muṣ'ab az-Zubayrī said, 'Mālik was one of the most handsome people in facial appearance, the most pleasant of them to the eye, purest of them in whiteness and most perfect of them in height and in excellent physique.'

One of them said, 'Mālik was a man of medium height,' but the first is better known.

Another said, 'I came to visit Mālik and I saw him wearing a wrapper, and his ears were large as if they were two palms of a man or less than that.'

Al-Ḥakam ibn 'Abda said, 'I entered the mosque of Madina when Mālik was there. His hair was parted.'

Aḥmad ibn Ibrāhīm al-Mawṣulī said, 'I saw Mālik with his hair gathered together.' They said, 'He did not dye it. He used 'Alī as a justification for that.' This is widely known about him. It is related that one of the governors of Madina asked him, 'Why don't you use hair dye, Abū 'Abdullāh?' He said to him, 'Is this what remains for you as part of justice?'

Ibn Wahb related that he thought that Mālik used henna. 'Abd ar-Raḥmān ibn Wāqid related the like of that, but did not say henna.

Al-Wāqidī said, 'Mālik lived for seventy years without dyeing his white hair or entering the bath-house.' One version has 'or shaving the back of his neck.'

His clothes, scent, finery, dwelling, food and drink

Muḥammad ibn aḍ-Ḍaḥḥāk said, 'Mālik had a handsome face and clean garments. He disliked variety in clothes.'

Khālid ibn Khidāsh said, 'I saw Mālik wearing a Persian embroidered shawl, a Turkish hat and good clothes from Marv. There were cushions in his house and his friends sat on them. I said to him, "Abū 'Abdullāh! Is this which I see something that you have started or did you find the people doing it?" He answered, "I saw the people doing it."'

Al-Walīd ibn Muslim said, 'Mālik did not wear silk nor did he think that it should be worn. He wore white. I saw him and al-Awzāʿī wearing green shawls and they did not think that there was any harm in wearing them.'

Bishr ibn al-Ḥārith said, 'I came to visit Mālik and saw him wearing a shawl worth five hundred dinars. He had placed its sides over his eyes somewhat resembling the kings.'

Ashhab said, 'When Mālik put on a turban, he used to put part of it under his chin, and let the ends of it fall between his shoulders.'

Ibn Wahb said, 'I saw Mālik wearing a light russet garment dyed from Aden. He said to us, "It is a dye which we like, but my people use too much saffron in it, so I abandoned it." He said to us, "I have not met anyone wearing these fine garments – rather they were wearing thick garments – except for Rabīʿa. He used to wear the like of this," and he pointed to a fine shirt from Aden which he was wearing.'

Az-Zubayrī said, 'Mālik used to wear good garments from Aden, Khorasanī garments, and fine quality white Egyptian garments. He put on fine scent, and he said, "I did not like for anyone to have Allah give him blessings and not see the traces of His blessing on him, particularly the people of knowledge." He used to say, "I like it when the Qur'an reciter wears white garments."'

Ibn Abī Uways said, 'I did not seek any ink at all on the garment of Malik.'

Ashhab said, 'Mālik used to use scent: musk and other types.'

Al-Wāqidī said, 'Mālik would sit in his home on cushions and rugs which were put out, and there was ease and comfort in the entire room for those of Quraysh, the Anṣār and notable men who came to him.'

Ashhab said, 'When Mālik put on kohl out of necessity, he would sit in his house. He disliked its use except for a reason.'

Ibn Nāfiʿ the elder, Muṭarrif and Ismāʿīl said, 'Mālik's signet-ring which he was wearing when he died had a black stone on which these lines were inscribed in elegant script: "Allah is enough for me and the best of guardians". He wore it on his left hand. Sometimes he came out to us when it was on his right hand. We do not doubt that he changed it to his right hand when he performed *wuḍū'*.'

Muṭarrif asked him about his choice of engraving and he replied,

'I heard Allah say: "They said, *'Allah is enough for us and the best of guardians'...*" (3:173)' Muṭarrif said, 'I changed my ring and made it like that. Allah knows best.'

Aḥmad ibn Ṣāliḥ said, 'Mālik did not possess much. He showed restraint outwardly when things were constricted. He did not own a house. He rented until he died.'

Al-Mahdī asked him, 'Do you have a house?' He said, 'No, Rabī'a told me that a man's lineage is his house.'

'Atīq ibn Ya'qūb said, 'Written on the door of Mālik was "*Mā shā-Allāh* (What Allah wills)". He was asked about that. He answered, "Allah says, '*Why, when you went into your garden did you not say, What Allah wills. There is no strength except by Allah'?*" (18:39) The garden is the house.'

Ibn al-Mundhir said, 'The house of Mālik ibn Anas where he lived in Madina was the house of 'Abdullāh ibn Mas'ūd. His place in the mosque was that of 'Umar ibn al-Khaṭṭāb. It was the place in which the bed of the Messenger of Allah ﷺ was placed in the mosque during his retreats, as mentioned by al-Uwaysī.'

Muṣ'ab said, 'Mālik used to sit with Nāfi', the client of Ibn 'Umar, in the *Rawḍa* both during and after Nāfi''s lifetime.'

Ibn Bukayr said said, 'Mālik was born at Dhū al-Marwa (a village) and his brother, an-Naḍr, sold linen goods. Mālik was a cloth merchant along with him. Then he sought knowledge. He stayed first at al-'Aqīq and then he went to Madina.'

Mālik was asked, 'Why do you stay at al-'Aqīq? It is difficult for you to get to the mosque.' He answered, 'It has reached me that the Prophet ﷺ liked it and would come to it, and that one of the Anṣār wanted to move from it nearer the mosque and the Prophet ﷺ told him, "Are your steps not counted for the reward?"'

Ismā'īl ibn Abī Uways said, 'Every day Mālik had two dirhams for his meat and he used to command his baker to make a lot of food for him and his family every Friday.'

Muṭarrif said, 'If Mālik had not found two dirhams a day with which to buy meat, he would have sold some of his property for that and done it. His pay was in his meat.'

Ibn Abī Ḥāzim said, 'I asked Mālik, "What do you drink, Abū

'Abdullāh?" He answered, "Sugar in the summer and honey in the winter."'

Mālik liked bananas and said, 'Neither the flies nor a black hand has touched them. There is nothing more like the dates of the Garden than them. When you look for it in the winter or the summer, you find it. Allah says, "*Its produce is constant.*" (13:35)'

Abū as-Samḥ Ṭalq ibn as-Samḥ said, 'I saw Mālik on an excellent mule with a fine saddle on it. He was wearing the best clothes, and a slave boy was walking behind him until he came to the door of his house. He entered mounted to the place where one alights, and then he got off and sat down. The slave took a handkerchief and wiped his leather socks and removed them.'

Qāḍī Abū al-Faḍl said, 'The famous reports from him differ about this as we will mention. He did not ride in Madina out of respect for the earth in which the Messenger of Allah ﷺ was buried.'

Muḥammad ibn Mālik said, 'My aunt was with Mālik in his house, and she prepared his fast-breaking for him which consisted of bread and oil.'

Mālik once cautioned [the caliph] Abū Ja'far al-Manṣūr, instructing him to look into the affairs of his subjects. He said to him, 'When your daughter weeps from hunger, don't you order the millstone to be moved so that the neighbours will not hear her crying?' Malik said to him, 'By Allah, only Allah knows this.' He said to him, 'I know this, so do I not know the states of my subjects?'

This, and Allah knows best, was in the beginning when he was constricted. There are many different stories which we have brought and which we will report about his different states in this world. It varied at different moments and states since the state of a man in his beginning is different from his state at the end. He lived for about ninety years as was already stated. He was an Imām in them for about seventy years who related, gave *fatwās*, and whose words were heard. His states changed at every moment with more majesty and he advanced every day in his height in excellence and leadership until his death. He was unique for years and obtained the leadership of the *dīn* and this world without dispute. Do not object then to what comes to you of reports about his different states. Allah is the One Who gives success.

His intelligence, character, manners, the excellence of his company and other good qualities

They said that when Mālik came, Rabī'a said, 'The man of intelligence has come.'

Ibn Mahdī said, 'I met four: Mālik, Sufyān, Shu'ba and Ibn al-Mubārak. Mālik was the most intelligent of them all.' He said, 'My eyes have not seen anyone who inspired more awe than Mālik nor who had a more complete intellect nor who wasstronger in *taqwā* nor who possessed a fuller mind than Malik.'

Hārūn ar-Rashīd said of him, 'I have not seen anyone with more intelligence than him.'

Ibn Wahb said, 'That which we learned from the *adab* (proper manners) of Mālik was more than what we learned of his knowledge.'

Aḥmad ibn Ḥanbal said that Mālik stated, 'I have never sat with a fool.' This is a matter from which others were not safe. Aḥmad ibn Ḥanbal said, 'There is nothing more sublime than this in the virtues of the men of knowledge.'

Abū Nūḥ and Muṣ'ab az-Zubayrī said, 'One day Mālik mentioned something and we asked him, "Who gave you this *ḥadīth*?" He answered, "We do not sit with fools."'

Ziyād ibn Yūnus said, 'By Allah, Mālik was the greatest of the men in manliness and had the best character. When he sat in an assembly, no one broke away from it until he got up. I saw that he was often silent, spoke little and he guarded his tongue.'

Ibn al-Mubārak said, 'Mālik was the most sociable of people and the one who was the quickest to abandon what did not concern him.'

Ibn Abī Uways said, 'Mālik possessed justice.' He said, 'There is nothing rarer in people than it, so I wanted to continue with it.'

Az-Zahrānī said, 'In the morning Mālik put on his garments and turban and none of his family nor his friends saw him without a turban, dressed in his clothes. No one at all saw him eat or drink where people would see him nor laugh or talk about what did not concern him.'

Ibn Fihr al-Miṣrī related that Abū Bakr ibn Isḥāq said, 'When the intellect of Abū 'Alī ath-Thaqafī was mentioned, he said, "That intellect was taken from the Companions and Followers. That is because Abū 'Alī stayed at Samarqand for four years learning those good qualities from Muḥammad ibn Naṣr al-Marwazī, and Ibn Naṣr learned them from Yaḥyā ibn Yaḥyā. There was no one in Khorasan with greater intelligence than him. He was asked about that and said, "I stayed to to learn and profit from his good qualities. They are the good qualities of the Companions and the Followers."'

Similarly Mālik was called, *'al-'āqil'* (the intelligent). They agreed that he was the most intelligent man of his time.

Zuhayr ibn 'Abbād said, 'Whenever I said to Mālik, "May Allah have mercy on you!" he replied, "and may Allah have mercy on you," and whenever I said to him, "May Allah give your health," he replied, "May Allah give you health" because of his excellent *adab*.'

They said, 'He was the best of people in character with his family and children. He said, "In that lies the pleasure for your Lord, wealth for your property and a staff for your own support. I heard that from one of the Companions of the Prophet ﷺ."'

'Abdullāh ibn 'Abd al-Ḥakam said, 'Mālik ibn Anas invited some students and I was among them. We went with him to his house. When we entered the house, he said, "Here is the lavatory and here is water." When we entered the room he did not enter with us. He came in later and brought us food. He did not bring the water before to wash our hands, but brought it afterwards. When the people left, I asked him about what I had see him do.

'He answered, "As for my telling you about the lavatory and water, I had invited you to be good to you. Perhaps you might have been pressed to urinate or something else, and not known where to go and would have been inconvenienced by that. As for my not going in to the room with you, perhaps I would have said, 'Abū so-and-so, sit here,' and 'Abū so-and-so, sit here,' and I might have forgotten one of you and he would have thought that there was dislike in that. Therefore I left you to take your seats and then I came to you. As for not bringing water before the food, washing before it is the custom of the Persians. There is a *ḥadīth* about using it afterwards."'

Ash-Shāfi'ī said, 'Mālik was asked about having an image in the room. He said, "There should not be."'

An Iraqi man said to him, 'Abū 'Abdullāh, there is an image in your room.' He exclaimed, 'I have lived in it since such-and-such a time and I have not seen it at all. Get up and scratch it off!' He took a lance and wrapped a rag around it and scratched it off.

Muṭarrif said, 'When Mālik entered his room, he would say, "What Allah wills. There is no power nor strength except by Allah." He was asked about that. He said, "Allah says, *'Why, when you entered your garden, did you not say: "What Allah wills. There is no strength but in Allah."'* (28:39) Your garden is your room."'

It is said that that was written on the door of Mālik. When he saw it, he wanted to be reminded to say that when he entered.

There are many different stories which we have told and will tell about his different states in respect of this world. It varied with time and indeed states change, for the state of a man at the beginning of his life is different from his state at the end of it.

THE BEGINNING OF HIS QUEST, HIS COURSE IN THAT, HIS PATIENCE IN IT AND HIS INVESTIGATION INTO THOSE WITH WHOM HE STUDIED

Muṭarrif reported that Mālik said, 'I told my mother, "I will go and write down knowledge." She responded, "Then come and put on the garments of knowledge," and she put tucked-up garments on me and placed a tether on my head and then she placed a turban above it. She said, "Go and write now."'

Mālik said, 'My mother used to put the turban on me and say, "Go to Rabī'a and learn proper manners (*adab*) from him before learning his knowledge."'

Ibn al-Qāsim said, 'The quest for knowledge compelled Mālik to destroy the roof of his house and sell its wood. Then this world later came to him.'

The like of this is related about Rabī'a.

Anas ibn 'Iyāḍ said, 'I sat with Rabī'a one day while Mālik was sitting with us. He was only known as Mālik, the brother of an-Naḍr. Then his desire to seek knowledge continued until we began to say, "An-Naḍr, the brother of Mālik." When Mālik was a student, he would shift with the shade of the tree so that he could finish what he wanted to finish. His sister said to her father, "This brother of mine does not go to the people." He said, "My daughter, he is memorising the *ḥadīth*s of the Messenger of Allah ﷺ."'

Mālik said, 'I had a brother the same age as Ibn Shihāb. My father put a question to us one day and my brother was right and I was wrong. My father said to me, "Have the pigeons distracted you from the quest of knowledge?" So I became angry and devoted myself to Ibn Hurmuz for seven years (one version has eight years) and I did not mix with anyone else. I used to put some dates in my sleeve and I gave them to his children and told them, "If anyone asks about the shaykh, say that he is busy."'

One day Ibn Hurmuz said to his slave-girl, 'Who is at the door?' She only saw Mālik. She came back and told him, 'It is only that ruddy-skinned one.' He said, 'Invite him. That is the man of knowledge of the people.'

Mālik used to wear short padded trousers to sit at the door of Ibn Hurmuz to protect himself from the cold of the stones there. It was also said, 'The cold of the courtyard of the mosque' and that was where Ibn Hurmuz sat.

Mālik said, 'When a man frequents a man for thirty years, he learns from him.' We thought that he meant himself with Ibn Hurmuz. Ibn Hurmuz made him swear not to mention his name in a *ḥadīth*.

Ibn 'Uyayna said, 'I saw Mālik ask Zayd ibn Aslam about a *ḥadīth* involving 'Umar being carried on a horse in the way of Allah, and he began to be friendly with him and to ask him about word after word, thing after thing. There was something difficult in Zayd's character.'

Ibn 'Abd al-Ḥakam said, 'Mālik said to me, "We used to come to Ibn Shihāb in his house among the Banū ad-Dīl and he had a good doorstep on which we used to sit, pushing each other and jostling until we went in to him."'

Mālik said, 'We used to sit with az-Zuhrī and Muḥammad ibn al-Munkadir. Az-Zuhrī would say, "Ibn 'Umar said such-and-such." Then after that, we sat with him and we would ask him, "That which you mentioned from Ibn 'Umar, who told it to you?" He replied, "His son, Sālim."'

Muṣ'ab said, 'Mālik used to lead Nāfi' from his house to the mosque. He had gone blind. He would question him and he would relate *ḥadīths*. The house of Nāfiʿ was in the vicinity of al-Baqīʿ.'

Mālik said, 'I used to go to Nāfiʿ, the client of Ibn ʿUmar, when I was a child with another boy. He would come down to me from some stairs of his, and sit with me and give me some *ḥadīths*.'

He said, 'I used to go to Nāfiʿ for half of the day. As long as the tree shaded me from the sun, I would wait for him to come out. When he came out, I left him alone for a time as if I had not noticed him. Then I would turn to him and greet him and then leave him again until he entered the courtyard. Then I would say to him, "What did Ibn ʿUmar say about such-and-such?" and he would answer me. Then I would withdraw from him. He was prone to be slightly irritable. I used to go to Ibn Hurmuz in the morning and I did not leave his house until it was night.'

Az-Zubayrī said, 'I saw Mālik in the circle of Rabīʿa wearing an earring in his ear. This indicated that he had persisted in his studies from his childhood as he said in the tradition of Nāfiʿ.'

Ibn Abī Zanbar said, "I heard Mālik say, 'I wrote down a hundred thousand *ḥadīths* with my own hand.'" Ibn Isḥāq related of him, "I did not write down a book from anyone in its way except from al-ʿAlāʾ."

Ibn Wahb related that he said, 'I have not written in these tablets at all.'

Aḥmad ibn Ṣāliḥ said, 'I looked at the books of Mālik and there was something like twelve thousand *ḥadīths*.'

ʿUbaydullāh ibn ʿUmar said, 'In general, what I heard from Ibn Shihāb and Mālik was review *(ʿarḍ)*. Mālik used to teach us and he taught us well.'

Ibn Mahdī said, 'Mālik was asked about his listening to az-Zuhrī and he said, "The least of that is review."'

Ibn Wahb asked him, 'Did you read knowledge to anyone?' He answered, 'No.'

It is related that he said, 'Az-Zuhrī visited us so we went to see him. Rabīʿa was with us. He gave us about forty *ḥadīths*, and then we went to him again the following day. He said, "Look for a book so I may give you *ḥadīths* from that. Do you think that you have retained any of the *ḥadīths* I gave you yesterday?" Rabī'a said to him, "Here is someone who will repeat to you all the *ḥadīths* you gave him yesterday." He asked, "Who is it?" He replied, "Ibn Abī 'Āmir." He said, "Go on." Then I repeated the forty *ḥadīths* he had given us. Az-Zuhrī then said, "I did not think that there was anyone capable of memorising in this way except for me."'

Mālik said in another version, 'I was at the *'Īd* prayer and I said, "This is the day on which Ibn Shihāb retires," so I left the place of the prayer and went and sat at his door. I heard him say to his slave-girl, "See who is at the door." She looked and I heard her say, "It is your ruddy-skinned friend, Mālik."'

'He said, "Bring him in," so I went in. He remarked, "I do not see you going to your home after the prayer." I answered, "No." "Have you eaten anything?" he asked. "No," I replied. He said, "Eat!" I replied, "I have no need of it." He asked, "What do you want then?" I said, "I want you to give me *ḥadīths*." He gave me seventeen *ḥadīths* and then said, "What use will it be to you if I give you *ḥadīths* and you do not remember them?" I said. "If you like, I will repeat them to you" and so I repeated them to him.'

One version has, 'He said to me, "Come on," so I brought out my slatesand he gave me thirty *ḥadīths*. I said to him, "More!" He told me, "That is enough for you. If you can relate these *ḥadīths*, you are one of the *ḥuffāẓ*." I retorted, "I have related them." He pulled the slates from my hand and then he said, "Speak then!" so I reported them and he repeated them to me. He said, "Get up. You are one of the vessels of knowledge," or he said, "You are the best repository of knowledge."'

It is related from him, 'Ibn Shihab gave me forty *ḥadīths*, one of which was the *ḥadīth* of the Verandah and I memorised them. Then I said, "Repeat them to me. I have forgotten the one over the forty." He refused, so I said, "Would you prefer that they are repeated to you?" He said, "Yes," so I repeated them and it was as I had memorised.'

In one version Ibn Shihāb said to him, 'I have not questioned a man of knowledge at all.' Then he said, 'We belong to Allah and to Him we return,' and remarked, 'The memory of people has become poor. I used to go to Sa'īd ibn al-Musayyab, 'Urwa, al-Qāsim, Abū

Salama, Ḥumayd, Sālim,' and he named a group. 'I went around to them listening to fifty to a hundred *ḥadīths* from each of them. Then I went and memorised all of them without mixing the *ḥadīths* of this one in the *ḥadīths* of that one.'

Mālik said in the version of Ibn Wahb, 'I used to sit with Ibn Shihāb and I took a thread with me. When he gave a *ḥadīth*, I tied a knot in the thread and then I returned to the house,' i.e. to write it down.

He said in the version of Ibn Zayd, 'When Ibn Shihab sat down for a gathering, he used to recount thirty *ḥadīths*. One day, he recounted *ḥadīths* and I made knots for his *ḥadīths*, but then I forgot one of the *ḥadīths*. I met him and I asked him about it. He asked, "Weren't you in the assembly?" I answered, "Yes." He said, "So what is wrong with you? Why did you not memorise it?" I responded, "I have thirty, but I missed one." He said, "The memory of people has evaporated. I did not entrust anything at all to my heart that I forgot. Come on then, what do you have?" I asked him and he informed me of it, and then I left.'

'Abd al-'Azīz ibn 'Abdullāh said that Mālik was asked if he had listened to 'Amr ibn Dīnār. He responded, 'I saw him relating *ḥadīths* and the people were writing while standing up. I did not like to write down a *ḥadīth* of the Messenger of Allah ﷺ while standing.'

Aḥmad ibn Ṣāliḥ said, 'Mālik went to 'Amr ibn Dīnār and he could not understand his words due to his missing front teeth. So he went to az-Zubayr's house and wrote with him.'

Az-Zubayrī said, 'Mālik passed by Abū az-Zinād when he was relating *ḥadīths*. He did not sit with him. I met him afterwards and I asked him, "What kept you from sitting with me?" He said, "The place was crowded and I did not wish to take a *ḥadīth* of the Messenger of Allah ﷺ while standing."'

It is related that this story involved him and Abū Ḥāzim.

Ibn Wahb said, 'Mālik was asked whether they used to use analogy in the assembly of Rabī'a and debate a lot with one another. He answered, "No, by Allah."'

Mālik said, 'Abū 'Ubayda ibn Muḥammad ibn 'Ammār ibn Yāsir said to us, "If you are taking the plain and simple, we will speak with you. If you are taking the elaborate, we will leave you."'

Ibn Abī Uways said, 'I heard Mālik say, "This knowledge is vital to the *Dīn*, so take care about those from whom you take it. I have met seventy people who said, 'The Messenger of Allah ﷺ said' within these pillars," and he pointed to the mosque, "and I did not take anything from them. Had any of them been entrusted with a treasure, they would have proved trustworthy, but they were not worthy of undertaking this business."'

Something similar is found in the version of Ibn Wahb, Ḥabīb and 'Abd al-Ḥakam.

Muṭarrif reported that he said, 'I met a group of the people of Madina, but I did not take any knowledge from them. Knowledge was taken from them and they were of various sorts. Some of them used to lie about a man in his *ḥadīths* while he did not lie in his knowledge. Some of them were ignorant about what they had. Some of them were suspected of poor reasoning, so I therefore abandoned them.'

According to the version of Ibn Wahb from him: 'I have met people in this city and if a Rain Prayer had been performed by them, they would have been given rain. They heard knowledge and many *ḥadīth*s, but I have not taken a *ḥadīth* from any of them because they bound themselves to fear of Allah and *zuhd* while this business (i.e. *ḥadīth* and *fatwā*) requires a man with *taqwā*, scrupulousness, safeguarding, proficiency, knowledge and understanding so that he will know what issues from his head and what he will reach tomorrow. As for a man without proficiency or recognition, there is no benefit through him. He is not a proof nor is he to be taken from.'

Ibn Kināna reported that he said, 'Sometimes a shaykh sat with us for most of the day and we did not take from him. We did not suspect him, but he was not one of the People of *Ḥadīth*.'

Mālik said, 'We used to crowd together on the steps of Ibn Shihāb until some of us would fall over one another.' He said, 'I had boxes of books which are now gone. If they had remained, I would have preferred that to my family and my property.'

One of them related from him that he said, 'I wrote a hundred thousand *ḥadīths* by my own hand.'

Mālik said, 'I came to Zayd ibn Aslam, and I heard the *ḥadīth* about 'Umar giving a horse to be used in the Way of Allah. I frequented him for days asking him and he gave me the *ḥadīth*. Perhaps he had some doubt or meaning in it, so I left it because he was one of those whom asceticism had distracted from *ḥadīth*.'

He was asked, 'Why do you not write from 'Aṭā'?' He replied, 'I wanted to take from him and I desired to look into his character and his business. Therefore I followed him until he came to the minbar of the Prophet ﷺ. He wiped the housing and the lowest step, i.e. of the minbar. I have not written from him since because that is one of the actions of the common people. The lowest step and the housing are something which the Umayyads repaired. When I saw that he did not distinguish between the minbar of the Prophet ﷺ and the rest of it and that he did what the common people did, I left him.'

Mālik related from another man from him. Perhaps he first left him because what he observed in him and did not recognise the reality of his excellence and knowledge. This is why he wanted to investigate him and to test him. When his state and knowledge were clear to him later and he had missed him, he took his knowledge from someone else.

Ibn 'Uyayna said, 'I did not see anyone better in taking knowledge than Mālik.' He said, 'May Allah have mercy on Mālik. There was none stronger in reviewing the men and the men of knowledge.'

Ibn al-Madīnī said, 'I do not know anyone who holds the same standing as Mālik in that.'

Aḥmad ibn Ṣāliḥ said, 'I do not know anyone stronger in his selection of the men and scholars than Mālik was. I do not know that he related from anyone in whom there was any doubt. He related from people who are not abandoned, not a single one.'

Ibn Wahb related that he said, 'I went to 'Ā'isha bint Ṭalḥa, but I thought her weak, so I did not take anything from her except "My father had a wash-tub from which he and all his family did *wuḍū'*."'

He said, 'Whenever I saw the man from the people of Madina who had *ḥadīths*, I wanted to take that from him. I did not see a place to take it, so I postponed it until he died and so I missed him.'

He said, 'I saw Ayyūb as-Sakhtiyānī at Makka in two *ḥajjs* and I did not write from him. On the third *ḥajj*, I saw him sitting in the courtyard of Zamzam. When the Prophet ﷺ was mentioned, he wept until I wished for mercy on him. When I saw that, I wrote from him.'

Ibn Wahb said, 'Mālik looked at al-'Aṭṭāf ibn Khālid and said, "It has reached me that you take from this one." He answered, "Yes." He said, "We only accept *ḥadīths* from the *fuqahā'*."'

The beginning of his prominence in knowledge, his sitting to give *fatwās* and teach, and people's need of him

Al-Layth said, 'We came to Madina and found 'Abd al-'Azīz ibn Abī Salama and Mālik on either side of Rabī'a, and 'Abd al-'Azīz was above him. Then I went there another time and Mālik was above 'Abd al-'Azīz.'

Muḥammad ibn Fulayḥ said, 'I was with Rabī'a and Mālik was sitting with him. Then he surpassed him and was needed, so he moved from the assembly of Rabī'a and knowledge was sought from him. I was one of those who moved to him from Rabī'a's assembly. We were a group, and my father commanded me to do that.'

Sufyān ibn 'Uyayna said, 'A question passed around the assembly of Rabī'a. Mālik was asked about it, and Rabī'a responded with some critical words. Mālik left in anger and sat alone at the *Ẓuhr* prayer and people sat with him. After *Maghrib* had been prayed, there were fifty or more gathered around him. In the morning there were many. He was seventeen at the time and the Imamate was known for him, and people had life then.'

Ibn al-Mundhir said, 'Mālik issued *fatwās* during the lifetime of Nāfi' and Zayd ibn Thābit.'

Ibn 'Abd al-Ḥakam said, 'Mālik issued *fatwās* along with Yaḥyā ibn Sa'īd.'

Ayyūb said, 'And Rabī'a and Nāfi'.'

'Āṣim ibn 'Umar said, 'We used to take from Mālik during the lifetime of Yaḥyā ibn Sa'īd.'

Ayyūb as-Sakhtiyānī said, 'I came to Madina while Nāfi' was still alive and Mālik had a circle.'

Muṣ'ab said, 'Mālik had a circle in the lifetime of Nāfi' which was larger than Nāfi''s.' One version has 'Rabī'a' in place of 'Nāfi''.

Shu'ba said, 'I came to Madina one year after the death of Nāfi', and Mālik had a circle at that time. Nāfi' died in 117 AH.'

Imām Abū Al-Faḍl said, 'All of this is sound since it has already been stated that Mālik sat for the people when he was seventeen years old. He was born in 93 AH according to the disagreement on that – either before it or somewhat after it. Nāfi' died when he was some twenty years old after he had already been sitting for people for two years.'

Ibn Wahb said, 'Mālik said to us one day, "The governor summoned me while I was young to present myself to the assembly. I delayed until Rabī'a came home and I told him and said, 'I have not attended until you came so that I could ask for your advice.' Rabī'a said to me, 'Yes.'"'

Ibn Wahb said, 'I said to him, "If he had not told you to attend, you would not have attended?" He replied, "I would not have attended.' Then he stated, "Abū Muḥammad, there is no good in the one who sees himself in a state which other people do not think him worthy of."'

In another version, 'When I attended the ruler with Rabī'a, I saw displeasure in his face. When we left, I said to him, "If you do not like for me to attend, I will not attend. I have learned from you." He replied, 'I do not dislike it. It is because he called someone to attend with us and you have more *fiqh* than him."

Mālik said, 'No one who desires to sit in the mosque to teach *ḥadīth* and *fatwā* can do so until he has consulted people of soundness and excellence and the people in charge of the mosque. Only when they consider him worthy of it may he sit there. I did not sit until seventy shaykhs of the people of knowledge had testified that I was ready to do so.'

Ibn Wahb said: 'A man came to ask Mālik about something and Ibn al-Qāsim promptly gave him a *fatwā*. Mālik turned on him with an angry expression and told him, "You dare to give *fatwā*, 'Abd ar-Raḥmān? I did not give a *fatwā* until I had asked myself whether I was ready to do so." When his anger had abated, he was asked, "Whom did you ask?" He replied, "Az-Zuhrī and Rabī'a."'

Mālik said, 'When the man questioned Rabī'a and he did not understand him, he said to him, "Ask this one." I would tell the asker, "He forbids you such-and-such."'

Ibn Bukayr and others said, 'The first of what made the *fiqh* of Mālik clear occurred when a man left a will at his death that he had married his two daughters to the two sons of his brother and stated that the bride-prices were to be taken. The man died and the governor, al-Ḥasan ibn Zayd, summoned some people. Among them were Ibn Abī Dhi'b, Ibn 'Imrān, Ibn Abī Sabra and Mālik when he was still young. He mentioned the problem to them and all of them said, "That is allowed."

'Mālik, however, remained silent and the governor asked, "What do you think, Mālik?" He answered, "That is not permitted." All of them got angry. Ibn Abi Dhi'b said, "He only wants to answer us back!" The governor said, "He is right and you are wrong. Why do you say this, Abu 'Abdullāh?" He replied, "Do you think that they should be given their husbands so each of the men can take one howdah and then each of them say, 'This is my wife rather than the other one'? Who would you decide she is for?"

'The people were silent and they said, "He is correct." The governor said, "So what do you think, Abu 'Abdullāh?" He replied, "The marriage is invalid unless each of the women is named for her specific man."'

Ibn al-Mājishūn said, 'Part of what showed the excellence of Mālik is that a thief was seized and he had in possession some wheat which he had stolen from the baskets of different persons until he had amassed a lot of wheat. He admitted that. The governor summoned those at Madina who included Rabī'a and Yaḥyā ibn Sa'īd. Mālik was with them despite his youth because they recognised his knowledge. When they started their assembly, the governor asked them about the case, and brought out the wheat. It was something like four ardebs (one ardeb = 24 *ṣā'*), and all of them thought that he should have his hand cut off. Mālik was silent.

'The governor said, "Speak!"

'He responded, "His hand is not cut off for it."

'Those who were there thought this very presumptuous and they asked him why he had made this statement. He told them, "Is not the hand cut off for only four dinars or more? If he steals what is equal to one dirham from this basket, and what is equal to one dirham from that one, this does not cause him to have his hand cut off." So the people left and the excellence of his knowledge was clear to them.'

Abū al-Ḥasan aṭ-Ṭālibī said, 'Ṣafwān ibn Sulaym, who was one of the lofty, excellent, discriminating shaykhs of Mālik, asked Mālik about a dream which he had experienced. Mālik at that time was a small boy. Mālik said to him, "Does someone like you ask someone like me?" He told him, "Do not worry, nephew. I dreamt that I was looking into a mirror."

'Mālik said to him, "You were looking at the business of the Next World and what will bring you near to your Lord."

'Ṣafwān said to him, "Today you are Muwaylik (little Mālik), and it you continue you will be Mālik. Fear Allah, Mālik, if you are able (*Mālik*). If not, then you will be destroyed (*hālik*)."

'Mālik said, "Before he used to call me Muwaylik, When he asked me, he said to me, 'O Abū 'Abdullah.' He was the first of them to give me that *kunya*."'

Aṭ-Ṭālibī said, 'His words, "Do not worry" indicate that he possessed what made him worthy to answer what he was asked.'

Qāḍī Abū al-Faḍl said, 'If he had not possessed that, he would not have asked him, and he would not have allowed himself nor delved into the knowledge of the unseen and played with prophethood.'

Al-Ḥārith said, 'Ibn Hurmuz advised Mālik and 'Abd al-'Azīz ibn Abī Salama that when they went to the ruler, they should be among the last to speak. Mālik kept to his advice. It has reached me that he attended the governor with Ibn Abi Dhi'b and his equals. The governor asked them for a *fatwā* about a man who had confessed that he had murdered with premeditation. They all gave a *fatwā* that he should be killed unless the guardians [of the deceased] forgave him. Mālik remained silent. The governor asked him and he answered, "I will investigate" with his head bowed. Then he asked him again and he said, "It is death until I investigate." They asked, "What will you investigate? A man has confessed that he murdered with premeditation. What is this?" He then asked, "Where is the killer who has confessed?" It was a very young lad. He said, "How long have you been in prison?" The answer was "Since such a time." So he had been imprisoned and confessed before he had reached puberty. This, and Allah knows best, means that his confession is not recognised and is retracted from him.'

Aḥmad ibn Ṣāliḥ said, 'Mālik was in three generations: a generation below him, another with him and another before him. There was none in three generations who was as excellent in knowledge as he was. He was the pinnacle of the three generations. Those who were above him were those born in 80 AH: Ibn 'Ajlān, Ibn Abī Dhi'b and their likes. With him were 'Abd al-'Azīz ibn al-Mājishūn, Ibn Abī az-Zinād, Sulaym ibn Bilāl and others. Below him were Ibn ad-Darāwardī, Ibn Abī Ḥāzim, Anas ibn 'Iyāḍ and their likes.'

Ibn al-Qāsim said, 'Mālik said to me, "Forty of us with turbans sat with Rabī'a, not counting those who did not put the turban on. We only know four of them. As for one of them, the kings overcame him," meaning Ibn al-Mājishūn.' (In one version, "He was preoccupied with questions which cause one to err" or words to that effect.) "As for the other (meaning Kathīr ibn Farqad), he died. As for the third (i.e. 'Abd ar-Raḥmān ibn 'Aṭā'), he exiled himself." He was silent about the fourth, and we knew that he meant himself.'

Abū Ḥanīfa was asked, 'What do you think of the boys of Madina?' He answered, 'The ruddy-skinned, blue-eyed one is noble among them,' meaning Mālik. One version has, 'I see scattered knowledge there, but one of them has gathered it. That is the white reddish lad.'

Ibn Ghānim said, 'I mentioned that to Mālik and he said, "He spoke the truth. I have met him, and I think that he is a man who possesses knowledge and understanding. But if only he had based it on a root!" meaning the tradition of the people of Madina.'

Ibn Abī Uways said that Mālik said, 'I came to Rabī'a one day and he asked me, "Who are the low, Mālik?" I replied, "Those who consume through their *dīn*." He asked, "Who are the lowest of the low?" I said, "Those who consume others through their *dīn*." He said, "Got it!" and he promoted me, may Allah be pleased with all of them.'

THE TESTIMONY OF THE RIGHTEOUS *SALAF* AND THE PEOPLE OF KNOWLEDGE THAT HE WAS AN *IMĀM* IN KNOWLEDGE OF THE BOOK AND THE *SUNNA*, HAD PRECEDENCE IN *FIQH* AND TRUTHFULNESS IN TRANSMISSION, AND THEIR PREFERRING HIM AND PRAISING HIM

In the chapter about the precedence for the school of Mālik, we have already mentioned the tradition which has come about him. We presented what is transmitted and what is understood in such a way that we cannot add anything to it. We mentioned the words of the early generations and the Imāms testifying that he had the imamate and precedence over others. So we will not go on at length to repeat that. We will mention here a good summary of these details. Allah is the One Who gives help.

One day, Ibn Hurmuz asked his slave-girl, 'Who is at the door?' She only saw Mālik and mentioned that to him. He said, 'Invite him in. He is the man of knowledge of Madina.'

Ibn Shihāb said to him, 'You are one of the vessels of knowledge' or 'You are the best repository of knowledge.'

Abū al-Aswad, the shaykh of Mālik, was asked in Egypt in 131 AH, 'Whose opinion should be taken in Madina after Rabī'a? Yaḥyā ibn Sa'īd is in Iraq.' He replied, 'The Aṣbaḥī lad.'

Sufyān ibn 'Uyayna said, 'Who are we in comparison to Mālik? We follow the tracks of Mālik.' He said, 'Madina (or he said, 'I only think that Madina') will go to ruin after Mālik.' He said, 'Mālik is the master of the people of the people of Madina.' He said, 'Mālik is the master of the Muslims.' He said, 'Mālik is the Imām.' He said, 'Mālik is the man of knowledge of the people of the Hijaz.' He said, 'Mālik is the Lamp. Mālik is the proof of his time.' When the death of Mālik reached him, he said, 'His like is not left' or 'His like is not left upon the earth.'

He said to one of them, 'Do you join me with Mālik? He and I are only as Jarīr said:

> When the three year old camel is roped with another camel,
> it cannot attack the slashing teeth of the young camels.'

Then he added, 'Who is like Mālik, following the tracks of those who have passed with intellect and proper manners (*adab*)?' He said, 'Mālik is the Imām in *Ḥadīth*.' He said, 'Mālik, the truthful, related to me.'

Upon receiving the news of Mālik's death, Ḥammād ibn Zayd wept until he began to wipe his eyes with a rag. He said, 'May Allah have mercy on Mālik! He had an important place in the *dīn*. I saw his opinion discussed in the assembly of Ayyūb.' In one version, 'Then Ḥammād said, "O Allah, give us a worthy successor after him!"'

Ash-Shāfi'ī said, 'When a tradition comes to you from Mālik, hold on to it tightly.'

He said, 'When a report comes to you, Mālik is the star.'

He said, 'When scholars are mentioned, Mālik is the star. No one reached the level that Mālik did in knowledge through his retention, his proficiency and his care. Whoever desires sound *ḥadīths* must have Mālik.'

He said, 'Mālik ibn Anas was my teacher. (One version has 'my master'.) There was was no one more gracious to me than Mālik. We took knowledge from him and we were one of Mālik's boys.'

He said, 'I have put Mālik between me and Allah as a proof.'

Muḥammad ibn 'Abd al-Ḥakam said, 'During his lifetime, when ash-Shāfi'ī was asked about something, he said, "This is the statement of the master" meaning Mālik. He mentioned the rules and the *sunan*.' He said, 'Knowledge revolved around three men: Mālik, al-Layth and Ibn 'Uyayna.'

He said, 'Mālik and Sufyān were comrades. Mālik is the piercing star which is not reached.' He said, 'If it had not been for Mālik and Ibn 'Uyayna, the knowledge of the Hijaz would have vanished.' It is also related: '...knowledge would not have been known in the Hijaz.'

Ash-Shāfi'ī said, 'I was talking with Muḥammad ibn al-Ḥasan one day and he said to me, "Our man (meaning Abū Ḥanīfa) knows more than your man meaning Mālik)." I asked him, "Do you want justice or self-importance?"

'"Justice," he replied.

'I said, "I ask you by Allah. There is no god but Him. Who is the one with the most knowledge of the Book of Allah and what abrogates and is abrogated?" He replied, "By Allah, your man."

'I asked him, "Who has the most knowledge of the *Sunna* of the Messenger of Allah ﷺ?" He repeated, "O Allah, your man."

'I said to him, "Only analogy remains." "Our man is better in analogy," he stated. I retorted, "Analogy is only achieved by means of these things, so on what basis do you draw your analogy? We claim for our man what you do not claim for your man."'

In one version, 'I said to him, "Analogy was not unknown for our man, but he safeguarded himself and made diligent investigation."' He meant that he based himself on those before him.

One of them said, 'I heard Baqiyya ibn al-Walīd say in a group of those studying *ḥadīth* and some shaykhs from the people of Madina, "There is no one on the face of the earth with more knowledge of the past or remaining *Sunna* than you, Mālik."'

'Abdullāh, the father of Muṣ'ab az-Zuhrī, said, 'Mālik ibn Anas is the master of the Muslims.'

Al-Layth mentioned him and said, 'Mālik, Mālik' raising his degree.

Al-Awzā'ī mentioned him and he was asked, 'What do you think of Mālik?' He said, 'I think that he is a man of knowledge.'

'Ubaydullāh ibn 'Umar said, 'The best successor for the people was Mālik.'

'Abd al-'Azīz said, 'Mālik is our master and our man of knowledge.'

Al-Layth said, 'I met Mālik in Madina and said to him, "I see that you are wiping the sweat from your brow." He replied, "I sweated with Abū Ḥanīfa. He is a *faqīh*, O Egyptian!" Then I met Abū Ḥanīfa and I said, "How excellent was the statement that man made about you!" He replied, "By Allah, I have not seen anyone swifter than him with the truthful answer and complete asceticism."'

Abū Yūsuf said, 'I have not seen any with more knowledge than three men: Mālik, Ibn Abī Laylā and Abū Ḥanīfa.'

Al-Bahlūl ibn Rāshid said, 'I have not seen anyone swifter to use an *āyat* from the Book of Allah in refutation than Mālik ibn Anas.'

Muṭarrif said, 'When Mālik was asked about a problem which had arisen, it was as if a Prophet were speaking on his tongue.' Muḥammad ibn 'Abd al-Hakam said, 'When Mālik spoke alone, no one spoke before him. His word was considered to be a proof when deciding a dispute because he was an Imām.' He was asked, 'What about ash-Shāfi'ī?' He answered, 'No.'

Al-Ḥakam said, 'I entered the mosque and I asked a group of those who were in the mosque, "Who is the one with the most knowledge of those in the mosque and the best of them?" They replied, "This standing one who is bowing," meaning Mālik.'

Wuhayb ibn Khālid said, 'He was one of the people with the most insight into *ḥadīths*. I came to Madina and I did not find anyone but that he knew some *ḥadīths* and did not know others except for Mālik and Yaḥyā ibn Sa'īd.' Wuhayb did not consider anyone to be equal to Mālik.

It is reported that al-Layth said, 'The knowledge of Mālik is the knowledge of one who is fearfully aware of Allah. The knowledge of Mālik was pure. Mālik was a trustworthy one for those of the people who took from him.'

Ibn al-Mubarak said, 'If it had been said to me, "Choose an Imām for the community," I would have chosen Mālik for it.' Abū Isḥāq al-Fazārī said, 'Mālik is a proof whose tracks many followers wish for.'

Ibn Mahdī said, 'Mālik possessed a greater understanding of *fiqh* than al-Ḥakam and Ḥammād.' He said, 'The Imāms of *ḥadīth* who are followed are four: Sufyān in Kufa, Mālik in the Hijaz, al-Awzā'ī in Syria and Ḥammād ibn Zayd in Basra.'

He was asked, 'Who has the most knowledge – Mālik or Abū Ḥanīfa?' He replied, 'Mālik has more knowledge than the master Abū Ḥanīfa.'

He said,'Ath-Thawrī is an Imām in *ḥadīth*, but not an Imām in the *Sunna*. Al-Awzā'ī is an Imām in the *Sunna* but not an imam in *ḥadīth*. Mālik is an *imām* in both of them.' (In *al-Jarḥ wa't-Ta'dīl*)

He once again to his companions. "'I will give you *ḥadīths* from one who is such that my eyes have never seen his like.' Then he said, 'Mālik related to us.' He said, 'Mālik had the best memory of the people of his time and Mālik did not err in *ḥadīth*.'

He said, 'There does not remain on the face of the earth anyone more trustworthy with the *ḥadīth* of the Messenger of Allah ﷺ than Mālik.'

He said, 'I do not put anyone ahead of Mālik in the validity of *ḥadīths.*' He said, 'I did not see anyone like Mālik and Ḥammād ibn Zayd. They used to seek reward from Allah in *ḥadīths.*'

Ya'qūb ibn Sufyān said, 'Leadership in knowledge, *fiqh* and proficiency reached Mālik, ath-Thawri and Ibn 'Uyayna.'

Ibn Ḥanbal said, 'Mālik was followed more than Sufyān.'

He was asked about when ath-Thawrī and Mālik differed in a transmission and which of them had the most understanding of the path of transmission. He said, 'Mālik is greater in my heart.'

He was asked, 'And when Mālik and al-Awzā'ī differ in the transmission?' He said, 'I prefer Mālik, even though al-Awzā'ī is one of the Imāms.'

He was asked, 'And Mālik and al-Layth?' He replied, 'Mālik.'

He was asked, 'Mālik and al-Ḥakam and Ḥammād?' He replied, 'Mālik.'

He was asked, 'And Mālik and an-Nakhā'ī?' He answered, 'Leave him with the people of his time.'

He said, 'Mālik is one of the masters of the people of knowledge. He is the Imām in *ḥadīth* and *fiqh*. Who is like Mālik, following the traces of those who have passed with intellect and proper manners?'

He was asked, 'If a man wishes the memorise the *ḥadīths* of a particular man, whose *ḥadīths* should he memorise?' He replied, 'The *ḥadīths* of Mālik. He is a proof between me and Allah.' He also gave that answer to a man who asked him, 'From what should I write *ḥadīths*?'

He was asked, 'If someone wants to look into opinion, whose opinion do you think he should look into?' He replied, 'The opinion of Mālik.' He said, 'May Allah have mercy on Mālik. He has an important place in Islam.' He said, 'There is no *ḥadīth* nor any words of Mālik that are not written down.' He said, 'Mālik was a man of verified memory, one of the firmest people in the *ḥadīths.*'

Abū Qudāma said, 'Mālik had the best memory of the people of his time.'

Yaḥyā ibn Sa'īd al-Qaṭṭān said, 'There is no one among the people with sounder *ḥadīths* than Mālik ('people' meaning al-Awzā'ī and the two Sufyāns). I prefer Mālik to Ma'mar. Mālik is the *imām* of the people in *ḥadīths.*' He also said, 'Mālik is the Amīr al-Mu'minīn in *Ḥadīth.*' 'Alī ibn al-Madīnī and Yaḥyā ibn Sa'īd also said that.

Yaḥyā said, 'Mālik was a *ḥāfiẓ*.' He said, 'Mālik is an *imām* to be followed.'

Yaḥyā ibn Ma'īn said, 'Mālik is noble in opinion, noble in knowledge. The earlier ones took from Mālik and thought him reliable. He was sound in *ḥadīths*. He was one of the proofs of Allah to His creation. He was the *imām* in *Ḥadīth*.' He said, 'He made him foremost among the people of az-Zuhrī.' He said, 'I have not seen anyone with greater retention of *ḥadīths* than him and Sufyān.'

He was asked, 'Do you consider Mālik or al-Layth higher?' He replied, 'Mālik. He was the highest and the firmest of the people of az-Zuhrī and the firmest of people in everything.'

He said, 'Mālik is one of the Imāms of the Muslims. His excellence and firmness in *ḥadīths* is agreed upon.'

He said, 'Mālik is the star of the People of *Ḥadīth* who refrain from the weak men. He is the transmitter from the sons of the Muhājirūn and the Anṣār.'

'Alī ibn al-Madīnī said, 'I have not put anyone over Mālik in the soundness of the *ḥadīth*. Mālik is the Amīr al-Mu'minīn in *ḥadīths*.'

He said, 'I will give you *ḥadīths* from such a one that your eyes have not seen (one version has 'my eyes') his like,' and he gave *ḥadīths* from Mālik.

He said, 'If it had not been that Allah Almighty sent the likes of Mālik, Shu'ba and al-Awzā'ī in every age, they would have inserted into the *ḥadīths* of the Messenger of Allah what was not in it.'

He said, 'Mālik and Ibn 'Uyayna are enough for you in memory and proficiency when they agree.'

Bakr ibn Aḥmad ibn Muqbil said, 'Mālik ibn Anas is the upright proof.'

Al-Bukhārī, Abu Zur'a ar-Rāzī, Muḥammad ibn 'Abd al-Ḥakam, Abū 'Abdullāh ibn ar-Rabī' and more than one said, 'Mālik ibn Anas is an *imām*.'

Ayyūb ibn Suwayd said, 'Mālik is the Imām of the Abode of the Hijra and the *Sunna*, and the truthful reliable one.' He said, 'I have not seen anyone more excellent in *ḥadīths* than him.'

Abū Ḥātim ar-Rāzī said, 'The reliable sources of the Muslims in whom there is no doubt are: ath-Thawri, Shu'ba, Mālik, Ibn 'Uyayna and Ḥammād ibn Zayd.'

Abū Zur'a ar-Rāzī said, 'He was asked about him and about Ayyūb and others in the companions of Nāfi'. He said, "Mālik and his leadership."'

He said, 'In *fiqh* Mālik is like the karyābūka [housekeeper?] who manages the business of the house and works for everything that will put it right.'

Saḥnūn said, 'When Ibn Ghānim read a book from the *Muwaṭṭā'* to us, a man asked him, 'Do you like this from the words of Mālik?' He threw the book from his hand and declared, 'Would it not be a deficiency in my intellect and my *dīn* if I should refute Mālik's words? I met the slaves and the people of scrupulousness and the *dīn* who were scrupulous about the smallest things and more: Sufyān and those with Sufyān, but these eyes have not seen one more scrupulous than Mālik."

[The caliph] Abū Ja'far al-Manṣūr said to him, 'You are the one with the most knowledge of the people of the earth (or the most knowing of all people)!' He exclaimed, 'No, by Allah!' Then he said to him, 'Indeed you are, but you conceal it.'

We find in another tradition from him, 'There does not remain on the face of the earth any with more knowledge than me and you.' He also said, pointing at him, 'The people will remain in blessing as long as this one remains with them.'

Al-Mughīra was asked about Mālik and 'Abd al-'Azīz. He said, 'They were not at all equal in knowledge. Mālik was higher than him.'

Ziyād ibn Yūnus said, 'The likeness of Mālik among scholars is like the *tharīd*-broth among dishes. It is equal to them, but they are not equal to it.'

At-Tustarī said, 'Abū 'Abdullāh az-Zubayr said while we were discussing the schools, that with the school of Mālik, he could manage without their schools, but there was none of their schools which would let him dispense with his school.'

Ḥumayd ibn al-Aswad said that Mālik said, 'For us, the Imām with the people after 'Umar ibn al-Khaṭṭāb was Zayd ibn Thābit, and the Imām of the people after Zayd ibn Thābit was 'Abdullāh ibn 'Umar.'

'Alī ibn al-Madīnī said, 'Twenty-one men who followed his opinion took from Zayd and established it: Qabīṣa, Khārija ibn Zayd, 'Ubayd ibn 'Abdullāh ibn 'Utba, Ibn Mas'ūd, 'Urwa ibn az-Zubayr, Abū Salama, al-Qāsim ibn Muḥammad, Abū Bakr ibn 'Abd ar-Raḥmān, Sālim, Sa'īd ibn al-Musayyab, Abān ibn 'Uthmān, and Sulaymān ibn Yasār.

'Then the knowledge of all these went to three men: Ibn Shihāb, Bukayr ibn 'Abdullāh ibn al-Ashajj and Abū az-Zinād. Then the knowledge of all these went to Mālik ibn Anas. Ibn Mahdī liked this *isnād* and favoured it.'

Muḥammad ibn 'Īsā said, 'One day the People of *Ḥadīth* were discussing the *fuqahā'* and they mentioned those who could not be discredited in memory and scrupulousness. They mentioned Ḥammād ibn Zayd, Mālik ibn Anas and Yazīd ibn Zuray'.'

'Abd ar-Raḥīm – and I think that he was Ibn 'Abdi Rabbih – said when Asad [ibn al-Furāt] went out to raid, 'I asked him about what he placed his reliance. He told me, "If you desire Allah and the Next World, you must have the knowledge of Mālik."'

Abū Isḥāq al-Jabanyānī said, 'The school is the school of the people of Madina, the school of Madina.'

Ibn Waddāḥ said, 'Yaḥyā ibn Ma'īn asked me, "Do you rely on the knowledge of Mālik?" I replied, "On the knowledge of Mālik." He said, "He is enough for you."'

Sa'īd ibn al-Ḥaddād said, 'Mālik was one of those firmly-rooted in Islam.' Abū Ṭālib said to him one day, 'And in knowledge, Abu 'Uthmān?' He replied, 'By Allah, he was firmer in knowledge than the unshakeable mountains.'

Ḥammād ibn Zayd said, 'I came to Madina when a caller was calling out, 'None gives *fatwā* and *ḥadīth* in the mosque of the Messenger of Allah ﷺ except for Mālik.'"

Ibn Wahb said, 'I went on *ḥajj* in 148 and a caller was calling out in Madina, "No one gives *fatwā* to the people except Mālik and Ibn Abī Dhi'b."' One version has 'Abd al-'Azīz in place of Ibn Abī Dhi'b.

'Abdullāh ibn al-Mājishūn said, 'The governor's messenger went out during the time of the *ḥajj* and called out, "No one gives *fatwā* to the people except for 'Abdullāh ibn 'Umar, Yaḥyā ibn Sa'īd and Mālik ibn Anas."' Ibn Kāsib mentioned something similar.

Ḥusayn ibn 'Urwa said, 'I heard a caller calling out in the days of the festival: "No one gives *fatwā* to the people except for Mālik, Ibn Abī az-Zinād and ad-Darāwardī."'

Al-Musayyibī said, 'It reached me that the governors of Madina used to not give permission to anyone to give *fatwā* except for Mālik and Ibn Abī az-Zinād '

Qāḍī Abu 'Abdullah at-Tustari said, 'It appears that these traditions come in one time after another, and Allah knows best, because of the difference of the generations of those connected to Mālik in them.'

We find in the story of the beginning of ash-Shāfi'ī when he wanted to study knowledge in Makka, 'I asked, "Who is known for this matter?" I was told, "Mālik in Madina."'

Ibn Abī Ḥāzim said, "Abd al-'Azīz ibn al-Mājishūn told me, "Take booty from Mālik. None remain who have met the people except for me and him."'

Sa'īd ibn Dāwūd said, 'There was none in the time of Mālik higher in the estimation of the people of Madina than Mālik.'

Another said, 'I have not seen anyone better in clearing things up than Mālik. Whenever he cleared some point up, I was increased in my preference for him.'

Ibn Hurmuz was asked, 'We question you and you do not answer us, but Mālik and 'Abd al-'Azīz question you and you answer them.' He replied, 'Some weakness has entered my body and I am not certain that some of that might not have entered into my intellect in the same way. When you people ask me about something, I answer you and you accept it. Mālik and 'Abd al-'Aziz look into it. If it is correct, they accept. If it is otherwise, they leave it.'

Muḥammad ibn Sa'd said, 'Mālik was a firm reliable trustworthy man of *fiqh* and scrupulousness, a proof, a man of knowledge.'

Abū 'Alī ibn Abī Hilāl said, 'An-Nasā'ī was asked about Mu'āwiya. He said, "Islam is a house and the Companions, may Allah be pleased with them, are its door. Whoever speaks badly about any of them has violated sanctity."' Abū 'Alī ibn Abī Hilāl said, 'And I say that Mālik is the ring of the door. Whoever touches the ring, desires to enter the house. May Allah be pleased with all of them.'

The rest of their testimony about his truthfulness and firmness in traditions and the position about his *mursal ḥadīth*s and his ensuring the reliability of those from whom he related:

Ibn Mahdī said, 'Mālik was firmer than 'Abdullāh and Mūsā ibn 'Utba in transmitting from Nāfi' and [firmer] than Ismā'īl ibn Umayya and than all people.' Yaḥyā ibn Sa'īd and Yaḥyā ibn Ma'īn stated something similar. Sulaymān ibn Ḥarb said, 'Mālik was worthy of that.'

Ibn Mahdī said, 'I prefer Mālik from Ibn al-Musayyab to Qatāda from Ibn al-Musayyab unless Qatāda said, "I heard."'

Ibn Wahb said, 'None is more trustworthy or reliable than Mālik.'

When the *mursalāt* traditions of the Sufyāns, ath-Thawrī, al-A'mash and others were mentioned to him, Yaḥyā ibn Sa'īd al-Qaṭṭān said about some of them, 'just like the wind' and 'like nothing'. He was asked, 'And the *mursalāt* of Mālik?' He said, 'I prefer them. There was no person sounder in the *ḥadīths* than him.' He put him at the foremost of the people of az-Zuhrī. He said, 'I prefer Mālik from Sa'īd to Sufyān from Ibrāhīm.'

Aḥmad ibn Ḥanbal said, 'Mālik is better in *ḥadīths* from az-Zuhrī than Ibn 'Uyayna and Mālik is the firmest of people in transmitting from az-Zuhrī.'

Aḥmad ibn Ṣāliḥ said, 'A third of the *ḥadīths* of Mālik have an *isnād*. This degree does not belong to any of his peers. Mālik's *ḥadīths* were something like 1200 *ḥadīths*, meaning that which I related from him and he told.'

Abū al-Qāsim al-Lālakā'ī said that 'Alī ibn al-Madīnī said, 'Mālik had something like a thousand *ḥadīths*.'

Aḥmad ibn Ṣāliḥ mentioned al-Layth and Sufyān and began to exalt them. He said, 'Each of them is an Imām.' He was asked, 'And when Sufyān and Mālik differ about az-Zuhrī, which do you prefer?' He answered, 'Mālik.'

Sufyān ibn 'Uyayna said, 'Mālik and Ma'mar took from az-Zuhrī by review (*'arḍ*) and I took from them orally.'

Ibn Ma'īn said, 'Had they written a book, they would have been firmer than him.'

Al-Bukhārī said, 'Mālik is the firmest of people relating from az-Zuhrī.'

Yaḥyā ibn ʿAbdullāh said to Abū Zurʿa, 'This is not from *zaʿzaʿa* (commotion) from *zawbaʿa* (whirlwind). You remove the veil and look at the Messenger of Allah ﷺ with his Companions in his presence: Mālik from Nāfiʿ from Ibn ʿUmar.'

Wakīʿ said, 'The reliable one told me,' referring to Mālik ibn Anas.

The like of that is related from al-Qāsim ibn ʿAlī and Aḥmad ibn ʿAlī.

Al-Ḥasan ibn ʿAlī said, 'We were with Wuhayb ibn Khālid and he reported a *ḥadīth* from Mālik and Ibn Jurayj. I said to a man, "Write down Ibn Jurayj and leave out Mālik" because he was alive at that time. Wuhayb heard that and said, "Do you say, 'Leave out Mālik'?" We do not know of anyone between the east and the west who is more trustworthy than Mālik is in *ḥadīths* in our opinion."

Ibn al-Madīnī said, 'I prefer Mālik from a man from Saʿīd ibn al-Musayyab to Sufyān from a man from Ibrāhīm. Mālik would only give *ḥadīths* from reliable people.'

Abū Dāwūd said, 'The soundest in *ḥadīth* of the Messenger of Allah ﷺ is Mālik from Nāfiʿ from Ibn ʿUmar, then Mālik from az-Zuhrī from Sālim from his father, then Mālik from Abū az-Zinād from al-Aʿraj from Abū Hurayra.'

He did not mention anything except from Mālik.

He said, 'The *mursalāt* of Mālik are sounder than the *mursalāt* of Saʿīd ibn al-Musayyab and than the *mursalāt* of al-Hasan. Mālik is the soundest of people in the *mursal* of al-Ḥasan. Mālik is the soundest of people in *mursal* traditions.'

Sufyān said, 'When Mālik says, "It has reached me," it is a strong *isnād*.'

Yaḥyā ibn Saʿīd said, 'The *mursalāt* traditions of Mālik are sound.' Yaḥyā said, 'One of our companions said, "The *mursalāt* of Mālik are [equivalent to having an] *isnād*."'

Ibn Wahb said, 'Mālik and al-Layth are counting as an *isnād*, even if they do not give the *isnād*.'

Ibrāhīm al-Ḥarbī said, 'Mālik only gave the *mursal* from someone reliable.'

Aḥmad ibn Ḥanbal was asked about the *ḥadīths* of Jaʿfar ibn Muḥammad. He said, 'What should I say about it when it is related from Mālik?'

Al-Athram said, 'I asked Aḥmad ibn Ḥanbal about 'Amr ibn Abī 'Amr, the client of al-Muṭṭalib. He said, "Mālik ibn Anas confirmed his business. He related from him, and al-Bukhārī mentioned him in his *Ṣaḥīḥ* and said, 'Mālik related from him.'"'

The consensus of the people about him and the great ones following him and their need of him

Mālik said in what Ibn Wahb and Ibn al-Qāsim related from him, 'There is no one from whom I transmitted knowledge except that he was compelled to me so that he asked me about the business of his *dīn*.'

Ibn Abī Ḥāzim said, 'I saw Zayd ibn Aslam standing while asking him for a *fatwā*.'

Mālik said, 'Yaḥyā ibn Sa'īd said to me when he left for Iraq, "Gather together a hundred of Ibn Shihāb's *ḥadīths* from me so that I can relate them from you." I wrote them down and I gave them to him. He asked me, "Can I relate them from you?" I answered, "Yes!" It was said to him, "Did he hear them from you?" He said, "He has more *fiqh* than that."'

Yaḥyā ibn Sa'īd said, 'Mālik and ath-Thawrī met. Ath-Thawrī was questioning.

Ma'n said, 'I saw ath-Thawrī crowding with us at Mālik's door.'

Matrūḥ ibn Shākir said, 'Ibn Shihāb, Rabī'a and Mālik sat. Ibn Shihāb posed a question and Rabī'a gave an answer on it while Mālik remained silent. Ibn Shihāb said to him, "Why haven't you answered?" He replied, "The master has answered," or something to that effect. Ibn Shihāb said, "We will not part until you answer!" So he answered differently to Rabī'a's answer. Ibn Shihāb said, "Let us return to the words of Mālik."'

Ad-Darāwardī said, 'While I was sitting with Yaḥyā ibn Sa'īd al-Anṣārī and Hishām ibn 'Urwa, I heard one of them say to the other, "How long will this man be among us while we do not go to him to listen to him or to take from him?" I said to myself, "A man to whom these two go to take knowledge is such that I should not be ignorant of him!" They got up and I got up with them. They came to Mālik's door and asked for his permission to go in. It was not long before we heard the falling of the cushions and he gave them permission to enter. They went in and I went in with them. They said, "Abū 'Abdullāh! Give us *ḥadīths* from Ibn Shihāb!"'

When Sufyān ath-Thawri was asked about the rare (*shādhdh*[1]) *ḥadīths,* he said, 'Leave them. The Ḥijāzī man forbade their use,' meaning Mālik.

Yaḥyā ibn Ma'īn said, 'Yaḥyā ibn Sa'īd al-Qaṭṭān listened to Mālik when Mālik was still a young man.'

Shu'ba said, 'I entered Madina in 117 AH, a year after the death of Nāfi' (a sounder version has 118 AH) and I saw that Mālik had a circle. When people disagreed about something they would look to him to see what he would say.'

Qāḍī Muḥammad ibn Aḥmad al-Baṣrī said, 'In this year, Shu'ba listened to Mālik and Mālik was about twenty years old at that time.'

Ibn Abi Uways said, 'All people espoused the opinion of Mālik ibn Anas, and the governor had a man with him to question him. It was the same with the *qāḍī* and the *muḥtasib.*'

Sa'īd ibn Manṣūr said, 'I saw Mālik performing *ṭawāf* while Sufyān ath-Thawrī was behind him learning from him as the child learns from his teacher. Whenever Mālik did something, Sufyān also did it to imitate him.'

Ibn 'Uyayna said, 'Where are we with Mālik? We followed the tracks of Mālik. When Mālik used a shaykh as a source, we would also do so.'

One of them said, 'I was with Ibn 'Uyayna when a man asked him about performing the *'Īd* sacrifice at night. Sufyan said, "There is no harm in it." I told him, "Ibn Wahb reports from Mālik that the sacrifice is not done at night. He recited, *'In specific days'* (22:28)." Ibn 'Uyayna shouted after the man and told him, "This man has informed me from Ibn Wahb that Mālik did not sacrifice at night!"'

He mentioned that Ibn Wahb was the one who related this statement of Mālik to Ibn 'Uyayna.

Ibn 'Uyayna said, 'When Mālik performed *ḥajj,* the *ṭawāf* was constricted by the number of people following his example.'

Yaḥyā said that ash-Shafi'ī said, 'I broke the fast at Madina with

[1] *Shādhdh* = a tradition from a single transmitter which contradicts another.

Mālik, and he went out to the *'Īd* and prayed. Then he left and looked at the people in the room of the Prophet ﷺ while he was standing at the door of the mosque. He said, "What is the matter with them?" They answered, "They went to greet the Prophet ﷺ." He returned to the square to the enclosure where the poor were fed during Ramaḍān and did not enter the mosque. I saw that the people had left the mosque to follow where he went.'

'Atīq ibn Ya'qūb said, 'The people of Madina did not agree on anyone after the Prophet ﷺ except for Abū Bakr and 'Umar. Mālik died, and we do not know of any of the people of Madina who did not agree about him before he died.'

Ḥumayd ibn al-Aswad said, 'The people of Madina did not imitate after the words of Zayd ibn Thābit as they imitated the words of Mālik.'

Ibn Abī Uways said, 'I was present at the Rain Prayer in the prayer place. When the Imām changed his cloak, Mālik stood up and changed the small dark cloak he was wearing. People stood up and changed their cloaks. When Mālik left, he was asked, "Is it part of the *sunna* of the Rain Prayer that when the Imām changes his cloak, the people stand up and change their cloaks?" He said, "They do not have to stand up. They can change them while sitting. I got up because my cloak was under me and I could not change it without getting up."'

Marwān ibn Muḥammad said, 'Mālik did not abandon a transmission from anyone unless it was weak.'

Ibn Kināna said that al-'Umari[1] said to Mālik, 'The people of the two Ḥarams have given me homage and you decide in favour of the injustice of Abū Ja'far (al-Manṣūr)?' Mālik said to him, 'Do you know what kept 'Umar ibn 'Abd al-'Azīz from appointing a virtuous man to succeed him?' He answered, 'No.' He said, 'The homage was made to Yazīd and 'Umar feared that if he gave the homage to another man, Yazīd would start a civil war and people would fight and so what was not correct would sow dissension.' Al-'Umari preferred Mālik's opinion.

[1] 'Abd al-'Azīz ibn 'Abdullāh ibn 'Umar, d. 171 or 172 AH. He rebelled with an-Nafs az-Zakiyya.

Sufyān said, 'Mālik was a lamp. Ath-Thawrī went on *ḥajj*. I performed *ṭawāf* with him. There was not a great number with him. Mālik came forward and performed *ṭawāf* of the house, and the *ṭawāf* was congested by the people because there were so many of them.'

When Mālik related from Yazīd ibn 'Abdullāh ibn al-Hādī, about a thousand camels travelled to Yazīd. In the morning, Yazīd looked at how many people had come to his door. He said, 'What is this?' He was told, 'Mālik has related from you.'

Dāwūd ibn Mihrān said, 'When I came to Madina, I attended a funeral prayer. There was not one of the Banū Hāshim, the Quraysh and the people who did not attend it. When the bier left, Mālik got up and the people got up when he got up. He went walking in front of it, and the people followed him and I did not see anyone behind the bier. Mālik was their Imām.'

Al-Layth said, 'I made supplication for Mālik in my prayer,' and he mentioned the need that people had for him in *fatwās*.

Ash-Shāfi'ī said, 'I saw al-Mughīra, Ibn Abī Ḥāzim and ad-Darāwardī adopting the school of Mālik.'

Ibn Wahb said, 'I asked 'Abd al-'Azīz ibn al-Mājishūn about a question and he said, "I cannot think of an answer to it. But ask Mālik and then tell me what he says." I asked him and he told me. He stated, "Mālik is our master and our man of knowledge."'

'Abd al-'Azīz ibn al-Mājishūn mentioned a question in which the statement of his father and that of Mālik disagreed. He said, 'I say that it is the statement of Mālik. I incline with Mālik where he inclines. He was given success.'

Khālid ibn Nizār said, 'Muslim ibn Khālid az-Zanjī visited Mālik and Mālik said to him, "Muslim! What are these things which have reached me about you in which you differ from the people of Madina?" He said, "Abū 'Abdullāh! May Allah make you thrive! I have gathered some things which I want to ask you about." Mālik said, "Let's have them! I want Allah to give you right guidance, but I dislike for you to differ from the people of Madina for other people."'

Muḥammad ibn al-Ḥasan ash-Shaybānī said, 'I stood at Mālik's door for two or three years to listen to him.' He used to say that he had heard more than seven hundred *ḥadīths* from him.

Yaḥyā ibn Yaḥyā at-Tamīmī said, 'I stayed with Mālik ibn Anas for a year after I had finished listening to him in order to learn his form and his qualities. They are the qualities of the Companions and the Tābi'ūn,' or something to that effect.

Muḥammad ibn 'Abd al-Ḥakam said, 'When ash-Shāfi'ī was asked about something, he would say, "This is the statement of the master," i.e. Mālik. He said about him, "Mālik is my master. Mālik is my teacher," and he took knowledge from him. There was no one more gracious to me than Mālik. I was one of the boys of Mālik, and I have put Mālik between me and Allah as a proof.'

Ibn Wahb said, 'If it had not been that Allah let us ask for *fatwā*s from Mālik and al-Layth, we would have been misguided.'

Mālik was asked about 'Abdullāh ibn 'Abd ar-Raḥmān al-Anṣārī from whom Ibn Sam'ān related *ḥadīths*. He said, 'I do not know him.' The people said, 'One of the men of Madina of the Anṣār? He relates from him and Mālik does not know him?' So the people suspected him.

'Alī ibn al-Madīnī said, 'When Mālik related *ḥadīths* from a man of the people of Madina who we did not know, he was a proof because he selected him.' 'Alī said, 'Mālik is my master among the people of Madina and Yaḥyā among the people of Iraq.'

One of those who wrote about his virtues related that Ibn Hurmuz passed by the house of one of the people of *Qadar* (free will) who was standing with a female client of his. Ibn Hurmuz said, 'So-and-so! You are on the road and this is not lawful for you!' He said, 'This is my house, my female client and my servants, so what can be blamed in someone like me?'He told one of his slaves, 'Tread on his belly,' and they trod on him so that he had to be carried back to his house.

People visited him, and Mālik was one of them. He began to complain and people prayed for him while Mālik was silent. Then he spoke. He said, 'You had no right to do this. You went to one of the men of the people of *Qadar* at the door of his house who had his servants and clients with him.' Ibn Hurmuz said to him, 'Do you think that I made a mistake?' He answered, 'Yes, by Allah,' and he mentioned the rest of the story.

When Ḥammād ibn Zayd came to Madina, none of the companions

of Mālik went to him. Ḥammād went and complained about that to him. He told him, 'I commanded them to do that.' He said, 'Why, Abū 'Abdullāh?' He said, 'Because you, people of Iraq, write things down in Madina from those whom we consider to have no standing in testimony, so we suspect that you do the same thing in your land.' Ḥammād returned and cast away most of his knowledge.

Saḥnūn said, 'A man of the people of Egypt came with their questions for Rabī'a and he found that he had died. He said, "I did not want to go back without finding answers. I saw a circle in the mosque who were delving into knowledge and I sat down with them and told them about my business. I said to them, 'If you have knowledge, then answer me so you can give me right guidance.' They all pointed out Mālik ibn Anas. He was at that time a young man sitting alone by a column. I did not leave any circle but that I sat down with them and I asked them and they all pointed him out to me. I came to him and told him about my news and that the people had pointed him out to me." He mentioned that he questioned him and whenever he told him a question, he wept and then he answered him.'

Saḥnūn said, 'He wept when he recognised it and knew that he was needed in it.'

Al-Maghāmī reported from 'Abd al-Mālik: 'I heard Muṭarrif and Ibn al-Mājishūn speaking about what Mālik said about women who are *umm walads* when they are demanded (by someone who claims a prior right over them so as to pre-empt the buyer's purchase) that they are taken along with the price of their children, until the mother of his child, Muḥammad, was demanded. The representative of the one who demanded her argued about her with Mālik's representative before al-Muṭṭalib, the governor of Madina. Al-Muṭṭalib said, "I do not think that there is anyone from whom I can seek advice in this matter except him." The representative of the appellant said, "Do you ask his advice in a matter which has happened to him?" Al-Muṭṭalib said, "Someone like him is not doubted. If his friend were present, we would ask for his advice," meaning Ibn Abī Salama.

'He asked for Mālik's advice on that and he said, "My opinion is as you know and it has taken place with people so that I saw the strong business applied to the mother of my child. She is being taken from my authority although I bought her from the market of the Muslims and she became pregnant immediately. I ransomed her with all my property and the one to whom the price was given was not wronged."

'He gave judgement by that. The people of Madina did not rejoice so much in anything as their joy at these *fatwās*.' Something similar is found in *ath-Thamāniyya* [*The Eight of Abū Zayd 'Abd ar-Raḥmān*] and *al-Wāḍiḥa*. That is the position of Ibn Kināna and Ibn al-Mājishūn.

Abū Muḥammad aḍ-Ḍarrāb and others said that a group of the shaykhs related from Mālik from whom he himself they related. They are:

Yaḥyā ibn Sa'īd al-Anṣārī
Abū al-Aswad ibn Nawfal
Ziyād ibn Sa'd
Ibn Shihāb
Hishām ibn 'Urwa
Rabī'a, and others besides them.

As for those of his comrades who related from him and died before or after him, they are numerous, like:

Ibn Jurayj
Ibn 'Ajlān
Ad-Darāwardī
'Abdullāh ibn Ja'far al-Madīnī
al-Layth
Nāfi' the reciter
'Abd al-'Azīz ibn al-Mājishūn
Sufyān ibn 'Uyayna and Sufyān ath-Thawrī
Ḥammād ibn Salama and Ḥammād ibn Zayd
Az-Zanjī
Abū Ḥanīfa
His two companions (i.e. ash-Shaybānī and Abū Yūsuf al-Anṣārī)
Wakī'
Shu'ba

Al-Awzā'ī and others whom we will mention later.

Someone else said in one version, 'These shaykhs and their likes relating from Mālik is a proof of his immense importance.'

Ja'far al-Firyābī said, 'I do not know anyone among the Imams and the lofty ones from those who died a long time before him related except for Mālik. Yaḥyā ibn Sa'īd died thirty-five years before him, Ibn Jurayj thirty years, al-Awzā'ī twenty years, ath-Thawrī eight years and Shu'ba seven years.'

Qāḍī Imām Abū al-Faḍl said, 'Abū Ḥanīfa died thirty years before and Hammām by more than that. Stranger still was az-Zuhrī. He died fifty-five years before Mālik.'

Abū al-Ḥasan ad-Dāraquṭnī said, 'We do not know anyone before or after who gathered what Mālik gathered: that is that two men related the same *ḥadīths* from him and there was about one hundred and thirty year gap between their deaths: Muḥammad ibn Shihāb az-Zuhrī was his shaykh and he died in 125, and Abū Hudhāfa as-Sahmī died after 250. They both related the *ḥadīth* of al-Furay'a bint Mālik from him about the residence of a woman in her *'idda*.'

His careful investigation into knowledge, *fatwās* and *ḥadīths*, and his scrupulousness and fairness in that

'Abd ar-Raḥmān al-'Umarī said: Mālik told me, 'Sometimes a question comes to me which keeps me from eating, drinking or sleeping.' I said to him, "Abū 'Abdullāh! By Allah, your words are etched in stone among the people. You do not say anything but that they learn from you." He said, "So who is better entitled to be like that than the person who is like this? I saw someone in a dream saying, 'Mālik is protected.'"'

Ibn al-Qāsim said that he heard Mālik say, 'I have been reflecting on one question for some twenty years and even now I still do not have an opinion on it.'

Ibn Mahdī said that he heard Mālik say, 'Sometimes a question comes to me and I remain sleepless about it for many nights.'

Ibn 'Abd al-Ḥakam said:'When Mālik was asked about a question, he told the asker, "Go away so that I can look into it." The man would go away and come back again several times about it. We spoke to him about that. He wept and said, "I fear that I will be asked such questions on a Day – and what a Day that is!"'

Qarrād said: 'When Mālik sat, he bowed his head and moved his lips with *dhikr* of Allah and he did not turn either to the right or the left. When he was asked about a question, his complexion changed. He was reddish with some paleness. He would grow pale and bow his head and move his lips. Then he would say, "What Allah wills. There is no power nor strength except by Allah." Sometimes he would be asked fifty questions and not answer any of them.'

One of them said: 'By Allah, when Mālik was asked a question, it was as if he was standing between the Garden and the Fire.'

He used to say: 'Whoever wants to answer a question should turn himself towards the Garden and the Fire before he answers. How will save himself in the Next World? Then he can answer.'

He said: 'Nothing is harder for me than when I am asked a question about the *ḥalāl* and the *ḥarām* because this is absolute in the judgement of Allah. I met the people of knowledge and *fiqh* in our land, and if one of them was asked such a question, it was as if death were dearer to him. But I see the people of this time desiring to discuss it and give *fatwā*. If they had understood what it is that they are heading for Tomorrow, they would have done little of this.

'As for 'Umar ibn al-Khaṭṭāb, 'Alī and 'Alqama, the best of the Companions, and the best generation to whom the Prophet ﷺ was sent, when questions came to them, they would gather together the Companions of the Prophet ﷺ and ask. Then and only then would they give a *fatwā* regarding it. The people of our time now pride themselves in their *fatwā*s and the knowledge they have.'

He said, 'It was not the way of the people nor of those who passed away before us who are followed and on whom Islam is based to say, "This is *ḥalāl* and this is *ḥarām*": they would say, "I dislike this" and "I think this." But as for the *ḥalāl* and the *ḥarām*, that is inventing things against Allah. I have heard the words of Allah: *"Say: 'What do you think about the things Allah has sent down to you as provision and which you have then designated as lawful and unlawful?'"* (10:59) because the *ḥalāl* is what Allah and His Messenger have made *ḥalāl* and the *ḥarām* is what they have made *ḥarām*.'

Mūsā ibn Dāwūd said: 'I have not seen any scholar who said more often, "I do not think it good" than Mālik. Sometimes I heard him say, "It is not like this in our city."'

Marwān ibn Muḥammad said, 'I used to see Mālik say to the man who asked him, "Go away so that I can look into the business."'

I said, 'The *fiqh* is from his mind and Allah only raised him up by his *taqwā*.'

Saḥnūn said: 'Mālik told us one day that he had reflected for twenty years on a single question.'

Ibn Mahdī said, 'A man asked Mālik about a question and he mentioned that he had been sent for that purpose on a six-month journey from Morocco. Mālik told him, "Tell the one who sent you that I have no knowledge of it." He asked, "Then who knows it?" He replied, "Whomever Allah has taught about it."'

A man asked him about a question which the people of the Maghrib had entrusted to him. He said, 'I do not know. We have not been tested with this matter in our land and we have not heard any of our shaykhs speak about it, so you can go back.' The next day the man came and he had loaded his baggage on a mule he was leading. He said, 'My question?' Mālik said, 'I do not know. What is it?'

The man said, 'Abū 'Abdullāh! I have left behind me people who say that there is no one on the face of the earth with more knowledge than you!' Mālik replied without any disquiet, 'When you return, tell them that I do not think that that is true.'

Another person questioned him and he did not answer him. The man said to him, 'Abū 'Abdullāh! Answer me!' He said, 'Bother you! Do you want to make me a proof between you and Allah? I first need to look to see where my deliverance lies and then I will deliver you.'

Ibn Abī Ḥāzim said that Mālik said, 'When a man is asked a question, he begins with himself in order to preserve himself.'

Al-Haytham ibn Jamīl said, 'I saw Mālik being asked about forty-eight questions and he said, "I do not know" in response to thirty-two of them.'

Khālid ibn Khidāsh said, 'I came from Iraq to Mālik with forty questions and he only answered five of them for me.'

Mālik said that Ibn 'Ajlān used to say when a man of knowledge erred, 'I do not know whether a mortal blow has been struck.' These words were related from Ibn 'Abbas.

Mālik said, 'I heard Ibn Hurmuz say, "A man of knowledge must bequeath to people who sit with him the words, 'I do not know' so that will become a basic principle in their possession which they can use. When one of them is asked about something he does not know, he can then say, 'I do not know.'"'

Ibn Wahb said, 'Mālik used to say about much of what he was asked, "I do not know."' 'Umar ibn Yazīd said, 'I asked Mālik about that and he said, "The people of Syria refer to Syria, the people of Iraq to Iraq, and the people of Egypt to Egypt. Perhaps I might refute the *fatwās* that they have been given."' Ibn Wahb said that he told al-Layth about that and he wept and said, 'By Allah, Mālik is stronger than al-Layth!' or words to that effect.

Ma'n ibn 'Īsā said that he heard Mālik say, 'I am a man who is sometimes right and sometimes wrong, so look into my opinion. Take all that agrees with the Book and the *Sunna* and leave all that does not agree with the Book and the *Sunna*.'

Ibn Abī Uways said, 'Mālik was once asked about twenty questions and he only answered one of them. Sometimes he was asked about a hundred questions and only answered five or ten. About the rest he said, "I do not know."'

Abū Muṣ'ab said, 'Al-Mughīra said to us, "Come let us get together and mention all that we still have about which we wish to question Mālik." We gathered that and he wrote it all down on a piece of paper and al-Mughīra took it to him to ask him the questions. He answered some and he after a lot of it, "I do not know."'

Al-Mughīra said, 'People, by Allah. Allah has not elevated this man by anything except *taqwā*. Who among you is asked about this and is prepared to say, "I do not know"?'

Ibn Wahb said, 'I asked Mālik about thirty thousand questions – events in his own lifetime – and he only answered a third or a half of them – or what Allah willed with "I do not know" or "I do not think it good."' He said, 'If a man had filled his page with Mālik's word, "I do not know," he could have done that before he had answered a question.'

Muṣ'ab said, 'My father sent me with my friend to Mālik with a question. He read it to him and he replied, "I cannot think of a good answer for it. Ask the people of knowledge."

Ibn Abī Ḥassān said, 'Mālik was asked about twenty-two questions in my presence and he only answered two of them after he had said many times, "There is no power nor strength except by Allah, the High, the Immense."'

A man would ask him about a question and he would say, 'Knowledge is vaster than this man.'

One of them said to him, 'Since you, Abū 'Abdullāh, say, "I do not know," who does know?' He said, 'Bother you! You do not know me. Who am I? What is my position that I should know what you do not know?' Then he used as a proof the words of Ibn 'Umar and said, 'This man, Ibn 'Umar, said, "I do not know. Who am I? Pride and seeking after leadership has destroyed people. This melts away very quickly."'

Another time he said, "Umar ibn al-Khaṭṭāb was tested with these things and he did not answer them. Ibn az-Zubayr said, "I do not know" and Ibn 'Umar said, "I do not know."'

Muṣ'ab said: 'Mālik was asked about a question and said, "I do not know." The asker said to him, "It is a simple matter and I want to tell the governor about it." The asker was a man of some merit, so Mālik got angry and said, "A light, simple question! There is nothing light in knowledge! Have you not heard the words of Allah, *'We will impose a weighty word on you'*? (73:5) All knowledge is weighty and especially what we will be asked about on the Day of Rising."'

One of them said, 'I never heard a more frequent remark from Mālik than, "There is no power nor strength except by Allah." If we wanted to leave our boards filled with his words, "I do not know." *'We have only been conjecturing. We are by no means certain'* (45:32)," we could have done it.'

Ibn al-Qāsim said, 'After the people of Madina, there are none with more knowledge of sales than the people of Egypt.' Mālik said, 'And from where did they learn them?' He replied, 'From you.' Mālik said, 'I do not know them, so how could they learn them from me?'

Mufaḍḍal ibn Faḍāla said, 'Mālik only counted with the same care as the cashier of the treasury.'

Ibn Abī Ḥātim said, 'I said to Ibn Ma'n, 'Mālik does not speak much." He replied, "That is due to his great discrimination."'

Mālik was asked about some *ḥadīths* in which things are put in a different order while the meaning remains the same. He said, 'As for what has come of the words of the Prophet ﷺ, a man must quote it as it has come. As for the words of other people, there is no harm in that.' He was asked, 'And the *ḥadīth* of the Prophet ﷺ where the *wāw* and *alif* is added while the meaning remains the same?' He answered, 'I prefer that it is slight.' Ibn 'Ufayr related the like of it from him.

Al-Qaṭṭān said, 'When Mālik died, I brought his books and I found a book in it from Ibn 'Umar although the *Muwaṭṭā'* only contained two *ḥadīths* from him.'

Ibn Wahb said that Mālik said, 'I listened to many *ḥadīths* from Ibn Shihāb which I did not relate at all nor will I relate them.' Al-Farawī said, 'I asked him, "Why?" He answered, "There was no action based on them."'

'Atīq ibn Ya'qūb said, 'Mālik said to me, "I took ten books from Ibn Shihāb, inside and out. There are some things among them which I have not related since I took them at Madina."'

A man said to Mālik, 'Ath-Thawrī gave us a *ḥadīth* from you about such-and-such.' He said, 'I gave a *ḥadīth* about such-and-such and such-and-such which I have not made known in Madina.'

Mālik's son said, 'When we buried Mālik, we entered his house and brought out his books. There were seven books containing the *ḥadīths* of Ibn Shihāb, filled both inside and out, and he had books – or boxes – containing the *ḥadīths* of the people of Madina. People began to read and they made supplication and said, "May Allah have mercy on you, Abū 'Abdullāh! We sat with you for a very long time and we did not see you mentioning any of what we have read!"'

We find in one version from his son, there is the opposite of this, 'We only found that he had one book in which there were *ḥadīths* from Ibn Shihāb which were written over others.'

It is related that Isḥāq ibn Bābayn said, 'In what Mālik left, we found two locked boxes which contained books. My father began to read them and weep. He said, "May Allah have mercy on you! You only desired the face of Allah by your knowledge! I sat with him for a very long time, and I did not hear him relate anything of what I have read."'

'Atīq ibn Ya'qūb mentioned that he entered Mālik's house after his death with his son and opened boxes filled with books, and he read them, and he mentioned something similar to that. Then he opened another box, and he brought out twelve thousand *ḥadīths* of az-Zuhrī, and he opened another and brought out seven books filled inside and out with the *ḥadīths* of the people of Madina. 'In them, I did not see what his companions mentioned during his lifetime.'

Aḥmad ibn Ṣāliḥ said, 'I looked into the roots of Mālik, and I found that they were something on the order of twelve thousand *ḥadīths*.' One of them said, 'That was the *ḥadīths* of the people of Madina at that time. Mālik only related a third or a fourth of them.' He said, 'Ibn Abī Uways has given that Mālik heard something like three hundred and fifty *ḥadīths* from az-Zuhrī. The books of Mālik were brought out to me in parchment except for Ibn Shihāb's book. I reckoned that there was about twelve thousand *ḥadīths*.'

Ash– Shāfi'ī said that Mālik was asked, 'Does Ibn 'Uyayna have *ḥadīths* which you do not have?' He said, 'If I were to relate to people all that I have heard, then I would have been an idiot!' In one version: 'Then I would want to misguide them. *Ḥadīths* have come from me such that I wish I would be whipped for every *ḥadīth* of them and I wish that I had not related them. I used to frighten people about the whips.' In another version, 'I wish that I had been struck with a whip for every question on which I spoke.'

Ad-Darāwardī reported, 'I said to him, "Tell me the *ḥadīth* of the skin on the head," and he replied, "No." I said to him, "Sufyān relates it from you." He said, "He spoke the truth. If I had given a *ḥadīth* to anyone, I would give it to him. The action in our city is not based on it and our friend does not live here."'

When he was told, 'This is a *ḥadīth* which no one except you has,' he would abandon it. If he was told, 'This is used by the people of innovation as a proof', he would also abandon it.

He was told, 'So-and-so relates *gharīb ḥadīth* to us.' He said, 'We flee from the *gharīb*[1].'

Abū Muṣ'ab said: Mālik was asked, 'Why do you not transmit *ḥadīths* from the people of Iraq?' He said, 'Because I saw that when they came to us, they took *ḥadīths* from unreliable people and I said, "So they are like this in their land."'

[1] *Gharīb*: unusual, a tradition traces uninterruptedly to the Prophet ﷺ, but only related by one of the *Tābi'ūn* or the *Tābi'ū't-Tābi'īn*.

He said, 'I have some *ḥadīths* such that if my head were to be beaten with a whip, I still would not relate them.'

Ibn 'Uyayna said, 'Mālik only conveyed the sound *ḥadīths*. He only gave *ḥadīths* from someone reliable.'

Ash-Shāfi'ī said, 'When Mālik doubted part of a *ḥadīth*, he threw all of it away.'

Ma'n said, 'I heard Mālik say, "I am a man who sometimes errs and sometimes is right, so investigate my opinion. Take all that agrees with the Book and the *Sunna* and leave all that does not agree with the Book and the *Sunna*."'

Ibn al-Qāsim, Ibn Wahb, and Ashhab reported something from him with with the same meaning. Not all that the man says, even if he is excellent, is to be followed and taken as a *sunna* and taken to the cities. Allah says, '*Give good news to My slaves who listen well to what is said and follow the best of it.*' (39:18)

Ashhab said, 'Mālik was asked about a question and answered it. Then he immediately said, "I do not know. We only have a supposition and that is the opinion. I am a man who is sometimes right and sometimes wrong. Not all that I say should be written down."'

Ashhab said, 'He saw me write down his answer to a question and he said, "Do not write it down. I do not know whether I will remain firm in it or not."'

Ibn Wahb said, 'I heard him say in what he was asked about the business of judicial decision, "This is the property of the Sultan." I heard him find fault with a scholar giving many answers so that he (i.e. the man who had sat for this) is questioned. The student of the book does it, while the man was sitting. When the scholar is asked about something, he hears it.'

When he was asked a lot of questions, he would refrain and say, 'That is enough for you. Whoever takes a lot makes mistakes.' He criticised doing a lot of that. He said, 'He spoke as if he were an excited camel. He says, "It is like this and it is like that" while he is roaring out everything.'

An Iraqi man asked him about a man who stepped on a dead chicken and an egg came out of it and then the egg broke and had a young chick in it. Could he eat it? Mālik said, 'Ask about what exists and leave what does not.'

Someone else asked him a similar question and Mālik did not answer him. He said, 'Aren't you going to answer me, Abū 'Abdullāh?' He replied, 'If you had asked me about something that would benefit you, I would have answered you.'

Ibn al-Mu'adhdhal said, 'Mālik was told, "Quraysh say that you do not mention their fathers and men of excellence in your assembly." Mālik replied, "We are speaking about something whose blessing we hope for."'

Ibn al-Qāsim said, 'Mālik used almost not answer us at all, and so his companions would resort to tricks. A man would present a question the answer to which they wanted to know as if it were a question of urgency, and then he would answer it."'

Mālik told Ibn Wahb, 'Be fearful of a lot of questions. This which you hear should not be related.' He told him, 'I hear it so that I will know it, not so that I will relate it.' Mālik told him, 'A man does not hear anything but that he speaks about it. Similarly, I have heard things from Ibn Shihāb which I have not given, and I hope that I will not do so for as long as I live.'

Al-Bayāḍī said that he said, 'I regret that I did not throw away more *ḥadīths* than I did throw out.'

Al-Qāsim ibn Mabrūr said to him, 'Abū 'Abdullāh, do you think that there are *ḥadīths* which are related from you and on which your opinion is not based by anything which you have confirmed?' He replied, 'If I had known at the beginning of my business what would be the end, I would not have done it, but it spread with the people. If someone asked me about it and I did not relate it to him with another *ḥadīth*, he would have made me a target.'

Bishr ibn 'Umar said, 'I once asked Mālik about a man and he said, "If he had been reliable, you would have seen him in my books."'

A man asked him about a question whose answer had defeated the people of Madina and he refused to answer. The man came again and Mālik still refused. He refused a third time. It seemed as if the man thought little of Mālik's knowledge. Someone came to the man in a dream and said to him, 'Do you think little of Mālik's knowledge? Go to him and question him. Even if your question is finer than a hair and harder than a stone, he will be given success in it by his seeking help with "Whatever Allah wills. There is no strength nor power except by Allah, the High, the Immense."'

Ashhab said, 'I saw someone saying in a dream, "Mālik clings to a certain phrase in his *fatwās*. It is such that if the mountains had come to him, it would have uprooted them. It is, *'It is what Allah wills. There is no strength but in Allah.'* (18:39)"'

Al-Qa'nabī said, 'I came to Mālik and found him weeping. I asked him about that and he said, "Who should weep more than I? I do not say anything without having it written down and carried off in all directions."'

Mālik said, 'I have only my own opinion in three questions.'

Description of Mālik's assembly, his disseminating knowledge, his preserving it and his respect for the *ḥadīths* of the Prophet ﷺ

Qāḍī 'Iyāḍ aid that al-Wāqidī and others said, 'Mālik would sit on cushions and rugs scattered in his room for the comfort of visitors from Quraysh, the Anṣār and other people. His assembly was one of gravity and forbearance. He was a noble dignified man, and there was no quarrelling nor clamour nor raised voices in his assembly. When he was asked about something, he answered the questioner and did not say to him, "From where did you get this?"

'Strangers would ask him about one or two *ḥadīths*, and he would answer them one after the other. Sometimes he gave permission to one of them to read to him. He had a scribe called Ḥabīb who copied out his books, and he would read them out to the assembly. None of those present came near him or looked into his book nor asked him out of their great awe and respect for him. When Ḥabīb made an error, Mālik pointed it out to him, but that was rare, and he himself did not read his books to anyone.

'He was like a sultan with a chamberlain who announced people to him. When people gathered at his door, the doorkeeper would seek his permission and he invited them inside. He first selected his companions. When he finished with the elite, then the common people were given permission to enter. This was widely known about the oral sessions of the companions of Mālik. They would recite to him, and many reports supported this. However, Yaḥyā ibn Bukayr mentioned that he heard the *Muwaṭṭā'* from Mālik fourteen times. He claimed that most of it was read by Mālik, although some of it was read out to him.'

Mālik was rebuked for giving preference to his companions. He replied, 'They are my companions and the neighbours of the Messenger of Allah ﷺ.'

Ismā'īl ibn Ḥammād said, 'I came to Mālik and saw him sitting in front of his room while his companions were sitting at the sides of the room. Abū Muṣ'ab, Ibn aḍ-Ḍaḥḥāk, Muṭarrif, al-Haydarī, 'Abd al-Malik, Ibn Maslama and other companions of his were sitting with Mālik. Their manner and *adab* were as if there were birds sitting on their heads.'

Ibn Ḥabīb said, 'When Mālik sat in an assembly, no one moved from him until he got up.'

Muṭarrif said,'When people came to Mālik, his slave-girl went out to them and said to them, 'The shaykh asks you, "Do you want *ḥadīths* or do you have questions?" If they said, "Questions," he would come out to them and give them *fatwā*s. If they said, "*Ḥadīths*," he would tell them, "Sit down," and he went into the bathroom and performed a major ablution, he put on some scent and a turban on his head and a dais would be set out for him. He went out to them dressed and scented, full of humility. He burned aloes wood until he had finished relating the *ḥadīth*s of the Messenger of Allah ﷺ.'

Yaḥyā said, 'We used to gather at his door. When we were all there, the person who gave permission would come and shout, "Let the people of Madina enter!" Then he gave permission to others. Mālik came in, greeted us and was silent and we remained silent for a time. When he saw that we crowded, he said, "Make yourselves remain still with dignity. It is a help for you yourselves and it will help the younger person know the right of the elder person."'

Another version has: 'When permission was given to us, the curtain by the column was lifted and we came in. He was sitting with his head inclined and remained so until the people took their seats. He raised his head and said, "*As-salāmu 'alaykum*".'

He supposed that Mālik used to do that so that none of the people – 'Alawites, 'Uthmanīs, or others – would come near him at the expense of others and believe that was their due. Therefore he left them alone until they took their seats. They each knew the rights of the others. During the time of the *ḥajj*, he put a doorman at the door to allow the people of Madina to come in first. When they had entered, he told the doorman, 'Retire.'

Ibn Qa'nab said, 'I have never seen an assembly with more gravity than the assembly of Mālik. It was as birds were on their heads.'

Ibn Abī Uways said, 'When Mālik sat down to relate *ḥadīths*, he would perform *wuḍū'* and sit on the front of his rug and comb his beard. He remained sitting with gravity and respect. Then he would relate *ḥadīths*. They asked him about that. He said, "I wanted to show respect for the words of the Messenger of Allah ﷺ. I only give *ḥadīths* when I am in a state of purity."'

He disliked giving *ḥadīths* while standing in the road or hastily. He said, 'I prefer to understand the *ḥadīths* of the Messenger of Allah ﷺ.'

Ibn al-Mundhir said, 'Mālik did not make room for anyone in his circle nor make anyone get up. He let each of them sit where the assembly ended.'

Muṭarrif and Ismā'īl said that Ibn Abī Uways said, 'Let those of you with forbearance and intelligence come near me.'

Ismā'īl said, 'Sometimes al-Qa'nabī would sit on his right.'

He said, 'Mālik only sat on a dais when he related *ḥadīths* from the Messenger of Allah ﷺ.'

Abū Muṣʻab said, 'Mālik only related *ḥadīths* while he was in a state of *wuḍū'* out of respect for the *ḥadīths* of the Messenger of Allah ﷺ.»

Muṣʻab ibn ʻAbdullah said, 'When Mālik was asked about *ḥadīths*, he got ready and performed *wuḍū'* and put on his garments. He was asked about that and he said, "It is the *ḥadīths* of the Messenger of Allah ﷺ."'

ʻAbdullāh ibn al-Mubārak said, 'I was with Mālik when he was relating *ḥadīths* to us when a scorpion stung him sixteen times. Mālik changed colour and grew ashen, but he did not stop the *ḥadīth* of the Messenger of Allah ﷺ. When he finished the assembly and the people split up, I said, "Abū ʻAbdullah, I have seen something wondrous from you today." He replied, "I was patient out of respect for the *ḥadīths* of the Messenger of Allah ﷺ."'

Yaḥyā ibn Yaḥyā al-Andalusī said, 'I was sitting with Mālik and two geckos fell on his head and went over his hat. Then they got near his neck until they went under his collar and came out from under his clothes, but he did not remove them or get up.'

Muṣʻab az-Zubayrī said, 'Ḥabīb would read to Mālik, and I was at his right and my brother was on his left. He was nearer to Mālik. He was older than me.'

Ḥabīb used to read two to two and a half pages to us every day. It did not reach three. People were in one area and they did not come near or look. When he had finished, the people would come to us and compare their books with our books.

Muṣʻab said, 'One day we went to stay with our father in al-ʻArṣa. We would go to Mālik in the evening. One day the rain fell and we did not go that night and he did not wait for us, but presented the subject to the people. We went to him the next day and said, "Abū ʻAbdullāh, yesterday the rain prevented us from attending your reading, so repeat it to us." He replied, "No. The one who seeks this business is steadfast in it."'

Ja'far ibn Ibrāhīm said, 'A friend of my father spoke to Mālik about whether I could listen to him, and he gave permission. I used to frequent him and I was rather conceited about my lineage from the Messenger of Allah ﷺ and my position. I went past the people to reach the cushion of Mālik and he did not move from it. It seemed to me that he did not notice me out of disdain for me and I complained about that to my father and some other people. They sent to him to question him about my honour and preference. He told the messenger, "In our opinion, he and other people are the same. These are – may Allah protect you! – assemblies of knowledge and the first person there is the one most entitled to it." I used to come when the circle had formed, and there was no room for me, so I would try to get as near as I could.'

Ibn Wahb said, 'When we sat with Mālik, people used to question each other. If they disagreed and wanted to raise the question to Mālik, one man joined him with a low voice full of respect and esteem, saying, "May Allah make you thrive! What do you say about such-and-such?" If the one who had gotten up, was correct, he told him, "May Allah give you success!" If it was the other, he told him that. The one he wished success knew that he was correct.'

'Abd ar-Razzāq said, 'While we were in the *Masjid al-Ḥarām*, we were told, "This is Mālik." So we met him entering by the door of the Banū Hāshim. He was wearing a cloak and a Yemeni shirt. He performed *ṭawāf* around the House and went out in the direction of Ṣafā. He prayed two *rak'ats* and sat down with his legs drawn up and his cloak wrapped around him. When he finished, we gathered around him as did the people of *ḥadīth*. When we sat down, he got up as if he was angry. We went to our shaykhs and they said, "What have you written down from Mālik?" We told them what we had done and they said, "That which you have done is unbearable for Mālik" The next day, we came one by one, were calm, and he related *ḥadīths* to us. He said, "What you did yesterday is what fools do."'

Khālid ibn Nizār said, 'I asked Mālik about something while he was reclining and he said, "Yaḥyā ibn Sa'īd related to me from Sa'īd ibn al-Musayyab..." Then he sat up and wrapped himself in his cloak and said, "I seek forgiveness from Allah!" I asked him about that and he said, "Knowledge is too sublime for that. I do not relate *ḥadīths* from the Messenger of Allah ﷺ while reclining."'

Ibn Bukayr said, 'A man went to Mālik and said, "Can I read?" He said, "Yes." He read, "Did Ibn Shihāb relate to you from Sālim?" Mālik said to him, "You are thick." Another man got up and said, "Ibn Shihāb related to you" without the question. Mālik said, "You have done well in this."'

Baqiyya ibn al-Walīd came to Mālik and the people said, 'Today we will profit from Abū Muḥammad.' He asked Mālik some questions which we wrote down. He asked him about six questions and Mālik answered them all. Then he asked him another question and Mālik said, 'You have done too much. Take the shaykh's hand.' Two people took him by the arm and led him out.

Ibn al-Mundhir said, 'Mālik had a circle in which the *fuqahā'* of Madina would sit. He did not make room for anyone nor did he make anyone get up. He let each of them sit wherever the assembly reached.'

Az-Zubayr related from his uncle Muṣ'ab and more than one person that when Hārūn ar-Rashīd went on *ḥajj*, he went to Mālik and asked his permission to enter. The chamberlain asked for permission to enter and then he gave him permission. One version has: 'Then he went out to him.' When he came out to him, he asked, 'Abū 'Abdullāh, what made you delay when you know my position?' One version has: 'You kept me at your door.'

He replied, 'By Allah, Amīr al-Mu'minin, I only performed *wuḍū'*. I knew that you only come to me for the *ḥadīths* of the Messenger of Allah ﷺ and I wanted to be ready for it.' He said, 'I know that Allah has not elevated you for no reason.' Hārūn ar-Rashīd took his hand and walked to the grave of the Messenger of Allah ﷺ and asked, 'Tell me about the place of Abū Bakr and 'Umar, may Allah be pleased with them.' He replied, 'Their place with him during his life was like their place with him after his death.'

Hāshim ibn 'Īsā said, 'When Hārūn [ar-Rashīd] came to Madina he summoned Mālik. Mālik said to him, "This knowledge has left you while you are the person most bound to esteem it. Part of your esteem for it is that you do not summon those who bear it to your doors." He said, "I will act accordingly, Abū 'Abdullāh."'

One of them said, 'Al-Mahdī went on *ḥajj* and came to Madina. Mālik came to him. Al-Mahdī showed some dutifulness and respect and ordered his sons Mūsā and Hārūn to listen to his books from him. They sent for Mālik, but he did not come to them so they informed al-Mahdī of that. He sent a message to Mālik: "Why didn't you come to them?"'

He replied, 'Amīr al-Mu'minīn! Knowledge is worthy of dignity and one comes to it.' He said, 'He has spoken the truth. Go to him.'

When they went to him, they said, 'Read to us.' He said, 'In this land one reads to the man of knowledge as the child reads to the teacher. When he errs, he informs him of that.'

They left him and told al-Mahdī. He sent to Mālik and said, 'You refused to come to them, so they went to you and now you refuse to read to them?' He replied, 'Amīr al-Mu'minīn, I heard Ibn Shihāb say, "We have gathered this knowledge from men in the *Rawḍa*: they are Sa'īd ibn al-Musayyab, Abū Salama, 'Urwa, al-Qāsim, Sālim,

Khārija, Sulaymān and Nāfi'. Then Ibn Hurmuz, Abū az-Zinād, Rabī'a and al-Anṣārī transmitted from them as well as the sea of knowledge, Ibn Shihāb. People read to these men and they did not read."'

Al-Mahdī said to his sons, 'Go and read. These men serve as models.' Their instructor used to read to them.

We find in one version of the story: 'When Mālik came to Hārūn, he rose from his seat and said to his sons, "Get up and sit before your uncle." They got up and sat in front of Mālik. He said, "Read to them." Mālik's colour changed. Then he turned to Hārūn and said, "Allah has only elevated you and put you in your place by knowledge, so do not be the first of those who abase the might of knowledge so that Allah abases your might."

'Hārūn turned to his sons and told them, "Get up. When your uncle leaves, go to his house and listen to him."

'When Mālik left, they rode to him and alighted and knocked at his door. He did not open it for them. They sat at the door with the wind blowing the dust of al-'Aqīq in their faces. When they despaired, they went away.'

Some said that Hārūn ar-Rashīd came to Mālik while Mālik was ill. He sent for Mālik to come to him so that he could ask him about a question. He replied, 'I am ill.' He said, 'I must meet you,' so he sent him a litter and he was carried by the hands of servants. When he arrived, al-Faḍl ibn ar-Rabī' went to him and asked him about a problem. Mālik exclaimed, 'You rascal! I was carried here to inform the Amīr al-Mu'minīn.' Al-Faḍl bent over to kiss him and show his respect for him. When he was brought to Hārūn, he asked him what he wanted.

Muṭarrif, Ibn Nāfi' and others – and some of them added others – said, 'When Hārūn came to Madina, he sent [Faḍl] al-Barmakī to Mālik and said, "Tell him: Bring me the book which you have written so that I can hear it from you." Mālik was grieved and saddened by that and said to al-Barmakī, "Give him my greetings and tell him:

Knowledge is visited and does not visit. One comes to knowledge and it does not come to one.'"

Al-Barmakī went to Hārūn and told him that and he got angry. Most of Mālik's companions advised him to go to Hārūn. Al-Barmakī said to ar-Rashīd, 'The people of Iraq will hear that you went to Mālik and he opposed you! Be firm with him until he comes to you.' Mālik came to him and greeted him without a book.

Hārūn ar-Rashīd asked him about this and Mālik said, 'Amīr al-Mu'minīn! Allah sent Muḥammad ﷺ to us and He commanded that he be obeyed and that his *Sunna* be followed and that we guard him in both life and death. He put you in this place by your knowledge, so do not be someone who demeans knowledge so that Allah will demean you. Allah! Allah! I have seen those who did not have your ability nor your lineage among the clients and other people who exalt this knowledge and respect it and esteem those who bear it. You are more fitted to respect this knowledge.'

He continued to repeat that until he wept. Then he said to him, 'Az-Zuhrī related to me, (and he mentioned the *ḥadīth* of Zayd ibn Thābit): "I was writing in the presence of the Messenger of Allah ﷺ: *'Those believers who stay behind are not the same as those who do jihād in the Way of Allah.'* (4:95) Ibn Umm Maktūm was with the Prophet ﷺ and said, 'Messenger of Allah! Allah has revealed the excellence of *jihād*. I am a blind man, so do I have any allowance?' The Messenger of Allah ﷺ answered, 'I do not know.' Zayd said, 'My pen was still wet and had not yet dried when the revelation descended on the Prophet ﷺ and his thigh fell against my thigh and mine was very nearly shattered by the weight of the revelation. Then he came out of it and said, "Write, Zayd! *'Other than those forced to by necessity.'*"'"'

'Amīr al-Mu'minīn, this is a single letter with which Jibrīl and the angels were sent a distance of 50,000 years until it descended on His Prophet ﷺ, so how should I not respect it and esteem it?' Hārūn said, 'Let us go to your home.'"

'Hārūn came to Mālik's house and Mālik entered, performed a major ablution, put on new clothes and scent, placed aloes-wood on the incense-burner and sat down. He said, "Come on then." Hārūn said, "Read to us." Mālik replied, "I have not read to anyone for some time." Hārūn said, "Then have the people leave so that I can read to you." Mālik answered, "When knowledge is kept from the common people for the sake of the elite, then the elite do not profit by it." Hārūn said, "So tell one of your companions to read it." He commanded al-Mughīra who read it to Mālik for him.'

One version has that the one who recited to him was Ma'n.

He said, 'Hārūn was leaning beside Mālik. When he began to read, he said, "Amīr al-Mu'minīn, Allah elevates whoever is humble for Allah."'

Abū Muṣ'ab said: Mālik said, 'Part of exalting Allah is to esteem the Muslim with white hair.' The Amīr got up and sat before him. When he had finished, he returned to his place.

Mālik said, 'After a time, ar-Rashīd said to me, "We showed humility for your knowledge and we benefited by it. The knowledge of Sufyān ibn 'Uyayna was humbled to us and we did not profit by it."' He used to come to them and give them *ḥadīths*.

They said, 'A man of Quraysh used to disparage Mālik and say, "What makes him greater than us?" When Hārūn ar-Rashīd came and sat with the people, they said to him, "This is Hārūn. Mālik will come in, so you go in and do what he does." They sent someone with him to observe. Mālik came forward, greeted and said, "Peace be upon you, Amīr al-Mu'minīn, and the mercy of Allah and His blessing. Your uncle Mālik ibn Anas – where should he sit?" He said, "He should sit right here."

'The man came forward after him and kissed Hārūn's hand. Hārūn said to Mālik, "What do you think about coming to your son and relating *ḥadīths*? (meaning the sons of Hārūn)." Mālik did not answer him at all until those with him had retired. Then he turned to him and said, "I ask you by Allah, Amīr al-Mu'minīn, are you the first one to bring about the abasement of knowledge at your hands?" He asked, "How is that?" He replied, "You know that one comes to the people of knowledge and they do not come." He told him, "You are right. They will come to you."

'Mālik left and Hārūn said, "This man which you blame me for – I have never seen a man with more intellect than him. I spoke to him before and he did not answer at all disliking that any of that come from him in that gathering. When I was alone, he brought out to me what was in himself. Take him such-and-such a reward."

'Afterwards they said to the Qurayshī man, "What did you see?" He answered, "That is a man who is protected."'

Muṭarrif said, 'Mālik came to Hārūn during one of the *ḥajjs*. Hārūn said to him, "I want you to come to me to read me your books." Mālik said, "One comes to knowledge and it does not come." He said, "Send me someone to copy it." He said, "Yes."'

Ibn Mahdī said, 'One day I walked with Mālik to al-'Aqīq from the mosque and I asked about *ḥadīths* and he scolded me.' In one version, 'He turned to me and said, "You are too good for this in my eyes. Do you ask me about the *ḥadīths* of the Messenger of Allah ﷺ while I am walking?"

'I said, "We belong to Allah." He only showed me that I had fallen in his estimation. When I sat in his assembly, I put myself far from him. He said, "Come over here." So I came near and he said, "I think that we have disciplined you in proper behaviour. Do you ask me about the *ḥadīths* of the Messenger of Allah ﷺ while I am walking? Ask about what you want here."'

Ibn Mahdī said, 'They questioned Mālik at the festival, while he was standing and he did not relate *ḥadīths* to them.'

Abū Muṣ'ab said, 'Qāḍī Jarīr ibn 'Abd al-Ḥamīd asked him about a *ḥadīth* while he was standing and he ordered that he put in jail. He was told, "But he is a *qāḍī*." He said, "The *qāḍī* ought to have more manners. Jail him." He was jailed until the following day.'

'Abdullāh ibn Ṣāliḥ said, 'Mālik and al-Layth did not deal with *ḥadīths* except when they were in a state of purity.'

Al-Qarawī said, 'When Mālik was with us, it was as if he were one of us. He was cheerful with us in conversation and we had the greatest humility towards him. When he began a *ḥadīth*, his words filled us with awe. It was as if he did not recognise us and we did not recognise him.'

When Hāshim ibn Jurayj[1] went on *ḥajj* when he was young, he came to Mālik ibn Anas,with two pages of his *ḥadīths* when the people had ridden off, and he said to him, 'Read these *ḥadīths*. The people have gone.' Mālik said, 'Does one of you wait until people have gone and then come and say, "Recite to me when the people have gone?"'

Hāshim turned to Mālik and said, 'May Allah make you thrive! If it is a need or a command which you command, I will go to obey you and I stand at your command and I rejoice in your submission in the circle of my people and I will use it to block my tribe. I commend you to Allah's protection. Farewell. To obey you is an obligation and your word is a judgement. I commend you to Allah's protection. Farewell.'

When he turned away, Mālik said, 'The like of this man truly seeks knowledge. Bring him back. He sent someone to look for him. He was brought and he recited to him and then he left.'

Al-Qarawī said, 'When people were strongly for Mālik, he was asked, "Could have some people who would repeat what you say so that the people could hear?" He said, "Allah says, '*O you who believe! Do not raise your voices above the voice of the Prophet.*' (49:2) Respect for him while he is alive and while he is dead are the same."'

Ibn Mahdī said, 'I was present with Mālik when a man came to him with a notebook and he asked him to give him permission and he did that.'

Ibn Wahb related from him that once he saw him do it and once he disliked it. He gave permission to pass it on (*munāwala*).

He wrote a hundred *ḥadīths* by Ibn Shihāb for Yaḥyā ibn Sa'īd al-Anṣārī, and he was asked, 'Did he read them to you?' He replied, 'He has too much understanding for that.'

[1] The famous scholar Ibn Jurayj.

Muṣ'ab said, 'I asked al-Mahdī if I could listen to his books. He said, "This is something lengthy for you, but I will write it down for you, make it correct and send it to you."'

Most of his business was that he was read to and he himself did not read.

Muṭarrif said, 'I kept Mālik's company for nineteen years. I did not see him recite the *Muwaṭṭā'* to anyone. I heard him strongly refute the one who said, "Reading (*'arad*) is not allowed."'

Ibn Bukayr stated that he heard the *Muwaṭṭā'* from Mālik himself more than once.

More than one person said to Mālik, 'Do you think that in what I recite to you, we can say, "He related to us" and "He reported to us"? He replied, "Yes, have I not devoted myself to you and I put its omissions and its errors right?"' He was asked, 'Is it permitted for the one who is present to say that?' He answered, 'Yes.'

In the hearing of Ibn Wahb, a man asked Mālik about the book which is read to him and then that person gives it to his friend and it spends the night with him, can he then have permission to relate it? He said, 'Yes.'

Mālik said in the hearing of Ibn al-Qasim, Ibn Wahb and others, 'I prefer reading to listening and it is firmer since that which is read becomes firm.'

A Khurasānī tried to provoke the Qāḍī of Madina against him. He said, 'I have come from Khurasan where we do not believe in presentation (*'araḍ*), but Mālik refuses to recite to us.' The Qāḍī decreed that Mālik should read to him. He was asked, 'Did he hit the right?' He replied, 'Yes.'

Al-Ḥārith ibn Miskīn said, 'One of the Hashimites spoke to Mālik during the festival days, asking him to read to him. He refused and said, "These are the days of the *Ḥajj*. When they are over, then you can read if you like." He grew angry and said, "Hārūn, the Amīr al-Mu'minīn, wanted you to do this and you agreed." Mālik said to him, "He wanted me to, but I did not do it."'

Al-Qaṭṭān said, 'Ibn Mahdī reading to Mālik resembled *ḥadīths* because he used to say, "I hear so-and-so say that he heard so-and-so say."'

Ibn al-Madanī said, 'I asked Yaḥyā, "Did Mālik dictate to you?" He replied, "I used to write in his presence."'

Muṣ'ab said, 'Mālik would see a man writing in his presence and he did not forbid him but he did not answer him nor let him consult him."'

Ashhab said, 'Mālik criticised using the book for knowledge and said, "I have not met anyone who did it."'

Al-Qaṭṭān said, 'I entered Madina in 44 AH, and Mālik's hair and beard were black then. People were silent around him, and none of them spoke out of esteem for him. No one gave *fatwā* in the assembly of the Messenger ﷺ except for him. I sat in his presence and I asked him, and he related to me. Then I answered him back and he refuted me. Then one of his companions made a sign to me and I fell silent.'

Ma'n said, 'Mālik would be careful about the *ḥadīths* of the Messenger of Allah ﷺ in the details of the *tā'* and the *yā'* and the like of that.'

Ibn 'Umayr related the like of it from him.

Ibn Wahb mentioned, 'When I went to 'Abd al-'Azīz ibn al-Mājishūn to listen to him, he told me, "Be careful not to tell Mālik that you came to me. Then he would not give you *ḥadīths*." It was as if he knew that he found him weak.'

Ismā'īl said that Muḥammad ibn Abī Ḥanīfa said, 'I came to Mālik and I saw him sitting in the front of his room while his companions were sitting on the sides of the room. Each of them had a place, so I stood at the door of the room. He asked, "Who are you?" I said, "So-and-so. I would ask about a matter." He said, "Approach" until he sat me down in front of his rug. When his companions saw that, they all got up from their seats and went out of the room. He asked me, "What did your father say about such-and-such?' I told him. He said, "What was his proof?" and he began to question me. I told him. He began to question me about the things of the school of Abū Ḥanīfa and his evidence. Then he said, "Ask," and I asked. He answered me. When I left, his companions returned to their seats.'

Al-Ḥasan ibn ar-Rabīʿ al-Bawwārī said, 'I was at Mālik's door, and a caller called out, "Let the people of the Hijaz enter." Only they entered. Then he called for the people of Syria, and then the people of Iraq. I was the last to enter. Ḥammād ibn Ḥanīfa was among us.He said, "Peace be upon you and the mercy of Allah." People made gestures to him with their hands that he should be quiet. He said, "Are we in the prayer so that we should not speak?"

'I heard Mālik say, "I ask Allah for the best" twice. Then he said, "Nāfiʿ informed us..." and then he reported twenty *ḥadīths.* Then he said, "Take them out," and the whips took us.'

Ash-Shāfiʿī said, 'I read the *Muwaṭṭā'* of Mālik and only those who understood knowledge and the one who sat with its people read it to him. I used to listen to Ibn 'Uyayna, az-Zanjī and other people of Makka, and none of reached in knowledge what Mālik reached in his retention, proficiency and care.'

'Abdullāh ibn Mutīʿ said, 'We came to Mālik and he related some *ḥadīths* to us and we asked him for more. He said, "Enough" and the whips took us.'

A man asked Mālik about a question and he did not answer. He asked him, 'Why don't you answer me?' He said, 'If you had asked about something that would help you, I would have answered you.'

Ash-Shāfiʿī said, 'I asked permission to come to Mālik, and I had wanted to listen to the *ḥadīth* of the skin of the head. I said, "If I put it first, I fear that he will think it long and not relate it to me. If I put it at the end, I fear that I will not have him convey it." So I put it after ten *ḥadīths*, and I began to ask him. When the ten had passed, he said, "That is enough for you," so I did not hear it.'

Bishr ibn Ādam said, 'Al-Aghlaf asked Mālik about a question and then about another question, but he did not answer it. He asked him why and Mālik said, "Boy! Take his hand and lead him to prison." He said, "I am the Qāḍī of the Amīr al-Mu'minīn!" He said, "That is worthless for you." He said, "I will not do it again." Mālik said, "Let him go."'

Ismā'īl ibn Bint as-Suddī said, 'I asked Mālik about the *ḥadīth* about the Messenger of Allah, may Allah bless him and grant him peace, trotting from the Stone to the Stone (in *ṭawāf*). I asked, "And its *isnād*?" He said, "Drag him out feet first."'

Ismā'īl al-Qawārīrī said, 'I came to Mālik and I asked him for *ḥadīths* and he gave them to me. I think that there were twelve *ḥadīths*, and so I asked him for more. Two black men were standing near him. They picked me up and put me out of his house into the road,' or words to that effect.

Ibn al-Ḥārith said, 'Ibn al-Mubārak and his companions came to Mālik and they said, "Abū 'Abdullāh! Give us *ḥadīths*, but only give us the *ḥadīths* of az-Zuhrī." Mālik said, "Take hold of them and remove them from me." The people got up. The following day Ibn al-Mubārak said to his companions, "Mālik will not complain if you do not listen to him at all, so return to the man." They came to him and when they took their seats, he rebuked them and gave them the *ḥadīths* of az-Zuhrī as they had wanted.'

Ibn Mushir said, 'Mālik would be asked one or two questions. When he was asked about a third, he said, "Take hold of his hand and put him out."'

Ibn Mahdī said, 'When Yaḥyā ibn Zā'ida wanted to go on *ḥajj*, he asked 'Abdullāh ibn Idrīs to write a letter for him to Mālik so that he could listen to him. There was some friendship between them and so he did that. He was listening to him one day when a man came to him and said, "Abū 'Abdullāh, what do you say about a man who bequeaths a hundred dirhams to his slave?" Mālik replied, "The bequest is allowed." Yaḥyā said to him, "Abū 'Abdullāh! Can he leave his property to his property?" Mālik looked at those with him and said, "'*You will know them by their ambivalent speech.*' (47:30) Do not return to me."'

Mālik's signs of nobility, awe, his inspiring appearance and his earnestness

The Qāḍī said that Ziyād ibn Yūnus said, 'I have never seen a scholar nor a man of worship nor a clever man nor governor who inspired more awe than Mālik, may Allah have mercy on him.'

Ibn al-Mājishūn said, 'I went to the Amīr al-Mu'minīn, al-Mahdī. There was only a servant between him and me, but he did not awe me the way Mālik awed me.' Ad-Darāwardī said something similar.

Sa'īd ibn Maryam said, 'I have not seen anyone who inspired more awe than Mālik. The awe he inspired was greater than the awe of the Sultan.'

Muṣ'ab az-Zuhrī said, 'I have never seen anyone who inspired more awe than Mālik: except the caliph.'

Sa'īd ibn Abī Hind said, 'I was never in awe of anyone in the way I was in awe of 'Abd ar-Raḥmān ibn Mu'āwiya – meaning the ruler of Andalusia – until I went on *ḥajj* and met Mālik. He filled me with an intense awe which made my awe of Mu'āwiya's son seem insignificant.'

Ibn Abī Uways and Abū Muṣ'ab said, 'No one at Madina was ready to say, "The Messenger of Allah ﷺ said," but Mālik was enough for him. When he was asked about it, he said, "What he said is sound" and left.'

Ismā'īl said, 'Ibn Kināna, Ibn Abī Ḥāzim, ad-Darāwardī and others listened with Mālik to the shaykhs and they abandoned *ḥadīths* from them out of their awe of him until he died. Then that spread among them.'

Al-Aṣmā'ī said, 'I did not stand in awe of any scholar as I stood in awe of Mālik until he made a grammatical mistake and then awe of him departed from my heart. I spoke to him about that and he said, "How would it have been if you had seen Rabī'a? We used to say to him, 'How are you this morning?' and he said, 'Well, well.'"'

Ibn Wahb said, 'I came to Madina and people asked me to question Mālik about hermaphrodites. They gathered around him and I was supposed to ask on their behalf. I was too awed to ask him and all who were in the assembly were too awed to ask the question.'

Hishām ibn 'Ammār said, 'I entered Madina and went to Mālik

ibn Anas. When my eye fell upon him, I was in awe of him until I was almost poleaxed.'

Ash-Shāfi'ī said, 'I have not been in awe of anyone as I had awe of Mālik ibn Anas when I looked at him.'

It is said that ath-Thawrī was in his assembly. When he saw the esteem which the people had for him and his respect for knowledge, he composed:

He refuses to answer, but that does not dispel the awe.
  The askers' heads are bowed.
The *adab* of gravity and the might of the Sultan meet.
  He is obeyed, but is not a Sultan.

Ibn Ḥanbal said, 'Mālik was inspired awe in his assembly. None answered him back due to their esteem for him.'

Ash-Shāfi'ī said, 'When Muḥammad ibn al-Ḥasan reported *ḥadīths* from Mālik in Iraq, his house was filled so it was cramped for him. When he gave them *ḥadīths* from other men of the shaykhs of Kufa, it was not filled very much. He used to say, "I do not know of anyone weaker in praise for your companions than you."'

Bakr ibn ash-Shurūd and others said (all meaning about the same), 'We came to Mālik ibn Anas and he began to relate *ḥadīths* to us from Rabī'a and we asked him for more of his *ḥadīths*. He said to us that day, "What will you do to Rabī'a who is sleeping in that arch?" We went to Rabī'a and woke him. We said to him, "You are Rabī'a from whom Mālik relates *ḥadīths*?" He replied, "Yes." We said to him, "How did Mālik succeed by you when you do not succeed by yourself?" He said, "Don't you know that a *mishkal* (small weight) from a government is better than bearing knowledge?"'

Ibn Ḥārith said, 'Mālik used to esteem knowledge which he had with great respect and he guarded himself from all aspects which could lessen it, and he was very awe-inspiring.'

Yaḥyā ibn Ḥassān said, 'I wrote down eight *ḥadīths* from Mālik one day and I was very happy indeed with them.'

Bishr al-Ḥāfī said, 'Mālik related *ḥadīths* to us and I ask forgiveness of Allah because one of the adornments of this world is that a man be able to say, "Mālik related *ḥadīths* to us."'

Ḥabīb said, 'I saw Mālik leaving al-Mahdī. He did not pass by anyone except that he rose for him and mentioned Allah.' He said, 'I remembered the *ḥadīth* which has been reported: "When they are seen, remember Allah."'

Another said, 'Mālik used to ask aḍ-Ḍaḥḥāk ibn 'Uthmān and Ibn Kināna about the expeditions. Then he reported *ḥadīths* from them in his assembly. People began to write that down from him and aḍ-Ḍaḥḥāk and Ibn Kināna also wrote with them. He heard most of that from the two of them."

Al-Qa'nabī said, 'I only suppose that Mālik reached what he reached by a secret which was between him and Allah. I saw him with a man standing in his presence as he would stand before a ruler.'

Ismā'īlibn Ya'qūb as-Sahmī said, 'One day I was sitting with Mālik ibn Anas when the people of the Ḥajj festival arrived. An Iraqi man sat down with him and asked him about a matter and he answered him. Then he asked him again and he answered him. Then he asked him yet again and he refused to answer. He said to him, "I have made a financial outlay and I have come in this fashion seeking right guidance, so guide me!" He said, "It has reached me that the Messenger of Allah ﷺ said, 'The one with no modesty has no belief.'" The Iraqi man said, "It has reached me that the Prophet ﷺ said, 'When the appearance of a man is rough, his *dīn* is very soft.'" A group of those sitting with Mālik jumped on the man, pulled off his turban and threw him on his back and choked him with it.'

Ashhab said, 'Mālik visited Muḥammad ibn 'Alī because he was ill, and nobility among the people accrued to him by virtue of Mālik's visit.'

'Abdullāh ibn Nāfi' az-Zubayrī said, 'I was reciting to Nāfi' ibn Abī Nu'aym after the *Ṣubḥ* prayer and I raised my voice and he chided me. He said, "Don't you see Mālik?" That was the first I knew of Mālik.'

This is also related from Ibn Wahb.

Yūnus ibn Tamīm said, 'I came to Madina in 160 AH and I went to Mālik. When I looked at him, I was filled with awe of him, so I remained hanging back for ten days. I complained about that to one of the people of Madina, and he told me, "Let your scribe ask for you about what you want. As for you yourself, I do not think that you are prepared to ask him because he inspires more awe than that in the breasts of people."'

'Abdullāh al-'Abbāsī said, 'When a man of their died, the people of Madina would say, "Take us to Mālik to console us."'

Muṣ'ab said, 'I saw Mālik sitting on a cushion and no one sat with him on it. Quraysh were seated. When a man of the Banū Hāshim came, he folded his leg and made him sit on his cushion and turned to him and did not turn to anyone until he had left.'

At-Tustarī remarked, 'This was in other than a gathering of knowledge.'

It was said that al-Makhzūmī was one of those who sat with him on his rug.

One of them said, 'Ibn Abī az-Zinād took Mālik to one of the governors of Madina and Mālik went to him at night to ask him to leave him alone. He let him enter his canopy and the people wondered at how he could trust him because of what was between them. He went to the governor and returned, saying, "I have restrained him." Then Mālik did not speak to him again until he died.'

One of the Ḥusaynīs said, 'I was staying with my wife in the days when I was visiting her and Mālik came to me while I was with my wife in the canopy. He asked for permission to enter and I disliked keeping him at the door until I got my wife out, so I left the canopy and dropped the curtain in front of my wife's face and sat in front of the canopy and gave him permission to enter. He came in and sat down and then said, "This man – meaning the governor – has imprisoned my slave. The night patrol has arrested him. Go to him and have him release him." I was too afraid to tell him about where my wife was or to make him come back, so I left him sitting there. I went to the governor who freed the slave. I brought him. When he saw me with the slave's hand, he met me and took the slave and left leaning on him. By Allah, he did not tell me, "May Allah repay you well."'

His following the *Sunna* and his dislike of innovated things and part of what is related from him about the beliefs of the people of the *Sunna* and discussion on the people of sects

The *faqīh* and *qāḍī* said, 'Mālik used to often cite the example:

"The best matters of the *dīn* is what is *Sunna*
and the worse of matters are innovated things."'

Ibn Ḥanbal said, 'Mālik followed the *Sunna* more than Sufyān did.'

Ibn Ḥanbal said, 'When you see a man who hates Mālik, know that he is an innovator.'

Abū Dāwūd said, 'I fear that he [such a person] has innovation.'

Ibn Mahdī said, 'When you see that a Hijazī loves Mālik ibn Anas, know that he is someone with the *Sunna*. When you see someone carping at him, know that he is the opposite.'

Ibrāhīm ibn Yaḥyā ibn Bassām said, 'I never heard Abū Dāwūd curse anyone at all except for two men. One of them was a man who he was told had cursed Mālik and the other was Bishr al-Marīsī' [who advocated the idea that the Qur'an was created].

Ma'n said, 'Mālik went to the mosque one day leaning on my hand. A man called Abū Ṭurayda – who was suspected of espousing *irjā'* – met him and said, "Abū 'Abdullāh! Listen to something from me. I would speak to you about it and argue with you and tell you what my opinion is."

'Mālik said to him, "Take care I do not testify against you." The man replied, "By Allah, I only want the truth. Listen, if it is correct, say yes or speak." He said, "If you defeat me?" He said, "Then you will follow me." He said, 'And if I defeat you?" He said, "Then I will follow you." He said, "And if a man comes and speaks to us and defeats us?" He answered, "We will follow him."

'Mālik said to him, "Abū 'Abdullah! Allah sent Muhammad with the *dīn*, but I see you shifting. 'Umar ibn 'Abd al-'Azīz said, 'Whoever makes his *dīn* a target for conflict shifts about a lot.'"'

Mālik said, 'There is no argument about anything in the *dīn*.'

Mālik said, 'Quarrelling and argument in matters of knowledge remove the light of belief from the heart.'

He said, 'Disputation hardens people's hearts and brings about rancour.'

Az-Zuhrī said, 'I saw Mālik when some people were arguing in his presence. He got up and changed his cloak, saying, "You are war."'

Al-Haytham ibn Jamīl said, 'Mālik, was asked, "Should a man with knowledge of the *Sunna* argue about it?" He answered, "No. He should inform people about the *Sunna* if they will accept it from him. Otherwise he should remain silent.'

Abū Ṭālib al-Makkī said, 'Mālik was the furthest of people from the schools of the *mutakallimūn*, the strongest of them in hatred for the Iraqis and the firmest of them in the *sunna* of the early generations among the Companions and the Followers.'

Sufyān ibn 'Uyayna said, 'A man questioned Mālik as follows: "'*The All-Merciful established firmly on the Throne.*' (20:4) How can He be established anywhere, Abū 'Abdullāh?" Mālik was silent for a long time until he began to sweat profusely. I had never seen Mālik grieve at anything the way that he did at these words. People began to look to see what position he would take. Then he regained his composure and said, "His 'being established' is well known. The 'how' of it is beyond our comprehension. Asking about it is innovation. Belief in it is obligatory. I think you are misguided. Get him out!" The man called out to him, "Abū 'Abdullāh! By Allah, and there is no god but He! I asked the people of Basra, Kufa and Iraq about this question, and I did not find anyone who dealt with it as successfully as you have."'

Abū Mus'ab said, 'Ibn Mahdī came to us and prayed and placed his cloak in front of the row. When the Imām gave the *salām*, the people stared at him and they stared at Mālik. He had prayed behind the Imām. When he gave the greeting, he said, "Are there guards here?" Two men came and he said, "Take the corner of this garment and jail him." He was jailed and it was said, "It is Ibn Mahdī!" He sent to him and said to him, "Do you not fear Allah and are you not fearfully aware of Him? You place your garment in front of you in the row and you distract people who are praying so that they look at it. You have innovated something in our mosque that we do not know! The Prophet ﷺ said, 'Whoever innovates something in our mosque has the curse of Allah and the angels and all people on him.'" Ibn Mahdī wept and promised that he would never do it in the mosque of the Prophet ﷺ or any other mosque.""

In the version of Ibn Mahdī, he said, 'I said to the guards, "Take me to Abū 'Abdullāh." They said, "As you wish." They took me to him. He said, "Abū 'Abd ar-Raḥmān, do you pray stripped?" I said, "Abū 'Abdullāh, it was a hot day as you saw, so my cloak felt heavy on me." He said, "By Allah, you did not mean by that to attack those who passed and oppose them?" I answered, "No, by Allah!" He said, "Release him."'

Sufyān ibn 'Uyayna said, 'I asked Mālik about someone who assumed *iḥrām* from Madina instead of assuming it from the *mīqāt*. He said, "This is opposing Allah and His Messenger. I fear trial for him in this world and a painful punishment in the Next. Have you heard not His words, '*Those who oppose his command should beware of a testing trial coming to them or a painful punishment striking them*' (24:63)? The Prophet ﷺ ordered that the *iḥrām* begin at the *mīqāt*."'

A man asked Mālik about something concerning inward knowledge. He got angry and said, 'Inward knowledge is only known by the one who knows outward knowledge. When he knows outward knowledge and acts by it, then Allah will open him to inward knowledge. That is only with the opening of his heart and its illumination.' Then he said to the man, 'You must have the pure clear *dīn* and beware the structures of the path, and you must take what you recognise and leave what you do not recognise.'

Ibn Wahb said, 'When one of the people of the sects (*ahwā'*) came to Mālik, I heard him say, "As for myself, I am on a clear sign from my Lord. As for you, you are a doubter. So go to the doubter like yourself and argue with him." Then he recited, "*Say: 'This is my way. I call to Allah with inner sight.'*" (12:108)'

Muṭarrif said, 'When one of the people of deviation and sects was mentioned in Mālik's presence, I heard him say, "'Umar ibn 'Abd al-'Azīz said, 'The Messenger of Allah ﷺ made a *Sunna* and the those in command after him made *sunan*. Taking it is tantamount to following the Book of Allah, the completion of obedience to Allah and strength in the *dīn* of Allah. No one after these can change the *sunan* nor look into anything which opposes them. Whoever is guided by them will be guided. Whoever seeks help by them is helped. If anyone leaves them to follow other than the path of the believers, Allah will assign him what he has taken and Hell will roast him. An evil return!' When Mālik uttered this, he shook with joy."'

A man asked Mālik, 'Who are the people of the *Sunna*, Abū 'Abdullāh?' He replied, 'Those who do not have any name by which they are known – who are not Jahmīs, Rāfidites (Shi'ites) or Qadarīs.'

Ibn Nāfi' and Ashhab – and one added to the other – said, 'I said, "Abu 'Abdullāh! '*Faces on that day will be radiant, gazing at their Lord.*'(75:22-23) Do they look at Allah?" "Yes, with these eyes," he replied.

'I said to him, "Some people say that one does not look at Allah and that *nadhira* (looking) means *muntadhira* (waiting) for the reward." He answered, "They have lied. One looks at Allah. Have you not heard what Mūsā, peace be upon him, said: '*Lord, show Yourself to me*' (7:143)? Do you think that Mūsā would ask his Lord for something impossible? Allah Almighty says, '*You will not see Me*' in this world because it is a transient realm. The eternal cannot seen by the temporal. When people go to the Abode of Eternity, they will look and see the eternal by the eternal. Allah Almighty said, '*No, on that Day they will be veiled from their Lord.*' (83:15)"'

Zuhayr ibn 'Abbād said, 'I asked Mālik, "What do you say about the two groups with us in Syria who disagree about belief and say that it increases and decreases?" He replied, "What they say is bad." I said, "They say that they fear hypocrisy in themselves." He repeated, "What they say is bad." I continued, "They say, 'We are believers if Allah wills.' Another group say that belief is the same and that the belief of the people of the earth is like the belief of the people of the heaven." He said, "Do not say that." I asked, "So what should the two groups say?" He replied, "They should say, 'We are believers' and then refrain from going beyond those words. The Prophet ﷺ said, 'I am commanded to fight the people until they say, "There is no god but Allah."' Allah says, *'Do not say, "You are not a believer" to someone who greets you as a Muslim.'* (4:94)"'

Zuhayr said, 'I said to him, "The two groups attack one another!" He said, "We belong to Allah and to Him we return" and was amazed. He told me, "The people began to pray towards Jerusalem for sixteen months and then they were commanded to pray to the Sacred House. Allah said, *'Allah would never let your faith go to waste'* (2:143) meaning their prayer towards Jerusalem." This *āyat* reminded me of the statement of the Murji'ites, "The prayer is not part of belief."'

Zuhayr said, 'Someone who asked the like of this came to Mālik and he commanded that he be expelled, and it seemed as if he were making fun of me.'

More than one person said, 'I heard Mālik say, "Belief is both statement and action which increases and decreases. Some of it is better than the rest." He said, "By Allah in the heaven whose knowledge is in every place."'

Ibn al-Qāsim said, 'Mālik used to say, "Belief increases," but refrained from mentioning decrease. He stated, "Allah mentioned its increase in more than one place. He did not speak about its decrease." Therefore he refrained from that.'

Mālik said, 'I am a believer, and praise belongs to Allah.'

Ibn Abī Uways said that Mālik said, 'The Qur'an is the Word of

Allah and the word of Allah is from Allah. There is nothing created in the Word of Allah.'

Another added from him, 'Whoever says that the Qur'an is created is an unbeliever. The one who hesitates is worse than him. He is asked to repent. If he does not, then strike off his head.'

According to Ibn Nāfi''s version, 'Someone who says that is flogged and jailed.'

In the version of Bishr ibn Bakr at-Tanīsī, 'He is killed and his repentance is not accepted.'

Al-Barmaki and at-Tustari among our shaykhs in Iraq said, 'The meaning behind the two replies is different. The one who is intelligent and a propagandist is killed and the other one is beaten.'

He was asked about the *Ḥadīth* of Descent [about Allah's descending every night]. He said, 'His command descends every day in the time before dawn. As for Allah Himself, He does not descend.'

Al-Walīd ibn Muslim said, 'I asked Mālik about these *ḥadīths* and he said, "Read them as they have come." It was said to him, "Ibn 'Ajlān related them." He stated, "He is not one of the *fuqahā'*."'

He said in the version of Ibn al-Qāsim and Ibn Wahb that he did not know these things. Mālik disliked to relate them to the common people who did not know their significance and their intellects did not reach it, so they would reject them or use them in other than their proper place.

A man came to Mālik and said to him, 'What do you say about the one who says, "The Qur'an is created?"' He cried, 'A *zindīq*! Kill him!' He said, 'Abū 'Abdullāh! These are not my words. They are words which I have heard.' He retorted, 'I have only heard them from you.'

Ashhab said, 'We were with Mālik when a man of the 'Alawites stood where he was. They were overcoming his assembly so he called to him, "Abū 'Abdullāh!" Mālik looked at him. When anyone called to him, he did no more than look at him with his head.'

'The seeker said to him, "I want to make you a proof in what is between me and Allah. When I come before Him and He questions me, I can say to Him, 'Mālik told me.'" He told him, 'Speak.' He asked, 'Who is the best of people after the Messenger of Allah ﷺ?' He replied, 'Abū Bakr.' The 'Alawite said, 'Then who?' Mālik answered, 'Then 'Umar.' The 'Alawite asked, 'Then who?' Mālik said, 'The wrongfully-slain caliph, 'Uthmān.' The 'Alawite said, 'By Allah, I will never sit with you!' Mālik said to him, 'That is your choice.''''

'Abd ar-Raḥmān ibn al-Qāsim said from him, 'I did not meet anyone but that he thought it best to abstain between 'Uthmān and 'Alī, but there is no doubt that Abū Bakr and 'Umar were better than the other two.'

Ibn Wahb added from him, 'This is what the people in the past held to.'

In Abū Muṣ'ab's version, 'Mālik was asked, "Who is the best of people after the Messenger of Allah, may Allah bless him and grant him peace?" He replied, "Abū Bakr." Then he asked, "Then who?" He said, "'Umar." Then he asked, "Then who?" He replied, "'Uthmān." He was asked, "Then who?" He replied, "People stop here. These are the best of the Companions of the Messenger of Allah ﷺ. He put Abū Bakr in charge of the prayer and Abū Bakr chose 'Umar. 'Umar gave the choice to six men and they chose 'Uthmān. Therefore people stop there."'

He added in one variant, 'Someone who seeks leadership is not equal to someone who does not seek it.'

In Ibn Wahb's variant, '"The best of people were Abū Bakr and 'Umar." I said, "Then who?" He stopped. I said, "I am a man you imitates you in my *dīn*." He said, "And 'Uthman."'

He added in Abū Muṣ'ab's version, 'Then people are equal.'

Al-Bazzāz said, 'I asked Abu 'Āṣim an-Nabīl about who had precedence among the *Salaf*. He said, "Ḥamza and Ja'far." I said, "We are dealing with the ten." He was silent. He said, "Mālik used to advance Ḥamza."'

Muṣ'ab az-Zubayrī and Ibn Nāfi' said, 'Hārūn (ar-Rashīd) entered the mosque and prayed. Then he went to the grave of the Prophet ﷺ and greeted him. Then he came to Mālik's assembly and said to him, "Peace be upon you and the mercy of Allah and His blessings." Mālik said to him, "And upon you peace, Amīr al-Mu'minīn, and the mercy of Allah and His blessings."

'Then he asked Mālik, "Does the one who curses the Companions of the Messenger of Allah ﷺ have any right to the booty?" He said, "No, nor any honour nor joy." He asked, "On what basis do you say that?" He said, "Allah Almighty says, '*So that by them He might infuriate the unbelievers.*' (48:29) Whoever criticises them is an unbeliever and an unbeliever has no right to the booty."

Another time, he uses as a proof for that the words of Allah, '*For the poor of the Muhājirūn …*' (59:8-10). He said, 'They are the Companions of the Messenger of Allah ﷺ who emigrated with him, and his Anṣār, and those who came after them. *"They say, 'Our Lord, forgive us and our brothers who preceded us in faith'"* Whoever attacks them has no right to it.'

Isḥāq ibn 'Īsā said, 'I saw a Maghribī man come to Mālik ibn Anas and say, "The sects before us are many, and I made it incumbent upon myself that if I saw you, I would follow what you command." Mālik therefore described to him the laws of Islam: prayer, fasting and the *ḥajj*. Then he said, "Take them and do not argue with anyone."'

Ibn Wahb and others said, 'Mālik was asked about the people who espouse *Qadar* and whether one should refrain from speaking to them. He said, "Yes, he should when he knows the position of such a person." He said, "We command him to what is correct and forbid him what is objectionable. We tell them of their opposition and we do not continue to speak with them nor pray over them nor attend their funerals. And I do not think that one should marry them."'

He added in another version, 'Allah says, "*A slave who is a believer is better for you than a man of the idolators.*" (2:221)'

He said in Ashhab's version, 'He should not pray behind them nor transmit *ḥadīths* from them. If you come across them in a port, remove them from it.'

Ibn al-Qāsim reported that he said, 'He should not greet them nor visit their sick.'

Al-Wāqidī said that he said: 'The testimony of a Qadarī who makes a claim is not allowed, nor that of a Khārijite nor a Rāfiḍite. It was related from Mālik that he forbade their testimony entirely. It is also related from him, "Only when he is a propagandist."'

Muṣ'ab said, 'A man asked Mālik, "Did Allah decree (*kataba*) foul actions for us?" He said, "Yes, before He created us. The one for whom that has been written must do it and go towards what has been decreed for him."'

Al-Karābīsī said, 'When Mālik was asked who the Qadariyya are, I heard him say, "Whoever says, 'Allah did not create acts of rebellion (i.e. the Mu'tazilites).'"'

Al-Qāsim ibn Muhammad said, 'I asked Mālik who the Qadariyya are and he said, "I asked Abū Suhayl as you have asked me and he said, 'They are those who say that they possess power (*istita'a*) so that if they wish, they obey [Allah]. If they do not wish, they rebel.'"'

Al-Farawī said, 'I heard the son of Abū Ḥanīfa say to Mālik, "We have an opinion which we would show you. If you think it is good, we will continue in it. If you think that it is bad, we will turn from it." He said, "We do not make anyone an unbeliever on account of a wrong action. The wrongdoers are all Muslims." He said, "I do not see any harm in it."'

Dāwūd ibn Abī Zanbar, Ibrāhīm ibn Ḥabīb and Ibn Nāfi' aṣ-Ṣā'igh said to him, 'Abū 'Abdullāh! This will lead the discussion to the point where it is said, "My *dīn* is the *dīn* of the angels and Jibrīl and Mikā'īl." He said, "No, by Allah! The *dīn* increases. Allah says, '*thereby increasing their faith with more faith.*' (48:4) And Ibrāhīm said, '*My Lord, show me how You give life to the dead*' (2:260) Increase in the *dīn* was confirmed."'

Ibn Wahb said that he heard Mālik say, 'The Murji'ites erred and said something terrible. They said, "Whoever burns the Ka'ba or does anything, no matter what, is a Muslim."' Mālik was asked, 'What do you think about them?' He said, 'Allah says, "*If they repent and establish the prayer and pay zakāt, they are your brothers in the dīn.*" (9:11)'

Ibn Wahb said, 'I heard Mālik when he was told, "The people of sects are using a *ḥadīth* as a proof against us: 'Every child is born on the *fiṭra* (natural form).'" He said, "Then use another *ḥadīth* as a proof against them: 'Allah knows best what you are doing.'"'

Ibn Nāfi' said that he heard Mālik say, 'If someone commits all the great wrong actions while he does not associate anything with Allah and then he is saved from these sects, I hope that he will be in the highest part of the Garden of Paradise because every wrong action between the slave and his Lord is based on hope. Every sect (*hawā*) which is not from Him is based on the hope that it will makes its follower fall (*hawā*) into the Fire of Hell.'

aṣ Mālik said, 'All the people of sects are unbelievers, and the worst of them are the Rāfiḍites[1].' It was asked, 'And the Nawāṣib?[2]' He said, 'They are Rāfiḍites. They abandoned (*rafaḍu*) the truth and directed (*naṣabū*) enmity and hatred towards it.'

He means that the four (caliphs) are the people of truth. Whoever rejects one of them has opposed the truth.

Mutarrif said, 'I saw Mālik being cupped on Wednesday and Saturday to refute what had been related about that.'

Mālik's worship, scrupulousness, fear, retirement ('*uzla*) and his supplications being answered

The Qāḍī said that az-Zubayr ibn Ḥabīb said, 'When the month began, I used to see Mālik staying up [in prayer] the first night of it, and I used to think that he did that in order to begin the month with that.'

[1] *Rāfiḍiyya* or *Rawāfiḍ*: originally a Shi'ite group in Kufa who wanted Zayd ibn 'Alī to condemn Abū Bakr and 'Umar. When he forbade them to speak against the Companions, they abandoned him.

[2] *Nāṣibiyya* or *Nawāṣib*: a group of Kharijites who consider it obligatory to violently hate 'Alī.

Fātima, the daughter of Mālik, said, 'Mālik used to pray his *ḥizb* every night. On the night of *Jumu'a*, he would stay up the entire night.'

Al-Mughīra said, 'I went out at night after the people had gone to sleep and I passed by Mālik. I saw him standing in prayer. When he finished the Fātiḥa, he began to recite, "*Fierce competition for this world distracted you*" (102) until he reached the verse "*you will be asked that Day about the pleasures you enjoyed.*" He wept for a long time, and he began to repeat it and weep. What I heard him saying distracted me from the need for which I had gone out. I remained standing there while he was weeping and repeating that until dawn. When dawn was clear, he went into *rukū'* and I went home. I performed *wuḍū'* and then went to the mosque. He was there in his place and the people were around him. I looked at him in the morning and his face was covered in a beautiful light.'

Muḥammad ibn Khālid ibn 'Utma said, 'When I saw Mālik's face, I would see the signs of the Next World in his face and when he spoke, I knew that the truth came from his mouth.'

Abū Muṣ'ab said, 'Mālik used to remain a long time in *rukū'* and prostration in his private prayers. When he stood in prayer, it was as if he were a dry piece of wood and no part of him moved at all. After he had been beaten, he was asked, "If you were to lighten this somewhat?" He said, "When someone does an action for Allah, he must do it well as Allah says, '*In order to test which of you is the best in action*' (67:2)."'

Ibn Wahb said, 'My eye has never seen one more scrupulous than Mālik ibn Anas.'

Ibn al-Qāsim mentioned that Mālik's servant said to him, "Today Mālik has spent some forty years praying the *Ṣubḥ* prayer with the *wuḍū'* of the *'Ishā'* prayer."

Ibn al-Mubārak said, 'I saw Mālik and saw that he was one of those who fear Allah. Allah elevated him by a secret between him and Him. That is because I often heard him say, "Whoever wants an opening to be opened for him in his heart and to be saved from the death throes and the terrors of the Day of Rising should do more actions secretly than he does openly."'

Something similar is related from Muṭarrif.

Ibn Mahdī said, 'By Allah, I have not seen anyone who had more awe of Allah in his heart than was in the heart of Mālik ibn Anas.'

One version has 'more majesty' in place of 'more awe'.

Ibn Abī Uways said, 'Mālik used to command what was correct and encourage it.'

Muṣ'ab ibn 'Abdullāh said, 'When the Prophet ﷺ was mentioned in Mālik's presence, he grew pale and he bowed over so that it was difficult for those who were sitting with him. One day he was asked about that. He said, "If only you knew, you would not object to what you see. I used to go to Muhammad ibn al-Munkadir who was the master of the reciters. Almost every time we asked him about a *ḥadīth*, he wept until we felt sorry for him. I used to go to Ja'far ibn Muḥammad (aṣ-Ṣādiq) and he used to joke and laugh a lot, but when the Prophet ﷺ was mentioned in his prsence, he turned pale."

'Mālik said, "I used to frequent him for a time. I only observed three states in him: either praying, fasting or reciting Qur'an. I did not even see him relate from the Messenger of Allah ﷺ except in a state of purity nor speak about what did not concern him. He was one of the men of knowledge, worship and asceticism who feared Allah, and I did not ever come to him but that he took the cushion out from under him and put it under me.' He began to recount his qualities and what he had seen of the qualities of other shaykhs of his in a long account."'

One of them said, 'I saw Mālik was silent. He did not speak nor look to the right or the left except when a man spoke to him. Then he would listen to him answer him with something simple. He was asked about that and said, "Are people toppled into the Fire of Hell for anything but this?" (and pointed to his tongue.) It has reached me that a man came to Abū Bakr aṣ-Ṣiddīq while he was pulling his tongue, saying, "This is what brought me calamities." Since he said that, then how is it with us unless Allah envelops us in His mercy?'

Mālik said, 'Whenever I found some hardness in my heart, I would go to Muḥammad ibn al-Munkadir and look at him once, and I would be admonished by that for days.'

Bishr ibn 'Umar said, 'Mālik did not laugh. He was asked about that. He said, "Laughter leads to foolishness, and it reached me that the laughter of the Prophet ﷺ consisted merely of a smile."'

Ibn Wahb said, 'Mālik had a handkerchief in his sleeve rolled up in four layers. When he prostrated, he prostrated on it. He was asked about that and said, "I did that so that the pebbles do not make a mark on my brow so that people would suppose that I stand up in prayer at night."'

Ibn Wahb said, 'Mālik did a lot of worship secretly at night and in the day when one saw him.'

Abū Bakr al-Uwaysī said, 'Mālik was always looking at a copy of the Qur'an for the two years before he died. He used to recite a lot and he would weep for a long time.'

Ibn Mahdī said, 'I heard Mālik say, "If I had known that my heart would be put right on a dung-heap, I would have gone and sat on it."'

Muṭarrif said, 'Mālik used to occupy himself with what other people did not impose and he said, "A scholar is not a scholar until he is like that, and until he makes himself attend to that which entails no wrong action in it if it is omitted."'

Ash-Shāfi'ī said, 'At Mālik's door I saw some of the horses of Khurasan (and it is said, of Egypt). I said to him, "How beautiful they are!" He said, "They are a gift from me to you." I said, "Leave one animal for yourself to ride on." He said, "I am too shy before Allah to walk with an animal's hoof on the earth in which the Prophet of Allah ﷺ is located."'

Abū 'Imrān aṣ-Ṣadafī said, 'I came to Mālik wearing wool clothes. He said, "Get him out!" I said, "Do not do it, Abu 'Abdullāh! I have come to you because you are one of the heirs of the Prophets." He said, "Leave him." I asked him about the stipends of the Sultan. He disliked them and I said to him, "You accept them." He said, "Do you want to return (laden) with my wrong action and your wrong action?" (ref. to 5:35)'

At-Tanīsī said, 'We were with Mālik while his companions were around him. A man from the Nāṣibiyya said, "We have people who are called Ṣūfiyya. They eat a lot and then they begin *qaṣīdas* and then they stand up and dance." Mālik asked, "Are they boys?" He said, "No." He said, "Are they mad?" He said, "No, they are people who are shaykhs and other men of intellect." Mālik said, "I did not hear that any of the people of Islam did this." The man said to him, "They eat and then they stand and begin to dance energetically. Some of them hit their heads and some of them hit their faces." Mālik laughed. Then he got up and went into his house. Mālik's companions said to the man, "You, person, are ill-omened for our companion! We have sat with him for about some thirty years and we have not seen him laugh except for this day."'

Yaḥyā ibn az-Zubayr said, 'Mālik said to me, "Do you and 'Abdullāh ibn 'Abd al-'Azīz retire (*'uzla*)?" I said, "Yes." He said, "You are hasty. This is not yet the time."'

He said, 'Then I met Mālik some twenty years later. He said, "This is the time."' Then he retired and kept to his house.

One of them said, 'Mālik did not attend the group prayer and *Jumu'a* for seven years.'

Muḥammad ibn 'Umar said, 'When Muḥammad ibn al-Ḥasan rebelled, Mālik kept to his house and did not leave it until Muḥammad was killed.' [This was Muḥammad ibn 'Abdullāh ibn al-Ḥasan an-Nafs az-Zakiyya.]

Al-Wāqidī and Muṣ'ab ibn 'Abdullah said, 'Mālik used to attend the mosque, attend the *Jumu'a* and the general prayers, visit the sick, answer the invitation and fulfil the rights for a time. Then he stopped sitting in the mosque and used to pray and then withdraw. Then he stopped visiting the sick and attending funeral prayers. He used to go to their friends and console them. Then he abandoned sitting with the people and conversing with them and praying in the Prophet's mosque, even on *Jumu'a*. He did not console anyone nor give anyone a right. He was asked about that and said, 'One is not prepared to mention what it is about.'

In one of the variants, 'There are certain excuses which are not mentioned.'

The people put up with all of that for him. They had great preference for him and intense respect for until he died.

'Atīq ibn Ya'qūb and Muṣ'ab said, 'When he was near death, he was asked why he had stayed away from the mosque.' 'Atīq ibn Ya'qūb said, 'He had stayed away from the mosque for two years before he died. He said, "If it had not been that I am in the last of the days of this world and the first of those of this world, I would not have told you. I have incontinence and I disliked to come to the mosque of the Prophet ﷺ without being in a state of purity, making light of the Messenger of Allah ﷺ and I did not want to mention my illness and therefore complain to my Lord."'

In another variant he said, 'Out of fear that I would see something disliked.'

In the version of Khalaf ibn Muḥammad, 'I was too weak for that.'

It was said, 'He had a hernia from the beating which he received and a smell came out of it and he said, "I dislike annoying the people of the mosque of the Prophet ﷺ."'

Ya'qūb ibn 'Abd ar-Raḥmān said, 'Mālik did not speak at sunrise or sunset.'

Ibn Wahb said, 'Mālik used to not give *fatwā* nor speak until the sun had risen.'

Marwān ibn Muḥammad and Sa'īd ibn al-Jahm asked, 'He used to glorify and remember Allah.' Marwān said, 'When the sun had risen, he got up for his circle and spoke with his companions.' The other said, 'He moved to his circle and said, "Peace be upon you."'

Muṭarrif said, 'I saw him one day while he was sitting in the mosque making supplication after the *Ṣubḥ* prayer. His face became pale while his supplication went on at some length. Someone came and asked him a question and stopped him. He turned to him in anger and said, "Does one of you come to a man while he is making supplication and Allah will open to him what He wills to open of it and its answer is certain? Then he cuts that off for him and it will never come back?"'

Ibn Abī Ḥāzim said, 'Some words passed between a man of

Quraysh and Mālik. Mālik said to him, "If you want to disgrace me, Allah will give power over you to someone who will drive you out of your houses in a bad manner."

'The Imām woke up when the people were in an uproar about the man. He had been expelled from the mosque and seized and a rope was put on his neck and he was taken to the Sultan's house. The Imām told the people about the dream and the man recounted his story and began to plead with Mālik. He said, "Let me be, O best of those who say, 'He related to me,' so Mālik asked for forgiveness for him."'

Abū Muṣ'ab said, 'I heard Mālik say, "I remember and there is not a single lock of hair on my face. There is none of us who enters the mosque except with a turban out of respect for the Messenger of Allah ﷺ."'

Bishr ibn 'Umar said, 'I went with Mālik from his house until he went into the mosque. He came to a circle and they made room for him in the front of it. He refused and sat down where the assembly ended. I said to myself, "This is a just man. Room was not made for anyone in his assembly nor does he sit in the front of the assemblies of people."'

Al-Ḥārith ibn Miskīn said, 'May Allah have mercy on Mālik! There was none who guarded knowledge more and was more patient in poverty and clinging to Madina. He was ordered to be given awards of three thousand dinars and he did not take in exchange another house for the one he was in, nor did he use any of it for agricultural revenues, land or trade.'

Ibn al-Qāsim said, 'Mālik had four hundred dinars with which he traded. From them, he supported himself and his well-being.'

Ibn Abī Uways said, 'Mālik used to look often at a copy of the Qur'an in the two years before he died. He recited a lot and wept profusely.'

Mālik's severity in establishing the *ḥudūd* of Allah

The Qāḍī said that al-Bahlul ibn 'Ubayda said, 'I was with Mālik when he was brought a man who was led by the neck. They said to him. "The governor sends his greetings to you and says to you, 'This man strangled a man and killed him.'" Mālik said, "Then strangle him until he dies as he did to him." They took him away and Mālik turned pale and he watched until a man came by and he told him that he had strangled him. His normal colour returned and Ibn Kināna asked him about that. He said, "Do you think that I regretted it? Rather I feared that one of the judgements of Allah Almighty would fall into disuse."'

'Abd al-Jabbār ibn 'Umar said, 'I was present with Mālik when the governor summoned him present in a group of people of knowledge and asked them about a man who had attacked his brother, seized him, pushed him into a well and took his cloak. The parents of the two lads were present. The group of the scholars said, "The choice is up to the parents whether to pardon or to take retaliation." Mālik said, "I think that his head should be cut off." The parents said, "Should our son be killed yesterday and then we suffer the loss of the other one today? We are the guardians of blood and we pardon!"

'The governor said, "Abū 'Abdullah! There is none except them to seek it and they have pardoned." Mālik said,""By Allah! There is no god but Him! I will never speak on knowledge at today unless you strike off his head!"

'He remained silent. He spoke and then did not speak. Madina was in turmoil and the people were shouting, "If Mālik is silent, whom will we ask and who will answer?" There was a great uproar. They said, "There is no one in the cities like him, and none stands in his place in knowledge and excellence!"

'When the governor saw his determination to be silent, he went to the lad and cut off his head. When his head fell, Mālik turned to those present and said, "He killed him by plundering when he took his brother's garment. I did not kill him in retaliation so that his parents could pardon him." The people left and their selves were at peace when they saw how he honoured his oath since that was known that he would not break it.'

Ḥafṣ ibn Ghiyāth said, 'Mālik ibn Anas was sitting with the governor when the people of the prison came before him. He said, "Cut off this one's head. Beat this one with a hundred lashes and that one with two hundred. Crucify this one." It was as if a book had come down on him.'

Ashhab said, 'One of the governors called Mālik to ask his advice in something and he came in and indicated that some people should have their hands cut off and some people should be killed. He came out to smiling and reciting, "*There is life for you in retaliation, people of intelligence.*" (2:179)'

HIS APHORISMS, ADVICE AND MANNERS

The *Faqīh* and Qāḍī said that Mālik said, 'Humility lies in fearful awareness and the *dīn*, not in clothing.'

He said, 'Humility lies in abandoning showing off and reputation.'

He said, 'The worst knowledge is what is unusual. The best knowledge is the clear knowledge which people have related.'

Zayd ibn al-Ḥasan said, 'I heard him say, "Asceticism in this world consists of good earning and little hope."'

He said, 'This world is the body's health and cheerfulness from blessing.'

He said, 'Humility lies in fearful awareness and the *dīn*, not in clothing.'

Ibn al-Mubārak related that he said, 'Whoever wants for an opening to be given to him in his heart should perform more actions secretly than he does openly.'

He said, 'Knowledge is not achieved by a lot of *riwāya*. Knowledge is a light which Allah places in the hearts.'

These words were related from Ibn Mas'ūd.

Ibn Wahb quoted him: 'Seeking knowledge is good for someone who is provided with its good. It is a portion from Allah. But you must look to what you have from the morning to the evening and cling to that.'

He said, 'Knowledge is a light which can only reside in a godfearing heart.'

Ibn 'Abd al-Ḥakam related, 'Mālik was asked about seeking knowledge and whether it an obligation. He said, "No, the one who will not profit by it does not seek it. He does not seek questions which cause one to err, conundrums and excess."'

In Ashhab's version: 'Mālik was asked about seeking knowledge and whether it was an obligation. He said, "By Allah, not every person is a scholar. Some of you are not commanded to seek it." Then he said, "That is not the case with all people."'

Ibn Wahb said that Mālik said, 'The best of matters are those which are clear and evident. If you are unsure about two things, then take the more reliable.'

He said to Ibn Wahb, 'Convey what you have heard and it is enough for you and you will not bear anyone on your back. It is said, "People are lost who sell the Next World for this world, and lost is the one who sells the Next World for this world when it belongs to someone else."'

He said, 'When a man is given knowledge and becomes a leader at whom people point, he should put dust on his head and detest himself when he is alone and he should not rejoice in leadership. When he lies in his grave and the earth is his pillow, all of that will be bad for him.'

He said to Abū Mushir, 'Do not ask about what you do not want so that you forget what you want. The one who buys what he does not need sells what he needs.'

He said, 'Part of the victory of knowledge is that you answer whoever asks you. The one who relates all that he has heard is not an Imām. Part of the victory of knowledge is that he speaks it before he is asked about it.'

He said, 'When a man is asked a question and he does not answer and it rushes away from him, that is an affliction which Allah has averted from him.'

He said, 'It is not sound for a bankrupt or a proud rich man to seek knowledge.'

He was asked, 'What is the best that a person can do?' He replied, 'Seek knowledge.'

He said, 'Were it not for forgetfulness, many people would be men of knowledge.'

He said, 'People are destroyed by interpretation (*ta'wīl*) of what they do not know.'

He was asked, 'Can a scholar err?' He replied, 'The good which he indicates is much. Who is there who does not have anything wrong in him? If only those who had nothing in them commanded what is correct, no one would have commanded what is correct.'

He said, 'Part of the business of the descendant of Ādam is that he does not know and then he knows. Have you not heard the words of Allah, "*If you have taqwā of Allah, He will give you discrimination* (8:29)"?'

He said, 'Wisdom is the touch of an angel on a person's heart.'

He said, 'Wisdom is a light which Allah casts into a person's heart.'

He also said, 'It has occurred to my heart that wisdom is *fiqh* in the *dīn* of Allah and a matter which Allah makes enter the hearts from His mercy and His bounty.'

He also said, 'Wisdom is reflection on the command of Allah and following it.'

He said in the hearing of Ibn Wahb and Ibn al-Qāsim, 'Wisdom consists of obedience to Allah and pursuing it and *fiqh* in the *dīn* and acting by it.'

Al-Farawī said, 'I heard him say, "When a man has no good in himself, people have no good in him."'

Ibn Wahb said, 'I heard him say, "There is no good in any of this world, even if it is abundant when the *dīn* of a man or his manly virtue (*murū'a*) is corrupted."'

He said, 'Learn knowledge before action.'

He said, 'Cleanliness of garments, good aspiration and manifestation of manly virtue is one of the forty odd parts of Prophethood.'

He said to one of his nephews, 'When you learn a knowledge which is part of obedience of Allah, its trace should be seen on you and its mark should be seen in you. You will learn tranquillity, forbearance and gravity by that knowledge which you have learned.'

He said, 'It is a duty for anyone who seeks knowledge to have gravity, tranquillity and fear. He should follow in the footsteps of those who have gone before. The people of knowledge should dispense with joking, particularly if they have some renown in knowledge.'

He said, 'The *adab* of Allah is the Qur'an. The *adab* of His Messenger is the *Sunna*. The *adab* of the righteous is *fiqh*.'

He said, 'A man's belief is not complete until he safeguards his tongue.'

He said to one of his companions, 'Do not fill your house with a lot of individuals unless it is by a necessary matter that you have in it. Do not sit in an assembly from whose knowledge you do not benefit.'

Sufyān said, 'I came to Mālik and said to him, "Knowledge is abundant." He said, "Knowledge is a tree whose root is in Makka, and its branches are in Madina, its leaves are in Iraq and its fruit is in Khurasan." He said, "Write, boy! This is one of the rare sayings of Mālik."'

Az-Zubayrī said, 'I said to Mālik, "There are some people who will obey if someone commands them. There are some people such that if I command them, I will be injured by them. The poets will satirise me and those who are in power will beat me and imprison me, so what shall I do?" He said, "If you are afraid and think that they will not obey you, then leave it and dislike it with your heart. You have the capacity for that. Command the one you do not fear and forbid him, especially if you desire the face of Allah by it. If you are like that, you will only see good from Allah, especially if there is some leniency in you. Do you not see that Allah told Mūsā and Hārūn, '*Speak gentle words to him*'? When you are harsh in your command, it is not accepted from you and then you will be exposed to what you dislike and you will leave the body of the people of the Qur'an and knowledge."'

He said in earshot of Ashhab, Ibn Wahb and Ibn al-Qāsim, 'Whoever is truthful in speech enjoys his intellect and what strikes the people of senility and dotage does not touch him.'

A man said to him, 'I am a dotard.' He said, 'Liars become dotards.'

Ibn al-Mubārak said, 'I heard him say, "A man is not righteous until he abandons what does not concern him and is occupied with what concerns him. When he is like that, Allah is about to open his heart."'

Ibn Abī Uways related that he said, 'If you desire of it what will be enough for you, then the least of livelihood will be enough for you. What is little and enough is better than what is a lot and distracting.'

Ibn Wahb said, 'I heard him say, "When anyone does without this world, Allah makes him speak by wisdom."'

Khālid ibn Ḥumayd said, 'I heard him say, "You must sit with someone whose words will increase you in your knowledge and whose actions will call you to the Next World. Beware of sitting with the one whose words entertain you and whose *dīn* causes fault in you and whose action calls you to this world."'

Ibn al-Qāsim said, 'Mālik mentioned the goal and its excellence. Then he said, "Beware of the goal by which you will be elevated." It was asked, "Why?" He replied, "You will be vain about it."'

Muṭarrif said that a man said to Mālik, 'Counsel me!' He said, 'When you desire some business of Allah's obedience, if you are able to do so, do not leave it for a single minute without doing it. You are not safe from events. When you desire to do other than that, then if you are able not to do it for a minute, then do so – perhaps Allah will make something happen to cause you to abandon it. When you are called to a matter which is not about a right, do not be too shy to say, "Allah Almighty says in His Book, *'Allah is not reticent with the truth.'*" (33:53) Purify your garments and clean them of acts of rebellion against Allah. You must have lofty and noble matters and fear base and inferior ones. Allah loves lofty qualities and dislikes base ones. Do a lot of recitation of the Qur'an and strive that not an hour of the day or night comes to you but that your tongue is moist with the remembrance of Allah. Do not give people power over yourself and then go where you like.'

He said, 'A slave does not conceal a secret good action but that Allah cloaks him in its cloak nor does he conceal a secret bad action but that Allah clothes him in its cloak.'

Mālik said to al-Qa'nabī, 'Whatever you play with, do not play with your *dīn*.'

He said to his nephews, 'If you want Allah to help you in this matter, then make do with little of it and learn *fiqh* from it.'

He said, 'No one has a lot of it and is then successful.'

Ibn Wahb said, 'Mālik said to me, "A man who is not safe from relating all he has heard is never an *imām*. Part of abasement is debasing knowledge with someone who is incapable of it."'

Ibn Nāfi' said that Mālik said, 'Everything is useful in excess except for words.'

Muṭarrif said, 'When one of the seekers of knowledge bade farewell to Mālik, he said to him, 'Fear Allah with respect to this knowledge and do not put it in a house of ruin. Spread it and do not conceal it.'

Muṣ'ab said, 'When Mālik heard about the death of a person, he said, "Praise be to Allah, the Lord of the worlds, who made us continue after him. O Allah, do not make him a trial for us!"'

Ibn 'Abd al-Ḥakam and Ibn Wahb said, 'I heard Mālik say, "The first acts of rebellion are pride, envy and avarice. Iblīs envied and was arrogant. He said, '*You created me from fire and You created him from clay.*' (7:12) Allah Almighty says, '*So eat of it wherever you like, but do not go near this tree.*' (7:19) Ādam was avaricious and so he ate from it."'

Abū Qurra said that he heard Mālik say, 'Whoever knows that his words are part of his actions speaks little. Words are part of action.'

Abū Qurra said, 'It is even stronger than action, and belief and disbelief are by it.'

Ibn Wahb said, 'I heard him say, "If someone is pleased with something, it is enough for him," meaning that contentment is beneficial for the people of scrupulousness.'

Mālik said, 'A man's foolish management is worse than his lack of it because he will use money after lacking it and then foolish management will not leave him anything.'

Ibn Wahb said, 'A man said to Mālik, "Counsel me!" He said, "I counsel you to do right actions and to eat what is good."'

He said that he heard him say, 'When Allah wants good for someone, He puts him in order. When Allah Almighty blesses His slave, His settles his affair for him. When He afflicts someone, He scatters his affair for him.'

I heard him say, 'Drawing near to the people of falsehood is destruction, and false words block the truth. Part of a man's happiness is that he is given success in good. Part of the misery of a man is that he continues to err.'

He said, 'I heard him say, "When the false overcomes the truth, there is corruption in the earth. Both a little of the false and a lot of it are destruction. Clinging to the truth is salvation."'

He said, 'I heard him say, "It is a duty for the seeker of knowledge to have gravity, tranquillity and fear, and that he follow in the tracks of those before him."'

He said, 'Part of the good manners of a scholar is that his laughter is only a smile.'

He said, 'Everything has a buttress and the buttress of a believer is his intellect. He worships his Lord according to what he understands.'

He said, 'Islam is vast. When you only desire the truth, then Islam is vaster still than that. It should not be made narrow.' He added in another place, 'when its limits (*ḥudūd*) are established.'

He said that he heard him say, 'It is said that a believer has good backing (*ma'ūna*), little provision (*mu'na*), and that the one who has left the right way is the opposite.'

He also heard him say, 'I used to hear him say that the man commits the error and so he is one who despairs of his action being good.' He added in the hearing of Ashhab, 'He turns frequently to Allah Almighty.'

Al-Qa'nabī said, 'I heard him say, "When a man praises himself, his radiance departs."'

Ibn Wahb said, 'I heard him say, "Speaking about these problematic questions increases blindness and corrupts a person."

'I also heard him say, "An excess of words disgorges a scholar, abases him and lessens him."'

He said that he mentioned discussion and the dialectic process of people and said, 'If someone does this, his radiance departs.' He used to dislike a lot of discussion and censured it. He said, 'It only exists among women and weak people.'

He said that it used to be said, 'So-and-so would be the best of men had not been that he speaks enough words for a month in a single day.'

Khālid ibn Khidāsh said, 'I said to Mālik, "Counsel me!" He said, "You must have *taqwā* of Allah and seeking knowledge with its people."'

Ibn al-Qāsim said, 'When we bade farewell to Mālik, he said, "Fear Allah and spread this knowledge. Teach it and do not conceal it."'

He said, 'This business will not be won until poverty is tasted in it.'

Abū Qurra said, 'I heard Mālik say, "Learn from a scholar, even the wearing of his sandals."'

Ashhab said, 'I heard him say, "There is no good in raising the voice in the mosque on knowledge or anything else. I came across people of old who used to criticise that."'

Ibn Wahb said from him, 'When there is a lot of discussion, there is error in it. When the answer is correct, there is little discourse.'

He used to say when he was asked for a *fatwā*, 'Speaking what is false blocks the truth.'

He said to Ibn Wahb, 'Have fear of Allah and confine yourself to your knowledge. No one confines himself to his knowledge but that he benefits and gives benefit. If you want what you seek from Allah, then be correct in what you use. If you want what will teach you this world, you possess nothing.'

We find in Mālik's letter to Abū Qurra: 'I think that it is correct to omit teaching the questions which are partially beneficial when there is harm in them which one fears will make the person who has it fall into error and discord. So how is it with other questions which are useless?'

Ibn Wahb said that Mālik said, 'Things are ugly when their places exceed them.'

He said, 'Seeking provision in the questionable is better than being in need of people.'

He said, '*Zuhd* (asceticism) in this world consists good earning and little hope.'

He said, 'There are four types of people in knowledge. There is a man who knows and acts by it and teaches it. His likeness in the Book of Allah is, "*Only those of His slaves with knowledge fear Allah.*" (35:28) There is a man who knows and acts by it and does not teach it. His likeness in the Book of Allah is, "*Those who hide the Clear Signs and Guidance We have sent down.*" (2:159) There is a man who does not know and does not act by it. His likeness in the Book of Allah is, "*They are only like cattle.*" (25:44)'[1]

He said, 'Part of the failing of a *qāḍī* is that when he retires, he does not return to where he sat when he studied.'

[1]There are only three mentioned.

Mālik gave a *fatwā* against one of the poets which the man did not like. He said to him, 'Abū 'Abdullāh! Do you think that the governor does not know this case in which you have given judgement against me? He sent us to you to put things right between us and yet you did not do it! By Allah, I will lacerate your flesh with satirical poetry!'

'You!' Mālik retorted to him, 'Do you know how you have described yourself? You have described yourself with insolent stupidity and baseness. They are two things which no one lacks. If you are capable of it, then bring other things of nobility and manly virtue before which heads are cut off!'

Ibn Wahb said that Mālik said, 'You are enough of an unjust man when you continue the argument.'

He said, 'The Arabs have sweet tongues.'

He said, 'The terrors of this world are three: travelling on the sea, riding a Arabian horse, and marrying a free woman.'

The *Muwaṭṭā'* and Mālik writing it

The Qāḍī said that Ibn Mahdī said, 'After the Book of Allah there is no book more beneficial for people than the *Muwaṭṭā'*.'

He said, 'I do not know of any of the knowledge of the people after the Qur'an which is sounder than the *Muwaṭṭā'* of Mālik.'

Ibn Wahb said, 'Whoever writes the *Muwaṭṭā'* of Mālik does not have to write anything else regarding the lawful and the unlawful.'

Ash-Shāfi'ī said, 'There is no book on knowledge on the earth more correct than the book of Mālik.'

He said, 'There is no book on the earth sounder than the book of Mālik. (One version has 'better'.) People have not written anything after the Qur'an more beneficial than the *Muwaṭṭā'* of Mālik. When a tradition comes from Mālik's book, it is in the Pleiades.'

Sa'īd ibn Abī Maryam said when his nephews were in Iraq: 'If they had collected knowledge in Iraq for their entire lives, they could not have brought a knowledge like Mālik's *Muwaṭṭā'*.'

He said in another transmission: 'They could not have brought a *sunna* agreed-upon different than what is in the *Muwaṭṭā'*.'

Ibn Ḥanbal said, 'How excellent is the *Muwaṭṭā'* for the one who takes on its *dīn*!'

Ad-Darāwardī said, 'I was sleeping in the *Rawḍa* between the grave and the minbar and I dreamt that the Prophet ﷺ left his grave leaning on Abū Bakr and 'Umar. He passed and then he came back. I went to him and said to him, "Messenger of Allah! From where have you come?" He said, "I went to Mālik ibn Anas and I set up the Straight Path for him."' He said, 'I went to Mālik and found him writing the *Muwaṭṭā'*. I told him the story and he wept.'

Abu Muṣ'ab related that Abu Ja'far al-Manṣūr[1] said to Mālik, 'Write a book for people to which I can direct them.' Mālik spoke to him about that. Al-Manṣūr said, 'Write it. There is no one today with more knowledge than you,' so he wrote the *Muwaṭṭā'* and still had not finished it when Abū Ja'far died.

Abū Muṣ'ab said that he heard Mālik say, 'I came to Abū Ja'far in the morning when the sun stood over the land. He had come from his property to his rug. There were two large horses standing on the rug from where I entered to where I left. They were trained to neither urinate nor defecate. Then a child came in and went back out. He said, "Do you know who this was?" I answered, "No." He said, "That is my son. He was frightened of your white hair."'

We find in another variant: 'He disliked the fact that you were sitting near me as he has not seen anyone except you do that. You are worthy of every good and qualified for every honour. (He had brought him close and his knee was touching his knee.) He continued to question me until the *mu'adhdhin* came to him for the *Ẓuhr* prayer. He said to me, "You are the most knowing of people." (In one version, "of the people of the earth".) I said, "No, by Allah, Amīr al-Mu'minīn." He said, "Yes, but you conceal that."'

According to one version: 'There is no one with more than you today after the Amīr al-Mu'minīn. If I last, I will write your books in gold ink, (In one version, 'as the copies of the Qur'an are written') and then I will hang them in the Ka'ba and make people follow them.'

He said, 'I said, "Amīr al-Mu'minīn, do not do it. My book contains

[1]The Abbasid caliph.

the *ḥadīth*s of the Messenger of Allah ﷺ, sayings of the Companions and sayings of the Followers, and the opinion is the consensus of the people of Madina whom I have not left. But I do not think that it should be hung in the Ka'ba."'

He said, 'Abū Ja'far said to him while he was at Makka, "Make all knowledge into one knowledge, Abū 'Abdullāh."' He said, 'I said to him, "Amīr al-Mu'minīn, the Companions of the Messenger of Allah ﷺ scattered throughout the lands and each of them made *fatwā*s in the city to which he went as he thought best. "'

In one version, 'So the people of the various regions each have a position, and the people of Madina have a position. The people of Iraq have a position in which they overstep their authority.'

He said, 'As for the people of Iraq, I do not take either my religious obligations or supererogatory actions from them. True knowledge is the knowledge of the people of Madina, so write down knowledge for people.'

According to one version, 'I told him, "The people of Iraq are not content with our knowledge."' Abū Ja'far said, 'Their common folk will be driven to it with the sword and their backs will be broken to it by whips.'

In one of them, 'Abū Ja'far said to him, "I have resolved to make copies of these books of yours and then I will send a copy to every city of the Muslims and I will command them to learn what is in them and not to leave it for things other than this knowledge of *ḥadīth*. I think that the root of knowledge is the transmission of the people of Madina and their knowledge."'

He said, 'I said to him, "Amīr al-Mu'minīn! Do not do it. The people have already made statements before us and they have heard *ḥadīth*s and have related transmissions, and each people have taken what came to them first and learned it and based their *dīn* on it from the different Companions of the Messenger of Allah ﷺ and others. To turn them from what they believe will be harsh, so leave people with what they have and what the people of each land have chosen from themselves." He said, "By my life, if you had complied with me in that, I would have commanded it."'

One version has that al-Manṣūr said to him, 'Abū 'Abdullāh, write down this knowledge and compose books and in them avoid the harsh ones of 'Abdullāh ibn 'Umar, the soft ones of Ibn 'Abbās and the odd *ḥadīth*s (with a single ascription) of Ibn Mas'ūd, and be content with the middle business and what the Imāms and Companions agree about.'

Al-Mahdī said that he said to him, 'Write a book that I will make the community adopt.' Mālik said to him, 'As for the region, i.e. Maghrib, I have spared you from it. As for Syria, al-Awzā'ī is there. As for the people of Iraq, they are the people of Iraq.'

'Atīq az-Zubayrī said, 'Mālik wrote the *Muwaṭṭā'* from some ten thousand *ḥadīth*s, and he continued to look at every year, and remove some from it until it remained this. Had he lived a little longer, he would have dropped it all.'

Al-Qaṭṭān said, 'The knowledge of the people was in increase, and the knowledge of Mālik in decrease. If Mālik had lived, he would have dropped all his knowledge,' meaning out of carefulness.

Sulaymān ibn Bilāl said, 'When Mālik wrote the *Muwaṭṭā'* there were four thousand *ḥadīth*s in it (or he said 'more than'). When he died, it had about one hundred *ḥadīth*s. He refined it year after year according to what he thought was right for the Muslims and more excellent in the *dīn*.'

Mālik said when the *Muwaṭṭā'* was mentioned to him, 'It contains the *ḥadīth*s of the Messenger of Allah ﷺ, the sayings of the Companions and the Followers and my opinion. I spoke by my opinion and with *ijtihād* and according to what I found with the people of knowledge in our land. I did not leave them for others.'

Abū Mūsā al-Anṣārī said, 'A fire occurred in a man's house and everything inside the house except for a copy of the Qur'an and the *Muwaṭṭā'*.'

Ibn Abī Uways said, 'Mālik was asked about "Your words in the books, 'The matter agreed upon' and 'the business with us' and 'I have met the people of knowledge' and 'I heard one of the people of knowledge'."

'His answer was: "When I often say 'my opinion' in books, by Allah, it is my opinion, but, by my life, it is not mere opinion since I heard it from more than one of the people of knowledge and excellence and the Imāms who are followed from whom I took knowledge. They are those who are fearful of Allah. That became too repetitive for me, so I said, 'my opinion' Their opinion is the same as my opinion when it is the same as the opinion of the Companions which they found them with and subsequently I found that with them. This is an inheritance which was passed on from generation to generation down to our time.

""'I think' is the opinion of the previous Imāms. As for 'the business with us', it is what the people with us do and on which judgements have passed and which both the ignorant and men of knowledge know. It is the same when I said, 'In our land'. When I said, 'one of the people of knowledge,' it is something I liked in the words of the scholars.

'"When I did not hear anything from them, I strove and investigated according to the school of those I have met until that I felt that I had reached the truth or close to it, so that it would not depart from the school of the people of Madina and their opinions, even if I had not heard that itself. I said that it was my opinion after *ijtihād* with the *Sunna* and the action of the people of knowledge who are followed and the practice which has been acted upon with us since the time of the Messenger of Allah ﷺ and the Rightly-guided Caliphs and those I have met. That is their opinion and I have not left it for that of any others."'

Aḥmad ibn 'Abdullāh al-Kūfī mentioned in his *History* that all that Mālik said in his *Muwaṭṭā'* as 'The matter which is agreed upon with us' comes from the decision of Sulayman ibn Bilāl. This is not correct.

He said, 'What is *mursal* in it from Ibn Mas'ūd was related by 'Abdullāh ibn Idrīs al-Awdī. What he gave as *mursal* from anyone else is from Ibn Mahdī.'

Ad-Darāwardī said, 'When Mālik said, "This is how I found the people of knowledge in our city" and "the matter with us", he meant Rabī'a and Ibn Hurmuz.

'Umar ibn Abī Salama said, 'There was no time that I read the General Chapter of the *Muwaṭṭā'* but that I saw a man in my sleep who said to me, "This is the *ḥadīth* of the Messenger of Allah, may Allah bless him and grant him peace."'

He said, 'When we came to Madina by an intermediary to Mālik, he told me, "Come tomorrow with the book of the *mudabbar* and the *mukātab*. They have agreed to read them." I spent the night and I saw someone saying while I was asleep, "Tomorrow the *ḥadīth* of the Messenger of Allah ﷺ will be read to Mālik." I went to Mālik and he had two scribes with him. When he saw me, he said to me, "What do you have with you?" I answered, "The *mukātab* and the *mudabbar*." He said, "It seems proper to them and they have agreed to recite the General Chapter." I mentioned the dream to him and Mālik told me, "It is true and it is the *ḥadīth* of the Messenger of Allah ﷺ."'

Ṣafwān ibn 'Umar ibn 'Abd al-Wāḥid said, 'We read the *Muwaṭṭā'* to Mālik over forty days. He said, "A book which I wrote in forty years. You have taken it from me in forty days. How little you understand in it!"'

Another said, ''Abd al-'Azīz ibn al-Mājishūn was the first to compile a *Muwaṭṭā'*. He used the words without the *ḥadīth*. When Mālik saw it, he said, "How excellent is what he does! If it had been me, I would have begun with traditions. Then I would have strengthened that with words."'

Then he resolved to write the *Muwaṭṭā'*. There were scholars in Madina at that time who worked on *Muwaṭṭā'*s. It was said to Mālik, 'You have occupied yourself with doing this book while people share with you in it and are also making ones like it.' He said, 'Bring them to me!' He looked at them and threw them away. He said, 'So you should know that what I want by it is the Cause of Allah.'

Muṭarrif said, 'Mālik asked me, "What do people say about my *Muwaṭṭā'*?" I replied, "The people are divided into two sorts of men:

a fulsome lover and a tepid envier." He said, "If you live long enough, you will see what Allah desires by it.'"

He said, 'It was as if those books were thrown in the wells, and after that nothing of them was ever mentioned.'

'Abd ar-Raḥmān ibn Zayd ibn Aslam said, 'When Mālik wrote the *Muwaṭṭā'*, he put the *ḥadīths* of Zayd at the end of the chapters. I asked him about that. He said, 'They are like a commentary for what is before them.'"

Abū Dāwūd said, 'It was said to Mālik, "There are no *gharīb ḥadīths* in your book."He said, 'You have made me happy.'"

Abū Zur'a said, 'Had a man been made to take an oath of divorce according to Mālik's *ḥadīths* which are in the *Muwaṭṭā'* all being sound, he would not break his oath. If he swore on the *ḥadīth* of something else, he would break it.'

Ibn Sawwār al-Jurmī said, 'I heard Mālik say, "The matter with us is like that" and I told Ibn Abi Dhi'b about it. He said, "It is not permitted for Mālik to say this. This is not from what he supposed." I told Mālik that and he said, "I do not consider the opinion of Ibn Abi Dhi'b. I consider the one I have met from the people of knowledge."'

What was said about the *Muwaṭṭā'* in verse

Part of that are the words of Sa'dūn al-Waraskhshī:

I say to the one who relates and writes down *ḥadīths*
  and travels the paths of *fiqh* and seeks its knowledge,
If you want to be called a scholar among the people,
  do not go beyond the knowledge that Yathrib contains.
Would you abandon one of its houses where Jibrīl,
  the angel brought near, came and went?
The Messenger of Allah died in it, and after him
  the Companions took on the discipline of his *Sunna*.
The body of knowledge split up among their followers
  and each man among them had a school in it.
Mālik purified and clarified it by formulating it for the people.
  From him comes what is sound in the testing and the measure.
He removed its illness by making the *riwāya* sound, and the
  verification of soundness contains the cure for the one with mange.

If it had not been that the light of the *Muwaṭṭā'*
shown to the one who sees
his blindness in the night, he would not have known where to go.
Hasten to the *Muwaṭṭā'* of Mālik before it vanishes. If it is missed,
there is no goal after it for the one who seeks the truth.
He entrusted every knowledge you desire in the *Muwaṭṭā'*.
The *Muwaṭṭā'* is the sun while the others are mere stars.
It is the root whose branch is wholesome because of its excellence,
and how could the branch not be good when the root is good?
It is knowledge with Allah after His Book. It contains
the language of truthfulness clearly proclaiming the truth.
Its traditions are distinctly stated in their clarity.
There is no one in the entire universe who denies them.
Part of the boast of the people of the Hijaz
is that the *Muwaṭṭā'* is loved in Iraq.
If anyone does not have the books of the *Muwaṭṭā'* in his house,
that house is bereft of success.
May Allah reward Mālik from us for the *Muwaṭṭā'*
with the best reward with which
a disciplined man of intelligence can be repaid.
It is good to acquire all that he related. The action of the one
who fears and dreads Allah is like that.
He surpassed the people of knowledge in life and death,
and examples are made about him for the people.
He only surpassed them by *taqwā* and fear
and since he was pleased for Allah and angry for Him.
His grave continues to quench the thirst of every visitor
with a torrent whose water spouts gush out
Which waters the graves around it other than his area, and what
is between them is full of luxuriant grass in the morning.
I do not begrudge you to drink as it drinks,
but the right of knowledge is more demanding and obligatory.

Abū Ṭāhir Aḥmad ibn Muḥammad al-Iṣbahānī said on that:

The most universal book in use for the *faqīh* is Mālik's *Muwaṭṭā'*.
There is no doubt in it.

Do not begin with anything to listen to except it be
from an *imām* who is pleasing.
Keep the company of the one who respects him
and avoid the books of all who slight him.

The Qāḍī said:

When the books of knowledge are mentioned,
the best of them is the *Muwaṭṭā'* of Mālik from Mālik's books.
Its *ḥadīths* are sounder and its *sunan* firmer
and it is the clearest of roads in *fiqh* for the traveller.
Isnāds like the firm mountains, sound,
and opinion like the lights of the interlaced stars.
It is as the glorious proof and the protection
whose guidance rescues from all destruction.
One is guided and follows it in every matter
and it contains the clarification of murky obscurities.
The consensus about it has preceded in every community
despite cantankerous enviers.
The first work to be corrected, it came out early
to teach the preservation of those paths.
By the writing down of what was obscure and excellent expression,
and the perfection of the organisation for those perceptions,
He came as one who adorns the sash and he purified the pure gold
with the purification of the smelter.
Take the knowledge of the *dīn* pure from it
and learn the Sharī'a of the blessed Prophet from it.
The grasping hand of the stingy should seize it.
Whoever is hindered from it perishes in disasters.

PEOPLE'S CONCERN FOR THE *MUWAṬṬĀ'* AND THEIR INTEREST IN IT

The Qāḍī said, 'People were not concerned with any of the books of *fiqh* and *ḥadīth* as they were concerned with the *Muwaṭṭā'*. Both friend and opponent agreed to give it precedence and prefer it and its transmission, and to advance its *ḥadīths* and consider them sound.'

We mentioned some of that in the chapter before it and we will mention a chapter about the glorious ones who related from Mālik.

As for those who were concerned with the discussion on its men and its *ḥadīths* and writing that, this comprises a number of the Mālikis and other people, and some of the People of *Ḥadīth* and Arabic, and many of them collected the *ḥadīths* of Mālik from the *Muwaṭṭā'* and other places.

One of those who wrote on that was Qāḍī Ismā'īl. He produced the *Muwaṭṭā'* with *isnād* from its men to Mālik ibn Anas from the copies of the *Muwaṭṭā'* of Mālik and all his *ḥadīths*. He wrote the *musnad* on the *ḥadīths* of Mālik, and he also wrote the witnesses of the *Muwaṭṭā'*.

Qāsim ibn Aṣbaḥ wrote the *Musnad* of the *Muwaṭṭā'* as did Abū al-Qāsim al-Jawharī.

Abū al-Ḥasan al-Qābisī wrote *al-Mukhlaṣ*.

Abū Dharr al-Harawī wrote the *Musnad* of the *Muwaṭṭā'*s.

Abū Bakr al-Qabbāb wrote the *ḥadīths* of Mālik.

Abū al-Ḥasan 'Alī ibn Khalaf as-Sijilmāsī wrote the *Musnad* of the *Muwaṭṭā'*, and 'Abdūs ibn Muḥammad related it from him.

Al-Muṭarriz did the same.

Abū 'Abdullāh al-Jīzī.

Aḥmad ibn Fahzād al-Fārisī

Qāḍī Abū Mufarrij

Ibn al-A'rābī

Musnad of the Ḥadīths of Mālik and his opinion by Muḥammad ibn Shurūsh as-Ṣan'ānī.

The *ḥadīths* of Mālik in the *riwāya* of Ibn Nāfi' az-Zubayrī

'Abd ar-Raḥmān an-Nasā'ī wrote the *musnad* of Mālik's *ḥadīths*.

Abū Muḥammad ibn 'Adī al-Jurjānī

Aḥmad ibn Ibrāhīm Jāmi' as-Sakawī

Qibdār ibn al-A'rābī

Ibn 'Ufayr

Abū 'Abdullāh as-Sirāj an-Naysābūri

Abū Bakr ibn Ziyād an-Naysābūrī

Abū al-'Arab at-Tamimī

Abū Ḥafṣ ibn Shāhīn

'Abd al-'Azīz ibn Salama

Abū al-Qāsim al-Andalusī

Abū 'Umar ibn 'Abd al-Barr

Qāḍī Ibn Mufarraj
Muḥammad ibn 'Ishūn aṭ-Ṭutayṭilī
Abū al-Qāsim al-Jawharī also wrote *Musnad* of the *ḥadīths* of Mālik outside the *Muwaṭṭā'*.
Abū Bakr Muḥammad ibn 'Īsā al-Ḥaḍramī
'Abd al-Ghanī ibn Sa'īd
Abū al-Faḍl ibn Abī 'Imrān al-Harawī
Abū al-Ḥasan ad-Dāraquṭnī wrote it also who also has a book on the different copies of the *Muwaṭṭā'*
Aflaḥ ibn Aḥmad on the gharib *ḥadīths* of Mālik
Ibn al-Jārūd
Qāsim ibn Aṣbagh
Abū al-Ḥasan ad-Dāraquṭnī has a book on the *ḥadīths* in which Mālik is opposed.
Al-Bazzār had a similar book
Muḥammad ibn Abi al-Muẓaffar, the *ḥāfiẓ*, has a book on what Mālik has of uninterrupted *ḥadīths*.
Abū 'Umar ibn Khaḍr aṭ-Ṭuṭaytilī wrote the *musnad* of the *Muwaṭṭā'* in the *riwāya* of al-Qa'nabī.
Ibrāhīm ibn Naṣr as-Saraqustī
Abū Bakr Aḥmad ibn Sa'īd ibn Fūḍakh al-Akhmīmī has the *musnad* of the *Muwaṭṭā'*,
Abū Sulaymān Muḥammad ibn 'Abdullāh ibn Zayd wrote the *musnad* of Mālik's *ḥadīths*,
Usāma ibn 'Alī ibn Sa'id al-Miṣrī
Mūsā ibn Hārūn al-Ḥammāl
Abū Nu'aym al-Ḥalabī al-Qalānisī
Qāḍī Abū Bakr ibn as-Salīm wrote the *Kitāb at-Tawṣīl* about what is not in the *Muwaṭṭā'*.
Abū al-Ḥasan ibn Abī Ṭālib al-'Ābir wrote *The Book of the Muwaṭṭā'*.
Abū Bakr ibn Thābit al-Kātib wrote *The Book of the Ends of the Muwaṭṭā'*.
Yaḥyā ibn Muzayn wrote a commentary on it and one on its causes called *al-Mustaqṣiyya*.
Muḥammad ibn Abi Zamanayn summarised its commentary in his book, *al-Maghrib*.

Ibn Muzayn wrote a book on its men.
Ibn Wahb has a commentary on it
As does 'Īsā ibn Dīnār,
'Abdullāh ibn Nāfi' aṣ-Ṣā'igh,
Ḥarmala ibn Yaḥyā,
and Muḥammad ibn Saḥnūn.
Ibn Ḥabīb and Muslim authored works on Mālik's shaykhs.
Al-Barqī wrote a book on the men of the *Muwaṭṭā'*
As did Abū 'Umar at-Talamankī
And Qāḍī Abū 'Abdullāh ibn al-Hadhdhā'
And Abū 'Abdullāh ibn Mufarrij
Al-Barqī wrote a commentary on its *gharīb*.
Ahmad ibn 'Imran al-Akhfash wrote a book on its *gharīb*
Abū al-Qāsim al-'Uthmānī al-Miṣrī has a commentary on its *gharīb*
Abū Ja'far ad-Dāwūdī has a book, *an-Nāmī*, on its commentary
Abū Marwān al-Qanāzi'ī wrote a famous book on its *gharīb*.
Abū 'Abd al-Mālik al-Būnī authored a famous book on its commentary.
Ibn Ḥawṭ has collected the *Muwaṭṭā'* from the *riwāya* of Ibn Wahb and Ibn al-Qāsim.
I saw that someone else had a *Collection* from the *riwāya* of Yaḥyā ibn Yaḥyā al-Andalusī and Abū Muṣ'ab.
Abū 'Umar ibn 'Abd al-Barr has two large famous books on its discussion and commentary on its meanings. They are in the *Kitāb at-Tamhīd* and the *Kitāb al-Istidhkār*. He has the *Kitāb at-Taqaṣṣī* on the *musnad* of his *ḥadīth*s and *mursal ḥadīth*s, and a book on the *ḥadīth*s of Mālik outside the *Muwaṭṭā'*.
Qāḍī Abū al-Walīd al-Bājī has his famous books on it: *al-Muntaqā*, *The Book of Oaths* and *The Book of Asking Fatwā*, which is incomplete. It is the largest and most comprehensive book. He also has a book on different copies of the *Muwaṭṭā'*.
Qāḍī Abū al-Walīd aṣ-Ṣaffār has *Kitāb al-Maw'ib* which is an incomplete commentary on it.
Qāḍī Muḥammad ibn Sulaymān ibn Khalīfa has his great commentary called *al-Muḥallā*.

Abū Bakr ibn Sābiq aṣ-Ṣiqillī has his commentary called *al-Masālik.*

Abū Muḥammad ibn Ḥazm aẓ-Ẓāhirī has a book on its commentary.

Our shaykh, Qāḍī Abū 'Abdullāh ibn al-Ḥājj, wrote a large work on its commentary, as our shaykh, the *faqīh* Abū al-Walīd ibn al-'Awwād, also wrote a book in which he brought the *Istidhkār* and *Tamhīd* together. He died before it was completed.

Abū Muḥammad ibn as-Sayyid al-Baṭalyūsī an-Naḥawī has a book on its commentary called *al-Muqtabas.*

There is *Tawjīh al-Muwaṭṭā'* by Abū 'Abdullāh ibn 'Ishūn aṭ-Ṭutayṭilī.

Abū Sa'īd 'Imrān ibn 'Abd Rabbih al-Ma'āfirī al-Andalusī, known as ad-Dabbāgh, has a work on the proofs of Muḥammad al-Aṣīlī and his writing on the chapters of the *Muwaṭṭā'* which I came across.

Abū al-Qāsim ibn al-Judd has a book on the commentary of the *Tamhīd.*

Ibn 'Abd al-Barr has something on the *ḥadīths* of the *Muwaṭṭā'*. Some of them ascribe it to Abū 'Abdullāh Mālik ibn Wuhayb.

Shaykh Ḥāzim ibn Muḥammad ibn Ḥāzim has his book called *al-Mushir* on the traditions of the *Muwaṭṭā'* which consists of forty sections.

There is a commentary done by a man of Córdoba known as Abū al-Ḥasan al-Ishbīlī on the *Muwaṭṭā'*. There is one by Ibn Sharāḥīl, and Abū 'Umar aṭ-Ṭalamankī has a commentary which he did not finish. It is the same with Qāḍī Abū 'Abdullāh ibn al-Hadhdhā'.

There is the commentary of the *musnad* of the *Muwaṭṭā'* by Qāḍī Yūnus ibn Mughīth, which is a commentary on the *Summary.*

Abū al-Qāsim al-Muhallab ibn Abī Ṣufra and his brother Abū 'Abdullāh wrote a commentary on it.

Abū Muḥammad ibn Yarbu', the *ḥadīth* scholar, one of those I have met, has a book discussing its *isnād* which he called *The Crown of Adornment and The Lamp of Desire.*

Abū Bakr ibn Mawhab al-'Anbarī did a commentary of the *Summary* in many volumes.

Those who related the *Muwaṭṭā'* from Mālik

They include:

'Abd ar-Raḥmān ibn al-Qāsim
'Abdullāh ibn Wahb
Muṭarrif ibn 'Abdullāh
Abū Muṣ'ab az-Zuhrī
Muḥammad ibn Idrīs ash-Shāfi'ī
'Abdullāh ibn 'Abd al-Ḥakam
Yaḥyā ibn Bukayr
Muḥammad ibn al-Ḥasan, the companion of Abū Ḥanīfa
Muṣ'ab ibn 'Abdullāh az-Zubayrī
His brother, Bakkār
His son az-Zubayr ibn Bakkār
Yaḥyā ibn Yaḥyā an-Naysābūrī
Yaḥyā ibn Yahyā al-Andalusī
Abū Qurra as-Siksikī
Muḥammad ibn Mubārak aṣ-Ṣūrī
'Abdullāh ibn Maslama al-Qa'nabī
'Abdullāh ibn Yūnus at-Tanīsī
Abū Hudhāfa as-Sahmī of Baghdad
Aḥmad ibn Manṣūr at-Tāmrānī
Qutayba ibn Sa'īd al-Khurāsānī
Ma'n ibn 'Īsā of Madina
'Atīq ibn Ya'qūb az-Zuhrī
Asad ibn al-Furāt al-Qarawī
Isḥāq ibn 'Īsā at-Tabbā' of Syria
Yazīd ibn Mu'annā of Baghdad
Ḥafṣ ibn 'Abd as-Salām of Andalusia
His brother, Ḥassān
Habīb ibn Abī Habīb, his scribe
Khalaf ibn Jarīr ibn Faḍāla al-Qarawī
Khālid ibn Nizār al-Aylī
Al-Ghāzī ibn Qays of Andalusia
Qa'rūs ibn al-'Abbas of Andalusia

Muḥarrar al-Madanī, whom I think was Ibn Hārūn ibn 'Abdullāh al-Hudayrī
Yaḥyā ibn Mālik
His daughter, Fāṭima
Yaḥyā ibn Ṣāliḥ al-Waḥḥāẓī of Syria
Yaḥyā ibn Muḍar of Andalusia
Sa'īd ibn al-Ḥakam ibn Abī Maryam of Egypt
Sa'īd ibn Kathīr ibn 'Ufayr of Egypt
Sa'īd ibn Abī Hind of Andalusia
Sa'īd ibn 'Abdūs of Andalusia
Sulaymān ibn Bard of Egypt
'Abd al-A'lā ibn Mushir of Damascus
'Abd ar-Raḥīm ibn Khālid al-Miṣrī
Suwayd ibn Sa'īd al-Ḥadathānī
Ismā'īl ibn Abī Uways
His brother, Abū Bakr
'Alī ibn Ziyād at-Tūnisī
'Abbās ibn Aṣbaḥ of Andalusia
'Īsā ibn Shajara of Tunis
Ayyūb ibn Ṣāliḥ al-Muzanī, living in Ramla
'Abd ar-Raḥmān ibn Hind of Toledo, Andalusia
'Abd ar-Raḥmān ibn 'Abdullāh al-Ashbūnī of Andalusia
Sa'īd ibn Dāwūd ibn Sa'īd ibn Sa'īd ibn Zanbar of Madina

The Qāḍī said, 'Those are the ones whom we have verified that they related the *Muwaṭṭā'* from him, and there is a text about that among the people of tradition and those who speak about the men.'

They also mentioned that Muḥammad ibn 'Abdullāh al-Anṣārī al-Baṣrī took the *Muwaṭṭā'* from him in writing.

And Ismā'īl ibn Ṣāliḥ took it from him by having it handed over (*munāwala*).

As for Qāḍī Abū Yūsuf, he related it from a man from him.

They mentioned that Hārūn ar-Rashīd and his sons, al-Amīn, al-Ma'mūn and al-Mu'tamin took the *Muwaṭṭā'* from him.

He mentioned that al-Mahdī and al-Hādī heard it from him and related it from him, and that he wrote the *Muwaṭṭā'* for al-Mahdī.

There is no doubt that the transmission of the *Muwaṭṭā'* was more than those men from the whole of his companions and famous transmitters. But we only mentioned those from whom we have a text that they heard it from him, and took it from him, or one whose *isnād*s reach to him in it.

The famous of the texts of the *Muwaṭṭā'* which are related or which I have found or are in the transmission of our shaykhs, or transmitted from him by people of different copies of the *Muwaṭṭā'* number about twenty versions. Some of them mentioned that there are thirty versions.

Success is by Allah, the Mighty and Exalted.

Mālik's books other than the *Muwaṭṭā'*

The Qāḍī said, 'Know, may Allah give you success, that Mālik had noble books related from him. Most of them were with sound *isnād*s in other fields of knowledge. However, none of them are well known except the *Muwaṭṭā'* nor were people assiduous in hearing it and transmitting it while he deleted from it, and gradually made it more concise. All of his works were related from him by the one who wrote them for him or asked him about them or by one of his companions, not all of whom related them.'

One of the most famous is his letter to Ibn Wahb about Qadar and the refutation of the Qadariyya. One of the best letters on this subject, it shows the vastness of his knowledge of the subject.

More than one of our shaykhs related it with their *isnād*s which lead back to Mālik. One of them was the *faqīh* Abū Muḥammad ibn 'Attāb who related it to us along with another from Ḥātim ibn Muḥammad from Abū 'Abdullāh Muḥammad ibn Danīr aṭ-Ṭutayṭilī from Abū al-Faraj 'Abdullāh ibn 'Abd al-Wārith from Muḥammad ibn Aḥmad ibn Sa'dūn from Muḥammad ibn Saḥnūn from 'Abd al-'Azīz ibn Yaḥyā al-Qurashī from Ibn Wahb.

Qāḍī Abū 'Alī aṣ-Ṣadafī told me about it from Qāḍī Abū al-Walīd al-Bājī from Abū Muḥammad ibn al-Walīd from Abū Muḥammad ibn Abī Zayd from Sa'dūn ibn Aḥmad al-Khawlānī from Muḥammad ibn al-Ḥakam from Ibn Wahb.

It has a sound *isnād* and all of them are reliable Imāms.

There is also his book on the stars, *The Reckoning of the Passage of Time and the Stages of the Moon*, which is a very good and useful treatise indeed. People rely on it in this subject and use it as a basis. Abū Muḥammad 'Abdullāh ibn Masrūr al-Qarawī relied on it in his book on this subject and began with its sections. The authors of the *Kitāb al-Isti'āb* included all of it along with Mālik's statements. They are Abū 'Abdullāh al-Mu'ayṭī and Abū 'Umar ibn al-Makawī in the *Collection* of their great book.

Sahnūn said, 'It is part of what 'Abdullāh ibn Nāfi' aṣ-Ṣā'igh alone transmitted. I heard it from Ibn Nāfi'.'

We find in our transmission from him by means of more than one of our shaykhs, it is from Abū al-Qāsim aṭ-Ṭarābulisī from Ibn Danīr from his father from 'Abd ar-Raḥmān ibn 'Īsā from one of his companions from Muḥammad ibn Maysur from Ibrāhim ibn Hilāl and Muṭarrif ibn Qays from Saḥnūn from 'Abdullāh ibn Nāfi' aṣ-Ṣā'igh from Mālik.

It is related from more than one from Abū 'Abdullāh ibn 'Attāb from Abū al-Qāsim Khalaf ibn Yaḥyā from Abū Ja'far Tamīm ibn Muḥammad from his father from 'Abd al-Jabbār ibn Khālid and Aḥmad ibn Abī Sulaymān from Suḥnūn.

Abū al-Qāsim said that Abū 'Abdullāh Muḥammad ibn Aḥmad ibn Khālid related it to us from his father from Ibrāhīm ibn Hilāl from Suḥnūn.

This is also a sound *isnād* which was related by men who are reliable.

There is also the treatise of Mālik in ten parts on *Judgements*, which he addressed to the *qāḍīs*. The *faqīh* Abū Isḥāq ibn Ja'far informed us about it from Ibn Sahl from Ḥātim ibn Muḥammad from Ibn Dīnār from Abū Ja'far ibn Raḥmān from Sa'īd ibn Sha'bān from Muḥammad ibn Yūsuf ibn Matrūh from 'Abdullāh ibn 'Abd al-Jalīl, the student of Mālik ibn Anas.

There is also his famous letter to Abū Ghassān Muḥammad ibn Muṭarrif on *fatwā*. It is related by Khālid ibn Nizār and Muḥammad ibn Muṭarrif, and he is one of the great men of Madina, an associate of Mālik. He related from Abū Ḥāzim and Zayd ibn Aslam, and reliable men related from him and considered him reliable.

Isḥāq ibn Sa'īd transmitted the sayings of Mālik in this letter. Part of it is in his book.

Part of that is his famous letter to Hārūn ar-Rashīd about proper manners and admonition. It was first related in Andalusia by Ibn Ḥabīb from its transmitters from Mālik. Then later it was related by Abū Ja'far ibn 'Awn Allāh and Qāḍī Abū 'Abdullāh ibn Mufarraj from Aḥmad ibn Zaydawayh ad-Dimishqī, although the *isnād* is not continuous.

Our shaykhs related that to us from Abū 'Umar aṭ-Ṭalamnakī from both of them. The *isnād* of this letter is not direct to us by this path. As for others, the Qāḍī and martyr Abū 'Alī and more than one of our shaykhs related it to us from Abū al-Ḥasan ibn aṭ-Ṭayyūrī al-Baghdādī from Abū al-Hasan al-'Ubaydī from Abū 'Umar ibn Ḥayawayh from Abū 'Umar 'Ubaydullah ibn 'Uthmān al-'Uthmānī from his father from 'Abdullāh ibn Nāfi' from Mālik.

Abū Muḥammad ibn 'Attāb also reported it to us from Abū 'Abdullāh ibn Nabbāt from Ibn Mufarraj from Abū Ja'far from Muḥammad ibn 'Abd al-Ḥamīd al-Farghānī from 'Uthmān ibn 'Abdullāh ibn Sa'īd ibn Sa'īd al-Mughīra al-'Uthmānī who said,

"Abdullāh ibn Nāfi' az-Zubayrī related it to us saying, "This is a letter which Mālik ibn Anas wrote to instruct the people.""

Abū 'Abdullāh ibn 'Attāb said, 'This *isnād* is weak, and there is no doubt that one of the men relating it is omitted from it.'

Some shaykhs did not acknowledge it: Qāḍī Ismā'īl, al-Abharī, and Abū Muhammad ibn Abī Zayd. They said, 'It is not sound, and its path to Mālik is weak, and it contains *ḥadīth*s which we do not recognise.'

Al-Abharī said, 'It contains *ḥadīth*s such that if Mālik had heard the one who gave them, he would have disciplined him. It contains unknown *ḥadīth*s which are in opposition to their root.'

They said, 'The things in it are not known to be in the school of Mālik and his opinion.'

Aṣbagh ibn al-Faraj also disliked it and swore that it was not Mālik's writing.

There is his treatise on the commentary of the unusual words of the Qur'an which Khālid ibn 'Abd ar-Raḥmān al-Makhzūmī related.

Abū Ja'far Ahmad ibn Sa'īd related it to us from Abū 'Abdullāh Muḥammad ibn Muḥammad ibn al-Ḥasan al-Maqqarī from Muḥammad ibn 'Alī an-Na'ālī al-Maṣīṣī from his father from Abū al-Ḥasan from 'Alī ibn Aḥmad ar-Razzār from Abū Bakr al-Ja'dī from Abū al-A'lā Aḥmad ibn Muḥammad ibn Hānī al-Bazzār from Yaḥyā ibn 'Atīk al-Qarawī from Khālid ibn 'Abd ar-Raḥmān al-Makhzūmī from Mālik.

Al-Khaṭīb Abū Bakr mentioned in his *Great History* that Abū al-'Abbās as-Sirāj an-Naysābūrī said, 'These are seventy thousand questions of Mālik,' and he pointed to some books put in order with him which he had written."

The Qāḍī said, 'They are his answers which his companions who were with the Iraqis had heard.'

There is a book called *Kitāb as-Sirr* which is also ascribed to Mālik as transmitted by Ibn al-Qāsim. We were given an *ijāza* for it by Abū Muḥammad ibn 'Attāb from Abū 'Umār ibn al-Hadhdhā' from his father 'Abdullāh from Abū al-Qāsim al-Ḥusayn ibn 'Ubaydullāh ibn Aḥmad al-'Uthmānī from Muḥammad ibn 'Abd al-'Azīz ibn Ṣāfī al-Harrānī known as al-Jarw from al-Ḥārith ibn Miskīn from Ibn al-Qāsim from Mālik.

As for his letter to al-Layth about the consensus of the people of Madina, we related it as well and we mentioned it at the beginning of the book with its text because it is short and we needed to mention it in its proper place. Allah is the master of success by His might.

Reports about Mālik with rulers and his admonishing them, his good position with the governors, visiting them and taking their stipends from them

The Qāḍī said, "Īsā ibn 'Umar al-Madanī was asked, "Did Mālik go to the governors?" He answered, "No, but they sent for him and then he went to them.""

Mālik was asked, 'Does one go to rulers when they are unjust and tyrannical?' He replied, 'May Allah have mercy on you! And where else will one speak the truth then?'

Mālik said, 'It is a duty for every Muslim (or man) in whose breast Allah has put any knowledge and *fiqh* to go to those with power to command them to do what is right and forbid them from doing what is wrong so that the station of a man of knowledge will be clear to others. If that is the case, then it is an excellence which is unsurpassed.'

'Atīq ibn Ya'qūb said, 'When Mālik came to the governor, he

admonished him and urged him to put the affairs of the Muslims in order. One day he came to Hārūn ar-Rashīd, and he urged him to see to the best interests of the Muslims. He told him, "It has reached me that 'Umar ibn al-Khaṭṭāb, in spite of his excellence and precedence, would blow on the common ashes of the fire under the pots until smoke came from his beard. People are pleased with you doing less than that."'

Once he came to Hārūn when there was a chess game set up in front of him and he was looking at it. Mālik stopped and did not sit down. He asked, 'Is this the truth, Amīr al-Mu'minīn?' He answered, 'No.' He said, *'What is there after the truth except misguidance?'* (10:32) Hārūn kicked it away with his foot, saying, 'It will never be set up in front of me again.'

He said to one of the governors, 'Investigate the affairs of the people. You are responsible for them. 'Umar ibn al-Khaṭṭāb said, "By the One in whose hand is my soul, if a camel had died from neglect on the banks of the Euphrates, I would think that I should be questioned about it on the Day of Rising."'

Al-Ḥasan said, 'I heard Mālik swear by Allah, "I have not gone to one of them (i.e. the rulers) except that Allah took away his awe from my heart so that I could tell him the truth."'

Khalaf ibn 'Umar said, 'I said to Mālik, "People keep saying that you go to the rulers." He said, "That is a burden on myself. I do it because otherwise he might consult those whom he should not consult."'

He said to another, 'If I had not gone to them, you would not see any *Sunna* of the Prophet ﷺ acted upon in this city.'

Ibn Wahb and Ibn 'Abd al-Hakam said that Mālik said, 'I came to Abū Ja'far and I saw that more than one of the Banū Hāshim kissed his hand twice and three times. Allah has provided me with restraint from that, so I did not do it.'

It is related that he was sitting with Abū Ja'far and Abū Ja'far sneezed and Mālik asked for mercy for him. When he went out, the chamberlain remonstrated with him and threatened him if he should do it again. When he sat with him another time and Abū Ja'far sneezed, Mālik looked at the chamberlain and then said to al-Manṣūr, 'What judgement do you want, Amīr al-Mu'minīn, the judgement of Allah or the judgement of Shayṭān?' He answered, 'The judgement of Allah, of course.' He said, 'May Allah have mercy on you.'

Ya'īsh ibn Hishām al-Khābūrī said, 'I was with Mālik when the messenger of al-Ma'mūn came to him (and ar-Rashīd was said instead, which is sound) to forbid him to relate the *ḥadīth* of Mu'āwiya and the quinces. Mālik recited the words of Allah Almighty, "*Those who hide what was sent down.*" (2:159) Then he said, "By Allah, I will relate it in this very room," and he plunged into it, saying, "Nāfi' related to us from Ibn 'Umar, 'I was with the Messenger of Allah ﷺ when he was given some quinces. He gave each of his Companions one while he gave Mu'āwiya three quinces. He said, "Give them to me in the Garden." The Messenger of Allah ﷺ said, "The quince removes the grief of the heart."'"'"

The author said, 'Mālik did not live to the time of al-Ma'mūn. He died before them, so it is weak to mention al-Ma'mūn here.'

Az-Zubayrī said from Mālik, 'When I came to Abū Ja'far (and he mentioned his story about making the people use his books, roughly the same as the previous story), he said, "I spoke to him about the people and I urged him to see to them. Then he began to ask me about my daughter and about my son and about my wife and I told him. He said, 'Do you think that I know your household and I do not know the affairs of the people?"

'Then he said to me, "Doubt from the governor of Madina or the governor of Makka or one of the governors of the Hijaz has made you uneasy about yourself or about someone else, or else bad conduct toward the people. Write that to me and I will do what they deserve to them. I have written this to my governors – that they should listen to you and obey all that you enjoin on them. So forbid them the reprehensible and command them to the correct and you will be rewarded for that. You deserve to be obeyed and heard." Then I went out and his gift reached me later.' He mentioned that it was five thousand and a good garment, and one thousand for his son, Muḥammad.

He said, 'When the eunuch brought him the garment, he placed it on his shoulder. That is the way they used to do it so that he would go out to the people with it. Mālik leaned away from him out of distaste for that. Abū Ja'far called to him, "Take it to the mount of Abū 'Abdullāh!"'

When the caliph al-Mahdī came to Madina, people came to him to pledge allegiance to him. When they took their places, Mālik asked for permission to enter and people said, 'Today Mālik will sit at the far end of the gathering.' When he came near and looked at the crowd of people, he said, 'Amīr al-Mu'minīn, where shall your shaykh, Mālik, sit?' He called to him, 'With me, Abū 'Abdullāh!' The people moved aside so that he was able to reach him and al-Mahdī lifted his right knee and made him sit down next to him.

He said, 'Then al-Mahdī was brought the jug and basin and washed his hands. Then he said to the boy, "Offer it to Abū 'Abdullāh." Mālik said, "Amīr of the Believers, this is not part of what is done. Remove it, boy!" So he ate with him without washing his hands.' The story is mentioned in the *Muwaṭṭā'*.

It is related that Mālik went to 'Abd al-Malik ibn Ṣāliḥ, the governor of Madina, and sat with him for a time. Then the governor called for food and water for washing. He said, 'Give it first to Abū 'Abdullāh.' Mālik said, 'Abū 'Abdullāh (meaning himself) does not wash his hands.''Why?' he asked. He replied, 'This is not what I found the people of knowledge in our land doing. It is the custom of the Persians, and 'Umar forbade the custom of the Persians. When 'Umar had eaten, he wiped his hand on the inside of his foot.'

'Abd al-Malik said to him, "Will you leave that undone, Abū 'Abdullāh?' He said, 'Yes, by Allah.' Ibn Ṣāliḥ did not go back to doing that.

Mālik said, 'I do not command the man not to wash his hands, but when he makes that like something which is obligatory for him, then I say no. Kill the *sunna* of the Persians and give life to the *sunna* of the Arabs. Did you not hear the words of 'Umar, may Allah have mercy on him, "Use the garments and mode of life of Ma'add (i.e. the Arabs), lead a rough life and walk barefooted. Beware of Persian customs."'

Ḥusayn ibn 'Urwa said, 'When al-Mahdī came to Madina, he sent Mālik a thousand dinars or three thousand dinars with ar-Rabī' [ibn Yūnus][1]. When he left him, Mālik said, "Slave-girl! Do not touch this money. I investigated carefully when I looked into the face of ar-Rabī' and I saw something I disliked in it. There is a reason behind this money."

'When al-Mahdī went on the *ḥajj*, he came to Madina and ar-Rabī' came to him later and said to him, "The Amīr al-Mu'minīn sends his greetings to you. He wants you to go with him to the City of Peace [i.e. Baghdad]." Mālik said to him, "Give my greetings to the Amīr al-Mu'minīn and tell him that the Messenger of Allah ﷺ said, 'Madina is better for you, if you but knew' and I have the money on the spot. Slave-girl, get it out!"

'Rabī' refused to accept it, but Mālik kept at him until he took it. Ar-Rabī' came to al-Mahdī and he was saddened by the return of the money. When it was time for the journey, the people accompanied him to see him off. He reached them and sent to Mālik and bade him farewell and did not command him to do anything. When he came to his home, he sent six thousand dinars to him, and he turned to those

[1] The chief minister of al-Mahdī.

who were present and said, "Whoever leaves something for Allah, Allah replaces it with better than what he left.'"

One of the governors said to Mālik, 'Why do you not dye [your hair] as your companions dye theirs?' Mālik said to him, 'Is all of justice remaining to you that I use dye?'

The people praised the governor of Madina in his presence before Mālik, and Mālik became angry and turned to him and said, "Beware lest these people beguile you through their praise of you. Whoever praises you and says something good about you which is not in you is about to speak of evil about you which is not in you. Be on your guard about your own purification of yourself or being pleased with what one of them says to your face. You know yourself better than them. It has reached me that a man praised another man in the presence of the Prophet ﷺ and the Prophet ﷺ said to him, 'You have cut his back' or 'his neck'. If he had heard it, he would not have prospered."

The Prophet ﷺ said, 'Throw dirt in the faces of those who praise.'

Abū Ja'far al-Manṣūr argued with Mālik in the mosque of the Prophet ﷺ and Abū Ja'far raised his voice. Mālik said to him, 'Amīr al-Mu'minīn! Do not raise your voice in this mosque. Allah taught manners to the people and said, "*Do not raise your voices above the voice of the Prophet.*" (49:2) He praised people and said, "*Those who lower their voices in the presence of the Messenger of Allah.*" (49:3) He censured people and said, "*Those who call to you...*" (49:4) Respect for him dead is the same as his respect while alive.' So Abū Ja'far submitted to that.

Abū Ja'far said to him, 'Shall I supplicate facing the *qibla* or facing the Messenger of Allah ﷺ?' Mālik said, 'Why would you turn your face away from him when he is your means and the means of your father Ādam to Allah Almighty on the Day of Rising? Face him, and ask him to intercede with your Lord for you. Allah says, "*If only when they had wronged themselves, they had come to you.*" (4:64)'

Usāma ibn Zayd said, 'When Abū Ja'far [al-Manṣūr] arrived, we went in submission to him, and we took our seats. While we were like that, Mālik came in and Abū Ja'far said to him, "Come here, Abū 'Abdullāh! Why have you left the sayings of 'Alī and Ibn 'Abbās and taken the words of Ibn 'Umar?"'

He told him, 'Because he was the last of the Companions of the Messenger of Allah ﷺ to die.' Al-Manṣūr said, 'Abū 'Abdullah! By Allah, there is no one remaining on the face of the earth with more knowledge than you and me. Take the statement of Ibn 'Umar and spare me the others.'

Muṣ'ab said, 'When al-Mahdī came to Madina, Mālik and other nobles of Madina met him some miles before it. When he saw Mālik, al-Mahdī turned to him, embraced him, greeted him and went along with him. Mālik turned to al-Mahdī and said, "Amīr al-Mu'minīn! You are now entering Madina, so pass by the people on your right and left. They are the descendants of the Muhājirūn and the Anṣār. Greet them. There are no better people on the face of the earth than the people or Madina nor any better place than Madina."'

He asked him, 'Why do you say this, Abū 'Abdullāh?' He replied, 'Because today no grave of any Prophet is known on the face of the earth except for the grave of Muḥammad ﷺ. Those who have the grave of Muḥammad ﷺ with them should have their excellence over others recognised.'

Al-Mahdī did what Mālik commanded him. When he entered Madina and alighted, he sent his mule to Mālik so he could ride it and come to him. He returned the mule and said, 'I am too shy before Allah to ride in the city where the corpse of the Messenger of Allah ﷺ is located.' He came to him on foot. He was ill, so he leant on al-Mughīra al-Makhzūmī, Ibn Ḥasan al-'Alawī and Ibn Abī 'Alī al-Lahabī. Those were the men of knowledge of Madina and their nobles. When al-Mahdi saw him, he said, "Glory be to Allah! He would not ride the mule out of respect for the Messenger of Allah ﷺ, so Allah sent these men for him to lean on. By Allah, if I had called them to this, they would not have answered me!'

Al-Mughīra said, 'Amīr al-Mu'minīn! We pride ourselves over the people of Madina because he has leant on us.'

Mālik asked for something to drink when he was with al-Mahdī, and he was brought a goblet which had a silver ring in its handle and refused to drink. He was brought a clay mug and he drank. Al-Mahdī called for the ring and pulled it out.

Ma'n said, 'Ibrāhīm ibn Yaḥyā al-'Abbāsī, the governor of Madina, came to Mālik on a camel while Mālik was young. Mālik remained seated and did not make room for him. Ibrāhīm sat on the smallest part of Mālik's rug. Mālik did not move, and spoke for an hour. Then he asked him, "What do you say, Abū 'Abdullāh, about someone in *iḥrām* who kills a louse?" He said, "He does not kill it." He said, "He killed it. What is its redemption?" Mālik said, "He does not do it." He said, "He did it." He said, "He does not do it." He said, "I tell you that he did and you say, 'He does not do it!'" He said, "Yes." Ibrāhīm got up in a fury and Mālik was silent for an hour. Then he said to us, "They want to play with the *dīn*. The *fidya* is owed by someone who kills it unintentionally. This man means to not leave a single louse on any of his entourage in his army."'

Ma'n said that Ibrāhīm asked Mālik to write him a book and he wrote it for him. Then Mālik came to him one day and Ibrāhīm said to him, 'I want you to write me a book to replace that book. It is lost.' Mālik said, 'It is not lost. May Allah put you right!' He said, 'Yes indeed. By your right, it is lost, so quickly make me a book like it.' He said, 'I will not do it.' He asked, 'Why?' He said, 'Because someone like you does not lose a book. Command someone to look for it and you will find it, Allah willing.'

Then he returned to him later. He said, 'Abū 'Abdullāh, do you know that we looked for the book and we found it?' He said, 'Praise be to Allah, You got it when you looked for it.'

'Atīq ibn Ya'qūb said, 'We went out with Mālik to the place of prayer for the *'Īd* and Mālik was walking. 'Abd al-Malik ibn Salih, the governor of Madina, went out with arms, flags and banners. Mālik looked at them and said, "We belong to Allah and to Him we return. The Prophet ﷺ and the Rightly-guided Caliphs were not like this."

'Word of that reached 'Abd al-Malik and he came to him in the place of prayer and said, "Abū 'Abdullāh! What did you dislike?" He answered, "What I saw with you. People come to the prayer submissive, humble, hoping for forgiveness. Yaḥyā ibn Sa'īd informed me that the Prophet ﷺ came on the Day of the Conquest among ten thousand or twelve thousand men, and he was riding in the middle of his camel on a saddle-cloth worth four dirhams with his head bowed. He said, 'The kingdom belongs to Allah, the One, the Conqueror.' He would come to the place of prayer for the *'Īds* and the Rain Prayer leaning on a staff or bow, humble, head bowed."'

'Atīq ibn Ya'qūb said, 'One day Mālik came to 'Abd al-Malik ibn Ṣāliḥ and he was angry with one of the people of Madina so that that had reached him. Mālik said to him, "Ka'b said to 'Umar, 'It is written in the Torah: Woe to the ruler of the earth from the Ruler of the heaven.' 'Umar said to him, 'Except the one who takes account of himself.' Ka'b said, 'All that is between them is "except for the one who takes account of himself."'"'

He admonished [the caliph] al-Manṣūr to look into the states of the people, and he said to him, 'Is it not the case that when your daughter weeps from hunger you make your servant move the millstone so that the neighbours will not hear her?' Mālik said, 'By Allah, no one knows this except Allah.' He told him, 'Could I know this and not know the state of the subjects?'

One of them said, 'When ar-Rashīd came to Madina (and another said, 'one of the caliphs'), he wanted to dismantle the Prophet's minbar and add to it. He asked Mālik, "What do you think?" He replied, "I do not think you should do it." He got angry and stated, "Mu'āwiya added to it." Mālik said, "At that time the minbar was firm. You have no security that its blessing will not leave if you dismantle it."'

One version has, 'If it collapses, people will see a bad omen in you and say, "It was by his hand that one of the traces of the Messenger of Allah ﷺ departed." He said, "May Allah give you a good reward," and he abandoned what he intended to do.'

He said, "Al-Mahdī asked for Mālik's advice in three things. One was the Ka'ba and whether he should dismantle it and restore it as it was. He advised him not to do it. Then whether he should dismantle the minbar and restore it as it was, and that was when he wanted all the minbars to be small compared to the minbar of the Prophet ﷺ. Mālik told him, 'It is made of tamarisk and nailed to their branches (i.e. those which Mu'āwiya added to it). I fear that if you dismantle it, it will be ruined and broken. If it had not been for that, I would think that should return it to its original state. He asked his advice regarding Nāfi' ibn Abī Nu'aym al-Qāri' (the reciter) and putting him ahead to lead the prayer. He indicated that he should not do it. He said, 'He is an *imām* whom I fear will have some inattention so that it will be recounted about him.'"

Ibn 'Abd al-Hakam said, 'Al-Mahdī asked permission to see Mālik, and he made him wait an hour and then gave him permission. He came in and said, "Amīr al-Mu'minīn! The family heard of your arrival and wanted to put their house in order."'

According to Sa'īd ibn Abī Zanbar, Mālik wrote a letter to one of the caliphs in which he admonished him:

'As for what follows, I am writing a letter to you in which I do not hold back right guidance and I do not omit counsel accompanied by praise of Allah Almighty and the exemplary manners of His Messenger ﷺ. So reflect on this using your intellect, turn your eyes to it, and devote your hearing to it. Understand it with your intellect and apply your understanding to it. Do not allow your mind to let it slip away. It contains excellence in this world and the good reward of Allah Almighty in the Next.

'Remind yourself of the throes of death and its grief, and what will happen to you when it comes, and what you know will follow after death: being presented before Allah Almighty, and then the Reckoning, and then remaining forever either in the Garden or the Fire. Prepare for it something to make the terrors of those sights and their distress easy for you to endure.

'If you were to see the people who incur wrath of Allah Almighty and the myriad punishments they are heading to and the severity of the vengeance of Allah, and if you were to hear their moaning in the Fire, their groaning with their livid faces, the length of their grief and their being turned over on their faces in its bottom levels where they cannot hear or see while they are calling out for utter and final destruction! And the most terrible thing of all for them is the pain when Allah Almighty turns away from them and their hope is cut off from Him and His answer to them after the long drawn-out sorrow is *"Slink away into it and do not speak to Me."* (23:108) If you remind yourself of this, nothing of this world will seem of any importance to you. You will want to be saved from that. You have no security from its terror.

Even if you were to offer all that the people of this world have to seek deliverance, that would be insignificant.

'If you were to see the people who obey Allah and what they are destined to receive by way of honour from Allah, their position of nearness to Allah Almighty, the freshness of their faces and the light of their colours, their joy in looking at Him, and having a place with Him and their rank in His sight along with nearness to Him, those things of this world which you seek and which appear immense in your eyes would then seem insignificant.

'Be careful not to allow your lower self to beguile you. Deal with your lower self before it gets the better of you and remember the distress it will feel when death alights. Contend with your soul for Allah Almighty while you still have time. If Allah permits, you will be able to bring benefit to yourself and avert the punishment from yourself before Allah takes charge of your Reckoning. Once it comes, you will not be able to avert from your soul that which it will hate nor bring any benefit to it. Give Allah Almighty a portion of your time by night and day.

'Your life decreases with the passing hours of the night and day. You are standing on the earth and it is insignificant for you. Whenever an hour of your term passes, the guardian angels do not neglect both minor and great actions until your page which Allah writes against you is filled.

'You must liberate your self if you love it and beware of what Allah Almighty has cautioned you. He said, "*Allah advises you to beware of Him.*" (3:28) Do not think that the small wrong action is insignificant when you know that Allah Almighty said, "*Whoever does an atom's worth of good will see it. Whoever does an atom's worth of evil will see it.*" (99:8-9) He said, "*He does not utter a single word, without a watcher by him, pen in hand.*" (50:18) Be heedful of the obligations of Allah Almighty and avoid the wrath of Allah. Beware of the call of the wronged and fear a day in which you will be returned to Allah. Peace.'

Ibn Nāfi' aṣ-Ṣā'igh said, 'Mālik wrote a letter to one of the caliphs in which he said:

"Know that Allah Almighty has singled you out for my warning to you by what good counsel I have given you previously. In it I have explained for you what I hope Allah will make a means of happiness for you and a matter which He will make your path to Him in Paradise. Therefore – may Allah have mercy on us and you! – it lies in what I have written to you about establishing the command of Allah and what Allah has said about being responsible for His flock. According to a *ḥadīth*, 'Guardians will be brought with their hands tied to their necks. Only justice will set them free.'"

"'Umar ibn al-Khaṭṭāb, may Allah be pleased with him, said, 'By Allah, if a lamb died on the bank of the Euphrates, I would think that Allah Almighty would ask 'Umar about it.' He went on *ḥajj* for ten years, and I am told that he only spent twelve dinars on his *ḥajj*. He would alight in the shade of a tree and carry his whip on his neck and go around in the markets to inquire about the news of those who were present and absent (from Madina).

"We are told that when he was struck down, those Companions of the Prophet ﷺ who were present praised him. He said to them, 'Deceived is the one who deceives. If I had any gold on the face on the earth, I would give it in ransom for the terror of what is coming.'

"'Umar, may Allah have mercy on him, was insistent on being corrected – even though the Prophet ﷺ had testified that he was one of the people of the Garden. In spite of that, he was fearful since he had taken the affairs of the Muslims upon himself. So then how is it with what you know? You must pay attention to what will bring you near to Allah and what will rescue you from Him tomorrow. Beware of a Day when only your actions will save you. You have an example in those who passed away before you. You must show fear of Allah. Make it your first consideration and read what I have written to you in all your moments. Make yourself take on its responsibilities and assume them. Model your good manners on it and ask Allah for success and right guidance if Allah Almighty wills.'"

'Abdullāh ibn Muslim al-Khayyāṭ said, 'When ar-Rashīd came, I put on my garment and went to Mālik. I said, "He can lean on me, and then because of him, I will receive some money from the Amīr al-Mu'minīn." Mālik came leaning on the arm of his son, Yaḥyā. He rewarded Mālik four thousand dinars and his son with five hundred, and a gift came to him from ar-Rashīd.'

A man of Khurasan said to him, 'Abū 'Abdullāh, what do you say about a man who has debts he owes to people and he gives to some and leaves some out. Can one take from him?' He said, 'When a man can spare the Muslims what the Muslims cannot do for themselves, it is taken from him. Yesterday I looked at the story of those kept confined until dawn.'

Al-Ḥārith said from Ibn al-Qāsim that Mālik used to say, 'As for the caliphs, there is no doubt (i.e. no harm in it). As for the others, does he possess anything?'

Ibn Abī Zanbar said, 'Hārūn [ar-Rashīd] rewarded Mālik with three thousand dinars. One of the men of asceticism said to him, "Abū 'Abdullāh! Do you take three thousand dinars from the Amīr al-Mu'minīn?" as if he thought that was a lot. Mālik said, "If it is the amount which he would have given if he had a just *imām* who was equitable to the people of virtue. I do not see any harm in it. I dislike the large amount which is not like what the recipient would merit."'

More than one person asked him about the reward of the Sultan. He said, 'Do not take it.' He said to him, 'But you accept it.' He said, 'Do you want to burden me with both my wrong action and your wrong action?'

He said to someone else, 'Have you come to make me weep for my wrong actions?'

Muḥammad ibn Maslama said, 'Mālik came to al-Mahdī who said to him, "Advise me!" He said, "I advise you to have fear of Allah alone, and to be kind to the people of the land of the Messenger of Allah ﷺ and his neighbours. It has reached us that the Messenger of Allah ﷺ said, 'Madina is the place of my *hijra* and my grave is in it and I was sent in it and its people are my neighbours. It is a duty for my community to guard my neighbours for me. If anyone guards them, I will be a witness for him (or an intercessor) on the Day of Rising. If anyone does not preserve my bequest for my neighbours, Allah will let him drink the mud of pus.'"'

Al-Mahdī gave a large gift and he himself went around the houses of Madina. When he wanted to leave, Mālik came to him and he said to him, 'Mālik, haven't I kept your advice which you gave me? If I am safe, I will not neglect them.'

Abū Muṣ'ab said, 'Mālik said to me, "I went to al-Mahdī and he mentioned Madina. I said to him, 'The Prophet ﷺ said, "I am commanded to a city which will eat up the cities. They call it Yathrib, and it is Madina. It drives out people as the blacksmith's furnace drives out the dross of iron."'" Al-Mahdī took a bit of wool from his rug and said, "By Allah, no, and I will assist them even with this."'

Mālik said, 'Then I went to Hārūn and he asked me about the people of Madina and I recounted to him what al-Mahdī had said, He asked me, "What did al-Mahdī say?" I told him and he said, "I am my father's son."'

Az-Zubayrī said, 'I heard Mālik say, "When Hārūn came, I met him and said, 'Amīr al-Mu'minīn, the people of Madina have a right, so show good concern for them.' He asked, 'What is their right then?' I replied, 'Do you know of a grave of a Prophet known on the face of the earth other than the grave of your Prophet Muhammad ﷺ?' He replied, 'No.' I said, 'If the people of Madina were to leave it, then you would be obliged to bring those who would live there and be in the vicinity of his grave and send provision to it.' He said to me, 'If all that I owned in this world was this cloak of mine, I would help them with it.'"'

Muṣ'ab and Ibn Abī Zanbar said, 'The governor of Madina asked Mālik for a *fatwā* on a question and he refused to answer him. He said, "How can I answer you when you have appointed Khaytham ibn 'Irāk over the Muslims?" He dismissed him and then he gave him a *fatwā*.'

Yaḥyā ibn Bukayr said, 'Ar-Rashīd broke an oath and he gathered the scholars together and they agreed that he should free a slave. He asked Mālik and he said, "Fast for three days." He said, "Why? Am I lacking when Allah Almighty says, *'And the one who does not find'* so that I am put in the position of one who lacks?" He replied, "Yes, Amīr al-Mu'minīn, all that is in your possession is not yours. You must fast for three days."'

'Abd ar-Razzāq said, 'Mālik came to Abū Ja'far and he said to him, "Who is at the door of the companions of Nāfi'?" He answered, "Mālik, 'Abdullāh ibn 'Umar and Ibn Abī Dhi'b." He said, "And he does not take that opinion about the *dīn*?" meaning the Qadar. He said, "Amīr al-Mu'minīn! Praise be to Allah who made us hear it from you! We would have weighed it against you."'

Al-Mufaḍḍal ibn Muḥammad ibn Ḥarb said, "Mālik and Qāḍī Ibn 'Imrān came to al-Manṣūr with the nobles of Madina. Whenever anyone wanted to go, Abū Ja'far presented his sleeve to him to be kissed. One of them said, 'Today I will follow this shaykh (i.e. Mālik). If he kisses the sleeve, I will kiss it. If he does not do it, I will notdo it.' Mālik got up and left without kissing it. I wanted to do that, but my knees would not hold me until I had kissed it."

Ma'n said, 'Mālik gave a *fatwā* for the governor of Madina to kill a man. The governor ordered him to be struck at the waist (i.e. cut in two). Mālik got ready to get up and said, "I will not sit in a place where anyone is harshly mutilated. Allah said, '*Strike the necks.*'" The governor said, "Sit down, Abū 'Abdullāh. Do not strike his waist. Strike his neck."'

Reports of Mālik with scholars and his debates with them

The Qāḍī said that 'Abd al-'Azīz ibn Yaḥyā said, 'When the Amīr al-Mu'minīn came to Madina accompanied by Abū Yūsuf and al-Barmakī, he went to Mālik wanting to put him down and humble him (meaning that Abū Yūsuf wanted to do that.) Yaḥyā al-Barmakī said, "Amīr al-Mu'minīn, Mālik compels the people to accept his opinion, and shows contempt for the opinion of the people of Iraq. If you get him together with Abū Yūsuf and the truth is in his hand, you will recognise that. If it is in the hand of the other one, then you will know that."

'The Amīr al-Mu'minīn sent his greetings to him and commanded him to come to him. Mālik wrote to him, "If the Amīr al-Mu'minīn wants to ask me about something problematic for him, I think that he could write about that to me and he will receive the answer. My body is weak and my feet cannot support me."

'Yaḥyā said to him, "People have heard that you sent to Mālik and he did not come to you. Write to him with resolution." He did that and Mālik came to him leaning on three of his companions: al-Mughīra al-Makhzūmī, 'Abd ar-Raḥmān ibn 'Abdullāh al-'Umarī and Sa'īd ibn Sulaymān al-Masāḥiqī al-'Āmirī.

'When they sat down – and those three at that time were the nobles of Madina and men of renown – Abū Yusuf came until he sat in front of Mālik and said, "Amīr al-Mu'minīn, will you give me permission to debate with Abū 'Abdullāh?" He said, "Debate with him."

'Abū Yusuf said, 'Abū 'Abdullah says, 'If a man takes an almond and promises to divorce if there is a pair in it and then breaks it with force so that he does not know what was in it, he has broken his oath."' Al-Musaḥāqi said, "Amīr al-Mu'minīn, will you give me permission to speak?" He said, "Yes."

'He said, "Abū 'Abdullah says something stronger than this. He says that if he breaks it gently and a pit comes out of it, he has broken the oath because he took an oath on what is unseen and which he did not know. Divorce is not something to be made into a game." The Amīr al-Mu'minīn said, "What he said is good."

'Abū Yūsuf said, "Abū 'Abdullāh says that if a man divorces his wife before he has come in to her and he has given her a hundred dinars for a bride-price, half of the dowry is not returned to him as Allah Almighty says." Al-'Umari said, "Amīr al-Mu'minīn, will you give me permission to speak?" He said, "Yes."

'He said, "Abū 'Abdullāh says a statement such that the Amīr al-Mu'minīn will not recognise anything else but it. It is the statement of his fathers and those of his predecessors who have passed away. That is if a man gives a dowry of a hundred dinars to his wife and she says, 'I will leave it with my parents and come to you without anything, she cannot do that unless she has spent that in the normal custom of the Muslims in her utensils and what is good for her. If he leaves her until she spent that in what she must have and then divorces her and tells her, "Sell what you have bought and bring me fifty dinars," he cannot do that unless it is something on which she squandered the dowry."' The Amīr al-Mu'minīn said, "What Abū 'Abdullāh says is good."

'Abū Yusuf said, "Amīr al-Mu'minīn, Mālik has turned people from their *dīn* and made them take on his opinion and made them ignorant of the business of the first of them and abandoned *ḥadīths* from the fathers of the Amīr al-Mu'minīn and his uncles."'

He mentioned the rest of his words and al-Mughīra's answer to him until Mālik gave the story of az-Zubayr which I will mention later. Ar-Rashīd sent four thousand dinars to him as a reward.

He mentioned that Mālik said to ar-Rashīd when he told him, 'Debate with him,' 'I do not think that he is one of the people of knowledge so that I can debate with him.'

In ash-Shāfi'ī's variant: 'A man of knowledge debates with another man of knowledge to inform the people of what is between them, or a man of knowledge teaches the people from him. As for Abū Yūsuf, Allah has put him far from that.'

That was distressing for ar-Rashīd and he became angry, so he said to him, 'How can he be one of the people of knowledge? These are the *ṣadaqāt* of the Messenger of Allah ﷺ and the *ṣadaqāt* of his Companions which remain.[1] The Muslims have inherited them generation after generation, but he is ignorant of them and does not know them.'

One variant has that he said, 'I ask you by Allah, Amīr al-Mu'minīn, does the Messenger of Allah ﷺ have a *waqf* which you take from and put where you like?' He answered, 'Yes.' He said, 'This one says that the *waqfs* are invalid.' Hārūn turned to Abū Yūsuf and said, 'What do you say?' He answered, 'Our man did not think so, but I do think so.' He added in one variant, 'From the third [of the estate of a deceased].' Ar-Rashīd turned away from him.

Al-Wāqidī said, 'When ar-Rashīd went on *ḥajj* and came to Madina, he wanted to have meeting between Mālik and Abū Yūsuf. He sent to Mālik to ask him to come to him. He sent to him "I cannot because of something wrong with my foot." He went to him, "Then we will send a mount to you." He said, "No, the mount is harder on me than walking." He said, "Then we will send a litter for you." He said, "That is a sort or renown which I dislike." He sent to him, "If you cannot come, we will come to you."

'When he heard that, he dressed and came to him, coming between two men. He came to him and the assembly was packed.

[1] Meaning *waqfs*.

People had taken their places and he gave the greeting. He disliked to sit where it ended so as to be last, and to make people move would be bad manners. He asked, "Where shall I sit, Amīr al-Mu'minīn?" He said, "Come to me, Abū 'Abdullāh," so he went up to him.

'When he was settled, Abū Yūsuf asked him a question about the pledge, but he did not answer him. He said, "Amīr al-Mu'minīn! Tell him to answer me!" He said, "Answer him," so he answered him. Abū Yūsuf said, "Why?" He was silent. He said, "Tell him to answer me." Ar-Rashīd said, "Answer him." Al-Mughīra got up and said, "Amīr al-Mu'minīn! There are those who can spare Abū 'Abdullāh the answer if the Amīr al-Mu'minīn will give permission." He said, "Who is that?" He replied, "Me." So he debated with him and al-Mughīra alone answered him, and he continued to debate until the assembly was over.'

Al-Wāqidī said, 'Yaḥyā ibn Barmak said to me, "I wished that the *mu'adhdhin* would hurry up the *adhān* to break up the assembly because of what Abū Yūsuf experienced from him."'

When they left, al-Mughīra asked Mālik, 'What did you think of my debate with the man?' He said, 'I think you got the better of him although you let up.' He asked, 'How is that?' He said, 'When you beat him with a question and overcame him, he brought you out to another one and was saved from you by that. You should not break from him in it until you finish with it.'

It is related that when Abū Yūsuf asked ar-Rashīd to debate with Mālik in his assembly, ar-Rashīd forbade him that and told him, 'Beware of the man of Madina!' He repeated the request to him many times, so he finally gave him permission. He opened the debate and Mālik began to say, 'Nāfi' related to us from Ibn 'Umar from the Prophet ﷺ.' Abū Yūsuf said, 'Al-Ḥasan ibn 'Umara related to us from al-Ḥakam and Abū Ḥanīfa from Ḥammād.'

When he did this a lot, Mālik said to him, 'What bad manners your people have taught you, Ya'qūb! Do I relate from Nāfi' from Ibn 'Umar from the Prophet ﷺ while you relate to me from al-Ḥasan ibn

'Umāra and Abū Ḥanīfa?' Ar-Rashīd cast him an angry look and indicated with his eye that he forbade him to object.

Muṭarrif's version reports that Abū Yūsuf asked Mālik about a man who took an oath not to ever pray a supererogatory prayer. Mālik said, 'I think that he should be beaten and disciplined until he prays unwillingly.'

Abū Yūsuf said to Hārūn ar-Rashīd, who had not been present, 'I asked Mālik about such-and-such and he said such-and-such.' He said, 'Do you think that, Abū 'Abdullāh?' He replied, 'No.' Abū Yūsuf said to him, 'Didn't you say that to me?' He said, 'Yes, but you are an Iraqī man. If I were to give you a *fatwā* to abandon the supererogatory, you would give people a *fatwā* to abandon the obligatory. I do not fear that for you (i.e. ar-Rashīd).' When he left, Abū Yūsuf went out leaning on him while Mālik was telling him, 'Go back' until he came to his house.

Dufāfa ibn 'Abd al-'Azīz said, 'I saw Abū Yūsuf ask Mālik about a question in the presence of ar-Rashīd, and he answered two or three times. Then it was time for the prayer, and ar-Rashīd went to the mosque and we went with him. I got together with Mālik and told him, "This man is trying to pick a quarrel with you and harass you, so do not answer him. The Amīr al-Mu'minīn will not dislike that." When we went, Abū Yūsuf returned and Mālik did not answer him. He said, "I supposed that he was seeking right guidance, and now I think that he is looking for a quarrel, so I do not answer him."'

One of them said, 'Abū Yūsuf asked ar-Rashīd to command Mālik to debate him and he said, "Debate him, Abū 'Abdullah." Mālik said,

"Knowledge is not like baiting beasts and cocks." Hārūn did not understand him and began to say, "Debate him." Mālik was silent.'

'Abd al-Malik ibn al-Mājishūn said, 'Our shaykh, Amīr al-Mu'minīn, is too esteemed for debate and discussion. We, his students, will take his place. We will debate him and speak to him. If the opinion is incorrect, he will not be silent on it. Hārūn said, "That then."'

When they debated, Abū Yūsuf mentioned a woman's dowry. He said, 'She can do what she likes with it. If she wishes, she can cast it aside and come in a shirt. If she likes, she can put it in the thread for a spinning top.'

Mālik said, 'If the Amīr al-Mu'minīn were to propose to a woman of his family and give her a bride price of a hundred thousand dirhams and she came to him in a shirt, he would not judge that she should do that. But he should command her to get utensils and prepare for him its like of what women use as goods.' Hārūn said, 'He is right.'

He said, 'He took *ḥadīths* until Abū Yūsuf said, "The Prophet ﷺ set out for al-Ghāya." Mālik said, "No, Amīr al-Mu'minīn! It is al-Ghāba. It is behind you."'

Abū Muḥammad az-Zuhrī said that Abū Yusuf said to Mālik, 'What do you say about the man who sends a dinar with a man and another man sends two dinars with him and then he mixes them and looses one dinar?' Mālik said, 'As for one, it belongs to the one with the two, and there is no doubt about it. As for the other one in which there is doubt, they should divide it.'

'Abd al-Malik ibn al-Mājishūn said, 'A man of the people of Iraq asked Mālik about the *ṣadaqa* of a *ḥabūs*, and he said, "When there is full and exclusive possession, it is carried out." The Iraqī said, "Shurayḥ says that there is no *ḥabūs* in the Book of Allah." Mālik laughed – and he did not laugh often – and said, "May Allah have mercy on Shurayḥ! He does not know what the Companions of the Messenger of Allah ﷺ did here."'

Sa'īd ibn Dāwūd ibn Abī Zanbar said, 'Hārūn came to Madina with Abū Yūsuf. Mālik came to him and greeted him while Abū Yūsuf was on the left of ar-Rashīd. His sons, al-Amīn and al-Ma'mūn, were beside him. When Mālik entered, Hārūn made a sign to his sons and said, "Get up before your uncle until he leaves (meaning Mālik)."'

Abū Yūsuf said, 'I came in and Mālik was wearing a garment of black cloth from Aden. By Allah, I have never seen one more excellent than him in it. Hārūn moved so that he made him sit with him on the dais.' It seemed that Abū Yūsuf envied him and asked him, 'What do you say, Abū 'Abdullāh, about the man in *iḥrām* who breaks a gazelle's middle incisor?' Mālik said, 'He has to do *fidya*.' Abū Yusuf laughed and said, 'Does a gazelle have a middle incisor then?'

Mālik raised his head to Hārūn and said to him, 'Glory be to Allah! I did not know that anyone could mention knowledge and then laugh. There is no gravity for knowledge or for the assembly of the Amīr al-Mu'minīn. I have answered him: if the gazelle is in a state where he has a tooth in place of a middle incisor and the man in *iḥrām* does it, then he has to do *fidya*. If not, you know of him what he knows. It is not necessary for people to know this nor is it obligatory for them. However, what do you say about the *imām* at 'Arafa when the Day of 'Arafat falls on Friday? Does he have to do the recitation aloud? It is obligatory for the Muslims to know this.'

Abū Yūsuf said, 'He does it aloud.'

Mālik said, 'You are wrong. By Allah, this is not wanting among the children of Makka and their blacks, let alone them themselves! When Friday occurs on 'Arafat, it is not said aloud. The sons have inherited that from the fathers from the Messenger of Allah ﷺ to this very time.'

Then he turned to Hārūn and said, 'Amīr al-Mu'minīn! A fool which asks the questions of fools! Do you appoint him over the affairs of the Muslims?'

He got up and when it was time to go, he returned to him leaning on al-Mughīra and al-Musaḥāqī and he greeted him. Abū Yūsuf turned to Hārūn and said, 'Amīr al-Mu'minīn, Abū 'Abdullāh does not report *ḥadīths* from the fathers of the Amīr al-Mu'minīn: 'Abbās, 'Abdullāh and 'Alī. He gives *ḥadīths* from Mu'āwiya, Marwān and his son and considers their *ḥadīths* as *sunan*.'

Mālik was silent. Al-Mughīra said, 'Amīr al-Mu'minīn, will you give me permission to speak?' He said, 'Speak,' he said.

He said, 'Abū 'Abdullāh relates *ḥadīths* from the fathers of the Amīr al-Mu'minīn – al-'Abbās and his son and from the sons of his uncle, 'Alī and his sons, and from the other sides of the Amīr al-Mu'minīn, Mu'āwiya, Marwān and his son. He does not relate *ḥadīths* from so-and-so, the meat seller nor so-and-so the slanderer, nor so-and-so, the barley owner. These are known men and there is no doubt in them,' meaning those from whom Mālik related. Abū Yūsuf bowed his head and was silent.

Mālik got up and said, 'Amīr al-Mu'minīn, the illness which I mentioned to you is present with me and Abū Yusuf is an idle man. The one who knows that time is passing and that death is coming acts differently than the way Ya'qūb acts.'

Sa'īd ibn Abi Maryam and Muṣ'ab ibn 'Abdullah said, 'Hārūn came to Madina with Abū Yūsuf. Mālik came and he raised him above Abū Yūsuf.'

Muṣ'ab said that Mālik asked, 'Where shall the shaykh sit?' Hārūn said, 'Wherever he likes.' He sat above Abū Yūsuf. He said to him, 'Ya'qūb, debate with Abū 'Abdullāh.'

Abū Yūsuf said, 'What do you say about a man who said to his wife, "You are divorced when the bowl is filled"?' Mālik bowed his head in silence for an hour. Then he lifted his head. Hārūn said to him, 'Answer him, Abū 'Abdullāh!'

Mālik said to him, 'Amīr al-Mu'minīn, I have examined his question in the Book of Allah, the *Sunna* of the Messenger of Allah ﷺ and the words of the Companions and the Followers, but I did not find any root in them for his question. There is no good in a knowledge which is not found in what I have mentioned.' Hārūn turned to Abū Yusuf and said to him, 'Ya'qūb, Abū 'Abdullah has uprooted your question.'

Muṣ'ab said that he said, 'Amīr al-Mu'minīn! He does not have anything in that. If he did have something, he would have answered,' and he laughed. Mālik looked at him and said, 'What bad manners your family has taught you! Do you laugh in the assembly of the Amīr al-Mu'minīn?' Abū Yūsuf was embarrassed.

Then the Amīr al-Mu'minīn asked Mālik about some questions which he answered and explained. There was a man called Sandal in the assembly who said, 'Abū 'Abdullāh sometimes errs and is sometimes not correct.'

Mālik remarked, 'People are like that.' Then he thought about his words and became very angry indeed and said, 'Amīr al-Mu'minīn! Allah says, *"Has the time not arrived for the hearts of those who believe to yield to the remembrance of Allah?"* (57:16) I did not think that any of the Muslims would mention Allah and the Messenger while his heart did not feel ill out of fear of them. Allah says, *"It is not for any man or woman of the believers."* (33:36) You do not recognise the due of the immensity of Allah and You have not recognised the due of the assembly of the Amīr al-Mu'minīn.'

Then he got up in anger and said, 'You are tested by Islam and the people of Islam are tested by you,' and left. That distressed Hārūn and he said to Abū Yūsuf, 'Get up and go after the shaykh and appease him.' He went out and found Mālik sitting in the shop of a friend which had a lamp. Abū Yusuf was riding an adorned horse with a group of people in front of him. He greeted him and said, 'What do you think of me, Abū 'Abdullāh?' Mālik looked at him and said, 'Like Caesar among his people.' He was ashamed and left.

Abū Muṣ'ab said that Abū Yūsuf said to Mālik, 'Do you give the *adhān* with *ar-tarjī'* when you do not have anything on it from a *ḥadīth* of the Prophet ﷺ?' Mālik turned to him and said, 'Glory be to Allah! I have never seen anything more extraordinary than this! It is called out in front of witnesses five times every day and sons have inherited it from the fathers from the Messenger of Allah ﷺ until this very day, and he needs so-and-so from so-and-so in it? This is sounder in our opinion than the *ḥadīth*.'

He asked him about the *ṣāʿ* and he said that it was five and a third *raṭls*. He said, 'Why do you say that?' Mālik said to one of his companions, 'Bring what you have of the *ṣāʿ*.' The people of Madina – or the common people of the Muhājirūn and Anṣār came and each of them had a *ṣāʿ* and stated, 'This is the *ṣāʿ* which I inherited from my father from my grandfather, the Companion of the Messenger of Allah ﷺ.' Mālik said, 'This well-known report is firmer with us than the *ḥadīth*.' Abū Yusuf retracted his words.

Ma'n said, 'Mālik came to Hārūn when Abū Yusuf was with him. Hārūn continued to bring him near until he took his hand and sat him at his side. He began to ask him, "Abū 'Abdullāh! Abū 'Abdullāh!" Abū Yūsuf asked him, "How old are you, Abū 'Abdullāh?" He turned from him and Hārūn told him, "This is our Qāḍī." So he turned away from him. Abū Yūsuf asked him about a question and he did not answer him. Hārūn told him, "Answer him." Mālik said to him while he was turning away from him, 'If you think that we have sat for the people of falsehood, come so that I can answer you."'

Ibn Ḥanbal said, 'Abū Yusuf asked Mālik about a question in the presence of Hārūn and he did not answer him. Abū Yūsuf said to Hārūn, "Tell him to answer me." Mālik said to him, "Your family has taught you bad manners."'

Muḥammad ibn 'Ajlān came to Mālik, and he was somewhat brisk. He said to him while he was standing, 'Tell me what you think about the *fatwā* that the Messenger of Allah ﷺ assumed *iḥrām* from Dhū al-Ḥulayfa?'

Mālik said to him, 'If you sit down, I will listen to your words.'

He sat down and Mālik said to him, 'Do you think if I were to say that the Messenger of Allah ﷺ assumed *iḥrām* from al-Bayḍā' would a person accept that and enter into what I say?' He answered, 'Yes.'

Mālik said, 'What would you think if I said that the Prophet ﷺ assumed *iḥrām* from the mosque? Would that not be outside the action of what you say? There is disagreement on that. The prudent course is the mosque of Dhū al-Ḥulayfa, and the *ḥadīth* about it is stronger. Ibn 'Umar said, 'This Bayḍā' here is part of the lies you forge against the Messenger of Allah ﷺ.' The place of Ibn 'Umar in Islam is what it is. He kept the company of the Messenger of Allah ﷺ and most of the transmission comes from him. He was with him in his company writing down his actions in order to do them and investigate them to such an extent extent that when he went on *ḥajj* and *'umra*, he would take care to be in one of the places where he knew that the hooves of the camel of the Prophet ﷺ stepped. He lived thirty-three years after him, and he related what the Companions of the Messenger of Allah ﷺ did.'

He continued to speak until his words were clear to Ibn 'Ajlān who then went to Mālik's head and kissed it.

Ḥāmid ibn Yaḥyā and others said – each adding to the other and we brought the complete report – that Mālik ibn Anas and 'Umar ibn Qays, known as Ṣandal, the brother of Ḥumayd ibn Qays, met in the presence of the governor of Makka. 'Umar was told, 'This is a man from Dhū Aṣbaḥ.' He said, 'I am a man from Dhū Amsā'.'[1] He turned to Mālik and said to him. 'What do you say about the one who breaks a gazelle's middle incisor?' He said, 'He owes what he destroyed.' 'Umar said, 'Sometimes he errs and sometimes he is not correct.' Mālik said, 'People are like that.' Then he understood.

[1] He is playing with *ṣubḥ* (morning) being the root of Aṣbaḥ and Amsā' coming from *masā'* (evening).

'Umar said, 'No, it is you who are like that.' Mālik turned to the governor and said, 'I did not think that the governor had jesters present in his assemblies." He asked, 'Who is this?' He was told, "Umar ibn Qays, the brother of Ḥumayd.' He said, 'If I had known that Ḥumayd had a brother like this, I would not have related from him.'

Abū Dāwūd as-Sijistānī said, "Umar ibn Qays was dropped because of this meeting.'

Another said, 'Mālik went on *ḥajj* and sat at the Mīzāb in the shade of the Ka'ba. There were a lot of people with him asking him for *fatwā*. Then someone came to ask him about the *ḥajj*. He said, "Do *Ifrād*! *Ifrād*! It is the *Sunna* of the Prophet ﷺ."'

'Umar ibn Qays went to him and stood by him. He said, 'Mālik! You are destroyed! You sit in the Ḥaram of Allah misguiding the *ḥajjis* of the House of Allah. You say, "Do *Ifrād*! *Ifrād*!" May Allah make you alone!' The people went to attack him and Mālik said, 'Leave the wretch alone. He is in evil from this. He drinks khondros wine.' One version has: 'He thinks that it is lawful to drink khondros wine,' i.e. an intoxicant made from *nabīdh*. One of them added, 'He sold a copy of the Qur'an and bought a dog.' 'Umar turned away and he was disgraced, and Allah abased him until the Day of Rising.

Abū Muṣ'ab said, 'The governor sent a young boy to Mālik. Witnesses had testified that he had stolen. Al-Mughīra had given a judgement that he be jailed and Ibn Abī Ḥātim that his hand be cut off. His hand was stretched out to be cut when the governor said, "Take him to Mālik." He was brought to him and a long story was recounted to him along with the strong testimonies. Then a witness passed by who testified that he had looked at him on the day that he stole and he found that he had reached puberty. He said, "Look for another witness with this one." Another witness was not to be found. He said, "I see that there is only one witness to his puberty and he did not look at him until he was uncertain. He does not have his hand cut off." The messenger asked him, "How many lashes do you think?" He answered, "Seventy-five. I would add more if he could bear it."'

Abū 'Abd ar-Raḥmān as-Surūjī came and went to Mālik and sat in front of him. Mālik was wearing a cloak from Aden which he had bought for five hundred dirhams. He asked him about a man who had died without performing the obligatory *ḥajj* of Islam and left a bequest for it and whether *ḥajj* be paid for from his property." Mālik said it could not. Abū 'Abd ar-Raḥmān said to him, 'This is not what our scholars say.' Mālik asked, 'What do your scholars say?'

He said, 'Hushaym told us,' and he mentioned the *ḥadīth*: 'The Prophet ﷺ heard a man saying, "*Labbayk* from Shibrama". The Prophet ﷺ said to him, "From yourself and then from Shibrama."'

Mālik said, 'Our scholars!' Our scholars! Who are your scholars? You relate to me from two mule-drivers. Allah Almighty says, "*Man will have nothing but what he strives for.*" (53:39)" Then he said, 'Make him get up.' They got him up and it seemed that if he had been silent, he could have listened to him.

Al-Ḥārith ibn Miskīn used to advise Mālik and 'Abd al-'Azīz and say, 'When you go to the Sultan, be the last to speak with him.'

Abū 'Amr said, 'By my life, Mālik kept to that. I heard that one of the governors summoned him in a group which included Ibn Abī Dhi'b. He presented a story to them which was read out. It concerned a man who had confessed that he had deliberately murdered someone. They all said, "We think that it is death and that he should be handed over to the man's guardians. If they like, they can kill him or pardon him." Mālik was silent. The governor said to him, "What do you say, Abū 'Abdullāh?" He said, "I would investigate." He bowed his head in thought and the governor began to urge him to speak. He said, "It is death until I investigate." The people said among themselves,

"What will he investigate? What think is this?" He raised his head and said, "Where is the confessed murderer?" It was a young man. Mālik asked, "When were you imprisoned?" He said, "Since such a time," and he had confessed before he had reached puberty.'

One of them said that Mālik and al-Awzā'ī met and debated. Al-Awzā'ī drew Mālik to the topic of the battles and *Sīra*, and was better than him. When Mālik saw that, he moved him to other matters of *fiqh*, and Mālik was better in them than him.

CONCERNING HIS ORDEAL

The Qāḍī said that Ibn Mahdī said, 'There is disagreement about who it was who flogged Mālik, the reason for which he was flogged and during whose caliphate he was flogged.'

It is said that Abū Ja'far forbade him to relate the *ḥadīth*: 'There is no divorce for the one who is compelled,' and then he secretly sent someone to question him about it and he related it in front of the people, and so he had him whipped.

Muṣ'ab said that he said, 'The one who forbade him was Ja'far ibn Sulaymān [the governor].'

Al-Wāqidī said, 'When Mālik was a leader and was listened to and his words accepted, people envied him and wronged him. When Ja'far ibn Sulaymān was appointed governor of Madina, they went to him and a lot of them came out against him in his presence. They said, "He does not think anything of this oath of homage to you. He takes a *ḥadīth* related by Thābit al-Aḥnaf that the divorce of someone under compulsion is not binding."

'Ja'far became angry and summoned him. He used what had been put before him as a proof against him and then he had him stripped and stretched out and flogged with a whip. He stretched his hands out until his shoulder was dislocated.'

In one version, 'He extended his hands until his shoulders were dislocated.'

There is disagreement about whether Muṣ'ab az-Zubayrī was involved in that.

Al-Jayyānī said, 'After the flogging, Mālik remained with his hands hampered. He could not lift them, and a terrible thing had been done to him. By Allah, after that beating, Mālik continued in elevation, height and esteem from the people until it was as if those lashes were adornments for him.'

It was said, 'This was in the time of ar-Rashīd, and the *fatwās* of Mālik were presented to ar-Rashīd.'

Abū al-Walīd al-Bājī said, 'When al-Manṣūr went on *ḥajj*, he offered Mālik retaliation from Ja'far ibn Sulaymān, and he sent him to him so that he could take retaliation from him, He said, "I seek refuge from Allah. By Allah, he did not lift the whip from me put that I made it lawful at that moment because of his kinship with the Messenger of Allah ﷺ."'

Another reported that he said, 'When I went to Abū Ja'far (al-Manṣūr) and he obliged me to come to him at the Festival, he said to me, "By Allah, there is no god but Him, I did not desire what happened nor did I know of it. The people of the two Ḥarams (Makka and Madina) will continue to profit so long as you are among them. I believe that you are a security for them from the punishment of Allah and that Allah has lifted a terrible blow from them because of you. They are the swiftest of people to rebel and I have commanded the enemy of Allah (the governor who ordered the punishment) to be brought from Madina to Iraq on a pack-saddle. I have ordered him to be imprisoned and humiliated. I must give him a punishment many times more than what you received from him!"

'I said, "May Allah preserve the Amīr al-Mu'minīn and increase his reward! I declared him free of responsibility for what happened and have said to him that I have pardoned him for it because of his kinship with the Messenger of Allah ﷺ." He said to me, 'And you, may Allah pardon you and your relations."'

Al-Farawī and al-'Umarī said – one adding to the other – that when Mālik was flogged and injured, he was carried out unconscious. The people came to him and he regained consciousness and said, 'I testify to you that I have put my flogger in the lawful.'

They visited him on the second day when he was recovering. We told him what he had heard from him, and we said to him, 'He has injured you.' He replied, 'I was afraid that I might die yesterday and I would meet the Prophet ﷺ and I would be ashamed before him that one of his family should enter the Fire because of me.'

Only a short passed before al-Manṣūr became angry with his flogger, and he flogged him and inflicted terrible injury on him. Mālik was told about that and he said, 'Glory be to Allah! Do you think that our portion of what happened to us is to gloat over him? We hope that he has a greater punishment with Allah than this and we hope that we have a greater pardon from Allah than this. Muḥammad ibn al-Munkadir, Rabī'a and Ibn al-Musayyab were flogged for what I was flogged. There is no good in the one who is not injured in this business.'

It was said, 'The one who did that to him was the governor Ja'far ibn Sulaymān and that Ja'far was the one who gave his governor the preceding punishment. The first is better known.'

Muṭarrif said that Ja'far ibn Sulaymān gave Mālik eighty lashes.

Ibn al-Qāsim said, 'Muṭarrif and Muṣ'ab said, "It was because of Muḥammad ibn 'Abd al-'Azīz az-Zuhrī that it was interpreted in the first fashion: that he had given people a *fatwā* that the one who gave homage under duress owed nothing."

'Muṭarrif said, "I saw the marks of the whip on his back, and it had cut him a lot. When he was extended by his hands by the rope, they dislocated his shoulder so that he was not able to straighten his cloak. When Ja'far was appointed to a position again, Mālik came to him and Ja'far asked him to put him in the lawful. He said, 'I was ignorant and made a mistake. By Allah, only the Qurashites flogged you.'"

'Mālik said to him, "Do you think that you wronged me then?" He replied, "Yes." He said, "Then you are in the lawful and may Allah be generous to you."'

Ibrāhīm ibn Ḥammād az-Zuhrī said, 'I saw Mālik holding one of his hands in the other.'

Mālik was told, 'This Ibn 'Abd al-'Azīz az-Zuhrī has stopped in the mosque.' He was the Qāḍī of Madina, and he was the one who wronged Mālik. Mālik said, 'What Allah wills. There is no power nor strength except by Allah.' Then he mentioned the ordeals of Muḥammad ibn al-Munkadir and Rabī'a. He said, "Umar ibn 'Abd al-'Azīz said, "I do not envy anyone who has not received harm in this matter."'

Ad-Darāwardī said, 'When Mālik was summoned to be flogged for the homage about which he gave a *fatwā* – and I was the nearest of people to him – I heard him say whenever the whip fell, "O Allah, forgive them. They do not know," until his flogging had finished.'

He mentioned that he gave a *fatwā* during the uprising of Muḥammad ibn 'Abdullāh ibn Ḥasan al-'Alawī, called al-Mahdī, that the homage to Abū Ja'far was not binding because it had been taken under duress.

Al-Layth said, 'I hope that Allah will raise Mālik a degree in the Garden for every lash.'

Ibn Bukayr had a different story than this and said, 'Ibn Bukayr said, "Mālik was flogged purely because he preferred 'Uthmān over 'Alī. The Ṭālibites did not give up until he was flogged."'

It was remarked to Ibn Bukayr, 'You differ from your companions. They say it was about the allegiance.' He replied, 'I know better than my companions.'

Aḥmad ibn Ṣāliḥ said, 'Mālik was flogged on account of the *ḥadīth* about a divorce before marriage being invalid. It had not been his opinion and then it was.'

Abū Dāwūd commented, 'Aḥmad did not do anything.'

Ibn Kināna said, 'He was flogged for saying that the oath to the Sultan was not binding and about handing over *zakāt* to them.'

Muṣ'ab said, "Ja'far ibn Sulaymān gave Mālik with thirty lashes. It is said that it was thirty odd. It is also said that it was sixty. Makkī ibn Ibrāhīm said that it was seventy lashes. It is said that it was some seventy odd lashes. It is said that it was one hundred lashes as reported from the transmission of al-Ḥārith from Ibn al-Qāsim.

Mālik said, 'There was nothing harder for me on the day I was flogged than a feeling in my breast. There was a tear in my wrapper through which my thigh showed, and I left it to Allah to renew the wrapper and not be left with my feeling.'

Muṣ'ab said, 'He was flogged in 146 AH.' It is also said that it was 147 AH.

Muḥammad ibn Khālid ibn 'Uthma said, 'We were with Ja'far ibn Sulaymān during his final illness when Ḥammād ibn Zayd came to him. He said to him, "Abū Ismā'īl! I have seen Mālik in a dream and I greeted him and he did not answer." I repeated it to him and he answered, "You and I have a position with Allah tomorrow," so I was sleepless because of that and it grieved me.' Ḥammād said to him, "Mālik is in a sublime place in Islam. There is only regret and asking forgiveness."'

One version has: 'That you set free' so he freed a slave for every lash of the whip.

Al-Aṣmā'ī said, 'I went back and forth between Ja'far ibn Sulaymān and Mālik until he made it lawful.'

Al-Mundhir said, 'It was a man of the Banū Makhzūm, a philologist, who incited Ja'far ibn Sulaymān against Mālik. He mentioned the report about his *fatwā* on the oaths, and Ja'far wrote to report that to the Caliph and he wrote to him to flog him. So he flogged him and stretched out his hands between the two pieces of wood. That is why he did not come to the mosque. A smell continued to come from his shoulder. Then Ja'far was dismissed and then appointed again and he honoured Mālik and tried to bring him near. Mālik kept his distance from him until he left him alone.

'He went on *ḥajj*, and while Mālik was at the Standing Place, Ja'far said to his companions, "Do not move." He went and Mālik was only aware of a man who had struck his litter with a whip. Mālik raised his head. He said, "Mālik, this is an immense day. Allah looks at His slaves and forgives them, so put me in the lawful for what I did to you." Mālik said, "No, by Allah, not until you and I meet before Allah," so he went back.'

The accuracy of his perception of character (*firāsa*) and his discernment regarding people

The Qāḍī said, 'Ash-Shāfi'ī possessed perception of character. He was asked about that and said, "I took it from Mālik."'

Asad ibn al-Furāt said, 'A friend of mine and I stayed with Mālik. When we wanted to go to Iraq, we visited him to bid him farewell. We said to him, "Advise us." He turned to my friend and said, "I advise you to be good to the Qur'an." He turned to me and said, "I advise you to be good to this community."'

Asad said, 'My friend did not die until he had turned to worship and the Qur'an.' Asad was appointed a *qāḍī*.

Ash-Shāfi'ī said, 'When I travelled to Madina and met Mālik and heard his words, he looked at me for a time – and he had perception of character. Then he asked me, "What is your name?" I replied, "Muḥammad." He said, "Muḥammad, be fearful of Allah and avoid acts of rebellion. That will give you a standing in the business."'

Someone else said, 'He had perception of character which did not err. One day he looked at three of his companions from North Africa: Ibn Farrūkh, Ibn Ghānim and al-Bahlūl ibn Rashīd. He said about Ibn Ghānim, "This is the Qāḍī of his land," and about al-Bahlūl, This is the man of worship of his land," and on Ibn Farrūkh, "This is the *faqīh* of his land."'

Anecdotes about him

The Qāḍī said that Ma'n said, 'Ibn Sarjūn, the poet, came to Mālik, may Allah have mercy on him, and said to him, "I have uttered some poetry which I want you to hear." He said, "No," thinking that he had satirised him. He exclaimed, "You will hear it!" and he recited:

Ask Mālik the *muftī* about diversion, singing
and love of attractive menstruating beauties.
He will give you a *fatwā* that I am correct and that
I divert the cares of the self from me by that.
Is there an offence in a lover who conceals love and passion?
Is there in the embrace of the one who is worn out with exertion?

Mālik was amused and laughed. It was rare that he laughed.'

Az-Zubayr ibn Bakkār said, 'Muḥammad ibn 'Abdullāh al-Asadī asked Mālik about a woman he wanted to marry and he told him the story. Mālik told him, "Wait. She is not lawful for you at the moment." So he said:

I will court her as much as I can, and I disagree with what
the sage of Madina, Mālik, tells me.
He says – while she is lawful – 'Wait!' If you only knew,
waiting is destruction for someone like me.
Do you forbid lovers to marry while, according to people's opinion,
you are a devout man?'

Muḥammad ibn al-Faḍl al-Makkī said, 'Mālik passed by a woman singer who was singing:

"You are my sister and you are the inviolable lady of my neighbour.
I have a duty to preserve the neighbours.
I am a guardian for the neighbour in what is hidden from me,
preserving the secrets which are hidden.

What do I care if there is a curtain lowered at the door
 or whether it remains without a curtain?"

'Mālik said, "If this had been sung around the Ka'ba, it would be permitted!"'

One version has, 'People of the house! Teach your girls the like of this!'

Mālik reported that Abū Ḥāzim said, 'The people of the *Jāhiliyya* were better neighbours that you are. The words of their poet are between us and you:

"My fire and the fire of my neighbour are the same,
 and before me, the pot is set down for him.
There is no harm done to a neighbour of mine whom I am near
 if he has no curtain on his door.
I am like a blind person. When my slavegirl goes out,
 then the curtain conceals my slavegirl."'

Mālik said, 'There is no harm in singing the like of this.'

Ibn Abī Uways said, 'I was walking with Mālik when a female client came carrying a jug of water, saying:

"I wish that I was the earth for Salmā
 and her feet walked on me.
I wish that I was the shift for Salmā
 and she would wear me behind her.
I wish that the servant of Salmā was sitting
 where I could see her."

'He asked me, "Ismā'īl, is it a man or a woman?" I said, "She is Ghazzāl, a servant of the Banu 'Umāra." He said, 'She has an eloquent tongue and good rendering."'

He said, 'Mālik heard me when I was reciting, "Bid farewell to Hurayra. The horsemen are departing." He stopped and I was not aware of it until I reached the words, "I became accidentally attracted to her... (from the *Mu'allaqa* of al-A'shā)." He said, "These are five which receive mercy."'

Muṭarrif said, 'One of the Kufans came to Mālik and stayed for about sixty or seventy days. He heard that number of *ḥadīths*, and he complained about that to Mālik, saying, "In Iraq we write more than this from a man of *ḥadīth* in a single hour."

'Mālik said to him, "Nephew, you have the mint in Iraq. It mints during the night and then brings it out in the day."

'Then Mālik added, "Iraq levies an army of dinars and dirhams against us, so now it begins to levy an army of *ḥadīths* against us."'

He was told, 'The people of Syria recite "Ibrāhām" [instead of Ibrāhīm].' He said, 'They must eat watermelon.'

Ibn Abī Maryam said, 'Mālik asked me, "Egyptian! Are there doors on your mosque?" I replied, "Yes." He said, "This is a jail, not a mosque!"'

Ibn Abī Uways reported that Mālik said, 'Ibn Shihāb az-Zuhrī came to Madina, and I went to him in the evening and I found him on the road to the mosque. He had his slave, Anas, with him. He had married him to a slave-girl of his, and he said to him, "How did you find your wife?" He replied, "Master, I found her like a garden." Ibn Shihāb said, "Praise be to Allah."

'I understood and laughed, and he questioned me. I said, "He says that he did not like her. There is expanse and coldness in the garden." He said, "Is it like that, Anas?" He said, "Yes, by Allah, master." He continued to laugh and repeat it until he missed the group prayer and prayed in his house.'

Ibn Abī Uways said, 'A man and his wife who were among the clients of Mālik came to Mālik, each of them complaining about the other. Mālik asked the man, "What do you have against her?" He said, "She laughs when I break wind." Mālik said, "Then keep your distance from her when that happens to you."

'The woman said, "It requires more than this. It is like the thunder of the autumn storms." Mālik said to her, "Stop up your ears with cotton." She said, "By Allah, if I were to put iron anvils in my ears, it would still penetrate." Mālik said, "Then go and laugh however you like." He said to the man, "You must eat wild thyme and keep doing that." Then he stopped doing that.'

A man who was a Jahmite asked Mālik about an oath he had sworn, and he gave him a *fatwā* that he had divorced his wife irrevocably. He said:

I shed the tears of my eye, which is moist,
  one tear coming after the other.
The unhappy one who weeps
  does not comprehend blame and rebuke.
The one with amulets weeps.
  The one who does not contest weeps.
The disconsolate one weeps in grief,
  and sheds floods of tears.

What is left after severing the rope with Umm Ma'mar?
One weeps for love and blames time.
But I will weep for her and the moments
in which I sported with her, drinking rain by her moments.
If it had not been for fear of Allah and death
which I will soon encounter
and what happens after death
when I will await the gathering,
I would have put to the test the cry of the supplicating Muslim
– for Allah knows the secret and what is aloud –
Against Mālik, the days in which Mālik gave you a *fatwā*
and did not test the contract nor any command from a Prophet.
If I had been given a choice of the severance of her
or the loss of my hand,
I would have chosen to have my hand cut off.
In the evening he gives me a *fatwā*
and claims that I must be composed
over my separation from Rāma or be patient.
Mālik is a tyrant in the daytime of Madina
and moves for my murder while he requests the reward.
I returned home and I carried out the counsel of Mālik
which takes over the heart and breast.
What do I care then when I am forbidden at the end
if the gravedigger cuts out a grave for me
When the tears of weeping for you are finished
and the tears of the eye cease to flow down one by one?

'Amr ibn Sulaymān said, 'Mālik saw a boy walking in a disliked manner. Mālik got up and began to walk at his side copying him. The lad stopped and Mālik asked him, "Is my manner of walking good?" He replied, "No." "Then why do you walk like that?" he asked. He said, "I will not do it again."'

Abū 'Awf 'Abd ar-Raḥmān ibn Marzūq said, 'I told 'Ubaydullāh ibn Muḥammad, the Qāḍī of Tarsus, that Bakr al-Muzanī had said, "The person who most deserves a slap is the one who eats food to which he has not been invited. The person who most deserves two slaps is the one to whom the master of the house says, 'Sit here,' and he says, 'No, there.' The person most entitled to three slaps is the one who says to the master of the house, 'Let the lady of the house eat with us.'"

'He said, 'I have something more extraordinary and more witty than this. One day Mālik was sitting and a friend of his asked permission to enter and he gave him permission. Mālik had a watermelon in the corner, and he put a handkerchief over it. The man came in and Mālik said to him, "Here, here!" He refused to sit anywhere except on the handkerchief and the watermelon burst apart under him. Mālik said, "May Allah have mercy on you! We know the faults of our house better than you."'

A man asked him about someone who said to another, 'Ass!' He said, 'Flog him.' He said, 'If he says to him, "O horse!"?' He said, 'You flog him.' Then Mālik said, 'Dim-wit, have you ever heard anyone say to another, "O horse"?'

Ibn Mahdī said, 'I said to Mālik, "Accompany me. I have stayed a long time, and I do not know what has happened to my wife after I left." He smiled and said, "Nephew, my family is near me, but I do not know what has happened to them after I left."'

Mālik's death and the visions which indicated his excellence with Allah

The Qāḍī said, 'We have already given the date of his death. The sound version is that it was in Rabī' al-Awwal, 179 AH, Sunday, after twenty-two days of illness.'

Ibn Kināna and Ibn Abī az-Zubayr washed him. His son Yaḥyā and his scribe Habib poured the water for them.

He was put down in his grave by a group of men, and he had left instructions in his will that he be shrouded in white cloth and prayed over in the place of the funeral prayer. 'Abd al-'Azīz ibn Muḥammad ibn Ibrāhīm ibn Muḥammad ibn 'Alī ibn 'Abdullāh ibn 'Abbās prayed over him, and he was the deputy for his father over Madina. He walked with his funeral procession and carried his bier. His shroud cost five dinars.

We have already mentioned some of the visions which indicated his knowledge and imamate in general, and we will be brief here according to the goal of what we did not mention before.

Bakr ibn Sulayman ibn aṣ-Ṣawwāf said, 'We came to Mālik ibn Anas in the evening in which he died, and we said, "Abū 'Abdullah, how do you feel?" He said, "I do not know how to say it, but tomorrow you will see the pardon of Allah which is not in the reckoning." Before we left he closed his eyes. It was said that he said the *shahāda* and then he said, "The business belongs to Allah both before and after."'

'Umar ibn Yaḥyā ibn Sa'īd al-Anṣārī saw Mālik in the night when he died (in a dream). He was saying:

Islam's support has been shaken in the morning.
In the early morning, the guide settles in the excavated grave.

The Imam of guidance still guards knowledge,
may the peace of Allah be upon him until the end of time.

He said, 'I woke up and wrote down the two verses by the lamp, and then the call came announcing Mālik's death, may Allah have mercy on him.'

Ḥabīb, Mālik's scribe, said, 'We were with Mālik the day he died amid a group of our brothers when Ibn Abī Ḥāzim came and said, "Abū 'Abdullāh, I saw a dream in the night which I want to tell you." He said, "Tell it." He said, "I saw the sky burst open and an angel came from it with a page in his hand, saying, 'Tribe of people! This is the freedom of Mālik from the Fire!'"

'Then our assembly was still when the governor of Madina, Ibn Abī Zaynab came in with his teacher. He said, "Abū 'Abdullāh! My teacher had a dream last night," and he mentioned something similar. Mālik said to him, "Abū Tammām got here before you."

'Then we left him. When we reached the door of the house, it was shut. We heard the criers and went back. It was not long before his son emerged, saying, "Allah has taken him to Him."'

Ash-Shāfi'ī said, 'My aunt said to me when we were at Makka, "I saw something wondrous last night." I asked, "What was that?" She said, "It was as if someone was saying, 'The man with the most knowledge on the earth died in the night.'" We took note of it and it was the night when Mālik died.'

Al-Ḥasan ibn Ḥamza al-Ja'farī said, 'I used to vilify Mālik. I spent my evening doing that, and I went to sleep. Then I saw that it was as if the Garden had opened. I said, "What is this?" They said, "The Garden." I said, "What are these rooms?"' They said, "The room above the room is for Mālik ibn Anas because he held people to their *dīn*." I did not disparage him afterwards and I began to write from him.'

Another man said, 'It was as if someone was saying, "Let the one who was truthful to Allah stand up." Mālik ibn Anas stood up.'

One of them said, 'I saw Mālik ibn Anas in a dream and I said, "Allah has given benefit by you and you have helped the people of your land." He replied, "By Allah, I only desired Allah through that."'

Asad ibn Mūsā said, 'I saw Mālik after his death and he was wearing a tall hat and green clothes. He was on a she-camel flying between the heaven and the earth. I said, "Abū 'Abdullāh! Aren't you dead?" He replied, "Yes." I asked, "What source did you go to?" He said, "I came before my Lord and He spoke to me face-to-face and said, 'Ask me and I will give to you. You were a blessing to your land.'"'

Al-Fuḍayl ibn 'Iyāḍ dreamt that he had entered the Garden. He said, 'While I was on its roads, I passed by Zayd ibn Aslam wearing a tall hat. I said, "Zayd!" He said, "Yes." I said to him, "Allah has made you dwell here and honoured you. Where is Mālik? I do not see him." He said, "Where is Mālik? Mālik is above." He continued to say "above" until his hat fell off.'

Another man saw him [in a dream] and asked him, 'What did your Lord do to you?' He replied, 'He forgave me.' He said, 'Why?' He said, 'For the words of 'Uthmān which he used to say when he saw a corpse, "Glory be to the Living who does not die."'

Ibn Abī Uways said, 'Yaḥyā ibn Yazīd an-Nuwaylī was one of the men of worship and asceticism. He did not speak to Mālik nor Ibn Abī Dhi'b nor Ibn 'Imrān. He wrote a letter to each of them in which he warned them about their turning towards this world. Mālikgave him a good answer. The other two spoke harshly to him.

'After Mālik's death, he came from al-Ghāba to Madina. No one stayed away from him. I was present one day when he was giving *ḥadīths* and there were a lot of people with him. Weeping, he was saying, "Last night I dreamt that I was in a place of palm-trees, gardens, greenery, castles and flowing rivers. I went to a castle which I thought was the best. When I went to enter it, there was a man at the door who stopped me from entering. He said, 'Wait until you are given permission.'

'"He went away and then he came back and let me in. There was a castle so beautiful that eyes have never seen its like. There was Mālik ibn Anas sitting in the middle of it. There was a copy of the Qur'an in his room and he was wearing the most beautiful green garments. When I stopped, I greeted him and asked, 'Aren't you dead?' He said, 'Yes indeed.' I said, 'By what did you come here?' He said, 'By the pardon of Allah and vast His mercy, not by my knowledge.'

'"I asked, 'What do you think about the case of this knowledge?' He answered, 'More of us are saved by hesitating in it.' I asked, 'Where is Zayd ibn Aslam?' (One version has 'Abd ar-Raḥmān ibn Zayd ibn Aslam) He lifted his head and pointed with his finger, saying, 'There that one is in 'Illiyūn with the weepers.'"

'His dream was on a paper before him with their answers to him. He read it to the people and wept and asked for mercy on Mālik in every assembly.'

Bishr ibn Bukayr said, 'I dreamt – or was shown – al-Awzā'ī and ath-Thawrī. They were in the Garden. I asked, "Where is Mālik?" He told me, "Mālik is higher." He lifted his head until his hat fell off.'

At-Tustarī said, 'Abū Zur'a was seen in a dream and was asked, "What did Allah do with you?" He said, "He said to me, 'You did a lot for Me, Abū Zur'a' (meaning that he quarrelled a lot with the people of false statements.) I said, 'Yes, Lord, they argued against You.' He said, 'Put him with Abū 'Abdullāh. Abū 'Abdullāh Mālik, ath-Thawrī and Ibn Ḥanbal.'"'

THE DREAMS OF THE PEOPLE OF KNOWLEDGE WHICH INDICATE HIS KNOWLEDGE AND BEING AN IMĀM

Ad-Darāwardī said, 'I dreamt that the Prophet ﷺ was sitting in the *Rawḍa* between the grave and the minbar by the old column. We went to him and I sat with him. Then Mālik came last of all and gave the greeting, and the Messenger of Allah ﷺ had him sit down beside him. Then he ﷺ removed his ring from his hand and turned it between his fingers and brought them together. There was none of us who was not looking at him. He took Mālik's hand and placed it on his finger. If he had been right for the caliphate, we would have said the caliph: but it was knowledge.'

This version is related from ad-Darāwardī in different words while meaning the same.

Another report has, 'I used to disparage Mālik. Then I saw the Prophet ﷺ in a dream and he said to me, "Cling to what Mālik ibn Anas commands you. He desires Allah by what is in it."'

Az-Zubayr ibn Ḥabīb said, 'I used to discuss Mālik. Then I dreamt that I saw the Prophet ﷺ at the old column, and I was with him. Then a man came to ask about some matter and the Prophet ﷺ said, "Go to Mālik and ask him. There is no one on the face of the earth with more knowledge than him."'

Muḥammad ibn Ramḥ said, 'I saw the Prophet ﷺ in a dream. I said, "Messenger of Allah, Mālik and al-Layth differ." The Messenger of Allah ﷺ said, "You must have what Mālik says. He has inherited and lives."' One version has 'inherited my good fortune.'

Al-Ḥasan ibn 'Alī al-Ashnānī said, 'The meaning of "my good fortune" is that "my good fortune" is Ibrāhīm the Friend, and he said, "My good fortune is my *dīn*."' It is said, 'my *Sunna*.'

From Ibn Ramḥ as well, 'I dreamt of the Prophet ﷺ while I was a young man and the people were gathered around him asking him. He said, "I have given Mālik a treasure and I commanded him to divide it between you."'

A man came to Mālik's assembly and asked, 'Which one of you is Mālik?' They answered, 'This one.' He greeted him and embraced him and drew him to his breast. He said, 'By Allah, I have seen the Messenger of Allah ﷺ sitting here last night and he said, "Bring Mālik." You were brought trembling. He said, "There is no harm intended for you, Abu 'Abdullāh. Sit down." You sat down. He said to you, "Open your bosom," and you opened it and he filled it with effulgent musk. He said, "Press it to you and spread it in my community."'

Mālik wept and said, 'The vision gives joy and does not deceive. If your dream is true, then it is knowledge which Allah has entrusted in me.'

Abū Hishām said, 'A man saw the Prophet ﷺ speaking on the minbar. When Mālik came, he said, "Mālik, take this purse and put it under my minbar."'

Abū Hishām said, 'That is the knowledge which he disseminated.'

Abū Bakr ibn Sa'dūn said, 'I prayed *Ḍuḥā* in Egypt and saw the Prophet ﷺ. I said, "Messenger of Allah, Mālik and al-Layth disagree about *Ḍuḥā*. Mālik says that it is twelve *rak'at*s and al-Layth says that it is eight." He struck his hand between my hips and said, "Mālik's opinion is the correct one."'

Khalaf ibn 'Umar said, 'I was with Mālik when Ibn Abī Kathīr, the Qur'an reciter of Madina, came to him. He had a page with him and he looked at it and put it under his prayer-mat. When he got up, I went to get up. He said, "Stay put."

'He gave me the paper and on it was: "Last night I dreamt that I was told, 'This is the Messenger of Allah ﷺ.' I came to the mosque and a corner of the grave had opened and the Messenger of Allah ﷺ was sitting while people were saying, 'Messenger of Allah, give to us. Messenger of Allah, who is for us?' He told them, 'I have put a treasure under the minbar and I have commanded Mālik to divide it between you, so go to him.' People went saying to one another, 'What do you think Mālik will do?' One of them said, 'He will aim for what the Messenger of Allah ﷺ commands him.'"'

He said, 'Mālik was afraid and wept. Then I went out and left him immediately.'

Yazīd ibn Yazīd an-Nufaylī said, 'In Marv, I saw the Prophet ﷺ [in a dream] and Mālik ibn Anas was walking in front of him carrying a candle.'

In another version: 'I dreamt that we were in the Garden and there was Mālik ibn Anas with a pillar of light between his hands.'

Ibn Abī al-Kirām said, 'One of your companions saw the Prophet ﷺ in a dream, and he was making a division. He said, "I spread out my hands to him and I said, 'Messenger of Allah, give to me!' He said, 'I have concealed something for you under this minbar of mine.' I said, 'What is it, Messenger of Allah?' He said, 'Mālik ibn Anas.'"'

Zayd ibn Dāwūd said, 'I dreamt that I saw the grave split open from the Messenger of Allah ﷺ and the people gathered to him and a crier cried for Mālik ibn Anas. Mālik came and he gave him something and told him, "Divide this between the people." I saw him give it to them. Then he stopped and we obtained the knowledge which he spread out.'

Another said, 'I had a difficult precise question in myself and I wanted to see the Prophet ﷺ in a dream so that I could ask him about it. I saw him and said, "Messenger of Allah, I have a subtle question which I want to ask you about." He said, "Go to Mālik and ask him about it. He will bring it out, even if it is finer than a hair."'

Ḥajjāj ibn Sulaymān ar-Ra'īnī said, 'I saw the Prophet ﷺ in a dream and I asked him about a question and he said, "Have I not stored up a treasure under my minbar and commanded Mālik to divide it for you?"'

Muḥammad ibn Abī Bishr said, 'Some people attacked Mālik while others attacked ath-Thawrī in the assembly of Ibn Ḥanbal. I left, and there was a sorrow in my heart that I could not describe. I spent the night and dreamt of a man who was the most handsome I had seen and had the most fragrant scent and cleanest garments. There was a man on his right and another man on his left. Both of them had a beautiful form, although his state was higher than both of them. He said, "Do you recognise me?" I replied, "I have never seen you before so that I could recognise you. When I saw your form and beautiful face I thought that you would be famous." He said, "I am your Prophet Muḥammad." I said, "May Allah bless you. By my father and mother, who is this?"

'He replied, "The Imām of my house, Mālik ibn Anas," and he pointed at the one on his right. "And this is the Imām of the people of Iraq, Sufyān ath-Thawrī," and he pointed at the one on his left. "I testify to their truthfulness. Love them, for I love them. By Allah, they did not utter an opinion but that they were correct in my *Sunna* regarding it, nor a counsel in which they strove but for all my community. If they are later than the first generation, it does not lessen their position because they clung to the *Sunna* and exact traditions. Have you got it?" I answered, "Yes."

'In the morning I went to Ibn Ḥanbal and told him. He said, "I wish that I had seen what you saw and got up in the morning without any food for the day! This, by Allah, is my opinion of them."'

One of them said, 'I dreamt of a man who said to the Prophet ﷺ, "With whom will we find your inheritance, Messenger of Allah?" He replied, "With Mālik ibn Anas."'

Ibn al-Qasim said, 'In Alexandria I dreamt that I stopped a falcon and forced it open and its inside was filled with a jewel. I asked Zayd ibn Shu'ayb to interpret my dream and he said to me, "Perhaps you related something of the search for knowledge?" I said, "That is so." He said, "Who did you mention?" I said, "Mālik." He said, "He is your falcon, and the falcon is the master of the birds. The jewel which you found inside it is the knowledge about which you asked."'

'Ammār ibn Zayd ibn al-Khashshāb said, 'I dreamt that I entered a city and I became lost in its streets, and I passed by some people and a shaykh stood up for me. He took my hand until he brought me out to a clear wide road. He said, "Take it." I asked about him and was told, "It is Mālik."'

Ibn al-Labbād said, 'I also heard that a man I knew who followed the school of Abū Ḥanīfa once dreamt of the Prophet ﷺ. He greeted him and shook his hand. He said, "I wanted to embrace him, but he turned away from me. I said to myself, 'I think that it is only because *nabīdh* is considered lawful.' Someone said, 'We would like to ask him what he follows.' He, peace be upon him, said, 'The truth is in the words of Mālik, not in what is beyond it.'" The man moved to Mālik's school and left his school.'

It is related that Mālik said to Ibn Hurmuz, 'I dreamt that I was looking into a mirror.' Ibn Hurmuz said, 'Whoever sees this, looks into the mirror of his *dīn*.' Then he said, 'Mālik, today you are owned (*mumlak*), so fear Allah in this community if you will be a master (*mālik*) for it.'

Al-'Āmirī said, 'I dream that while I was in the mosque when it was crowded by his people, suddenly the Messenger of Allah ﷺ came out of his tomb with a bottle of musk in his hand. He stopped and said, "Which of you is Mālik?" Mālik got up and said, "Here I am, may my father and mother be your ransom, Messenger of Allah." The Messenger of Allah ﷺ said, "Take this," and he gave him the bottle, "and divide it between the people."' Al-'Āmiri went to recount it to Mālik. Mālik said to him, 'Do not tell me. I have seen the like of what you saw.'

Ibrāhīm ibn Yaḥyā said, 'I went to sleep and I dreamt that the sun was eclipsed and that darkness was over the earth so that the people could not see one another. I said to a man at my side, "Is it the Resurrection then?" He said, "Why would it not happen when the man of knowledge of Madina has died?" I asked, "Who is it?" "Mālik," he replied. I woke up in alarm and found that he had died.'

Ibn Muzāḥim said, 'I dreamt of the Prophet ﷺ and asked, "Messenger of Allah, whom should we ask after you?" He replied, "Mālik ibn Anas."'

Ibn al-Qāsim said, 'While I was asleep, someone came to me and said, "If you desire knowledge, then you must have the man of knowledge of knowledge of all horizons." "Who is that?" I asked. He told me, "This Shaykh. Look at him."

'I looked and there was a ruddy tall shaykh with a good beard. I woke up. Most of Shawwāl had passed, so I took a rental to go to Makka and did the *ḥajj*. When I came to Madina, I did a *ghusl* and entered the mosque of the Prophet ﷺ. I looked and there was the man with the description which I had dreamt. It was Mālik. I told him about what was said to me about him, "the scholar of the horizons". I stayed with him.'

One of them had a dream that the people had gathered in the Alexandria desert to shoot at the target which all of them missed. Then a man shot and hit it. He asked, 'Who is this?' It was said, 'Mālik ibn Anas.'

THE FINAL ESTATE OF MĀLIK

Ibn al-Qāsim said, 'Mālik died with a hundred turbans, not to mention other things.'

Ibn Abī Uways said, 'What was in the house of Mālik was sold on the day he died, may Allah have mercy on him: the dais, saddles, rugs, cushions stuffed with feathers and other things – for about five hundred dinars.'

Muḥammad ibn Khalaf said, 'Mālik left five hundred pairs of sandals. One day he wanted to wear a Qūmisī garment, and he had not passed the night until he had seven of them sent to him.'

Yaḥyā ibn Yaḥyā an-Naysābūri gave him a gift. I found in the writing of one of our reliable shaykhs that what was left of it was sold for eighty thousand.

Abū 'Umar said, 'He left in coin two thousand dinars and sixty dinars and twenty-nine dinars and one thousand dirhams. They were gathered in his inheritance of some thirty-three hundred odd dinars.'

What was said about Mālik in poetry in his lifetime and after his death

The Qāḍī said, 'Part of the famous lines about that are the words of Ibn al-Mubārak:

"Silent, since silence adorns its people
and the opening of the sealed virgin words.
He contained what the Qur'an contains of every wisdom,
and good manners were his in flesh and blood."'

Ibn Munādir said:

'Whoever desires instruction,
I have instruction for both the old and young.
Take from Mālik and from Ibn 'Awn.
Do not relate the *ḥadīths* of Ibn Dāb.'

'Abdullāh ibn Sālim al-Khayyāṭ said:

'He refused to answer, and it has no effect
on awe; the askers' chins are lowered.
The manners of gravity and the might of the Sultan meet.
He is more awesome, but is not a sultan.'

They recited by Abū al-Mu'āfī about Mālik – one adding to the other – and some of it is mentioned by Abū al-Mu'āfī:

The loss of knowledge lies in the loss of Mālik.
Mālik remains with the sound state among us.
If it had not been for him, many rights would not have been established. If it had not been for him,
the paths would have been blocked for us.
He establishes the correct truth both secretly and openly.
He guides just as the Milky Way guides.
We went to him in the evening desiring the light of his fire,
and the powerless curbed bickerer kept close.
He brought an opinion for us by whose like one is guided
like a string of pearls whose adornment is ingots.

At-Tustarī related that Mālik let Abū al-Mu'āfī invalidate the one who testified against him, so al-Mughīra testified against this. When Mālik died, he said, 'Do not say to a people...' In one variant:

'Do not say to a people, "Greetings, Welcome to you."
For the one who asks about a *fatwā*, Mālik has died.'

Az-Zubayr recited an elegy of Mālik to Ibn al-Mu'āfī or Ibn Abī Mu'āfī:

Do you not say to a people who are delighted at the loss of Mālik:
'Was not knowledge lost when Mālik died?'
What is wrong with me that I do not weep for the loss of Mālik
since the loss of one of the people who has died is dear?
What is wrong with me that I do not weep for the loss of Mālik?
The paths are closed to us with his loss.

Aṣbagh quoted a woman who elegised him:

I have wept copious tears for the loss of Mālik.
The paths have been closed to us with his loss.
What is wrong with me that I do not weep for him
when the Pleiades and the Milky Way have wept for him?
I have sworn by what Quraysh gave on the morning of the tenth
when the *ḥajj* practices are fulfilled:
Malik was the best vessel of knowledge in *fiqh*.
When the loss is reckoned by people, he is dead.

Abū Muḥammad aḍ-Ḍarrāb quoted from one of them:

When scholars are counted one day,
 Mālik is the light in knowledge.
People master the pinnacle of the scholars.
 They are but like the earth while he is the heaven for them.

Another composed:

The *faqīh* of the two Ḥarams is Mālik.
 When he gives a command, he is obeyed.

Ṭālib ibn ʻIṣma al-Andalusī said:

Mālik is the Imām of mankind in guidance and the path,
 as well as in *fiqh* and traditions which cannot be reached.
His opinions in *fiqh* flash their light, and the paths
 are made easy by their clarification.
The light of his traditions guides the slaves
 just as the radiant Milky Way guides them.
He has the highest part and the remnant
 from the pinnacles of knowledge
and portions and ends in all people.

Az-Zubayr also recited to Abū al-Muʻāfī:

Mālik ransomed a people who hoped for his death. If he had died,
 there would have been no substitute or successor among them.
The knowledge of the *dīn* takes on a straight light
 with the *isnād* of reliable people from the *Salaf.*
When the bows of the archers were bent,
 the end of the shooting and goal is him.
They shot the arrow which he had feathered for them,
 and their knowledge is strong in both arm and hand.
No arm among them resists his victory when an arm is firm
 for them by the fingers of the hand.

It was said that when Mālik heard this poem, he exclaimed, 'Allah is the One Who is asked for help.'

Muḥammad ibn Abī Zayd said to someone who disagreed with what Mālik said:

'You overstep in lowering the stars of the heaven,
  and this is the false hope.
You desire the Imām of guidance, Mālik,
  and he is the firm mountain.
There is no trace of the atom on a stone, and its effort
  in standing upright in the supererogatory.
Without your acquisition from Mālik,
  beware of this disappointed hope.
You are far beneath the one you desire,
  as distant as the piercing star.'

'Abd as-Salām ibn Sulaymān said:

'Mālik visited me, and later I did not care
  who visited me and who did not visit me.'

Abū Muṣ'ab recited to one of them:

'Whoever did not sit with Mālik since he appeared
  and sits with someone else is ignorant.'

At-Tustarī recited to Muḥammad ibn 'Abd ar-Raḥmān al-Baghdādī, known as Abū al-Ḥasan aṣ-Ṣāliḥī, an elegy of Mālik in the form of a *qaṣīda* which begins:

He completed the goal of his sorrow and so he is sad
  and his eyes were wet to the edge of the night.
He looked with belief at the weak part of the *dīn*, and spent
  sleepless nights while the eyes were slumbering.
He saw that the days of passion will not return
  and love is lost in the station of white hair.
No diversion is praised, nor easy life returns nor is
  forbearance censured nor ignorance beneficial.
Remember that knowledge denies passion and the signs
  of grey hair startle him with terrors.

After this there are many verses in which he mentioned Madina. He said:

The Ḥaram of the Messenger of Allah is in it and his security,
and filth and the Dajjāl are barred from it.
The belief of the lands will seek refuge in it when
abominable times appear among them.
From it Allah brought His *dīn* to the lands.
Similarly, all belief returns to the Abode.

Then he said after some verses:

Allah gave a drink of what the Prophet Muḥammad embraced
of the earth, from what the shedding clouds which give drink
To the *Rawḍa* of *taqwā* to the *qibla*
by which the moon of *taqwā* arrives and bows,
To the best of the Companions and Followers by whom
the armour reaches the Book,
And excellent is the grave in which the shroud of Mālik is located,
and its high and low places,
The best Imām of knowledge and the star whose light
comes flashing in the page of the *dīn*.
The contractor of guidance among us and the lamp of our *dīn*.
By his words the truth and right guidance occur
From the handhold of Islam inside his hand. It is the firm handhold
and comes out openly with the truth,
One who is from the best of people and knowledge in his guidance,
and from him are its pillars and Sharī'a.
Even if you were not a companion among us by Allah's decree,
you would still follow the unlettered one by the truth.
You put the *dīn* of the Prophet Muḥammad upright for us, and
his neighbours and in-laws since the time you were an adolescent.
Your knowledge is the highest knowledge
in branch and articulation.
Similarly every knowledge below it is humbled to it.
When the *adhān* reverberates, their hearts come
and listen to him with listening necks.
There is no knowledge for the one
who does not listen to Mālik's words
and the one whose heart does not believe him is lost,

Not guided by the proof from the knowledge of Mālik
 and what his reports and summaries pave.
By my life, we inherited pure knowledge from him,
 and now the houses have become wastelands, desolate of you.
You transmitted to us from the lamps of our *dīn* by the success
 of a Lord whose wide gift overflows.
If you are not among us, your knowledge is still among us
 and we defend it and fight for it against criticism
With every proof from Book and proof of it
 from the places of the hearts of the believers.
The earth of people will weep and the people above it
 and the stars rising the air will weep.

At-Tustarī related that Abū al-Mu'āfī was jailed by the governor of Madina, al-'Abbās ibn Muḥammad, on a matter put before him, and he wrote a poem to Mālik in which he said:

The life of knowledge is in the life of Mālik.
 Mālik remains with the correct state among us.

When he finished reciting the verses, we saw modesty in Mālik's face and then he bowed his head and lifted it and stated, 'Allah has made the obligations obligatory and He has made the *ḥadd* punishment of adultery stoning when the man is *muḥṣan* and a hundred lashes when he is not *muḥṣan*. There is eighty lashes when a *muḥṣana* woman is slandered. When he steals that for which the hand is cut off, it is cut off. I have not heard that Allah commanded imprisonment for any of His *ḥadd* punishments.' That was put before al-'Abbās and he went to Mālik to question him. He said, 'Today, after three months, I think that the door should be opened for him and what has passed should be allowed,' and he went on his way.

Al-Mu'āfī composed opposing the Qurayshites who have a *fatwā* that he should be imprisoned:

Mālik has ransomed a people who desired his death …

Ibn Abī Sulayman, one of the Banū Khuḍra, recited about Mālik:

How can the one who shuns his assembly understand Allah and be
increased in *fiqh* when he is coarse towards his *fiqh*?
O end of the people of *fatwā* when they strive!
Yet they compare you by a gauge to the foolish ones.
You are what is left when our remnant becomes bent,
not the one who made an opinion for sixths from fifths.

The *faqīh* Muḥammad ibn 'Ammār al-Kilā'ī al-Būraqī also said in a *qaṣīda*:

Be a Mālikī in these schools,
Madinan with the firm *Sunna*.
Madina is the best for the one who rides the mount and the place
where the revelation of the Lord of the worlds fell.
The Prophet is there, and the best of company and
most of them are buried there.
There is no doubt about Mālik, the pleasing,
and that he travelled the Clear Path.
We looked in the schools, but we did not see any school
like Mālik for those that seek.
His school is following, not innovation,
as the noble follows the noble ones.
I have every correct striver,
but Mālik is among those who go first.
The proof indicates what is correct.
It is stated with those who are precise.

The *faqīh* Abu Ḥafṣ ibn 'Abd an-Nūr aṣ-Ṣiqillī, known as Ibn al-Hakkār, said on that:

'I reflected on the knowledge of pleased ones with intelligence.
The best of them is the one who
has no diversion in his seriousness.
Part of his *fiqh* is derived from his *ḥadīth*.
He related it with sound *riwāya* and selected.
Mālik is only guidance. That is why communities
from all the Arabs and non-Arabs were guided by him.'

He also said:

'Mālik is the light which illuminates for us by his knowledge
so that we throw light on the darkness of the shell.
He does not start with the asker by the promise to spend time on it
nor to pass on the leaves and pages
Or answer an answer and then follow it with contradiction,
but rather with an opinion which is not disputed.'

The *faqīh* Abū al-Faḍl ibn an-Nawawī said on that:

'The Aṣbaḥī Imām is
one of the radiant stars.
Allah preserved the *hadith* by Him.
He counted him as one of the memorisers.
His opinions acted freely
in unique beginnings.
He walked following the guidance
on which the brother of the firm walked.
The people of Madina were guided by them
and they are the highest transmitters.
After analogy,
he unravelled obscure events.
He sought the noble things
and was level above the noble lofty things.
His lights shone
towards the distant lands.
From them it struck one who would agree
to the correct and to guidance.
Musk makes the selves pleased with it
among the scents.'

The Qāḍī said:

'O you who ask about the one
whose guidance and *sunan* are praised:
seek knowledge of *fiqh* and the *Sunna*
and you will be guided.
Fix your heart and make it strong on ice which does not
allow it to contain doubt or the appearance of conflict.

Travel the path of those who obtained intelligence and *taqwā*.
They are clearly beautiful, secret and public.
They are the Imāms and Poles.
They were not deceived and they did not
take their *dīn* for a paltry price and fraud.
The Companions of the best of mankind,
the best of his religion,
the best of the generations, the stars of time and age:
Whoever is guided by their guidance is guided.
They are salvation for those after them
from the throes of seditions.
Their followers are following right guidance.
They are the people of intelligence,
fearful awareness, knowledge and cleverness.
He chose for this *dīn* the one with knowledge to be imitated
which is famous in Syria and the Yemen.
He enclosed their roots and then his tracks were followed
on a road to every pure meaning.
Mālik the pleasing is the most excellent of them without a doubt,
the Imām of the Abode of guidance, revelation and *Sunna*.
Take their knowledge from him if you are a follower
and leave the vanities like the dreams of sleep.
He is imitated in the traditions which are relied on,
besides the one who is not trusted in them.
He is imitated in *fiqh* and in opinion he was one
whose guidance was imitated in that time:
The man of knowledge of the whole earth by what the testimony
of the Chosen with excellence and favours expressed,
The one to whom people repaired from all parts of the earth:
the mounts were exhausted and the bodies of camels lean,
Who let creation drink his love, and it flowed in the hearts
as water flows in the tree branch.
Every man goes on at length speaking about his virtues, even
if their tongues are incapable of eloquence in the description.
Gifts from his Lord enveloped him as well as His pleasure
like the rain or heavy-laden massed rain clouds.

His grave is good and the drifting of the heavy rain
gives His mercy to the abode of those eyes.'

The famous transmitters from Mālik among his shaykhs and associates who died before him or near to that

The Qāḍī said, 'We compiled the transmitters of Mālik by the letters of the alphabet as we explained to you at the beginning of the book. We compiled thirteen hundred names of them. We have mentioned some of them in this book of ours in three generations of *fuqahā'* since it is the goal of this book.

'In this book, we wanted to mention something about the famous men who related from Mālik among his shaykhs, associates, the great ones who took from him and the famous ones among all people in order to demonstrate his immense position in his time and the fact that all obeyed him and recognised his due. We were content with the names and deaths of the earlier ones without information and story.

'At the end of this chapter, we will return to our goal which is to organise his companions, the *fuqahā'*, and to mention their news as we stipulated at the beginning of the book, Allah willing.'

Those who related from Mālik among his shaykhs and associates from whom he learned and related

Among the Tābi'ūn

Muḥammad ibn Muslim ibn 'Ubaydullāh ibn Shihāb az-Zuhrī. He related from him the *ḥadīth* of al-Furay'a bint Sinān about divorce. He died in 124 AH, fifty-five years before Mālik.

Abū al-Aswad, the orphan of 'Urwa. He died close to the time of az-Zuhrī's death.

Ayyūb ibn Abī Tamīma as-Sakhtiyānī. He died in 121 AH, forty-nine years before Mālik's death.

Rabī'a ibn Abī 'Abd ar-Raḥmān. He died in 136 AH. It is also said 142 AH. He related the *ḥadīth* of the *mut'a* from him and other things.

Yaḥyā ibn Sa'īd al-Anṣārī. He related a lot from him from the *ḥadīths* of Ibn Shihāb. He died in 143 AH. It is said 144 AH. That was thirty-six years before Mālik.

Mūsā ibn 'Uqba. He died in 141 AH. He related from him the *ḥadīths* of the prohibition about selling dates before their soundness was evident.

Abū Muḥammad al-Ḥasan ibn Ismā'īl aḍ-Ḍarrāb and others who related from Mālik mentioned that among his shaykhs who related from Mālik among the Tābi'ūn were:

Hishām ibn 'Urwa who died in 146 AH.

Others mentioned among them were:

Zayd ibn Aslam and his questioning him,

Yazīd ibn 'Abdullāh ibn Qusayṭ al-Laythī.

From other than the Tābi'ūn among the Shaykhs of Mālik from whom he related in his *Muwaṭṭā'* and elsewhere, and who related *ḥadīths* from him:

'Amr ibn al-Ḥārith al-Miṣrī. He died thirty years before him.

Zayd ibn Abī Unaysa al-Jazarī. He died fifty-five years before him in the year that Ibn Shihāb died. However, he died as a young man of thirty-six years. Al-Bukhārī said all of that. Mālik related from him in the *Muwaṭṭā'* and he related a *ḥadīth* from Mālik, 'Whoever has an act of injustice towards his brother...'

Nāfi' al-Qārī' (the reciter) ibn Abī Nu'aym who died ten years before him. Mālik recited the Qur'an with him.

Muḥammad ibn 'Ajlān.

Ziyād ibn Sa'īd

Sālim ibn Abī Umayya, Abū an-Naḍr, the client of 'Umar ibn 'Ubaydullāh.

Yazīd ibn 'Ubaydullāh ibn Usāma ibn al-Hādī. He died forty years before him. He related from him: 'None of you should milk the cow of his brother without his permission.'

'Umar ibn Muḥammad ibn Zayd ibn 'Abdullāh ibn 'Umar ibn al-Khaṭṭāb. He related the *ḥadīth* about *mut'a* marriage and other things from him.

Another generation of the great among the generation of his later shaykhs

Among the followers of the Tābi'ūn and those who died some time before him from whom Mālik did not relate, but who related from Mālik included his contemporaries and those who died some time before him:

Muḥammad ibn 'Abd ar-Raḥmān ibn Abī Dhi'b al-Qurashī. He died twenty years before him.

'Abd al-Mālik ibn Juṛayḥ. He died thirty years before him.

Muḥammad ibn Isḥāq, the author of *al-Maghāzī*. He died about thirty years before him. Abū Muḥammad aḍ-Ḍarrāb mentioned that he related from him and there is some disagreement about that.

Muḥammad ibn Isḥāq al-Madanī is another man who related from Mālik without doubt.

Sulaymān ibn Mahrān al-A'mash. He died thirty-one years before him.

Another generation of his peers who related from him

Among the Imāms and famous men whose deaths were near to him and were his peers in listening with him to his shaykhs were many. Some of them died many years before him:

Sufyān ibn Sa'īd ath-Thawrī of Kufa who died about twenty years before him.

Al-Layth ibn Sa'd of Egypt who died about four years before him.

Shu'ba ibn al-Ḥajjāj who died twenty years before him.

Abū 'Amr al-Awzā'ī who died twenty-three years before him.

Ibrāhīm ibn Tahmān of Herat

Ibrāhīm ibn Muḥammad Abū Isḥāq al-Fazarī who died eight years before him.

Ibrāhīm ibn Muḥammad ash-Shāfi'ī of Makka

Anas ibn 'Iyaḍ, Abū Ḍamra, of Madina, who died twenty years after him

Usāma ibn Zayd al-Laythī

Juwayriyya ibn Asmā' of Basra. He died thirteen years after him.

Jarīr ibn 'Abd al-Ḥamīd ad-Dabbī, the Qāḍī of Rayy

Ḥammād ibn Salama of Basra

Ḥammād ibn Zayd of Basra who died the same year as him.

Sufyān ibn 'Uyayna of Makka who died eleven years after him.

Abū Hanīfa of Kufa who died thirty years before him.

His son Ḥammād

Qāḍī Abū Yūsuf, his companion, who died three years after him.

Ja'far ibn 'Awn al-Makhzūmī of Kufa

Ḥafṣ ibn 'Umar ibn Maysara aṣ-Ṣan'ānī

Al-Ḥasan ibn Ziyād al-Lu'lu'ī of Kufa

Ḥamīd ibn 'Abd ar-Raḥmān ar-Rawāsī of Kufa who died twenty years later

Rawḥ ibn al-Qāsim al-Baṣrī

'Abbād ibn 'Abbād al-Muhallabī who died a year after him.

Fulayḥ ibn Sulaymān of Madina who died twelve years before him.

His brother Hārūn al-Aylī

Qāḍī Muḥammad ibn 'Imrān aṭ-Ṭā'ī

Muḥammad ibn Abī Ṣabra who died seven years before him

Muḥammad ibn Ismā'īl ibn Abī Fudayk

Ismā'īl ibn Ibrāhīm ibn 'Aliyya of Basra who died thirteen years after him.

Sharīk ibn 'Abdullāh the Qāḍī who died two years before him.

Muḥammad ibn al-Ḥasan

Ismā'īl ibn Ja'far ibn Abī Kathīr al-Qārī' of Madina

His brother Muḥammad

Mūsā ibn A'yan al-Jazarī who died two years before him.

Aḍ-Ḍaḥḥāk ibn 'Uthmān ibn 'Abdullāh al-Ḥizāmī the elder

His brother, 'Uthmān

His son, aḍ-Ḍaḥḥāk 'Uthmān ibn aḍ-Ḍaḥḥāk the younger. He was one of the great Companions. This al-Aṣghar died a year after Mālik.

'Abdullāh ibn Ja'far of Madina who died a year before him.

Muslim ibn Khālid az-Zanjī who died a year before he died.

'Abd al-'Azīz ibn Abī Salama al-Mājishūn who died about twenty years before him.

Wakī' ibn al-Jarrāḥ who died some time after him.

Nafi' ibn Yazīd of Egypt

Al-Mughīra ibn 'Abd ar-Raḥmān al-Khuzāmī who died a year before his death.

Ma'mar ibn Rāshid who died twenty-six years before him.

Warqā' ibn 'Umar

Ibrāhīm ibn Muḥammad ibn Abī Yaḥyā

'Abdullāh ibn Lahī'a al-Miṣrī who died five years before him.

Ḥafs ibn Maysara aṣ-Ṣan'ānī who died two years after Mālik.

'Abd ar-Raḥmān ibn Zayd ibn Aslam who died three years after him.

Wahb ibn Khālid al-Baṣrī who died fifteen years before him.

Yūnus ibn Yazīd al-Aylī who died twenty years before him.

'Abdullāh ibn Idrīs al-Awdī

Abū 'Awn 'Abdullāh ibn 'Awn ibn Arṭiyān of Basra who died about twenty years before him.

Al-'Aṭṭāf ibn Khālid al-Makhzūmī

Mu'āwiya ibn Ṣāliḥ al-Ḥimṣī, the Qāḍī of Andalusia, who died about ten years before him.

Another generation after them

Among those who related knowledge from him among the famous Imams and those who studied *fiqh* with him and sat with him among the bulk of the scholars outside of these men (some of them shared shaykhs with him and some of them achieved importance in his lifetime and gave *fatwā* in his time):

From the people of Madina:

Al-Mughīra ibn 'Abd ar-Raḥmān al-Makhzūmī who died seven years after him.

Sulaymān ibn Bilāl who died four years before him.

'Abd al-'Azīz ibn Abī Ḥāzim who died five years after him.

Muḥammad ibn Idrīs who died three years after him.
'Uthmān ibn Kināna who died six years after him.
'Abd al-'Azīz ad-Darāwardī who died six years after him.
Muḥammad ibn Muṭarrif, Abū Ghassān
Zakariyā' ibn Manẓūr
Yaḥyā ibn 'Abd al-Malik al-Hudayrī
Muḥadd ibn Maslama al-Makhzūmī

From the people of Iraq and Syria

'Abdullāh ibn al-Mubārak who died two years after him.
Yaḥyā ibn Sa'īd al-Qaṭṭān and his death was after him.
'Abd ar-Raḥmān ibn Mahdī the same.
Muḥammad ibn al-Ḥasan, the companion of Abū Ḥanīfa who died eight years after him.
Al-Ḥasan ibn Ziyād al-Lu'lu'ī, his companion
Ḥafṣ ibn Ghiyāth

From the people of the Hijaz and the Yemen

Qāḍī Abū Qurra Mūsā ibn Ṭāriq

From the people of Egypt

'Abd ar-Raḥīm ibn Khālid who died eight years before him.
'Uthmān ibn al-Ḥakam who died forty-five years before him.
Sa'd ibn 'Abdullāh who died six years before him.
Zayd ibn Shu'ayb who died seven years after him.
Ṭulayb ibn Kāmil al-Iskandarānī whose name was 'Abdullāh.

From the people of Kairouan

Al-Bahlūl ibn Rāshid who died four years after him.
'Alī ibn Ziyād the same
Abū Mas'ūd ibn Ashras
'Abdullāh ibn Farrūkh who died four years before him.
Qāḍī Abū Muḥriz, Muḥammad ibn 'Abdullāh
'Abdullāh ibn Abī Ḥassān al-Yaḥṣubī of Madina
Qāḍī 'Abdullāh ibn Ghanim who died two years after him

according to what ash-Shirāzī mentioned. The sound version is that he died ten years after him.

From the people of Andalusia

Muḥammad ibn Yaḥyā an-Naysābūrī
Ḥafṣ ibn 'Abd as-Salām as-Saraqusṭī
Ziyād ibn 'Abd ar-Raḥmān ibn Muḥammad
Ja'far ibn Muḥammad
Sa'īd ibn 'Abdūs
Sa'īd ibn Abī Hind who died about thirty years before him.

From the people of Syria

Al-Walīd ibn Muslim who died four years before him.

The famous ones after those:

Another generation

From among those who took *fiqh* and *ḥadīths* from him, and who are classified after him from the earliest in years from him, and we have presented them roughly alphabetically and in order. Allah is the One Who is asked for help.

Chapter of *Alif*

Aḥmad ibn Muḥammad ibn Mālik, his grandson
Aḥmad ibn Abī Bakr az-Zuhrī, Abū Muṣ'ab, of Madina
Aḥmad ibn Naṣr ibn Mālik al-Khuzā'ī
Aḥmad ibn Muḥammad ibn al-Walīd al-Azraqī of Makka
Aḥmad ibn Manṣūr al-Ḥarrānī
Aḥmad ibn 'Abdullāh ibn Yūnus al-Yarbū'ī of Kufa
Aḥmad ibn Ismā'īl ibn Nabīh as-Sahmī, Abū Hudhāfa
Aḥmad ibn Ḥātim ibn Maḥshī al-'Uṭāridī of Basra
Aḥmad ibn Ḥātim aṭ-Ṭawīl of Baghdad
Aḥmad ibn Faraj aṭ-Ṭā'ī of Kufa
Aḥmad ibn Ṭayyiba al-Jurjānī
Aḥmad ibn Mūsā
Aḥmad ibn Yaḥyā al-Kindī al-Aḥwal

Aḥmad ibn Ibrāhīm al-Mawṣūlī
Aḥmad ibn Abī Sakīna al-Ḥalabī, and it is said that his name is Muḥammad.
Aḥmad ibn Sulaymān al-Ja'nānī
Aḥmad ibn Yazid al-Wartanī of Harran
Aḥmad ibn Yaḥyā al-Mundhir al-Qurashī
Aḥmad ibn Muḥammad al-'Ablī of Barqa

*

Ismā'īl ibn Dāwūd al-Khuzā'ī of Madina
Ismā'īl ibn Abī Uways of Madina
Ismā'īl ibn Ḥarb aḍ-Ḍabbī al-Wārī
Ismā'īl ibn 'Ayyāsh
Ismā'īl ibn Ḥammād Abī Ḥanīfa of Kufa
Ismā'īl ibn Ibrāhīm Abū Sa'īd al-Aqra'
Ismā'īl ibn Yaḥyā ibn 'Ubaydullāh at-Tamīmī of Kufa
Ismā'īl ibn Maslama ibn Qa'nab
Ismā'īl ibn 'Īsā al-Fazarī
Ismā'īl ibn 'Umar Abū al-Mundhir al-Wāsiṭī
Ismā'īl ibn Rāshid aṭ-Ṭabarī
Ismā'īl ibn Ibrāhīm at-Tarjumānī of Baghdad
Ismā'īl ibn Ziyād ad-Dūlābī of Baghdad
Ismā'īl ibn Rajā' Abū Mu'ādh of Ramla

*

Ibrāhīm ibn 'Umar ibn Abī al-Wazīr of Basra
Ibrāhīm ibn Ḥammād ibn Abī Ḥāzim az-Zuhrī
Ibrāhīm ibn Muḥammad ibn Abī Ḥāzim al-Aslamī
Ibrāhīm ibn al-Mukhtār ar-Rāzī
Ibrāhīm ibn Muḥammad ar-Rabī' as-Sulamī
Ibrāhīm ibn Zayd al-Aslamī
Ibrāhīm ibn Rustam al-Khwārizmī
Ibrāhīm ibn 'Īsā al-Khuzā'ī
Ibrāhīm ibn Zayd at-Taflīsī
Ibrāhīm ibn 'Alī at-Tamīmī
Ibrāhīm ibn Isḥāq at-Tamīmī of Kufa
Ibrāhīm ibn Hirāsa ash-Shaybānī Abū Isḥāq of Kufa
Ibrāhīm ibn Hārūn al-Laythī of Madina

Ibrāhīm ibn Bashīr of Makka
Ibrāhīm ibn Yūsuf of Balkh
Ibrāhīm ibn Ḥibbān al-Anṣārī
Ibrāhīm ibn Ḥabīb ibn Yūnus of Madina
Ibrāhīm ibn 'Īsā Sabalān of Baghdad
Ibrāhīm ibn Ziyād Sabalān of Baghdad

*

Ayyūb ibn Sulaymān al-A'war of Egypt
Qāḍī Ayyūb ibn Yūnus Abū Ghassān, a Marwazī
Ayyūb ibn Suwayd ad-Daylī
Ayyūb ibn 'Ammār ibn Abī Unays of Madina
Ayyūb ibn Hānī al-Ju'fī of Kufa

*

Asad ibn Mūsā of Egypt
Asad ibn 'Umar al-Balkhī, the companion of Abū Ḥanīfa, of Kufa
Asad ibn al-Furāt al-Qarawī

*

Isḥāq ibn 'Īsā aṭ-Ṭabbā' of Syria
Isḥāq ibn Muḥammad al-'Adawī
Isḥāq ibn Muḥammad al-Musayyibi ar-Rūmī
Isḥāq ibn 'Īsā ibn bint Dāwūd ibn Hind
Isḥāq ibn Yūnus, the brother of Abū Muslim al-Mustamlī
Isḥāq ibn Ibrāhīm of Madina
Isḥāq ibn al-Furāt, the Qāḍī of Egypt
Isḥāq ibn Bishr al-Bukhārī
Isḥāq ibn Muqātil al-Kāhilī of Kufa
Isḥāq ibn Manṣūr ibn Ḥibbān of Kufa
Isḥāq ibn Ibrāhīm aṭ-Ṭabarī
Isḥāq ibn Ibrāhīm ibn Saṭṭās of Yemen
Isḥāq ibn Ibrāhīm, Abū Ma'mar of Basra

*

Ashhab ibn 'Abd al-'Azīz, whose name was Miskīn
Aṣram ibn Hawshab Abū al-Hishām, the Qāḍī of Hamdan
Aswad ibn 'Āmir Shādhān
Umayya ibn Khalaf of Basra, the brother of Hudba
Ādam ibn Abī Iyyās of Ashkelon

Isrā'īl ibn Rawḥ
Azdād ibn Mūsā of Baghdad
Idrīs ibn Yaḥyā al-Khawlānī of Egypt

THE LETTER BĀ'

Bishr ibn al-Mufaḍḍal of Egypt
Bishr ibn 'Umar az-Zahrānī of Basra
Bishr ibn Ādam of Baghdad
Bishr ibn Yazīd al-Azdī of North Africa
Bishr ibn Bakr al-Azdī ad-Dimishqī
Baqiyya ibn al-Walīd of Hums
Bashshār ibn Dirāṭ of Rayy
Bakkār ibn 'Abdullāh az-Zubayrī of Madina
Burayd al-Mughannī of Baghdad
Bikr ibn 'Abdullāh ibn ash-Shurūd of San'a
Bihr ibn 'Abdullāh of Basra
Bahlūl ibn Ṣāliḥ of Kairouan

THE LETTER THĀ'

Thābit ibn Ya'qūb ibn Hurmuz of Egypt

THE LETTER JĪM

Ja'far ibn Muḥammad ibn Bishr ibn Jarīr
Ja'far ibn 'Awn ibn Ḥārith al-Makhzūmī
Ja'far ibn Zayd as-Sahmī of Madina
Al-Jārūd ibn Yazīd, Abū aḍ-Ḍaḥḥāk of Khurasan
Jamīl ibn Yazīd
Jabir ibn Madrīq al-Ḥarrī

THE LETTER ḤĀ'

Al-Ḥasan ibn Sawwār al-Baghawi of Basra
Al-Ḥasan ibn Yaḥyā Abū al-Malik ad-Dimishqī
Al-Ḥasan ibn Muḥammad ash-Shaybānī of Kufa
Al-Ḥasan ibn Muḥammad al-Ashyab
Al-Ḥasan ibn Muḥammad al-'Abdi as-Sudūsī of Basra
Al-Ḥasan ibn al-Ḥasan ibn 'Aṭiyya al-'Awfī of Kufa

Al-Ḥasan ibn 'Alī al-Ḥulwāni al-Khallāl of Baghdad
Al-Hasan ibn Rāfi' al-Bawārī of Basra
Al-Ḥusayn ibn 'Abdullāh al-'Ajalī
Al-Ḥusayn ibn al-Walīd an-Naysābūrī
Al-Ḥusayn ibn 'Urwa al-Baṣrī
Ḥammād ibn Wāqid aṣ-Ṣaffār of Basra
Ḥammād ibn Khālid al-Khayyāṭ of Baghdad
Ḥammād ibn Mas'ada of Basra
Ḥammād ibn Usāma, Abū Usāma of Kufa
Ḥammād ibn Sawwār of Jurjan
Ḥammād ibn 'Abd al-Malik of Barqa
Ḥafṣ ibn Yaḥyā as-Sarkhasī
Ḥafṣ ibn 'Umar ibn Maymūn al-Aylī
Ḥafṣ ibn Sulaymān as-Samarqandī
Ḥafṣ ibn Sulaymān Abī Ḥafṣ al-Harawī
Ḥafṣ ibn 'Umar ibn 'Ubayd aṭ-Ṭanāfasī of Kufa
Ḥafṣ ibn 'Umar al-Ḥawḍī
Ḥabīb al-Lālī, his trustee in Madina
Ḥabīb ibn Abī Ḥabīb, his scribe in Madina
Ḥassān ibn 'Abd as-Salām of Andalusia
Ḥassān ibn Ghālib ibn Nujaym al-Fārisī
Ḥajjāj ibn al-Minhāl of Basra
Ḥajjāj ibn Sulaymān ar-Ra'īnī
Ḥātim ibn Sulaymān ibn al-Qazzāz al-A'raj
Ḥātim ibn 'Uthmān of Kairouan
Ḥamza ibn Yazīd al-Harawī
Ḥamza ibn Ziyād aṭ-Ṭūsī
Al-Ḥārith ibn Manṣūr of Wasit
Al-Ḥārith ibn an-Nu'mān ibn Abī an-Naḍr
Al-Ḥārith ibn Asad al-Qafsī
Ḥayyūn ibn Ṣāliḥ of Egypt
Ḥakkām ibn Sulaymān ad-Dārānī
Ḥabbāb ibn Ḥabla of Baghdad
Ḥanẓala ibn 'Āmir al-'Abdī
Ḥarmala ibn 'Abd al-'Azīz ibn ar-Rabī' ibn Sabra
Ḥajj ibn al-Muthannā

The Letter Khā'

Khalaf ibn Hishām al-Bazzār al-Maghribī of Baghdad
Khalaf ibn Jarīr ibn Faḍāla of Kairouan
Khalaf ibn Ḥajjāj al-Azraq of Kufa
Khalaf ibn Ayyūb of Balkh
Khalaf ibn Mūsā of Balkh
Khalaf ibn Khalīfa Abū Aḥmad al-Ashjā'ī of Basra
Khālid ibn 'Abd ar-Raḥmān, Abū al-Haytham of Khurasan
Khālid ibn Khaddāsh of Basra
Khālid ibn 'Uthmān al-'Uthmānī
Khālid ibn Mukhallad al-Ghaṭūnī of Kufa
Khālid ibn Yazīd al-'Umarī of Madina
Khālid al-'Abdī of Egypt
Khālid ibn Ḥamīd, Abū Ḥamīd al-Mahdī
Khālid ibn Najīḥ
Khālid ibn Sālim
Khālid ibn Yazīd al-Fārisī al-Lu'lu'ī of Kairouan
Khālid ibn Nizār who related his *Risāla* to Muḥammad ibn Muṭarrif
Khālid ibn Sulaymān Abū al-Mu'ādh al-Balkhī
Khallād ibn Yazīd al-Arsalī of Basra
Khallād ibn Yazīd al-Makkī
Khālid ibn 'Abd ar-Raḥmān
Khārija ibn Muṣ'ab ibn al-Hajjāj, a Sarkhasī
Khasīb ibn Nāsiḥ of Egypt
Khirāsh ibn ad-Daḥrāḥ
Khalīl ibn Kurayz of Kufa

The Letter Dāl

Dāwūd ibn az-Zibraqān of Basra
Dāwūd ibn 'Abdullāh ibn Abī al-Kirām al-Ja'farī of Madina
Dāwūd ibn Mihrān ad-Dabbāgh
Dāwūd ibn 'Abd al-Jabbār
Dawud ibn Sa'īd ibn Abī Zanbar of Madina
Dāwūd ibn Sulaymān ibn Fulayḥ of Madina
Dāwūd ibn Manṣūr, the Qāḍī of Madina

Dāwūd ibn Ibrāhīm al-Qazīnī
Dāwūd ibn 'Uthmān at-Tamīmī of Andalusia
Di'bil al-Khuzā'ī, the poet

The Letter Dhāl

Dhu'ayb ibn 'Umāma as-Sahmī of Madina
Dhū an-Nūn ibn Ibrāhīm al-Akhmīmī of Egypt

The Letter Rā'

Rabī'a ibn 'Abdullāh ibn Ya'qūb
Ar-Rabī' ibn ar-Ruka ibn ar-Rabī' ibn 'Aliyya al-Fazarī of Kufa
Rawwād ibn al-Jarrāḥ of Ashkelon
Rawḥ ibn al-Qāsim of Basra
Rawḥ ibn 'Ubāda of Basra
Rabāḥ ibn Zayd of Yemen
Rabāḥ ibn Thābit of Kairouan

The Letter Zāyy

Zayd ibn Yaḥyā ibn 'Ubayd of Damascus
Zayd ibn al-Ḥabbāb al-'Uklī of Kufa
Zayd ibn Abū az-Zurqā' of Mosul
Zayd ibn al-Ḥasan of Egypt
Zayd ibn 'Awn
Zayd ibn Dāwūd of Madina
Zayd ibn Bishr of Egypt who lived in North Africa
Ziyād ibn Yūnus of Egypt
Ziyād ibn 'Abdullāh aṭ-Ṭulayṭilī
Ziyād ibn al-Haytham
Zakariyā' ibn Nāfi'
Zakariyā' ibn Yaḥyā as-Sutūrī
Zakariyā' ibn Yaḥyā ibn al-Ḥakam al-Qarawī
Zakariyā' ibn Darīd al-Ash'ath
Zuhayr ibn 'Abbād ar-Rawāsī
Zuhayr ibn Muḥammad of Makka
Az-Zubayr ibn Bakkār az-Zubayrī
Az-Zubayr ibn Ḥabīb ibn Thābit az-Zubayrī

Zanbar ibn Abū al-Azhar
Zama'a ibn 'Abdullāh ibn Rabī'a
Zurāra ibn 'Abdullāh of North Africa
Zabbān ibn Ḥabīb ibn Zabbān
Zahra ibn Ma'bad
Ziyād ibn Sa'd

THE LETTER ṬĀ'

Ṭalḥa ibn Yaḥyā ibn an-Nu'mān az-Zuraqī of Madina
Ṭāhir ibn Midrār aṭ-Ṭanāfisī of Kufa
Ṭāhir ibn 'Amr of Nasib
Ṭufayl ibn 'Abdullāh an-Anṣārī
Ṭalq ibn Ghanm of Kufa

THE LETTER ṢĀD

Qāḍī Ṣāliḥ ibn Bayān as-Sayrāfī
Ṣāliḥ ibn Muḥammad al-Khwārizmī
Ṣāliḥ ibn 'Abdullāh at-Tirmidhī
Ṣāliḥ ibn 'Abdullāh al-Qayrawāni
Ṣabāḥ ibn 'Abdullāh, Abū Bishr of Basra
Ṣabāḥ ibn Muḥārib ad-Dārī
Siqlab ibn Ziyād of Kairouan
Aṣ-Ṣalt ibn Muḥammad ibn Himām al-Khārikī of Basra
Ṣadaqa ibn 'Abdullāh as-Samīn of Damascus
Ṣakhr ibn Muḥammad al-Ḥājibī

THE LETTER ḌĀD

Aḍ-Ḍaḥḥāk ibn 'Uthmān ibn aḍ-Ḍaḥḥāk of Madina
Aḍ-Ḍaḥḥāk ibn Mukhallad ibn Abū 'Āṣim an-Nabīl of Basra
Ḍamra ibn Rabī'a of Ramla
Ḍimām ibn Ismā'īl of Egypt

THE LETTER KĀF

Kāmil ibn Ṭalḥa al-Jahdarī of Basra
Kathīr ibn Hishām
Kathīr ibn al-Walīd

The Letter Lām

Layth ibn Khālid al-Khurāsānī
Layth ibn 'Āṣim al-Qatabānī, Abū Zurāra

The Letter Mīm

Muḥammad ibn Mālik, his son
Muḥammad ibn Idrīs ash-Shāfi'ī of Makka
Muḥammad ibn Fulayḥ of Madina
Muḥammad ibn Ṣadaqa of Fadak
Muḥammad ibn aḍ-Ḍaḥḥāk ibn 'Uthmān ibn aḍ-Ḍaḥḥāk al-Khuzāmī of Madina
These four in order related from Mālik and kept his company.
Muḥammad ibn Ḥabīb al-Lawnī of Syria
Muḥammad ibn 'Umar al-Wāqidī of Baghdad
Muḥammad ibn an-Nu'mān ibn Shibl of Egypt
Muḥammad ibn 'Abdullāh aṣ-Ṣan'ānī
Muḥammad ibn Khālid ibn Ḥarmala al-Basri
Muḥammad ibn 'Abdullāh ibn al-Qāsim al-'Umayrī
Muḥammad ibn 'Abdullāh al-Ghādī
Muḥammad ibn Abī Nūḥ al-Murādī of Baghdad
Muḥammad ibn 'Abdullāh az-Zubayrī of Kufa
Muḥammad ibn Salama al-Ḥarrānī
Muḥammad ibn 'Abd ar-Raḥmān ibn ar-Raddād
ibn Raddād of Madina
Muḥammad ibn Yazīd al-Anṣārī
Muḥammad ibn Mūsā al-Anṣārī, Abū Ghaziya
Muḥammad ibn Yūnus ibn Mu'ādh al-Qurashī of Basra
Muḥammad ibn Sulaymān, nephew of Dāwūd al-Ḥarrānī, Buma
Muḥammad ibn Khālid ibn Ghanma of Basra
Muḥammad ibn Khālid al-'Umarī of Madina
Muḥammad ibn Khālid al-Jundī
Muḥammad ibn Ja'far ibn Ṣabīḥ of Egypt
Muḥammad ibn Ḥātim ibn Ṣabīḥ of Khurasan
Muḥammad ibn 'Abdullāh ibn Raysān
Muḥammad ibn Ṣāliḥ ibn Fayrūz, a Mawruzī
Muḥammad ibn al-Ḥasan ibn Khālid at-Tirmidhī

Muḥammad ibn ʻAbdullāh ibn al-Muthannā al-Anṣārī, the Qāḍī of Basra
Muḥammad ibn ʻAbdullāh ibn Sinān al-Ḥārithī
Muḥammad ibn ʻAbdullāh ar-Raqqāshī, the father of Abū Qilāba of Basra
Muḥammad ibn ʻAwn az-Ziyādī
Muḥammad ibn Ibrāhīm ibn Abī Sukayt al-Ḥallī
Muḥammad ibn Ayyūb ar-Raqqī
Muḥammad ibn Jaʻfar al-Juʻfī of Madina
Muḥammad ibn Jaʻfar al-Ghanawī of Basra
Muḥammad ibn Jaʻfar al-Warkālī
Muḥammad ibn Mukhallad Abū Muslim ar-Raʻīnī of Syria
Muḥammad ibn Shujāʻ ibn Nabhān al-Khurāsānī
Muḥammad ibn Salām al-Madanī
Muḥammad ibn Isḥāq al-Lu'lu'ī
Muḥammad ibn Muḥammad ibn Ismāʻīl ibn ʻUbayd, the brother of Ḥuwayra, a Basran
Muḥammad ibn Usāma of Madina
Muḥammad ibn al-Ḥajjāj al-Makhzūmī
Muḥammad ibn al-Ḥajjāj al-Muḍfir of Baghdad
Muḥammad ibn Muṣʻab al-Furqasānī of Syria
Muḥammad ibn Ramḥ of Egypt
Muḥammad ibn Muʻāwiya an-Naysābūrī
Muḥammad ibn Zanbūr ibn Abī al-Azhar al-Makkī
Muḥammad ibn ʻAbd ar-Raḥmān ibn Shurūsh of Sanʻa
Muḥammad ibn al-Mubārak aṣ-Ṣūrī
Muḥammad ibn Abi Kathīr ibn Abī ʻAṭā' as-Sanʻānī
Muḥammad ibn Muḥammad al-Muqaddasī
Muḥammad ibn Yasūmā of Qarawan
Muḥammad ibn ʻAmr al-ʻAnawī
Muḥammad ibn Sakīn ibn ar-Riḥāl
Muḥammad ibn Yaḥyā ibn ʻAbd al-Hamīd, Abū Ghassān of Madina
Muḥammad ibn Bilāl of Baghdad
Muḥammad ibn Abī Bilāl
Muḥammad ibn Muslim al-Madanī

Muḥammad ibn Ja'far al-Mawānī
Muḥammad ibn 'Umar ibn 'Aṭā' al-Balghāwī of Damietta
Muḥammad ibn Mūsā ar-Ra'īnī of Barqa
Muḥammad ibn Marwān aṣ-Ṣadafī of Kufa
Muḥammad ibn Zayd al-Anṣārī
Muḥammad ibn Muzāham al-Marwazī
Muḥammad ibn Abī al-Khaṭīb of Antioch
Muḥammad ibn 'Umar ibn al-Walīd
Muḥammad ibn 'Īsā aṭ-Ṭabbā'
Muḥammad ibn al-Mughira al-Makhzumi
Muḥammad ibn Abī Muqātil
Muḥammad ibn Ḥayyān, Abū al-Aḥwaṣ al-Baghawī
Muḥammad ibn 'Uthmān ibn Rabī'a ar-Rā'ī
Muḥammad ibn Yaḥyā al-Iskandarānī
Muḥammad ibn Ḥarb ibn Sulaymān al-Makkī
Muḥammad ibn Ḥarb ibn Qaṭn ibn Qabīṣa al-Hāji' of Basra
Muḥammad ibn Sa'īd an-Nasā'ī of Andalusia
Muḥammad ibn Ḥarb al-Abrash
Muḥammad ibn 'Īsā ibn al-Qāsim ibn Samī'
Muḥammad ibn Abī 'Uthmān of Egypt
Muḥammad ibn al-Faḍl of Makka
Muḥammad ibn Salama al-Ḥarrānī
Muḥammad ibn 'Uthmān ibn Khālid al-'Uthmānī
Muḥammad ibn Abī al-Muṭī' of Egypt
Muḥammad ibn Abī al-Wazīr of Basra
Muḥammad ibn Aḥmad ibn Ḥammād Raghba of Egypt
Muḥammad ibn 'Imrān ibn Abī Laylā of Kufa
Muḥammad ibn Bukayr ibn Wāṣil al-Ḥaḍramī of Baghdad
Muḥammad ibn 'Attāb Abū Labīd as-Sarkhasī
Muḥammad ibn Khalaf al-Balkhī
Muḥammad ibn Bishr at-Tanīsī
Muḥammad ibn Yaḥyā al-Aslamī of Egypt
Muḥammad ibn al-Ḥakam al-Lakhmī of North Africa
Muḥammad ibn Mu'āwiya al-Aṭrābulisī
Qāḍī Muḥammad ibn Bashīr of Andalusia
Muḥammad ibn 'Abd al-A'lā Abū al-Khaṭṭāb of North Africa

Muḥammad ibn Rabī'a al-Ḥaḍramī of Tripoli
Muḥammad ibn 'Abdullāh ibn Ḥakam of Barqa
Muḥammad ibn 'Abdullāh ibn Qays of Barqa
Muḥammad ibn 'Alīm
Muḥammad ibn Ismā'īl of Homs and Madina
Muḥammad ibn Mukhallad al-Ḥaḍramī
Muḥammad ibn Qan'ab of Madina
Muḥammad ibn al-Ḥasan ibn Anas of San'a
Muḥammad ibn 'Abdullāh al-Maṭmāṭī of Andalusia
Muḥammad ibn Zakariyā' ibn Yaḥyā al-Ma'āfirī of Alexandria
Mūsā ibn Ja'far al-Ja'farī
Mūsā ibn A'yan al-Jazarī
Mūsā ibn Muḥammad al-Anṣārī of Kufa
Mūsā ibn Muḥammad ibn 'Aṭā' al-Balghāwī, known as Abū Ṭāhir al-Muqaddasī
Qāḍī Mūsā ibn Dāwūd aḍ-Ḍabbī, of Tarsus
Mūsā ibn Salama of Egypt
Mūsā ibn 'Abdullāh ibn Abī 'Alqama al-Qarawī
Mūsā ibn Ibrāhīm al-Marwazī
Mūsā ibn Ibrāhīm al-'Uthmānī
Mūsā ibn Abi Bakr al-Bakrī
Mūsā ibn Tamīm of Egypt
Mu'āfī ibn 'Imrān aẓ-Ẓuhrī of Mosul
Mukhallad ibn Yazīd al-Ḥarrānī
Muḥammad ibn Abān al-Bannā'
Mukhallad ibn Khidāsh of Baghdad
Marwān ibn Muḥammad aṭ-Ṭāṭirī
Marwān ibn Muḥammad as-Sanjārī
Mansur ibn Abi Muzāḥim of Baghdad
Manṣūr ibn Salama Abū Salama al-Khuzā'ī of Basra
Manṣūr ibn Ya'qūb ibn Abī Nuwayra of Kufa
Manṣūr ibn Ismā'īl at-Till of Harran
Muḥriz ibn 'Awn of Basra
Muḥriz ibn Salama al-'Adawī
Muḥriz al-Madanī
Mu'allā ibn Manṣūr ar-Rāzī

Mu'allā ibn al-Faḍl al-Baṣrī
Mālik ibn Ismā'īl Abū Ghassān of Kufa
Mālik ibn Sulaymān al-Harawī
Mālik ibn Ḥuwayṣ al-Harawī
Mālik ibn Ibrāhīm an-Nakhā'ī
Mālik ibn 'Uthmān al-Ma'āfirī, Abū Ṭālib of Kairouan
Mālik ibn Hārūn al-Aswānī
Al-Mughīra ibn al-Ḥasan, the uncle of Sa'īd ibn 'Ufayr
Al-Mughīra ibn Siqlāb of Harran
Al-Mughīra ibn al-Ḥasan al-Hāshimī of Madina
Maslama ibn Sulaymān of Andalusia
Maslama ibn 'Alī ibn al-Ḥasan of Syria
Ma'n ibn 'Īsā
Muṭarrif ibn 'Abdullāh
Makkī ibn Ibrāhīm al-Ḥanẓalī of Balkh
Maḥmūd ibn Maymūn of Kufa
Munabbih ibn 'Uthmān of Damascus
Miskīn ibn Bukayr of Harran
Mujā'a ibn az-Zubayr
Ma'mar ibn Khālid ar-Surūjī
Mufaḍḍal ibn Faḍāla of Egypt
Mufaḍḍal ibn Ṣadaqa
Ma'mar ibn Sulaymān of Basra
Mūsāyyab ibn Sharīk
Muqatil ibn Ibrāhīm of Syria
Mahdī ibn Ibrāhīm of Syria
Mahdī ibn Hilal
Muṣ'ab ibn 'Abdullāh az-Zubayrī
Muṣ'ab ibn 'Uthmān az-Zubayrī
Muṣ'ab ibn Ibrāhīm al-Qurashī
Mihrān ibn Abī 'Imrān ar-Razī
Maysar ibn Ismā'īl al-Ḥalabī
Mubārak ibn Mujāhid, Abū al-Azhar ar-Rāzī
Minjāb ibn al-Ḥārith of Basra
Mirdas ibn Muḥammad ibn Abī Bilāl al-Ash'arī
Manī' ibn Mājid, Abū Maṭar of San'a

Mu'āwiya ibn Hishām al-Anṣārī of Kufa
Mas'ada ibn al-Yasa' of Kufa
Mu'āwiya ibn Ḥafṣ as-Sabī'ī of Hums
Mu'āwiya ibn al-Faḍl al-Qarawī
Mandal ibn 'Ali al-'Anazī
Mughīth ibn Budayl, a Sarakhsī
Al-Mundhir ibn 'Alī al-Makhzūmī of Madina
Al-Māḍī ibn Muḥammad ibn Mas'ūd of Basra
Marḥūm ibn 'Abdi-l-'Azīz al-'Aṭṭār of Basra
Muslim, and it is said Salm, ibn Maymūn al-Khawwāṣ of Syria
Muṭarrā al-Aqra' al-Qarawī

THE LETTER NŪN

An-Nu'mān ibn 'Abd as-Salām al-Iṣbahānī
An-Nu'mān ibn Busl of Basra
Nūḥ ibn Abī Maryam, Abū 'Iṣma of Balkh
Nūḥ ibn Yazīd al-Mu'addib of Baghdad
Nūḥ ibn Maryam
An-Naḍr ibn Shumayl, a Marwazī
An-Naḍr ibn Shabkal of Makka
An-Naḍr ibn Ṭāhir of Basra
Naṣr ibn Bāb of Khurasan
Naṣr ibn Ṭarīf of Basra, Abū Khawla
Naṣr ibn Ibrāhīm
Nāfi' ibn Yazīd of Egypt
Nu'aym ibn Ḥammād of Khurasan

THE LETTER 'AYN

'Abdullāh ibn Nāfi' aṣ-Ṣā'igh of Madina
'Abdullāh ibn Nāfi' az-Zubayrī of Madina
'Abdullāh ibn Maslama al-Qa'nabī of Basra
'Abdullāh ibn Wahb of Basra
'Abdullāh ibn al-Ḥakam of Egypt
'Abdullāh ibn 'Uthmān ibn Abī Rawwād of Basra
'Abdullāh ibn 'Awn al-Kharrāz of Baghdad
'Abdullāh ibn Muḥammad ibn Abī al-Wazīr of Ta'if

'Abdullāh ibn Maymūn al-Wammām of Balkh
'Abdullāh ibn 'Uthmān al-Ma'āfirī of Qarawan
'Abdullāh ibn 'Abbād al-Baṣrī, the nephew of Ḥammād ibn Salama
'Abdullāh ibn 'Abd al-Wahhāb al-Jumaḥī
'Abdullāh ibn 'Anbasa al-'Uthmānī
'Abdullāh ibn 'Amr ibn Umayya aḍ-Ḍamrī
'Abdullāh Ibn Umayya an-Naḥḥās
'Abdullāh ibn Ibrāhīm al-Ghifārī of Madina
'Abdullāh ibn 'Amr al-Fihrī
'Abdullāh ibn Idrīs al-Ja'farī
'Abdullāh ibn Ibrāhīm al-Bayyāḍ
'Abdullāh ibn 'Abd al-Malik
'Abdullāh ibn Yazīd al-Qaṣīr of Makka
'Abdullāh ibn al-Ḥārith al-Makhzūmī of Makka
'Abdullāh ibn 'Uthmān ibn Isḥāq ibn Sa'd ibn Abī Waqqāṣ
'Abdullāh ibn 'Alī ibn Mihrān of Kufa
'Abdullāh ibn Ḥakam, Abū Bakr az-Zāhirī
'Abdullāh ibn Dāwūd al-Kharībī of Basra
'Abdullāh ibn Dāwūd at-Tammār of Wasit
'Abdullāh ibn Numayr al-Hamdānī of Kufa
'Abdullāh ibn al-Walīd al-'Adanī
'Abdullāh ibn Sa'īd ibn 'Abd al-Malik ibn Marwān of Madina
'Abdullāh ibn ar-Rabī'
'Abdullāh ibn Muḥammad ibn Abī Farwa
'Abdullāh ibn Muṭī' of Baghdad
'Abdullāh ibn Muslim ibn Rashīd al-Hāshimī
'Abdullāh ibn Rabī'a al-'Adanī of Maṣṣīṣā, their client
'Abdullāh ibn Muslim
'Abdullāh ibn Muḥammad ibn 'Umāra al-Qaddāḥ
'Abdullāh ibn Wāqid al-Ḥarrānī
'Abdullāh ibn al-Jarrāḥ al-Mursābī
'Abdullāh ibn 'Īsā ibn 'Aṭā' ibn Yasār of Madina
'Abdullāh ibn Muḥammad al-Buqaylī of Harran
'Abdullāh ibn Rajā' al-Makkī of Basra
'Abdullāh ibn Suwār al-'Anbarī, the Qāḍī of Egypt

'Abdullāh ibn Mālik al-Khuzā'ī
'Abdullāh ibn Yūsuf at-Tanīsī
'Abdullāh ibn Muḥammad ibn Hamīd ibn al-Aswad, the nephew of Ibn Mahdī
'Abdullāh ibn Mus'ab ibn Thābit az-Zubayri
'Abdullāh (and it is said 'Abd ar-Raḥmān) ibn Yaḥyā ibn Sa'īd al-'Udhurī of Madina
'Abdullāh ibn 'Umar ibn al-Qāsim al-'Umarī
'Abdullāh ibn Mu'ādh of San'a
'Abdullāh ibn an-Naḍr ibn Anas ibn Mālik of Basra
'Abdullāh ibn Abī Ḥassān of Kairouan
'Abdullāh ibn Ṣāliḥ, the scribe of al-Layth
'Abdullāh ibn as-Samḥ of Egypt
'Abdullāh ibn Muḥammad al-Bayṭārī of Egypt
'Abdullāh ibn Ḥammād al-Khawlānī of Barqa
'Abdullāh ibn Abī Ghassān al-Qarawī
'Abdullāh ibn 'Abd al-Ḥamīd al-Ḥanafī of Basra
'Abdullāh ibn 'Uthmān, Abū Ṭālib al-Abzārī
Qāḍī 'Abdullāh ibn 'Abbād
'Abdullāh ibn Dāwūd aṭ-Ṭayālisī
'Abdullāh ibn 'Abd al-Jalīl, his teacher
'Abd ar-Raḥmān ibn Ḥāzim ar-Ramlī
'Abd ar-Raḥmān ibn al-Qāsim of Egypt
'Abd ar-Raḥmān ibn Muḥammad al-Muḥāribī
'Abd ar-Raḥmān ibn 'Amr al-Ḥarrānī
'Abd ar-Raḥmān ibn 'Abdullāh ibn 'Umar al-'Umarī
'Abd ar-Raḥmān ibn 'Abdullāh Abū Sa'īd al-Hāshimī of Makka
'Abd ar-Raḥmān ibn Abi Ja'far ad-Dimyāṭī
'Abd ar-Raḥmān ibn Muḥammad al-Muḥammadī of Madina
'Abd ar-Raḥmān ibn Muslim ibn Wāqid
'Abd ar-Raḥmān ibn Ghazwān Qirād, Abū Nūḥ
'Abd ar-Raḥmān ibn al-Mughīra al-Khuzāmī
'Abd ar-Raḥmān ibn Dabīs al-Malā'ī of Kufa
'Abd ar-Raḥmān ibn Yūnus al-Ja'farī of Kufa
'Abd ar-Raḥmān ibn Yaḥyā Raysān of Baghdad
'Abd ar-Raḥmān ibn Muqātil, Abū Sahl, the uncle of al-Qa'nabī

'Abd ar-Raḥmān ibn al-Mubārak al-'Ayshī
'Abd ar-Raḥmān ibn Ibrāhīm ar-Rāssī
'Abd ar-Raḥmān ibn al-Jahm of Kairouan
'Abd ar-Raḥmān ibn Zayd ibn Aslam of Madina
'Abd ar-Raḥmān ibn 'Abdullāh al-'Umarī of Nishapur
'Abd ar-Raḥmān ibn Hind of Andalusia
'Abd ar-Raḥmān ibn Mūsā al-Huwārī of Andalusia
'Abd ar-Raḥmān ibn 'Abdullāh al-Ishbūnī of Andalusia
'Ubaydullah ibn 'Abd al-Majīd, called 'Abdullāh, Abū 'Alī al-Ḥanafī of Basra
'Ubaydullah ibn Sufyān al-'Awāmī of Basra
'Ubaydullah ibn Muḥammad ibn 'Ā'isha at-Tamīmī
'Ubaydullah ibn 'Amr al-'Umawī
'Ubayd ibn Ḥayyān of Damascus
'Ubayd ibn Qurra of Baghdad
'Ubayd ibn 'Ubaydullāh ibn 'Utba, a Marwazī
'Ubayd ibn 'Abd ar-Raḥmān al-Yamānī
'Ubayd ibn Hisham al-Ḥalabī al-Qalānisī, Abū Nu'aym
'Abd al-'Azīz ibn 'Imrān az-Zuhrī
'Abd al-'Azīz ibn 'Abd al-Malik al-Uwaysī
'Abd al-'Azīz ibn Yaḥyā of Madina
'Abd al-'Azīz ibn 'Abdullāh al-Unaysī
'Abd al-'Azīz ibn Abi Rajā'
'Abd al-'Azīz ibn Yaḥyā al-Hāshimī, their client, of Madina
'Abd al-'Azīz ibn 'Abdullāh al-'Āmirī of Baghdad
'Abd al-'Azīz ibn Abi Rawwād of Khurasan
'Abd al-Malik ibn al-Mājishūn
'Abd al-Malik ibn Maslama al-Qa'nabī of Basra, the brother of 'Abdullāh
'Abd al-Malik ibn Maslama al-Qurashī of Egypt
'Abd al-Malik ibn Ziyād an-Naṣībī
'Abd al-Malik ibn Qarīb al-Aṣma'ī
'Abd al-Malik ibn Yazīd al-Ḥarazī
'Abd al-Malik ibn 'Amr ibn 'Āmir al-Qa'dī
'Abd al-Malik ibn 'Abd al-'Azīz an-Nasā'ī, Abū Naṣr at-Tammār
'Abd al-Malik ibn Mihrān ar-Rifā'ī

ʿAbd al-Malik ibn Abī Karīma, the Qāḍī of Kairouan
ʿAbd al-Malik ibn Muzammil al-Qarqashānī
ʿAbd al-Malik ibn al-Ḥakam ar-Ramlī
ʿAbd as-Salām ibn Salama ibn Yazdād of Madina
ʿAbd as-Salām ibn Ṣāliḥ Abū'ṣ-Ṣalt al-Harawī
ʿAbd al-Ḥamīd ibn Sulaymān al-Khuzāʿī, the brother of Fulayḥ ibn Sulaymān, of Madina
ʿAbd al-Ḥamīd ibn ʿAbd ar-Raḥmān ibn Farwa
ʿAbd al-Ḥamīd ibn Yaḥyā of Madina
ʿAbd al-Ḥamīd ibn Yaḥyā
ʿAbd al-Ḥamīd ibn Ṣāliḥ al-Burjumī of Kufa
ʿAbd al-Wahhāb ibn Nāfiʿ of Madina
ʿAbd al-Wahhāb ibn ʿAṭā'al-Khaffāf al-ʿAjlī of Basra
ʿAbd al-Wahhāb ibn Mūsā az-Zuhrī
ʿAbd al-Karīm ibn Rawḥ ibn ʿAnbasa
ʿAbd al-Karīm ibn Aʿyan of Egypt
ʿAbd al-Aʿlā ibn Ḥammād an-Narsī of Basra
ʿAbd al-Aʿlā ibn Mushir of Damascus
ʿAbd ar-Raḥmān ibn Sulaymān ar-Rāzī
ʿAbd ar-Raḥīm ibn Mūsā al-ʿAttād
ʿAbd ar-Raḥmān ibn Wāqid al-Wāqidī of Baghdad
ʿAbd al-Raḥīm ibn Ashras of Qarawan
ʿAbd *al-Kabīr* ibn ʿAbd al-Majīd Abū Bakr al-Ḥanafī
ʿAbd al-Jabbār ibn ʿUmar al-Aylī of Syria
ʿAbd al-Majīd ibn Abī Rawwād of Makka
ʿAbd al-Ghaffār ibn Dāwūd ibn Mihrān of Harran
ʿAbd al-ʿAẓīm ibn Ḥabīb ibn Raʿbān Abū Bakr al-Ḥumṣī
ʿAbd al-Razzāq ibn Himām of Sanʿa
ʿAbd al-Quddūs ibn al-Ḥajjāj, Abū al-Mughīra of Hums
ʿAbd al-ʿAẓīm ibn ʿAbdullāh ath-Thaqafī
ʿAbd al-Jabbār ibn Saʿīd al-Masāḥiqī
ʿAbd al-Mutaʿālī ibn Ṣāliḥ
ʿAbd al-Aḥad ibn Abī Zarrār al-Ghassānī
ʿAbd al-Ḥakam ibn Maysara al-Marwazī
ʿUmar ibn Hārūn al-Balkhī
ʿUmar ibn Rāshid, and it is said, ʿAmr, the client of Abān ibn ʿUthmān

'Umar ibn 'Iṣām of Madina
'Umar ibn Ibrāhīm ibn Mālik al-Farawī of Kufa
'Umar ibn Muḥammad ibn Yaḥyā 'Umar ibn Abī Salama ibn 'Abd ar-Raḥmān of the Hijaz
'Umar ibn Ayyūb al-Madanī
'Umar ibn Qays ibn Maysara ar-Rāzī
'Umar ibn Khālid of Egypt
'Umar ibn Ayyūb al-Barqī
'Umar ibn Ayyūb al-Ma'āfirī of Qarawan
'Umar ibn Sumayk, also called Samk, who related from as-Sahmī
'Umar ibn Sa'īd, Abū Dāwūd of Kufa
'Uthmān ibn 'Umar ibn Fāris of Basra
'Uthman ibn 'Amr ibn Sāj al-Ḥarrānī
'Uthman ibn 'Abd ar-Raḥmān aṭ-Ṭawā'ifī of Harran
'Uthman ibn Sa'īd ibn Kathīr al-Ḥumsī
'Uthman ibn Khālid al-'Uthmānī
'Uthman ibn 'Abdullāh al-Qurashī
'Uthman ibn 'Abdullāh aṭ-Ṭayyibī
'Uthman ibn Ṣāliḥ ibn Ṣafwān of Egypt
'Uthman ibn 'Abdullāh ibn Muḥammad al-Āmadī
'Alī ibn Ziyād, the *faqīh* of Tunis
'Alī ibn Ziyād, the *muḥtasib* of Alexandria
'Alī ibn al-Jarūd an-Naysābūrī
'Alī ibn Abā 'Alī al-Lahabi
'Alī ibn Hishām ibn al-Barīd of Kufa
'Alī ibn 'Ubaydullāh ibn Muḥammad ibn 'Umar ibn 'Alī ibn Abī Ṭālib
'Alī ibn Yūnus al-Balkhī
'Alī ibn 'Abd al-Ḥamīd al-Ma'ī of Kufa
'Alī ibn al-Ḥakam al-Marwazī
'Alī ibn al-Ḥasan ibn Abān ar-Rāzī Kirā'
'Alī ibn Abī Bakr al-Aslamī of Rayy
'Alī ibn Thābit al-Jazarī
'Alī ibn Muḥammad Abū al-Ḥasan al-Madā'inī al-Akhbārī
'Alī ibn al-Ja'd al-Jawharī of Baghdad
'Alī ibn ar-Rabī' ibn ad-Da'ī al-Fazarī of Kufa

'Alī ibn Muḥammad ibn al-Ḥasan al-'Alawī
'Alī ibn Yūsuf al-Baṣrī
'Alī ibn Sālim al-Jumaḥī
'Alī ibn Qutayba ar-Rifā'ī
'Alī ibn Sa'īd, the *mu'adhdhin,*
'Alī ibn Sa'īd at-Tirmidhī
'Alīibn 'Īsā al-Ghassāni
'Alī ibn Ma'bad ibn Shaddād al-'Abadī of Egypt
'Alī ibn Hārūn ar-Rassī
'Alī ibn al-Ḥasan ash-Shāmī of Ṣa'īd
'Alī ibn Zādawayh
'Alī ibn Abī al-Wazīr
'Alī ibn Yūnus al-Qarawī
'Alī ibn Mu'dim ibn al-Mu'dim of Basra
'Alī ibn Sa'd, Abū Dāwūd al-Ḥafrī of Kufa
'Umar ibn 'Imrān al-Madanī
'Umar ibn 'Uthmān az-Zuhrī of Madina
'Abbās ibn Abī Salama of Madina
'Abbās ibn al-Walīd al-Qurashī of Egypt
'Abbās ibn Nāṣiḥ al-Jazīrī of Andalusia
'Abbās ibn al-Walīd al-Fārisī of Tunis
'Amr ibn Ḥafṣ al-Aylī
'Amr ibn al-Haytham al-Qaṭī'ī of Basra
'Amr ibn Ḥakkām of Basra
'Amr ibn Muḥammad al-'Anqadī of Kufa
'Amr ibn Abī Salama of Tanis
'Amr ibn Marzūq of Basra
'Amr ibn Ziyād at-Tūtānī
'Amr ibn Yazīd of Egypt
'Amr ibn Marwān al-Aylī
'Amr ibn Ziyād al-Bāhilī of Egypt
'Amr ibn Muḥammad al-'Uthmānī
'Īsā ibn Zayd ibn 'Alī al-Ḥasanī
'Īsā ibn Ja'far al-Ja'farī
'Īsā ibn Yūnus ibn Abī Isḥāq as-Sabī'ī
'Īsā ibn Maymūn al-Makkī

'Īsā ibn Mūsā Ghanjār of the Hijaz
'Īsā ibn Minā Qālūn of Madina
'Īsā ibn Muslim aṣ-Ṣaffār
'Īsā ibn Khālid al-Yamāmī
'Īsā ibn Wāqid al-Ḥanafī
'Īsā ibn Abī Fāṭima ar-Rāzī
'Īsā ibn Shajara at-Tūnisī
'Īsā ibn Mūsā ibn Ḥamīd of Madina
'Īsā ibn Yūnus ar-Ramlī
'Īsā ibn Khālid of Damascus
'Āṣim ibn Muḥajja' Abū ar-Rabī' al-Basri
'Āṣim ibn Abī Bakr az-Zuhrī, Abū Ḍamra of Madina
'Āṣim ibn 'Alī ibn 'Āṣim al-Wāsiṭī
'Āṣim ibn 'Abd al-'Azīz al-Ashja'ī
'Uqba ibn Khālid as-Sakūnī of Kufa
'Uqba ibn 'Alqama al-Ma'āfirī of Marw
'Uqba ibn Ḥassān aṣ-Ṣaḥarī
'Uqba ibn 'Abdullāh al-Ḥamīdi, a Marwazī
'Uqba ibn Muḥammad al-Marwazī
'Āmir ibn Ṣāliḥ ibn 'Abdullāh ibn az-Zubayrī of Madina
'Āmir ibn Abī Ja'far of Andalusia
'Āmir ibn Mayyār
'Āmir ibn 'Abdullāh al-Ghāfiqī
'Abbād ibn Kathīr
'Abbād ibn 'Abbād al-Muhallab, Abū Mu'āwiya of Basra
'Abbād ibn Ṣuhayb Abū Bakr aṭ-Ṭā'ī
Al-'Alā' ibn 'Abd al-Jabbār of Makka
Al-'Alā' ibn Kathīr of Egypt
'Adī ibn Ḥātim ibn al-Faḍl, Abū Ḥātim al-Baṣrī
'Umāra ibn Zayd ibn 'Alī ibn Maṭar ar-Rahāwī
'Imrān ibn Abān al-Wāsiṭī
'Amr ibn Yazīd ibn Jarjīs al-Fārisī of Egypt
'Aṭṭāb ibn Khālid al-Makhzūmī
'Atīq ibn Ya'qūb ibn Ṣādiq az-Zubayrī
'Umayr ibn 'Ammār al-Hamdānī of Kufa
'Umāma ibn 'Amr as-Sahmī

'Awn ibn 'Umāra of Egypt
'Afīf ibn Sālim of Mosul
'Affān ibn Sayyār al-Jurjānī
'Anbasa ibn Dāwūd of Qarawan
'Ubayda ibn 'Uthmān of Damascus

THE LETTER GHAYN

Ghiyāth ibn Ibrāhīm
Ghiyāth ibn al-Musayyab
Ghassān ibn Mālik
Al-Ghāzī ibn Qays of Andalusia

THE LETTER FĀ'

Fuḍayl ibn 'Iyāḍ of Makka
Fityān ibn Abū as-Samḥ of Egypt
Fuḍayl ibn Ṣāliḥ al-Ma'āfirī
Al-Fuḍayl ibn Dukayn, Abū Nu'aym of Kufa
Al-Faḍl ibn Ghānim, the Qāḍī of Baghdad
Al-Faḍl ibn Yaḥyā ibn al-Murawwaḥ, of Anbara
Al-Faḍl ibn al-'Abbās
Al-Faḍl ibn Manṣūr
Faḍl ibn Isḥāq
Fayyāḍ ibn Muḥammad ar-Raqqī
Faraḥ ibn Marzūq, Abū Muslim
Fihrī ibn Ḥibbān al-A'ṭaf of Basra
Furāt ibn Zuhayr ibn Abī 'Īsā al-Jazarī
Fiṭr ibn Ḥammād ibn Wāqid aṣ-Ṣaffār of Egypt
Fiṭr ibn Muḥammad al-Kuwārī

THE LETTER QĀF

Qāsim ibn Ma'n ibn 'Abd ar-Raḥmān al-Mas'ūdī of Kufa
Qāsim ibn al-Ḥakam ibn Aws of Madina
Qāsim ibn Yazīd al-Jarmī
Al-Qāsim ibn 'Abdullāh al-'Umarī
Al-Qāsim ibn Nāfi' of Madina
Al-Qāsim ibn Sulaymān aṭ-Ṭā'ifī

Qutayba ibn Sa'īd of Khurasan
Qays ibn ar-Rabī' of Kufa
Qaṭn ibn Ṣāliḥ of Damascus
Qudāma ibn Shihāb
Qudāma ibn Muḥammad ibn 'Uthmān
Qar'ūs ibn al-'Abbās of Andalusia

The Letter Sīn

Sa'īd ibn 'Ufayr of Egypt
Sa'īd ibn al-Jahm of Egypt
Sa'īd ibn 'Uthmān of Egypt
Sa'īd ibn al-Ḥakam ibn Abī Maryam
Sa'īd ibn Dāwūd ibn Abī Zanbar of Madina
Sa'īd ibn Miskīn ibn Abī az-Zard
Sa'id ibn Hishām of Madina
Sa'īd ibn Mūsā of Syria
Sa'īd ibn Abī Hilāl
Qāḍī Sa'īd ibn 'Abd ar-Raḥmān al-Jumaḥī
Sa'īd ibn 'Abd al-Jabbār al-Karābīsī of Egypt
Sa'īd ibn Sālim al-Qaddāḥ
Sa'īd ibn Salām ibn Sa'īd al-'Aṭṭār of Makka
Sa'īd ibn 'Abd al-Ḥamīd ibn Ja'far of Basra
Sa'īd ibn Manṣūr of Makka
Sa'īd ibn Muḥammad, called Ibn Mūsā, al-Azdī
Sa'īd ibn 'Amr az-Zubayrī
Sa'īd ibn Ma'n of Madina
Sa'īd ibn 'Īsā
Sa'īd ibn Manṣūr of Balkh
Sa'īd ibn al-Mughīra aṣ-Ṣayyād of Maṣṣīṣa
Sa'īd ibn aṣ-Ṣabbāḥ of Nishapur
Sa'īd ibn 'Awn of Basra
Sa'īd ibn 'Abd al-Jabbār, Abū Ḥammām of Homs
Sa'īd ibn 'Amr ibn az-Zubayr az-Zubayrī of Madina
Sa'īd ibn 'Abd ar-Raḥmān al-Masāḥiqī of Madina
Sa'īd ibn 'Abd ar-Raḥmān ibn Ja'far of Basra
Sa'īd ibn Maysara, Abū Hubayra of Kufa

Sulaymān ibn Bard of Egypt
Sulaymān ibn Dāwūd aṭ-Ṭayālisī
Sulaymān ibn Ja'far of Egypt
Sulaymān ibn Dāwūd az-Zahrānī
Sulaymān ibn Ḥayyān, Abū Khālid al-Aḥmarī of Kufa
Sulaymān ibn Sa'īd al-'Usfānī
Sulaymān ibn Maḥbūb al-'Abadānī
Sulaymān ibn Abī Badī' of Egypt
Sulaymān ibn 'Īsā as-Sijzī
Sulaymān ibn Yazīd, Abū al-Muthannā of Madina
Salama ibn al-Ghabbār of Damascus
Salm ibn Qutayba ash-Sha'īrī of Basra
Salm ibn al-Mughīra al-Azdī of Kufa
Suwayd ibn Sa'īd al-Ḥarthānī of Kufa
Suwayd ibn 'Abdullāh
Suwayd ibn 'Abd al-'Azīz ad-Dimishqī
Suwayd ibn Muḥammad of Kairouan
Sahl ibn Ḥammād, Abu 'Attāb ad-Dallāl of Basra
Sahl ibn Muzāḥim al-Marwazī
Sahl ibn Ziyād al-Bāhilī
Suhayl ibn 'Amr
Suhayl, and it is said Sahl, ibn Qudāma al-Ḥāṭibī
Salām ibn Wāqid
Suwaylim ibn Yūnus of Baghdad
Surayḥ ibn an-Nu'mān
Suwār ibn 'Ammār of Ramla
Sinān ibn 'Abdullāh
Suhaym, his servant
Salama ibn 'Abdullāh ibn Ka'b
Sālim al-Qaddāḥ of Egypt
Salama ibn Ziyād ibn Yūnus of Egypt

The Letter Shīn

Shu'ayb ibn Yaḥyā of Alexandria
Shabbāba ibn Sawwār, from Mada'in
Shu'ayb ibn Isḥāq of Damascus

Shu'ayb ibn Ḥarb, Abū Ṣāliḥ of Baghdad
Shu'ayb ibn al-Layth ibn Sa'd of Egypt
Shajara ibn 'Abdullāh ibn 'Īsā of Kairouan
Shajara ibn 'Abdullāh of Andalusia

The Letter Hā'

Al-Haytham ibn 'Adī aṭ-Ṭā'ifī of Baghdad
Al-Haytham ibn Jamīl of Antioch
Al-Haytham ibn Khārija of Khurasan
Al-Haytham ibn Ḥabīb ibn Ghazwān, Abū Sālim of Khurasan
Al-Haytham ibn 'Abdullāh al-Qurashī al-*Faqīh*
Al-Haytham ibn Khālid al-Khashshāb of Kufa
Al-Haytham ibn Yamān, Abū Bishr ar-Rāzī
Hishām ibn 'Abd al-Mālik, Abū al-Walīd aṭ-Ṭayālisī of Basra
Hishām ibn Bahrām al-Madā'inī
Hishām ibn 'Ammār as-Sulamī of Damascus
Hishām ibn 'Abdullāh ar-Rāzī
Hishām ibn Isḥāq ibn 'Amr, Abū Rabī'a of Egypt
Qāḍī Hishām ibn Yūsuf aṣ-Ṣan'ānī
Hishām ibn al-Qāsim, Abū an-Naṣr of Baghdad
Hishām ibn Muḥammad ar-Rib'ī
Hani' ibn al-Mutawakkil of Alexandria
Hayyāj ibn Bisṭām of Herat
Hammām ibn Muslim
Hushaym ibn Bashīr of Baghdad
Hārūn ibn Ṣāliḥ aṭ-Ṭā'ifī
Hārūn ibn 'Abdullāh az-Zuhrī, the Qāḍī of Baghdad
Hārūn ibn Ma'rūf of Baghdad

The Letter Wāw

Warqā' ibn 'Amr as-Sukūnī, a Madā'inī
Al-Walīd ibn Salama aṭ-Ṭawwāfī
Al-Walīd ibn Kathīr
Wahb ibn al-Mubārak, Abū Sab'
Wahb ibn 'Aṭiyya of Basra

Qāḍī Wahb ibn Wahb, Abū al-Bakhtarī
Wabara ibn Dāwūd of Andalusia

THE LETTER YĀ'

Yaḥyā ibn Mālik, his son
Yaḥyā ibn Yaḥyā at-Tamīmī of Nishapur
Yaḥyā ibn Yaḥyā al-Laythī of Andalusia
Yaḥyā ibn Bukayr of Egypt
Yaḥyā ibn Muḍar of Andalusia
Yaḥyā ibn Sa'īd ibn Abān, an Umawī
Yaḥyā ibn ibn Sulaymān aṭ-Ṭā'ifī
Yaḥyā ibn Ayyūb al-Miṣrī
Yaḥyā ibn Abī Zā'ida of Kufa
Yaḥyā ibn 'Abdullāh ibn Sālim al-'Umarī of Madina
Yaḥyā ibn Naṣr ibn Ḥājib al-Qurashī
Yaḥyā ibn 'Abdullāh ibn aḍ-Ḍaḥḥāk al-Bābilī
Yaḥyā ibn 'Abd aṣ-Ṣamad ibn Ma'qil ibn Wahb ibn Munabbih aṣ-Ṣan'ānī of Syria
Yaḥyā ibn Ḥamza ad-Dimishqī
Yaḥyā ibn Muḥammad al-Fihrī
Yaḥyā ibn Thābit al-Jundī
Yaḥyā, his scribe
Yaḥyā ibn al-Mubārak aṣ-Ṣan'ānī
Yaḥyā ibn Ṣāliḥ al-Waḥḥāẓī of Syria
Yaḥyā ibn Ibrāhīm ibn Dāwūd ibn Abī Qabīla of Madina
Yaḥyā ibn Muḥammad ibn Abī Qabīla of Madina
Yaḥyā ibn Salām al-Baṣrī, living in North Africa
Yaḥyā ibn 'Abdullāh ibn Ghaylān al-Jawharī of Baghdad
Yaḥyā ibn as-Sakan
Yaḥyā ibn 'Abd al-Ḥamīd al-Ḥamā'ī of Kufa
Yaḥyā ibn Quza'a al-Qurashī of Madina
Yaḥyā ibn Abī 'Umar al-'Adanī
Yaḥyā ibn Abī Bakr al-Kirmānī
Yaḥyā ibn al-Mutawakkil al-Bāhilī
Yaḥyā ibn Muḥammad al-Ḥārrī of the Hijaz
Yaḥyā ibn 'Anbasa al-Baghdādī

Yaḥyā ibn Ḥassān al-Ḥarrānī, known as at-Tanīsī
Yaḥyā ibn Maslama ibn Qan'ab
Yaḥyā ibn 'Abbād and Abū 'Abbād
Yaḥyā ibn Rāshid
Yaḥyā ibn aḍ-Ḍarīs
Yaḥyā ibn Kathīr of Madina
Yaḥyā ibn Muḥammad ibn 'Abbād as-Sijzī
Yaḥyā ibn Naḍla ibn Sulaym al-Khuzā'ī of Madina
Yaḥyā ibn al-'Iryān al-Harawī
Yaḥyā ibn Yazīd ibn Ḍimār al-Murādī of Alexandria
Yaḥyā ibn Sābiq of Madina
Yaḥyā ibn 'Abbād az-Zubayrī of Madina
Yaḥyā ibn Kathīr al-Mustamilī
Yūsuf ibn 'Awn of Kufa
Yūsuf ibn 'Amr ibn Yazīd ibn Daḥsaraw of Egypt
Yūsuf ibn Shu'ayb al-Lādhiqī
Yūsuf ibn Yūnus, Abū Ya'qūb al-Afṭas of Syria
Ya'qūb ibn al-Walīd al-Murrī
Ya'qūb ibn Ibrāhīm al-Ḥaḍramī
Ya'qūb ibn Ibrāhīm ibn Muṭarrif
Ya'qūb ibn Isḥāq ibn Abī 'Abbād al-Qilzimī
Ya'qūb ibn Kāsib of Madina
Yūnus ibn Yaḥyā ibn Nabāta of Madina
Yūnus ibn Muḥammad of Baghdad
Yūnus ibn Hārūn of Syria
Yūnus ibn 'Abdullāh ibn Sālim al-Khayyāt, the paternal relative of Mālik
Yūnus ibn 'Abdullāh al-Laythī al-'Umarī of Basra
Yūnus ibn Tamīm of Egypt
Yazīd ibn Abī Ḥakam al-'Umarī
Yazīd ibn Ibrāhīm at-Tustarī of Basra
Yazīd ibn Hārūn al-Wāsiṭī
Yazīd ibn Hārūn, the brother of Khālid al-Aṣbaḥī, and it is said aṣ-Ṣabbāḥ
Yazīd ibn Marwān, al-Khallāl of Baghdad
Yazīd ibn Mughlis al-Bāhilī

Yazīd ibn Wahb, Abū Mawhab of Syria
Yazīd ibn Muḥammad al-Jumaḥī of North Africa
Yazīd ibn 'Abd al-A'lā ibn Suwayd al-Ḥabshānī
Ya'īsh ibn Hishām al-Qarmasā'ī of Syria

NAMES WITH KUNYA

Abū Bakr ibn 'Abd al-'Azīz ibn 'Abdullāh ibn 'Umar ibn al-Khaṭṭāb
Abū Bakr ibn Shu'ayb al-Madanī
Abū Bishr ibn Maslama ibn Qa'nab
Abū Ḥammād ibn Sālim
Abū al-Ḥārith ibn Ṣalatān of Egypt
Abū Muḥammad al-Makhzūmī of Madina
Abū Ṭalḥa, the Qāḍī of Madina
Abū Ṭālib, 'Uthmān al-Ma'āfirī of Kairouan. He, and Allah knows best, is Abū Ṭālib al-Abzāzī, and you will become aware of him, and there is some dispute about him.
Abū Muḥammad al-Ḥakamī of Madina
Abū Mūsā the Qāḍī. I think that it is Hārūn az-Zuhrī, but the *kunya* of that man is known as Abū Yaḥyā, and Allah knows best.
Abū al-Muṭarrif ibn Abī al-Wazīr of Basra
Abū 'Ali, the companion of Muḥammad ibn al-Ḥasan
Abū Naṣr ath-Thammār of Kufa
Abū Naḍla al-Uwaysī
Abū's-Samḥ, and it is said Abū as-Samḥā', the father of Fityān of Egypt
Abū Sahl, the nephew of 'Utba ibn Muḥammad al-Yamānī
Abū Sa'īd, the client of the Banū Hāshim
Abū al-Haytham al-'Abdī
Abū Sawwār, and it is said Ibn Sawwār, al-Jawnī
Abū Qubayl 'Abdullāh ibn Mālik
Abū Maslama al-Khuzā'ī
Abū Sulayman al-Balkhī, the scribe of Ibn ar-Rimāḥ

The Imam and Qāḍī said, "We have mentioned in these letters, along with the preceding biographies, some of the names of those who transmitted *fiqh* and *ḥadīth* from Mālik among the great men and shaykhs before him, with him and after him, and the famous transmitters. There are about one thousand names.

We have left out many of those who were not famous for that or those who were unknown, and it was not known who they were or who did not have a *riwāya* mentioned from him, except about a state or description of a story, or someone who is mentioned in his *riwāya* while his *riwāya* is not sound according to the people who know tradition.

We have summarised that from another book of ours which compiles all of his transmitters which we have already mentioned. We confined ourselves in it to only mentioning their names and identifying them without turning to what they related from him or any of their reports since the reports about the *fuqahā'* among them will come in full detail after this section, Allah willing. The others are not our aim in this book. We were not occupied with it which would bring us out of its proper course and would be incompatible with the demands of its biography and chapters.

Allah is the One Who is asked for help, and He is enough for us and the Best of Protectors.

The Beginning of the *Ṭabaqāt* (Generations)

The *faqīh* and Qāḍī, Imam Abū al-Faḍl 'Iyāḍ ibn Mūsā ibn 'Iyāḍ, may Allah be pleased with him, said:

Now I will begin to arrange the intended generations according to well-known conventions. We found that the companions of Mālik among the *fuqahā'* can be arranged in three ranks:

The first rank are those who had prominence in knowledge during his life and whose deaths occurred near the time of his death.

The second are people after the first rank who were known for being with him a long time and keeping his company and were famous after him because of the *fiqh* they learned from him and their transmission.

The third are the people who kept his company when they were young and continued for a time after him, and they were near the followers of his followers. They were distinguished by the honour of having sat with him and the virtue of having listened to him.

We organised them in this way and we brought those after him, group by group. Allah is the Master of success.

The First Generation of the Companions of Mālik

THE PEOPLE OF MADINA AMONG THEM

Al-Mughīra ibn 'Abd ar-Raḥmān al-Makhzūmī

Az-Zubayr ibn Bakkār said, 'He is al-Mughīra ibn 'Abd ar-Raḥmān ibn al-Ḥārith ibn 'Abdullāh ibn 'Ayyāsh ibn Abī Rabī'a ibn al-Mughīra ibn 'Abdullāh ibn 'Umar ibn Makhzūm.'

Abū al-Qāsim al-Lālakā'ī said, 'It is also said about his lineage that he is 'Ibn 'Abd ar-Raḥmān ibn al-Ḥārith ibn 'Ayyāsh.' Al-Bukhārī stated that.

It is said that he is: 'Ibn 'Abd ar-Raḥmān ibn 'Abdullah ibn 'Ayyāsh, and his *kunya* was Abū Hashim.'

He said, 'His mother was Qurayba bint Muḥammad ibn 'Umar ibn Abī Salama ibn 'Abd al-Asad al-Makhzūmī.'

He listened to his father, Ibn 'Ajlān, 'Abdullāh ibn Sa'īd ibn Abī Hind, Hishām ibn 'Urwa, Mūsā ibn 'Uqba, Abū az-Zinād, Yazīd ibn Abī 'Ubayd and Mālik.

His sons, 'Abd ar-Raḥmān and 'Ayyāsh, related from him as did Muṣ'ab ibn 'Abdullāh, Abū Muṣ'ab az-Zuhrī, Ibrāhīm ibn Ḥamza az-Zubayrī, Qutayba ibn Sa'īd, Yaḥyā ibn Bukayr, Sa'īd ibn Abī Maryam, Ibn Mahdī, Ibn Kāsib and ad-Darāwardī.

Abū Zur'a said, 'There is no objection to him, but I prefer al-Mughīra in relating from Abū az-Zinad over that of his son.'

Al-Bukhārī related from him.

Yaḥyā said that he is trustworthy.

Ahmad ibn Ḥanbal said that there is no objection to him.

His position in knowledge and praise for him

Az-Zubayr stated, 'Al-Mughīra was the *Faqīh* of Madina after Mālik.'

Abū 'Umar ibn 'Abd al-Barr said, 'In the time of Mālik and after him *fatwā* was directed to al-Mughīra and Muhammad ibn Dīnār. 'Abd al-Malik ibn al-Mājishūn related that Ibn Abī Ḥāzim was the third of them in that, along with 'Uthmān ibn Kināna and Nāfi'.'

Ibn Bukayr said, 'Al-Mughīra gave *fatwās* during Mālik's lifetime. Al-Mughīra has a few books on *fiqh* in people's possession.'

Al-Wāqidī said, 'Al-Mughīra was the *Faqīh* of the people of Madina after Mālik.'

Another said, 'At the beginning of his affair, there was some disagreement between al-Mughīra and Mālik. Then it ceased and he sat with him.'

Muḥammad ibn 'Abdullāh al-Bakrī said, 'I saw al-Mughīra come to Mālik and he would sit near him in the gathering, and none like him was higher in the gathering.'

Another said, 'In Mālik's assembly, he had something like a bench on which he sat. Al-Makhzūmī was at his side and no one else sat with him if al-Makhzūmī was absent.'

Az-Zubayr said, 'The Amīr al-Mu'minīn Hārūn ar-Rashīd offered the office of *qāḍī* of Madina to him. Its salary was 4000 dīnārs, but he turned it down. Ar-Rashīd insisted on imposing that on him. He said, "By Allah, Amīr al-Mu'minīn, I would prefer for Shayṭān to throttle me than for me to be appointed to the office of *qāḍī*." Ar-Rashīd said, "There is nothing after this," and he excused him and rewarded him with a thousand dīnārs.'

Al-Wāqidī said, 'When ar-Rashīd brought Mālik and Abū Yūsuf together and Mālik refused to debate with him, al-Mughīra stood up and said, "Amīr al-Mu'minīn, here is one who will spare Abū 'Abdullāh the need to answer if the Amīr al-Mu'minīn will grant permission." He asked, "Who is it?" "Me," he replied. He gave him permission and al-Mughīra debated him on the question of the security pledge (*rahn*). He was the *faqīh* of the people of Madina after

Mālik, and his argument was stronger than that of Abū Yūsuf. They debated until *Maghrib* and then they went out.

'When they went out, al-Mughīra asked Mālik, "What did you think of my debate with the man?" He said, "I think that you got the better of him although you left something." He asked, "What is it?" He said, "When you got the better of him in a question and it was tight for him, he took you off to another question and was saved from you through that. You should not part with him until it is finished."'

His anecdotes and news

Az-Zubayr ibn Bakkār said, 'Ad-Darawārdī studied with al-Mughīra, and he began to speak disliked ungrammatical Arabic. He said to him, "Bother you, Darawārdī! You should put your language right before you seek this business!" He added, "We have no respect unless the tongue matches it."'

Abū Bakr al-Khaṭīb related that Ibn al-Mājishūn said, 'My father and his companions went to [the caliph]al-Mahdī in Madina. They included al-Mughīra ibn 'Abd ar-Raḥmān, Abū Sā'ib and the nephew of al-Aḥwaṣ. He said to them, "Compose for me," and 'Abd al-'Azīz ibn al-Mājishūn composed:

"People have a full moon in the sky which they see while you are
a luminous full moon for us on the earth.
By Allah, O moon of the heaven and its light! You think
that you are equal to a bare tenth of Mālik!
The moon is only less than your face withdrawing in the darkness.
You appear when it is absent and gives light.
My eye has not looked at a full moon rising while
you are walking in clothes so you enchant."

'The nephew of al-Aḥwaṣ composed:

"Kilāba said, 'What is this?' I told her, 'This is why they claim
that you are one of his enemies.
I am a man relentless in love, so it grieved me
until I became worn out and until illness made me thin.'"

'Al-Mughīra composed:

"Distance shot at my heart and it caused pain and it cried out.
 There was a shout announcing departure, and I listened.
The caravan-chanter sang of distance and the branch was split
 and the deprived heart became miserable.
It is enough sorrow from the passage of time that I see distance
 but cannot repel distance.
I was ignorant of distance before the separation.
 O, you are far away! How wicked and heinous!"

'Abū as-Sā'ib composed:

"I listen to the one who calls for the love of Laylā so that
 the breasts of the mounts aim for her and listen.
My dear friend, if Laylā abides, I abide,
 and if she parts, then we will part with her.
If Laylā is established in the land of her enemy, then it is a refuge
 for us, by Allah, even if we are confused."

'Al-Mahdī said, 'By Allah, I will enrich you!' and he gave the four 10,000 dinars.

Al-Mughīra said, 'I used to ask Mālik about what he said and the source for what he said. One day, he prayed at my side and said to me, "Abū Hashim, you are dear to me and you ask me about things in which I do not give the people an answer. If I answer you, they will be bold towards me, and I prefer that you do not do it. Rather write down whatever questions you want and send them to me under your seal and I will answer what I am able to, Allah willing,"

'So I went away happy and said to our companions, "Write down questions." So we wrote them in half a scroll and I sealed them and sent them to him. It remained with him for four months, and then it came to me after that with his seal. He had answered a third of the questions. On the rest of them he said, "I do not know."'

Mālik went to [the caliph] ar-Rashīd with him, leaning on al-Mushāqī and 'Abd ar-Raḥmān ibn 'Abdullāh al-'Umarī. Perhaps Ibn Maslama was with al-Mughīra. They had been very much apart before this.

When al-Mughīra sat for the people at that time, Mālik was told, 'Al-Mughīra has opened his house to people and people have come to him.' He replied, 'The people are not stupid.'

It is mentioned that Abū al-Ma'āfī presented him with his poem, *al-Kāfī*, when he had been jailed. Mālik let him challenge those who had testified against him. He spoke a poem beginning, 'Say to a people whose joy is Mālik's absence...'

Al-Mughīra was born in 124 AH and died, according to az-Zubayr and his uncle, Muṣ'ab, in 188 AH.

Al-Bukhārī and Ibn Waḍḍāḥ said that it was in Safar, 186 AH.

Al-Bukhārī said that it was Wednesday, 7 Safar.

His son: Abū al-Qāsim 'Abd ar-Raḥmān ibn al-Mughīra

Abū al-Qāsim al-Lālakā'ī said that he related from Mālik and his father.

Ibn al-Mundhir al-Ḥizāmī and 'Abd ar-Raḥmān ibn Shayba related from him.

‘Abd al-‘Azīz ibn Abī Ḥāzim

The name of Abū Ḥāzim was Salama ibn Dīnār. He is the lame *faqīh*, a client of Aslam. Ibn Sha‘bān said that he was a client of the Banū Layth. He has more than one *kunya*: Abū Tammām and Abū at-Tammām. Abū Isḥāq gives his *kunya* as Abū ‘Abdullāh, but the first is sounder. Another said it is Abū al-Yamān. That is an misreading for Abū at-Tammām, but Allah knows best.

He studied *fiqh* with Mālik from Ibn Hurmuz. He listened to his father and al-‘Alā’ ibn ‘Abd ar-Raḥmān, Zayd ibn Aslam, Suhayl ibn Abī Ṣāliḥ, Thawr ibn Zayd, Yazīd ibn al-Hādī and Mālik. He was one of his esteemed companions.

Ibn Wahb, Ibn Abī Uways, Qutayba ibn ‘Abd al-‘Azīz al-Uwaysī, Ibn Mahdī, Qāḍī Hārūn az-Zuhrī, Ibn al-Madīnī, al-Qa‘nabī, Yaḥyā ibn Yaḥyā at-Tamīmī and Muṣ‘ab az-Zubayrī related from him.

Ibn Ma‘īn said that he was truthful, reliable and that there was no objection to him.

An-Nasā’ī said, ‘There is no objection to him.’ Abū Ḥātim ar-Rāzī said, ‘He has sound *ḥadīth*s.’

He and Abū Zur‘a said, ‘He knew more *fiqh* than ad-Darāwardī, and ad-Darawārdī knew more *ḥadīth*s than him.’

Ibn Ḥārith said, ‘He was the Imām of the people in knowledge after Mālik. Ibn Waḍḍāḥ related that from one of them. He was consulted along with Mālik.’

Aḥmad ibn Ḥanbal said, ‘He was not known for studying *ḥadīth*s except for the books of his fathers. He listened to them. He was a man who studied *fiqh*.’

It used to be said that there was no one in Madina with more *fiqh* than him after Mālik.

He said, 'It is said that the books of Sulaymān ibn Bilāl came to him but he did not hear them from him; he related from some people while it was not known that he listened to them.'

It was said that Muṣ'ab ibn 'Abdullāh was told, 'Abū 'Abdullāh ibn Abī Ḥāzim is weak except in his father's *ḥadīths*.'

He said, 'They said it! As for Ibn Abī Ḥāzim, he listened to Sulaymān ibn Bilāl. When Sulaymān died, he left his books to him. They were in his possession and a mouse urinated on them and some of them were lost. He used to read what was clear and leave what he did nor recognise. As for his father's *ḥadīths*, he memorised them.'

Al-Bukhārī and Muslim transmitted from him.

Ibn Ḥanbal said, 'He used to study *fiqh*, and after Mālik there was no one in Madina who had more *fiqh* than him.'

Muṣ'ab said, 'Ibn Abī Hazim was a *faqīh*.' Ibn as-Sukkarī said that he was a reliable man of Madina. Ibn Numayr said that the like of it.

Ad-Darāwardī said, 'He testified before the Qāḍī of Madina who asked, "What is your name?" He replied, "'Abd al-'Azīz ibn Abī Ḥāzim." He said, "The name is one of good character, but I do not know the face." He obliged the one for whom he testified to bring someone who knew his face. He noted, "Scholars recommend that."'

The author said, 'A similar story occurred with Ibn al-Qāsim, and it is more likely by his obscurity and the rareness of his connection to the judgeship. As for Ibn Abī Ḥāzim, he was too famous at Madina and the assemblies of its notable men to not be recognised.'

Ash-Shīrāzī related that Mālik said about him, 'He is a *faqīh*.'

Mālik said, 'Some people, including Ibn Abī Ḥāzim, will not be touched by the punishment." He said, "Madina is only defended by Ibn Abī Ḥāzim.'

Ibn Abī Ḍamra and others said, 'People mentioned death in Mālik's presence and he wept. We said to him, "When death comes to you, whom do you think we should seek shelter in and consult?" He replied, "There are some people of whom Ibn Abī Ḥāzim is one, so start with his opinion, and I hope that you will be successful."'

Ad-Dāwūdī related that Mālik was asked when he was near death, 'Who do you think we should have?' He answered, 'Abū Tammām', meaning Ibn Abī Ḥāzim.

Ibn Mahdī said, 'A man asked Mālik about a question and he did not answer him in it. He said to him, "Who shall we ask, Abū 'Abdullāh?" He replied, "Ask Ibn Abī Ḥāzim. He is the best man."'

Ibn Fulayḥ said to Mālik, 'The souls go in the morning and return, so to whom do you command, Abū 'Abdullāh?' He said, 'To Ibn Abī Ḥāzim.'

Abū Muṣ'ab said, 'Mālik and 'Umar ibn Ḥusayn were sitting with the governor, and he was raising his voice over 'Umar while he had some gentleness. When he died, Ibn Abī Ḥāzim sat in his place and he raised his voice over Mālik. Mālik said, "One day in exchange for another."'

Ibn Sha'bān and others said, 'He died suddenly in Madina during a prostration which he made in the *Rawḍa* of the mosque of the

Prophet ﷺ on Friday in the last prostration in Ṣafar, 185 AH.' Az-Zubayr and others said that as well.

Ibn Sa'd, al-Jārūdī, al-Qutabī and al-Bājī said that it was 207 AH.

Al-Bukhārī also mentioned that he died in 182 AH, and he was born in 107 AH. He used to use henna.

ʿAbd al-ʿAzīz ad-Darāwardī, Abū Muḥammad

He is ʿAbd al-ʿAzīz ibn Muhammad ibn ʿUbayd ibn Abī ʿUbayd, and it is said al-Andarāwardī as well, from Daraward in Persia.

Ibn Saʿd said: ʿDarāward is a town in Khurasan.' Ibn Abī Khaythma and others mentioned it. He was a client of the tribe of Juhayna, and he lived there. It is also said that he was a client of Bark ibn Wabara, the brother of Kalb ibn Wabara from Quḍāʿa who was born there.

He related from Hishām ibn ʿUrwa, ʿUbayd ibn ʿUmar, al-Aʿlā ibn ʿAbd ar-Raḥmān, Muḥammad ibn Isḥāq, Suhayl ibn Abī Ṣāliḥ, Thawr ibn Yazīd, Ḥumayd aṭ-Ṭawīl, ʿAmr ibn Yaḥyā al-Māzinī, and Muḥammad ibn ʿAbdullāh ibn Ḥasan al-Mahdī, and he kept the company of Mālik. He was mostly interested in *ḥadīth*s.

Ibn Wahb, Abū Nuʿaym, al-Qaʿnabī, Qutayba, Abū Muṣʿab and Yaḥyā ibn Yaḥyā related from him.

Muslim related from him and al-Bukhārī used his testimony.

Ibn Maʿīn said that there is no objection to him, and what is related in his book is firmer than what he memorised.

Ibn Abī Hazim and Muṣʿab said, ʿMālik used to think that ad-Darāwardī was trustworthy.'

Ibn Bukayr and Aḥmad ibn Ṣāliḥ said that he is trustworthy.

Al-Kūfī said, ʿHe is trustworthy, but he used to use ugly ungrammatical Arabic.'

Ibn Ḥanbal said, ʿWhen he gave *ḥadīths* from his book, he was sound. When he gave *ḥadīths* from people, he was weak.'

The position of an-Nasāʾī about him varies. Once he said that he is sound and there is no objection to him, and another time he said that he is not like that.

Muṣ'ab said, 'He was not a master of *fatwās*. He was a master of *ḥadīths*.'

Muḥammad ibn Sa'd said, 'He was reliable with a lot of *ḥadīths* while he did make mistakes.'

Ash-Shāfi'ī said, 'I think that al-Mughīra, Ibn Abī Ḥāzim, and ad-Darāwardī followed the school of Mālik.'

Ibn Ḥabīb counted him in his *Ṭabaqāt* among the *fuqahā'* of Madina after Mālik.

Muṣ'ab and Ibn Dīnār said, 'Hārūn commanded the governor of Madina to put the two best men in Madina in charge of collecting the *zakāt* which Hārūn had appointed for the people of Madina. At that time, he did not find anyone better than ad-Darāwardī and Salama ibn 'Ikrima al-Makhzūmī. The governor read them Hārūn's letter, and they refused. He wrote to Hārūn and he replied, "By Allah, if we appoint our worst men as agents, they think that it is part of our injustice and tyranny. If we appoint our best men, they refuse us. Flog each of them with thirty lashes every day until they accept it."

'Salama had been worn out by worship and nothing remained in him. The governor said to them, "By Allah, you are some of the most lofty people of Madina in my opinion, and by Allah, I will carry out the letter of the Amīr al-Mu'minīn against you unless you undertake it!"

'Salama wept and said to ad-Darāwardī, "By Allah, if I am beaten thirty lashes, I will die!" Ad-Darāwardī said to him, "Woe to you, Salama. It is better for you to die under the whip than the Fire!"

'Salama said, "By Allah, you have felt the whips and do not worry about them!" The people spoke to ad-Darāwardī and said, "It is *ṣadaqa* for the poor and you are rewarded for it." They both undertook it.'

Hārūn had sworn against ad-Darāwardī before this regarding an office he wanted him to undertake. He had refused. He swore that he would beat him unless he undertook it. Ad-Darāwardī took an oath, so Hārūn beat him with thirty-two painful lashes, but he did not undertake it.

He died in 186, and it is said 185, and it is also said in 187 AH, in Madina.

Zakariyā' ibn Manẓūr ibn Tha'laba

It is said that he is ibn 'Uqba ibn Tha'laba ibn Abī Mālik al-Quraẓī al-Anṣārī, Abū Yaḥyā. He was Malik's companion and was a great one among his companions. He listened to him, and with him to Zayd ibn Aslam, Abū Ḥāzim and Hishām ibn 'Urwa, and he listened to Ibn Abī Sabra, 'Ubaydullāh ibn 'Umar, Muḥammad ibn 'Uqba, 'Aṭṭāf ibn Khālid, Thābit ibn Yazīd al-Muḥāribī and 'Umar ibn Ḥusayn.

'Abdullāh ibn 'Abd al-Wahhāb, 'Abd al-'Azīz al-Uwaysī, Hārūn ibn Ma'rūf al-Ḥajibī, Muḥammad ibn Zabāla, Abū Ibrāhīm at-Tarjumānī, Isḥāq ibn Abī Isrā'īl, 'Abbād ibn Mūsā al-Khatlī, Abū Thābit al-Madanī, Hishām ibn 'Ammār, Ibrāhīm ibn al-Mundhir, 'Atīq ibn Ya'qūb and Qāḍī Hārūn ibn Yaḥyā related from him and studied *ḥadīths* with him.

Yaḥyā ibn Ma'īn said, 'There was some irascibility in him. He was of no consequence. He was not reliable. He was weak.'

Abū Ḥātim said, 'He was not strong, but weak in *ḥadīths* which are disliked. His *ḥadīths* were not written down.'

Abū Zur'a said, 'He was not strong, weak in *ḥadīths* which were disliked.'

Yaḥyā ibn Ma'īn mentioned that he lived in Baghdad. He said, 'There is no objection to him.'

Aḥmad ibn Ṣāliḥ said the like of that about him.

Al-Khaṭīb said that what is said about Yaḥyā him differs.

Ibn Rishdīn said, 'He was appointed *qāḍī*, and Hārūn encouraged him to leniency in a judgement he gave.' He added, 'He is not reliable.'

Ibn Rishdīn said, 'I asked Yaḥyā about him and he said, "There is no objection to him." I said to him, "I did not think that you had a good opinion of him." He replied, "There is no objection to him. They claimed that he was one who came uninvited."'

Ibn Ḥanbal said, 'Zakariyā' ibn Manẓūr is a shaykh,' and said that he was lax.

Ibn al-Madīnī said that he is weak. Al-Fallās, an-Nasā'ī and as-Sājī said something similar.

Ad-Dāraquṭnī said that he is abandoned and Muḥammad ibn Sa'd said that he was deficient.

Muḥammad ibn Dīnār

He was Muḥammad ibn Ibrāhīm ibn Dīnār al-Juhanī, a client of theirs (Juhayna). It is said that he was from the children of Dīnār ibn an-Najjār.

His *kunya* was Abū 'Abdullāh. Qāḍī Abū al-Walīd said, 'That is how the People of *Ḥadīth* ascribed him.'

The *faqīh* 'Abd ar-Raḥmān ibn Dīnār said in his transmission from him: 'Muḥammad ibn Ibrāhīm ibn 'Abdullāh ibn Dīnār.'

He related from Ibn Abī Dhi'b, Mūsā ibn 'Uqba, Yazīd ibn 'Ubayd and 'Abd al-'Azīz ibn al-Muṭṭalib, and he kept the company of Mālik and Ibn Hurmuz.

Ibn Wahb, Muḥammad ibn Maslama, Abū Muṣ'ab az-Zuhrī, Ya'qūb ibn Muḥammad az-Zuhrī and others related from him.

Ibn 'Abd al-Barr said, 'He used to give *fatwā* to the people of Madina with Mālik and 'Abd al-'Azīz and after them. He was a *faqīh* who was distinguished in knowledge in transmission and care.'

Ibn Ḥabīb said, 'He and al-Mughīra had the most *fiqh* of the people of Madina.'

Ibn Abī Ḥātim ar-Rāzī said, 'He was one of the *fuqahā'* in the time of Mālik. He was reliable.' Yaḥyā said that he is trustworthy.

Al-Bukhārī said, 'He is known in his *ḥadīths*.' Al-Bukhārī related from him.

Ashhab said, 'I did not see anyone with more *fiqh* among the companions of Mālik than Ibn Dīnār.'

Ibn Sha'bān said, 'I do not think that he meant other than the people of Madina.'

Ibn Ḥārith said, 'He was one of the old and great companions of Mālik. He shared with him in some of his men.'

Ibn al-Qāsim said, 'He was one of the great companions of Mālik. He is Ibn Dīnār.'

Ash-Shāfi'ī said, 'I did not see anyone with more *fiqh* among the young men of Mālik than Ibn Dīnār.'

Ash-Shīrāzī said, 'He studied with Mālik from Ibn Hurmuz.'

Al-Ḥārith ibn Miskīn said, 'Ibn Dīnār was one of those who were old among the companions of Mālik.'

He said, 'A man came to Mālik one day after the *Ṣubḥ* prayer, and Mālik did not speak until sunrise. Then the man sat as long as Allah willed. Then he got up to go and Ibn Dīnār said to him, "What do you want?" He told him and Ibn Dīnār gave him an opinion. When Mālik had finished the supererogatory prayer, he said, "Muhammad! Do you give *fatwās*?" He said, "May Allah make you thrive! The man did not hope to hear from you and got up to go, and I feared that he would go in ignorance so I gave him a *fatwā* according to what I know of your school." Mālik said to him, "You are hasty."'

Saḥnūn said, 'Mālik, 'Abd al-'Azīz ibn Abī Salama and Muḥammad ibn Dīnār frequented Ibn Hurmuz and questioned him and he answered Mālik and 'Abd al-'Azīz, but he did not answer the other one. Ibn Dīnār confronted him, and he said to him, "Why do you regard as lawful what is not lawful for you?" and he mentioned the story to him.

'He said to him, "I am old and I fear that my intellect will be hindered as my body is hindered. Mālik and 'Abd al-'Azīz are two young men of knowledge who ask about something and I answer them. They accept what they think is the truth and they leave what they think is error. When I answer you and those like you, you simplyaccept it."'

He, may Allah have mercy on him, died in 182 AH.

‘Uthmān ibn ‘Īsā ibn Kināna

Ibn Sha‘bān said, “His *kunya* was Abū ‘Amr. Kināna was the client of ‘Uthmān ibn ‘Affān.”

Abū ‘Umar ibn ‘Abd al-Barr said that he was one of the *fuqahā’* of Madina. He took from Mālik and opinion dominated him, and he had no renown in the field of *ḥadīth*s.

Ash-Shīrāzī said, ‘Mālik summoned him present to debate Abū Yūsuf in the presence of [Hārūn] ar-Rashīd, and he is the one who sat in the circle of Mālik after his death.’

Ibn Bukayr said, ‘There was no one more precise nor who studied more with Mālik than Ibn Kināna. When Mālik wearied of checking the book with us, he would sometimes hand it to Ḥabīb, his scribe, and sometimes to Ibn Kināna. He is the one who sat in the assembly of Mālik after his death. It is said that Yaḥyā ibn Mālik first sat in it, and then after Ibn Kināna, ‘Abdullah ibn Nāfi‘ aṣ-Ṣā’igh.’

Another said, “Ibn Kināna was one of those whom Mālik singled out with permission in the gathering of people at his door. He called him by his name, as well as Ibn Zanbar and Ḥabīb al-Lāl, known as Bābayn. When they entered, then others of those he considered elite entered, and then permission was given to the common people.’

Yaḥyā said, ‘Ibn Kināna sat at the right of Mālik and did not leave him.’

Ibn Mufarraj and Ibn al-Qurṭubī said that Ibn Kināna died in 186 AH.

Ibn Saḥnūn and Ibn al-Jazzār said that he died in 185 AH.

Ibn Bukayr said that there was ten years between the death of Ibn Kināna and Mālik. He died in Makka during the *ḥajj*.

'UTHMĀN IBN AḌ-ḌAḤḤĀK AND HIS SONS

Qāḍī Abū al-Fadl said, 'He is 'Uthmān ibn aḍ-Daḥḥāk ibn 'Uthmān ibn 'Abdullāh ibn Khālid ibn Ḥizām.' Ibn Abī Ḥātim added, 'Ibn Hakīm ibn Ḥizām ibn Khuwaylid ibn Asad ibn 'Abd al-'Uzzā ibn Qaṣṣī with the *kunya*, Abū 'Uthmān.'

Az-Zubayr said: 'He and his son, aḍ-Ḍaḥḥāk ibn 'Uthmān ibn aḍ-Ḍaḥḥāk were among the great companions of Mālik. They both sat with him. He related this from 'Uthmān.'

Ibn Ghānim, Ibn Nāfi', aṣ-Ṣā'igh and Anas ibn 'Iyāḍ listened to him.

He related from his father, ath-Thawrī, al-Qaṭṭān, Zayd ibn Ḥabbāb and Anas ibn 'Iyāḍ.

He related from Mālik, Sālim ibn Abū an-Naḍr, Nāfi', Bukayr ibn al-Ashajj and 'Abdullāh ibn 'Urwa.

Muṣ'ab ibn 'Abdullāh said, 'He was the foremost man of Quraysh in Madina regarding the poems of the Arabs and their tribal wars. He had manliness, virtue and *fiqh* and was one of the great Companions of Mālik.'

His mother was Umm 'Abdullāh bint 'Abd ar-Raḥmān ibn 'Abdullāh ibn Khālid ibn Ḥizām.

He had a brother named aḍ-Ḍaḥḥāk, and he related knowledge from him, and Ibn Abī Ḥātim mentioned him.

Az-Zubayr said, 'His son, aḍ-Ḍaḥḥāk, was a man of knowledge among Quraysh at Madina in their history, poetry and battles, as well as the poetry of the Arabs and their tribal wars and the history of the people.'

Ibn Ma'īn was asked, 'How was he in *ḥadīth*?' He replied, 'There is no objection to him.' He said, 'He is reliable and his father 'Uthmān was also reliable.'

Ibn Abī Numayr said, 'He was a reliable man of Madina. There is no objection to him. There is some disagreement about his *ḥadīths*.'

Ibn Ḥanbal said, 'He is a reliable man of Madina.'

Abū Zur'a said, 'He is not strong.'

Abū Ḥātim said, 'His *ḥadīths* are written down but not used as authoritative.'

His son, Muḥammad ibn aḍ-Ḍaḥḥāk, was also one of the companions of Mālik. He related a lot from him and sat with him. Az-Zubayr said that he died while still a young man when his manly virtue was clear, and he took after his father in knowledge and manners. He was praised.

His mother was Arwā from the Banū 'Āmir ibn Sa'sa'a. Az-Zubayr related a lot from him and Ibrāhīm ibn al-Mundhir.

His son, Aḥmad ibn Muḥammad was a companion of al-Wāqidī. Al-Wāqidī said, 'This youth, i.e. Aḥmad, was one of five whom I sat with to seek knowledge as you relate: he, his father, his grandfather aḍ-Ḍaḥḥāk ibn 'Uthmān, his father, 'Uthmān ibn aḍ-Ḍaḥḥāk, and his father, aḍ-Ḍaḥḥāk ibn 'Uthmān ibn 'Abdullāh.'

When ar-Rashīd appointed 'Abdullāh ibn Muṣ'ab ibn Thābit ibn 'Abdullāh ibn az-Zubayr governor of Yemen, he sent aḍ-Ḍaḥḥāk ibn 'Uthmān to 'Abdullāh as his successor to him there, and he paid him a thousand dinars every month until he came to him. Ar-Rashīd spoke to him, and gave him provision for his journey in the amount of forty thousand dirhams, and it was a praiseworthy journey.

He said when in Yemen:

I say to my companion when my patience is short
    and my heart yearns for the Hijaz,
By my life, I love al-'Aqīq and what is near it more
    than Ṣala' and Ṣahar.

Ṣala' and Ṣahar are two places in the Yemen.

Az-Zubayr said, 'My uncle Muṣ'ab said, "I think that it was one of the two houses. The first was his and the other belonged to someone else. Someone other than my uncle related them both."'

Aḍ-Ḍaḥḥāk died in Makka coming from the Yemen on the day before 'Arafat in 186 AH. Al-Mundhir ibn 'Abdullāh al-Ḥizāmī said to elegise him:

My eyes shed tears which overcome my composure in that
    and my insides feel weak
For aḍ-Ḍaḥḥāk. I think that he was rare
    and the dove wept for him along with my weeping.
Do not keep back tears for anything. Perhaps the tears will
    cool the heat of my ailment.

Sa'īd ibn Sulaymān al-Masāḥiqī

The Qāḍī said that he is Sa'īd ibn Sulaymān ibn Nawfal ibn Masāḥiq ibn 'Abdullāh ibn Makhrama.

Ibn Sha'bān said, 'Sa'īd ibn 'Abd ar-Raḥmān al-Masāḥiqī is not one of the transmitters of Mālik. That is Ibn Sulaymān.'

He was among those who sat with Mālik and his companions. Mālik went to ar-Rashīd leaning on him, al-Makhzūmī and al-'Āmirī.

Sa'īd ibn 'Abd ar-Raḥmān al-Jumaḥī took from him as well, and Ibn Sha'bān also mentioned him.

Az-Zubayr said, 'Al-Masāḥiqī was one of the masters of Quraysh in intellect, steadfastness, beauty, poetry, literature and eloquence. He was precise in his judgement.'

Ibn Sha'bān said, 'He was one of the notable companions of Mālik in Madina.'

Qāḍī Abū Bakr ibn Muḥammad ibn Khalaf, known as Wakī', said in *The Ṭabaqāt of the Judges*, 'He was the first *qāḍī* whom al-Mahdī asked to judge in Madina. Then he dismissed him. Later al-Hādī appointed him to that. Ar-Rashīd confirmed him at the beginning of his reign.'

Ibn al-Mājishūn said, 'Sa'īd ibn Sulaymān testified in the presence of Ibn 'Imrān aṭ-Ṭalḥī who was the *qāḍī* and he rejected his testimony. When Sa'īd was appointed, Ibn 'Imrān testified in his presence and

Sa'īd looked at his testimony and thought for awhile. Then he said to the scribe, "Allow his testimony, Ibn Dīnār. A believer does not take out his anger (on anyone).'"

Al-'Abbās ibn Muḥammad wrote to Sa'īd ibn Sulaymān when he was moving to the Hijaz and to his property in al-Jafr:

> Isn't it to Najd and the coolness of its waters,
> to a change of place when the returner is hot?

He said to him, 'Add to it.' Sa'īd said,

> The station of man in seeking wealth is to be
> rarely at the door of the Amīr al-Mu'minīn.

Al-Muṣ'ab ibn 'Abdullāh mentioned this story in his book.

He said, 'When he came to ar-Rashīd – and he was devoted to al-'Abbās ibn Muḥammad ibn 'Abdullāh ibn 'Abbās – he stayed with him. He began to move to Madina and to his property at al-Jafr in the area of Ḍariyya. He complained in the presence of al-'Abbās. Al-'Abbās began to make fun of him and kept him from going to the *ḥajj*.'

Muṣ'ab said, 'Al-'Abbās wrote to my father about a house to make fun of Sa'īd and said to him, "Increase him with a house for us," and he mentioned the first house. However, he said, "*ḥajj*" instead of "*ḥawl*" (change of place).'

He said, 'My father added it, and he mentioned the second house and said "*ḥawl*" instead of "*al-mar*"'. It is sounder and more appropriate to the meaning.

Al-Masāḥiqī said:

I said to the one with the old feud, 'Welcome' when he met me,
so he greeted and saluted.
I gave him the appearance of pleasure outwardly,
and I brought him until he came near and was close.
I lifted a firm palm to attack and by it,
I vented the grudge of the one who was angry.

He said to 'Amr ibn 'Abd ar-Raḥmān al-'Āmirī:

I tested the brotherhood of all people, O 'Amr,
and I tested until my testing gave me judgement.
I did not see that people's love lies in other than their pleasure.
Whoever stabs or censures is not a true friend.
Pardon the one you love and do not be difficult to him.
When toil is great, drinks are clouded.
Here you are in both love and hate. Sometimes one side appears
from a friend after the other side.

Ibn al-Jarrāḥ composed these two lines in *The Book of Paper* for his son, 'Abd al-Jabbār:

We have an assembly in which we rejoice
in the presence of cares and sorrow.
What it has of friendship is censured except for
the tenderness of heart for the homeland.

His son, 'Abd al-Jabbār will be mentioned in the following generation, Allah willing.

Muṣ'ab said that Sa'īd died while he was with al-'Abbās. His mother was Amat al-Wahhāb bint 'Umar ibn Masāḥiq.

SULAYMĀN IBN BILĀL

Abū Ayyūb, as al-Bukhārī said. Muslim said: It is also said that his *kunya* isAbū Muḥammad, and that is what al-Wāqidī said.

He was a client of 'Ubaydullāh ibn Abī 'Atīq, who is Muḥammad ibn 'Abd ar-Raḥmān ibn Abī Bakr aṣ-Ṣiddīq.

Ibn Ḥārith and Ibn Qutayba said, 'He was a client of al-Qāsim ibn Muḥammad of Madina. He listened to Yaḥyā ibn Sa'īd, Zayd ibn Aslam, 'Abdullāh ibn Dīnār, Rabī'a, Sharīk ibn Abī Numayr and Ṣāliḥ ibn Kaysān.'

Ibn Idrīs and Khālid ibn al-Mukhallad, al-'Aqaḍī, Ibn Wahb, Yaḥyā ibn Yaḥyā an-Naysabūrī, Ashhab, Ibn al-Qāsim, al-Qa'nabī, and his sons, Abū Uways and Yaḥyā ibn Ḥassān, related from him.

Ibn Ma'īn said, 'He is reliable. He has the most transmission from Yaḥyā ibn Sa'īd and I prefer him to ad-Darāwardī.'

Ibn Ḥanbal said, 'He was the scribe of Yaḥyā ibn Sa'īd. He was disparaged by the people of Madina since he was in charge of the market.'

Abū 'Umar ibn 'Abd al-Barr said, 'He was one of the trustworthy men of Madina.'

Ibn Ḥanbal and an-Nasā'ī said that he is trustworthy.

Ibn Qutayba said, 'He was radiant and beautiful.'

Muḥammad ibn Yaḥyā said, 'He had better memory than ad-Darāwardī.'

Abū Ḥātim said that he is mediocre.

Abū Zur'a said, 'I prefer him to Hishām ibn Sa'īd.'

Ibn Mahdī said, 'I regret that I did not take from him.'

Al-Bukhārī and Muslim related from him.

Ibn Ḥabīb counted him in his *Ṭabaqāt* in the generation to which *fiqh* went in Madina after Mālik's generation. And he shared with Mālik in many of his men. He was one of the most glorious and elite of his companions. He was the first to sit with him when he withdrew from Rabī'a's assembly and made an assembly for himself.

Muṭarrif said, 'Mālik said to us, "When I formed a circle from the assembly of Rabī'a, Sulaymān ibn Bilāl and I sat in the corner of the mosque. When Rabī'a got up, he turned to us and said, 'Mālik! You are playing with yourself. You are dancing and Sulaymān ibn Bilāl is applauding you. You have gone to the extent of setting up an assembly. Return to your place.'"'

We mentioned this entire story and its cause in the reports about Mālik.

Sulaymān ibn Bilāl was in charge of the market of Madina. Aḥmad ibn Ṣāliḥ al-Kūfī said that he was appointed as its *qāḍī*. Ibn Qutayba said, 'He was put in charge of its *kharāj*.' The first is sounder.

One of them said, 'When Mālik said, "The matter with us" and "The matter which is agreed upon with us," he meant what the judgement was in the time of Sulaymān ibn Bilāl.' This is not sound. We have explained this topic in the reports about Mālik.

Sulaymān ibn Bilāl undertook the office of *qāḍī* in Baghdad for [Hārūn] ar-Rashīd. He died while he was in charge of it and ar-Rashīd led the prayer over him. That was in 176 AH, three years before Mālik died.

Al-Bukhārī said, 'He died in 177 AH.' Ibn Qutayba said 172 AH. Muḥammad ibn al-Muthannā said 173 AH.

MUḤAMMAD IBN MUṬARRIF

Abū Ghassān al-Laythī al-Madanī, his companion. Mālik wrote his letter of *fatwā* to him, and he related from him.

Al-Bukhārī related that Isḥāq said he was Muḥammad ibn Ṭarīf. Al-Bukhārī said that the first is sounder. He was a man of Madina who lived in Ashkelon.

He listened to Zayd ibn Aslam, Abū Ḥāzim, Muḥammad ibn al-Munkadir, and Mālik shared with him in many of his men.

Ibn al-Mubārak, Yazīd ibn Hārūn, Ibn Abī Yaḥyā, 'Īsā ibn Yūnus, and 'Alī ibn 'Ayyāsh listened to him.

Abū Ḥātim said that he is trustworthy.

Ibn Ma'īn, an-Nasā'ī, al-Bazzār and Ibn as-Sukkarī said, 'There is no objection to him.'

Ibn Abī ar-Raqqī said, 'We accepted his *ḥadīths* because reliable men related from him.'

Yaḥyā ibn Kathīr ibn Dirham

Abū 'Imran, and it is said that his *kunya* is Abū al-Hayyāj. It is also said that it is Abū al-Haddāj, but the first is better known. That is the statement of al-Bukhārī. He was a client of the 'Umarites.

Ad-Dāraquṭnī, Ibn Sha'bān and Ibn Mufarraj mentioned him among the transmitters of Mālik.

Ad-Dāraquṭnī and Ibn Sha'bān said that he is from Madina. Ibn Mufarraj said he was Egyptian. Al-Bukhārī and others said that he was from Basra.

Ibn 'Ufayr said, 'He was one of the great early companions of Mālik and Ibn Sufyān related from him from Sa'īd, 'Abd al-'Azīz ibn Muslim and Abū Ḥafṣ ibn al-'Alā'.'

Ibrāhīm related from him. Al-Bukhārī and Muslim transmitted from him. Abū Ḥātim said that he is sound in *ḥadīths*.

FROM THE PEOPLE OF YEMEN

Yaḥyā ibn Thābit

He was one of the early companions of Mālik and was a soldier.

Aḥmad ibn Khālid said, "Ubayd ibn Muhammad al-Kashuri said to us, "Yaḥyā ibn Thābit was one of the earliest companions of Mālik. He was the first who laid out his book for him.'"

Aḥmad ibn Khālid related from Ibn al-Kashūrī that 'Abdullāh ibn aṣ-Ṣabbāḥ said: 'Yaḥyā ibn Thābit related from Mālik who said, "I heard Rabī'a say: 'It is not lawful for anyone who has a capacity to gain knowledge not to seek it,' meaning his intelligence."'

Another said, 'He was the scribe of Mālik at first.'

FROM THE PEOPLE OF THE EAST

ʻAbdullāh ibn al-Mubārak

He was a client of the Banū Tamīm, then the Banū Ḥanīfa, a Marwazī, and his *kunya* was Abū ʻAbd ar-Raḥmān.

He listened to Ibn Abī Laylā, Hishām ibn ʻUrwa, al-Aʻmash, Sulaymān at-Tamīmī, Ḥumayd aṭ-Ṭawīl, Yaḥyā ibn Saʻīd, Ibn ʻAwn, Mūsā ibn ʻUqba, the two Sufyāns, al-Awzāʻī, Ibn Abī Dhiʼb, Mālik, Maʻmar, Shuʼba, and Ḥaywa ibn Shurayḥ, and he studied with Abū ʻAmr ibn al-ʻAlāʼ, al-Layth and others.

Ibn Mahdī, ʻAbd ar-Razzāq, Yaḥyā ibn al-Qaṭṭān, Ibn Wahb and others related from him.

Ibn Wahb said, ʻIbn al-Mubārak listened to all our shaykhs except ʻAmr ibn al-Ḥārith.ʼ

Ash-Shīrāzī said, ʻHe learned *fiqh* with Mālik and ath-Thawrī, and he was the first of Abū Ḥanīfaʼs companions. Then he left him and abandoned his *madhhab*.ʼ

Ibn Waḍḍāḥ said, ʻIn the end, he avoided mentioning Abū Ḥanīfa in his books, and he did not read his work to people.ʼ

His position in knowledge and praise for him

Abū Isḥāq al-Fazārī said, ʻIbn al-Mubarak was the Imam of the Muslims.ʼ Al-Fazārī used to sit in front of him and ask him questions.

Shuʻba said, ʻNo one from his area was like him.ʼ

Ibn Mahdī said, ʻI met four *fuqahāʼ*: Mālik, Shuʻba, Sufyān and Ibn al-Mubārak. (One variant has ʻḤammādʼ in place of ʻShuʼbaʼ.) I did not see anyone with better counsel for the community than Ibn al-Mubārak. If Ibn al-Mubārak did not acknowledge a *ḥadīth*, then we would not acknowledge it.'

Ibn Mahdī was asked about him and ath-Thawrī and which of them was better. He answered, 'Ibn al-Mubārak.'

He was asked, 'And if the people disagree with you?' He replied, 'The people have not made any tests. I have not seen the like of Ibn al-Mubārak.'

He said, 'Ibn al-Mubārak related to us, and he was unique.'

When the death of Ibn al-Mubārak was announced to Sufyān ibn 'Uyayna, he said, 'May Allah have mercy on him. He was a man of *fiqh*, knowledge, worship, asceticism, generous, brave and a poet.'

He also said, 'No one has come to us like Ibn al-Mubārak and Ibn Abī Ziyāda.'

Muḥammad ibn al-Mu'tamir said, 'When ath-Thawrī died, I asked my father, "Who is the *faqīh* of the Arabs?" He replied, "Ibn al-Mubārak."'

Al-Awzā'ī said to Abū 'Uthmān al-Kalbī about him, 'If I had seen him, I would have been delighted.'

'Alī said, 'He is reliable.'

Abū Ḥātim said, 'He is an Imām.'

Abū Zur'a said, 'He combined *fiqh*, manly virtue, courage, generosity, and other things.'

Dāwūd al-'Aṭṭār said, 'He is a man who came to us from the east.'

An-Nasā'ī said, 'There was not known in the time of Ibn al-Mubārak anyone more glorious or higher than him nor anyone who had more virtues than he possessed.'

Salām ibn Muṭī' said, 'No one like him came in the east afterwards. I prefer Ibn al-Mubārak to ath-Thawrī.'

Ibn Waddāḥ said, 'I listened to a group of the people of knowledge state:"Knowledge, *taqwā*, *ḥadīths*, recognition of the men, poetry, generosity, worship and scrupulousness were combined in Ibn al-Mubārak."'

The beginning of his quest, the cause of his asceticism, and some of his virtues and knowledge

Qāḍī Abū al-Faḍl said that aṣ-Ṣadafī mentioned; 'When Ibn al-Mubārak came of age, his father sent him fifty thousand dirhams to use for commerce. He sought after knowledge until he had spent the money. When it was gone, his father met him and said, "What have you bought?" He brought out his books for him and said, "This is my trade." His father went into the house and gave him thirty thousand dirhams more and said, "Take this and follow your trade with them," and he spent them.'

Ibn al-Mubārak said, 'I studied manners for thirty years and I studied knowledge for twenty years.'

Ibn Ḥanbal said, 'In the time of Ibn al-Mubārak, there was no one who sought after knowledge more than him. He went to the Yemen, Egypt, Syria, the Hijaz, Basra and Kufa, and to whomever related knowledge and was worthy of it. He wrote from young men and old men. He omitted what was rare. He gave *ḥadīths* from books.'

Ibn Waḍḍāḥ said, 'Ibn al-Mubārak related about twenty-five thousand *ḥadīths*. He was asked, "Up until when did you study knowledge?" He said, "I hope that you will find me doing that until I die."'

Abū 'Amr said in his book on the *Ṭabaqāt of the Reciters*, 'He mentioned that he used to recite with the difference, "*that your son was made to steal* (*surriqa*)." [12:81, instead of *saraqa*]'

Yaḥyā ibn Yaḥyā al-Laythī said, 'A man with good deportment came one day to Mālik. I used to see Mālik say to him, "Come here."

'Then he made room for him in his assembly, and I had not seen Mālik make room for anyone else. He sat Ibn al-Mubārak near him. Sometimes Mālik was asked about a question and he answered it. Then he would lean over to the man and say to him, "What do your companions say about it?" The man would reply softly so we could not hear or understand. I saw him do that for some days, and I admired the good manners of the man. I did not see him ask about anything until he departed. He was content with what he heard and Mālik told us, "This is Ibn al-Mubārak, the *faqīh* of Khorasan."'

One day Ibn al-Mubārak prayed at the side of Abū Ḥanīfa. Ibn al-Mubārak began to lift his hands in each *takbīr*. Abū Ḥanīfa said to him, 'Do you want to fly?' He replied, 'If I had wanted to, I would have flown in the first one.'

He said, 'The true ascetic is the one who is not delighted when he gets this world and is not sad if he lacks it.'

Ibn Shāhīn said, 'Ibn al-Mubārak was with Ḥammād ibn Zayd to greet him. The People of *Ḥadīth* went to Ḥammād to ask Ibn al-Mubārak to give them *ḥadīths*. Ibn al-Mubārak said, "Glory be to Allah! Should I recount *ḥadīths* while you are present?" He said, "I beg you to do it," or words to that effect. He said, "Abū Ismā'īl Ḥammād ibn Zayd related to us," and did not give any *ḥadīths* except from him.'

Ibn al-Mubārak used to say, 'The beginning of knowledge is the intention, then listening, then understanding, then action, then preservation, and then spreading it.'

It was said, 'He went on *ḥajj* one year and on expeditions the following year. Whenever he came to a city, he said to its shaykhs among the people of knowledge who had little, "Whoever wants to go on *ḥajj*, come out with me. Their provision will be enough for them." He did the same when he went on expeditions.'

Aḥmad ibn Shujā' said, 'I saw the travel provisions of Ibn al-Mubārak on a cart,' or he said, 'on two carts.'

We find in the book of Abū 'Amr aṣ-Ṣadafī: '[Hārūn] ar-Rashīd came to the port, and al-Fazārī and Faraj Abū Sulaymān went to Ibn al-Mubārak and both of them said to him, "Hārūn [ar-Rashīd] has arrived and he wants to meet you and greet you." He said, "Then I will to speak to him without restraint."

'One of them said to the other, "Let us go. Perhaps what the other dislikes will come from him because of us."'

Al-Fasawī the Worshipper said, 'I was with Ibn al-Mubārak on a raid on a cold, rainy night. He wept and I said, "Are you weeping on account of the like of this?" He said, "I am weeping for the previous nights which did not have the like of this hardship so that we could be rewarded for them."'

Ibn al-Musayyab said, 'Ibn al-Mubārak sent seventy thousand dirhams to Abū Bakr ibn 'Ayyāsh and said, "Use it to stop the lack of censure of you."'

Nu'aym ibn Ḥammād said, 'Ibn al-Mubārak used to stay in his house a lot. He was asked, "Are you isolating yourself?" He replied, "How can I isolate myself when I am with the Prophet ﷺ and his Companions?"'

He related that Iblīs came to Ibn al-Mubārak when he was doing *wuḍū'* and said, 'You did not wipe.' He answered, 'I did wipe.' He repeated, 'You did not wipe.' He said, 'You are a claimant, so present your proof.'

Manṣūr ibn 'Ammār said, 'Three had their livers broken by fear: al-Fuḍayl, 'Īsā ibn Yūnus and Ibn al-Mubārak.'

Ibn al-Mubārak said to one of his companions, 'Do not neglect a Day which Allah has mentioned in sixty-three places in His Book.'

A man said to Ibn al-Mubārak, 'Yesterday I read the entire Qur'an in a single *rak'at*.' Ibn al-Mubārak said, 'But I know a man who did not cease to recite "*Rivalry*" (102) yesterday until the *Ṣubḥ* prayer. He could not get past it,' i.e. himself.

He and another man mentioned that Ibn al-Mubārak was asked about the beginning of his quest for knowledge. He said, 'I was a young man who drank *nabīdh*-wine, loved wealth and rejoiced in those foul things. I invited some brothers of mine to a garden when the apples and other fruits were ripe, and we ate and drank until we were overcome by drunkenness and sleep. I woke up at the end of the period before dawn. I took up the lute which I played and composed:

Is it not time that you had mercy on us
and defied the critics and censors?

'Then it did not answer me with what I wanted. When I repeated it to it, it spoke to me as a man speaks, "*Has the time not arrived for the hearts of those who believe to yield to the remembrance of Allah?*" (57:16) I said, "Yes, Lord."

'I broke the lute and spilled out the *nabīdh*, and repentance came by Allah's favour with its realities, and I directed myself to knowledge and worship.'

He related that 'Abdullāh ibn al-Mubārak entered Kufa when he was intending to go on the *ḥajj*. There was a woman sitting on a rubbish-heap plucking a duck. It occurred to him that it was carrion. He stopped on his mule and said to her, 'Woman! Is this duck carrion or sacrificed?' 'Carrion, she replied. He demanded, 'Then why are you plucking it?' She answered, 'So that my family and I can eat it.'

He said, 'Woman! Allah Almighty has forbidden you carrion while you are in a land like this!' She said, 'Man, go away.' They continued to exchange words until he asked her, 'Where in Kufa do you live?' She said, 'In the quarter of the Banū so-and-so.' He asked, 'By what is your house known?' She said, 'The Banū so-and-so.'

He left her and went to the inn. Then he asked about the tribe and they directed him to it. He said to a man, 'You will have a dirham if you come with me to the place.'

He went until he came to the tribe which the woman had mentioned. He said to the man, 'Go.' Then he went to the door and knocked on the door with a stick that he had. The old woman said, 'Who is it?' He said to her, 'Open the door.' She opened it part way. He said, 'Open it all the way.' Then he got off his mule and hit it with the stick and the mule went into the house. Then he said to the woman, 'This mule and the provision, money and clothes on it is yours, and you will have what is *ḥalāl* from it in this world and the Next.'

Then Ibn al-Mubārak remained hidden until the people returned from the *ḥajj*. Some of the people of his land came to him to greet him and congratulate him on the *ḥajj*. He turned to say to them, 'I had an illness and did not go on *ḥajj* this year.'

One of them said, 'Glory be to Allah! Did I not leave you my goods with you while we were at Minā and we were going to 'Arafat?' Another said, 'Did you not buy for me in the same way?' He turned to say, 'I do not know what you are saying. As for myself, I did not go on *ḥajj* this year.'

He dreamt of someone saying in the night to him, "Abdullāh, rejoice! Allah accepted your *ṣadaqa* and He sent an angel in your form who performed the *ḥajj* on your behalf.'

Some of his aphorisms, poetry and wit

He said:

Fight your tongue. The tongue is quick to kill a man.
  The tongue is the postman of the heart.
It shows a man's intellect.

He said:

I see that some people are content with the least of the *dīn*,
  but I do not see them pleased with what is meagre in this life.
Be wealthy with Allah, free of the world of the kings,
  as the kings are free of the *dīn* with their worldly things.

He also said:

If it had not been for the Community,
  we would not have any roads,
and the weakest of us would be loot for the strongest of us.

He said:

People's enjoyment of worship and *taqwā* is the sweetest bliss,
  not the pleasure of wine.
They enjoy it for all their lives, and they, by Allah,
  have provision until they reach the graves.
In an instant they obtain might and *taqwā*.
  Does not the enjoyment of life lie in piety and steadfastness?

A young man used to keep Ibn al-Mubārak's company every day and he listened to a little from him every day. Then Ibn al-Mubārak travelled and he travelled with him. A man came to Ibn al-Mubārak in his house and Ibn al-Mubarak related many *ḥadīth*s to him. The young man felt upset and wrote to him:

I was a visitor of yours in your land,
and today I am a comrade on a journey.
Those are two great rights joined together.
It is not like a bird who alights and departs.

Ibn al-Mubārak wrote to him:

The fruit of the end of patience is sweet,
and the taste of it increases as with patience.
In patience there lies a virtue between us,
so force the self to it and you will persevere.

He said:

I see every life as unhappy and miserable
except planting the spear in the shade of the horse
And standing in the dark nights, vigilant,
guarding the people in the furthest outpost.

A man came to Ibn al-Mubārak and said to him, 'May Allah be pleased with you! Describe for me those who are wild and distracted by love of Allah.' He replied, 'They are as I will tell you:

Alert, on mounts as if they were a caravan desiring to pass,
so they are moved.
Their limbs are restrained from every foul action.
Truthfulness is their school, as well as asceticism and fear.'

Another person asked him to describe the fearful. He said:

When the night is darkest, they endure it,
and night travels from them while they are bowing in prayer.
Fear dispelled their sleep, so they stood
while the people with security were sleeping peacefully in this world.

While they are prostrating under the darkness,
their groan pierces the ribs.
Mute in the day by the length of their silence,
they have tranquillity originating from their humility.

He also composed:

Seize the two *rak'ats* of nearness
if you are free and at rest.
When you desire to speak about the false,
replace it with glorification.
Seizing silence is better than plunging,
even if you are eloquent in speech.

He saw Abū al-Atāhiyya wearing wool and said:

O reciter who wears wool and becomes one
who is counted among the ascetics,
Cling to the frontier and worship there.
There is no house of worshippers in Baghdad.
Baghdad is a place for kings.
Hunting is a residence for the reciter.

Part of his recommended poetry is:

Bring your food near and give it to the one who enters
and entreat the one who refuses and thank the one who eats.
Do not fail the goal, ashamed of having little.
You are not honouring time.

Ibn al-Mubārak has a lot of poetry on more than one subject. He has a short poem in *rajaz*-metre on the Companions and the Followers and long *qaṣīdas* on standing firm and *jihād* which are well known. He wrote the *Kitāb ar-Raqā'iq* which is famous, and *The Book of the Objectives of Jihād*.

Ibn al-Mubārak was asked, 'Who are the people?' He answered, 'The scholars.' He was asked, 'Who are the kings?' He replied, 'The men of asceticism (*zuhd*).' He was asked, 'Who are the rabble?' He answered, 'Harthima and Khuzayma ibn Ḥāzim.' It was asked, 'Who are the fools?' He said, 'Those who sell their portion of Next World for the worldly portion of someone else.'

He used to say, 'The trace of ink on the garment of the master of *ḥadīth* is better than the perfume on the bride's garment.'

He was asked, 'Which of the people has the best state?' He said, 'The one who devotes himself to his Lord.'

Ibn al-Mubārak said, 'I passed by a weaver when I had broken the throng of my sandal and he met me with a strap. I asked, "Did you do it for pay?" He said, "Yes." When I passed by him, I leaned towards him and greeted him. Then I missed him and found that he had closed his shop. I asked one of the neighbours about him. I said, "If he is sick, I will visit him. If he is busy, I will help him. If he is poor, I will share with him."

'They said, "We have no knowledge of him." I asked permission to enter his house and he came out to me. I asked him, "What has kept you from your shop?" He said to me, "You, Ibn al-Mubārak. People see you inclining to me, so they have put a shirt on me which I do not have anything of."

'I took hold of his sleeve and went with him to the graves. I said, "This is the grave of so-and-so. His business was such-and-such. This is the grave of so-and-so. His business was such-and-such."

'He said to me, "Ibn al-Mubārak, I do not know what you are saying. The true man is not the man whom the tongues describe and the man is not the man whom the eyes see. The true man is the one whom Allah veils in his life and makes him enter the grave veiled and then He brings him out on the Day of Rising when there is no abasement or rebellion on him. That is the true man."'

Abū Bakr al-Khaṭīb related that al-Ḥasan ibn 'Īsā ibn Māsarjis used to pass by Ibn al-Mubārak while al-Ḥasan was still a Christian. Al-Ḥasan had one of the most beautiful faces. He asked about him and was told, 'He is a Christian.' He said, 'O Allah, provide him with Islam.' Allah answered his supplication and al-Ḥasan became an excellent Muslim and travelled in quest of knowledge. He was one of the scholars of the community and one of those who travelled in quest of knowledge and the *Sunna* in all regions and people took from him with scrupulousness, intellect and reliability.

One of the men who kept the company of Ibn al-Mubārak inclined to this world and kept the Sultan's company. He met him one day and greeted him. He said to him, 'My brother!

Eat rice, wheat and barley bread,
  and, O person! be far from the ruler's abode!
May Allah guide you!
  So do not visit it! Avoid it! They are false sparks.
They take away the *dīn* and bring you near to great wrong action.'

The man was ashamed and left the ruler's company and returned to his company.

His school in *riwāya* and *ḥadīths*

Ibn al-Mubārak disliked *tadlīs*[1] in *ḥadīths.* One of the Sufis who had heard him say that one of the transmitters was weak, said to him, 'Abū 'Abd ar-Raḥmān, do you slander?' He said, 'Be quiet. If we do not clarify, who will know the true from the false?'

Ibn al-Mubārak died in Hit, returning from a naval expedition and was buried in Hit in Ramadan in 181 AH.

Al-Bukhārī said that he was born in 118 AH.

When death was near, he told Naṣr, his freedman, 'Put my head on the earth.' Naṣr wept. He said, 'Why do you weep?' He said, 'I remember what you had in it of blessing and now you are dying a stranger and a pauper.' He told him, 'Be quiet. I asked Allah to let me live the life of the rich and to make me die the death of the poor.'

[1] Not mentioning in the tradition the one from whom he heard it, but rather mentioning the highest authority, thus inducing the opinion that he had heard it from him.

Then he said, 'Put me down and do not address me again unless I speak again. Put me down so that it is my last words.'

Abū Bishr ibn Qan'ab said, 'I saw someone saying in a dream, "'Abdullāh ibn al-Mubārak, so-and-so and so-and-so are in the Highest Part of Paradise."

FROM THE PEOPLE OF EGYPT

ʿUthmān ibn al-Ḥakam al-Judhamī ibn Naḍra

He was famous among the Egyptian followers of Mālik.

Ibn Shaʿbān said, 'He was the first to bring the knowledge of Mālik to Egypt.'

Ibn Abī Maryam said, 'Egypt did not rear anyone more noble than 'Uthmān ibn al-Ḥakam.'

Ibn Abī Ḥātim said, 'I asked my father about him and he said, "He was a shaykh who is not precise."'

Al-Amīr said, 'He was a *faqīh* with famous transmissions from Mālik.'

Ibn Mufarraj said that he had about seventeen *ḥadīths* from Mālik.

He related from Muḥammad ibn Zayd ibn al-Muhājir ibn Qunfud, Mūsā ibn 'Uqba, Zuhayr ibn Muḥammad, Yūnus ibn Yazīd, Ibn Jurayḥ and 'Ubaydullāh ibn Muḥammad.

Saʿīd ibn Abī Maryam, Abū Zurʿa, and 'Abd al-Aḥad ibn al-Layth related from him. Ibn Wahb related a lot from him in his *Muwaṭṭā'* and in the *Mudawwana*.

Abū ar-Rabīʿ ar-Rishdīnī said in the book, *The Worshippers of Egypt:* 'Al-Layth ibn Saʿd indicated that 'Uthmān ibn al-Ḥakam should be appointed *qāḍī* or some other office. 'Uthmān learned of that and said, "Layth, you have shot the arrows of death at me. Do not ever speak to me again after today."'

Al-Layth came to visit him when he was ill and he said, 'Turn my face to the wall.'

Ibn al-Mufarraj and Ibn al-Jazzār that he died in 163 AH.

Ibn Shaʿbān said in 136 AH. The first is better known.

ʻAbd ar-Raḥīm ibn Khālid ibn Yazīd

He was a client of the Jumaḥ tribe. Abū Amr al-Kindī said, 'He was a client of Abū aṭ-Ṭabīʻ, the client of 'Uthmān ibn Wahb al-Jumaḥī of Alexandria and his *kunya* was Abū Yaḥyā.'

Ad-Dāraquṭnī said, "Abd ar-Raḥīm and 'Uthmān ibn al-Ḥakam were the first to bring the legal questions of Mālik to Egypt.'

Ash-Shīrāzī said, 'He was one of the associates of Ibn Abī Ḥāzim and his like. Ibn al-Qāsim learned *fiqh* with him in Egypt before he journeyed to Mālik. He combined asceticism and knowledge. He related the *Muwaṭṭā'* from Mālik. Al-Layth and Ibn Wahb related from him. Ibn Wahb related from Saʻīd ibn Abī Ayyūb from him.'

Ibn Bukayr said, 'It reached me that Mālik used to like him and that he was a *faqīh*.'

Ibn al-Qāsim said, 'We were talking to 'Abd ar-Raḥīm ibn Khālid about the belief of an unbeliever and his return to Islam along with what Allah mentions in His Book, *"Say to those who disbelieve that if they stop, they will be forgiven what is past"* (8:38) and the wrong actions of the people of Islam.

'He said, "I hope that the people of Islam will have a better state than the people of disbelief. It has reached me that the repentance of the Muslim is like Islam after Islam."'

His father Khālid was one of the *fuqahā'* and qaḍīs of Egypt. He related from 'Aṭā', Abū az-Zubayr, al-Layth, Ibn Lahīʻa, and al-Faḍl. Abū Zurʻa thought him trustworthy. Abū Ḥātim said, 'There is no objection to him.'

Ibn al-Qāsim said to Mālik one day, 'There are no people with more knowledge of sales than the people of Egypt.' Mālik said, 'From where do they have this?' He answered, 'From 'Abd ar-Raḥīm.'

Ar-Rishdīnī mentioned that 'Abd ar-Raḥīm said, 'My father sent me for something he needed and a man came and he asked him about a question and he answered him about it. The man said to him, 'Allah has helped the community through your life. I heard him say to himself when he did not see me, "Khālid, client of Abū aṭ-Ṭabī', Allah has helped the community by extending your life. Who would you be if it were not for the blessing of your Lord? Who would you be if it were not for the veiling of your Lord?" He wept. When he sensed me, he was silent.'

Ar-Rishdīnī said, 'Idrīs said to me, "When 'Abd ar-Raḥīm died, he recognised the orphanhood of Ibn Shurayḥ."'

He died in 163 AH. Al-'Umarī, Ibn Sha'bān and al-Jazzār said that. That was in Alexandria in 153 AH. (sic)

Sa'd ibn 'Abdullāh ibn Sa'd al-Ma'āfirī

Abū 'Amr. It is said: Abū Muḥammad or Abū 'Uthmān. He was one of the associates of 'Abd ar-Raḥīm, one of the great companions of Mālik in Egypt.

Ibn al-Qāsim, Ibn Wahb, Ibn 'Ufayr, Ibn Bukayr and others listened to him.

Ash-Shīrāzi said, 'Ibn Wahb and Ibn al-Qāsim studied *fiqh* with him.'

Ibn al-Qāsim said, 'I did not go to Mālik before I had learned his words.'

Saḥnūn said, 'He means that he learned fthat rom 'Abd ar-Raḥīm, Ṭulayb and Sa'd, and they were the most reliable companions of Mālik in his opinion.'

Ibn Bukayr said that he was trustworthy.

Ibn Ḥārith said, 'He was praiseworthy and trusty, and he made Ibn al-Qāsim a guardian of his daughter along with Ibn Wahb.'

Ibn Sha'bān said, 'He is the one who helped Ibn Wahb with his books.'

Ibn Ḥārith said, 'He was the teacher of Ibn al-Qāsim in worship.'

Sulaymān ibn Dāwūd al-Mahrī said in his book, 'Fatḥ ibn Ḥammād informed me: "I met al-Layth ibn Sa'd when I came from Alexandria. He asked, 'How did you leave our brothers in Alexandria?' I told him, 'Sa'd ibn 'Abdullāh has died.' He repeated it and said, 'If people were on one river-bank and Sa'd and I were on the other bank, I would hope that I would be with him for a long time.'''

Ibn Ḥārith said that he was trusty, excellent.

After his death, Sa'd's daughter was engaged to a rich man whom the people of the *dīn* censured. Ibn Wahb said, 'I will marry her to him.' Ibn al-Qāsim said, 'No, I will not marry her to him.' He added, 'Do you think that if Sa'd had been alive, he would have done it?' Ibn Wahb answered, 'No.' He said, 'We will do as he would do.'

Sa'd quoted from Mālik, 'A *faqīh* does not have to give hospitality nor compensation,' meaning a gift, 'nor testimony between two.'

Ibn Waḍḍāḥ said, 'Muḥammad ibn Yaḥyā and others informed me that Ibn al-Qāsim gave seventy dinars to Sa'd, his teacher, Mālik's companion'

He died in Alexandria in 173 AH.

Zayn ibn Shu'ayb ibn Kurayb al-Ma'āfirī

Al-Khāmirī (from al-Akhmūr, a sub-tribe of Ma'āfir). Abū 'Abd al-Mālik. It is said that he was 'Abū 'Abdullāh' as Amīr Abū Naṣr said. He was an Egyptian of Alexandria.

He related from Mālik, Qāsim al-'Umarī, Usāma ibn Zayd and others.

Ibn Wahb, Sa'īd ibn Talīd, Ibn Bukayr, Murra al-Burlisī and 'Abd al-A'lā ibn 'Abd al-Wāḥid related from him.

Ibn Sha'bān said, 'When Mālik missed him, he would enquire, "How is the virtuous shaykh?"'

He was an excellent *faqīh* who worshipped a lot and he used to interpret dreams. He was the one who interpreted the dream of Ibn al-Qāsim which we will mention in his reports.

Al-Ḥārith ibn Miskīn said, 'Zayn was one of the lofty companions of Mālik.'

Sulaymān ibn Dāwūd al-Mahrī related from his uncle Abū al-Aṣbagh, 'I was with Zayd ibn Shu'ayb in a guard-post. He would sleep at the beginning of the night and then he did not sleep until morning. He acted as guard in the middle of the night and the end, the middle of it being the hardest part there is. Before dawn, two people arrived.

We saw him like that. They went to his face while he was lifting his hands and supplicating, and then he turned his palms upward. He was asking Allah and seeking refuge with Him until dawn.'

He said, 'I went to Makka,' and he mentioned some of his excellence.

Al-Ḥārith ibn Miskīn related that a man asked Zayn ibn Shu'ayb about anal intercourse. Zayn took one of the pillows of the guard-post and hit him on the head with it.

He said, 'Zayn was one of the high companions of Mālik.'

Ad-Dāraquṭnī said that he died in Alexandria after 180 AH.

Al-Amīr said it was in 184 AH and another said that it was in 189 AH.

ʿAbd al-Ḥakam ibn Aʿyan ibn al-Layth al-Qurashī

He was a client of Quraysh. It is also said that client of ʿUthmān ibn ʿAffān. It is said that he was the client of ʿAnbar, a woman among the clients of ʿUthmān. It is said that he was the client of Rāfiʿ, the client of ʿUthmān. Ibn Shaʿbān said that.

He was the father of the Banū ʿAbd al-Ḥakam, the *fuqahā'* of Egypt.

ʿAbd al-Ḥakam's *kunya* was Abū ʿUthmān. He transmitted from Mālik on the questions of the *mudabbar* and other things.

Ibn al-Qāsim related a question from in the *Mudawwana.*

Ibn Abi Ḥātim said, 'He related from Abū Ḥanīfa al-Yamānī and Ibn Wahb. ʿAbdullāh ibn Ṣāliḥ, the scribe of al-Layth, and Ibn al-Qāsim related from him.'

One of them said, 'He had intellect and good manners. Death came to him before he became proficient in the school of Mālik. He and his father lived in Alexandria. He said that they originated from Ayla.'

Ibn Bukayr said, 'He used to joke with people.'

He reported his name in the history of Aḥmad ibn Saʿīd. He called him ʿAbd al-Ḥakam ibn Aʿyan.

He died in 171 AH.

Ṭulayb ibn Kāmil al-Lakhmī

One of the great companions of Mālik and those who sat with him. His *kunya* was Abū Khalid. He was also called 'Abdullāh. He has two names. Abū Sa'īd, the grandson of Ibn Yūnus stated that in his *History*. He originated from Andalusia but lived in Alexandria.

Ibn al-Qāsim and Ibn Wahb related from him.

Ibn al-Qāsim studied *fiqh* with him before his journey to Mālik with Sa'd and 'Abd ar-Raḥīm.

Ibn Ḥārith said, 'In his opinion, they were the most reliable of the companions of Mālik.'

Ibn Waddāḥ said, 'Ṭulayb ibn Kāmil was noble. He was one of the Arabs of Lakhm. He was an Egyptian from Alexandria. Saḥnūn said that.'

Ibn Sha'bān mentioned 'Abdullāh ibn Kāmil among the Egyptians and Ṭulayb ibn Kāmil among the people of Alexandria. He made them into two men, but they are one man as was already mentioned.

Ṭulayb died in Alexandria in 173 AH during Mālik's lifetime.

Abū as-Samḥ 'Abdullāh ibn as-Samḥ

Ibn Usāma ibn Zanbar, a client of the Banū 'Āmir ibn 'Adī from Tujīb. He was an Egyptian, the father of the *faqīh,* Fityān. That is how his *kunya* and his lineage were given by Abū 'Amr al-Kindī in the book, *The Notable Clients of Egypt*, among those who related from Mālik. He said: 'Abū as-Samḥ was a *faqīh.* Ibn Bukayr related from him, and he related from 'Uqayl ibn Khālid and others.'

Ibn Sha'bān said, 'Abū as-Samḥ was the father of Fityān who related from Mālik.'

Ibn Waḍḍāḥ gives his *kunya* as 'Abū as-Samḥā''.

Ibn Ḥazm aṣ-Ṣadafī said that Saḥnūn said that he saw Abū as-Samḥā' in a dream and he said: 'The best action would be success [or *ḥajj* in one variant] if it were not for the watering-places.'

The author said that Abū as-Samhā' was not the father of Fityān. Fityān's father was the Abū as-Samḥ who was mentioned.

In the Book of Ḥajj in the *Mudawwana* under the question of an *imām* who remembers a prayer which he forgot, Ibn al-Qāsim described him as having *fiqh* and reliability. He said: 'A man asked me about this question and what Mālik said on it. He was one of the people of *fiqh* and his transmission was trustworthy. I informed him that Mālik related that the prayer is broken for those following him as it is for him. I do not know him until I was told. This man is Abū as-Samḥ, the father of Fityān.'

Al-Kindī said that Abū as-Samḥ was born in 125 AH and died in 182 AH.

Khālid ibn Ḥumayd ibn Abī Tha'laba

It is also said that his name was Abū Ḥumayd Khālid ibn Abī Tha'laba. He was a client of Bahra, and was from Alexandria.

Al-Kindī said, 'He was a *faqīh* among the companions of Mālik. Hānī ibn al-Mutawakkil and Sa'īd ibn Sābiq ibn 'Āmir related from him.'

He was born in 113 AH and died in 169 AH.

Yaḥyā ibn Azhar, Abū 'Abdullāh, a client of Quraysh

Al-Kindī said, 'He was a *faqīh* among the great companions of Mālik. He was dominated by worship.'

Al-Ḥārith said, 'Ibn Azhar was one of the best Muslims and early companions of Mālik.'

'Abd ar-Raḥīm ibn al-Qāsim said, 'The worshippers came to Yaḥyā and they looked closely at his prayer because of its beauty.'

Another said, 'He was an orphan and he had some property in the Treasury. When he was an adult and took his property, he gave about four hundred dinars of it for the *zakāt* of those years.'

Sulaymān ibn al-Qāsim said, 'Yaḥyā left a thousand dinars like someone who is fearful about it. He bought some goods and they grew and were sold for a thousand after he died.'

He died in 161 AH during Mālik's lifetime.

Mūsā ibn Salama ibn Abī Maryam, a client of Abū aḍ-Ḍubay'

He was the uncle of Sa'īd ibn Abī Maryam. He was one of the people of Egypt who was most devoted to seeking knowledge.

He died in 163 AH during Mālik's lifetime.

FROM THE PEOPLE OF NORTH AFRICA

Qaḍī ʿAbdullāh ibn Ghānim

Ibn al-Faraḍī said: He is ʿAbdullāh ibn ʿUmar ibn Ghānim ibn Shuraḥbīl ibn Thawbān ibn Muḥammad ibn Shurayḥ ibn Sharāḥīl ibn al-Ḥanaf ibn Ayman ibn Dhī al-Qamiṭ ibn Qazw ibn Dhī Raʿīn. His *kunya* was Abū ʿAbd ar-Raḥmān. That is how Ibn Shaʿbān, Ibn Ḥārith and Abū al-ʿArab gave his lineage.

Al-Bukhārī said in the *History*, "Abdullāh ibn ʿUmar an-Numayrī from Yūnus ibn ʿAbdullāh. He listened to ath-Thawrī and Ḥajjāj ibn Minhāl.' He said in the *Ṣaḥīḥ* that ʿAbdullāh ibn ʿUmar an-Numayrī reported to him the *Ḥadīth* of the Lie from Yūnus in the ʿChapter of the Those who were Present at Badr'.

Ibn Mandara said, 'This ʿAbdullāh is Ibn Ghānim al-Afrīqī from whom al-Qaʿnabī and Ibn al-Qāsim related.'

Abū al-ʿArab at-Tamīmī said, 'He was firm, reliable, a just *faqīh* in his judgement.'

Abū Alī ibn Abī Saʿīd said in *The Book of the Clear Words on the News of the Maghrib*, 'Ibn Ghānim was a perfect and eminent man of *fiqh*. He had clear language, fine eloquence, and insight into Arabic and the transmission of poetry. Beautiful verses were composed by him, although he had a stammer. His father was well known among the Arabs of North Africa and their sons before the arrival of ʿAbbasid partisans.'

Another said, 'He was one of the people of knowledge, the *dīn*, intellect, scrupulousness, humility, eloquence and purity of style.'

Abū Saʿīd ibn Yūnus said, 'He was one of the firm reliable ones. Abū Ḥātim did not recognise him because his land was so far away. Therefore he said that he was unknown.'

Ash-Shīrāzī said, 'Ibn Ghānim was one of the peers of Ibn Abī Ḥāzim and his associates.'

The author said: 'Ibn Ghānim listened to Ibn An'am and Khālid Abū 'Imrān and he travelled to the Hijaz, Syria and Iraq. He listened to Mālik and supported him, and he listened to Sufyān ath-Thawrī. 'Uthmān ibn aḍ-Ḍaḥḥāk, Isrā'īl ibn Yūnus, Dāwūd ibn Qays and others. Al-Qa'nabī and others listened to him.'

Ibn 'Imrān said, 'Mālik held Ibn Ghānim in great esteem. When Ibn Ghānim came, Mālik sat him at his side and asked him about the news of the Maghrib. When Mālik's companions saw him, they said, "The Maghribī has distracted him from us." When he was appointed a qaḍī, Mālik informed his companions of that and was happy about it.'

It is said that Mālik offered to marry his daughter to him and have him live with him. He refused to reside there and said to him, 'If you send her to Kairouan, I will marry her.'

He had what he heard from Mālik written down and devoted himself to that. There are questions from him in the *Collection* and he listened to the *Muwaṭṭā'*.

He said, 'A man brought a document to Asad in the handwriting of Ibn Ghānim. Asad began to show it and tap it with his finger. He said, "There is no one with more *fiqh* than him."'

Sulaymān ibn 'Imrān said, 'Ibn Ghānim was perfect, complete, eloquent, very clear, with good correct reading. If it had not been for his stammer, no one would have matched the fluency of his tongue.'

Aḥmad ibn al-Jazzār said, 'This stammer has remained from his birth until our time.'

Asad said that Ibn Ghānim was a *faqīh*.

Ma'mar said, 'Ibn Ghānim read the books of Abū Ḥanīfa to us on Friday one day. When news of his death reached Ibn Ghānim, he said, "We belong to Allah and to Him we return," and he prayed for mercy on him. Then he said, "I used to support this matter."'

Ibn Ghānim said, 'When I went with al-Bahlūl ibn Rāshid to Sufyān ath-Thawrī (and 'Abdullah ibn Farrūkh was with them), he said, "Let the one of you who has the most eloquent tongue read. When I hear ungrammatical Arabic, it does something to my heart," so I read to him until we left him. He did not correct me in a single letter.'

Abū al-'Arab said, 'The virtues of Ibn Ghānim are numerous.'

Ibn Ḥārith mentioned that 'Alī ibn Abī Ziyād used to speak badly of him and to slander him in his books. He said, 'He has not supported Allah.'

Saḥnūn and Dāwūd ibn Yaḥyā related *ḥadīth*s from him.

His being appointed *qāḍī* and his conduct

Ash-Shīrāzī said, 'Hārūn ar-Rashid appointed Ibn Ghānim *qāḍī* of North Africa. It is also said that it was the governor of North Africa, Rawḥ ibn Ḥātim al-Muhallabī, who appointed him. Ibn Farrūkh, the *faqīh*, indicated that he should be the *qāḍī* after he himself refused the appointment.'

It is said that Abū Yūsuf told Rawḥ when he went to Kairouan, 'There is a young man in Kairouan called 'Abdullāh ibn Ghānim. He knows *fiqh*, so appoint him *qāḍī* of North Africa.'

He was appointed in Rajab, 171 AH, when he was forty-two years old during the lifetime of Mālik, may Allah have mercy on him. When Mālik heard about his appointment, he was happy about it and told his companions about that. When Ibn Abī Ḥassān came to him, he asked Ibn Abī Ḥassān about that and he told him about it. He told him, 'There is no one better than him.'

Hārūn ar-Rashīd corresponded with him, and it is thought that his appointment as *qāḍī* originated from him.

Ibn Ghānim's companions argued about his appointment as *qāḍī*. Some of them said, 'It originates from the 'Abbasid partisans below the Amīr al-Mu'minīn himself.' Abū 'Uthmān ibn 'Uthmān al-Ma'āfirī said that his wife should be trebly divorced and his slaves set free if anyone other than the Amīr al-Mu'minīn had appointed Ibn Ghānim.

Then he went to Ibn Ghānim and told him what he had sworn. He said to him, 'Abū 'Uthmān, what is the bride-price of your wife?' He said, 'Two hundred dinars.' He said, 'What is the price of your slaves?' He said, 'One hundred dinars.' He said, 'Take it. Your wife is clear of you and your slaves are free.

Ibn Ghānim remained *qāḍī* until his death. His appointment lasted about nineteen years.

When he was *qāḍī*, Ibn Ghānim used to send this same Abū 'Uthmān to Mālik with his questions. When disputed issues came to him, he accepted Mālik's answers regarding them. He used to write to Ibn Kināna and take the answers which he had from Mālik. He also wrote to Abū Yūsuf.

As-Sūri said, 'Ibn Ghānim continued to rise in his judgements and commands. It was part of the honour of his successor that when he wrote a letter to Ibrāhīm ibn al-Aghlab[1], he said about it. 'I will not open your letter until the letter of Ibn Ghānim is with your letter.' Ibrāhīm was the person with the greatest courtesy and respect for him.'

[1] Governor of North Africa for the Abbasids and founder of the Aghlabid dynasty.

Ibn Ghānim used to wear the best clothes. He appointed a day for the lawsuits of the women in which he would sit to investigate them. On that day he would wear skins and coarse and tattered clothes and would keep his eyes on the ground. Someone who did not know him would not have doubted that he was blind and remove the curtain and book from him.

He used to pray night-prayers. When he had finished and sat in the *tashahhud* at the end of it, he presented each litigant for whom he intended to judge to his Lord and said in his intimate conversation [with Him], 'O Lord, so-and-so is fighting so-and-so and he claims such-and-such against him, but he rejects his claim. I asked him for a clear proof and he brought a clear proof to testify on behalf of what he claimed. Then I asked him for testimony [by witnesses] and he brought me those who testified to that. I asked about them secretly and they were mentioned and I am about to take what is due him from his friend as it is clear to me that he has that due. If I am correct, make me firm. If I am not correct, then avert me. O Allah, do not leave me! O Allah, make me safe!' He continued to present the litigants to his Lord until he had gone through all of them.

Ibn Ghānim is the one who made a *waqf* of the protected areas at the ports of North Africa for those of the *ribāṭ* guarding the port.

When Ibn Ghānim sat in place, the litigants would hand him bits of paper on which their cases were written. One day he found a piece of paper which contained the case of the mule-drivers. He summoned them and they told him that Abū Hārūn, a client of Ibrāhīm ibn al-Aghlab the elder, the man in power, had purchased some mules from them for four hundred dinars, but had not paid them anything. Ibn Ghānim closed his office and went to Ibrāhīm who had given him leave to come to him without permission. When the *qāḍī* arrived, he cleared his throat. Then he said to him, 'Come in,' and he went in and did as he usually did.

Ibrāhīm asked him, 'What is the story?' He mentioned the case of the wronged parties to him, so he summoned Abū Hārūn who admitted it. He said, 'Leave it until the *kharāj*-tax comes in. I have sent for it.'

Ibn Ghānim said, 'I will not go until you pay them their money.' He did not go until he had paid them.

One day the governor, Ibrāhīm ibn al-Aghlab summoned Ibn Ghānim and read to him the letter of ar-Rashīd and ordered him to summon a man called Ḥātim al-Abzārī. It said that he owed Faraj, the client of the Amīr al-Mu'minīn, was owed a debt of ten thousand dinars. He had commanded Ibrāhīm to take it and send it with a Khurāsanī messenger to him. He said to him at the end of the letter, 'Summon Qāḍī Ibn Ghānim and summon the one who is sought that he might tremble in fear.'

When Ibrāhīm finished reading the letter, he asked Ibn Ghānim, 'Have you heard what it contains?' He replied, 'Yes.'

Ibn Ghānim said, 'And am I summoned to say something about what the letter contains?' Ibrāhīm said, 'Why else would I command your presence then?'

He said, 'The first thing in that is that the messenger should confirm with two witnesses that the Amīr al-Mu'minīn appointed him to take the money if it is sound, and that the money belongs to the Amīr al-Mu'minīn or his client.' The messenger said, 'Would the Amīr al-Mu'minīn write what is false?'

He said, 'I seek refuge with Allah! The Amīr al-Mu'minīn is too noble to take money which is not lawful for him, but things can become broken up below him'' The Khurasānī said, 'What do you say, Amīr?' He answered, 'What the *qāḍī* says.' He endured it and Ibn Ghānim got up and brought al-Abzārī with him. Ibrāhīm said, 'How excellent he is! How penetrating his insight is and how effective his resolve!'

One day Ibn Ghānim was riding with Ibrāhīm when Ibrāhīm's animal was a faster walker, so Ibn Ghānim turned his beast around and returned to his house. Ibrāhīm criticised him for that. Ibn Ghānim said, 'May Allah put the governor right! The carrying out of the judgements of the *qāḍī* is according to his rank. If I assisted you and spurred my animal on, my turban would have fallen off and the children would have played with it!'

He rode with him another time and Ibrāhīm crossed a field, so Ibn Ghānim did not ride on with him.

He came to him one day while Ibrāhīm was holding a jar which contained a little oil. He said, 'How much do you think this is worth, Qāḍī?' He answered, 'A small amount. How much is it?' Ibrāhīm said, 'Such-and-such a price.' Ibn Ghānim asked, 'What is it?' He said, 'Poison.' He said, 'Can I see it?' Ibrāhīm gave him the jar and he deliberately hit it with a staff in the gathering and smashed it.

One day Ibrāhīm invited him to go up the minaret and he refused. He said, 'We will violate the sanctity of the Muslims!' He did not climb up with him.

He came to Ibrāhīm one day when a letter from Hārūn ar-Rashīd had come to him. Ibrāhīm read his letter and then gave it to Ibn Ghānim who read it and returned it to Ibrāhīm. Ibrāhīm said to him, 'Let me have your letter to read.' He answered, 'I will not do it.' Ibrāhīm said to him, 'So why did you read my letter?' He replied, 'You gave it to me and extended your hand with it, so I did not want to refuse it. The Amīr al-Mu'minīn has concealed for me in his letter what I do not want anyone to see.'

Ibrāhīm said to him, 'Do you not know that Ibrāhīm, the governor of North Africa, will kill 'Abdullāh, the *qāḍī*?' He said, 'He mentioned that, but you are not that governor. It is your son. I am not that *qāḍī*. He is another one.' It happened that the report was confirmed later in the case of the *qāḍī*, Abū al-'Abbās 'Abdullāh ibn Ṭālib. The governor Ibrāhīm ibn Aḥmad ibn Ibrāhīm killed him after this. He was poisoned in prison. The discussion on that will come later. Allah willing.

Ibn Ghānim said, 'I was in the assembly of Ibrāhīm ibn al-Aghlab when Ibrāhīm entered. The others in the room stood up for him. Then Ibrāhīm sat down in anger and said to me, "Abū 'Abd ar-Raḥmān, what kept you from standing up as your brothers stood up?" I said, "Amir, Mālik informed me from Nāfi' that Ibn 'Umar said that the Messenger of Allah ﷺ said, 'Whoever wants for men to present themselves to him standing should take his seat in the Fire.'" Ibrāhīm bowed his head and was silent.'

Riyāḥ ibn Yazīd az-Zāhid passed by Ibn Ghānim while was the *qāḍī*. He had a measure of oil in his hand. Ibn Ghānim said to him, 'I will carry it for you.' Riyāḥ said, 'As you like.' So he picked up the measure for him and he took him through the assemblies of the people. He went through the stores of the merchants until he reached his house. Riyāḥ said to him, 'I did this because it has reached me that you are self-important, and I wanted to abase you.' Ibn Ghānim blessed him for it.

Riyāḥ ibn Yazīd would come every Friday to Ibn Ghānim and

make supplication for him. He was thin. One day he came to make supplication for him and made Ibn Ghānim laugh. Riyāḥ continued his supplication and Ibn Ghānim continued to laugh until Riyāḥ got up. His companions censured Ibn Ghānim for that and said to him, 'Is someone like Riyāḥ laughed at?' Ibn Ghānim told them, 'Let me be. My worry is that if my enemy knew the blessing we have in him, he would want to stop him doing what you saw,' or words to that effect.

Then on Friday, Riyāḥ came and began to supplicate for Ibn Ghānim with more friendliness and humility than he had had. When he had given his supplication, Ibn Ghānim said to him, 'May Allah repay you with good, Abū Yazīd.' Riyāḥ said to him, 'I knew that what came from you was provoked by the enemy in order to cut off what blessing we have in it.'

One day he passed by the market when al-Bahlūl ibn Rāshid was buying some meat from a butcher. Ibn Ghānim dismounted and embraced him and brought his animal near to him to demonstrate his respect for him. Al-Bahlūl refused, and Ibn Ghānim entreated him. He said to him, 'I have bought some meat.' He said, 'Shall I carry it for you?' Al-Bahlūl said, 'I have too much esteem for you that you go walking.' He said, 'Then I will ride behind you.'

So al-Bahlūl rode on the saddle and the *qāḍī* rode behind him on the rump of the animal and carried the meat. They went through the middle until they reached the house of al-Bahlūl and the people were amazed at his humility and honour.

The rest of his reports and his generosity and forbearance

Al-Baṣrī said, 'He mentioned that a son of Ibn Ghānim came to him from his teacher and Ibn Ghānim asked him about his *sūra* [that he had learned]. He recited it to him and he did it well, so he gave him about twenty dinars. When the child took them to the teacher, he refused them and thought badly of the child. He brought them to Ibn Ghānim and Ibn Ghānim said to him, "Perhaps you think that they are too few?" He said, "No." Ibn Ghānim said to him, "One letter of what you taught him is equal to this world and what it contains."'

He mentioned that Ibn Ghānim gave a judgement against a man called Ibn Zur'a. That infuriated Ibn Zur'a and he met Ibn Ghānim on the road to his estate and cursed him. He said to him, 'O doer, O son of a woman-doer' and went to great lengths to insult him. Then after that Ibn Ghānim met him on the road to his estate and Ibn Ghānim greeted him and took him with him to his garden. He bought some food and sat with him. Ibn Zur'a asked for forgiveness and admitted his error to him. He said, 'As for this, I did not do it so that I could argue with you in the presence of Allah. Yet if you get anything disliked from me in this world, that will not be the case.'

We find from another path of transmission: 'The army was lodged in the house of Ibn Zur'a after he had abused him and they filled it with weapons. He went to Ibn Ghānim. When he got near the door, he remembered what he had done and said, "Can I ask for his help after I have abused him?" So he left, and when his situation became oppressive for him, he went back to him. When he got near, he retreated again. Then he came back yet again. When Ibn Ghānim saw him, he said, "Welcome, Ibn Zur'a," and made room for him. He said to him, "What has brought you?" and he told him. Ibn Ghānim said, "Boy, bring my cloak and sandals!" He put them on and went to the governor. He asked him to remove the army from his house and he did so.'

Ibn Ghānim went out with a group of people to his house with Sulaymān ibn Zur'a. He brought out his utensils and pots. He got down and food was brought to them. There was *kunafa*[1] in it. One of the men split the butter towards his direction and Ibn Zur'a said, '*Did you scuttle it so that its owners might be drowned?*' [18:71] Ibn Ghānim said, 'Is this mocking the Book of Allah! I will never speak to you again!' and he went back to Kairouan.

The poet Abū al-Muḍarrijī satirised Ibn Ghānim and the *qāḍī* heard about that. He was annoyed by it and the poem became famous. Ibn Ghānim was told, 'You only have Abū al-Wazn. He can counter him with all he dislikes.' Abū al-Wazn was a jester with weak poetry.

He was brought to him and Ibn Ghānim said to him, 'It has reached me that you have a fear-reaching voice and we need someone to call the prayer in the mosque.' He said to one of his servants, 'Pay Abū al-Wazn five *qafīzs* of wheat, fifty *qafīzs* of oil and one hundred dirhams until we can investigate his business.' When Abū al-Wazn took that, he said to the one who brought him to the *qāḍī*, 'By Allah, a story! I am not fit to be a *mu'adhdhin*.' He told him about the matter and he said, 'That is enough.'

One day he went to Ibrāhīm ibn al-Aghlab in a group of poets. He looked at the governor and then composed:

> I and I, and I and I, and the people of my house find the matter distressing

Then he pointed to Abū al-Muḍarrijī and said:

> Abū al-Muḍarrijī, your poet, farts on verse whenever he composes it.

The Qāḍī said, 'After this ugly verse we left him because of his indecency and coarseness. It was one of the three verses about him.'

The governor and those present laughed. The other poet was defeated and knew from where it had come. He went to Ibn Ghānim to apologise and to swear to him that he would never satirise any of the people of his house. Ibn Ghānim only indicated that he did not know anything of the case. He asked him to restrain Abū al-

[1] Vermicelli baked in sugar, butter, cream or cheese, and honey.

Wazn from him and he commanded that. Ibn al-Aghlab said, 'No, by Allah! Not until he is given the same as you were given when you satirised him,' and he ordered the like of that.

Ibn Ghānim used to frequently recite these two verses:

When my span of life leaves me,
the weepers will not weep much.
I will be forgotten and my friendship will be forgotten,
and after me the friend will speak to the friend.

Ibn Ghānim had a brother called Sa'd. He listened to his brother 'Abdullāh and wrote from him.

Ibn Ghānim had two exalted sons: Abū 'Amr Ghānim and Abū Sharāḥīl.

Abū Sharāḥīl was a notable *faqīh* of scrupulousness, *adab* and poetry. He studied with the people of Kufa and inclined to their opinion. He died when he was thirty-six. He was born in 209 AH.

Ibn Ghānim's son had the *kunya* Abū 'Abd ar-Raḥmān and he was the one who uttered a poem in which he boasted of his pride:

We were appointed to the office of *qāḍī* of the west for twenty *ḥajj*s (years).
One who found it weak respects justice with us.
Our father carried out the trust in people
and made his subjects equal in justice and boasted its *dīn*.
May Allah bless him in his resting-place
and let him drink from the rain of the white clouds.

His death

Qāḍī Abū al-Faḍl said: 'Abū al-Walīd al-Mahdī al-Laghawī came to Ibn Ghānim in his final illness. He said to him, "May Allah raise you from your bed from this illness to recovery and rest! May He return you to health and the well-being which you had! May the health and well-being last long! May Allah put you right! Be patient under the judgement of your Lord. Allah loves the one who is thankful for His blessings."

'Ibn Ghānim said, "It is death and the end to which creation arrives and what must take place. The one who is patient in it is rewarded better than being apprehensive about that which is unavoidable." Then he made an example:

"Is there anyone who is immortal? Do we not die?
Is there any disgrace in death, O people?"'

He died in Rabī' al-Ākhir in 190 or 196 AH from a hemiplegia which afflicted him. It was said, 'His eyesight had failed.' The first state is sounder and has witnesses – like the poetry of his grandson who said, "We were appointed to the *qāḍī*ship of the west for twenty *ḥajj*s (years)." He was appointed *qāḍī* in 171 AH at the age of forty-two. He died while he was still *qāḍī* as we stated. He was born on the same night as al-Bahlūl.

One of them mentioned that a voice was heard at his death, but they could not see the speaker. It said:

The wolves have roared after their long howling
when the grave embraces him.

It is said that one of them saw him in a dream.

When he died, Ibn al-Aghlab wept over him and sat on his chair waiting for his own time to come. Ibn Ghaffāl, the uncle of Ibrāhīm ibn al-Aghlab, stood with him by his grave. He was deeply grieved by his loss. Ibrāhīm asked him about that and he said, 'He was a loving friend to me.'

Ibrāhīm said, 'By Allah, we did not make any appointment in North Africa nor grant security until he had died.'

He had resolve (*himma*). When he died, his clothes were appraised for a thousand dinars.

'Alī ibn Ziyād at-Tūnisī al-'Absī

Abū al-Ḥasan. It is said that he came from the non-Arabs. He was born in Tripoli and then moved to Tunis where he resided.

Ibn Sha'bān and others said, 'He is from the tribe of 'Abs.'

Abū al-'Arab said, "Alī ibn Ziyād was from the people of Tunis. He was reliable, trustworthy, excellent, devoted to worship, proficient in *fiqh*, one of those who feared Allah in spite of his prominence in *fiqh*.'

He listened to Mālik, Sufyān ath-Thawrī, al-Layth ibn Sa'd, Ibn Lahī'a and others. Before this, he listened to Khālid ibn Abī 'Imrān in North Africa. There was none like him in North Africa in his time.

Al-Bahlūl ibn Rāshid, Saḥnūn, Asad ibn al-Furāt and others listened to him.

He related the *Muwaṭṭā'* from Mālik and he wrote down what he had heard from Mālik three times.

Abū Sa'īd ibn Yūnus said, 'He was the first to bring the *Muwaṭṭā'* and the *Collection* of Sufyān to the Maghrib. He explained the words of Mālik to them when they did not know them. He had gone to the Hijaz and Iraq in search of knowledge. He was Saḥnūn's teacher in *fiqh*.'

Ash-Shīrāzī said, 'Saḥnūn studied *fiqh* with him. He had books on his school and he learned *fiqh* with Mālik. He wrote *The Book of the Best of those I have adorned.*'

Saḥnūn said, '*The Book of the Best of those I have adorned* has its root in Ibn Ashras, although we heard it from Ibn Ziyād. He used to read it to al-Ma'āfī. He knew al-Ma'āfī better than Ibn Ashras.'

Ibn Waḍḍāḥ said, 'I asked him, "Was he greater than Ibn Ashras?" He replied, "Their business was the same, but Ibn Ashras sometimes listened when 'Alī was absent. Then 'Alī would study that with al-Ma'āfī.'"

There were three books: sales, marriage and divorce. He heard the three books from Mālik.

Abū al-Ḥasan ibn Abī Ṭālib al-Qayrawānī al-'Ābid said in *Kitāb al-Khaṭṭāf*, 'When 'Alī ibn Ziyād wrote a book on sales, he did not know what to call it. He was told in a dream, "Call it '*The Best of those I have adorned*'."'

Ḥabīb, Saḥnūn's brother, dreamt, 'Take *The Book of the Best of those I have adorned* in gold. It is the truth with Allah.'

Asad said, 'Al-Makhzūmī and Ibn Kināna said to me, "No one came to us from one of the lands who unveiled this business to us as 'Alī ibn Ziyād did."' Ibn Kināna's version has: 'Who unveiled Mālik to us from the root sources.'

Saḥnūn said, 'None of the people of North Africa was ahead of him.' He also said, 'Al-Bahlūl ibn Rāshid did not reach the strap of the sandal of 'Alī ibn Ziyād.'

Saḥnūn said, 'Al-Bahlūl came to 'Alī ibn Ziyād and listened to him and took refuge in him, i.e. in his knowledge and gnosis. He corresponded with him at Tunis to ask his opinion in the business of the *dīn*. When the people of knowledge at Kairouan disagreed in a question, they wrote about it to 'Alī ibn Ziyād so that he could teach them what was correct.'

He said, "Alī was the best of the people of North Africa in exact knowledge.'

Saḥnūn said, 'If the Tunisians had been asked, they would have given a more extensive answer more than the Egyptians,' referring to 'Alī ibn Ziyād and Ibn al-Qāsim.

Another variant has: 'If 'Alī ibn Ziyād had sought what the Egyptians sought, none of them would have been above him nor any of them close to him.'

Ibn al-Ḥaddād said, 'That is a statement about his superiority to them in it.'

Saḥnūn said, 'North Africa did not give birth to anyone like 'Alī ibn Ziyād.' He used to say, 'The Egyptians are only above him by the abundance of what they heard. This is because I examined his secret and public, but I only examined the public part of the Egyptians.'

Asad said, "Alī ibn Ziyād was one of the critical companions of Mālik. I used to call on him with my father.'

In one version: 'I would call on my teacher after the prayer, and I began with 'Alī ibn Ziyād because he was the first from whom I learned knowledge.'

Al-Balkhī said, 'There was no one present in the time of 'Alī ibn Ziyād with more *fiqh* than him nor with more scrupulousness. Saḥnūn did not consider anyone equal to him among the scholars of North Africa.'

Ibn Ḥārith said, "Alī was reliable, trustworthy.'

His virtues and excellence

One of them said, 'I saw 'Alī ibn Ziyād standing at a column in Kairouan mosque. He wanted to say, "*Allāhu akbar*", but trembled in fear of Allah. Then he struggled and said the *takbīr* while he was ashen.'

Ibn al-Labbād mentioned that Saḥnūn said, 'One of the *qāḍīs* of North Africa died and the Caliph's messenger came to North Africa and gathered the scholars together and asked their advice about whom to appoint as *qāḍī* over North Africa. He went to Tunis and sent its governor to 'Alī ibn Ziyād. 'Alī pretended to be ill and the governor told the messenger of the caliph about that. The messenger said to him, "A governor of a land and the messenger of the caliph are sent to a common man and he does not bother to come!"

'The governor went with him to 'Alī. When they entered, they found that he had turned his face to the wall. The governor said to him, "Abū al-Ḥasan! This is the Caliph's messenger to ask your advice about a *qāḍī* to appoint over North Africa."

'He turned his face towards the *qibla* and said, "By the Lord of this *qibla*! I do not know anyone who deserves to be *qāḍī*. Leave me!"'

Rawḥ ibn Ḥātim sent for him to appoint him *qāḍī* and he came to him. Al-Bahlūl and the right-acting men came to the door of the house of the ruler when they heard that he was coming. 'Alī came to him walking, wiping the sweat from his brow. They said to him, 'What have you done?' He said, 'May Allah guard! He is praised!' Al-Bahlūl said to him, 'What made you resolve on it?' He replied, 'Did I not refuse it?' So it seemed proper to him. He went to Tunis on his donkey and they bade him farewell.

A man came to al-Bahlūl and said to him, 'I dreamt that I saw a candle enter the gate of Tunis until it entered the house of the Banū Darrāj.' He asked, 'Do you know the house?' 'Yes,' he replied.

They accompanied the man until he brought them to the house. They made enquiries and found that 'Alī had entered it before dawn. Al-Bahlūl came to him. 'Alī rose for him and greeted him. Al-Bahlūl began to ask him about questions.

When Saḥnūn arrived, 'Alī came to him at this room with the *Muwaṭṭā'*. He said to him, 'By Allah, I will only hear it read to me in your room because my brother, al-Bahlūl, wrote to me that you are one of those who seek knowledge for Allah.'

I saw this story with someone other than Saḥnūn. We find in it: "Alī ibn Ziyād and al-Bahlūl ibn Rāshid died in 183 AH.'

Another man among the great companions of Mālik had a similar name. He had his *kunya* and his name and was named with his lineage. That was Abū al-Ḥasan 'Alī ibn Ziyād al-Iskandarānī. He will be mentioned in his generation, Allah willing.

ʻAbd ar-Raḥīm ibn Ashras

Abū al-ʻArab said, ʻHe was an Anṣārī from the Arabs of the people of Tunis. His *kunya* was Abū Masʻūd.ʼ He did not name his lineage.

Al-Mālikī called him al-ʻAbbās. He said, ʻHe was a client of the Anṣār. Abū Saʻīd ibn Yūnus said that. He said, "His name was ʻAbd ar-Raḥmān."ʼ

That is what Ibn Fihr said. Al-Mālikī thought it more likely that his name was al-ʻAbbās. He said, ʻHe was an excellent reliable man.ʼ

He listened to Mālik ibn Anas and Ibn al-Qāsim.

ʻAbd ar-Raḥmān related the *ḥadīths* of the *Muwaṭṭāʼ* from him. He said, ʻI read among the men of Ibn Wahb: Abū al-Ashras ʻAbd ar-Raḥmān ibn Ashras al-Maghribī at-Tūnisī.ʼ

Perhaps he was a brother of Abū Masʻūd. His *kunya* was Abū Masʻūd. Ibn Shaʻbān clarified this. He said from him, ʻHe is Abū Masʻud ʻAbd ar-Raḥmān ibn al-Ashras. It is also said that the name is ʻAbd ar-Raḥīm.ʼ

Saḥnūn said, "Alī ibn Ziyād was the best of people of North Africa in exact knowledge. Ibn Ashras had the best memory of transmission. He was strong in commanding the correct and forbidding the bad.ʼ

Ibn Yūnus aṣ-Ṣadafī said, ʻIbn Ashras related from Mālik and ʻAbdullāh al-ʻUmarī. Ibn Wahb, Saʻīd ibn Talīd, Mahdī ibn Jaʻfar and ʻImrān ibn Hārūn in Egypt related from him.ʼ

Mūsā ibn Muʻāwiya said, ʻI was with al-Bahlūl ibn Rāshid when Ibn Ashras came to him. Al-Bahlūl asked him, "What has brought you?" He replied, "The misfortune of a man whom the Sultan sought. I have concealed him and I have taken an oath to divorce my wife three times claiming that I have not hidden him."

'Al-Bahlūl said to him, "Mālik says that he breaks his oath which was based on his wife." Ibn Ashras said, "I have heard him say it. I want other than this." He answered back, "I only have what you have heard."

'He repeated it to him three times. Each time, al-Bahlūl repeated the first statement to him. On the third or fourth time, he said to him, "Ibn Ashras, evil is how you serve the people when they come to you with their misfortunes! You say, 'Mālik said. Mālik said.' Then, when misfortunes befall you, you seek allowance in them. Al-Ḥasan said, 'He does not break it.'"

'Ibn Ashras said, "Allah is greater! Al-Ḥasan limited it," or words to that effect.'

The *qāḍī* said, 'That is how I transmitted it from the book of Ibn Ḥārith and I saw it in his handwriting.'

Another said, 'Ibn Ashras went back to his wife and he was the one with the question.'

Al-Bahlūl ibn Rāshid

Abū 'Amr. He was one of the people of Kairouan. Muḥammad ibn Aḥmad at-Tamīmī said, 'He was a reliable man with *ijtihād* and scrupulousness, someone whose supplication was answered. There is no doubt about that. He had a lot of knowledge.'

He listened to Mālik, ath-Thawrī, 'Abd ar-Raḥmān, Ziyād, Yūnus ibn Yazīd, Ḥanẓala ibn Abī Sufyān, Mūsā ibn 'Alī ibn Rabāḥ, al-Layth ibn Sa'd and al-Ḥārith ibn Nabhān.

He was first busy with worshipping. When people needed him in knowledge, he listened to the *Muwaṭṭā'* from Ibn Ziyād and Ibn Ghānim, and he heard the *Lesser Collection* of Sufyān from Abū al-Khaṭṭāb and Abū Khārija and the *Great Collection* from 'Alī ibn Ziyād. People wrote a *Collection* from him and he undertook to give them *fatwā*s.

Saḥnūn, 'Awn, al-Ja'farī, 'Abd al-Muta'ālī, Khālid ibn Ziyād, Abū Sinān, Yaḥyā ibn Salām, and others of his associates and those after him listened to him.

Abū 'Abdullāh al-Jadalī said, "Abdullāh ibn Maslama al-Qa'nabī also related from him. He said, "Al-Bahlūl ibn Rāshid related to us and he is one of the pillars of the Maghrib.'"

Yazīd al-Faqīr related from him and Mālik ibn Anas looked at him and said, 'This is the devout worshipper of his land.'

Some cases reached Mālik from Ibn Ghānim. He asked, 'What does the pale one say about it?' meaning al-Bahlūl. 'What does the Persian say on it?' meaning 'Abdullāh ibn Farrūkh.

Sa'īd ibn al-Ḥaddād said, 'There was no one in this land who established the *Sunna* more than al-Bahlūl in his time and Saḥnūn in his time.'

Abū Ḥātim said, 'He is trustworthy. There is no objection to him.'

Al-'Uqaylī said, 'He was a shaykh from the people of the Maghrib. There is no objection to him. 'Alī ibn al-Madīnī said the like of that.'

Isḥāq ibn al-Barqī said, 'Bahlūl was one of the companions of Mālik, an excellent man.'

Abū Bakr al-Mālikī said, 'Al-Bahlūl was one of the people of excellence, knowledge and scrupulousness. He was known for that as well as worship and *ijtihād*.'

Saḥnūn said, 'Al-Bahlūl was a virtuous man, but he did not possess the *fiqh* that others had. I imitated him in abandoning giving the greeting to the people of sects.'

The virtues of al-Bahlūl, his scrupulousness, humility, good qualities and the rest of his reports

Abū Isḥāq al-Barqī said, 'Al-Bahlūl ibn 'Amr said, "I have not seen anyone with more fear of Allah than al-Bahlūl ibn Rāshid."'

Saḥnūn said, 'We used to frequent al-Bahlūl and we learned proper conduct from him.'

Someone else said, 'A letter was given to al-Bahlūl and he opened it. It said in it: "From a woman of Samarqand in Khurasan." She had made fun of a man and no one but her had made fun of him. Then she repented to Allah and asked about the worshippers in his land. Four were described to her: Bahlūl in North Africa was one of them. "I ask you by Allah, Bahlūl, to ask Allah to make me continue in what he has opened to me."' He said, 'The letter fell from his hand and he fell on his face. He began to weep until the letter stuck to the mud from his tears. Then he said, "Bahlūl! Samarqand in Khurasan! Woe to you from Allah if He does not veil you!"'

Saḥnūn said, 'Rabāḥ had renown. When he died, that went to al-Bahlūl. That was only due to something hidden which he possessed.'

Two women passed by him while he was delousing himself. One of them said to the other, 'This is Bahlūl.' She said, 'It is better for you to hear about al-Mu'īdī than to see him'[1] Al-Bahlūl said, 'This one has recognised me.'

One day a man called him a hypocrite and al-Bahlūl said to him, 'I have informed it of that,' i.e. informed himself, 'and it rejected me and did not accept it. Your testimony and my knowledge agree about it.'

Al-Bahlūl had some food and then prices rose, so he sold it and then ordered that a fourth of a *qafīz* be bought for him. He was asked about that and said, 'We rejoice when people rejoice and we are sorrowful when they are sorrowful.'

A group said that al-Bahlūl went out once making for the mosque. When he was opposite the governors castle, the ruler's servants came out of the kitchen carrying pots. They said to him, 'Come!' and placed a board with some pots on it on his head. When the people saw him, they leapt up on every side and wanted to attack the servants. They apologised, saying that they did not recognise him. He said, 'I did it myself. The believer must abase himself. Afterwards it will only bring good rewards.'

One of them said, 'I saw al-Bahlūl going to his house wearing a rough silk hat, embroidered shawl and a Tustarī shirt and sandals from Ṭā'if.'

[1] A proverb which refers to someone whose fame is greater than his reality.

'Awn said, 'Al-Bahlūl prepared some food and invited a group of his friends to it. They asked him, "Why did you do it without a reason?" He replied, "I feared that I would be one of the Berbers. When something new comes to you, let one of you inform me. I am not one of them."'

Al-Bahlūl was generous. It reached me that he did not retain more than five hundred dirhams.

Al-Ḥaddād said, 'My mother informed me, "I went to al-Bahlūl when I was a child. When he saw me, he said, 'Blessed is Allah! He has removed the doubtful by her!' and he gave me a hundred dirhams."'

His slave-girl said, 'I spent thirty years with al-Bahlūl. I did not ever see any remove his garment from his body nor ever see him praying a supererogatory prayer. He would come and lie down with me as the mother lies down with her child. Then he would enter the lavatory and prepare for the prayer. Then he went up to his room and lock it. I did not know whether he was alive or dead although I once did hear him fall towards the end of the night. I thought that he had grown heavy with sleep and fallen.'

He mentioned that a young man was studying with him and then engaged in impudent behaviour. Al-Bahlūl heard about that and it grieved him. One day when he was sitting, the lad came holding a mandolin and al-Bahlūl recognised that. Then he thought and said, 'Perhaps he is going to break it.'

After that, al-Bahlūl went to his house and invited him and greeted him and asked him what had kept him from him and began to admonish him until the young man turned to good and left what he had been doing. He clung to al-Bahlūl and Allah gave him profit from him and he had some importance.

Abū 'Uthmān ibn al-Ḥaddād said, 'It reached me that one day al-Bahlūl was visiting and he had his friend, Riyāḥ ibn Yazīd the ascetic, with him. Then al-Bahlūl's brother came from the desert and began to talk extensively about the news of the rain and the crops. Al-Bahlūl disliked and grew pale out of sorrow for Riyāḥ since he knew that he disliked mention of this world and its means. When his brother did a lot of that, Riyāḥ got up and began to say to Bahlūl, "You have fallen from my eye. This world is mentioned in your assembly and you do not object or change it."

'Al-Bahlūl said, "If I have not fallen from the eye of Allah, I do not care about from whose eyes I have fallen." Riyāḥ went to his head to kiss him and said, "Yes, by beloved Bahlūl. You do not care about whose eyes you fall from if you have not fallen from the eye of Allah."'

Bahlūl came to Qāḍī Ibn Ghānim at *Maghrib* in Ramaḍān. He brought the water near so that those who were present could wash. They washed and al-Bahlūl washed but did not eat. Qāḍī Ibn Ghānim spoke to him about that. He said, 'Am I am a sultan? Is my food unlawful? Are you not fasting?'

Al-Bahlūl began to apologise to him and say, 'It is food whose like I do not find in my house. If you burden me, it will be oppressive for me. I dislike to be burdened to do what is oppressive for me' Ibn Ghānim repeated his first words. Al-Bahlūl apologised and did not add anything to his first words until the people had finished and left, and then al-Bahlūl left.

Ibn al-Labbād mentioned that a man asked al-Bahlūl a question and he answered him about it. Then he said, 'Go to the Persian' (i.e. Ibn Farrūkh) 'and ask him.' He went to him and he questioned him and he answered him with a similar answer as that of al-Bahlūl. He went to al-Bahlūl and asked him about it as well. He said, 'Did I not direct you to Ibn Farrūkh?' He said, 'Yes, and he answered me.'

Bahlūl said, 'Perhaps you prefer some people to others?' meaning himself. 'By Allah, if wrong actions had had a scent, you would not have sat with me nor I with you."' He said, 'Ibn Farrūkh is the good dirham, and I am the counterfeit dirham.'

Bahlūl said, 'I met Riyāḥ ibn Yazīd at the well of Zamzam and a Khurasani was with him. They took water from the Zamzam well. They put it in some *sawīq*-mush, and I looked and it was honey. They said, "Do not mention what you have seen." I did not do so until he had died.

Ibn al-Ḥaddād said, 'The people of the drovers had twenty dinars with al-Bahlūl. He had twenty dinars with Dahnūn. A beggar came to him and he said to Dahnūn, "Give him one of the twenty dinars," and he gave it to him. Then the drovers came to him and he said to him, "Bring me the nineteen dinars." He told Dahnūn to go after them. He found twenty dinars and said to Dahnūn. "There is no god but Allah. I see that you do not count well."'

Sulaymān ibn Sālim said, 'Mughīth ibn Riyāḥ went to Bahlūl and told him of his determination to go on the *ḥajj*. He said to him, "Have you not already been on *ḥajj*?" He replied, "Yes, but I yearn for the Ḥarām, the House of Allah and for the grave of the Prophet ﷺ." He said to him, "How much did you prepare for your departure?" He told him, "A hundred dirhams." He asked him, "Would you come to me with them and let me spend them in places and guarantee for you ten accepted *ḥajj*s by Allah?"

'Mughīth brought him the bag and he left it under him and sat with him. He continued to give five and then from the bag. He said to this one, "Marry with it and live on the rest." To that one, "Spend it on your family." To the other, "Veil your face with it," until it was gone. After that, a virtuous man dreamt that someone came to him twice during the night and said, "Go to Mughīth and tell him that Allah has fulfilled Bahlūl's guarantee." The man told him that.'

Abū Zarjūna said, 'I dozed on a Friday night and I was hit with a club. I told al-Bahlūl about that on the following day. He applied himself to asking me to put the action of that man in the lawful. I said, "They did it what they did and then I should put them in the lawful?"

'He said to me, "Is it easy for you that a barrier should come between your Muslim brother and the Garden on your account?" He kept on at me until I put them in the lawful.'

He said, 'Harthama ibn A'yan, the governor of North Africa, came in his retinue to the mosque of al-Bahlūl ibn Rāshid. Bahlūl was leaning against a post in front of the door of the mosque. Harithma leaned over in the saddle and told one of those with him, "Give him the bag with the dirhams and tell him: 'The governor tells you to divide them up.'"

'The messenger came to him and al-Bahlūl said to him, "The governor is stronger in dividing them than me."'

Saḥnūn said, 'A man asked al-Bahlūl about a question when I was with him and he answered him incorrectly. I spoke to him about that. He said, "Do you not find that those young men injure us?"

'When a group agreed with me, I went out to 'Alī ibn Ziyād. I went out to him and while I was with him, al-Bahlūl's letter came to him. He gave it to me and I said, "This is the question on which he disagreed with us." He said to me, "What do you say?" I said, "Al-Bahlūl said the like of this." He asked, "Who disputed with him?" I said, "I said such-and-such on it." He said, "You were right and he was wrong. Write that to him from me." Then he said to me, "Hold fast to this man. He is righteous."'

Ibn al-Ḥaddād said from his father, 'Bahlūl was one of the most jealous of people. No other man except him entered his house.'

One of his companions said, 'I came to him while his young daughter was with him. She was wearing a dyed garment. He said to me, "I do not love anything the way I love her. I wish that I could offer her to my Lord." Then I left him and then returned to him and people had gathered at his door. I asked and was told, "His daughter has died." I went in to him and comforted him. When he I turned, he caught up to me and said to me, "By Allah, do not mention what I said (i.e. his wish) as long as I am alive."'

Zakariyā' ibn al-Ḥakam said, 'I said to al-Bahlūl, "Abū 'Amr, this recitation which is recited from you, is it something which you relate from the *Salaf* or is it something of your own opinion?" He answered, "I did not take it from anyone. However, I was travelling with my teacher and he ordered me to go to Musāfir ibn Sulaymān al-Wā'iẓ at the mosque when the reciters were reciting to him, and I stopped with him and enjoyed that. Then I took account of myself and said, "I will engage myself," so I began to take a known assignment from my teacher. When I finished it, I went to his assembly and I benefited from it and the sweetness of that and its benefit has remained in my heart until now." Then he said, "If those reciters come to me, I listen to them. If they are absent, I did not send for them."'

A man mentioned to Bahlūl that he saw the sun and the moon enter inside him and Bahlūl gave him an opinion that he would die. He recited, '*The sun and the moon are fused together. On that Day, man will say, "Where can I run?"*' (75:9-10)

His following the *Sunna*, avoiding the people of sects, and his friendship and enmity for Allah

Bahlūl went out to his companions one day and he had covered his little finger. His wife had asked him for something and he had tied his little finger with a thread so that he would remember it. Then he said, 'I have concealed it so that I will not innovate.' He covered his finger so that no one would see it and imitate him. Then he met one of his companions and confided the matter to him. Ibn Farrūkh, his friend, asked him about that and he came to him to inform him that 'Abdullah ibn 'Umar used to do that. So Bahlūl took the wrapper off his little finger. He said, 'Praise be to Allah who did not make me one of those who made an innovation in Islam!'

Ibn al-Ḥaddād said, 'Abū Sinān said to me, "Sometimes I heard Bahlūl from your house when he was shouting. He said, 'The *Sunna*! The *Sunna*!' and he was insistent about it."'

Saḥnūn said, 'I came to Bahlūl one day when a man from the people of sects was at his door. He asked me about the shaykh and I did not answer him. The shaykh was listening. When I entered, I greeted him but he did not answer me and turned away from me. When people left, I knelt in front of him and asked him, "What is my story?" He replied, "A man from the people of sects greeted you and asked about me." I said to him, "By Allah, I did not answer him at all. He said, 'Welcome!' and greeted me." He said to me, "By this the true is known from the false."'

Ibn al-Ḥaddād said, 'The *faqīh* Abū Muḥriz al-'Iraqī came to al-Bahlūl to visit him when he was ill. That was mentioned to al-Bahlūl and he said, "Tell him: if you continue with your opinion, then do not come near us."'

Saḥnūn said, 'It was al-Bahlūl I imitated in abandoning greeting the people of sects.'

One of them said, 'Bahlūl gave two dinars to one of his friends with which to buy some oil which he found sweet for him. He mentioned to the man that a Christian had some of the sweetest oil around. The man went with the two dinars and informed the Christian that he wanted sweet oil for al-Bahlūl.

'The Christian said, "We will seek nearness to Allah by al-Bahlūl as you seek nearness to Him by him." For two dinars, he gave him enough of that oil as he would give of a low oil for four dinars. Then he came to al-Bahlūl and told him the story. al-Bahlūl said to him, "You have fulfilled one need, so fulfil another for me and return the two dinars to me." He said, "Why?"

'Al-Bahlūl replied, "I remembered the words of Allah Almighty, *'You will not find people who believe in Allah and the Last Day having love for anyone who opposes Allah and His Messenger.'* (56:22)I feared that I would eat the oil of the Christian and then find love in my heart for him so that I would become one of those who oppose Allah and His Messenger by turning to a little of this world."'

His inquisition and his death

The Qāḍī said, 'Al-Bahlūl was subjected to the Inquisition at the hands of al-'Akkī[1], the governor of Kairouan who was told: "He is in your power and his business is weak." So he commanded he be brought and the people gathered with him. That increased his wrath against him. He brought out the army against them who dispersed them. Then he commanded that al-Bahlūl be stripped and flogged. A group threw themselves at him and were beaten. He was beaten with about twenty lashes and imprisoned. When he was distressed and taken away, some people with veiled faces met him and asked him advice about rising up and rescuing him. He began to say, "No, no."'

One of them said, 'We were in a raid with one of the caliphs. We were with him among twelve thousand people of the ports. Every day he granted two of our needs. When we heard that al-'Akkī had flogged al-Bahlūl, the army was disturbed. We went to the caliph's door and asked for a need. We said, "We make all that we need help for al-Bahlūl. News has reached us that al-'Akkī has flogged him." The chamberlain said, "Fear Allah for al-'Akkī's blood, If this were to reach the caliph, he would kill him. How could al-Bahlūl be beaten and the people of North Africa not rebel?"'

Part of what provoked al-'Akkī against him was that he gave a present to the King of Byzantium. The (Greek) despot asked him for some arms, iron and copper. When he wanted to send that to him, Bahlūl protested that he should refuse that and admonished him about it since it was not permissible for him.

[1] Muḥammad ibn Muqātil al-'Akkī, governor for the Abbasids.

Abū Zarjūna said, 'I was with al-Bahlūl when he was flogged. I heard the weeping of a man inside the door. It was Ibn Farrūkh. He sat in front of it, weeping. Al-Bahlūl said to him, "Why are you weeping, Abū Muhammad?" He answered, "I weep for a back flogged unjustly." He said, "Allah decrees and determines."'

After that al-'Akkī regretted what he had done and asked Ibn Ghānim, 'Can you show him to me?' He replied, 'As for him coming to you, no. But I will invite him and you can look from where you can see him.' He did that. When he saw him, he began to say, 'Blessed is Allah. It is as if he were Sufyān ath-Thawrī in his business.'

Al-'Akkī was very soon dismissed in disgrace and Tammām ibn Tamīm was appointed governor.

It is related that when his feet were stretched to be bound, he said, 'This flogging is part of the affliction from which I ask Allah well-being.'

The jailor came to him in al-'Akkī's prison and treated him, and he gave him a dinar and gave some dirhams to the one with him. He did that with them for three days. Whenever they came to him, he gave that to them. His companions feared for his need when he came out. They said to the jailor, 'He is well. Do not visit him.'

When al-Bahlūl kept him waiting, his friends asked after him and it was as if he understood them. They said to him, 'A dinar a day.' He said, 'What of it?'

Ḥafṣ ibn 'Umāra, one of his companions, said to him, 'I heard that ath-Thawrī said, "The truthfulness of the truthful is perfect when he does not own what is in his hand."' Al-Bahlūl fell on his hands and kissed them. He said, 'I ask you by Allah if you heard it from him?'

The flogging which he had received healed except for the trace of one lash which festered. It became an ulcer and was the cause of his death, may Allah have mercy on him.

Al-Bahlūl said, 'I remained for thirty years saying in the mornings and evenings, "In the name of Allah with whose name nothing in the earth or the heaven is harmed. He is the Living, the Knowing," etc., and I forgot one day with al-'Akkī and so I was tested.'

He mentioned that al-'Akkī sent him clothes and a purse, but he did not accept that from him. When he refused it, he asked him to make it lawful. He said to him, 'Not a lash fell on me but that I asked forgiveness for you, you wretch.'

In one variant, 'My hands were not released from the bonds but that I put you in the lawful.'

He died in 183 AH. Saḥnūn said that it was thirty-five days after 'Alī ibn Ziyād, and more than one person stated that.

Furāt said, 'He died in 202 AH and was born on the same night as 'Abdullāh ibn Ghānim in 128 AH.'

Abū Muḥammad 'Abdullāh ibn Farrūkh al-Fārisī

He was the *faqīh* of Kairouan in his time. Abū Bakr al-Mālikī mentioned in the *Kitāb Riyāḍ an-Nufūs* that he was born in Andalusia in 125 AH. Then he moved to North Africa and lived at Kairouan and its vicinity. Sulaymān ibn 'Imrān mentioned roughly the same in what Ibn al-Jazzār related from him in *Kitāb at-Ta'rīf.*

His name in Andalusia was 'Abdūs and a man among those who knew him by that name called him that in Kairouan mosque . He said to him, 'I beseech you by Allah to remember me in this land.' Then he travelled to the east and met a group of scholars and *ḥadīth* scholars like Zakariyā' ibn Abī Zā'ida, Hishām ibn Ḥassān, 'Abd al-Malik ibn Jurayḥ, al-A'mash, ath-Thawrī, Mālik ibn Anas, Abū Ḥanīfa and others. He listened to them and studied *fiqh* with them.

Abū Bakr said, 'He relied on Mālik ibn Anas in *Ḥadīth* and *fiqh* and was famous for his keeping his company. He studied *fiqh* with him, but he inclined to investigation and proof. Sometimes he inclined to the statement of the people of Iraq in what seemed to him to be clearly correct. Then he moved to North Africa and resided in Kairouan and taught people knowledge and related *ḥadīths* to them. People benefited from him. Then he travelled a second time and came to Egypt and then he died there as we will mention.'

Ibn al-Jazzār said in *Kitāb Ṭabaqāt al-Quḍāt*: 'Ibn Farrūkh was a *faqīh* of great scrupulousness who travelled in search of knowledge. He corresponded with Mālik ibn Anas about some cases which he answered.'

Ibn Ḥārith said, 'Ibn Farrūkh was one of the shaykhs of North Africa and one of those who travelled to Mālik. He listened to him and corresponded with him and Mālik answered him. Saḥnūn used to say of him, "He did not state the fundamental sources. He was asked about a question and would answer it with different positions about it."'

His being praised for knowledge, intellect and the *dīn*

Abū Bakr said, 'He was a virtuous, excellent man of scrupulousness, humble, with little awe of kings. He did not fear the censure of any critic in Allah, and kept apart from the people of innovations. He had great memory of *ḥadīths* and *fiqh*.'

Abū al-'Arab said, 'He was one of those who travelled to seek knowledge. He met Mālik, Sufyān ath-Thawrī and others. He used to correspond with Mālik and he answered his questions for him. He was a reliable man in his *ḥadīths* and asked to be exempt from the office of *qāḍī*.'

Ibn Abī Maryam said, 'He was the most pleasing of people on the earth in my opinion.'

Muslim related from him in his *Ṣaḥīḥ*.

Al-Bukhārī said, 'Ibn Abī Maryam listened to 'Abdullāh ibn Farrūkh. He was both recognised and unknown. He was a Khurasānī man who lived in the Maghrib.'

'Abdullāh ibn Wahb said, 'Ibn Farrūkh came to us in 196 AH after the death of al-Layth ibn Sa'd. We hoped that he would remain after him, but it was only a short time until he died. I put it on myself to go to his funeral only if I could stand over his grave to supplicate for him.'

Al-Mālikī said, 'It was a great misfortune among the people of knowledge when he died in Egypt. They said, "We hoped that he would be a successor to al-Layth." They respected him and believed that he was an Imām.'

He said, 'Mālik ibn Anas respected and esteemed him.'

Aṭ-Ṭaḥāwī related that Ibn Farrūkh came to Madina, put on his garments and went to the grave of the Prophet ﷺ and greeted him. Then he went to Mālik. When Mālik saw him, he met him with the greeting and stood up for him. He almost never did that with most people. Mālik had a place in his assembly where he sat and al-Makhzūmī was at his side which was known. Mālik did not invite anyone to sit in him, but he made him sit in it and asked him about his situation and when he had come.

He informed him that he had come at that very moment.

Mālik said, 'You have spoken the truth. If you had come earlier, I would have known it and I would have come to you.'

Mālik did not answer a question when 'Abdullāh was present without saying, 'Abū Muḥammad, answer!' He would answer and Mālik would state, 'It is as he has said.'

Then Mālik turned to his companions and said, 'This is the *Faqīh* of the Maghrib.'

We find in another report that he came to Mālik and sat with him on a bench. An individual from the people of the Maghrib came to him with some questions on injuries which were read to him. Mālik said, 'Answer them, Abū Muḥammad! They are the people of your land.' Ibn Farrūkh said, 'In your presence?' He said, 'Yes, I adjure you.'

The question was about a man being hit on his head and groins so that the meninex of his brain was affected and his mind lost, as well as his sight, hearing and teeth. His testicles hung until they reached his knees. Ibn Farrūkh said, 'There is blood-wit due for loss of hearing, sight, mind and teeth. He should sit in a tub which has cold water in it on a cold night. If his testicles contract and return to their place, there is nothing owed for them. If not, there is full blood-wit for them. If one of them contracts, there is half of the blood-wit owed for them.' The asker said, 'Is this your answer, Abū 'Abdullāh?' He replied, 'This is my answer.' Ibn Farrūkh related this story about him and Mālik.

Abū al-'Arab said that Abū 'Uthmān al-Ma'āfirī said, 'I brought Mālik some questions from Ibn Ghānim and he asked me, "What does the pale one say about them?" meaning al-Bahlūl ibn Rashid. "What does the Persian say on them?" meaning Ibn Farrūkh. Then he wrote answers and he wrote at the end of the letter, "The *dīn* of Allah is easy when its limits (*ḥudūd*) are established."'

Ibn Ḥārith said, 'The fact that Mālik asked about his words and the words of al-Bahlūl in the question indicates that he knew that they were the people of *fatwā* of Kairouan in his time. He did not ask about the words of Ibn Ziyād and Ibn Ashras because they were not at Kairouan. They were at Tunis with the debate of Ibn Ghānim and 'Alī ibn Ziyād.'

Al-Bahlūl ibn Rāshid respected Ibn Farrūkh and imitated him in what he had in matters of the *dīn*. He mentioned that he debated Zafar ibn al-Hudhayl in the assembly of Abū Ḥanīfa. Zafar made light of him for being a North African. but Ibn Farrūkh continued with him until he had stopped him. Abū Ḥanīfa said to Zafar, 'Allah did not lighten what you had.'

His asceticism, worship, scrupulousness, and establishing the truth

Ibn Qādim said, 'Ibn Farrūkh performed a lot of night prayers. His night prayer was done at the end of the night.'

Aḥmad ibn Yazīd said, 'When the army received their stipends, 'Abdullāh ibn Farrūkh locked up his store for those days until what was in their hands had gone.'

Ibn Qādim said, 'The people sought blessing in the company of Ibn Farrūkh and they sat for him on the road when he left his house. They walked with him and took the opportunity to invite him and receive admonition until he reached the mosque. He said to whoever was with him, "Enter, may Allah have mercy on you." He did not enter until none of them remained with him.'

Al-Jadalī related that Rawḥ ibn Ḥātim[1] sent for Ibn Farrūkh to appoint him *qāḍī*. When he came to him, he told him, 'It has reached me that you were thinking of rebelling against us.' He replied 'Yes.' That was hard on Rawḥ. Then Ibn Farrūkh said, 'That was with 317 men, the number of the companions of Badr, each of them better than me.' Rawḥ said, 'We hope that you will never attack us.'

Then he offered him the office of *qāḍī* and he refused. He sat him in the mosque and commanded the litigants to speak to him. He began to weep and said to them, 'Have mercy on me, Allah will have mercy on you.'

Someone else mentioned that when he refused, he commanded that he be bound and carried to the roof of the mosque. He was asked,

[1] Abbasid governor of North Africa.

'Do you accept?' 'No,' he answered. He was about to be thrown off. When he saw their resolve, he said, 'I accept.'

He sat in the mosque with guards. Two litigants came to him. He looked at them and wept for a long time. Then he raised his head and said to them, 'I ask you by Allah to release me from yourselves. Do not be the first to give me an evil omen.' They had mercy on him and left him. The guards informed Rawḥ about that and he said, 'Go to him and tell him, "Indicate to us whom we should appoint, or accept it yourself."'

He said, 'It is 'Abdullāh ibn Ghānim. I think that he is a young man who has care and is concerned with the questions of the office of *qāḍī*, so you must have him. He knows the measure of judgement.' So Ibn Ghānim was appointed. Ibn Ghānim used to ask his advice in many of his affairs and judgements. Ibn Farrūkh was apprehensive about that. He said to him, 'Nephew! I did not accept a governor, shall I then accept a *wazīr*?' Ibn Ghānim persisted with him and pressed him. When Ibn Farrūkh saw that, he went to Egypt to flee from that out of scrupulousness, and he died there.

He was one of the people most adverse to the office of *qāḍī*. He used to say, 'I asked Abū Ḥanīfa, "What kept you from accepting the office of *qāḍī*?" He answered me, "Ibn Farrūkh, *qāḍī*s are of three sorts: a man who swims well and then the sea overcomes him after a long time. It might be that he swims, but he very nearly becomes exhausted and drowns. Then there is a man who is not a strong swimmer and he swims a little and then drowns. Then there is a man who does not swim, but throws himself into the water and drowns immediately."'

Saḥnūn said, 'Ibn Ghānim and Ibn Farrūkh disagreed about the man whom a unjust governor appoints to the office of *qāḍī*. Ibn Ghānim permitted that he be appointed and Ibn Farrūkh rejected it.

They wrote about that to Mālik. When Mālik read the letter, he said to the messenger, "Has Ibn Ghānim been appointed?" He replied, "Yes." Mālik said, "We belong to Allah and to Him we return. Did he not flee? Why did he not run away until his authority was cut off? The Persian was right and the one who claims that he is an Arab was wrong."'

Yazīd ibn Ḥātim, the governor, asked him about the blood of fleas on clothes and whether it was allowed to pray in them. He told him, 'I do not see any harm in it.' Then he said in the presence of his messenger, 'They ask us about the blood of fleas and they do not ask us about the blood of a Muslim which is spilled!'

He once went out to pray over a funeral, and there was Isḥāq, the son of the governor Yazīd ibn Ḥātim. He had set his dogs upon a gazelle to chase it. When he went, he asked him to stop and said, 'Young man, I saw you do such-and-such now. I do not like that from you because the Prophet ﷺ forbade it.'

Isḥāq gave in to him and told him, 'You have spoken the truth, Abū Muḥammad. May Allah repay you well. By Allah, I will never do that again.'

Ibn Qādim said, 'Ibn Farrūkh washed the dead of the weak people with humility and did not delegate that to anyone else, and he would carry them to their graves.'

His journeying and seeking

Al-Mālikī mentioned that he travelled early on and met the shaykhs and *fuqahā'*.

He said, 'There he listened to Abū Ḥanīfa in many questions

which were not recorded. It is said that it amounted to about nineteen thousand questions.'

He said, 'In the journey, he met Mālik and studied *fiqh* with him. He listened to him, and as for his previous report with Mālik, that was in his second journey after he left Kairouan.'

He mentioned that he said, 'A brick fell from the highest part of the house of Abū Ḥanīfa on my head when I was with him, and it bled. He said, "Choose the blood-money or three hundred *ḥadīths*." I answered, "The *ḥadīths*," and he gave me *ḥadīths*.'

He said, 'When I came to Kufa and there was a lot of dictation from what had been heard from al-A'mash, I asked about him. I was told, "He is angry with the People of *Ḥadīth* and he swore that he would not let them listen for a time."

'I used to go often to the door of his house hoping to reach him. Then one day his door opened and a slave-girl came out of it. She said to me, "What are you doing at the door?" I told her my news. She asked, "Where is your country?" I answered, "North Africa." She relaxed with me and said, "Do you know Kairouan?" I replied, "I am one of its people." She asked, "Do you know the house of Ibn Farrūkh?" I said, "I am him." She looked at me intently and said, "'Abdullāh?" I said, "Yes."

'She was a slavegirl whom we had sold when she was young. Then she went to al-A'mash and said to him, "My master whom I told you about is at the door." He commanded that I be admitted and I went in and he gave me a room in front of his house and I listened to him and he gave me *ḥadīths*.'

His taking on the *Sunna* and following it, and the rest of his reports

Abū al-'Arab said, 'Ibn Farrūkh wrote to Mālik to inform him that there were a lot of innovations in his land. He wrote some words for them to use in refuting them.'

Mālik wrote to him saying to him, 'If you think that of yourself, I fear that you will slip or be destroyed. Only the one who is exact and knows what he is saying to them should refute them. Then they will be unable to twist it for him. There is no harm in this person. As for someone else, I fear that he will speak to them and err, and then they will carry on in their error or take something from him and so be increased in persistence in that.'

Muḥammad ibn Saḥnūn said, 'The Mu'tazilites laid claim to Ibn Farrūkh in our presence. One of my father's friends who kept the company of Abū Khārija[1], said to me: 'Abū Khārija alighted us him and I asked him about Ibn Farrūkh and what he was accused of. He said, "Who said this? By Allah, there is no god but Him! With these two eyes, I have not seen a young man worship Allah more than Ibn Farrūkh!"

'Then he said, "By Allah, I was with him when he was asked about the Mu'tazilites. He said to the one who had asked, 'What is your question about the Mu'tazilites? The curse of Allah is upon the Mu'tazila before the Day of the *Dīn*, on the Day of the *Dīn*, and after the Day of the *Dīn* and for the entire length of all time.' He asked him, 'And when there are right-acting people among them?' He replied, 'Woe to you! Is there a right-acting man among them?'"'

Saḥnūn said, 'One of the companions of al-Bahlūl died, and he, Ibn Ghānim and Ibn Farrūkh were present. They prayed over him. Then the funeral bier of Ibn Ṣakhr, the Mu'tazilī, came. They said to Ibn Ghānim, "The funeral prayer!" He said, "Every living thing dies. Bring me my animal." The like of it was said to Ibn Farrūkh and he said the same thing. The like of it was said to al-Bahlūl and he also

[1] Abū Khārija 'Anbasa ibn Khārija al-Ghāfiqī, who lived in a *ribāṭ* in Ounga.

said the same thing. They left without praying over him. That was part of what Ibn Farrūkh was known for.'

Before this, he had thought about attacking the unjust rulers when those who commanded the correct and forbade the bad gathered together amounting to the number of the people of Badr. Then he went to Egypt and the people made a party based on him. He turned to the one who had made him a party and said, 'I testify that I have retracted what I said about attacking the unjust Imams. I repent to Allah of it.'

He made an agreement with some people in the time of [the governor] al-'Akkī to attack him. Al-'Akkī was a bad man. When they were to gather at the gate of Tunis, Ibn Farrūkh went to the allotted place but they failed to come. The only ones to fulfil the agreement were Muḥammad ibn Manūtā of the people of Madina and Qāḍī Abū Muḥriz from the Iraqis. So he went back.

Saḥnūn said, 'I went with my brother Ḥabīb when he used to listen to Ibn Farrūkh. When I saw him joking with the students, my heart was changed to love of him.'

He mentioned that a man invited him and gave him food and then gave him *nabīdh* to drink. He used to hold the opinion of the people of Iraq regarding it. He drank it and then his face went red. The one who had invited him said, 'Did you not tell us that good deeds fall from the face of a man when his face goes red from *nabīdh*?' Ibn Farrūkh said to him, 'We have no need of your food.'

His death

He, may Allah have mercy on him, died in Egypt after he had returned from the *ḥajj*. That was in 175 AH, and 176 AH is also said. He was buried in the Muqaṭṭam.

'Abdullāh ibn Wahb said, 'Ibn Farrukh came to us in 176 AH when he was fifty-five. It is said that he was sixty years old. He dyed his hair with henna. He was only here for a short time before he died, may Allah Almighty have mercy on him.'

FROM THE PEOPLE OF ANDALUSIA

Sa'īd ibn 'Abdūs

He was one of the people of Toledo and was known as al-Judayy (the Pole-Star). He met Mālik and listened to the *Muwaṭṭā'* from him. He was the *muftī* of his land in his time, and he was heard.

His father was 'Abdūs, the client of Hishām ibn al-Ḥakam by emancipation. It is also said that he was the client of al-Ḥakam. He died in 180 AH, according Ibn al-Faraḍī's book.

Ibn Ḥārith said, 'Isḥāq ibn Ibrāhīm mentioned to me that he was one of the people of knowledge and *fiqh*. He was the *muftī* of his land. He was appointed *qāḍī* of Toledo. His father 'Abdus looked after amīr al-Ḥakam who was the one who set him free. He was an excellent man of *taqwā*. The business of the people of Toledo was settled at his hands and he made it at peace with al-Ḥakam.'

The author said, 'This is what those men mentioned about his being set free. The sound version is that he was set free by 'Abd ar-Raḥmān ibn Mu'āwiya and the contract of his emancipation existed in Toledo. He is the one who gave asylum to Yaḥyā ibn Yaḥyā when he fled from Córdoba in the affliction of the people of ar-Rabaḍ [sfter the rebellion]. He protected him from al-Ḥakam ibn Hishām until he gave him safe-conduct and apologised to him.'

Ibn Waḍḍāḥ said that he met him in Toledo.

Al-Ghāzī ibn Qays

He was one of the people of Córdoba, an Umayyad with the *kunya* Abū Muḥammad. He travelled and listened to the *Muwaṭṭā'* from Mālik. He listened to Ibn Abī Dhi'b, Ibn Jurayj, al-Awzā'ī, Thawr ibn Zayd, and Muḥammad ibn Wardān. He was the first to bring the *Muwaṭṭā'* of Mālik and the recitation of Nāfi' to Andalusia according to what Abū 'Amr al-Muqri' stated.

He said, 'He saw Mālik ibn Anas when he was reading out the *Muwaṭṭā'*. He recited the Qur'an with Nāfi' ibn Abī Nu'aym, the Qur'an reciter of Madina. He knew the *Muwaṭṭā'* by heart. He took immense knowledge to Andalusia and Allah helped its people through him.'

The reciter used to go forward and back and repeated that to him.

One day the reciter changed the order of the chapters of the *Muwaṭṭā'* so that the people could ascertain al-Ghāzī's memory, and he objected to that on his part. He said, 'If you do it again, do not read to me. You just want people to see what we have,' meaning its memorisation.

His son related from him as well as Ibn Ḥabīb, Aṣbagh ibn Khālid and 'Uthmān ibn Ayyūb.

It is said that he was offered the office of *qāḍī* but refused it.

Aṣbagh said, 'I heard him say, "By Allah, I have not told a single lie since the time I did *ghusl*. If it had not been for what 'Umar ibn

'Abd al-'Azīz said, I would not have said it. 'Umar did not say it as a boast nor showing off nor did he say it except in order to be imitated."'

Qāḍī al-Muṣ'ab ibn 'Imrān sought his advice in the death of Ṣa'ṣa'a ibn Salām.

He was educated in philology in Córdoba before his journey and because of it he was the Imām of the people in Qur'anic recitation.

Abū 'Amr al-Muqri' said, 'He was good and excellent, a man of knowledge, disciplined, reliable, trustworthy.'

Aḥmad ibn 'Abd al-Barr said, 'He was a noble man of intellect who related many *ḥadīth*s and studied *fiqh* in legal questions. He was a leader in the science of the Qur'an, one who recited the Qur'an at night and prayed a lot at night. He died before 199 AH.'

It is related from him that he used to say, 'There is no day that comes but that it says, "I am a new creation. There is a witness to what is done in me. Take from me before I vanish." When that day goes, it falls in prostration to Allah and says, "Praise be to Allah who did not make me the Terrible Day."'

Al-Ghāzī had two sons:

'Abdullāh. He was one of the people of knowledge of Arabic and conveying the recitation of Nāfi'. He listened to his father and Thābit, and his son Qāsim related from him. He died in 230 AH.

Muḥammad, Abū 'Abdullāh, was a master of Arabic and language. He travelled and met ar-Rayyāsī and Abū Ḥātim. He died in Tangier during his journey. When death was near, he said:

Praise be to Allah, then praise be to Allah! What is death
to the one who forgets or is heedless?
What wonder does a man with two eyes see
when leaving this world for Allah?

Ziyād ibn 'Abd ar-Raḥmān, known as Shabṭūn

He was from Córdoba and was the ancestor of the Banū Ziyād there. He has the *kunya* Abū 'Abdullāh.

He is Ziyād ibn 'Abd ar-Raḥmān ibn Zuhayr ibn Nāshira ibn Lūddān ibn Yaḥyā ibn Aḥṭab ibn al-Ḥārith ibn Wā'il al-Lakhmī. It is said that he was one of the descendants of Ḥāṭib ibn Abī Balta'a.

He listened to the *Muwaṭṭā'* from Mālik. He has a book of listening on *fatwā*s from him known as 'Samā' Ziyād'.

He listened to Mu'āwiya, the son of Qāḍī Ṣāliḥ Ziyād who was his son-in-law and married to his daughter, 'Abdullāh ibn 'Uqba, al-Layth ibn Sa'd, Sulaymān ibn Bilāl, 'Abdullāh ibn 'Abd ar-Raḥmān, 'Abd ar-Raḥmān ibn Abī az-Zinād, 'Abdullāh ibn 'Umar al-'Umarī, Yaḥyā ibn Ayyūb, Abū Mash'ar, Mūsā ibn 'Alī, Muḥammad ibn 'Abdullāh ibn 'Umar al-Laythī, al-Qāsim ibn 'Abdullāh, Ismā'īl ibn Dāwūd, Hārūn ibn 'Abdullāh, Muḥammad ibn Abī Salām al-'Umarī, Abū Ma'mar, the companion of Anas, 'Abd ar-Raḥmān ibn Abī Bakr ibn Abī Mulayka, Ibn Abī Dāwūd, Sufyān ibn 'Uyayna, 'Umar ibn Qays and Ibn Abī Ḥāzim.

Yaḥyā ibn Yaḥyā related from him the *Muwaṭṭā'* and what he had heard from Mālik before his journey from Andalusia. Ziyād indicated to him that he should travel to Mālik while he was alive and to learn from him, and so he did that.

Ziyād was one of the first people to bring the *Muwaṭṭā'* of Mālik to Andalusia. He learned *fiqh* by listening to it. Then Yaḥyā ibn Yaḥyā related it.

Yaḥyā ibn Yaḥyā said, 'Ziyād was the first of the people to bring the knowledge of the *sunan* to Andalusia and the questions of the *ḥalāl* and the *ḥarām*, and aspects of *fiqh* and judgements. He was the first to be acquainted with the *sunna* about turning the cloaks inside out in the Rain Prayer. The one in charge of leading the prayer (*ṣāḥib aṣ-ṣalāt*) at that time was al-Muṣ'ab ibn 'Imrān. He disliked that. He said, "This is delirium."'

Yaḥyā said, 'After that I went to the east and I met Mālik ibn Anas, al-Layth ibn Sa'd and others. I found that the *sunna* of turning the cloaks was known with them and well-spread.'

Ash-Shīrāzī said, 'The people of Madina called Ziyād the "*Faqīh* of Andalusia."'

Ibn Ḥārith related that he undertook two journeys. The last of them was when Mu'āwiya ibn Ṣāliḥ went with him.

Abū Bakr al-Mālikī related that Ziyād came to Madina and went to Mālik when he had Ibn Kināna with him. Ibn Kināna did not recognise him. Ibn Kināna asked him about what land he was from and he mentioned it. He asked him, 'Who is the *faqīh* of your land?' He replied, 'I am,' or something like that. Ibn Kināna gave him a streamof questions, and what he did not like came from him. He said, 'If there are people who give you mastery, there is loss,' and quoted the verse [of a poem].

Mālik told him, 'You have offended the man and shown bad manners.' When the assembly was firm for Ziyād, Ibn Kināna put him through some questions, and he had a sea which burst from him. He knew then that what had come from him at first was due to his awe of the assembly.

His excellence and righteousness

When Qāḍī Mu'āwiya ibn Ṣāliḥ sent something to Ziyād – and he was the father of his wife – to his house, he did not eat any of it.

Ziyād was a man of great devotion and scrupulousness. Hishām tried to tempt him with accepting the office of *qāḍī* and he refused it and fled. Hishām said, 'Would that all people were like Ziyād so that I could be spared people who desire this world.' He granted him security so he returned to Córdoba.

Hishām used to say, 'I testify to people and I did not see a man who concealed his asceticism more than he showed it with the exception of Ziyād.'

Yaḥyā ibn Isḥāq mentioned that when Hishām came to power, he was told, 'What you want will only be properly achieved unless you appoint Ziyād as *qāḍī*.' He sent to him and he refused, but Hishām insisted on it. Ziyād said to the wazīrs, 'If you have resolved on it, then I will tell you how I will begin, and (I swear an oath) that I will walk to Makka (if I fail). If you appoint me and anyone comes to me complaining of you, I will take from you what he claims and return it to him. I will demand the clear proof from you because of what I know of your injustice.' So they left him and he was excused. Yaḥyā ibn Yaḥyā was asked, 'Is this the method of the office of *qāḍī*?' He answered, 'Yes, in the case of the one who is known for injustice and perfidy.' They indicated that he should be excused.

Amīr Hishām preferred Ziyād, honoured him, trusted him and withdrew with him and asked him about the matters of the *dīn* to which he applied himself. He adopted his opinion and went to extremes in obeying him. He sent money to him to give out as *ṣadaqa*. Sometimes he went to him at night, so he came out to him and greeted him and spoke with him.

Aṣ-Ṣadafī mentioned that he was offered to take money to divide and he refused.

It is mentioned that he was present with Hishām one day when he became angry with one of his elite of him who had sent him a letter which he disliked. He commanded that his hand be cut off. Ziyād said, 'May Allah put the Amīr right. Mālik ibn Anas gave me a *ḥadīth* in a report going directly to the Prophet ﷺ: "If someone restrains his rage when he is able to act on it, Allah will appoint for him security and faith on the Day of Rising."'

The Amīr's anger was stilled and he said to him, 'By Allah, did Mālik relate this to you?' Ziyād answered, 'By Allah, Mālik related that to me.' The ruler commanded that they spare the servant's hand and he forgave him.

It is mentioned that Ziyād was riding with Amīr al-Ḥakam and Ziyād had his son riding on his mount behind him. They were leaving a funeral. The conversation with the Amīr lasted until they reached al-Qantara. He heard the *mu'adhdhin* and Ziyād stopped talking. He said, 'Pardon to the Amir! May Allah put him right! We were in a conversation which this caller to Allah Almighty has opposed. It is not permitted to turn from it. It is more fitting to be answered. If we meet again, we will be able to complete the conversation if we need to.' He saluted him and entered the mosque from the al-Qantara door and the Amīr went on to the castle.'

Yaḥyā said, 'Ziyād was unique in his time in aceticism and scrupulousness. Hishām came to him at night with his elite and knocked on the door. He went out in alarm and opened it to him and greeted him and asked him why he had come. He said, "To seek to be alone with you. This is good wealth," and he indicated some money a boy was carrying, "I want to draw near to Allah by it and I have come to you so that you can put it were you think best."

'Ziyād said to him, "You should find the one who is the most upright for you in that and who knows its people." He named some people among the virtuous for him. Hishām refused any except him, but he could not make him do it. Hishām was embarrassed and removed his money, saying, "O Allah, I intend to obey you with the like of this!"'

Ḥabīb said, 'We were sitting with Ziyād when a letter came to him from one of the kings he had singled out. He wrote on it and then sealed the letter and the messenger took it. Ziyād said, "Do you know what the author of this letter asked? He asked about the pans of the scales of actions on the Day of Rising and whether they are made of gold or silver. I wrote to him, 'Mālik related to me from Ibn Shihāb that he said that the Messenger of Allah ﷺ said, "When the Islam of a man is good, he leaves what does not concern him." It will come and then you will know.'"'

Ziyād had a humorous anecdote mentioned about him with his son-in-law, Mu'āwiya ibn Ṣāliḥ. That is that he wanted to look at a woman before her marriage was completed as some people did. It is also said that it was after the completion of the marriage, and that is more likely for his situation. At the end of the story, he made an appointment with the people of the house that he would come to them at night without the knowledge of Mu'āwiya. He came and hid himself in the portico of the house. Mu'āwiya went out, sensing restlessness and movement from his horse towards where Ziyād was. He disliked that and called for a lamp. When he looked, Ziyād had retired into one of the corners of the portico. He did not do more than say, 'Treat our guest well,' and left.

He listened to a book from Mālik, and to his general chapter.

Ibn 'Attāb said, 'It is *The Book of the Gharīb* which contains much knowledge.'

Yaḥyā ibn Yaḥyā said, 'I read the oral report of Ziyād to Ibn Nāfi' and Ibn al-Qāsim. Ibn al-Qāsim rejected a question from it and said to me, "Ziyād has lied about Mālik! He did not hear this from him at all!" I took the book and folded it and put it in my sleeve. He said, "Read." I replied, "I consider Ziyād too noble to be accused of the like of this." Ibn al-Qāsim was ashamed and said, "Read! By Allah, I will never repeat the like of it," so I read.'

Muḥammad ibn 'Īsā al-A'shā had a bad opinion of Ziyād. He used to say, 'I have eaten sweet apples, drunk light grapes and urinated in stagnant water since such a time so that Allah would make me forget the knowledge of Ziyād and remove it from my heart, but I did not forget it. So I shall cling to all that I knew he had forgotten.' He was asked, 'Why?' He said, 'Because Ziyād was nothing. His knowledge was inane.'

He died in 193 AH, or it is said 194 AH or 199 AH.

He was born in Córdoba. Among them were a number of the people of majesty, excellence, judgement, knowledge and good.

Sa'īd ibn Abī Hind, Abū 'Uthmān

He came from Toledo and lived in Córdoba. He met Mālik ibn Ana,s and he was the one whom Mālik called the 'Wise (al-Ḥakīm)'. Aḥmad ibn 'Abd al-Barr said that.

Ibn Lubāba said, 'His name was 'Abd al-Wahhāb.'

One of them said, reporting from Ibn Ḥārith, ''Abd ar-Raḥmān ibn Abī Hind al-Aṣbaḥī from the people of Toledo. His *kunya* was Abū Hind. He listened to Mālik and was respected by him. He called him "The Wise man of Andalusia." He went and took up residence in Córdoba. One of the caliphs appointed him a *wazīr*.'

The like of that is found in the book of Abū Sa'īd aṣ-Ṣadafī. He gives his *kunya* as Abū Zayd. He said that he died in 200 AH.

Another mentioned that the reason for his being appointed a *wazīr* was that he was tested in his truthfulness. He never told a lie at all. One of the wazīrs of that moment said, 'I will make him lie.' He waited until he dozed off. Then he said to him, 'Have you slept, Abū Hind?' He answered, 'Yes.' So he did not win what he wanted from him by people's habit of denying this.

This story is ascribed to someone else after him. Perhaps there are two stories, but Allah knows best.

I read in *The Book of the Qāḍīs* by Ibn Ḥārith that he is Sa'īd ibn 'Abd ar-Raḥmān ibn Abī Hind al-Asbaḥī. He was appointed the *qāḍī* of Toledo.

He said, 'He mentioned to me that Abū 'Abd ar-Raḥmān ibn Abī

Hind was one of the scholars and he went on a journey in which he met Mālik. After his journey he was appointed the *qāḍī* of Toledo.'

Another said, "Abd ar-Raḥmān ibn Abī Hind, Abū Hind al-Asbaḥī aṭ-Ṭulayṭilī. He related the *Muwaṭṭā'* from Mālik.'

Qāḍī Abū al-Walīd al-Faraḍī and Muḥammad ibn Ḥārith said, 'I do not know whether they were two or one. It is said that Ibn Abī Hind died during the time of Hishām ibn 'Abd ar-Raḥmān[1], but Allah knows best.'

Aḥmad ibn Sa'īd said, 'Ibn Abī Hind – and he did not give him name – was an excellent man of intelligence. He had good behaviour and esteem.'

Ibn Waḍḍāḥ said, 'Ibn Abī Hind was a sharif and Mālik used to ask about him. He would say, "What did the wise one in Andalusia do?" because of something he heard him say. That was one day when Mālik said, "How excellent is silence and what an adornment for its people!" Ibn Abī Hind said, "Does everyone wish to be silent, Abū 'Abdullāh?" Mālik liked what he said.'

It is said that he said to him, 'Silence adorns what is after it.'

A man intimated in the presence of the Amīr 'Abd Ar-Raḥmān that he was guilty of eye-service. Sa'īd said, 'May Allah put the Amīr right! He thinks that we have a bad secret while maintaining a public face. Doesn't the Amīr, may Allah Almighty exalt him, think that the secret of a man would corrupt his outward?'

He saw people looking at some people who had been clothed by the amīr, admiring their clothes, and remarked, 'They have only taken that for a cheap price,' meaning they have debased their *dīn* for that.

[1] The Umayyad Amīr of Córdoba from 172 AH to 179 AH.

Yaḥyā ibn Yaḥyā related from him and Ibn Wahb reported from Mālik that Ibn Abī Hind said, 'I found silence harder than speaking.'

Yaḥyā ibn Yaḥyā said, 'I heard Ibn Abī Hind say, "I have not been in awe of anything as I was of 'Abd Ar-Raḥmān ibn Mu'āwiya[1]. When I went on *ḥajj* and I came to Mālik, I experienced such an intense awe of him that it made the awe of Ibn Mu'āwiya seem insignificant."'

He said, 'There was a son of a shaykh who did not own any of his father's property. He said to him one day, "Father, give me something from Mālik." He said, "Have I appointed anything of it apart from you? You ride, dress and eat as I do." He said, "I want you to tell me something of it." He said, "I am prevented from that since it is said, 'The intellect of a man is disparaged as his property is disparaged.'"'

Aḥmad said, 'Sa'īd ibn Abī Hind died at the beginning of the reign of 'Abd Ar-Raḥmān ibn Mu'āwiya, much before the death of Mālik.'

[1] The first Umayyad Amīr.

Yaḥyā ibn Muḍar al-Qaysī (and it is said al-Yaḥṣubī)

He was one of the people of Córdoba, Abū Zakariyā'. It is also said that he is Abū Bakr. He was a Syrian by origin. He was one of the great *fuqahā'* of Córdoba. He listened to Sufyān ath-Thawrī and Mālik ibn Anas and related the *Muwaṭṭā'* from him.

Mālik related a story from Sufyān at-Thawrī from him that 'clustered acacias' (59:59)[1] refers to the banana. He said, 'Yaḥyā ibn Muḍar, the *faqīh* of Andalusia, told me that as reported from Sufyān.'

'Abdullāh ibn Wahb and Yaḥyā ibn Yaḥyā related from him before this journey. He was a man of perfect knowledge, one with opinion.

Yaḥyā ibn Yaḥyā spoke to one of the great men who told him, 'The Amīr has granted my request to make the *fuqahā'* sit with him when he judges Ibn Bashīr, and he wants you to sit with him.' Yaḥyā said to him, 'If you must act, then you must have our shaykh, Yaḥyā ibn Muḍar.'

The Amīr al-Mu'minīn, al-Ḥakam ibn Hishām ibn 'Abd ar-Raḥmān ibn Mu'āwiya ibn 'Abd Al-Mālik ibn Marwān crucified him among those he crucified because of uprising on the part of those who wanted to rise against him and depose him in 189 AH.

They objected to many matters which their Amīr had done in his pleasures and other things, and they wanted to depose him. They

[1] *Ṭalḥ mandūd. Ṭalḥ* is also the banana tree.

consisted of a number of notable *fuqahā'*, great scholars, virtuous men, important people and their shaykhs. They brought a cousin of his and they resolved to attack with the cousin and advance him, but he betrayed them to the Amīr who was acquainted with his soundness because he had brought his scribe and reliable person into a dome of his and put the curtain in front of them on a day when the group had arranged to meet with him. When they were present, he began to question them about those who were with them in this business while the scribe was writing it down, until one of them grew suspicious about the frequency of his questions. It was said that he heard the squeaking of the pen behind the curtain, and they uncovered the scribe and understood what the business was. They were defeated and hurried to leave. Those who were quick were saved and those who remained were seized. Among those who were saved were Yaḥyā ibn Yaḥyā and 'Īsā ibn Dīnār. Yaḥyā ibn Muḍar was among those who were seized. The Amīr commanded that they be crucified on the side of the river of Córdoba. They numbered seventy-two men among the *fuqahā'* and people of virtuous action.

It is said that he crucified one hundred and forty men.

Something else was said in the commentary of this story.

What he did to them caused pain in the hearts of the people and they turned against him again and continued to wait to attack him until they carried out the famous uprising in the Battle of Rabaḍ in which they were utterly defeated in 202 AH.

The Middle Generation

FROM THE PEOPLE OF MADINA

ʿAbdullāh ibn Nāfiʿ

He was a client of the Banū Makhzūm and was known as aṣ-Ṣā'igh. His *kunya* was Abū Muḥammad. Al-Bukhārī said that.

He related from Mālik, Ibn Abi Dhi'b, Husayn ibn ʿAbdullāh ibn Ḍamīra and Ibn Abī az-Zinād, and he learned *fiqh* from Mālik and his peers.

Aḥmad ibn Ḥanbal said, ʿHe held the opinion of Mālik and was the Muftī of the people of Madina following the opinion of Mālik. He was not a master of *Ḥadīth*, and he did not have that in *ḥadīth*s. He was weak in that.'

Abū Zurʿa ar-Rāzī said, ʿThere is no objection to him.'

Al-Bukhārī said, ʿHis *ḥadīth*s were both known and unknown, and his book is sounder.'

Muḥammad ibn al-Ḥusayn said, ʿI asked Abū ʿAbdullāh about him and he said that he is reliable.'

Ibn Lubāba said, ʿThe People of *Ḥadīth* advance Ibn Nāfiʿ over the companions of Mālik in *ḥadīth*s and reliability.'

Ibn Ghānim said, ʿI asked Mālik, "Who has this business after you?" He answered, "A man among my companions." A one-eyed man came in, and it was Ibn Nāfiʿ. He said, "This one."'

Ash-Shīrāzī said, ʿHe was deaf and illiterate and could not write.'

He said, ʿI kept the company of Mālik for a year in which I did not write down anything from him. I memorised it.'

He is the one to whom Saḥnūn and the great companions of Mālik listened. He is the one whose oral transmission was accompanied by that of Ashhab in *al-'Utbiyya*. It is not as Abū 'Abdullāh ibn 'Attāb claimed in his *Index* about him being Ibn Nāfi' az-Zubayrī. What we mentioned is not denied. That is why he was counted among the shaykhs of Andalusia in its oral transmission. In the oral tradition of the two shaykhs, they name Ashhab and Ibn Nāfi' aṣ-Ṣā'igh. He is the one they mentioned, and his transmission in the *Mudawwana* is precious.

Ashhab said, 'I was never present at an assembly of Mālik but that Ibn Nāfi' was present. I did not listen but that he listened. However, he did not write.' Ashhab would write both for him and for himself.

We find in the *Mudawwana* that Mālik asked Ibn Nāfi' about a *ḥadīth* from Ḥusayn ibn 'Abdullāh ibn Ḍamīra on recitation in the two *rak'at*s of *Fajr*. Ibn Nāfi' said, 'I related it from him.' Mālik liked that and approved of it. He said, 'We were with this and nothing of it reached me.' He sat in Mālik's seat after Ibn Kināna.

Ibn Waḍḍāḥ said, 'He was the best of the Egyptian and Alexandrian companions of Mālik in worship. Ibn Nāfi' was a virtuous man, but those ones were above him.'

Muḥammad ibn Sa'īd said, 'He clung to Mālik very strongly and did not put anyone ahead of him. He was below Ma'n.'

Saḥnūn said, 'Ibn Nāfi' was a virtuous man. He was impatient and his father was a dyer. When he was young, he put the vowels at the end. When he was in one of the gardens of Madina one day, he heard a man recite the Qur'an. He exclaimed, "This one recites the Book of Allah while I am occupied in this garden!" and he went back and clung to the mosque.'

He had a commentary on the *Muwaṭṭā'* and Yaḥyā ibn Yaḥyā related it from him. Ibn Ḥabīb and Ibn Ḥārith counted him among those who succeeded Mālik in Madina in *fiqh*.

Mujāhid ibn Musa said, "Abdullāh ibn Nāfi' aṣ-Ṣā'igh said, "I have sat with Mālik for thirty years (or thirty-five years) both morning and night. Sometimes I come t midday, and I did not see him read the *Muwaṭṭā'* to anyone.""

He died in Madina in Ramadan in 186 AH.

Muḥammad ibn Maslama ibn Hishām

Az-Zubayr said, 'He is Muḥammad ibn Maslama ibn Muḥammad ibn Hishām ibn Ismā'īl ibn al-Walīd ibn al-Mughīra ibn 'Abdullāh ibn 'Umar ibn Makhzūm.'

This Hishām was the governor of Madina to whom the *mudd* of Hishām is ascribed, and the one from whom the contract of the slave was mentioned in his khuṭba.

Muḥammad related from Mālik and learned *fiqh* from him. He also related from aṣ-Ḍaḥḥāk ibn 'Uthmān, Ibrāhīm ibn Sa'īd and al-Hudayrī.

Abū Ḥātim said, 'He was one of the *fuqahā'* of Madina among the companions of Mālik and among them he had the greatest knowledge of *fiqh*. He was trustworthy.'

Muḥammad ibn Maslama had books of *fiqh* which were used.

Qāḍī at-Tustarī said, 'He is trustworthy and a trusted source.'

Ash-Shīrāzī said, 'He had both knowledge and scrupulousness.'

He said, 'When Mālik came to ar-Rashīd, he came between two men of the Banū Makhzūm: al-Mughīra on his right and Ibn Maslama on his left.'

Al-Bukhārī said, 'Muḥammad ibn Maslama was asked, "What is the opinion of so-and-so who came to all the lands except Madina?" He replied, "It is because he is one of the dajjāls. The Prophet ﷺ said, 'Neither the Dajjāl nor the plague will enter it.'"'

He died in 216 AH.

Muṭarrif ibn 'Abdullāh ibn Muṭarrif ibn Sulaymān ibn Yasār al-Yasārī al-Hilālī

Abū Muṣ'ab. It is also said that he is Abū 'Abdullāh. He was a client of Maymūna, the Umm al-Mu'minīn.

His great grandfather Sulaymān was an early scholar, famous for his knowledge and *fiqh*.

He and his brothers, 'Aṭā', 'Abdullāh and 'Abd al-Mālik, the Banū Yasār, acted scribes for Maymūna, the Umm al-Mu'minīn. He took knowledge from all of them, and their *walā'* belonged to the Banū 'Abbās. Maymūna gave their *walā'* to 'Abdullāh ibn al-'Abbās.

Al-Bukhārī said, 'He was the client of Umm Salama, Umm al-Mu'minīn, may Allah be pleased with her.'

Abū 'Umar aṣ-Ṣadafī remarked, 'This is a misapprehension which I do not recognise. He was, in fact, the client of Maymūna, Umm al-Mu'minīn, may Allah be pleased with her.'

Ibn Ḥārith called him 'al-Aslamī'.

Ismā'īl ibn Isḥāq mentioned in *al-Mabsūṭ*, 'Al-Aslamī related from Mālik,' but he did not name him.

Muḥammad ibn Sa'īd said, 'Muṭarrif ibn 'Abdullāh ibn Yasār. Yasār was the scribe of a man of Aslam. 'Abdullāh ibn Abī Farwa paid for him and freed him. He was one of his supporters and he was reliable.'

Qāḍī Abū al-Walīd al-Bājī said, 'Muṭarrif the *faqīh*, the companion of Mālik, who was his nephew. Muṭarrif was deaf. He related from

Mālik, Ibn Abī az-Zinād, 'Abd ar-Raḥmān ibn Abi al-Mawālī and 'Abdullāh ibn 'Umar al-'Umarī.'

Abū Zur'a, Abū Ḥātim, Ibrāhīm ibn al-Mundhir, ad-Dhihlī, Ya'qūb ibn Shayba, and al-Bukhārī transmitted from him and he related from him in his *Ṣaḥīḥ*.

Ash-Shīrāzī said, 'He learned *fiqh* from Mālik, 'Abd al-'Azīz ibn al-Mājishūn, Ibn Abī Ḥāzim, Ibn Dīnār, Ibn Kināna and al-Mughīra.'

Ibn Ma'īn said, 'Muṭarrif was reliable.'

Ibn Waḍḍāḥ said, 'In his opinion, he was better than Ibn Abī Uways.'

Al-Kūfī said, 'He is trustworthy.'

Aḥmad ibn Ḥanbal said, 'They used to put him first among the companions of Mālik.'

Abū Ḥātim said, 'I prefer Muṭarrif to Ismā'īl ibn Abī Uways, and Muṭarrif was an unsupported truthful man.'

Ibn Ma'īn was asked, 'Is Muṭarrif like al-Qa'nabī and Ma'n?' He replied, 'All of them are reliable men.'

Az-Zubayr said, 'Muṭarrif said, "I kept the company of Mālik for seventeen years. I did not see him read the *Muwaṭṭā'* to anyone. He used to criticise writing down knowledge to us. He said, 'I did not know anyone among the people of our land nor among those in the past who wrote (it).'"'

'He was asked, "What should we do then?" He said, "You should memorise as they memorised and act as they acted until your hearts are illuminated, and that will spare you writing. 'Umar ibn al-Khaṭṭāb, may Allah be pleased with him, disliked that. He said, 'A book is not written along with the Book of Allah.'"'

Ibn Waḍḍāḥ said, 'I saw that Saḥnūn did not admire Muṭarrif.'

Abū al-'Arab said, 'Muṭarrif was tried regarding the [createdness of the] Qur'an in the time of the caliph al-Ma'mūn.'

Al-Bukhārī said, 'He was born in 139 AH and died in Madina in 220 AH. Ibn Abī Khaythama and Muḥammad ibn Sa'īd, "At the beginning of it."'

Ad-Dāraquṭnī said, 'In Ṣafar of it.' Another said, 'In 214 AH.' Ibn Waḍḍāḥ said, 'In 219 AH.' It is said that he was about eighty years old.

'ABD AL-MĀLIK IBN 'ABD AL-'AZĪZ IBN 'ABDULLĀH IBN ABĪ SALAMA

His *kunya* was Abū Marwān, and Abū Salama's name was Maymūn. Al-Lālakā'ī stated that. It is also said that it was 'Dīnār'. Al-Bājī said that. He was a client of the Banū Taym from Quraysh and then of the family of al-Munkadir.

Al-Mājishūn[1] is Abū Salama according to what al-Lālakā'ī said.

Muḥammad ibn Sa'īd ad-Dāraquṭnī said, 'He is Ya'qūb ibn Abī Salama, the brother of 'Abdullāh.'

Al-Bājī said, 'Al-Mājishūn' means "rosy" in Persian.'

Ad-Dāraquṭnī said, 'He was called that because of some redness in his face.'

Ibn Khālid related from one of them that they were among the people of Isfahan and then they moved to Madina. They used to meet one another and said, 'Shūnī? Shūnī?' meaning 'How are you?' They gave him a nickname because of that.

Ibn Ḥārith related that Mājish was a place in Khurasan from which they originated.

'Abd al-Mālik was an eloquent *faqīh*. He issued *fatwā*s in his time until his death, as did his father before him. He was a *faqīh*, son of a *faqīh*.

Muṣ'ab said, "Abd al-Mālik was the *muftī* of the people of Madina

[1] Al-Mājishūn is 'Abd al-'Azīz.

in his time. He was blind. It is said that he went blind at the end of his life. His house was a house of knowledge and the best house in Madina.'

His grandfather was 'Abdullah. He related from Ibn 'Umar and others. Muslim transmitted from him.

His grandfather's brother was Ya'qūb ibn Abī Salama. He also related from Ibn 'Umar.

There was 'Umar ibn 'Abd al-'Azīz. Muslim also related from him.

There was also Yūsuf ibn 'Abd al-'Azīz, the brother of 'Abd al-Mālik. Az-Zubayr ibn Bakkār gives *ḥadīth*s from him.

One of them was Yūsuf ibn Ya'qūb ibn 'Abdullāh ibn Abī Salama. He related from Ibn al-Munkadir and az-Zuhrī. Al-Bukhārī and Muslim related from him, and Ibn Ḥanbal and Ibn al-Madinī and others transmitted from him.

There was also his brother, 'Abd al-'Azīz ibn Ya'qūb Abū al-Aṣbagh. He also related the *mursal ḥadīth*s from Ibn al-Munkadir which Ibn Ḥanbal related from him.

Scholars' praise and esteem for him and his excellence

Ash-Shīrāzī said, 'He learned *fiqh* with his father, Mālik, Ibn Abī Ḥāzim, Ibn Dīnār, Ibn Kināna and al-Mughīra.'

He was eloquent. He related that when ash-Shāfi'ī conferred with him, he did not inform the people about much of what they said because ash-Shāfi'ī had been taught manners with Hudhayl in the desert, and 'Abd al-Mālik had learnt manners among his maternal uncles from the Banū Kalb in the desert.

Qāḍī Yaḥyā ibn Aktam said, "Abd al-Mālik was a sea which buckets do not perturb.'

'Abd al-Mālik said, 'I came to al-Mundhir ibn 'Abdullāh al-Makhzūmī when I was young. When I spoke and he understood some good Arabic from me, he asked me, "Who are you?" I told him. He told me, "Seek knowledge. You have your shoes and water-skins with you."'

Ibn al-Mu'adhdhil said, 'Whenever I remember that the earth ate the tongue of 'Abd al-Mālik, this world becomes insignificant in my eyes!'

He was asked, 'Where is your tongue in relation to the tongue of your master, 'Abd al-Mālik?' He replied, 'When his tongue was faulty, it was far more alive than my tongue when it is quick.'

Ibn Ḥārith said, 'He was one of the eminent *fuqahā'*. Saḥnūn praised him and preferred him. He said, "I want to travel to him and to read these books to him. What he allows of it, I will allow, and what he rejects, I will reject." Ibn Ḥabīb praised him a lot and used to elevate him in understanding over most of the companions of Mālik.'

Ibn al-Mawwāz said, 'I was with him after my uncle until the letter of the Amīr al-Mu'minīn reached him, asking him about some things. When the reader read it to him, he said to him, "Take the letter and write its answer." He dictated to him until he sealed it and sent it to the messenger.'

Ibn Sha'bān said, 'Al-Ma'mūn wrote to him to appoint him a *qāḍī*. He was blind, and refused that.'

He was told, 'If you go to Iraq, your eyesight could be healed. There are people who could cure it. You can look into your property.' He had a boy with him who shared some commerce with him. He said, 'I will not leave Madina.'

He mentioned that he was brought a cupper to cup him for his sight. He told him, 'You put such-and-such on your back lying down.' He refused. He said, 'I would not touch that whose reward Allah has made the Garden by hindering one of the obligations of the prayer.'

Ibn Ḥārith said, 'He had a rebellious self. Mālik spoke a harsh word to him one day, and he left him for an entire year. That was because he asked Mālik about the difference between two questions and Mālik said to him, "Do you know the house of Ibn Qudāma?" It was a house in which the young men played with doves. It is said that he alluded to the prison by it.'

Scholars used to prefer him in the science of *waqf.* Qāḍī Ismā'īl said that 'Abd al-Malik knew the position of Mālik regarding *waqf*s.

He used to say after he lost his sight, 'Come on and ask me about the difficult questions!' Qāḍī Ismā'īl mentioned some of his words in *al-Mabsūṭ*. Then he said, 'How lucid were his words and wonderful his details and little his excess!'

Many people and exalted Imams learned *fiqh* with him, like Aḥmad ibn al-Mu'adhdhal, Ibn Ḥabīb and Saḥnūn.

Qāḍī Ibn Aktam said, 'I have not seen any man like 'Abd al-Malik. If he had had people to question him – and he was one of those whose books were heard – four hundred volumes (or two hundred volumes) could have been written down from him." The transmitter was unsure of the number.

An-Nasā'ī said, 'The *fuqahā'* of the cities from the companions of

Mālik among the people of Madina include 'Abd al-Malik ibn al-Mājishūn. 'Abd al-Mālik ibn al-Mājishūn said much about *fiqh* and other things.'

Ibn Ḥārith said, 'He had extensive language. He has a book containing what he heard, and it is well-known. His book which he wrote at the end on *fiqh* was related from him by Yaḥyā ibn Ḥammād as-Sijilmasī. He also had a treatise on belief and predestination and the refutation of those who say that the Qur'an is created and that humans have the capacity (to create actions)."

His position on that about which people differ and his following the *Sunna*

Abū Muṣ'ab az-Zuhrī said, 'The Qur'an is not created.' He added, 'That is the statement of 'Abd al-Malik ibn al-Mājishūn.'

Saḥnūn wrote to 'Abd al-Malik to mention to him what occurred in a discussion on anthropomorphism and the Qur'an, and he asked him to answer for him. 'Abd al-Malik wrote to him, 'From 'Abd al-Malik ibn al-Mājishūn to Saḥnūn ibn Sa'īd. Peace be upon you. I praise Allah to you. There is no god but Him. As for what follows, may Allah give us and you success in obeying Him. You asked about some questions which are not the business of the people of knowledge, and knowledge about what is not known. Those who passed before from the beginning of this community are enough for you. They followed with the best, and they did not plunge into any of it. One approaches the *dīn* like a virgin in her tent. It is not said to her, "How?" or "From where?" Follow as they followed. Know that it is the greatest knowledge. A man does not wish to speak of any of this lest he disbelieves and so falls into the fire of Hell.'

'Abd al-Mālik said, 'If al-Marīsī[1] had been taken, his neck would have been severed.'

He said, 'I heard the scholars I met say, "The Qur'an is the word of Allah, the Majestic, the Mighty, and it is not created."'

The Qāḍī, may Allah be pleased with him, said, 'We mentioned all of this and we extracted it from the books of the reliable Imams to refute and invalidate what al-Bājī related differently about his faults which is not sound about him and which is not recognised, and it is more fitting to leave it.'

Ibn al-Labbād mentioned that Qāḍī Yaḥyā ibn Aktam was with 'Abd al-Malik on his seat and they were discussing the school of the people of Iraq and the people of Madina, and they were debating that. Ibn Aktam said, 'Abū Marwān, we travelled to Madina for knowledge, desiring it, but in Madina you are not concerned with it. The one who travels seeking it is not like the one who is in it and then slackens.'

'Abd al-Malik said, 'O Allah, forgiveness! Abū Muḥammad, summon for me 'Umāra, the *mu'adhdhin* from the people of Sa'd!' An old shaykh came and he said to him, 'For how long have you given the *adhān*?' He replied, 'For seventy years. I have given the *adhān* with my fathers, my uncles, and my grandparents. This *adhān* which I give today is that *adhān* which they told me that they had given with Ibn Umm Maktūm.'

'Abd al-Mālik said, 'If you say, "You have slackened and left this *adhān* of the Prophet ﷺ! Do you think that we do not pray? You have opposed us in it and there are other things more suited with which you can oppose us.'

Ibn Aktam was ashamed and did not mention that he had refuted him.

[1] Bishr ibn Ghiyāth al-Marīsī, a *mutakallim* with extreme views and known for spreading the idea that the Qur'an is created.

The rest of his reports and his death

He mentioned that Ibn Abī Isḥāq asked Ibn al-Mājishūn about a question and he answered it and then he refuted him and he answered him back. When that went on for a long time, he told him, 'Get out. I am too skilled for you to refute questions against me.'

He told Saḥnūn about that and he told him, 'Yes, he is too skilled to be refuted.'

'Abd al-Malik said, 'A man of Quraysh was a friend of mine. There was some reckoning between him and his guardian, so he sat me down with the man and then spoke with the guardian. The guardian said, "I took such-and-such and I spent such-and-such for you." The Qurayshī retorted, "You did not spend anything."

'He said to me and my friend, "Testify to what you heard from him. He is denying me my due." I said, "No, by Allah, we do not testify to it and we did not sit for this."

'He said, "Go with us to Mālik. If he commands you to testify, then testify," I said, "Even if he were to command, I still would not testify because I did not sit to give testimony."

'We went to Ibn Abī Ḥāzim and he told him the story. He said to me, "He has no testimony from you." Then we went to Mālik and we mentioned the story to him and he told me, "'Abd al-Malik, do not testify."'

The author said: 'In our opinion, there is disagreement on this source and there is disagreement on the interpretation of Mālik's words about it. It is like that if he had concealed them so that they could testify to what they heard or if he made them sit for the accounting with the precondition that they would not testify. The sound version of all that is that they testify, whether or not he gives permission if they have grasped all his words.'

Aṭ-Ṭālibī related in *Kitāb al-Bustān*, "Abd al-Mālik was excellent in dream interpretation. A man consulted him, saying that he had dreamt that his hand was a gold sword and he was brandishing it and it folded back. He said to him, "What you dreamt was good, may I be your ransom!"

'He was intent on him telling him [its interpretation]. So he said, "A boy who will be born to you who is a hermaphrodite," and that was the case.'

Abū 'Umar ibn 'Abd al-Barr said, "Abd al-Malik was very fond of listening to music, improvised and otherwise.'

Aḥmad ibn Ḥanbal said, 'He came to us with someone who was singing with him.'

Ibn Ma'īn said, 'He came to us and we heard the sound of his musical instruments. Allah knows best, but this is why he is not related from in the *Ṣaḥīḥ*.'

He said, 'When 'Abd al-Malik came to us from Iraq, he asked about it and he said:

"They are what you wish of noble men,
but faithfulness there is rare.
He says, 'You only see beauty,'
what was he says is not true."'

It is related that he said, 'I listened to some witty words and I only had a shirt, so I gave it to the one who said it and asked my Lord to clothe me. We were in Madina and the man spoke to me and dictated them to me and he mentioned the report with the wittiness. I asked him to repeat it and he did not do it. He said, "I will not give you my wit and manners.'"

'Abd al-Malik died in 212 AH. It is also said that it was 214 AH. It is said that was when he was about sixty years old.

ʿAbdullāh ibn Nāfiʿ az-Zubayrī, the younger, Abū Bakr

Az-Zubayr said: 'He is ʿAbdullāh ibn Nāfiʿ ibn Thābit ibn ʿAbdullāh ibn az-Zubayr ibn al-ʿAwwām al-Asadī al-Qurayshī, known as the younger. He was the *faqīh* and companion of Mālik.'

He had another brother named ʿAbdullah, known as the older. He was one of the people of excellence and the *dīn*, but he was not a *faqīh*.

Az-Zubayr said: 'Their father was Nāfiʿ, one of the people with the most worship in his time. He fasted for fifty years of his life.'

Yaḥyā ibn Miskīn said, 'I did not see anyone who took longer in the prayer than he did. He loved this son, ʿAbdullāh the younger.'

Musʿab said, 'He would come to him while he was praying and he would supplicate for him, and he saw that the blessing of his support reached him.'

This ʿAbdullah listened to Mālik and ʿAbdullah ibn Muhammad ibn Yaḥyā ibn ʿUrwa.

His son Aḥmad related from him as well as from ʿAbbās ad-Dūrī, az-Zubayr ibn Bakkār, ad-Dihlī, Hārūn al-Ḥammāl, Yaʿqūb ibn Shayba, Yaḥyā ibn Yaḥyā al-Andalusī, Ibn Razīn al-Qarawī, ʿAbd al-Mālik ibn Ḥabīb, and others. He was younger than Ibn Nāfiʿ aṣ-Ṣā'igh, and the one who did not reach that related from him.

Ibn Ma'īn said about him, 'Truthful. There is no objection to him.'

Al-Bukhārī said, 'His *ḥadīths* are known and in order.'

Al-Bazzār said, 'He is trustworthy.'

Muslim transmitted from him.

Mundhir ibn Sa'īd said, 'Ibn Nāfi' is an Imām whom no one accuses of innovation.'

Az-Zubayr said, 'He died while he was one of the esteemed figures among Quraysh in guidance, *fiqh*, and integrity. He fasted constantly and took it on himself.'

Aḍ-Ḍarrāb said, 'Az-Zubayrī kept the company of Mālik for forty years.'

The author said, 'We will clarify the error in this. The most likely position is that if this story is true, it refers to Ibn Nāfi' aṣ-Ṣā'igh.'

'Abdullāh ibn Nāfi' said, 'The first of what I knew of Mālik is that one day I was reading to Nāfi' ibn Abī Nu'aym after the *Ṣubḥ* prayer. I raised my voice and he chided me, saying, "Have you not seen Mālik?"'

'Abdullah ibn Nafi' the younger said, "Abdullah ibn Nafi' the older said to me, "If you take a close friend in your life, then take him as a firm support."'

Ibn Nāfi' said, 'There was a man among the people of az-Zubayr who cursed 'Abdullāh ibn Muṣ'ab ibn Thābit who did not disparage him back. 'Abdullāh ibn Muṣ'ab sent me two dinars every new moon and commanded me to give them to him. He said, "I do not want him to know that I have sent them."

'When Ibn Muṣ'ab died, he found that I was late and so I informed him. He began to supplicate for him. He cut me off, so I said:

"You cursed a man on whose honour censure left no impression,
but you did not know what he did.
When you were certain about what he did, then you began today
to talk ignorance and rashness towards me.
I did not have a wrong action, nor did Ibn Mus'ab
except that we brought what is more excellent.'"

Ibn al-Labbād related that a man asked Ibn Nāfi' and he said, 'I left the mosque and I took some pebbles secretly.' He said, 'Throw them away.' He said, 'They say that they cry out.' He said, 'Tell them to cry out until their throats burst.'

He noted, 'There was some irascibility in his character and I did not know which Ibn Nāfi' had this story. In my opinion, the most likely is that the one in this story is Ibn Nāfi' aṣ-Ṣā'igh. He is the one who is described with what is mentioned in that.'

He died in Muḥarram in 216 AH. Az-Zubayr stated that.

Al-Bukhārī said: 210 AH. One story has around 210 AH.

Az-Zubayr said that he was seventy years old.

This refutes what aḍ-Ḍarrāb said because according to this, he lived for thirty-six years after Mālik's death. There remained thirty-four years of his life. Part of it was his childhood, and after it, he kept Mālik's company. Allah knows best.

Ma'n ibn 'Īsā ibn Yaḥyā ibn Dīnār al-Qazzāz

He used to sell raw silk (*qazz*). He was the client of Ashja', Abū Yaḥyā.

He related from Mālik, Ibn Abi Dhi'b, Ibn Ṭahmān, Mu'āwiya ibn Ṣāliḥ, Makhrama ibn Bukayr, Ibn Abī Uways and others.

Aḥmad, Ibn al-Madīnī, Ibn Ma'īn, al-Ḥumaydī, Isḥāq ibn Mūsā al-Anṣārī, Ibn Numayr, Ibrāhīm ibn al-Mundhir, Abū Bakr ibn Abī Shayba, Saḥnūn ibn Sa'īd, 'Abdullāh ibn Ja'far al-Barmakī, Dhu'ayb ibn 'Umāma as-Sahmī, Abū Khaythama and others related from him.

Ash-Shīrāzī said, 'He was Mālik's stepson, and he is the one who read the *Muwaṭṭā'* to him for ar-Rashīd and his sons. He used to lay his head on his doorstep and he did not speak anything but that he wrote it down. He counted him among the *fuqahā'* of his companions and Ibn Ḥabīb counted him among those who were successors to Mālik in *fiqh* in Madina.'

Ibn Ḥārith said, 'He had recognised oral reports from Mālik which Ibn 'Abdūs mentioned in *al-Majmū'a*.'

He said, 'He was one of the great companions of Mālik.'

Abū 'Īsā at-Tirmidhī also mentioned many of his oral reports and transmissions from Mālik in his *Collection*. He said at the end of his book that all of what he included from Mālik is from the transmission of Ma'n.

Ibn 'Abd al-Barr said, 'He was one of the people who clung the most to Mālik. He used to lean on him when he left the mosque until he was called "the support of Mālik".'

Yaḥyā said, 'He is trustworthy. Al-Bukhārī and Muslim related from him.'

Abū Ḥātim ar-Rāzī said, 'The most reliable of the companions of Mālik and the firmest of them was Ma'n. I prefer him to Ibn Nāfi' and Ibn Wahb.'

Muhammad ibn Sa'īd said, 'He was reliable with many *ḥadīths*, trusty, firm.'

Ash-Shāfi'ī said that al-Ḥumaydī said, 'One whose like your eyes have never seen related to me: Ma'n ibn 'Īsā.'

Yaḥyā was asked about firmness in reporting from Mālik. He replied, 'Al-Qa'nabī and Ma'n.'

Ibn al-Junayd said, 'I asked the son of Ma'n, "Did Ma'n have anything other than the *Muwaṭṭā'*?" He answered, "Something small."'

'Alī ibn al-Madīnī said, 'Ma'n transmitted to us forty thousand questions which he had heard from Mālik.'

Ma'n said, 'Mālik did not answer any of the Iraqis until I was the one who asked about it.'

Ibn Bukayr said, 'Ma'n sold silk. He was tall.' Muḥammad ibn Sa'd said, 'He had some slaves who were weavers.'

Ibn Bukayr said, '"Ma'n used to say, "Mālik related to me." It was said, "How can you say this when people read to him?"'

He said, 'I used to bring *ḥadīths* on pages. Then I said, "Abū 'Abdullah, read me this *ḥadīth*," and he would read it and then I would leave it for some days and then I would come to him with another page.'

Ibn Waḍḍāḥ said, 'Some people went to Ma'n in Madina to ask permission to come to him in his house. While they were like that, a black man came where they were in order to enter the house. They asked him to ask for permission for them to enter. He went inside and called out, "Ma'n!" and he answered him. He informed him [about them] and he gave permission and they entered.

'They said to him, "May Allah put you right! We were amazed at this black man calling your name." He answered, "In addition to that, he is my property." They said, "This is greater still!" He said, "What do you mean? Was he calling me with better than my name which Allah is pleased for me to have?" It was as if he thought that what he had done was good.'

Al-Bukhārī said: 'Ma'n died in 198 AH.' It is said that that was in Shawwāl in Madina.

Ismā'īl ibn Abī Uways

His *kunya* is Abū 'Abdullāh, as al-Bukhari said.

Al-Lālakā'ī, al-Jurjānī, Abū Khaythama, Yaḥyā ibn Ma'īn, and Ma'n ibn 'Īsā said: 'The name of Abū Uways was 'Abdullāh ibn 'Abdullāh ibn Uways ibn Abī 'Āmir al-Aṣbaḥī. He was a nephew of Mālik ibn Anas, both by way of his maternal aunt and paternal uncle, and the husband of his daughter.'

Ibn Sha'bān said, 'The name of Abū Uways was 'Abd al-'Azīz ibn 'Abdullāh.'

Someone else said, 'His name was Uways ibn Mālik ibn 'Abdullāh ibn 'Abdullāh,' but the first is sounder.

Abū Uways was one of those who listened to knowledge and transmitted from Ibn Shihāb, Ibn al-Munkadir, Hishām ibn 'Urwa, and others.

Aḥmad ibn Ḥanbal said, 'They claim that his oral transmissions and those of Mālik were the same thing. He listened to people in the Hijaz and Iraq.'

Al-Qa'nabī and others related from him.

There is disagreement about him. Aḥmad ibn Ḥanbal and Abū Dāwūd praised him while Ibn al-Madīnī thought him weak and Yaḥyā ibn Ma'īn deemed his *ḥadīth*s to be weak. But he said, 'He was a righteous man.' He once said, 'He is trustworthy.' Once he said, 'There is no objection to him and he is a truthful man, but he is not authoritative.' He once said, 'He is not trustworthy.'

Abū Ḥātim said, 'He writes out his *ḥadīth*s and is not used as authoritative.'

Abū Zur'a said, 'A righteous man, but with *tadlīs* (see footnote no.1) in *ḥadīths*.'

Abū Dāwūd said, 'He is reliable and memorised the *ḥadīths* of his land.'

Abū Nu'aym said, 'He came to us and some slave-girls were with him,' i.e. singers. Al-Fallās said that there is some weakness in him. In their opinion, 'he is one of the people of truthfulness.'

Ya'qūb ibn Shayba said, 'He was truthful, a righteous man whose *ḥadīths* tend to be weak.'

An-Nasā'ī said, 'He is not strong.'

Ad-Dāraqtuṭnī said, 'There is something amiss in some of his *ḥadīths*.'

He died in 169 AH.

Ismā'īl listened to his father, his brother, his uncle Mālik, Ibrāhīm ibn Sa'īd and Sulaymān ibn Bilāl, and he read with Nāfi' ibn Abī Nu'aym. He has a text from him, and he was the last to relate from him in Madina.

Qutayba, Aḥmad ibn Ṣāliḥ, Ibn Kāsib, adh-Dhihlī, Qāḍī Ismā'īl, his brother Ḥammād, Abū Ḥātim as-Sijistānī, Ibn Khaythama, Ibn Ḥabīb and Ibn Waḍḍāḥ related from him.

Ḥāfiẓ Abū Aḥmad al-Karābīsī said, 'His uncle Mālik listened to him, and al-Bukhārī and Muslim transmitted from him.'

Abū Ḥātim ar-Rāzī said, 'He is considered to be truthful, but he was negligent.'

Ibn Ḥanbal said, 'There is no objection to him.'

Ibn Ma'īn once spoke about him outside the subject of truthfulness. Once he said, 'He and his father stole *ḥadīths* [meaning they took them in an invalid manner].'

An-Naḍr ibn Salama al-Marwazī called him a liar. He said, 'He gave *ḥadīths* from Mālik with the questions of Ibn Wahb.'

Ibn 'Adī said, 'He related *gharīb ḥadīths* from his uncle, Sulaymān ibn Bilāl, and others which are not followed. People reported *ḥadīths* from him. Ibn Maʿīn and Aḥmad praised him. Al-Bukhārī related many *ḥadīths* from him. He is better than his father except that was negligent. An-Nasāʾī spoke about him.'

Aṣ-Ṣadafī quoted him: 'I sat with my uncle Mālik from 158 AH until he died. That was twenty-one years.'

Ibn Waḍḍāḥ related from him, and praised him. He mentioned that he had strong words about anyone who said that the Qur'an was created. He related many *ḥadīths* and much *fiqh* from Mālik.

Ismāʿīl said, 'I went to Sufyān after the death of my uncle, and he came near where I was sitting. He mentioned my uncle and made supplication for him, mentioned his excellence and states and what people had obtained from him. He wept. Then he said, "Ask me what you wish by the position of your uncle." I said, "*Ḥadīths* are what I want to hear from you." He said to me, "Which do you prefer: that you read or that I read to you?" I said, "I will read. It makes it firmer for me." He said, "So do then," and I began to read.

'Some people from Iraq said, "Abū Muḥammad, you read and we will all listen." He said, "Ask him. I prefer him in this assembly because of the position of his uncle." They spoke to me and I refused them. I read and they shouted, saying, "We will not listen!" He said to them, "So do not listen. What will I do for you?" They began to shout and say, "May Allah not give you benefit by him!" or words to that effect.'

Ibn Waḍḍāḥ said, 'A man questioned Ibn Abī Uways when he was sitting in the *Rawḍa* inside the mosque. He said to him, "May Allah have mercy on you! What do you say regarding the Qur'an? There is some disagreement among us regarding it."

'He grew angry and said, "I have lived until I am asked this, or it is mentioned in my assembly! I ask you by Allah, and the grave and the one who is in it, and the minbar and the one above it (and he appointed at both of them), will you leave me or shall I leave you? This is part of what is not mentioned in my assembly.'"

Ismāʿīl died in 226 AH, and it is said 227 AH.

His brother, Abū Bakr 'Abd al-Ḥamīd ibn Abī Uways, known as al-A'shā

He related from his father, his brother, his uncle, Ibn 'Ajlān, Ibn Abī Dhi'b and Sulaymān ibn Bilāl.

He read to Nāfi' the reciter, and he had good Arabic and recitation.

Al-Bukhārī and Muslim transmitted from him. Aḥmad ibn Ṣāliḥ al-Miṣrī, his brother Ismā'īl, Ibrāhīm ibn al-Mundhir, Isḥāq ibn Mūsā, Sulaymān ibn Bilāl, 'Abd ar-Raḥmān ibn 'Abd al-Mālik ibn Shayba, and Muḥammad ibn 'Abd al-Ḥakam related from him.

Yaḥyā said, 'He is trustworthy in what Ibn Abī Ḥātim, al-'Uqaylī and others related.'

Ibn Sha'bān said, 'He and his brother had what is not unknown from Mālik: the *Muwaṭṭā'* and other things. It is related that Mālik said to them, "I see that you two love this business. If you want Allah to benefit you by it, have a little of it and learn *fiqh* in it." Yaḥyā ibn Bukayr mentioned, "Only good has reached me from him. He had a lot of knowledge."'

Aḥmad at-Tamīmī said in *The Book of Inquisitions* that Mūsā ibn al-Ḥasan said, 'I heard Abū Bakr ibn Abī Uways and Muṭarrif ibn 'Abdullāh. They were summoned to the inquisition about the Qur'an in Madina. When the Book was read to them, Abū Bakr said, "Is there rejection of Allah after some seventy years and company with Mālik while the men of knowledge were abundant?" He was told, "Let your house be your prison."'

He said, 'He kept the company of Nāfi' the reciter for twenty-four years and I only left him in his house. *Ḥadīth* dominated him.'

Ibn Shāhīn said, 'Ibn Ma'īn used to think that all the people of the house of Abū Uways were very weak.'

He died in 202 or 203 AH. It is also said 201 AH.

Dāwūd ibn Sa'īd ibn Abī Zanbar

Al-Ḥākim said, 'He was a Qurayshī. He kept Mālik's company and related many *ḥadīth*s and much *fiqh* from him. It is said that he was one of his trustees. He had a lot of *ḥadīth*s. A group of the companions of Mālik related from him: like Muḥammad ibn Maslama, Ibn Nāfi' and others. Ibn Abī Uways praised him highly.'

Al-Ḥākam said, 'He was the first to take *fiqh* from Mālik.'

Someone else said, 'He was one of those whom Mālik singled out for the permission to be among the first to come to him. He was one of his trustees.'

His son, Sa'īd ibn Dāwūd whose *kunya* was Abū 'Uthmān.

Ad-Dāraquṭnī said, 'He also related a text from Mālik and single *ḥadīth*s which only he had from Abū az-Zinād, az-Zuhrī, Hishām ibn 'Urwa and Thawr ibn Ziyād.'

Ibn Abī Ḥātim said, 'Sa'īd lived in Baghdad and came to Rayy. He related the *Muwaṭṭā'* from Mālik. Abū Ḥātim ar-Rāzī spoke about him and said that he is not strong.'

'Abd ar-Raḥmān ibn Abī Ḥātim said, 'Aḥmad ibn Manṣūr ar-Ramādī and Muḥammad ibn 'Umar ad-Dārī related *ḥadīth*s from him. My uncle related from him. Ibn Abī Ḥātim and Ya'qūb ibn Shayba related from him.'

Al-Bukhārī said, 'Sa'īd ibn Dāwūd az-Zanbarī.' It is said, 'Ibn Dāwūd. A man of Madina who lived in Baghdad.'

Al-Ḥākim counted him among the weak and said, 'He fabricated *ḥadīth*s from Mālik.'

Al-Bukhārī used his testimony in the *Ṣaḥīḥ*.

Yaḥyā ibn 'Abd al-Mālik al-Hudayrī

His *kunya* was Abū Zakariyā'. Ad-Dāraquṭnī said, 'He is Yaḥyā ibn 'Abd al-Mālik ibn Hārūn ibn 'Abdullāh ibn Ibrāhīm ibn 'Abdullāh ibn Muḥriz al-Hudayrī at-Tamīmī.'

Someone else said, 'He was a descendant of Rabī'a ibn 'Abdullāh al-Hudayrī, famous for his keeping company with Mālik and transmission from him in *ḥadīth*s and legal questions. He has transmissions from him which Qāḍī Abū Yaḥyā az-Zuhrī related from him. He learned *fiqh* from him.'

Ash-Shīrāzī said that az-Zubayr ibn Bakkār related from him.

He died in 206 AH. It is also said that it was in 208 AH.

Sa'īd ibn 'Amr ibn az-Zubayr ibn 'Umar ibn az-Zubayr ibn al-'Awwām al-Asadī al-Qurayshī

Az-Zubayr mentioned him in his Jamhara. He related from Mālik ibn Anas and 'Abd ar-Raḥmān ibn Abī az-Zinād. He was among those who sat with Mālik and was one of his companions. He was put in charge of the police in Damascus for 'Abbās ibn Muḥammad ibn Ibrāhīm.

Az-Zubayr ibn Bakkār and Qāḍī Wakī' (from his father az-Zuhrī) said – and they added to one another while the account of az-Zuhrī is more complete: 'When Abū al-Bakhtarī Wahb ibn Wahb was appointed over Madina, he summoned Sa'īd ibn 'Amr so that he could put him in charge of the police. He refused. Wahb swore that he would beat him and imprison him and not release him as long as he was in power. So he accepted the post and put on the black and girded on his sword and Wahb gave him a hundred dinars. He said to him, "Pray *'Ishā'* with the people." He did that. When Sa'īd went to his house, Wahb's messenger was with him with the hundred dinars. He said, 'Put it in that window.' He regretted his appointment.

'Abū al-Bakhtarī wanted to confirm the business and he sent to him, "Lead the people in the *Ṣubḥ* prayer, for I am ill." He refused. The next morning he went to the mosque and sat in it.'

Az-Zubayr said, 'He was appointed the Qāḍī of Madina. In the morning, he sat in the courtyard and sent for three of the *fuqahā'* of Madina. They were Abū Zayd al-Anṣārī, Muṭarrif ibn 'Abdullāh and

'Abd al-Mālik ibn al-Mājishūn. He said to them, "Allah has provided me with thirty dinars. I will divide them between you. Each of you has ten and I have appointed you successor, Abū Zayd." Abū Zayd said to him, "Ten dinars should be increased, but I am too weak for me to follow you."

'He said to 'Abd al-Mālik, "As for you, I will make you my scribe." He said, "Ten a month is desirable, but I have weak sight and cannot write properly."

'He said to Muṭarrif, "I will appoint you over the *ṭawāf*." Muṭarrif was annoyed. He told him, "If I had been appointed to your position, I would not have accepted it. How can I act for you over the *ṭawāf* then?"

'He said, "I will not leave you alone until I am excused."'

Wakī' said, 'He sent for Abū Ghaziyya al-Anṣārī, Muṭarrif, 'Abd al-Mālik and Ibn Nāfi' aṣ-Ṣā'igh. He said to Muṭarrif, "I put you in charge of the prison." He said to Abū Ghaziyya, "I appoint you over the market." He said to 'Abd al-Mālik, "I appoint you to be my scribe." He said to Ibn Nāfi', "I appoint you over such-and-such," and he mentioned the like of that.

'They went to Wahb and mentioned that to him. He sent for him and when he came to him, he told him to leave them alone. Sa'īd said to him, "It is not for you to object to me and forbid me because of their dislike." He said, "Do not be hasty."

'Sa'īd swore that he would not act unless he left him alone and without objecting to appointing those he thought best. Wahb said to him, "Put down your sword, remove the black and return our money." He commanded that he be driven out by the neck while he was saying, "Allah is greater!" The messenger caught up him and asked for the hundred dinars. He asked him, "Where did you put it?" He said, "In the window where you told me." He said, "Look for it where you put it." He took it and left.

'Sa'īd ibn 'Amr spoke on that:

"Did that Wahb ibn Wahb think that I would follow him
when he was arrogant in his power?
When Wahb was arrogant in his folly and increased
in his pride, arrogance and innovation,
I left them behind as an arrow leaves. He did not appoint and esteem the slave
in what lies disgrace and bad character."'

His brother, al-Walīd ibn 'Amr

Az-Zubayr said, 'He was a noble man. One of the governors of Madina appointed him. He was one of the companions who sat with Mālik.'

One of our companions mentioned that he wrote out the *Muwaṭṭā'* for Mālik, and Allah knows best whether he did a fair copy.

Ibrāhīm ibn Hārūn ibn Muḥammad ibn Ilyās ibn Abī an-Naḍr al-Laythī

Az-Zubayr said, 'He was one of those who sat with Mālik, and memorised from him and joined together the various fields of of knowledge: he was a man of intellect with a good brain.'

Someone else said: 'He had perfect memory. Az-Zubayr related from him.'

Zayd ibn Dāwūd

Muṭarrif said, 'Zayd ibn Dāwūd, who was one of our excellent companions, related to me: "I dreamt that the grave split open from the Messenger of Allah ﷺ and I saw him sitting up. The people had gathered to him, and a crier called out for Mālik ibn Anas. He came to the Messenger of Allah ﷺ. He gave him something and told him, 'Divide this between the people.' Then I saw him giving it to them. It was musk." We interpreted that as the knowledge which Mālik spread among the people.'

Abū Zayd al-Anṣārī

His name was Muḥammad ibn Zayd ibn 'Abd ar-Raḥmān ibn Zayd ibn Ḥārith. That is how the Qāḍī Wakī' gave his lineage.

He was one of those who transmitted from and sat with Mālik. He was one of the *fuqahā'* of Madina and their *muftī* from the people of the Anṣār. He was appointed their *qāḍī* in the days of the Mubayyiḍa[1] partisans when Muḥammad ibn Sulaymān ibn Dāwūd entered Madina. When the Abbasids were restored, he was returned. Then in the days of the caliph al-Ma'mūn, he was appointed twice: before Abū Muṣ'ab and after him.

Qāḍī Wakī' mentioned that.

Muṣ'ab said, 'Al-Ma'mūn appointed him *qāḍī* of Madina in 220 AH.'

There are some rare transmissions from him in the book of Ibn Ḥabīb.

Ibn Ḥabīb listened to him.

[1] The Mubayyiḍa (wearers of white) were the 'Alid partisans who followed Ḥusayn ibn 'Alī (a descendant of Ḥasan) in a revolt in Madina. Muḥammad ibn Sulaymān, an uncle of al-Hādī, defeated them in the Battle of Fakhkh.

ʿAbd al-Jabbār ibn Saʿīd ibn Sulaymān al-Masāḥiqī

His lineage was already mentioned in the first generation when his father was mentioned.

He was one of the companions of Mālik and those who sat with him.

ʿAbd ar-Raḥmān ibn Abī Ḥātim said, 'His *kunya* was Abū Muʿāwiya. He related from Abū az-Zinād, Yaḥyā ibn Muḥammad ibn Hānī and Ibn Wahb. Abū Zurʿa related from him.'

Muṣʿab said, 'He had the most beautiful face in Quraysh and the most excellent tongue. He was appointed head of the guard of Madina and also appointed as its *qāḍī*. His mother was the daughter of ʿUthmān ibn az-Zubayr ibn ʿAbdullāh ibn al-Walīd ibn ʿUthmān ibn ʿAffān.'

Muḥammad ibn al-Jarrāḥ said in *Kitāb al-Waraqa*, 'He was literate and witty, a man of Madina.'

Wakīʿ said, 'He was one of the companions of Mālik and Ibn Abī az-Zinād. He was one of the people of literature. Qāḍī Ismāʿīl and others related from him. He was appointed the *qāḍī* of Madina in 202 AH.'

He said:

I let it be heard marred, so I dismissed it and I tread on it
with my sandal without a stammer.
It did not come again. It was as the past
and the winds made the dust cover it.

He has:

The business of the beautiful women is the same.
  The examples are exactly the same.
Make your heart be steadfast with death:
  they sever the necks of men.

Az-Zubayr recited to him:

I gave a client good counsel while his inside is starved
  and his consciousness hates me.
He is embarrassed and friendly when I meet. When I am absent
  or turn away, he indulges himself in attacking my honour.
If I had so wished, the fingertips would have clung to a repentant,
  and trampled on him when he is treacherous in the track of denial.
But one of my hands does not find a way
  to let part of me reach the other.
I overlook it without weakness in that whose like,
  by my life, one does not overlook.

Al-Ḥasan ibn Zayd spoke to him one day when al-Ḥasan had been put in charge of the police of Madina. He censured him about something, 'I want to part from you completely with no going back after it.' Al-Masāḥiqī said to him, 'Then, governor, I say:

"I have parted so that I do not care a date-pit,
  even if my neighbours are separated on the noble.
I have withdrawn myself into distance while my eye sleeps
  to the separation of the beloved."'

Az-Zubayr said, 'He died in 226 AH when he was eighty-three. He was a Shaykh of Quraysh.'

Ḥabīb al-La''āl

He was known as Bābayn. He was one of the early companions of Mālik and one of those who sat with him and were special to him. He was one of those he let come to him first and made him one of the elite. He was one of his trustees.

One of them said about him, 'Ibrāhīm ibn Ḥabīb. I think that he was the son of so-and-so,' and he mentioned that Mālik made him a trustee.

Ibn Sha'bān mentioned them both together.

He also mentioned Isḥāq ibn Ibrāhīm ibn Ḥabīb Bābayn. I found that he had a story about the death of Mālik ibn Anas: 'Isḥāq ibn Bābayn found two locked boxes containing books among the things that Mālik left. My father began to read them and weep. He said, "May Allah have mercy on you. You desired Allah by your knowledge. We sat with you constantly over a long time, and I did not hear you give any *ḥadīth*s of these I have read."'

I think that the correct form is Abū Isḥāq.

Qāsim ibn Asbagh said, 'Ibrāhīm ibn Ḥabīb was a reliable man among the companions of Mālik. He was a trustee of Mālik, may Allah Almighty have mercy on him.'

Ḥabīb ibn Abī Ḥabīb

His name was Abu Ḥabīb Marzūq. It is also said that his name was Razīq. He was Mālik's scribe and reader, and it was by his reading that people heard the *Muwaṭṭā'*. He was a Madinan who later moved to Egypt. Some of them counted him among the Egyptians because he died there.

He related other things than the *Muwaṭṭā'* from Mālik: *fiqh*, many *ḥadīth*s and other things.

Ibn Ḥanbal, Ibn Ma'īn, an-Nasā'ī and Abū Ḥātim ar-Rāzī thought him weak. They called him a liar and censured him.

Ibn Ma'īn said, 'Ḥabīb was the one who was in Egypt. He read to Mālik and did it quickly for the people and would read two pages. They asked him about that in Egypt. He said, "It is nothing." Ibn Bukayr listened to his recitation and said that he has the worst recitation.'

Ibn Abī Khaythama said, 'I mentioned to Muṣ'ab what was mentioned that Ḥabīb used to turn two pages. He said, "We used to read two pages," denying what had been mentioned about that.'

Muṣ'ab said, 'Mālik said to us, "Bring Ḥabīb. Give to Ḥabīb." He lived with Mālik.'

Mus'ab said, 'Ḥabīb used to read to Mālik while I was on the right hand of Ḥabīb any my brother Abū Bakr was on his left. He was nearer to Mālik than me because he was older than me. Every day

Ḥabīb read two pages or two pages and a bit. He took two dinars in each presentation from every person, and we gave him more.'

Ḥabīb said, 'Ad-Darāwardī, Ibn Kināna and Ibn Abī Ḥāzim gave me a dinar to ask Mālik about three to whom they had listened (relating) from Mālik while Mālik did not give *ḥadīth*s from them. They were afraid of taking *ḥadīth*s from them because of that. I went to him after *Ẓuhr* and only these three were with him. He said to me. "This is not your time."

'I said, "Yes, but there is neither flour nor *sawīq* in the house, and some people gave me a dinar to ask you why you did not relate from so-and-so, so-and-so and so-and-so." He bowed his head and said to me, "I do not like you being used for me. I only took knowledge from its people.' He indicated that people should refrain from asking me."'

Yaḥyā ibn Yaḥyā said, 'I gave Ḥabīb a bribe of a thousand dirhams to place me with Mālik so I heard a thousand *ḥadīth*s with him.'

He died in Egypt in 228 AH.

Muḥammad ibn aḍ-Ḍaḥḥāk ibn 'Uthmān al-Ḥizāmī

He was one of the people who sat with Mālik. He related from him, and from his father, aḍ-Ḍaḥḥāk. Ya'qūb ibn Ḥamīd ibn Kāsib related from him.

He was already mentioned where his father and grandfather were mentioned in the first generation. The rest of his reports are there. Az-Zubayr said, 'He died a youth, and followed his father in knowledge and good manners.'

Abū Ghaziyya Muḥammad ibn Mūsā ibn Miskīn al-Anṣārī

He was one of the Banū Māzin ibn an-Najjār, one of the descendants of Usāma ibn Zayd on the female side. He was one of the companions of Mālik and those who took his position. He transmitted.

He was appointed *qāḍī* in Madina. He listened to Ibn Abī az-Zinād.

Muḥammad ibn Sa'd said, 'He had transmission, knowledge, and investigation into *fatwā* and *fiqh*.'

Al-Bukhārī said, 'He was counted among the people of the Hijaz. He had some *munkar* transmissions.'

In one of the texts of the *Great History*, al-Bukhārī said that he is reliable. I found that in the handwriting of our shaykh, the *qāḍī* and martyr, may Allah Almighty have mercy on him.

Ya'qūb ibn Muḥammad related from him.

He died in 207 AH. Al-Bukhārī said that.

Muṣ'ab ibn 'Abdullāh ibn Muṣ'ab ibn Thābit ibn 'Abdullāh ibn az-Zubayr ibn al-'Awwām

He is Abū 'Abdullāh al-Qurashī al-Asadī. That is how al-Bukhārī and others give his lineage. He was the uncle of az-Zubayr ibn Bakkār.

He related the *Muwaṭṭā'* and other things from Mālik. He was known for keeping his company. His transmission of the *Muwaṭṭā'* is well-known. He listened to his father and Mālik ibn Anas and their sort among the people of Madina. Abū Khaythama and his son and Yaḥyā ibn Ma'īn wrote from him. He was the man of knowledge among Quraysh in respect of lineage, poetry and news, and a sharif of great esteem with both the elite and the common, and he was a witty poet.

Aṣ-Ṣadafī said, 'Muṣ'ab ibn 'Abdullāh az-Zubayrī, Abū 'Abdullāh, the master of genealogy and the companion of Mālik.'

Yaḥyā ibn Ma'īn said that he is reliable.

Some of his reports

Muṣ'ab said, 'My father told us, "Seek knowledge. If you do not have money, it will bring you money. If you have money, it will give you beauty."'

Ibn Abī Khaythama said, 'I said to Muṣ'ab ibn 'Abdullāh, "Those people say that the Qur'an is the Word of Allah. Then they stop and say, 'Whoever says that it is created has innovated. Whoever says that it is not created has innovated.' They use you as a proof and claim that you make this statement and that Mālik said it."

'He responded, "I seek refuge with Allah. Not I! I merely say 'the Word of Allah' and then I remain silent. My heart inclines to the fact that it is not created, but I am silent because it has reached me that Mālik said, 'I dislike discussion about the *dīn*.' The people of our land continue to hate the doctrine of Qadar and the opinion of the Jahmites and all that resembles it. I only like to speak about what entails action. As for discussion about Allah, I prefer to remain silent about these things because the people of our land forbade discussion about anything that does not have some action resulting from it. Isḥāq ibn Abī Isrā'īl debated me and said, 'I do not say such-and-such nor such-and-such. I do not say that with any doubt. Rather, I am silent as the people before me were silent.' So I recited to him my poem in which I spoke on the Wāqifa[1] and he wrote it down from me and I liked it. It is:

"Will I sit after my bones tremble,
 and death is nearer than what is next to me?
Will I argue with every contentious opponent
 and make his *dīn* a target for my *dīn*?
Will I abandon what I know for the opinion of another
 when opinion is not like certain knowledge?
What do I have to do with argument
 when it is confusion which veers to the left and the right?
The truth is not hidden.
 It is beautiful like the blaze of the clear dawn."

The poem is longer than this.'

Some of his witticisms

Ibn al-Jarrāḥ mentioned in *Kitāb al-Waraqa* that he said, 'I came to Aḥmad ibn Hishām and he said, "Abū 'Abdullāh, Ibrāhīm al-Mawṣulī made you notorious when he said:

Muṣ'ab and Ṣabāḥ criticised it,
 so we rebelled against Muṣ'ab and Ṣabāḥ.
They censured what they censured and they grew weary,
 so we had rest from them and they rested."

[1] Those who would not say whether or not the Qur'an was created, refusing to engage in debate about it.

'I said, "He only made us famous for a good business. He made us command the correct and forbid the objectionable. What he made you notorious for is more famous still when he said:

Pure wine, fine. The pledge of a year
  and a year is in the jugs.
We passed the quenching cup around in the deep of the night
  until every darkness vanished.
The horn of the sun continued until it showed us the fatigue
  we related of Aḥmad ibn Hishām."

'He nearly fainted.'

He died at the end of Shawwāl in 238 AH. Ibn Khaythama said that: 'He was seventy-six or seventy-seven. He was older than my father.'

‘Atīq ibn Ya‘qūb

Ibn Ṣādiq ibn Mūsā ibn ‘Abdullāh ibn az-Zubayr ibn al-‘Awwām al-Qurashī al-Asadī, Abū Bakr. His mother was Ḥafṣa bint ‘Atīq ibn ‘Amr ibn ‘Abdullāh ibn az-Zubayr. He was one of the elite of Mālik and those who took his position and who had a lot from him and knew his life and qualities.

He said, ‘I heard Mālik say, “A man must teach his family and children and those for whom he has a duty. The Prophet ﷺ said, ‘All of you are shepherds and those over whom you have charge with your manners and your character until they have your manners and follow that which you have so that they will be a help for you in obeying Allah.’”’

We mentioned in the reports of Mālik that he entered Mālik’s house after his death and what he found of *ḥadīth*s there and the fact that he had not seen any of it in what he had mentioned to his companions during his lifetime.

Muḥammad ibn Sa‘d, the scribe of al-Wāqidī, said in his *History*, ‘He clung to Mālik and wrote the *Muwaṭṭā’* and other things from him. He also clung to ‘Abdullāh ibn al-‘Umarī and withdrew and then returned to Madina. He was one of the best Muslims. He died in 227 or 228 AH.’

AMONG THEIR NUMBER OF THE MAKKANS OF THE PEOPLE OF THE HIJAZ

MUḤAMMAD IBN IDRĪS ASH-SHĀFI'Ī

Muḥammad ibn Idrīs ibn al-'Abbās ibn 'Uthmān ibn Shāfi' ibn as-Sā'ib ibn 'Ubaydullāh ibn 'Abd Yazīd ibn Hāshim ibn al-Muṭṭalib ibn 'Abd Manāf ibn Quṣayy. His mother was from Azd.

He was born in greater Syria at Gaza, and it is also said that it was in the Yemen in 150 AH. He was taken to Makka and lived there, and he alternated between the Hijaz, Iraq and other places. Then he went to Egypt and stayed there.

He related from Mālik, Muslim ibn Khālid, Ibn 'Uyayna, Ibrāhīm ibn Sa'd, Sa'īd ibn Sālim, Ismā'īl ibn 'Aliyya, Yaḥyā ibn Ḥassān, ad-Darāwardī, Ibrāhīm ibn Abī Yaḥyā, Marwān ibn Mu'āwiya, Ibn Abī Rawwād, Ibn Abī Salma, ath-Thaqafī, Ibn Abī Fudayk, Fuḍayl ibn 'Iyāḍ and from his uncle, Muḥammad ibn Shāfi'.

Aḥmad ibn Ḥanbal, al-Ḥumaydī, Abū aṭ-Ṭāhir ibn as-Sirāj, Ḥarmala ibn Yaḥyā, al-Buwayṭī, al-Muzanī, ar-Rabī' the *mu'adhdhin*, Yūnus ibn 'Abd al-A'lā, Abū Thawr, az-Za'frānī, Aḥmad ibn Sinān al-Wāsiṭī, Muḥammad ibn al-Ḥakam, Ibn Akhī ibn Wahb and Hārūn al-Aylī related from him among others.

THE BEGINNING OF HIS QUEST AND HIS MEMORY

Ash-Shāfi'ī said, 'I was in the *kuttāb* listening to the teacher dictating to the child, and so I memorised what he said. My mother did not have anything to give to the teacher. I was an orphan. The teacher was pleased with me as I followed him when he stood. They used to write and before the teacher had finished the dictation, I had memorised all of that.'

One version has: 'One day he said to me, "It is not lawful for me to take anything from you."

'When I left the *kuttāb*, I would gather pottery, palm-stumps and the shoulder-blades of camels. I wrote *ḥadīth*s on them. I would go to the *Dīwān*s and seek assistance. I wrote on them until I filled the wells which my mother had with that.'

Then he listened to his uncle in Makka and Muslim ibn Khālid az-Zanjī and other Makkans.

He said: 'Then I left Makka and stayed with the tribe of Hudhayl where I learned their words. They had the best Arabic among the Arabs. I remained there among them for seventeen years, travelling when they travelled and alighting when they alighted. When I returned to Makka, I began to recite poetry and mentioned the literature, reports and battles of the battles of the Arabs. A man from the Zubayrīs passed by me and said to me, "O Abū 'Abdullāh! It is grievous to me that there is no *fiqh* along with this eloquent clear Arabic and intelligence so that you would satisfy the people of your time."

'I asked, "Who is there to whom I can go?" He told me, "This Mālik is the master of the Muslims today." That touched my heart and I applied myself to the *Muwaṭṭā'* and I asked to borrow it and I memorised it in nine nights.' (Imām Abū al-Ma'ālī al-Juwaynī mentioned from him that he had memorised it in three nights.)

'Then I went to the governor of Makka and I took his letter to Mālik as well as his letter to the governor of Madina to ask Mālik about my business. When I came to Madina, I took the letter to the governor of Madina and I told him, "Send for Mālik to come to you and recommend me to him."

'He said, "When I ride to him with you with my retinue to his door, we will sit there until the wind beats our faces with the dust of 'Aqīq and he will give us permission."

'When we had prayed *'Aṣr*, he rode with me to him. I went with him until we reached al-'Aqīq and his house. He got down with those who were with him and sat at his door. A slave-girl came out to them and said, "The Shaykh says to him, 'If you want questions, then write them on a paper and he will answer them for you.'" He said to her, "Tell him that the governor has written to me about a need."

'She went to him and was away a long time. Then he turned to me and said, "Did I not tell you?" "Yes," I answered.

'Then Mālik came out and sat down and said, "What Allah wills," so the governor gave him the letter. When he reached the place of intercession, he threw it out of his hand and said, "Glory be to Allah! The knowledge of the Messenger of Allah ﷺ begins to be taken through intermediaries!"'

'I saw that the Governor was too in awe of him to speak to him, so I went forward to him and said, "May Allah make you thrive! I am a man who seeks you, and this is my state and this is my story." When he heard what I had said, he looked at me for a time. He had discrimination (*firāsa*). He asked, "What is your name?" I answered, "Muḥammad."

'He told me, "Muḥammad, be fearfully aware of Allah and avoid acts of rebellion. You will have some importance in the business." Then he said, "Yes, and gladly. Come tomorrow and bring someone to read the *Muwaṭṭā'* to you." I said, "I can undertake the reading."'

'I came to him the next day and began the recitation while the book was before me. Then I began to be in awe of Mālik and wanted to stop the recitation. He liked my recitation and said, "By Allah, lad, do more." So I read it to him in a few days. Then I stayed in Madina until he died, may Allah have mercy on him.'

One variant reports that when Mālik looked at the letter, he said, 'Who is he?' The governor told him, 'This one.' He looked at him and bowed his head. Then he said, 'How is knowledge proper for the one who is not ill from fear of Allah? When he is like that, then Allah is about to benefit him by knowledge.' The governor said to him, 'He seeks you.' When he heard that, he regained his composure and mentioned the like of that.

Muṣ'ab az-Zubayrī said, 'Ash-Shāfi'ī came to Madina. He was sitting in the mosque reciting the poetry of the poets. He had very good expressions and clear eloquent Arabic and he knew the meanings. My father said to him one day, "Are you content with yourself by being a Qurayshī to be a poet in what you have?" He said to him, "What should I do then?"

'He said,'"Learn *fiqh*. The Messenger of Allah ﷺ said, 'When Allah desires good for someone, He makes him learn *fiqh* in the *dīn*.'" He asked, "Where will I have that?" He replied, "Mālik ibn Anas is the master of the Muslims." He said, "Take me to him."

'We came to Mālik and he sat with him and he told him about his honour and his business and he brought near and close to Mālik and he began to listen to him.

'After some days, ash-Shāfi'ī said to my father, "When Mālik says, 'our business' and 'that which is with the people of our land' and 'that which the Imāms of the Muslims of right guidance have,' what is that?"

'He told him. "They have the Messenger of Allah ﷺ and then Abū Bakr, 'Umar and 'Uthmān who died in Madina."'

Ash-Shāfi'ī left what he had and listened to the *Muwaṭṭā'* from Mālik and Mālik rejoiced in him. Then ash-Shāfi'ī went to Iraq and clung to Muḥammad ibn al-Ḥasan and debated with him on the school of the people of Madina. He wrote his book and there he composed his previous statement there. That is the book of az-Za'frānī.

His following Mālik and his acknowledgement of him

The words of ash-Shāfi'ī about him already been mentioned in the reports about Mālik as has much of his praise for him.

Ash-Shāfi'ī said, 'Mālik ibn Anas is my teacher.' One variant has: 'My master. I learned knowledge from him. When scholars are mentioned, Mālik is the star. There was no one who was more generous to me than Mālik and I took knowledge from him.'

He said, 'I am one of the lads of Mālik.'

He said, 'I have made Mālik a proof in what is between me and Allah.'

Muḥammad ibn 'Abd al-Ḥakam said, 'Ash-Shāfi'ī continued to take the position of Mālik and not oppose him except as some of his companions opposed him until the young men overcame him. Thaṭ moved him to what he added to Mālik. Otherwise all the time when he was asked about something, he would say, "This is the statement of the master."'

Qāḍī Hārūn ibn 'Abdullāh az-Zuhrī said, 'Ash-Shāfi'ī was with me at Gaza in the same house. He wrote his books at night. I said to him, "You tire yourself. You stay awake and you use up the oil and write books in which you oppose the school of Mālik and the people of Madina. Who will look at them?"

'He told him, "Allah will send notable people to it from the people of this east and they will have more of the Book and the *Sunna*."'

Qāḍī Abū 'Abdullāh at-Tustarī said, 'Qāḍī Abū al-'Abbās ibn Surayj ash-Shāfi'ī told me, "I said to Abū Isḥāq Ibrāhīm ibn Ḥammād, 'The difference between Mālik and ash-Shafi'ī is less than what is between Abū Yūsuf and Abū Ḥanīfa. He used as a proof what Mālik believed in the question of the khul' of the third. He said, "I only give *fatwā* and judge by the words of Mālik."'"'

Abū al-'Abbās ash-Shāriqī related that Abū Isḥāq ash-Shīrāzī said to him, 'Ash-Shāfi'ī is only counted as one of the companions of Mālik. If one were to compare his differences with him with that in which he differed from 'Abd al-Malik and others among his companion, it is less,' or words to that effect.

Scholars' praise for him because of his knowledge and excellence

Muḥammad ibn 'Abd al-Ḥakam said, 'My father told me, "Cling to this shaykh (i.e. ash-Shāfi'ī). I have not seen anyone with more insight into the roots of knowledge," or he said, "the roots of *fiqh*."'

Muḥammad said, 'If it had not been for ash-Shāfi'ī, I would not know what I know. It is that which analogy taught me. He had the *Sunna*, tradition, excellence, eloquence and sound firm intelligence.'

Ibn 'Uyayna said about him, 'He was the most excellent of the young men of his time.' When something regarding *tafsīr* or *fatwā* was posed to Ibn 'Uyayna, he would say, "Ask this one, " meaning ash-Shāfi'ī.'

Muslim ibn Khālid az-Zanjī, his shaykh, said to him when he was a young man of fifteen (and it is said eighteen), "It is time that you gave *fatwā*, Abū 'Abdullāh.'

Yaḥyā ibn Sa'īd al-Qaṭṭān said, 'I used to make supplication for ash-Shāfi'ī in my prayer because of the words he showed which were sound from the Messenger of Allah ﷺ.'

Aḥmad ibn Ḥanbal said, 'No one carries an inkwell from the People of *Ḥadīth* who does not owe ash-Shāfi'ī a favour.'

He said, 'We used to curse the People of Opinion and they would curse us until ash-Shāfi'ī came and brought us together.'

He said, 'I did not know the abrogated and the abrogating *ḥadīth*s until I sat with him.'

Aḥmad ibn Ḥanbal said to Isḥāq ibn Rāhawayh, 'Come, I will show you a man whose like your eyes have never seen.' He showed him ash-Shāfi'ī.

He said, 'He told me, "Sit with him, shaykh."

'I said, "His age is close to ours. Shall I leave Ibn 'Uyayna and al-

Maqburī?" He said, "Bother you! That one is not to be missed and that other one can be missed."'

Ibn Ḥanbal said, 'Ash-Shāfi'ī had the most *fiqh* of people in respect of the Book of Allah and the *Sunna* of His Messenger ﷺ. He did not devote a great deal of time to seeking *ḥadīths*.'

When he had seen him, he stated, 'This is a mercy from Allah for the community of Muḥammad ﷺ.'

One of them said, 'I said to Aḥmad, "You have abandoned Sufyān while he has followers and gone to ash-Shāfi'ī!" He told me, "Be quiet! If you miss the knowledge of *ḥadīths* which you can find in various places, it will not harm either your *dīn* or your intellect. If you miss the intellect of this young man, I fear that you will never find it. I have not seen anyone with more *fiqh* than him regarding the Book of Allah."'

Aḥmad [ibn Ḥanbal] said, 'Ash-Shāfi'ī was like the sun for this world and well-being for people, so see which of those two can be replaced.'

Aḥmad said, 'It has reached me that the Prophet ﷺ said, "Allah will send a man to this community at the beginning of every hundred years to put the business of its *dīn* right." He added, "We frequented him and we only saw good."'

Ibn Ma'īn said to Ṣāliḥ ibn Aḥmad ibn Ḥanbal, 'Is your father not embarrassed? I saw him with ash-Shāfi'ī when ash-Shāfi'ī was mounted while he was walking. I saw that he had taken hold of his stirrup.'

Ṣāliḥ said, 'I spoke to my father and he told me, "Tell him: 'If you want to learn *fiqh*, then take hold of his other stirrup.'"'

Isḥāq said, 'There was none who spoke but that ash-Shāfi'ī had more adherence and fewer errors.'

Isḥāq said, 'Ash-Shāfi'ī is the Imām.'

Abū 'Ubayd said, 'I have not seen a man at all more perfect than ash-Shāfi'ī.'

Hārūn said, 'I have not seen his like. If he had debated about this column which is made of stone asserting that it is made of wood, he would have proved it by his sheer ability in debate.'

Abū Thawr said, 'In my opinion, ash-Shāfi'ī had more *fiqh* than ath-Thawrī and an-Nakhā'ī.'

Another said, 'I did not see Muḥammad ibn al-Ḥasan esteem any of the people of knowledge as he did ash-Shāfi'ī.'

Hilāl ibn al-'Alā' said, 'Ash-Shāfi'ī opened the locks of knowledge.'

Az-Za'frānī said, 'I have not seen anyone at all with better Arabic nor more knowledge than ash-Shāfi'ī. He used to read some of every poetry to him and he knew it.'

Ibn Hishām said, 'Ash-Shāfi'ī was a proof in language and he was consulted in Egypt about men's lineage. Ash-Shāfi'ī said to him after an hour, "Leave this. It will not escape you or us. Tell us about the lineage of women." When they began that, Ibn Hishām remained silent. He noted, "I did not think that Allah created the like of this man."'

An-Nasā'ī said, 'He is one of the scholars, a reliable trustworthy one.'

Yūnus said, 'Hijaz did not produce the like of ash-Shāfi'ī. He was asked, "How did you take from him?" He said, "We fell short, and his death came quickly. Had he remained alive, there would have been obtained from his knowledge what none of the people of knowledge in his time obtained."'

He said, 'The people of Iraq had not seen the like of ash-Shāfi'ī. Had we compared the intellects of all people to his intellect, their intellects would have drowned in his intellect and those who understood what ash-Shāfi'ī said. This is the goal. He used to speak to people according to their understanding.'

Al-Muzanī said, 'Ash-Shāfi'ī wrote *The Book of Racing and Shooting.* He had insight into that. What knowledge did he base it on?'

He said, 'Had we understood all that ash-Shāfi'ī said, we would have brought you varieties of knowledge from him, but we did not understand.'

A man asked him about opinion and he said, 'Where are you in relation to the book of ash-Shāfi'ī?'

Al-Aṣmā'ī said, 'I saw Muḥammad ibn Idrīs and I saw a *faqīh* of knowledge and good recognition with a sweet tongue who gave proof and recognised. It was only sound for the front of a throne or the top of the minbar. I do not know that I helped him with one letter more than another, but I benefited from him so much that if a man had memorised only a little of it, he would have been a scholar.'

Another said, 'Ash-Shāfi'ī continued studying the science of Arabic and the battles of people for twenty years, and he was asked about that. He said, "I only intended it as help in *fiqh*."'

Az-Za'frānī said, 'The men of literature and the scribes used to attend his assembly in Baghdad to listen to his beautiful expressions and excellent clear Arabic. I did not see nor did anyone see his like during the time of ash-Shāfi'ī.'

Abū Ya'qūb al-Buwayṭī said, 'I saw people in Egypt, Syria, Iraq, Kufa, Basra and Hijaz from every type of the scholars of the Qur'an, *fiqh*, the Arabic language, *Sīra*, *kalām*, and the battles of the Arabs, and I did not see anyone like ash-Shāfi'ī. In my opinion, he had more scrupulousness than any I have seen to whom scrupulousness is ascribed.'

Ash-Shāfi'ī said, 'I wanted for people to learn what is in my books and not ascribe any of it to me.'

Ayyūb ibn Suwayd said, 'I did not think that I would live to see the like of ash-Shāfi'ī. I have never seen the like of this man,' and he met many people.

Ash-Shāfi'ī said, 'I wanted people to learn what is in my books, and not to ascribe any of it to me.'

Suwayd ibn Sa'īd said, 'We were with Ibn 'Uyayna in Makka, Ash-Shāfi'ī came and sat and Ibn 'Uyayna related an affecting *ḥadīth* and ash-Shāfi'ī fainted. It was said to Sufyān, "Ibn Idrīs has died!" He said, "If he has died, he has died the best of the people of his time."'

Aḥmad ibn 'Abdullāh said, 'He is reliable, a master of opinion and speech who does not have *ḥadīth*s. He leaned towards the Shi'a.'

There is a lot of praise for ash-Shāfi'ī. His excellence is well-known. However, there is what is reported from Yaḥyā ibn Ma'īn when he spoke a lot about him and spoke badly of him. The like of that is reported from 'Alī ibn al-Madīnī, Yūnus, al-Ḥasan ibn Mukarram, Muḥammad ibn 'Abd al-Ḥakam and others.

The dispute between Yūnus and Muḥammad in that was already mentioned. I think that it was because of Yaḥyā's words and those of the people of the *Ṣaḥīḥ* who abandoned his *ḥadīth*s, and did not include a single letter from him and why that was the case. There is no dispute that he was an Imām in *fiqh*. He was weak in *ḥadīth*s because he related from those who were considered weak, as Muḥammad ibn 'Abd al-Ḥakam stated, 'He related from liars and innovators. However, he himself is free of that.'

The Ḥāfiẓ Abū Bakr ibn Thābit wrote *The Book of the Proof on ash-Shāfi'ī*, and confirmed him in the *Ṣaḥīḥ*.

The Qāḍī said, 'After this, we will mention some of his following the *Sunna* which will verify what we said and will invalidate other things, if Allah Almighty wills.'

There are many reports about ash-Shāfi'ī and his virtues are reported. Ar-Rabī' said to the one who asked him to recount his reports to him, 'If I were to tell you about the days of ash-Shāfi'ī, I could not bring them all in a year.'

The traditions transmitted about him, his following the *Sunna*, and his School about which there is disagreement

Abū Hurayra related that the Prophet ﷺ said, 'O Allah, guide Quraysh! Their man of knowledge will fill the entire earth with knowledge. O Allah, as You made them taste punishment, make them taste favour!'

Ar-Rabī' said, 'Ash-Shāfi'ī said, "The Qur'an is the Word of Allah and is not created. Whoever says that it is created is an unbeliever."'

Muḥammad ibn 'Abd al-Ḥakam was asked, 'Is ash-Shāfi'ī an innovator or a liar?' He said, 'If we disagree with him, we must not say what we do not know about him. He was the furthest of people from that.'

He was asked, 'Did he hesitate about the Qur'an?' He answered, 'I do not know of that. He was free of that,' or a similar statement.

Ibn Ḥanbal said, 'Ash-Shāfi'ī is trustworthy, a master of opinion and *kalām*. He does not have *ḥadīth*s and he has some Shi'ite inclination.'

Ash-Shāfi'ī was told, 'There is some Shi'ism in you.' He asked, 'How?' They said, 'You show love for the family of the Prophet.'

He said, 'People! Did the Messenger of Allah ﷺ not say, "None of you will believe until I am more beloved to him than his children and his parents and all people" and "My friends and my near kin are the godfearing."? Then it is mandatory for me to love my near kin and my maternal relatives when they are among the godfearing. So is it not part of my *dīn* that I love the near kin of the Messenger of Allah ﷺ who are like that? He himself used to love them.'

Then he recited:

O rider! Stop at the pebbled ground at Minā and call out
to the dweller in its low mountains and heights
Before dawn when the *ḥājjī*s flow out to Minā,
overflowing like the clap of the overflowing gulf:
'If love for the family of Muḥammad makes one a Rāfiḍite,
then the two tribes of jinn and men testify that I am a Rāfiḍite.'

Ash-Shāfi'ī used to say to Aḥmad [ibn Ḥanbal] and Ibn Mahdī, 'You know more *ḥadīth*s than me. If it is sound, then tell me that, and I will take it.'

Al-Buwayṭī said, 'Ash-Shāfi'ī used to follow the qualities of the Messenger of Allah ﷺ.'

His generosity and the rest of his reports and his excellent qualities

Ash-Shāfi'ī went from Yemen to Makka and he had ten thousand dinars with him. He struck up a tent outside of Makka and people came to him. He did not leave it until he had divided all of it up. When he entered Makka, he borrowed what he spent.

Ar-Rabī' said, 'I did not see any day come to him but that he gave *ṣadaqa* in it. In the months of Ramaḍān, he gave a lot of *ṣadaqa* of clothes and dirhams. He fed the poor. A man mended his button and he gave him a dinar and apologised to him. Another man handed him his whip and he gave him a purse of dinars and he said, "This is all we have with us."'

Ar-Rabī' said, 'We heard of the generous and we thought that some of the people there with us in Egypt were among them. As for the like of ash-Shāfi'ī, we have not seen nor heard of anyone like him in his time. When a man asked (something) of him, his face became red out of modesty before the asker.'

Once he entered the bath-house and gave the master a lot of money. He dropped his whip and a man handed it to him, so he gave him fifty dinars.

Ash-Shāfi'ī recited when he left for Egypt:

My brother, I see myself yearning for Egypt, and before it lies
the land of desert and wastelands.
By Allah, I do not know whether I am going to ease and wealth
or whether I am going to the grave.

The author said, 'He went to both of them together, may Allah have mercy on him.'

Sa'd ibn 'Abdullāh ibn 'Abd al-Ḥakam said, 'When ash-Shāfi'ī came to Egypt, he came to us in great need. My brother Muḥammad went to one of the wealthy men in the land and said to him, "A man from our companions and from the people of our school of Quraysh has come to us in need, so command what will change his situation." He commanded five hundred dinars for him. In the evening, we met with my father and he said, "One ought not to be content with the like of this from so-and-so." My brother said to him, "Help us in it." He did and made it a thousand.'

Ash-Shīrāzī said, 'It is said that Ibn 'Abd al-Ḥakam gave ash-Shāfi'ī a thousand dinars from himself and took a thousand from one of his friends and a third thousand from another two men. Ash-Shāfi'ī died with Ibn 'Abd al-Ḥakam.'

Sa'd said, 'Ash-Shāfi'ī stayed with Muḥammad and did not leave him. He came to him every day in the morning. Sometimes he did not find him in the house and he would ask where he had gone and then go to him. He used to take two sections of the books of Mālik from our books. They would remain with him that day and the night. Then he would come when he had finished them and he would return them and take another two.'

It is related in his reports that he said, 'While I was going around seeking *ḥadīth*s in the Yemen, I was told, "There is a woman whose waist goes to the bottom of the body and the top is two separate bodies with four hands and two heads (i.e. they were Siamese twins)." I wanted to see her as I did not think that possible. I spoke to her and came to her and found her as she had been described. By my life, two bodies were clashing and fighting and making peace and eating and drinking.

'Then I left her and withdrew. I returned after some time and asked about her. I was told, "One body has died, and its lower part was tied to a firm rope and left until it wasted away. Then it was cut off and buried."

'I saw another person after that who came and went in the road.'

The author said, 'There is debate about the marriage of a person like this. They are two sisters without any doubt who are joined together by one body. The genitals are shared. When it is according to what is described of their different characters and desires, that it clearer. Allah Almighty knows best.'

Ibn 'Abd al-Ḥakam said, 'It is related that when the mother of ash-Shāfi'ī was pregnant with him, she dreamt that Jupiter left her private parts until it divided in Egypt. Then a splinter of it stopped in every land. It was interpreted to mean that he was a man of knowledge whose knowledge was particular to the people of Egypt and then it spread out from it in the lands.'

Ar-Rabī' said, 'Ash-Shāfi'ī used to finish the Qur'an every night. In Ramaḍān, he finished it every night and then he finished every day as well.'

He said, 'He gave a *fatwā* when he was fifteen. He used to pray at night until he died.'

When ash-Shāfi'ī went to az-Za'frānī, he stayed with him. Az-Za'frānī used to write down for a slave-girl what flavours were proper for his food each day. Ash-Shāfi'ī called the slave-girl one day. He looked in the paper and added a flavour which he desired. When the food was brought, az-Za'frānī did not recognise the flavour which he had not commanded. He questioned the slave-girl and she told him. When he looked at the paper and found that in the handwriting of ash-Shāfi'ī, he freed the slave-girl out of joy at that.

One day the People of *Ḥadīth* pestered him and he said to them, 'Do not make me say to you what Ibn Sīrīn said to a man who pestered him, "If you burden me with what I cannot do, character which delights you from me will hurt you."'

It is related that ash-Shāfi'ī wore perfume and his slave boy would bring him a scent every day to wipe on the column against which he sat. There was a man of asceticism at his side, and he went to some human dung and put it in his own moustache to counter was he did. He deemed it worthless.

When ash-Shāfiʿī smelled the odour, he said, 'Smell your sandals.' Then he said, 'Smell each other.' They found that on the man. Ash-Shāfiʿī said, 'What prompted you to do what you did?' He said, 'I saw your pride and I wanted to humble myself to Allah.'

Ash-Shāfiʿī said, 'Take him to the prefect of police to bind him until we leave.' When ash-Shāfiʿī went out, he commanded that he be given thirty lashes. He said to him, 'I think this is for your ignorance.' Then he ordered forty and told him, 'This is for your bringing human dung into the mosque.'

Some of his wisdoms and manners

Ash-Shāfiʿī said, 'Whoever undertakes to be a *qāḍī* and does not become poor is a thief. Whoever learns the Qur'an has immense value. Whoever writes *ḥadīth*s strengthens his proof. Whoever investigates *fiqh* has noble value. Whoever looks into language refines his nature. Whoever looks into reckoning has sound opinion. Whoever does not protect himself does not benefit from his knowledge.'

He was asked, 'How are you this morning?' He answered, 'How is the one in the morning who seeks Allah by the Qur'an, the Prophet ﷺ by the *Sunna* and memorisation of what he said, Shayṭān by acts of rebellion, time by its passage, the self by its appetites, the family by nourishment, and the Angel of Death by his spirit being taken?'

He said, 'The best form of proof is that whose meanings shine, whose clear points are precise and in which the hearts of the listeners rejoice.'

He said, 'Nature is the earth and knowledge is the seed. Knowledge is achieved only by seeking. When the nature accepts, it flourishes and becomes fourfold, and its meanings branch out.'

He said, 'Knowledge is ignorance with the people of ignorance and ignorance is ignorance with the people of knowledge.' He recited:

The station of the fool in relation to the *faqīh*
  is like the station of the *faqīh* in relation to the fool.
This one does without while near to that,
  and that one is more ascetic than him in it.

Ash-Shāfi'ī asked to borrow some books from Muḥammad ibn al-Ḥasan. He refused to lend them to him, so he wrote to him:

Say to the one you did not think is notable,
  who does he see like him?
Knowledge refuses for its people forbid its people.
  Perhaps he will spend it to his people by his knowledge.

Muḥammad ibn al-Ḥasan then allowed him to use what he wanted of them.

Ash-Shāfi'ī frequently recited:

I have humbled myself to them to honour it by them.
  The self will not be honoured by the one to whom he does not abase it.

Al-Muzanī said, 'I heard ash-Shāfi'ī say, "A man mentioned another man and said, 'By Allah, he fills the eye with beauty and the ear with clarification.'

'"The man said to him, 'Repeat it, may Allah have mercy on you.' He said, 'I will repeat it to you, by Allah, without conflicting testimony or amusing you or increasing it.'"'

His trial and his death

Al-Faḍl ibn ar-Rabī' said that he was sent for by ar-Rashīd at a time in which no one was sent for. He said, 'I came to him in the assembly of his elite and there was a sword in front of him and his face was glowering. He told me, "Faḍl! Go to this Hijāzī Muḥammad ibn Idrīs and fetch him to me! If you do not bring him, I will do to you what I want to do with him!"

'I went to him and found him praying in the mosque of his house. He turned from his prayer. I said, "Respond to the Amīr al-Mu'minīn." He said, "In the name of Allah," and moved his lips.

'Then I got up and went before him while he was following me until I reached the castle. I was hoping that he had gone to sleep, but he was seated and said, "What did the man do?" I replied, "He is at the door." He said, "Perhaps you have alarmed him?" I answered, "No." He said, "Bring him in."

'When he came in, ar-Rashīd moved from his seat for his, his face brightened and he smiled at him, shook his hand, and embraced him. He told him, "Abū 'Abdullāh! Have we no rights over you except that you come to us by a messenger?" He gave a soft apology. He said, "We have commanded four thousand dinars for you."(One variant has "twenty thousand".) He said, "I will not accept it." 'He said, "I insist that you take it. Faḍl! Carry it with him."'

Al-Faḍl said, 'When I went, I said to him, "By that which saved you from him and changed his wrath into pleasure, what did you say when you came to him and came in to him?"

'He said, "Yes. I said, "'Allah bears witness that there is no god but Him as do the angels and the people with knowledge, upholding justice. There is no god but Him, the Almighty, the Wise,' (3:18) the Lord of the Mighty Throne. O Allah! I seek refuge with the light of Your absolute purity and the might of Your pureness and the blessing of Your majesty from every disaster and infirmity or any event which occurs except for something that brings good, O Most Merciful of the merciful! O Allah, You are my refuge and I seek refuge by You and You are my shelter, so I seek shelter in You, O You to whom the necks of the tyrants are abased and the power of the Pharaohs is humbled! I seek refuge with Your generosity from Your wrath and from forgetting Your remembrance and from You dishonouring me or revealing my secret. I am in Your protection in my night and my day, my start and my departure, my sleep and my repose. Make Your praise my blanket and Your mention my password. There is no god but You, disconnecting Your face and exalting the glory of Your absolute purity. Protect me from Your punishment and Your wrath and strike the pavilions of Your preservation over me and give me good which Your knowledge surrounds and avert from me the evil of what Your knowledge surrounds, and make me safe from the terrors of the Day of Rising, O Most Merciful of the Merciful!"'

Faḍl said, 'I did not enter (the presence) of a sultan when I made this supplication but that he smiled at me, embraced me and honoured me.'

Another version reports that al-Faḍl asked him about what he used for supplication, and he said, 'Yes, it is what Mālik related to me from Nāfiʿ from Ibn ʿUmar that the Prophet ﷺ used for supplication on the Day of the Confederates: "O Allah! I seek refuge with the light of Your absolute purity and the might of Your pureness and the blessing of Your majesty from every disaster and infirmity,'" and he mentioned the like of what was already mentioned.

Ash-Shāfiʿī died in Egypt with ʿAbdullāh ibn ʿAbd al-Ḥakam, and he made him the executor.

Ar-Rabīʿ said, 'We were sitting in the circle of ash-Shāfiʿī shortly after his death, and a bedouin stopped with us and then asked, "Where is the moon and the sun of this circle?" We answered, "He has died, may Allah Almighty have mercy on him."

'He wept deeply and said, "May Allah have mercy on him and forgive him. How often his clarification opened the locked proof and his debate guided to the clear proof and washed shame from blackened faces and made the blocked doors wide through opinion!" Then he left.'

He died in Egypt on Thursday. It is said that it was on Friday night, at the end of Rajab in 204 AH. The Banū ʿAbd al-Ḥakam buried him in their graves, and the governor of Egypt prayed over him. He, may Allah have mercy on him, had a sparse beard which he dyed.

FROM THE PEOPLE OF YEMEN

Abū Qurra Mūsā ibn Ṭāriq as-Siksikī

His *kunya* was Abū Muḥammad, and Abū Qurra was his title. Al-Ḥusayn ibn Muḥammad al-Ghassānī al-Ḥāfiẓ said that. He said, 'I related it from the writing of Ibn Fuṭays.'

Amīr Abū Naṣr said in *Kitāb al-Ikmāl*: 'Abū Qurra Mūsa ibn Ṭāriq al-Janadī, related to Janad, a part of the Yemen.'

Ibn Sha'bān said, 'He was from the people of Zabīd from the family of Khaṣīb and was their *qāḍī*.

They said that he related countless *ḥadīths* and questions from Mālik. He related the *Muwaṭṭā'* from him.

Abū Qurra has his book *al-Kabīr* and his book, *al-Mabsūṭ*, and a known oral transmission in *fiqh* from Mālik which 'Alī ibn Ziyād al-Ḥajabī related from him there.

Ṣāmit ibn Mu'ādh also related from him, and Abū Qurra was the Qāḍī of Zabīd.

Abū 'Amr al-Maqburī said in *The Book of the Reciters*, 'Abū Qurra recited with Nāfi'. He related from Ismā'īl al-Qāsim, Mūsā ibn 'Uqba, Mālik, Ibn Jurayj and Ibn 'Uyayna.'

'Alī ibn Ziyād al-Ḥajabī, Muḥammad ibn Yūnus az-Zubaydī, Ibn Ḥanbal and Ibn Rāhawayh related from him.

Abū Ḥātim said, 'He was truthful and Ibn Ḥanbal praised him a lot.' Ibn Abī Dāwūd said that he is trustworthy.

Muḥammad ibn Ḥāmid ibn 'Abd ar-Raḥīm ibn Sharūs

He was called ash-Sharūsī aṣ-Ṣan'ānī, one of the companions of Mālik. He had the *Muwaṭṭā'* from him and *The Book of Oral Transmissions of Questions* in three parts.

Abū 'Alī al-Ḥasan ibn Aḥmad ibn Abī aṭ-Ṭayyib aṣ-Ṣan'ānī related from him.

The Qāḍī said about him, 'I saw his *Muwaṭṭā'* from Mālik. It was strange and not known to people with different copies of the *Muwaṭṭā'*. This is why they did not mention anything from him. Allah knows best. They mentioned other things than the *Muwaṭṭā'* from Ibn Sharūs.'

FROM THE PEOPLE OF BASRA AND IRAQ AND FURTHER EASTERN LANDS

‘Abdullāh ibn Maslama ibn Qa‘nab at-Tamīmī

Abū ‘Abd ar-Raḥmān al-Ḥārithī al-Qa‘nabī. He came from Madina and he lived in Basra. He was considered to be a Basran.

He related from Mālik, Ibn Abī Dhi’b, his father, Makhrama ibn Bukayr, Shu‘ba, al-Layth, ad-Darāwardī, al-’Umarī, the two Ḥammāds, and Sulaymān ibn Bilāl.

Abū Zur‘a, Abū Ḥātim (both of Rayy), ‘Alī ibn ‘Abd al-‘Azīz, adh-Dhihlī, Aḥmad ibn Sinān, Muḥammad ibn Sahl ibn ‘Askar, ar-Ramādī and Abū Dāwūd as-Sijistānī related from him. Al-Bukhārī and Muslim transmitted from him.

Ḥāfiẓ Abū ‘Alī al-Ghassānī related from him. He said, ‘I stayed close to Mālik for twenty years until I read the *Muwaṭṭā’* to him.’

His virtues and praise

Ibn Shāhīn said in what he related from al-Ḥunaynī, ‘We were with Mālik, may Allah have mercy on him, when a man came and told him that al-Qa‘nabī had come. He said, “Welcome to his imminent arrival!” He said, “Take us to the best of the people of the earth so that we can greet him.” He got up and greeted him.’

Abū Zur‘a said, ‘I did not write from anyone who was loftier in my eyes.’

Abū Ḥātim said, ‘I prefer al-Qa‘nabī to Ibn Abī Uways. He was from Basra and was trustworthy, a proof.’

He said, ‘I have not seen anyone with more humility than him. We asked him to read the *Muwaṭṭā’* to us and he said, “Come to the morning.”

‘We said, “We are sitting with al-Ḥajjāj.” He asked, “And when you finish?” We said, “We go to Muslim ibn Ibrāhīm.” Then he asked, “And when you finish?” He said, “Then it is *Ẓuhr* and we go to Abū Hudhayfa.” He asked, “And after *‘Aṣr*?” We answered, “We go to Ḥāzim.” He asked, “And after *Maghrib*?”

'We used to go to him at night, and he would come out to us and he had on felt cloth with nothing under it. In the summer it was very hot indeed and we read to him while it was on his body. If he had wanted to, he could have given a lot.'

Hārūn ibn Isḥāq said, 'I did not see anyone who desired Allah by his knowledge except for al-Qa'nabī.'

Ibn Ma'īn said about him, 'That came from spending many dinars.'

He said, 'His brothers are trustworthy men as you like.'

He said, 'The firmest people in Mālik are him and Ma'n.'

He said once, 'The firmest of them is al-Qa'nabī.'

Aḥmad said that he is trustworthy.

Al-Kūfī said that he is a trustworthy righteous man.

Sa'īd ibn Manṣūr said, 'We say – or it is said – that no one whom Allah has created does *ṭawāf* of the House better than al-Qa'nabī.'

Ibn Mufarraj said, 'He was a Basran, trustworthy, a man of worship.'

'Abdullāh ibn Dāwūd said, 'Al-Qa'nabī related to me, and by Allah, in my view he was better than Mālik.'

Ibn Abī Uways said, 'When Mālik sat, he said, "Let those of judgement and intelligence among you follow me."' He said, 'Usually al-Qa'nabī sat to the right of him.'

'Abdullāh ibn 'Abd al-Ḥakam said, 'I was with 'Abd ar-Razzāq and he scolded me once and refused to write for me. I spent the night in sorrow and I saw the Prophet ﷺ. I told him my story with 'Abd ar-Razzāq. He told me, "Write from four." I asked, "Who are they, Messenger of Allah?" He mentioned al-Qa'nabī and three other men with him.'

Abū 'Umar ibn 'Abd al-Barr counted him among the *fuqahā'* of the companions of Mālik and he related a lot from Mālik.

Al-Qa'nabī had four brothers: this 'Abdullāh, Ismā'īl, Yaḥyā and 'Abd al-Mālik. They are the Banū Maslama. All of them related from Mālik.

Aḥmad ibn al-Haytham said, 'When we came to al-Qa'nabī, he came out to us and it was as if he was looking down at Hellfire.'

Al-Bukhārī said that he died in 220 or 221 AH.

What is verified by Ibn Mufarraj and Abū Ismā'īl at-Tirmidhī is that he died in 221 AH in Makka on Saturday. It was not in the last days of Muḥarram.

Abū Ismā'īl at-Tirmidhī said, 'It was not at the end on Thursday. It is said that it was the Day of 'Āshūrā'. Ibn al-Jazzār stated that in the *Kitāb at-Ta'rīf.*'

ʻAbd ar-Raḥmān ibn Mahdī ibn Ḥassān al-ʻAnbarī

The *kunya* of Ibn Mahdī was Abū Sa'īd, and he was a client of the tribe of Azd. He was a Basran. He listened to the two Sufyāns, the two Ḥammāds, Mālik, Shuʻba, ʻAbd al-ʻAzīz, Sharīk, Hammām, Abū ʻAwāna, Ziyāda, ad-Dastawānī, and others.

Ibn Wahb, Ibn Ḥanbal, Yaḥyā, Zuhayr, Ibn al-Madīnī, the sons of Ibn Shayba, Isḥāq, Abū ʻUbayd, Abū Thawr, his son Mūsā, ʻAbd ar-Raḥmān, Yaḥyā ibn Saʻīd, and others related from him. Al-Bukhārī and Muslim transmitted from him. He clung to Mālik and took much *fiqh* and many *ḥadīth*s as well as the science of [ascertaining the reliability of] men from him. He has stories with him.

Ibn al-Madīnī said, ʻIbn Mahdī took the view of Mālik and Mālik took the view of Sulaymān ibn Yasār. Sulaymān ibn Yasār took the view of ʻUmar ibn al-Khaṭṭāb, may Allah be pleased with him.'

Aḥmad ibn ʻAbdullāh ibn Ṣāliḥ said, ʻThe *Risāla* of ash-Shāfiʻī was begun by Ibn Mahdī, and ash-Shāfiʻī finished it.'

Abū Isḥāq ash-Shīrāzī that ash-Shāfiʻī wrote the *Risāla* with Ibn Mahdī and I think that it is the most likely. He used to sit with ash-Shāfiʻī and keep his company with Aḥmad ibn Ḥanbal. Ash-Shāfiʻī used to say to them both, ʻTell me about whatever *ḥadīth*s I have which are sound and I will follow them because you know more *ḥadīth*s than I do.'

It is said that Mālik only gave him *mursal ḥadīth*s from Ibn Masʻūd, so he took them from Ibn Mahdī.

Scholars' praise of him and his excellence

ʻAlī ibn al-Madīnī said more than once, ʻHad I been taken and put between the Corner and the Maqām, I would have sworn by Allah that I did not see anyone at all with more knowledge of *ḥadīth*s than Ibn Mahdī.'

He also said, 'Ibn Mahdī had the most knowledge of people.' Ibn Mahdī told me, 'I frequented Ḥammād ibn Zayd for a time, and I did not have any need of him.'

Ibn Ḥanbal said, 'Ibn Mahdī is one of the lodes of truthfulness.'

He said, 'He is firmer in certainty than Wakī'.'

Aḥmad ibn Sinān said, 'Ibn Mahdī always had scrupulousness. When Ḥammād ibn Zayd looked at Ibn Mahdī in his assembly, his faced beamed.'

Abū Ḥātim said, 'Ibn Mahdī was excellent, trustworthy, one of the lodes of truthfulness, a man of right of right action, sound. When Sufyān was near death, he said to Ḥamīd's client, "Go to Ibn Mahdī and bring him to close my eyes." Sufyān said, "My books at Kufa are with an old person. If you can get them, I want Ibn Mahdī to look them over."'

'Alī ibn al-Madīnī said, 'I went to Kufa and concerned myself with the *ḥadīth*s of al-A'mash and collected them. When I went to Basra, I met Ibn Mahdī and I greeted him. He said, "Bring me what you have." I said, "No one can tell me anything at all from al-A'mash."'

He said, 'He became angry and said, "These are the words of the people of knowledge? And one who is precise in knowledge and understands it? The like of you says this? Do you have anything with you on which you can write?" I replied, "Yes."

'He said, "Write!" I said, "Tell it to me. Perhaps I already have it." He said, "I will only dictate to you what you do not have."' He said, 'He dictated thirty *ḥadīth*s which I had not heard at all. Then he said, "Do not do it again." I answered, "No."'

'Alī said, 'Then after a year, Sulaymān came and said, "Take us to Ibn Mahdī so that we can outshine him today about *ḥajj* practices." Sulaymān was the companion of ours who had the most knowledge about the *ḥajj*.'

He said, 'We went and came to him and greeted him and sat down before him. He said, "Bring what you have. I think that you, Sulaymān, are the one with something to say."

'He said, "Yes, no one can tell us anything about the *ḥajj* at all."

'He confronted him with the like of what he confronted 'Alī. Then he said, "Sulaymān, what do you say about a man who finishes all the practices except *ṭawāf* of the House and then sleeps with his wife?" Sulaymān dashed in and related, "They part where they meet and they meet where they part." He said, "Then when do they meet and when do they part?"

'He said, "Sulaymān was silent." He said, "Write." He began to teach him questions and dictate to him until we wrote down thirty questions and he related a *ḥadīth* and two *ḥadīths* in each question. He said, "I asked Mālik, and I asked Sufyān and 'Abdullāh ibn al-Ḥasan."'

He said, 'When I got up, he said, "Do not do that a second time."'

He turned to Sulaymān and asked, 'What has come to us from the loins of this Mahdī?'

A man came to Ibn Mahdī and said, 'Abū Sa'īd, there is a *ḥadīth* which al-Hasan related from the Prophet ﷺ: "Whoever laughs in the prayer should renew his *wuḍū'* and redo the prayer."'

'Abd ar-Raḥmān said, 'This was only related by Ḥafṣa bint Sīrīn from Abū al-'Āliyya from the Prophet ﷺ.' The man asked him, 'Why do you say this, Abū 'Abdullāh?'

He said, 'When you go to the money-changer with your dinars and he tells you, "It is in disorder," you can say, "What do you say that? Explain it to me." He said, "This *ḥadīth* is only related by Ḥafṣa bint Sīrīn. Hishām ibn Ḥassān heard it from her. He was in the house with her and al-Hasan related it. Al-Ḥasan said, 'The Messenger of Allah ﷺ said it.'"'

He was asked, 'From where did az-Zuhrī hear it?' He replied, 'Sulaymān ibn Arqam used to frequent al-Ḥasan and az-Zuhrī. He heard it from al-Ḥasan and he mentioned it to az-Zuhrī. Az-Zuhrī said, "The Messenger of Allah ﷺ said..."'

Aḥmad ibn Ṣāliḥ said that Ibn Mahdī only related from reliable men. He said, 'All that Mālik gave of *mursal ḥadīths* from Ibn Mas'ūd, he took from Ibn Idrīs. What he had from other than Ibn Mas'ūd, he took from Ibn Mahdī.'

Yaḥyā ibn Sa'id said, 'I prefer to listen to the oral transmission of Ibn Mahdī asleep than to one who dictates to another,' or words to that effect.

His nephew said, 'My uncle wrote *ḥadīth*s for me and then corrected them later, and I read them to him.

'I spoke to him about that. He said, "I thought that doing that would lower the reputation of justness of its transmitters, so they would become my litigants before Allah. He would say, 'Did you see me? Do you know me? Did you hear my words?'"'

Ibn Mahdī fell ill and Ḥammād ibn Zayd visited him among his companions. He went out saying, 'I used to have hopes of you for the people of this land,' twice.

Al-Qaṭṭān said, 'What Ibn Mahdī read to Mālik is firmer than what people heard from him.'

Ibn Mahdī said, '*Ḥadīth*s were written from me in the circle of Mālik.'

Ibn Abī Ṣafwān said, 'If Mālik had written from him, it would not have harmed him.'

Ibn al-Mubārak said, 'Whoever met Ibn Mahdī without taking his portion from him has skimped.'

He also mentioned him and said, 'This is a man who increased in good every day since we met him.'

Muḥammad ibn 'Abdullāh ibn as-Sakūnī said that he is reliable.

Abū Dāwūd said, 'The trustworthy man, 'Abd ar-Raḥmān ibn Mahdī, related to us.'

The rest of his reports and his death

Ibn Ḥanbal said, 'Ibn Mahdī came to us in Baghdad when he was forty-six or forty-five, and he used henna.'

Ṣāliḥ ibn Aḥmad said, 'Ibn Mahdī and Abī Dāwūd aṭ-Ṭayālisī devoted themselves to memorisation. As for Ibn Mahdi, he did not die until he had white leprosy and Abū Dāwūd the other type of leprosy.'

Ibn al-Labbād said, "Abd ar-Raḥmān ibn Mahdī used to sell jewels and his father was a miller.'

Al-Bahlūl ibn Rashīd said, 'I did not regret anything as I regretted the book which I saw Ibn Mahdī present to Sufyān ath-Thawrī. Sufyān liked it.' Aṣ-Ṣamādiḥī said, 'When I came to Ibn Mahdī, I mentioned it to him and he brought it out for me *Kitāb as-Sunna wa-l-Fitan* from his books.'

Ibn Mahdī said, 'I frequented Ḥammād ibn Zayd for three years. A year did not go by without any benefit.'

It was said to Ibn Mahdī, 'So-and-so has made a book to refute the Jahmites.' 'Abd ar-Raḥmān said, 'Does he refute them with the Book of Allah Almighty and the *Sunna* of His Messenger Muhammad ﷺ?' They said, 'No, rather with opinion and intellectual reasoning.' He said, 'He has erred. He refutes innovation with innovation.'

Al-Qāsim ibn Salām said, 'I entered Basra in order to listen to Ḥammād ibn Ziyād and he had died. I complained about that to Ibn Mahdī and he said to me, "Whatever you are outstripped in, do not be outstripped in fear of Allah."'

Al-Qawārīrī said, 'I saw 'Abd ar-Raḥmān ibn Mahdī speaking on the minbar and his father Mahdī was on the other step and his grandfather Ḥassān was above the top of the highest step while he was speaking to the people.'

Al-Fallās said, 'I saw Ibn Mahdī on Friday and he came and sat outside of the circle and Yaḥyā said to him, "Come into the circle."

'He said, "You related to me from Ibn 'Ajlān from 'Amr ibn Shu'ayb from his father from his grandfather that the Prophet ﷺ forbade circles on Friday before the Imām has come out."

'Yaḥyā said, "I saw Ḥabīb ibn ash-Shahīd, Hishām, and Ibn Abī 'Arūba making circles then." Ibn Mahdī said, "It reached those people that the Prophet ﷺ said it, so they did it." Yaḥyā was silent.'

Ibn al-Madīnī said, 'Ibn Mahdī was asked about the *ḥadīth* which Ma'n related like that, and he said that it was an error and that it must be incorrect from such-and-such an aspect. So it was investigated and found to be as he had said.'

Ibn Mahdī said, 'If anyone flees from leadership, it follows him. If anyone seeks it, he does not obtain it.'

Ibn Mahdī died in Basra in Jumādā al-Ākhira in 198 AH when he was sixty-three.

It is said that he was born in 135 AH. And it is said 134 as well as 136 AH. He had a son who related from him called Ibrāhīm from whom Aḥmad ad-Darūqī related.

Muḥammad ibn 'Umar ibn Wāqid al-Wāqidī

He was a client of the Banū Sahm ibn Aslam His *kunya* was Abū 'Abdullāh. He was from Madina, but is counted among the people of Baghdad. He lived in Baghdad and was appointed *qāḍī* there by the caliph al-Ma'mūn over al-Mahdi's army, the eastern side, and put in charge of the prayer at Rusafa. He had been appointed *qāḍī* for ar-Rashīd before that.

He related many *ḥadīth*s, *fiqh*, and questions from Mālik. In the *ḥadīth*s reported from him there are many *munqaṭa'* and *gharīb ḥadīth*s. It is the same in his reported legal questions which are unknown according to his school and no one else has them. People spoke about them, and Ahmad, Yaḥyā, Ibn Numayr, an-Nasā'ī and others rejected him. He had vast knowledge and much recognition, being a noble man of literature, with knowledge of *Ḥadīth*, *Sīra* and historical reports.

Aḥmad ibn 'Abdullāh ibn Ṣāliḥ said, 'I did not see anyone with greater memory of *ḥadīth*s than he had. Ibn al-Mubārak spoke on him.'

Muḥammad ibn Sa'd, his scribe, said in his *Great History*: 'He had knowledge of the expeditions and of *Sīra*, the conquests, the differences of the people regarding *ḥadīth*s, judgements, their consensus and the writing of books.'

He related that Qāḍī Wakī' said, 'Al-Wāqidī was one of the people to whom one turns in knowledge.'

Aḥmad was asked about him and said, 'We called from the seas of al-Wāqidī. He claimed that he had ten thousand *ḥadīth*s from Ma'mar which no one else had. We looked at those with whom were the earliest that Ma'mar sat with, and we found that he did not have this.'

Ibn al-Barqī said that he is a liar.

An-Nasā'ī said that he is not reliable, and his *ḥadīth*s are not written down.

Ibn Ma'īn said that his *ḥadīth*s are nothing, and that his *ḥadīth*s are not written down. He was asked, 'Why do you not attack his name?' He said, 'I am too shy before his son who is my friend.'

Aḥmad ibn 'Abdullāh al-Kūfī said, 'I wrote a lot from him and he is trustworthy. I did not see anyone with more memory than him. I wrote about sixty thousand *ḥadīth*s from him. It reached me that Ibn al-Mubārak said to him, "Do not make these two *ḥadīth*s *marfū'*. They are not *marfū'*." He insisted on them and people said that he is a liar.'

Ibn al-Jārūd said, 'They abandoned him.'

Abū 'Amr al-Muqri' mentioned him in the *Ṭabaqāt of the Reciters.* He related recitation from Nāfi' ibn Abī Nu'aym, 'Īsā ibn Wardān, and Sulaymān ibn Muslim ibn Ḥibbān, and he listened to Ma'mar ibn Rashīd and his son related from him as well as his scribe, Muḥammad ibn Sa'd.

Some of his reports, his generosity and concerning his death

Muṣ'ab ibn 'Abdullāh said, 'I spoke to al-Wāqidī about appointing a man from the people of Madina as agent over some of the agencies in which allowances were paid out. He sent me a bag which contained a hundred or two hundred dirhams. I said, "I did not tell you to send it." He said, "What will he spend until he is appointed?"'

Muḥammad ibn Sa'd said, 'Al-Wāqidī saw me sorrowful. He said to me, "Do not be sad. Provision comes from where you do not reckon. Once I was poor so that I sold my work-horse. Yaḥyā ibn Khālid found me slow. I apologised to him and he became aware of my condition and commanded five hundred dinars for me. I took them to the house and I was using them to pay off the debts and for the family when a man of the people of Madina came to me who was one of the descendants of Abū Bakr. He had been the victim of highway robbery. He complained to me of his situation so I gave him what was left over and did not purchase a work-horse.

"'"Yaḥyā found me slow and I told him the tale and he sent to the Bakrī man and he said, "Yes, I took the dinars from him. When I took them to the house, so-and-so the Anṣārī came to me and complained to me of his state and so I gave them to him."

"'"Yaḥyā went to the Anṣārī and he told him the story and he was astonished by the generosity. Then he commanded a thousand dinars for me and the like of it for the Bakrī and the like of it for the Anṣārī, and five hundred for my wife because of her sorrow when I gave the dinars to the Bakrī.'"

Qāḍī Hārūn ibn 'Abdullāh said, 'Al-Wāqidī presented a sheet of paper to al-Ma'mūn in which he mentioned that he was overcome by debts and his lack of patience in it. Al-Ma'mūn wrote on the back of it: "You are a man in which there are two qualities: modesty and generosity. As for generosity, it is that which releases what you have. As for modesty, it is that which prevents you from informing us about what you have. We have commanded such-and-such for you. If we have hit what you want, then increase your expanse. If we did not hit what you want, then your crime is on yourself. You related a *ḥadīth* to me when you were in charge of the *qāḍī*s of ar-Rashīd from Muḥammad ibn Isḥāq from az-Zuhrī from Anas that the Messenger of Allah ﷺ said to az-Zubayr, 'O Zubayr, the treasures of provisions are opened in front of the Throne. Whoever has a lot, Allah has made it a lot for him and whoever has a little, Allah has made it a little for him.'"

'Al-Wāqidī said, "I had forgotten this *ḥadīth*. It is what you have mentioned to me. I would like to be given some of its reward."

'Hārūn said, "It has reached me that his reward was two hundred thousand dirhams."'

Al-Wāqidī said, 'I had had two friends. One of them was a Hāshimī. We found ourselves in straitened circumstances and my wife said to me, "We will be patient in hardship and difficulty. As for our children, they wound my heart. If you would look to see if there is anything you can use for them to put their situation right."

'I wrote to my Hāshimī friend and asked him for some expansion from what he had. He sent me a sealed bag and mentioned that there were two thousand dirhams in it. It was not long before the other friend wrote to me and mentioned a complaint similar to mine, so I sent him the bag as it was. Then I went to the mosque and spent the night in it out of shame before my wife. Then I returned and she thought that what I had done was good. Then my Hāshimī friend turned up and he had a bag like the first one with him. He said, "Tell me the truth about this business." and I told him.

'He said, "You sent to me and I only had what I sent you. Then I wrote to our mutual friend to ask him for some charity and he sent me my bag with my seal."'

He said, 'We shared the thousand and divided it into three parts after we sent a hundred dirhams to the woman. News of that reached al-Ma'mūn and he summoned me and I explained the matter to him. He commanded seven thousand dinars for me: two thousand for each us and one thousand for the woman.'

He mentioned something similar in another variant of this story, and that al-Barmakī sent to him and said to him, 'Yesterday I saw you in a dream in a state which indicated hardship, so inform me about your business.' He mentioned the story to him. He said, 'Which of you do you think is the more generous?' He commanded three thousand dirhams for him, and two thousand for them, and he invested me as a *qāḍī*.' Al-Ma'mūn was not mentioned.

Al-Wāqidī said, 'I met Ash'ab one day and he said to me, "Ibn Wāqid! I have found a dinar! What should I do with it?"

'I replied, "Announce it!" He said to me, "Glory be to Allah! You are only in error in your knowledge!" I said, "What is correct then,

Abū al-ʿAlā'?" He said, "I will buy a shirt with it and then announce it." I said, "Then no one will recognise it." He said, "That is what I want."'

The author said, 'This is how I found this report from him, and I do not know who this Ashʿab was. Ashʿab aṭ-Ṭammāʾ was before the time of al-Wāqidī. He listened to Sālim ibn ʿUmar.' The people of this subject said, 'He is only known by this name.'

Al-Wāqidī died in Baghdad while he was the *qāḍī* of the army of al-Ma'mūn on Monday night of the 11th of Dhū al-Ḥijja in 207 AH. He was buried on the following Tuesday. He was seventy-eight years old.

He was born in 130 AH.

Muḥammad ibn Samāʿa prayed over him and he made al-Ma'mūn his executor. He accepted this task and took care of his debts.

Yaḥyā ibn Yaḥyā ibn Bukayr ibn 'Abd ar-Raḥmān at-Tamīmī

Al-Ḥanẓalī, as he was a client of Ḥanẓala. It is also said that he was the client of the Banū Minqar ibn Sa'd ibn 'Amr ibn Tamīm an-Naysābūrī.

He related the *Muwaṭṭā'* from Mālik. It is said that he read it to him. This is what the *ḥadīths* from him indicate in *Ṣaḥīḥ* Muslim and elsewhere. He stayed with him for a time to follow him. In his book, *al-Muntaqā*, Abū 'Umar ibn 'Abd al-Barr counted him among the *fuqahā'* of the companions of Mālik.

He related from al-Layth, the two Ḥammāds, Abū 'Awāna, Ibn Lahī'a, Ibn 'Uyayna, Hushaym, Ibn Al-Mubārak, Zuhayr ibn Mu'āwiya, Sulaymān ibn Bilāl and others.

Abū 'Umar said, 'He had property in Nishapur and a portion of *fiqh*. He was reliable, safe, and trustworthy. A group of the people of our land and other Imāms related from him: like Isḥāq ibn Rāhawayh, adh-Dhihlī, al-Bukhārī and Muslim. They both (i.e. al-Bukhārī and Muslim) transmitted a lot from him in the *Ṣaḥīḥ*.'

Ibn Khallād ar-Rāmahurmī said in his book *al-Fāṣil*, 'Yaḥyā travelled to Egypt, Syria, Yamana and Iraq. Ibn Hanbal used to praise him and say, "Khurasan has not produced the like of him since Ibn al-Mubārak. Part of his scrupulousness was that he doubted a lot in *ḥadīths* to such an extent they called him 'the Doubter'. A great deal of his excellence and precision is mentioned." Abū Ḥātim ar-Rāzī mentioned the like of that, and Abū Zur'a ar-Rāzī praised him and considered him trustworthy.'

Isḥāq ibn Rāhawayh said, 'I did not write down knowledge from anyone more trustworthy in my opinion than him and al-Faḍl ibn Mūsā as-Sinānī.'

He said, 'Yaḥyā was a man of intellect.' He said, 'Yaḥyā is firmer than Ibn Mahdī.' He said, "I have not seen the like of Yaḥyā ibn Yaḥyā, and I do not see any opinion like his own."

Muḥammad ibn Muslim said, 'I saw the Prophet ﷺ in a dream. I asked, "From whom should I write down knowledge?" He replied, "From Yaḥyā ibn Yaḥyā."'

Abū Aḥmad ibn 'Adī said, 'He was one of the worshippers and an excellent man.'

Yaḥyā ibn ash-Shahīd said, 'I did not see a man of *ḥadīth* more scrupulous than Yaḥyā ibn Yaḥyā nor any with better clothes than him.'

Abū Bakr ibn Isḥāq said, 'There was no man in Khurasan with more intelligence than Yaḥyā ibn Yaḥyā. He took these qualities from Mālik ibn Anas, may Allah Almighty have mercy on him. He was asked about that. He said, "I stayed in order to learn his qualities. They are the qualities of the Companions and the Followers."'

Abū Aḥmad ibn 'Adī said in his *Collection*, 'It is said that Isḥāq ibn Rāhawayh owed a debt. He went from Marw to 'Abdullāh ibn Ṭāhir at Nishapur. He entrusted the people of *ḥadīth* to (go to) Yaḥyā ibn Yaḥyā about his business. He asked, "What do you want?"

'They replied, "For you to write a paper to 'Abdullāh ibn Ṭāhir." 'Abdullāh was the Amīr of Khurasan at that time.

'Yaḥyā said, "I have not ever written to him." They pressed him, so he wrote on a paper, "'Abdullāh ibn Ṭāhir. Isḥāq ibn Rāhawayh is one of the men of knowledge and correctness."

'Isḥāq took the paper to him. When he came to the door, he said to the chamberlain, "I have a paper from Yaḥyā ibn Yaḥyā for the governor." The chamberlain came to Ibn Ṭāhir and said, "A man at the door claims that he has a paper from Yaḥyā ibn Yaḥyā for the governor." He said, "Yaḥyā ibn Yaḥyā?" He said, "Yes."

'He said, "Bring him in." He brought him in and handed him the paper. At-Ṭāhir kissed it and sat Isḥāq at his side and paid his debt of thirty thousand dirhams and put him among his companions.'

Yaḥyā did not frequent him. Yaḥyā ibn Yaḥyā was one of those who were well-off.

He mentioned that he gave Mālik a gift which Mālik sold in his legacy for 80,000.

Al-Bukhārī said, 'He died midday on Wednesday at the end of Ṣafar, 226 AH.'

FROM THE PEOPLE OF SYRIA

AL-WALĪD IBN MUSLIM IBN ABĪ AS-SĀ'IB

Abū al-'Abbās, a client of the Banū Umayya of Damascus.

Ibn Sha'bān said, 'He has what is too much to count from Mālik: the *Muwaṭṭā'*, legal questions and many *ḥadīths*. He related from Mālik, Ibn Jurayj, al-Awzā'ī (and he was one of his elite), al-Layth, ath-Thawrī, Ibn 'Uyayna, Nāfi' al-Qāri', Yaḥyā ibn al-Ḥārith az-Zamārī, Ibn Lahī'a, 'Abd ar-Raḥmān ibn Yazīd, Maslama ibn 'Alī, 'Amr ibn Jābir, Yazīd ibn Jābir, Abū Bakr ibn Abī Maryam and others. He related ten *ḥadīths* from Sharīk.'

Al-Lālakā'ī said, 'Al-Layth, al-Ḥumaydī, Aḥmad ibn Ḥanbal, Abū Khaythama and others related from him.'

Isḥāq ibn Rāhawayh also related from him as well as Hishām ibn 'Ammār, and Ṣafwān ibn Ṣāliḥ. Al-Bukhārī and Muslim transmitted from him.

Abū Mushir said, 'May Allah have mercy on Abū al-'Abbas. He was concerned with knowledge.'

Aḥmad said, 'He is trustworthy in *ḥadīths*.' Yaḥyā said, 'He used *tadlīs* (concealment of source).'

Aḥmad said, 'No one else related more *ḥadīths* from the *ḥadīths* of the Syrians and from Ismā'īl ibn 'Ayyāsh.'

Al-Walīd said, 'I came to Makka when Muhammad ibn Ibrāhīm was in charge of it. He shortened the prayer at Minā and 'Arafa while Sufyān repeated the prayer and Ibn Jurayj performed the full prayer.

'I came to Madina and I mentioned that to Mālik. He told me, "The governor was right and Sufyān and Ibn Jurayj were wrong." I think that al-Awzā'ī said something similar.

'I came to Egypt and I mentioned that to ash-Shāfi'ī and he told me, "The governor, al-Awzā'ī and Mālik were wrong and Sufyān and Ibn Jurayj were right."

'As for Mālik, he thought that the prayer was shortened for someone performing *ḥajj*, even if he was one of the people of Makka as the governor did. Al-Awzā'ī said that the people with him from Makka and the others shortened it. According to ash-Shāfi'ī, the Makkans extend it to perform it in full. That is the position of ath-Thawri, Ibn Ḥanbal and the People of Opinion.'

Al-Khaṭṭābī said about Sufyān repeating the prayer, 'It was because he did not think that someone doing an obligatory prayer should pray behind someone doing a supererogatory one. In his opinion, the prayer of the governor was obligatory when he shortened it. He was Makkan. Sufyan re-did the prayer. This is different from what was mentioned from him about doing it in full. In his variant from Mālik, there is the rare (*shādhdh*) and unusual (*gharīb*).'

Aḥmad said that he is trustworthy.

Aḥmad ibn Ṣāliḥ al-Kūfī said, 'Al-Bukhārī, Ibn Abī Khaythama and Ibn Waḍḍāḥ said that he died in 195 AH when he coming back from the *ḥajj*, at Dhū al-Marwa.'

Ibn Sha'bān and others said that he died in Muḥarram of 194 AH. He was born in 119 AH.

Abū Mushir 'Abd al-A'lā ibn Mushir al-Ghassānī ad-Dimishqī

Abū 'Amr al-Muqrī' said that he was one of the Banū Ka'b ibn Hind.

Ibn Sha'bān said, 'He related the *Muwaṭṭā'* and other questions and many *ḥadīth*s from Mālik.'

Ibn Abī Ḥāzim said, 'He listened to Sa'īd ibn 'Abd al-'Azīz, 'Abdullāh ibn al-'Alā' ibn Zayd, and Khālid ibn Yazīd ibn Ṣāliḥ.'

Ibn Abī al-Ḥawārī, Abū Zur'a ad-Dimishqī, Yaḥyā ibn Ma'īn and Abū Ḥātim related from him.

Ibn Ma'īn said, 'Since the time I left my land, I did not see anyone more like the shaykhs whom I have met than Abū Mushir. He was trustworthy.'

Abū Ḥātim said, 'I did not see anyone from whom we wrote the sound who was firmer than him. He is an Imām and al-Bukhārī transmitted from him.'

Ibn Waḍḍāḥ said, 'He was excellent, trustworthy. Muḥammad ibn Yūsuf as-Sukūnī an-Nasā'ī and Abū Dāwūd related from him.'

Az-Zubayrī said, 'He recited the Qur'an with Nāfi' and Ayyūb ibn Tamīm.'

Abū Zur'a, ad-Dimishqī and Abū 'Ubayd ibn Salām related from him.

Ibn Mufarraj said, 'Abū Mushir was the master of the people of Syria, their *faqīh* and their man of worship.'

Ibn Ma'īn said that he is trustworthy. Al-Kūfī also stated that he is trustworthy.

'Abd al-Baqī ibn al-Ḥasan said, 'After Ibn Dhakwān, being the *imām* of the reciters went to Abū Mushir.'

A man asked Abū Mushir about a question but he did not answer him. Then he repeated it to him and he did not answer him. He was asked about that. He said, 'I heard Mālik say, "Part of the abasement of knowledge is to answer everyone who questions you."'

Section on his reports and rare sayings

Abū Mushir was asked about the *ḥadīth*s of Baqiyya. He said, 'Be careful about the *ḥadīth*s of Baqiyya and be cautious about them. They are pure.'

He had written on his signet-ring, 'Abū al-'Alā', say the truth.'

Engraved on his brother's ring was: 'You are finished, so get up.' When his companion grew burdensome for him, he would give him his seal to show him its engraving.

Muḥammad ibn 'Abddikān would not let him come to him, so Abū Mushir wrote to him:

I come to you for consent for you, but the veils and curtains
did not give me permission for you.
You know that I did not want any desire except
for brotherhood, knowledge and manners.
The veil which cuts you off is not a hope for me.

The sky hopes when it is veiled.

Ibn 'Abddikān, may Allah have mercy on him, answered him,

If you would be compensated by the best, I would say as Ibn Aws said,
'There is manners in asking for forgiveness.'

Hārūn ibn Mūsā said, "I came to Abū Mushir, and he was lying on his back chanting the words of the poet:
The youth rejoices at what preceded of fear of Allah
when the disease arrives which kills him.

His inquisition

Mūsā ibn al-Ḥasan said, 'I heard Abū Mushir when al-Ma'mūn sent him to Isḥāq ibn Ibrāhīm in Baghdad. Isḥāq had a group summoned for him so that he could read the document of the inquisition which al-Ma'mūn had written about the creation of the Qur'an, the denial of the Vision (of Allah) and the punishment of the grave, and that the Balance does not have two scales, and that the Garden and the Fire are not created.

'When the document was read out to Abū Mushir, he said, "I deny all that is in this document of yours. It is far from the assembly of Mālik, ath-Thawrī and the shaykhs of the people of knowledge. I will not reject Allah after some ninety-one years. I will not say that the Qur'an is created nor will I deny the punishment of the grave nor that the Balance has two scales nor that Allah will be seen on the Rising nor that Allah Almighty is on His Throne and that His knowledge encompasses everything. The Qur'an was sent down with that and the tradition which the people of knowledge have transmitted brings that. If they were suspected in what they say, they would have been suspected in the Qur'an. They are the ones who transmitted the Qur'an and the *Sunna* from the Prophet ﷺ."

'He was dragged by his feet and thrown into the most cramped of prisons. He did not last very long until he died, may Allah Almighty have mercy on him. There were so many people present at his funeral that only Allah can count them.'

Abū Dāwūd said, 'He was taken to the inquisition, but did not reply.'

Abū Ja'far aṭ-Ṭabarī said, 'Abū Mushir was carried in chains to al-Ma'mūn to undergo the inquisition about the Qur'an and he did not answer. Al-Ma'mūn called for a sword and a leather mat to execute him. When he saw that, he said, "Created," so he left him and did not kill him. He had him travel to Baghdad in Rabī' al-Ākhir in 218 AH and he was imprisoned and it was not long before he died at the beginning of Rajab of that same year.'

Al-Balkhī related that when al-Ma'mūn came to Damascus, Abū Mushir was mentioned to him and he was described as having knowledge and *fiqh*. Therefore he summoned him and debated with him about the Qur'an. Then he asked him about the Prophet ﷺ and whether he said the *shahāda* when he married. He replied, 'I do not know.' He asked whether the Prophet ﷺ had shaved his head and he said, 'I do not know.'

So he cursed him and made him get up. Al-Ma'mūn did this to him out of his animosity to him because he had opposed him about the Qur'an. Whoever says, 'I do not know' is just.

Abū Mushir was asked about a man who misreads, errs and makes *ḥadīth*s obscure. He said, 'Make his business clear.' He was asked, 'Is that a fault?' He said, 'No.'

He died, according to aṭ-Ṭabarī, al-Barqānī and al-Bukhārī, in 228 AH.

Ibn Mufarraj said in 210 AH. He was born in 149 AH. Al-Bukhārī said the like of it.

Marwān ibn Muḥammad ibn Ḥassān al-Asadī

Aṭ-Ṭaṭarī of Damascus. He kept the company of Mālik and related many *ḥadīths* and questions from him, and also from al-Layth ibn Sa'd, Sa'īd ibn 'Abd al-'Azīz and Mu'āwiya ibn Salām.

Ibn Waḍḍāḥ said, 'Marwān ibn Muḥammad was a great man of excellence.'

Ibn Ma'īn said, 'There is no harm in aṭ-Ṭāṭarī.' He said, 'He was a Murji'ite.' Ibn Ma'īn said, 'Whoever was a Murji'ite in Damascus wore a turban. Whoever was not a Murji'ite in Damascus did not wear a turban.'

Al-Bukhārī said, 'He was called aṭ-Ṭāṭarī because his garment was ascribed to it.'

He listened to Mu'āwiya ibn Salām. Muslim transmitted from him in the *Ṣaḥīḥ* as did Abū Dāwūd and the other Imāms, although some of them considered him weak.

Al-Haytham ibn Khārija, Maḥmūd ibn Khālid, Aḥmad ibn Abī al-Ḥawārī, ad-Dārimī, Aḥmad ibn Abī al-Azhar an-Naysābūrī, and Salama ibn Shabīb related *ḥadīths* from him.

It is related that he said, 'Three are not trusted in a debt: a Sufi, a story-teller, and an innovator who refutes the people of sects.'

His son, Ibrāhīm ibn Marwān ibn Muḥammad, related from his father. Abū Ḥātim ar-Rāzī wrote from him. He said that he is truthful.

Al-Bukhārī said that Marwān died in 210 AH. Another said in 216 AH.

Isḥāq ibn 'Īsā ibn Najīḥ, Abū Ya'qūb, known as Ibn aṭ-Ṭabbā'

There are three brothers: Muhammad, Yusuf and Isḥāq.

Isḥāq listened to Mālik ibn Anas and kept his company and he listened to Sharīk ibn 'Abdullāh, 'Abd ar-Raḥmān ibn Zayd ibn Aslam and Abū Ḍamra Anas ibn 'Iyāḍ.

His nephew Muḥammad ibn Yūsuf, Aḥmad ibn Ḥanbal, Isḥāq ibn Bahlūl, Ya'qūb ibn Shayba, 'Abbās ad-Dūrī, al-Ḥārith ibn Salama, al-Ḥasan ibn Mukarram, and Muslim ibn al-Ḥajjāj related from him. He transmitted from him in his *Ṣaḥīḥ* as others did.

Al-Khaṭīb Abū Bakr said, 'At the end of his life he moved to 'Udhna, and he lived there until he died.'

Ṣāliḥ ibn Muḥammad was asked about him and said that there is no objection to him. He is truthful.

Muḥammad ibn Sa'd said, 'Isḥāq aṭ-Ṭabbā' the *faqīh* died in 215 AH.'

Ibn Nāfi' said in 214 AH.

Abū Bakr al-Ḥāfiẓ said, 'The first version is sounder.'

FROM THE PEOPLE OF EGYPT

‘Abdullāh ibn Wahb ibn Muslim al-Qurashī

He was a client of Quraysh, a client of Yazīd ibn Rayḥāna. It is also said that he was a client of the Banū Fihr. Al-Bājī stated that.

Ad-Dāraquṭnī said, ‘He was a client of Yazīd ibn Rayḥāna, a client of Yazīd ibn Anas al-Fihrī.’

Abū ‘Umar al-Kindī said, ‘He was a client of Yazīd ibn Rayḥāna, a client of the family of Shaybān ibn Muḥārib ibn Fihr.’

He said, ‘They disagree about his *walā’*. It is said that Ibn Rayḥāna was a client of a woman of the Anṣār from the Banū Bayāḍa. Her husband was a Fihrī.’

Another said, ‘His *walā’* reverted to his sons because of her.’

Al-Bukhārī said, ‘He was a client of Rayḥāna.’

Ibn Abī Ḥātim said, ‘A client of Ibn Rayḥāna, a client of Fihr.’

Ibn Sha‘bān and Ibn ‘Abd al-Barr said, ‘Rayḥāna was the client of Abū ‘Abd ar-Raḥmān Yazīd ibn Anas al-Fihrī.’

Al-Kindī said, ‘They claim that Ibn Wahb was sometimes called al-Anṣārī and sometimes al-Qurashī. Then he remained “al-Qurashī”. Ibn ‘Ufayr mentioned something similar.’

Ibn Bukayr said, ‘I found his testimony in a deed as al-Anṣārī.’

Abū aṭ-Ṭāhir said, ‘His grandfather, who was a Berber, became Muslim’

He related from Mālik, al-Layth, Ibn Abī Dhi’b, Yūnus ibn Yazīd, ath-Thawrī, Ibn ‘Uyayna, Ibn Jurayj, Ibn An‘am, ‘Abd al-‘Azīz ibn al-Mājishūn, Yaḥyā ibn Ayyūb, and about four hundred shaykhs from the Egyptians, Hijazis and Iraqis. He recited Qur’an with Nāfi‘, and al-Layth related from him and clearly stated his name.

It is said that Mālik related the *ḥadīth* of the *'urbān* (down payment) from him from Ibn Lahī'a.

Some of the people who related from him were Aṣbagh ibn al-Faraj, Saḥnūn, Aḥmad ibn *Ṣaḥīḥ*, Ibn Bukayr, Yūnus, Abū aṭ-Ṭāhir, Qutayba, Ibn 'Ufayr, al-Waqqār, al-Qarāṭīsī, al-Ḥārith ibn Miskīn, the Banū 'Abd al-Ḥakam, Ḥarmala, Abū Muṣ'ab az-Zuhrī and others.

Ash-Shīrāzī said, 'He learned *fiqh* with Mālik, 'Abd al-Mālik ibn al-Mājishūn, Ibn Abī Ḥāzim, Ibn Dīnār, al-Mughīra, and al-Layth.'

Ḥarmala said, 'I listened to Ibn Wahb say, "I met 360 scholars. If it had not been for Mālik, I would have been misguided in knowledge."'

He said, 'I met more than twenty men of the companions of Ibn Shihāb.' Al-Layth gave many *ḥadīth*s from Ibn Wahb.

Abū aṭ-Ṭāhir said, 'Ibn Wahb listened to Mālik some ten years before Ibn al-Qāsim. He kept Mālik's company from 148 AH until he died. Ibn Wahb was not present at his death as he had gone on *ḥajj*.'

Ibn Waḍḍāḥ said, 'Ibn Wahb went on *ḥajj* in 144 AH. He first met Mālik there and he only listened to one question from him. He listened to al-Muthannā ibn aṣ-Ṣabbāḥ in Makka. The question which he heard from Mālik was about joining the two evening prayers during rain. The governor had sent to ask him about that. There was a light rain, and he ordered them to be joined together.'

Ash-Shīrāzī said, 'Ibn Wahb kept the company of Mālik for twenty years.'

Ibn Waḍḍāḥ said, 'He sought knowledge young when he was sixteen.'

Ibn Saḥnūn mentioned that he said, 'He sought knowledge when he was seventeen.'

His place in *fiqh* and *ḥadīth*, and his praise by lofty scholars

Abū 'Umar said, 'They say that Mālik did not write anyone down as a *faqīh* except for Ibn Wahb.' Ibn Waḍḍāḥ said, 'He used to write to him, "to 'Abdullāh ibn Wahb, the *faqīh* of Egypt."'

Ash-Shīrāzī said, 'Mālik used to write to him, "to Abū Muḥammad, the *muftī*."' Abū aṭ-Ṭāhir related the like of that, He added that he did not do this for anyone else.

Mālik said, 'Ibn Wahb is an Imam.' He said, 'Ibn Wahb is a man of knowledge.' He once looked at him and said, 'What a young man! If only it had not been for having too much.'

Aḥmad ibn Ḥanbal said, 'Ibn Wahb was a sound scholar, a *faqīh* of much knowledge.'

He also said, 'Ibn Wahb was sound in *ḥadīth*s from his shaykhs from whom he related. He distinguished the oral from what was read, and one *ḥadīth* from another *ḥadīth*. How sound are his *ḥadīth*s! How much he knew the names! However, those who took from him were not precise, with the exception of Hārūn ibn Ma'rūf.'

Yūsuf ibn 'Adī said, 'Among people, I met a *faqīh* who is not a man of *ḥadīth*, and a man of *ḥadīth* who is not a *faqīh*, except for 'Abdullāh ibn Wahb. I saw that he was a man of *ḥadīth*, a *faqīh*, and a man of asceticism.'

Abū Muṣ'ab said, 'When we doubted something about Mālik's opinion after his death, Ibn Dīnār, al-Mughīra and the great companions would write to Ibn Wahb and his answer would reach us.'

Ibn Ḥanbal said, 'He informed us about the opinion of Ibn Abi Ḥāzim which was read to him to Ibn Wahb as the opinion of Mālik.'

Qāḍī Hārūn az-Zuhrī said, 'The companions of Mālik in Madina disagreed about Mālik's words after his death. They waited for the arrival of Ibn Wahb and they accepted his opinion.'

Ibn Waḍḍāḥ said, 'The people of the Hijaz needed Ibn Wahb in the science of the Hijaz, and the people of Iraq needed him in the science of Iraq. He had much knowledge.'

When his death was announced to Ibn 'Uyayna, he asked for mercy on him and said, 'The Muslims in general are afflicted (by his loss) and I in particular am afflicted.'

Ibn Rishdīn said, 'Ibn Wahb had much more knowledge than Ibn al-Qāsim.'

Mālik said when he had left him, 'This is how it is with the people of knowledge when he sees one to whom he is humbled.'

Sufyān said to him, 'You are Ibn Wahb the Egyptian?' He answered, 'Yes.' He said to him, 'I have known your place in Islam since something about you reached me.'

Yaḥyā ibn Ma'īn said that Ibn Wahb was trustworthy.

Aḥmad ibn Khālid said, 'Ibn Wahb was one of the great men of excellence and one of those who were precise and excellent.' Ibn al-Qāsim used to say, 'The most trustworthy of my companions told me,' meaning him.

Ibn Rishdīn said, 'Al-Ḥasan ibn Thawbān said to me when he saw him, "If this young man lives, he will be the Imām of this age if Allah Almighty wills."'

Aḥmad ibn *Ṣaḥīḥ* said, 'None of those Allah created was greater in respect of Mālik than Ibn Nāfi' and Ibn Wahb. Aḥmad preferred Ibn Nāfi'. Ibn Wahb had precedence in abundant knowledge and many questions. Mālik did not speak about anything but that Ibn Wahb wrote it down. Ibn Wahb was tolerant to the shaykhs. If he had adopted the manner that Mālik did, it would have been better for him.'

Aḥmad ibn *Ṣaḥīḥ* said, 'The *ḥadīth*s of Ibn Wahb numbered a hundred thousand. I did not see anyone with more *ḥadīth*s than him. I have seventy thousand of his *ḥadīth*s.'

Abū Zur'a said, 'I looked at about eighty thousand *ḥadīth*s from the *ḥadīth*s of Ibn Wahb. I did not see any *ḥadīth*s of his that was without a root. He was trustworthy and he had more *fiqh* than Ibn al-Qāsim.'

Al-Kūfī said, 'He was trustworthy, the master of *Sunna* and traditions, and a man of right action.'

A man asked 'Alī ibn Ma'bad about a question when he was posted in Alexandria. He said, 'I would not answer in place which contains Ibn Wahb, so go to him and ask him.'

Muḥammad ibn al-Ḥusayn said, 'Ibn Wahb in his time was the man of *ḥadīth* of his land, and he was a man of right action and worship.'

Muḥammad ibn 'Abd al-Ḥakam and Ibn Bukayr said, 'Ibn Wahb knew more *fiqh* than al-Qāsim. However, his scrupulousness prevented him from giving *fatwā*.'

Ibn Waḍḍāḥ said, 'Ibn Wahb knew the rites of the *ḥajj* and Ibn al-Qāsim knew sales-transactions.'

Abū Ḥātim ar-Rāzī said, 'I prefer Ibn Wahb to Ibn Nāfi' and al-Walīd ibn Muslim. He has much sounder *ḥadīth*s than al-Walīd. Ibn Wahb was sound and truthful in *ḥadīth*s.'

Ibn Ma'īn and an-Nasā'ī said that Ibn Wahb is trustworthy.

Ibn Ma'īn said that he is trustworthy although he related from weak men.

He was asked, 'Why did you leave Ibn al-Qāsim and relate from Ibn Wahb?' He said, 'Ibn al-Qāsim was excellent, but Ibn Wahb is a master of traditions.'

Al-Bukhārī and Muslim transmitted from him.

Abū Muṣ'ab respected Ibn Wahb and listened to his questions from Mālik. He used to say, 'He is sound.'

Aṣbagh said, 'Of the companions of Mālik, Ibn Wahb has the most knowledge about the *sunan* and the traditions (*āthār*).'

'Abd ar-Raḥmān ibn Muḥammad as-Sahmī said, 'I saw Mālik in a dream riding a mule. I took hold of its rein to ask him about the difference in his words, and he refused to answer me. He said, "Was it as if you asked about pearls and hidden jewels?" I answered, "Yes." He said, "You must have the old book of Ibn Wahb."'

Al-Ḥārith said, 'Ibn Wahb combined *fiqh*, transmission and worship. He was an Imām. He was provided with love from scholars and favour from Mālik and others. I did not ever come to him but that I had good benefit from him.'

Abū Zayd ibn Abī al-Ghamr said, 'I heard Ibn Wahb say, "I went on twenty-four *hajj*s. In them I met Mālik."' Abū Zayd said, 'We called Ibn Wahb the Repository of Knowledge.'

Ḥarmala said, 'I saw the letter of Mālik "to Ibn Wahb, the *muftī* of Egypt."'

They said, 'There was no one that Mālik did not rebuke except for Ibn Wahb. He used to love and respect him.'

Ibn al-Qāsim said, 'If Ibn 'Uyayna had died, camels would have beaten to reach Ibn Wahb. None had written knowledge as he wrote it.'

Yūnus said, 'I only saw Abū al-Ḥasan al-Iskandarānī speak to Ibn Wahb, saying, "Uncle." When the shaykhs saw Ibn Wahb, they were humble towards him.'

Abū aṭ-Ṭāhir said, 'Ibn Wahb was asked about some new questions. He said, "Will I leave the previous questions which we read to him while he was devoted to them so that sometimes he would erase something from my book for me?"'

His nephew said, 'I was posted with him in Alexandria in a *ribāṭ*. People gathered to him to ask him about the spread of knowledge. He said to me, "This is a land of worship. Rarely do I prepare myself to be with what people are occupied."

'He stopped sitting for them in the times in which he used to sit. He turned to worship and guarding. After two days, a man came and informed him, "I dreamt that I was in an immense mosque like the Masjid al-Ḥarām and the Prophet ﷺ was in it. Abū Bakr was on his right and 'Umar was on his left. You were in front of him. There were candles in the mosques giving off the most radiant and strongest of light. When you feared for one of the candles, it went out. The Messenger of Allah ﷺ said to you, 'Get up, Abū 'Abdullāh, and light it.' So you lit it. Then another was like that. Then I remained some days and I saw that all of the candles wanted to go out. Abū Bakr said, 'Messenger of Allah, do you see these candles?' He ﷺ replied, 'This is the action of 'Abdullāh,' meaning putting them out."

'Ibn Wahb wept and the man said to him, "I have come to give you good news. If I had known that it would sadden you, I would not have come to you."

'He said, "It is good. I am admonished by this dream. I thought that worship was better than spreading knowledge."

'He left much of his work for the sake of knowledge and kept himself for them to read to him and question him.'

His school in transmission

Ibn Wahb said, 'Everything in my books (books ascribed to Mālik) I have heard from him.' He had a special relation with him.

Ibn Wahb said, 'I asked Mālik to leave me something which he would read to me, so he did that. I was with him reading to him when 'Abd aṣ-Ṣamad al-Hāshimī, the governor of Madina, asked permission to come to him. He asked him for the like of what I had asked him, and he refused him. He said, "The caliph wanted me do this, but I did not grant his request." I said to myself, "How can he not use me as a proof against him?"'

Ibn Wahb said, 'I was writing in the presence of Mālik when the *iqāma* for the prayer was given (in one version has 'the *mu'adhdhin* gave the call to prayer'), and there were books scattered in front of him. I went to quickly gather them up and he told me, "Slow down! What you are called to is not better than what you are in if the intention is sound."'

Ibn Wahb said, 'Mālik asked me, "What kept you from me from some nights?" I replied, "I had inflamed eyes." Mālik said, "I suppose you are someone who writes at night?" I answered, "Yes." Mālik shouted for a slavegirl, "Bring some of that kohl for my Egyptian friend, Ibn Wahb!"'

Ismā'īl ibn Qa'nab said, 'I was with Ibn Mālik, and a gift would come to Mālik by day and he would give it to Ibn Wahb at night.'

Ibn Wahb said, 'I entered the mosque and there were people crowding around Ibn Sam'ān. Hishām ibn 'Urwa was seated. I said, "I will listen to this one and then go to him." When I had finished, he got up and went to his house. It was said, "He is resting." I said, "I will go on *ḥajj* and then come to him again." When I returned, he had died.'

Ibn Wahb was told, 'Ibn al-Qāsim disagrees with you on certain things.' He replied, 'Ibn al-Qāsim came to Mālik when he was weak. I came to Mālik when he was a strong young man who took my book and read it. Sometimes he would find an error in it and take up a rag in his hand and dip it into the water and erase it and write for me what was correct.'

Ibn Wahb said, 'If it had not been that Allah rescued me with Mālik and al-Layth, I would have been misguided.' He was asked, 'How is that?' He said, 'I had a lot of *ḥadīth*s that made me bewildered. I used to read that to Mālik and al-Layth and they would tell me, "Take this and leave that."'

Nu'aym ibn Ḥammād said, 'Ibn Wahb appointed Tuesday for strangers. They would read to him. The one who entered would come and he still had some of the book which he read. He said, "Let him come to me." He would answer him. He did that to more than one person. Then he would go to him and ask him about *ḥadīth*s. He said, "Now is the time this is heard." He said, "We will read it to you." We said, "We read to Abū Muḥammad." If it was read and we were present, we said, "It was read to Abū Muḥammad while he were present." He was lenient with good character. He said, "We did not take the *ḥadīth* as you wish."'

Muḥammad ibn 'Abd al-Ḥakam said, 'The books of Ibn Wahb were sold after his death for three hundred dinars (one version has three hundred and sixty). Our companions were numerous and my father was his trustee and no one disliked that. If it had not been that he advised one of them not to increase, I would have had more.'

It is related that he gave eighty dinars of her price to one of his two wives and did not leave a child as heir. This reckoning is more than the first, and Allah knows best. He mentioned it in *al-Mabsūṭ*.

Abū Zayd said, 'Ibn Wahb, Ibn al-Qāsim and Ashhab agreed that when I took the book from the man of *ḥadīth*, I should say, "He informed me."'

It was said to Ibn Hanbal who praised him for his *ḥadīth*s, 'Is it not a bad form of taking?' He said, 'Yes, but when I looked at his *ḥadīth*s and what he took from his shaykhs, I found them to be sound.'

Other reports

Ibn Wahb said, 'The beginning of my business was in worship before seeking knowledge. Shayṭān made me fond of the mention of 'Īsā, peace be upon him, and how Allah had created him. I complained about that to a shaykh and he said, "Seek knowledge." That was the reason for my quest.'

Ḥusayn ibn 'Āṣim said, 'I was with Ibn Wahb when a beggar stopped at the circle. He said, "Abū Muḥammad! The dirham which you gave me yesterday is counterfeit." He said, "So-and-so, our hands are empty." The beggar became angry and said, "May Allah bless Muḥammad! This is the time about which it is said that only the hypocrites bring *ṣadaqa* for this community!"

'A man from the people of Iraq got up and dealt the wretch such a slap that he fell on his face. Then he began to shout. "Abū Muḥammad! Imam of the Muslims! He does this to me in your assembly?!" Ibn Wahb asked, "Who did this?"

'The Iraqi answered, "I did it, may Allah make you thrive! by the *ḥadīth* in which the Prophet ﷺ said, 'If someone defends the flesh of a believer from a hypocrite who slanders him, Allah will protect his flesh from the Fire. You are our lamp and our light whom he has slandered before our faces!'"

'He said, "I will tell you the *ḥadīth* that the Prophet ﷺ said, 'There will be wretches at the end of time called the immoderate who will not do *wuḍū'* for the prayer nor do a *ghusl* for *janāba*. People will go out to their mosques and their festivals and ask Allah for His favour and they will leave asking people (meaning for their rights from people). They do not think that Allah has any right over them.'"'

Ibn Wahb used to say, 'Whoever makes a promise and says, "Allah willing" does not owe anything.'

Ibn Wahb asked for some kohl from Mālik. He told his slavegirl, 'Give me some kohl for my Egyptian friend.' He said, 'They brought him one or two tubes.'

Ar-Rabī', the companion of ash-Shāfi'ī, said, 'We went to 'Abdullāh ibn Wahb to listen and a group of people gathered at his door. He got up to open the door. When he opened it, we crowded in to enter. He fell and wounded his face. He said, "This only levity and lack of gravity! With the like of this, by Allah, I will not let you listen to a single letter today!" Then he sat, and we sat as well. When he saw the stillness we had, he said, "Where is the tranquillity of knowledge? I will do expiation for my oath and let you listen today." So he did expiation and let us listen.'

Ibn Wahb looked at a man who was fermenting cheese. He said to him, 'It hardens the heart, weakens the sight, and makes a lot of lice.'

Ibn Wahb said, 'I used to pray in the mosque in Alexandria. I heard al-'Alā' ibn Kathīr say to his companion, "Who among you will present himself to this young man and marry him to his daughter?" based on his perception of him.'

Saḥnūn said, 'Ibn Wahb made a vow to never fast the day of 'Arafa. That was because once he fasted the heat and the thirst became intense for him in the Standing. He said, "The people were waiting for mercy and I was waiting to break the fast!"'

Ibn Wahb said, 'Mālik said to me, "Do not allow any of the People of the Book to teach the Muslims."' Ibn Wahb said, 'My teacher was a Christian.'

Yaḥyā ibn Yaḥyā said, 'I heard Ibn Wahb report a *ḥadīth* which said, "After one hundred and twenty years, it will be better for one of you to teach a puppy than for him to teach a child." I objected about that to him.

'He said, "Abū Muḥammad, I do not think that you are in what Allah has brought you from His favour. You were only born after this time." He told me, "Yes."

'By Allah, he did mention the *ḥadīth* again until I parted from him.'

Yaḥyā said, 'If anyone is safe from the fault of having too much, it is Ibn Wahb who is safe from it.'

An-Nasā'ī said, 'There is no objection to him except that he was terribly easy going in taking (knowledge).'

Ibn Sa'd said, 'He used *tadlīs*.'

Sa'īd ibn Manṣūr said, "Abdullāh ibn Wahb listened with us to the shaykhs. He used to go to sleep in the assembly and then he would take the books from some of us and write them down.'

They said, 'He was the first in Egypt to distinguish between "he related to us" and "he informed us."'

His worship, asceticism, fear and his death

Abū 'Umar said, 'Ibn Wahb was a man of right action, fearful of Allah.'

Another said, 'He went on *ḥajj* often.'

Saḥnūn said, 'Ibn Wahb said that he divided his time into three portions: one third was for *ribāṭ*, one third to teach the people in Egypt, and one third for the *ḥajj*. They mentioned that he went on *ḥajj* thirty times.'

Ibn Wahb said, 'I imposed on myself that whenever I slandered a man, I would fast a day. That was easy for me. So I imposed on myself that whenever I slandered a person, I would give a dirham in *ṣadaqa*. That was burdensome for me, so I abandoned slander.'

Abū Ja'far al-Aylī said that Ibn Wahb said, 'There was no night that passed but that I was terrified of it and I remembered the terror of the Next World in it.'

When he was sought after to act as a *qāḍī* of Egypt, he hid with Ḥarmala ibn Yaḥyā for a year and some months.

Ḥajjāj ibn Rishdīn said, 'One day I looked down at him from my room which was opposite him. He said to me, "Abū al-Hasan, when I hope to be gathered in the party of the men of knowledge can I be gathered in the party of the *qāḍīs*?"'

His nephew said, 'I did not see anyone with more asceticism in this world than him. Part of his building fell down and he did not put it right nor build anything and I did not see anyone with more firm resolution than him.'

He said, 'I saw 'Abdullāh ibn Wahb have *The Book of Terrors* read to him in his house which he related had reached him from Abū Hurayra. Abū Usāma saw him weeping, so they too began to weep. Then Abū Usāma got up with that page while Ibn Wahb was weeping while the reader was reading. Ibn Wahb was sobbing in a loud voice so that I supposed that it could be heard for fifty yards. He continued like that until he leaned over the wall against which he was reclining. Then he was carried to his house and he remained in this state without regaining consciousness until he died. We thought that he had had a heart attack.'

Yūnus said, 'Ibn Wahb said, "The People of *Ḥadīth* asked me to let them listen to the description of the Garden and the Fire, but I do not think that I can capable of that."

'When he sat for them and they read the description of the Fire to him, he passed out. Water was sprinkled on his face and it was said, "Read the description of the Garden to him.' He still did not come around. He remained like that for twenty-two days. A doctor was summoned for him. He looked at him and said, 'This man has had a heart attack."'

He died in Egypt in 197 AH according to Aḥmad ibn Ṣaḥīḥ and Abū 'Umar al-Kindī.

Ibn al-Jazzār said that it was Sunday, the 25th of Sha'bān.

It was said 198 AH. It was said 195 or 196 AH. Al-Bājī said it was 190 AH. The first is more sound and well-known.

Ibn Saḥnūn said, 'The firm position is that he died in 196 AH when he was seventy-two years old. It is also said that he was seventy-six and it is said eighty.'

He was born in Egypt in 125 AH. It is said 125 AH.

Abū Isḥāq said, 'He was three years older than Ibn al-Qāsim, and he lived for five years after him.'

His nephew said, 'When Ibn Wahb died, a man dreamt on that night that it was said to him, "Four hundred scholars have died tonight." When he woke up, he heard a call announcing a death and asked about it. It was said, "Ibn Wahb has died."'

He said that Ibn Wahb related from four hundred scholars.

Aṭ-Ṭabbā' said, 'When they washed Ibn Wahb they found a fresh date in his mouth. 'Abbād, the Governor of Egypt, prayed the funeral prayer over him.'

Abū Bashīr ibn Qa'nab said, 'On the night Ibn Wahb died, I dream that the table of knowledge was taken away.'

Aṭ-Ṭabbā' and others said, 'I sold his books after his death and it reached five hundred dinars.'

Muḥammad ibn 'Abd al-Ḥakam said, 'Ibn Wahb made my father the trustee to pay for the expiation of oaths, and he commanded him to pay the creditors two *mudd*s each, and he made Ibn al-Qāsim a trustee in it by giving a *mudd* each.'

He wrote many books of great merit and immense benefit. Among them are his oral reports from Mālik in thirty books, the great *Muwaṭṭā'*, *The Book of the Commentary on the Muwaṭṭā'*,*The Book of Sales*, *The Book of 'No Hāma*[1] *nor Ṣafar*[2]*'*, *The Book of Ḥajj Rites*, *The Book of Raids*, and *The Book of the Ridda.*

He had a brother called 'Abd ar-Raḥmān who was the father of Aḥmad and 'Abd al-'Azīz.

He also had a brother whose name was 'Amr ibn Wahb. It was said, 'He had *ḥadīth*s but I did not know him.'

He died in Muḥarram, 197 AH according to Ibn Yūnus.

He had a son called Ḥamīd. Al-Kindī mentioned that he was accepted by the *qāḍī*s of Egypt. Aṭ-Ṭaḥāwī stated, 'There was some idleness in him.'

[1] An owl or night bird which frequents the grave, reputed to come from the unavenged dead demanding vengeance (a belief of the *Jāhiliyya*).

[2] A serpent in the belly which bites a man when he is hungry. Another *Jāhiliyya* belief.

‘Abd ar-Raḥmān ibn al-Qāsim al-‘Utaqī

Abū ‘Umar al-Kindī said in his book, *The Notables of the Clients of Egypt*, that his *kunya* was Abū ‘Abdullāh. He is ‘Abd ar-Raḥmān ibn al-Qāsim ibn Khālid ibn Janāda. That is how ad-Dāraquṭnī and al-Amīr settled his name. Al-Bājī related it as ‘Jabāra’ but that is a mistake. He was a client of Zabīd ibn al-Ḥārith al-‘Utaqī. Zabīd is located in the desert of Ḥimyar. Those “*utaqa*” were a group who were from the area of Ḥimyar, from Sa‘d al-‘Ashīra, and from Kināna of Egypt and others.

Ibn Waḍḍāḥ said, ‘His roots were from the city of Ramla in Palestine from greater Syria. He lived in Egypt.’

Ad-Dāraquṭnī said, ‘There was a mosque in Egypt known as the mosque of al-‘Utaqā’.’

Ibn al-Ḥārith said, ‘It is ascribed to the slaves from Ta’if who reached the Prophet ﷺ who made them free men.’

His father was in the *Dīwān* (chancellery) and Ibn al-Qāsim inherited from him the money which he spent for his journey to Mālik. He gave Sa‘d ninety dinars of it. I have heard that he spent all his inheritance for that purpose.

He related from al-Layth, ‘Abd al-‘Azīz ibn al-Mājishūn, Muslim ibn Khālid az-Zanjī, Bakr ibn Muḍar, Ibn ad-Darāwardī, Ibn Zabīd, Ibn Abī Ḥāzim, Sa‘d, ‘Abd ar-Raḥīm, ‘Uthmān ibn al-Ḥakam, and others.

Aṣbagh, Saḥnūn, ‘Īsā ibn Dīnār, al-Ḥārith ibn Miskīn, ‘Īsā ibn Talīd, Yaḥyā ibn Yaḥyā al-Andalusī, Abū Zayd ibn Abī al-Ghamr, Muḥammad ibn al-Mawwāz, Abū Thābit al-Madīnī, and Muḥammad ibn ‘Abd al-Ḥakam related from him. Most of the transmissions of Muḥammad ibn al-Mawwāz and Ibn ‘Abd al-Ḥakam were from a man from him. Al-Bukhārī transmitted from him.

Praise for him by esteemed men

Al-Kindī said, 'Ibn al-Qāsim was mentioned to Mālik and he said, "May Allah preserve him! His metaphor is a sack filled with musk."'

Ad-Dāraquṭnī said, 'Ibn al-Qāsim, the companion of Mālik, was one of the great men of Egypt and their *fuqahā'*.'

Abū 'Umar ibn 'Abd al-Barr said, 'Opinion (*ra'y*) dominated him, and he was a man of right action, poor, patient. His transmission from him in the *Muwaṭṭā'* is sound with little error. He was accurate in what he related from Mālik with excellent precision. Mālik was asked about him and about Ibn Wahb. He said, "Ibn Wahb is a man of knowledge and Ibn al-Qāsim is a *faqīh*!"'

Ibn Ma'īn said that he is trustworthy. Abū Zur'a said, 'He is trustworthy, a man of right action. He had about three hundred volumes of questions from Mālik. Asad asked him about them.' He mentioned the rest of the story which will come later.

An-Nasā'ī said, 'Some of the *fuqahā'* of the cities of Egypt were 'Abd ar-Raḥmān ibn al-Qāsim and Ashhab ibn 'Abd al-'Azīz.'

An-Nasā'ī said, 'Ibn al-Qāsim was reliable, a man of right action. Glory be to Allah! How excellent are his *ḥadīth*s from Mālik and how sound! He does not differ in a single letter, and no one related the *Muwaṭṭā'* from Mālik firmer than Ibn al-Qāsim. In my opinion, none of the companions of Mālik were like him.'

He was asked, 'And Ashhab?' He said, 'Not Ashhab nor anyone else. He was a wonder of excellence, asceticism, sound transmission, excellent awareness and good *ḥadīth*s. His *ḥadīth*s attest to him.'

Ibn Wahb said to Ibn Thābit, 'If you desire this affair, namely Mālik's *fiqh*, you must have Ibn al-Qāsim. He devoted himself to it while we were occupied with something else.'

It is by this path of transmission that Qāḍī Abū Muḥammad 'Abd al-Wahhāb al-Baghdādī preferred the questions of the *Mudawwana* by the *riwāya* of Saḥnūn from Ibn al-Qāsim because of Ibn al-Qāsim's connection to Mālik and his keeping his company for a long time, not mixing with anyone else with him except for something insignificant. Then Saḥnūn was also with Ibn al-Qāsim in this way in addition to the excellence and knowledge that they both possessed.

Yaḥyā ibn Yaḥyā said, 'Ibn al-Qāsim was the youngest of the

people of Mālik in Egypt in age and the youngest of them in seeking and the one among them with the most knowledge of Mālik and their most trustworthy in him.'

Ibn Ḥārith said,'"He was the person with the most *fiqh* of the school of Mālik.' He said, 'We heard the shaykhs preferring Ibn al-Qāsim over all of his companions in the science of sales transactions. Mālik told him, "Be fearful of Allah. You must disseminate this knowledge."'

Abū 'Abdullah ibn Abī Ṣufra said, 'None like him sat with Mālik,' i.e. any like Ibn al-Qāsim. He said, 'Al-Asīlī used to say that about him.'

Al-Ḥārith ibn Miskīn said, 'Ibn al-Qāsim possessed asceticism, knowledge, generosity, courage and his supplication was answered.'

Aḥmad ibn Khālid said, 'Ibn al-Qāsim only had the *Muwaṭṭā'* and what he heard from Mālik. He memorised it well.'

Aḥmad said, 'However, he was not good at recitation. The reciter was absent one day and he needed to recite. He had not finished a page before his face grew red and he could not do anything. He said, "Look for someone to recite to you," and he cast the book aside.'

Ashhab was asked about Ibn al-Qāsim and Ibn Wahb. He said, 'If the foot of Ibn al-Qāsim had been cut off, it would have had more *fiqh* than Ibn Wahb.' What was between Ibn al-Qāsim and Ashhab was very wide, but that did not prevent him from saying the truth about him.

Abū aṭ-Ṭāhir said, 'My uncle (who was one of those who strive and one of the people of knowledge) informed me, "I dreamt that someone was saying, 'Only Ibn Wahb and Ibn al-Qāsim give *fatwā* in the school.' Then I dreamt the like of that a year later."'

Ibn Waddāḥ said, 'None like Ashhab, Ibn al-Qāsim and ibn Wahb went to Mālik. Ashhab knew the *fiqh* concerning wounds, Ibn al-Qāsim knew sales, and Ibn Wahb knew the rules of the *ḥajj*.'

Abū Isḥāq ash-Shīrāzī said, 'He combined *fiqh* and scrupulousness, and he kept the company of Mālik for twenty years, and he learned *fiqh* with him and his peers.'

Al-Ḥārith said (and he mentioned Ibn al-Qāsim and his being content with the knowledge of Mālik): 'He listened to some *ḥadīth*s from Sufyān and wrote them on his boards. Then he listened to something from Mālik and erased that and wrote down what he had heard from Mālik.'

Al-Ḥārith said, 'I said to Ibn al-Qāsim, "Inform me of the vision which I heard that you saw in such-and-such a year." He said, "Do not tell it to anyone. I dreamt that it was as if it was said to me, 'Allah prays on you and on Sa'īd ibn Zakariyā,' i.e. Sa'īd al-Ādam."'

One of them said that Ashhab stood at the grave of Ibn al-Qāsim. He said, 'May Allah have mercy on you, Abū 'Abdullāh! We used to leave a lot fearing your criticism, so we will be destroyed after you.'

The beginning of his quest and his behaviour in that

Ibn Waḍḍāḥ said, 'Ibn al-Qāsim listened to the Egyptians and the Syrians. He sought knowledge when he was older, and he did not go to Mālik until he had listened to the Egyptians. He spent a thousand *mithqāls* in his journey to Mālik.'

Saḥnūn said that he said, 'I did not go to Mālik until I had learned his words.'

He said to his son Mūsā ibn 'Abd ar-Raḥmān, 'Shall I tell you how I sought knowledge?' He answered, 'Yes.'

He said, 'I had a brother and he argued with a man and then went to the Sultan. I followed him until we reached the Sultan. He ordered my brother to be put in prison and I followed him. I entered the mosque wearing Sindī sandals and clothes dyed red. When the people formed circles to study knowledge, I was startled by them and distracted from going to my brother. I returned to the house and I got some shoes and a different cloak than the first one, and I came to the mosque and I sat in it alone looking at the people. Then I left and fell asleep. Someone came to me and said, "If you love knowledge, then you must have the man of knowledge of the horizons." I said, "Who is the man of knowledge of the horizons?"

'I was told, "This shaykh." There was a tall ruddy shaykh with a good beard. Then I woke up and the month of Shawwāl had passed. I hired (someone to take me) to Makka and I performed the *ḥajj* with the people. When I came to Madina, I had a *ghusl* and entered the mosque. I looked and there I was at the Ṣuffa as I had been shown in the dream. There was Mālik ibn Anas and the people around him were reading to him. I recognised that it was he who was called the man of knowledge of the horizons to me in the dream, so I devoted myself to him.'

Aṣbagh said that Ibn al-Qāsim said, 'I took the *ḥadīth*s of the Egyptians and it occurred to me to seek the science of *fiqh*, so I went to Abū Shurayḥ. He was a wise man of right action. I sought his counsel and I said, "I want to go to Mālik."

'He told me, "How excellent is *fiqh*! Its people will strip you of pride. But seek, because the pillow of knowledge is better than the pillow of ignorance."'

'Then he said, "Then I went to sleep after that and I dreamt that there was an eagle which swooped on my head. (Another said that it was a falcon fluttering over his head or in his room.) He took it and opened its belly. Someone said to him, 'Do not squander its insides. What it contains is a jewel.' (In one variant, 'I began to swallow it until I was brought to him.')" The dream was interpreted by Abū Shurayḥ. Another said, "By a man who had insight into dream interpretation called Zayn ibn Shu'ayb." He said, "The falcon is the master of the birds and the jewel is knowledge. This is a scholar whose knowledge you are commanded to take if you come to him."'

We find in the account of Aṣbagh: '"The eagle is the master of the birds and the scholar is the master of the people. If your dream is true, you will come to the knowledge of a scholar, so be fearful of Allah, Abū 'Abd ar-Raḥmān." He commanded me to go to Mālik and to stay with him.' He went to Mālik and listened to him and stayed with him.

In one variant reports that it was said to him, 'Perhaps you spoke to yourself about seeking knowledge?' He said, 'Yes.' He said, 'Whom did you mention?' He answered, 'Mālik.' He said, 'He is your falcon which you have hit upon.'

Ibn al-Qāsim said, 'I used to listen to three *ḥadīth*s from Mālik every night before daybreak until he left for the mosque, not to mention what he let people hear in the daytime.'

In one variant, 'I would come to Mālik in the darkness before day and ask him two, three, or four questions. I used to experience expansion of the breast at that time. I would come every day before dawn. Once I laid my head on his doorstep and my eyes were overpowered and I fell asleep. Mālik went out to the mosque while I was not aware of him. A black girl of his kicked me with her foot and said to me, "Your master has gone out. He is not heedless as you are heedless. Today he is forty-nine, and he has always prayed the *Ṣubḥ* prayer with the *wuḍū'* of the *'Ishā'* prayer."' The black girl thought that he was his master because he frequented him so much.

We find in another report: 'I took up residence at the door of Mālik for nineteen years. I did not sell nor buy anything in that time."' He said, 'While I was with him, I was told, 'meet a *ḥajj*i of Egypt." There was a young veiled man who came to us and greeted Mālik. He asked, "Is Ibn al-Qāsim among you?" I was pointed out. He began to kiss my eyes and I felt a good fragrance from him. It was the fragrance of the child and it was my son. Ibn al-Qāsim had left his mother while she was pregnant with him. She was his cousin. His name was 'Abdullāh. He had given the mother a choice when he set out by the length of his residence, and she chose to remain.'

People did not mention 'Abdullāh ibn 'Abd ar-Raḥmān ibn al-Qāsim among his children and we will mention them. Perhaps he died as a young man before him, and Allah knows best.

Abū Zayd said, 'I heard Ibn al-Qāsim say, "No one was stingy in his knowledge and then successful. I was present at the assembly of Mālik and I listened to him. If my companions were not present, they would ask me what I had heard and I would tell them. If they were present and I was not and then I asked them, they would not tell me."'

Ibn al-Qāsim said, 'It was as if I and Ashhab were going to two different scholars," because of the difference of their transmissions.'

Aṣ-Ṣamadāḥī said, 'It is for this reason that I stopped listening to Ashhab.'

Aṭ-Ṭālibī said that when Ibn al-Qāsim returned to Egypt, the people gathered around him in the mosque. Al-Layth asked about that and was told, 'This is Ibn al-Qāsim!' He said, 'Allah and the Muslims refuse that.'

That night he dreamt that an unseen voice was blaming him for that, and he woke up and said, 'Allah and the Muslims do not refuse that.' Then he came to the mosque and told the people around him about his dream.

Ibn al-Qāsim listened to twenty books and the 'Book of Questions on Sales on Credit' from Mālik.

His excellence, worship, asceticism and scrupulousness, and his *karāmāt* and some reports about him

His son Mūsā said, 'My father (who commanded us to pray and do good) said to us, "When I was eighteen, I completed the Qur'an in a single day," and I reckoned that he said "a day and a night."'

Al-Ḥārith ibn Miskīn said, 'I heard Ibn al-Qāsim say, "O Allah, keep this world from me and keep me from it by that by which You guard Your virtuous slaves." He was a marvel in his scrupulousness and asceticism.'

Another said, 'It was mentioned that he testified before one of the *qāḍī*s of Egypt who did not recognise him. He asked someone to declare that he was a just witness due to his obscurity and withdrawal. He went out saying, "Allah declares just and pure whomever He wills" until he recognised him. When he recognised him, he gave judgement by his testimony and the oath of the appellant. He was an Iraqi and did not have that opinion, but he did that by the excellence of Ibn al-Qāsim.'

It was said, 'He testified with one of the *qāḍī*s and the Qāḍī said, "The name is just but I do not know the person. Bring someone who knows him by sight." He did not used to go to the *qāḍī*s.' He said, 'He was busy with worship and self-restraint.'

Saḥnūn said, 'Mālik was the teacher of Ibn al-Qāsim in knowledge. His teacher in worship was Sulaymān ibn al-Qāsim.'

Ibn al-Qāsim said of both of them, 'Two men whom I followed in my *dīn*: Sulaymān in scrupulousness and Mālik in knowledge.'

He mentioned that one of the wealthy men of Egypt wanted him to marry his daughter. He would pay for him and take every expense upon himself. He said, 'Let me seek counsel.'

He sought counsel with his uncle, Sulaymān ibn al-Qāsim. He said to him, 'Do you want him to have eunuchs serve you while you are wearing silk and riding horses, and bowls are presented to you morning and night?' He replied 'No.' He said, 'You did not occupy yourself with the money of so-and-so?' So he abandoned that.

Asad said, 'Ibn al-Qāsim used to recite the entire Qur'an twice every day and night. He forwent the recitation when I came to him out of the desire to give life to knowledge.'

When it was said to Yaḥyā ibn Yaḥyā, 'It has reached us that Ibn al-Qāsim used to not eat Egyptian wheat.' He retorted, 'They lied. He and Mālik only ate of it. I met Ibn al-Qāsim coming from the market of Egypt and he had with a porter with some food. I asked him and he said, "It is some food I have purchased." I put my hand in it to see it. It was wheat mixed with a lot of barley. I asked, "Isn't there any better than this?" He told me, "Abū Muḥammad, I am content with little. What will be enough for me from this world for myself, so I will try to be content by it."'

Yaḥyā said, "I heard Ibn al-Qāsim say, "I have not lied since I tied on my wrapper," meaning forbearance.' Yaḥyā said, 'I was not created for that.'

Yaḥyā said, 'He heard two men from the people of Andalusia from Ibn al-Qāsim and they had written from him. When he gave a *fatwā*, they told him, "Testify for us to what we have heard from you to some people from our land." He disliked that and said, "There is no good in a people when the people of their land do not believe them in what they transmit to them except when it is by a clear proof."'

Yaḥyā said, 'When Asad read the *Asadiyya* (*Mudawwana*) to Ibn al-Qāsim, Ashhab put his hand on the like of it, and he opposed him in most of it.' The *faqīh* and Qāḍī Abū al-Fadl, 'Iyāḍ, may Allah have mercy on him, said, 'It is known as the *Mudawwana* of Ashhab, and *The Book of Ashhab*.' I said to Ibn al-Qāsim, 'Abū 'Abdullāh. If you look at these books, your companion has opposed you. Confirm what he does not press you with and look again into what he opposed you about.'

He said, 'I will do it if Allah Almighty wills.'

When I called on him about that some days later, he said to me, 'Abū Muḥammad, I looked at your treatise and I found my answer for a day in which I will answer Allah alone. I hope that I will be successful. My answer now would disparage my friend and I fear that I will not be successful in the Next World, so I have left it.'

Yaḥyā said, 'During the length of time he was read to, his finger was raised while he was supplicating Allah Almighty for success and soundness.'

He said, 'One day we were speaking with Ibn al-Qāsim about this matter. All of us said, "Scrupulousness is the strongest of what there is in this *dīn*." Ibn al-Qāsim said, "I do not think that that is the case." I asked him, "Abū 'Abdullāh, how is that?" He said, "We are commanded and we are forbidden. If someone does what he is commanded and leaves what he is forbidden, that is the most scrupulous of people."'

It was said to him, 'Abū 'Abdullāh, what is heavy for others is light for you. What thing do you find the heaviest of this business?' He replied, 'I have not found anything heavier for me than enduring the hours of the night.'

Yaḥyā ibn Yaḥyā ibn 'Umar related from one of them: 'I was at the *'Īd* prayer with 'Abd ar-Raḥmān ibn al-Qāsim. When we left, Ibn al-Qāsim entered the mosque and prayed. Then he prostrated for a long time until I feared that I would miss lunch with my family. I went near to him and heard him say, "My God, turn Your slave to what hinders him for this day! Turn 'Abd ar-Raḥmān to You hoping for Your forgiveness on this immense day. If you do, how excellent, and if you do not, O my woe and my grief!"

'He said, "I put a mark on his clothes and then I went to my family and I sat with them and I had intercourse and slept. Then I went to the mosque and I found him exactly as I had left him."'

Yaḥyā said, 'Ibn al-Qāsim went out to the *ḥajj*. When he was at al-Abwā', a slavegirl came to him who was like the most beautiful of slavegirls. He gave her something and she said, "I do not want this. I want from you what comes from a man to a woman." He put his head between his knees and began to weep. His companions came to him when he was like that. They questioned him and he told them (the story). They began to weep. He said to them, "Why are you keeping?" They said, "Had we been tested with the like of what you are tested, we would not have been safe from the temptation."'

Ibn al-Qāsim dreamt of Yūsuf ﷺ. He said to him, 'There was a marvel in your affair with the wife of the 'Azīz.' Yūsuf said to him, 'Your business with woman at al-Abwā' was more amazing. I inclined and you did not incline.'

From the book of the *faqīh*, Abū Marwān ibn Mālik al-Qurṭubī is that Ibn al-Qāsim said, 'I went to Alexandria and had a deposit with me. We anchored in a perilous place and I preferred to remain awake in order to guard the deposit. In the middle of the night, there was a white man on a grey mule. He split the sea until he stopped at the ship and said to me, "Sleep, Ibn al-Qāsim, we will guard you."'

Ibn al-Qāsim told Ibn al-Ḥārith, 'Do not tell anyone during my lifetime.'

Another variant reports that the deposit was ten thousand and that the horseman said to him, 'My Lord has sent me to you to guard this trust for you, so sleep in safety.' When I awoke, I looked at him going around us. It was his habit for three nights until he reached Alexandria.'

Yaḥyā ibn Yaḥyā said, Ibn al-Qāsim went to one of the deserts of Egypt. He became thirsty. One of its kings had gone out for a walk. It had just been a short time when his animals stopped and refused to budge. He hit them, but they would not get up. He said to someone who was with him, "What is this about? Investigate!" They looked and said, "There is a person." He said, "Question him." They questioned him and he said, "I am thirsty." They let him drink and then the animals went on.'

'Īsā ibn Dīnār said, 'I was at Alexandria with Ibn al-Qāsim in the *ribāṭ*. He had a man with him who was close to him. While we were in the ship on the 27th of Ramaḍān, a man from the people of the ship said, "I will tell you something immense which I have dreamt just this hour," and he told him. He said to his companion, "If what he says is true, then it is the Night of Power." He mentioned that the sign of that would be the sweetness of the sea water. They leaned over the front of the ship and I saw them drinking. They then turned to the qibla and I got up and went to the place from where they had come and I drank and found it to be sweet."'

Al-Ḥārith said, 'Ibn al-Qāsim did not accept the stipends of the Sultan. He had a debt, but he got from reading that which would settle it.'

He said that he used to say, 'There is no good in nearness or proximity to the rulers.' At first he used to go to them and then he abandoned that.

Ibn Waḍḍāḥ said, 'Ibn al-Qāsim used to only sit with one or two. There was no benefit for him for people nor for his parents nor his son nor himself in any of the matters of this world except knowledge. Ashhab and Ibn Wahb used to sit in a group and needs would be fulfilled by them and they would help people.'

Saḥnūn said, 'Often I heard him say, "Beware of the bondage of the free men." He was asked about that and replied, "Many brethren." He did not go to anyone's funeral and he did not leave the mosque. He mentioned the *ḥadīth* of Sulaymān ibn al-Qāsim, "Do not burden yourself for another what you will not burden for yourself."'

He said, 'The cause of Ibn al-Qāsim's death was that he did *ghusl* with cold water of two *mudd*s and he did not want any of it heated for him because it was illegal seizure by one of the Umayyads.'

Saḥnūn said, 'One day I stood in the Masjid al-Ḥarām to drink water. Ibn al-Qāsim said, "From where are you drinking?" I said, "Can I not have the booty of a drink of water?" He said, "What booty is there in Makka? It is *ṣadaqa*."'

Saḥnūn said, "Abd aṣ-Ṣamad al-Atrābulisī bought a slavegirl for Ibn al-Qāsim and then another. He did not take have other than these two until he died. When the first one died, he sent to him to buy him a slavegirl from the Sicilians when they arrived. He bought her for him and sent her to him. She was the mother of his two sons, who will be mentioned later. This 'Abd aṣ-Ṣamad was one of the devout worshippers who stayed at the outpost of Tripoli.'

Ibn Waḍḍāḥ said, 'He made for the Sicilians because they had no treaty.'

He said, 'Abū Muḥammad ibn Abī Zayd related that Ibn al-Qāsim used to give half of his food as *ṣadaqa*. He would make it into small squares and when the beggar stopped him, he gave him a small cube as he had made it. He sold half of this food for the year and bought with it dates to give to the beggars, date by date.'

Abū Muḥammad said, 'It was as if he thought that this was the least for the responsibility and the purest amount since he feared to turn away the beggar without anything. This is by the measure of the intention.'

Ibn Wahb said when Ibn al-Qāsim died, 'He was my brother and my companion in this mosque for forty years. I did not ever come in the evening or the morning to this mosque but that I found that he had preceded me to it.'

It is related that while Ibn al-Qāsim was having the *Muwaṭṭā'* read to him, he stood up for a long time and then sat down. He was asked about that. He said, 'My mother came to ask me for something, and she stood up and I stood up when she stood up. When she went up, I sat down.'

Furāt said that Saḥnūn said, 'When I went on *ḥajj*, I accompanied 'Abdullāh ibn Wahb. Ashhab and Ibn al-Qāsim were with him. When I alighted, I went to 'Abd ar-Raḥmān to ask about the time of the journey. Ibn Wahb and Ashhab told me, "If you would speak to your companion (and ask) him to break the fast with us one night." I spoke to him and he said, "This is burdensome for me." I said to him, "By what will people know my position with you?"

'He responded to my request, and I went to them and told them. When it was time for the feast, he got up and I went with him to the people. I found that Ashhab had submitted to him and brought some food on a great tray. Ibn Wahb had prepared less than that. Ibn al-Qāsim gave the greeting and then sat down. Then he looked around. There was a plate with some flour on it. He took it in his hand and moved the spices to one side and licked the salt three times. He knew that the root of the salt of Egypt was good. Then he stood up and said, "May Allah bless you."'

Saḥnūn said, 'I was too embarrassed to get up. Ashhab spoke and thought that the business was terrible. Ibn Wahb said, "Leave him, leave him."'

Abū al-Faḍl, the client of Najm, said, 'Ibn al-Qāsim used to eat twenty *mudd*s of flour a month measured by *mudd* of the Prophet ﷺ. He was a *faqīh* and a man of worship.'

Another said, 'Because he allocated his food to one third of the *mudd* of barley a day.'

He mentioned that one of the people of knowledge and good came from Iraq who wanted to meet him. A man came to him about that and he set a time for that. When he asked him for permission to enter, Ibn al-Qāsim said to him, 'I have investigated that and I saw that pride had affected him so he would acclaim me and I would promote him. Spare me that.'

The Egyptians used to say to the Kufans, 'Mention the virtues of Sufyān. We will mention the virtues of Ibn al-Qāsim,' and so they would be silent.

Ibn Waḍḍāḥ said, 'The people of Andalusia carried gossip between Ibn al-Qāsim and Ashhab until they destroyed what was between the two of them. Ashhab swore that he would walk to Makka if he ever spoke again to Ibn al-Qāsim. Then he regretted that and wanted to walk to Makka. When Ibn al-Qāsim heard that, he said, 'He will break his oath and walk and I will walk with him.' So they walked together and performed the *ḥajj* and 'Īsā ibn Dīnār was with them.'

Yaḥyā said, 'I heard Ibn al-Qāsim curse two men from the people of Andalusia who had come between him and Ashhab. I heard him say, "O Allah, may their running be against them and do not benefit them with their carrying." When they died, that was known about them.'

It was said" 'Ibn al-Qāsim and Ashhab used to differ about the words of Mālik on a question, and each of them swore to reject the other's statement. They questioned Ibn Wahb and he told them that Mālik had said both things. They then went on *ḥajj* to fulfil the oath which they had broken.'

His death

Ibn Saḥnūn and others said that Ibn al-Qāsim died in Egypt on Friday night on the 9th of Ṣafar, 191 AH, three days after he had returned from Makka. It is said that it was six days, and we have mentioned the reason for that. He was ill for six days and died when he was sixty-three. It is said that he died in 192 AH when he was sixty.

Al-Kindī and ash-Shīrāzī said that he was born in 132 AH. Abū aṭ-Ṭāhir and ibn Bukayr both said that.

Abū 'Umar ibn 'Abd al-Barr and Ibn Ḥārith said that he was born in 128 AH and he left two sons who will be mentioned.

Al-Kindī mentioned 'Umar ibn al-Qāsim, the brother of 'Abd ar-Raḥmān ibn al-Qāsim. He said, 'He was accepted by the *qāḍī*s and he was excellent.'

Amīr Abū Naṣr said, 'He had some carelessness.'

Ibn al-Qāsim was seen in a dream after his death. He was asked and reported about the good he had met. He was asked, 'Why?' He said, 'By virtue of the two *rak'at*s which I prayed in Alexandria.' He was asked, 'And the legal questions?' He said, 'No,' and made a gesture with hand to indicate that he found them to be empty dust.

'Alī ibn Ma'bad said, 'I saw him in a dream and I asked him, "How did you find the legal questions?" He said, "Faugh." I said to him, "What is the best that you found?" He replied, "The *ribāṭ* in Alexandria."'

'Abdullāh ibn 'Abd al-Ḥakam said, 'I reflected on the loneliness of the grave until I was told, "Is there not a model in Ibn al-Qāsim?"'

'Abdullāh ibn 'Abd al-Ḥakam said, 'I used to dream that it was as if I were dead and I was afraid of death. It became very intense indeed. I was told, "Are you not pleased to be with the Prophets, the truthful ones, the martyrs and the righteous? What excellent companions they are! And with 'Abd ar-Raḥmān ibn al-Qāsim?'"

Abū 'Amr Ashhab

He is Ashhab ibn 'Abd al-'Azīz ibn Dāwūd ibn Ibrāhīm al-Qaysī al-'Āmirī al-Ju'dī from the descendants of Ju'da ibn Kilāb ibn Rabī'a ibn 'Āmir. His name was Miskīn. Ashhab was his title, and his *kunya* was Abū 'Amr.

He related from Mālik, al-Layth, al-Fuḍayl ibn 'Iyāḍ, Sulaymān ibn Bilāl, Ibn Lahī'a, Yaḥyā ibn Ayyūb, Bakr ibn Muḍar, ad-Darāwardī, and al-Mundhir ibn 'Abdullāh al-Khuzāmī.

Al-Ḥārith ibn Miskīn, Yūnus aṣ-Ṣadafī, the Banū 'Abd al-Ḥakam, Abū aṭ-Ṭāhir, Sa'īd ibn Ḥassān, and Saḥnūn ibn Sa'īd related from him among those who are too numerous to count and constitute a group.

Ash-Shīrāzī said, 'He learned *fiqh* with Mālik, the Madinans and the Egyptians.'

Abū 'Amr al-Muqri' said, 'He recited to Nāfi'.'

Ash-Shāfi'ī said, 'I did not see anyone with more *fiqh* than Ashhab, if it had not been for some rashness in him. There was rivalry between him and Ibn al-Qāsim. Leadership in Egypt came to him after the death of Ibn al-Qāsim.'

Saḥnūn said, "Ibn al-Qāsim said to me, 'If you desire this knowledge after me, then seek it with Ashhab.'

Asad said, 'I came to Ibn al-Qāsim and he said to me, "I am occupied with myself and I have put the Next World before me. But you must have Ibn Wahb." So I went to him and he said, "I am a master of traditions, so go to Ashhab."'

Ḥāfiẓ Abū 'Amr said, 'Ashhab was a *faqīh*, a noble man with excellent investigation, one of the precise Mālikīs. He was the scribe of the *kharāj* tax of Egypt, and he was trustworthy in what was related from Mālik. He wrote a book on *fiqh* which Sa'īd ibn Ḥassān and others related from him.'

Abū 'Umar al-Kindī said in *The Book of the Qāḍīs* of Egypt: 'Ashhab was in charge of the legal questions of Qāḍī al-'Umarī in Egypt.'

Muḥammad ibn 'Abd al-Ḥakam said, 'Ashhab had a hundred times more *fiqh* than Ibn al-Qāsim.'

Ibn Lubāba said, 'In our opinion, it is not as he stated. He said that because Ashhab was his teacher and shaykh.'

Abū 'Umar said, 'Both of them were his teachers and shaykhs. He knew best.'

The author said, 'Muhammad ibn 'Abd al-Hakam did not listen to Ibn al-Qāsim. The proof for this will come. I do not know how Abū 'Umar has this when he has such precedence in the subject.'

Saḥnūn was asked about them and which of the two had the most *fiqh*. He said, 'They were like two horses in a race. Sometimes this one was successful and that one disappointed, and sometimes that one was successful and this one failed.'

Saḥnūn said, 'The scrupulous transmitter related to me from Ashhab in his oral reports.'

He said, 'May Allah have mercy on Ashhab. He was the most truthful and the most fearful of Allah Almighty. He did not add a single letter.'

Ibn 'Abd al-Hakam said to him one day, 'You should keep a little back.'

He said, 'I know what you are saying. If I had done that, I would have been nobler in the eyes of people and I would have stopped some of what they say. By Allah, I will never do anything by which I do not desire Allah!'

Saḥnūn used to accord Ashhab scrupulousness in his oral transmission while he did not listen to him. He listened to him via Ibn Nāfi'.

Ibn Waḍḍāḥ said, 'The oral report of Ashhab is closer and more likely than that of Ibn al-Qāsim. The number of his oral reports is twenty.'

Ibn Waḍḍāḥ said, 'When we heard him, and Ibn Ḥimyar from Muḥammad ibn 'Abd al-Ḥakam ibn as-Sukkarī who used to sit with Muḥammad ibn 'Abd al-Ḥakam and listen to our recitation, said, "I want it to be repeated to me." He said to me, "You have heard it!"

'He said, "I did not intend to hear it. He ﷺ said, 'Actions are by intentions.' I heard that he had very good questions. If I had wanted to bring out a *ḥadīth* on every question of them, I could have done it."'

Saḥnūn said, 'No one debated with Ashhab but that he was compelled by the proof until he retracted his statement. He would come to us in the circle of Ibn al-Qāsim. He spoke on the roots of knowledge, explained and gave the argument. Ibn al-Qāsim was silent and did not refute a single letter. Ashhab used to speak to us. When Allah provided him with that, a man spoke to him about a question, he raised his eyes to him, the question was impossible. He used to wear a black hat. He commanded them, to the correct and forbade them the objectionable.' He said, 'Then he listened to him from Muḥammad ibn 'Abd al-Ḥakam.'

Ibn 'Abd al-Barr said, 'Ash-Shāfi'ī did not find any of the companions of Mālik in Egypt except Ashhab and Ibn 'Abd al-Ḥakam. Ash-Shāfi'ī and Ashhab used to keep each other's company in Egypt. They would discuss *fiqh* and they were close.'

Abū 'Umar mentioned him with 'Abdullāh ibn 'Abd al-Ḥakam among those who took from ash-Shāfi'ī among the great companions of Mālik. He meant that ash-Shāfi'ī and Ashhab debated one another.

Ashhab wrote his book, al-*Mudawwana* and Sa'īd ibn Ḥassān and others related it from him. It is a great respected book with much knowledge.

Ibn Ḥārith said, 'When the *Asadiyya* was completed, Ashhab took it and corrected it for himself and supported some of it. He brought a noble book. It reached me that when that reached Ibn al-Qāsim, he said, "A foolish community does the like of this!" meaningthat he found a complete book and then built on it.'

Ashhab sent to him, 'You scooped from one spring and I from many springs.' So Ibn al-Qāsim answered him back, 'Your springs are turbid and my spring is clear.'

He had *The Book of the Disagreement about Qasāma* and a book on the virtues of 'Umar ibn 'Abd al-'Azīz.

Something of his virtues, generosity and reports

Saḥnūn said, 'Ashhab wrote to a man who had attacked him, "As for what follows, I was only prevented from writing to you to avoid intensifying what you are doing because I dislike to direct you to rebel against Allah. Know that I delight in your good deeds as you graze sheep in green pasturage. Peace."'

One day Ashhab sat in Makka for Ibn al-Qāsim, and a man asked him about a question. 'Abd ar-Raḥmān spoke on it. Ashhab's face altered at that and he said, 'It is not like that.' Then he began to explain and offer proof in it. Ibn al-Qāsim said to him, 'But the shaykh says that, may Allah preserve you!' meaning Mālik. Ashhab said, 'Even if he had said it sixty times.' Ibn al-Qāsim did not refute him.

Ashhab said, 'I went to al-Fuḍayl to seek his counsel about going to the governor and how one should approach him. No one went to him who was more direct in command and prohibition than I was when I went to him. Sometimes he accepted and the Muslims benefited from that.

'He told me, "You are a man who asks me about yourself in particular because you do not go to them nor love them nor love the one who loves them."'

Ibn Waḍḍāḥ said that Ashhab used to say, 'Scrupulousness is employed concerning doubtful things. As for grave sins, everyone is fearful of them.'

Ashhab said, 'My father ordered me to make a watering site in a place which he named. I built it many times, but some neighbours who envied me there always destroyed it. One day I felt grieved by that, and I sat there weeping and thinking. I heard a voice from the desert say, "*We desired to show kindness to those who were oppressed in the land* (28:5)." I moved my beast towards the sound, but did not see anyone. I returned to my place and heard the voice. I stood up but did not see anyone. I returned to sitting and the voice was repeated for yet a third time, and I knew that I was the one who was meant. I praised Allah and I made the intention to seek knowledge. I built it and entrusted it to someone who would guard it for a wage. No one returned to ruin it.'

A similar story is also related by al-Layth ibn Sa'd when he built his house, and Allah knows best.

He said, 'I did not pass by it for a few years until those and other people of my land had need of me.'

Ibn Abī Maryam said, 'When we saw Ashhab off to the *ribāṭ*, he did not have half a dirham. He did not die before he had spent ten *mithqāl*s every day at his table. He had opening in this world.'

Saḥnūn said, 'There was a famine in Egypt, and I saw him spending dinars in *ṣadaqa* from morning to night. He gave as *ṣadaqa* what he had of food.'

Saḥnūn mentioned from him that he saw him giving a thousand dinars as *ṣadaqa* every day."

Ibn al-Jazzār mentioned in *Kitāb at-Taʿrīf* that Ibn al-Qāsim stopped speaking to Ashhab because he took responsibility for the earth of Egypt. A man asked Ibn al-Qāsim about the contract of the earth of Egypt. He said, 'It is not allowed.' He was told, 'Ashhab grants it.' Ibn al-Qāsim said to him, 'Do what Ashhab does and you can assume responsibility for the mosque!'

He mentioned that a man asked Ashhab about ploughing the earth of Egypt. He said, 'It is not allowed.' The man said to him, 'You plough in it' He said, 'Shall I burden myself and you as well?' So he asked Ibn Wahb about it and he forbade it. He said to him, 'Ashhab does it.' He said, 'Give us another like Ashhab to care for our orphans and be kind to our weak ones and you will be allowed to plough our mosque.'

Saḥnūn said, 'He gave *ṣadaqa* many times over its rent.'

Saḥnūn said, 'We were present with Ashhab on the Day of ʿArafat in the mosque of Egypt. It was their custom to stand in their mosque until the sun set, i.e. for *dhikr* and supplication, as the people of ʿArafat did there. He used to pray sitting, namely in the supererogatory prayers, and there was a bag at his side from which he gave to beggars. I looked and there was a dinar in the hand of the beggar which he had been given. I mentioned it to him and he said to me, "Don't we give from the beginning of the day?"'

Yūnus mentioned that he said, 'Ashhab claimed that he heard Sulaymān as-Sā'iḥ saying in one of the mosques of the desert, "O Allah, Your slave Sulaymān is hungry and has not eaten for three days." When he finished, he heard him chewing. "I did not want to go to him and embarrass him. The mosque had two doors. He went out the front and we entered from the other door. There were date pits and a discarded date, so I ate it and I remained protected for ten days without eating or drinking."'

Saḥnūn said, 'Ashhab came across Ibn al-Qāsim one day. Ashhab was wearing clothes that were ragged and there was an easy-gaited mule under him. Ibn al-Qāsim said, "*We have made some of you a trial for other to see if you will be steadfast.*" (25:20) Then he was silent for a time and then said, "O Lord, we will be patient. We will be patient."'

This story and its words are ascribed to al-Muzanī. The Banu al-Ḥakam passed by him in their retinue in Egypt, but Allah knows best.

It is related that a man of the people of Iraq met Ashhab. The Iraqi said to him, 'You consider anal intercourse with men lawful.' Ashhab said to him, 'You consider it *ḥarām*. Come. I swear by Allah that I have not done it. You swear the like of it to me.' The Iraqi did not do that.

He mentioned that while Ashhab was with his companions, he heard a man admonishing a thief, and he got up and took up his weapons and went out to follow him. He was asked about that, 'It is not befitting for the like of you.' He said, 'I do not take on any other character than what Allah has naturally disposed me to.'

HIS BIRTH AND HIS DEATH

Ibn 'Abd al-Barr and Abū 'Amr al-Muqri' said, 'Ashhab was born in 140 AH.' Ibn Ḥazm aṣ-Ṣadafī related that from Abū aṭ-Ṭāhir.

Ash-Shīrāzī related that he was born in 150 AH. He died in Egypt in 204 AH in the month of Rajab. It is also said that it was the 23rd of Sha'bān.

Ash-Shīrāzī said, 'A month after ash-Shāfi'ī.' Ibn 'Abd al-Barr said, 'By eighteen days.' It is also said that it was by twenty-three days. This is famous in the date of his death.

Abū 'Alī al-Baṣrī said in *Kitāb al-Mu'arrib*, 'It is said that he died in 203 AH.'

Muḥammad ibn 'Abd al-Ḥakam said, 'I heard Ashhab pray for ash-Shāfi'ī to die. I mentioned that to him and he recited the quotation:

"Some men desire that I die.
If I die, that is a path in which I am not alone.
Tell the one who desires the opposite of what has passed to prepare for another like it. It is as if he is cut off."

'Ash-Shāfi'ī died and Ashhab purchased a slave boy who was a cook from his property. Then he died eighteen days after him. Then I purchased the boy from what Ashhab left. People tried to keep me from buying him and I was told to leave him. The two men of knowledge were buried within about ten days. I bought him and ignored the bad omen.'

Ar-Rabī' ibn Sulaymān related that he said, 'We heard Ashhab say in his prostration, "O Allah, make ash-Shāfi'ī die. Otherwise the knowledge of Mālik will vanish." That reached ash-Shāfi'ī and he began to recite the two verses.'

Muḥammad ibn Ḥafṣ al-Ma'āfirī said about Ashhab's illness, 'I dreamt that someone was saying to me, "Muḥammad!" I answered him and he said:

"Those who were spoken about in their parting have departed.
I wish that the land would burst with its people."

'I said to my wife, "I fear nothing more than the death of Ashhab." I went out and he had died.'

Another said, 'We slept at midday and I dreamt that a voice said:

"At your service for Islam from the one who weeps.
They are almost destroyed and the contract is not yet old.
This world has escaped and the best of it turned away
and the one who is alarmed by the threat is bored by it."

'I went to the mosque and the death of Ashhab, may Allah Almighty have mercy on him, was announced.'

Yūnus said, 'I came to Ashhab in his final illness. He said to me, "Yūnus!" I said, "At your service!" He said, "Look at what is here,' and he pointed to his books. What I have gathered of ḥajjs on this weak body. I can only find rest by taking the Qur'an and putting it on my breast."'

He said. 'His books were in a basket with large volumes.'

Sa'īd ibn Kathīr ibn 'Ufayr ibn Muslim

Abū 'Uthman al-Anṣārī al-Miṣrī. He listened to the *Muwaṭṭā'* from Mālik and kept his company. He mostly was concerned with science of *Ḥadīth* and the science of reports. He was a scholar in the field of the reports of people and he wrote a history. He listened to al-Layth ibn Sa'd, Ibn Lahī'a, Ya'qūb ibn Ibrāhīm and Ibn Wahb. He was one of the shaykhs of Egypt in his time.

Yaḥyā ibn Ma'īn said that he was reliable. Abū Ḥātim said that he was truthful, but not firm. He used to read the books of people.

Al-Bukhārī, Muslim, Isḥāq and aṣ-Ṣāghānī related from him. Muslims and al-Bukhārī transmitted from him.

When al-Ma'mūn came to Egypt and the scholars were summoned to be present, Sa'īd ibn 'Ufayr was among them. Al-Ma'mūn askedhim, 'Is this the Egypt about which Allah said what He said?' and he began to demean it.

Ibn 'Ufayr said to him, 'Amīr al-Mu'minīn, this is the Egypt which Allah destroyed. What do you think it was before the destruction? Allah Almighty says, "*We utterly destroyed Pharaoh and what his people made and the buildings they constructed.*" (7:137)' Al-Ma'mūn asked, 'Who is the speaker?' He was told, 'Sa'īd ibn 'Ufayr, Mālik's companion.'

He said, 'Sa'īd, what do you say about the one who says, "(I swear by an oath) to walk to Makka"?' He replied, 'Then he must walk.' Al-Ma'mūn said to him, 'Mālik was as stupid as the billy-goat on this question.' Sa'īd said, 'More stupid than the billy-goat is the one who listens to the billy-goat,' meaning his father, ar-Rashīd, when he swore that Mālik had given him a *fatwā* that he must walk and he walked.

Al-Ma'mūn was speechless with anger at that. They were like that when there was a complaint about two (government) agents. He said, 'Sa'īd, what do you say about them?' He said, 'Two unjust tyrants.' He said, 'Have they expropriated anything from you or wronged you?' He said, 'No.' He said, 'Then how can you testify against them?' He said, 'Just as I testify that you are the Amīr al-Mu'minīn before I saw you.'

Ibn 'Ufayr said, 'I heard someone say in a dream, "Allah is not concerned with the master of the *riwāya* of the story. He is concerned with the one with a heart and perception."'

He was born in 147 AH and died in 226 AH. Knowledge remained in his house for a long time.

Ibn 'Ufayr had two sons:

'Ubaydullāh

Abū al-Ḥārith Asad

Abū al-Ḥārith related from his father, Ibn Wahb and ash-Shāfi'ī. He died in Ṣafar, 260 AH.

Ibrāhīm ibn 'Ubaydullāh, his grandson, Abū Isḥāq, known as aṣ-Ṣayrafī. He related *ḥadīth*s as well. He died in 275 AH.

Al-Ḥusayn ibn Yazīd ibn Asad ibn Sa'īd, Abū 'Abdullāh. It is said Abū 'Alī. He died in Shawwāl, 328 AH.

Abū 'Amr ibn Yaḥyā, the client of the Banu Umayya

He was known as al-Khawlānī, one of the companions of Mālik. He died at the beginning of 211 AH. Worship dominated him.

Al-Mufaḍḍal ibn Faḍāla

He is al-Mufaḍḍal ibn Faḍāla ibn 'Ubayd, Abū Mu'āwiya al-Ḥumaydī al-Qitbānī. Qitbān is a tribe from Ra'īn. Al-Mufaḍḍal is related to it.

He related from Ibn 'Ajlān, Yūnus ibn Yazīd and 'Aqīl ibn Khālid.

Abū 'Abdullāh al-Jīzī said in his book on the Qāḍīs of Egypt: 'Al-Mufaḍḍal was one of the people of excellence and the best people.'

Ibn Shāhīn said that he was a truthful man. His son, Faḍāla, Qutayba ibn Sa'īd, Ḥassān al-Wāsiṭī, Ibn Bukayr, Ḥajjāj and Yūnus ibn Muḥammad related from him. Al-Bukhārī and Muslim transmitted from him in their *Ṣaḥīḥ* volumes.

Abū Ḥātim said that he is truthful. Yaḥyā ibn Ma'īn said that he is not that.

Abū Zur'a said, 'He wrote his *ḥadīth*s down.'

He had a brother called 'Abdullāh ibn Faḍāla. Ibn Yūnus said, 'I do not know that he had any transmission.'

Muḥammad ibn Sa'd said, 'He was appointed over the *qāḍī*s and was praised and had *ḥadīth*s which are *munkar*.'

His behaviour and his reports

Al-Mufaḍḍal was appointed Qāḍī of Egypt twice. Once was in 168 AH and then he was dismissed in 169 AH. Then he was reappointed when Abū aṭ-Ṭāhir al-Kharamī was dismissed in 174 AH, and al-Mufaḍḍal remained *qāḍī* until the beginning of 179 AH.

Al-Jīzī said, 'He was the first of the *qāḍī*s of Egypt to last a long time. When a decision in anything was difficult for him, he wrote that to Mālik so that his answer would come to him and he could act according to it.'

Another said, 'He gave *fatwā* according to the position of Mālik.'

Ibn Shāhīn said, 'When a man came to him who had broken his hand or foot, he set it. He used to make millstones.'

Abū al-Ḥasan ibn Ḍamḍam said, 'It reached me that this supplication reached al-Mufaḍḍal ibn Faḍāla. He said, "O Possessor of majesty and nobility, by the sanctity of the light of Your noble face, I ask You for sound eyesight, long life in good action and wide provision without owing any favour to anyone in it, so give!" three times.'

Al-Jīzī mentioned that he said, 'I wrote to Mālik about the *ḥabūs* of Ibn Abī Mudrik, and I meticulously transcribed it out for him letter by letter, and I informed him that those who sought it and allowed it were the sons of the sons. They used as evidence the fact that Qāḍī Khayr ibn Nu'aym wrote an authorisation for them to the last of them. The last was one of them. In addition to that, the *qāḍī*s permitted had it. They did not judge that it should go to the females of the sons nor others as inheritance. Other people offered the argument that someone setting up a *ḥabūs* does not mention it being for the last person in the *ḥabūs* and after the extinction of the sons, it is not diverted to any of the aspects of the *ḥabūs* in the way of Allah.

'He wrote to me, "I have looked at the *ḥabūs* of Ibn Abī Mudrik and in it I found an argument for the one who wants it to revert to inheritance. I found in the letter of Ibn Abī Mudrik which his sons brought me and confirmed and carried out, that the house is a *ḥabūs* for his sons, and one-third of the rest of its produce after the domicile of the house is for the way of Allah." He mentioned the like of that about a mill.'

Ibn al-Jarrāḥ, the author of *Kitāb al-Waraqa*, mentioned that Isḥāq ibn Ma'bad, the poet, used to argue in the presence of al-Mufaḍḍal in Egypt. He came to him one day and he had satirised him with two verses. They are:

Fear Allah and listen at that time, Mufaḍḍal!
  You will be questioned about the rendering of judgement.
Some people say you admire their words.
  Does a *qāḍī* have long variegated poetry?

He wrote it down and put it in his sleeve along with his (note) of injustice and went to him. In his presence, he put his hand in his sleeve to bring out the paper of injustice for the Qāḍī. He brought out the page of satire. When he read it, he returned it to him and said, 'O Allah, forgiveness! This is not for us, may Allah have mercy on you!'

Al-Mufaḍḍal died in 181 AH.

Fityān ibn Abī as-Samḥ

He was a client of Tujīb, and his lineage was already given.

Abū al-Ḥasan ad-Dāraquṭnī and others said, 'He is Abū al-Khiyār of Egypt. He related from Mālik. He was one of his great companions who were partisans of his school.'

Ibn Ḥārith said that his *kunya* was Abū as-Samḥ.

Abū 'Amr al-Kindī said in *The Book of the Notable Clients of Egypt*, 'One of them was Abū al-Khiyār Fityān ibn Abī as-Samḥ. His name is 'Abdullāh ibn as-Samḥ ibn Usāma ibn Zanbar, and he was a client of the Banū 'Āmir ibn 'Adī of Tujīb He was a *faqīh* and one of the companions of Mālik.'

Ibn Waḍḍāḥ gives his father the *kunya* of Abū as-Samḥā'. His father was already mentioned in the first generation. He was also one of the companions of Mālik.

Ibn Wahb said, 'He used to purchase for Mālik what he needed. He had ten questions from him, and he answered them. He went to Mālik once and asked him about some questions and he answered him. Then he added more and he answered him. Then Mālik said, "*If the hypocrites and those with sickness in their hearts do not desist...*" (33:60)'

Another said, 'Fityān used to serve Ibn al-Qāsim.'

Abū 'Amr said in what he related that he provoked dissension in debate. There was a debate between him and ash-Shāfi'ī about whether a free man is sold to settle a debt. Ash-Shāfi'ī said, 'He is sold.' Fityān said, 'He is not sold.' Fityān said to him, 'If he keeps to this, he will do such-and-such to you.'

He mentioned from Muḥammad ibn 'Abd al-Ḥakam that Fityān spoke to ash-Shāfi'ī in a rude manner in a debate after which they parted. As-Sarī ibn al-Ḥakam, the governor of Egypt, sent to ash-Shāfi'ī and asked him to inform him about what had reached him regarding the business. It is said that ash-Shāfi'ī told him and that as-Sarī flogged Fityān. Muḥammad said, 'I saw the caller calling out, "This is the repayment of the one who curses the Messenger of Allah ﷺ." Fityān was saying, "I seek refuge with Allah from that!"'

Abū Yazīd said, 'I was present with them both when they debated in a manner I would not like to repeat. Then some words passed between them until the Imāms were mentioned. Fityān said, "Mālik informed me that the Imām is only an Imām when he meets the preconditions of Abū Bakr aṣ-Ṣiddīq, may Allah Almighty have mercy on him, who said, 'I am in charge of you and I am not the best of you. However, the strongest of you is weak with me until I take what is due from him. The weakest of you is strong with me until I take his right for him. I follow and I do not innovate. If I do well, then help me. If I deviate, then stand up to me.'" Ash-Shāfi'ī offered some things in argument which I will never mention. That reached as-Sarī and he flogged Fityān. The people of the mosque rushed at ash-Shāfi'ī, so he went into his house and did not emerge from it until he died.'

He said that as-Sarī said, 'If another had testified in my presence to the like of what ash-Shāfi'ī testified against him, I would have beheaded him (i.e. Fityān).'

Aṭ-Ṭaḥāwī said, 'Abū Zayd was among those who were present at their quarrel. There was an argument between him and Fityān regarding the *zakāt* due on cattle. Fityān said, "It is *zakāt* like that of camels," and he used things to prove that until they attacked each other. Abū Zayd was one of those who went to as-Sarī with ash-Shāfi'ī. It is said that he testified against him.'

He heard Fityān say, "Allah is between me and ash-Shāfi'ī. I will not put ash-Shāfi'ī in the lawful."

Ad-Dāraquṭnī said, 'Ash-Shāfi'ī was suspected in the business of Fityān. He was questioned about that. He said, "By Allah, I did not mention it at all to the ruler. I heard it from him. If I had testified to it against him, his blood would have been lawful."'

Another said, 'Due to ash-Shāfi'ī's divergence from Mālik and his excess in that, enmity increased between the Mālikīs and the Shāfi'īs in Egypt. They attacked ash-Shāfi'ī and wanted to exile him. The governor set a term for him during which he died.'

Ibn Ḥārith said, 'He was born in 125 AH and died in 232 AH.'

Isḥāq ibn al-Furāt ibn al-Ja'd ibn Sulaym

Abū Nu'aym. He was a client of Mu'āwiya ibn Khadīj al-Kindī, the Qāḍī of Egypt.

Ibn Wazīr said, 'He was one of the great companions of Mālik. He met Abū Yūsuf and took from him.'

Al-Kindī said that he was a *faqīh*.

Ash-Shāfi'ī said, 'I have not seen anyone in Egypt with more knowledge of people's disagreements than Isḥāq ibn al-Furāt.'

He was appointed *qāḍī* in Egypt in 184 AH. He was both harsh and kind.

Ash-Shāfi'ī said, 'I indicated to one of the governors that he should appoint Isḥāq ibn al-Furāt as *qāḍī*. I said to him, "He can select and he knows the disagreements between those who have passed."'

Aḥmad ibn Sa'īd al-Hamdānī said, 'Isḥāq ibn al-Furāt recited the *Muwaṭṭā'* of Mālik to us from his memory. He did not omit a single letter of it as far as I know.'

He was dismissed from the office of *qāḍī* at the beginning of 185 AH. He was the first of those who were clients (*mawālī*) to be appointed in Egypt.

Al-Kindī said that Ibn Abī Ḥāzim said, 'Isḥāq ibn al-Furāt, the Qāḍī of Egypt. He related from Yaḥyā ibn Ayyūb and Mu'ādh ibn Muḥammad al-Anṣārī.'

Muḥammad ibn 'Abd al-Ḥakam, Yaḥyā ibn Naṣr and 'Īsā ibn Aḥmad al-'Asqallānī related from him.

Abū Ḥātim said, 'He is not famous.' Al-'Uqaylī said, 'There is no objection to him.' Al-Kūfī said that he is trustworthy. He died in 205 AH. It is also said that it was 204 AH. He was born in 135 AH.

Sulaymān ibn Bard ibn Nujaym at-Tujībī

He was a client of Tujīb. His *kunya* was Abū ar-Rabī'. He related the *Muwaṭṭā'*, *fiqh* and other things from Mālik.

Abū Ḥātib said that Sulaymān ibn Bard was one of the *fuqahā'* of Egypt. He counted him in his *Ṭabaqāt.*

Muḥammad ibn 'Abd al-Ḥakam said, 'The *Muwaṭṭā'* which Ibn Bard heard is the soundest *Muwaṭṭā'*.'

Abū 'Amr al-Kindī mentioned him in *The Book of the Qāḍīs* and *The Book of the Clients.* He said, 'He was accepted by the *qāḍī*s of Egypt. In the time of Ibn Bard, there was no more to be seen with more knowledge of judgements and its methods than him. He supported the business of 'Īsā ibn al-Munkadir during the time when 'Īsā was *qāḍī* in Egypt. The situation of Ibn al-Munkadir did not become unsettled until Ibn Bard died and 'Abdullāh ibn al-Ḥakam was appointed over the legal questions of Ibn al-Munkadir.'

Miqdām ibn Sa'īd said, 'I did not see anyone with more knowledge of judgement and its rank than Sulaymān.'

He died in 210 AH. It is also said 212 AH. He left a legacy of knowledge among his descendants in Egypt. Some of them continued to be in the forefront of the Mālikīs in every generation as will be mentioned."

Ibn Abī Dulaym and others mentioned Sulaymān ibn Bard among the transmitters of Mālik with the Alexandrians. He mentioned Abū ar-Rabī' Sulaymān ibn Sa'īd ibn Sulaymān ibn Bard among the Egyptians, but no one else mentioned him. That is an error. And Allah Almighty knows best.

Yūsuf ibn 'Amr ibn Yazīd ibn Yūsuf ibn Khurkhusan al-Fārisī

Ḥāfiẓ Abū Nasr wrote it as 'Khurkhusan'. Ibn Abī Dulaym said, 'Khurkhusru.' That is how al-Kindī wrote it. His *kunya* was Abū Yazīd. He listened to Mālik, and he listened to Ibn Wahb and other companions of his. He was one of the excellent companions of Mālik with asceticism and excellence.

Another said, 'His age was near to that of those. He mentioned Ibn Ḥabīb in their generation.'

Muḥammad ibn 'Abd al-Ḥakam related from him.

Sa'īd al-Ādam said that he is a trustworthy righteous man.

Al-Kindī said, 'He was a *faqīh* in *fatwā*, one of the trustees of ash-Shāfi'ī. He was injured in his eye and his beard filled his chest.'

Al-Ḥārith ibn Miskīn said, 'Yūsuf did not accept the stipends of the Sultan. He had a debt and died without leaving enough to pay the death.'

Yūsuf said, 'We kept the company of Mālik when we were young men occupied with grammar. We did not disapprove of his language.'

Al-Ḥārith said, 'Ashhab ibn Yūsuf ibn 'Amr (and I rather think that it was Yūsuf although the transmitter is doubtful about it) put it upon himself to go to one of the governors with fifty dinars of *ṣadaqa*. He used to come to them and then he abandoned that.'

Muḥammad ibn 'Abd al-Ḥakam was asked about reciting with chanting. He said, 'Mālik disliked that. My father and Yūsuf ibn 'Amr and others were in ash-Shāfi'ī's house. One of them said to him, "Read '*ar-rāhib* (the monk)' or the like of this and my father found that word repugnant." Yusuf said, "*Come, read 'On the Day Allah gathers the Messengers together*' (5:109), the story of the monks."'

Qāḍī Muḥammad ibn Lahī'a summoned our companions to a mashūra (legal query) and Abū Yūsuf ibn 'Amr was part of it. Yūsuf said, 'Do not call us present if so-and-so is present in your assembly. He is not one of those who are pleasing.'

Abū ar-Rabī' ar-Rishdinī said, 'Yūsuf ibn 'Amr used to say to Yaḥyā ibn Bukayr, "Take us to Rishdīn ibn Sa'd. Perhaps our hearts will be softened." They would go to him, and his house was that of a righteous man.'

Abū ar-Rabī' said, 'I heard Yūsuf ibn 'Amr say, "By Allah, there is no god but Him! This world is not good for anything of what Allah created except asceticism in it."'

Muḥammad ibn 'Abd al-Ḥakam said, 'His father, ash-Shāfi'ī, Ibn Bukayr and a group of our companions were in the house of Yūsuf ibn 'Amr preparing a wedding-feast for them. There was entertainment and drums, and none of them objected to that.'

Yūnus said, 'Yūsuf became very ill. Then he began to recover and he wanted some fresh dates. One of his family brought some for him from the market. He ate them and his appetite for them overpowered him. Before he would not eat anything until he had investigated its source. When he had finished eating, he went to sleep and woke up in fear and asked the one who brought them where they had come from. He said, "I do not know anything except that I bought them in the market." He sent him to investigate it and was told, "They are fresh dates from Hilwan."

'Yūsuf said, "I dreamt that it was as if I came to some dung beetles and, Allah knows best. but there was something in the earth of Hilwan."'

He died in Ṣafar of 205 AH. He was born in 105 AH. His sons will be mentioned later, Allah willing.

Sa'īd ibn Hishām ibn Ṣāliḥ al-Makhzūmī

He was from Basra and lived in Fayyum. Al-Ḥārith ibn Miskīn said that he was one of the companions of Mālik. This was already mentioned.

Ibn Sha'bān said, 'He has the *ḥadīth* with an *isnād* from Mālik: "Do not curse time." Al-Ḥārith ibn Miskīn related from him.'

Al-Ḥārith said, 'An 'Umarī *qāḍī* came to Egypt as if he were a brand of fire. He would sit for the people from the morning prayer until night. He had a good manner and upright business. Ibn Wahb, Ashhab, and all the people of knowledge attended his assembly. He said, "Help me and show some of the people of the land who are pleasing by whom I can help those who are pleasing [to Allah]."'

Sa'īd said, 'He wrote to me to ask me to be his deputy in Fayyum and help him. He wrote to my companions to request them to ask me that and to inform me about his soundness and his straightness. The matter was difficult for me and I did not know what to do. I heard an unseen speaker saying, "*Do not rely on those who do wrong so that the Fire afflicts you.*" (11:13)

'I said, "It is clear to me and I am warned.' I resolved not to enter into anything. I wrote to my companions to leave me alone. If they did not, I would move away." So he wrote to some of them to apologise.'

Sa'īd ibn al-Jahm ibn Nāfi'

He was a client of al-Ḥārith ibn Dāḥir al-Aṣbaḥī, then as-Suḥūlī. He is Abū 'Uthmān al-Jīzī. He lived in Giza. Abū 'Amr al-Kindī mentioned him and said that he was a *faqīh* from the people of Mālik. He was one of the trustees of ash-Shāfi'ī. The *qāḍīs* of Egypt accepted his testimony.

Al-Amīr said, 'His word was accepted. We do not know that he had *isnād* for more than one *ḥadīth*.'

He related from Ibn 'Ufayr and ar-Rabī' ibn Sulaymān.

Abū ar-Rabī' ar-Rishdīnī and al-Ḥārith ibn Miskīn related from him.

Al-Kindī said, 'When Sa'īd ibn al-Jahm testified with al-'Umarī, al-'Umarī gave *ṣadaqa* and set people free out of joy at his testimony.'

Abū ar-Rabī' ar-Rishdīnī mentioned him in *The Book of the Slaves of Egypt*. He said, 'He stopped speaking after Yūsuf ibn 'Amr. He was one of Mālik's companions. I saw him and sat with him.'

Sa'īd ibn al-Jahm said, 'Abū Shurayḥ, 'Abdullāh ibn Shurayḥ and 'Amr ibn al-Ḥārith joined the prayer in the mosque, i.e. in Egypt. Abū Shurayḥ said to 'Amr ibn al-Ḥārith, "What do you say about a man who inherits lawful property and then wants to give it all to Allah for the sake of asceticism in this world and for desire for what is with Allah?" He answered, "He does not do it."

'Abū Shurayḥ said, "Glory be to Allah! He does not do it! He does not go without and being ascetic in this world?"

"Amr ibn al-Ḥārith said, "The behaviour which Allah taught His Prophet ﷺ is better than that. He, may He be exalted! said to His Prophet ﷺ, 'Do not keep your hand chained to your neck.' (17:29) He gives away part of it and keeps part it."

'Abū Shurayḥ said, "What *fiqh* you have, Abū Umayya! Be ascetic in this world, Abū Umayya!" 'Amr said, "Supplicate to Allah for me, Abū Shurayḥ!"' He died in 209 AH.

Qāḍī Abū al-Mas'ūd ibn Muḥammad ibn Mas'ūd al-Ghāfiqī

Abū Ya'qūb said, 'And he is called 'Abd al-Mālik. They mentioned him among the transmitters from Mālik and counted him among those who spoke his words among the scholars of Egypt.'

He died in 182 AH.

Abū al-Ḥasan 'Alī ibn Ziyād al-Iskandarānī

One of the famous transmitters of Mālik and one of the people of good and asceticism. He was known as al-Muḥtasib (supervisor). He was not famous as one of the *fuqahā'* of the people of Mālik. However, he did transmit from Mālik in *ḥadīth*s and legal questions. He related from Mālik the rejection of of anal intercourse with women.

One of the transmitters of Mālik said, 'I was present with 'Alī ibn Ziyād who questioned Mālik. He said, "With us in Egypt, Abū 'Abdullāh, some people relate from you that you allow anal intercourse with women." Mālik said, "They have lied about me. May Allah make you thrive!"'

We mentioned him in the chapter on 'Alī ibn Ziyād at-Tūnisī in the previous generation. We mentioned his reports and virtues there.

FROM THE PEOPLE OF NORTH AFRICA

Asaḍ ibn al-Furāt ibn Sinān

He was a client of the Banū Sulaymān ibn Qays and his *kunya* was Abū 'Abdullāh.

Abū al-'Arab said in his *Ṭabaqāt* and Abū 'Alī al-Baṣrī in his *Collection* that he was from Nishapur in Khurasan.

One of them said, 'He was born in Harran in Diyarbakr.'

It is said that his father died while his mother was pregnant with him.

He learned the science of the Qur'an from some of the reciters. Then he visited 'Alī ibn Ziyād in Tunis and stayed with him and studied his *fiqh*. He then travelled to the east and listened to the *Muwaṭṭā'* and other things from Mālik ibn Anas. Then he went to Iraq and met Abū Yūsuf, Muḥammad ibn al-Ḥasan and Asad ibn 'Amr. He wrote from Yaḥyā ibn Zā'ida, Hushaym, al-Musayyib, Abū Sharīk, Abū Bakr ibn 'Ayyāsh and others. Abū Yūsuf took the *Muwaṭṭā'* of Mālik directly from him.

Yaḥyā ibn Isḥāq mentioned that he said, 'Muḥammad ibn al-Ḥasan took it from me.'

I do not know how this can be. Muḥammad listened to the *Muwaṭṭā'* from Mālik and also heard many *ḥadīth*s directly from him. Muḥammad said, 'I stayed with Mālik for three years, and I heard more than seven hundred *ḥadīth*s from him.'

Asad said, 'My mother dreamt that grass was growing on my back from which livestock grazed. It was interpreted for her as knowledge being conveyed from me.'

Events in his journey

Asad said, 'When I left for the east and arrived in Madina, I went to Mālik. In the morning, his doorman went out and let the people of Madina enter, and then the people of Egypt, and then the people in general. I used to enter with them. When Mālik saw my desire for knowledge, he told the doorman, "Let the Qarawī man enter with the Egyptians."

'After a day or two, I said to him, "I have two friends and I am distressed at entering before them," and he commanded that they enter with me.

'Ibn al-Qāsim and others had me question Mālik. When he answered me, they told me to say to him, "If such-and-such happens…" He was annoyed with me for a day and said, "This is *silsila bint sulaysala* (chain, daughter of a little chain): If such-and-such happens, then such-and-such. If you want that, then you must go to Iraq."

'When I said farewell to him when I went to Iraq, I came to him with my two friends (Ḥārith at-Taymī and Ghālib, the son-in-law of Asad), we said to him, "Counsel us."

'He told me, "I counsel you to have fear of Allah the Immense, to keep to the Qur'an, and to have good counsel for this community." This was because of Mālik's insight into him, and Asad was appointed *qāḍī* after this.'

He said, 'He said to my friends, "I counsel you to have fear of Allah and to have the Qur'an."'

He said, 'When I bade farewell to Ibn al-Qāsim, he told him, "I counsel you to have *taqwā* of Allah and the Qur'an and to spread this knowledge."'

Sulaymān ibn Khālid said, 'When Asad heard the *Muwaṭṭā'* from Mālik, he said to him, "Let me listen to more." He replied, "What people have is enough for you."'

When Mālik spoke on a question, he wrote it down for his companions. Asad thought a business was lengthy and he travelled to Iraq.

He said, 'When I arrived in Kufa, I went to Abū Yūsuf and found him sitting with a young man. He was reading a question to him. When he finished it, he said, "I wonder what Mālik says on it?" I answered, "He says such-and-such."

'He looked at me. It was like that on the second day and it was the same on the third day. When the people broke up, he called me and said, "Where are you from? From where have you come?"'

'I told him and he asked, "What are you seeking?" I answered, "That by which Allah will give me benefit." He turned to the young man who was sitting there and said, "Keep him with you. Perhaps Allah will give you benefit from him in this world and the Next."

'I went out with him to his house. It was Muḥammad ibn al-Ḥasan. I stayed with him until I was among the debaters among his companions.'

Asad said, 'I said to Muḥammad ibn al-Ḥasan, "I am a stranger and I hear little from you." He said, "Listen with the Iraqīs in the daytime and then come to me alone at night. You will spend the night with me and I will let you listen." When he saw I was drowsy, he splashed water on my face.

'He saw me drinking the water of the road one day and said to me, "Do you drink it?" I told him, "I am a traveller." In the night, he sent eighty dinars to me and said, "I did not know that you were a traveller until now."'

When he wanted to go to North Africa, he did not have enough money to take him there. He mentioned that to Muḥammad ibn al-Ḥasan who told him, 'I will mention your affair to the governor.' Ibn al-Ḥasan mentioned him and mentioned his situation to him.

Then he said to Asad, 'Go to the chamberlain on such a day and he will admit you to him. Know that when you lower yourself, they lower you.'

Asad went and asked permission to enter and was given permission. He went in until he reached a place where he was commanded to sit down. The servant who had brought him in came and brought him a covered table and placed it in front of him.

Asad said, 'I reflected on it and said to myself, "I think that this is only disparagement." I said to the servant, "Is this what you have brought or is it from your master?" He said, "My master commanded me to bring it."

'I said, "Your master is content with this? That his guest should eat without him? By Allah, this is some kindness from you and I want to repay your for it." I had forty dirhams in my pocket, and it was all that I had. I gave them to the servant and told him, "Remove your table."

'He did that and informed his master. It reached me that he said, "A free man, by the One Who is the only God!"

'Then he said to the servant, "Admit him." I came to him and found him on a seat. His teacher was at one side and a third seat was empty. He commanded me to sit on it, so I sat. He began to question me and I answered him. When it was close tothe time for my departure, he wrote a paper for me and sealed it and gave it to me. He said, "Take this paper to the master of the *Dīwān* and return to me."

'I took the paper and scorned it. I met Muḥammad the next day and I questioned him and informed him about it. He said, "Take the paper there now." I did so and the master of the *Dīwān* gave me 10,000 dirhams. I told Muḥammad ibn al-Ḥasan. He told me, "If you return to the people, you will become their servant. There is help for you in what you have taken."'

Asad said, 'Muḥammad asked me to accompany him to Makka. I appeared to dislike this, and his companions said to me, "We wish that we could buy this for 10,000 dirhams (i.e. travelling with him to Makka)." So I accompanied him. I used to ask him about what he wanted. Sometimes I asked him when he was praying and he would recite aloud to inform me that he was praying. I said, "You are distracted from me by the prayer when I have travelled through the lands to you?" He stopped and answered me.'

Muḥammad ibn Ḥārith, Abū Isḥāq ash-Shīrāzī and Yaḥyā ibn Isḥāq (adding to one another) said, 'Asad travelled to Iraq and he studied *fiqh* with the companions of Abū Ḥanīfa. Then the death of Mālik was announced and Iraq was in turmoil at the news of his death. Asad said, "By Allah, there is no circle in Iraq except that Mālik is mentioned in it. All of them say, 'Mālik, Mālik. We belong to Allah and to Him we return.'"'

Asad said, 'When I saw the intensity of their feeling and their agreement in that, I mentioned that to Muḥammad ibn al-Ḥasan while he was looking at them. I said to him in order to test him, "Why do you mention Mālik so much if he contradicts you so much?"'

Asad regretted what he had missed from Mālik and resolved to move to his school and he went to Egypt.

Abū Isḥāq did not mention Asad among those who took from Mālik nor state that he had listened to him. He mentioned him among the followers of his companions. I think that that did not reach him. However, the fact that he took directly from him is famous and sound.

Ibn Ḥārith said that Asad said about that, 'If I missed being with Mālik, I did not miss being with his companions.'

The books, *al-Asadiyya* and *al-Mudawwana*

Abū Isḥāq ash-Shīrāzī said, 'When Asad arrived in Egypt, he went to Ibn Wahb and said, "These are the books of Abū Ḥanīfa," and he asked him to respond to them according to the school of Mālik, but Ibn Wahb was too scrupulous to do so and refused. So he went to Ibn al-Qāsim and he responded to what he had asked for, and he answered him in what he remembered that Mālik had said, and in what he was unsure of, he said, "I imagine," "I suppose" and "I think". In part of it, he said, "I heard him speak on such-and-such a question, and your question is similar to it." In part of it, he spoke based on his own *ijtihād* based on what Mālik had said. Those books were called *al-Asadiyya*.'

Abū Zur'a ar-Rāzī said, 'Asad asked Muḥammad ibn al-Ḥasan about them. Asad said, "I used to write out at night in the hotel the questions of the Iraqis based on the analogy of the words of Mālik. I took them in the morning and I asked him about them. Sometimes we disagreed and debated on the analogy of the words of Mālik in them. Sometimes I retracted and took his words, and sometimes he would retract and accept my words."'

He said, 'Ibn al-Qāsim told me, "I used to do the entire Qur'an twice in a day and night. I have reduced it by one for you out of the desire to give life to knowledge."'

He said, 'When I wanted to depart for North Africa, Ibn al-Qāsim gave me what he had heard from Mālik and told me, "Sometimes I answered you while I was distracted. Examine this book. If it disagrees with the answer which I gave you, then drop that answer." The people of Egypt desired these books and they wrote them down from me.'

He said, 'They are the books of the *Mudawwana*, and I wrote them down and people took these books from Ibn al-Qāsim.'

Sulaymān ibn Sālim said, 'When Asad came to Egypt, he met with 'Abdullāh ibn Wahb and he asked him about a question and he answered it with the *riwāya*. He wanted to come to him and Ibn Wahb said to him, "It is enough for you when we give you the *riwāya*."

'Then he went to Ashhab and he answered him. He asked, "Who said this?" Ashhab replied, "This is what I say." Some heated words passed between them. 'Abdullāh ibn al-Ḥakam asked Asad, "What do you have to do with this? He gave you his answer. If you wish, accept it. If you wish, leave it."

'He returned to Ibn al-Qāsim and questioned him and he answered him. He came to him and he answered him until Asad has finished asking. Ibn al-Qāsim said to him, "More, Maghribi! Say: 'from where did you say it?' so that I can make it clear for you."

'Asad stood up in the mosque and said, "O tribes of people! If Mālik has died, this is Mālik!"

'He used to question him every day until he had written down sixty books from him. That is the *Asadiyya*."'

He said, 'The people of Egypt asked him for them, but Asad refused them. They took him to the *qāḍī* who said to them, "What means do you have against him? A man asked a man and he answered him. That lies in what is between them, so ask him as he asked him." They went to the *qāḍī* to ask him to grant their need to copy them out. He asked him for that and he agreed to it, so they copied them until they finished that. Asad took it to Kairouan and the people wrote it down.'

Abū Isḥāq said, 'Asad obtained leadership in Kairouan through those books.'

Another said, 'People disliked it when he brought these books. They said, "He has brought us 'I imagine,' 'I suppose it,' and 'I think', and left the traditions and what the *Salaf* said."'

He said, 'Do you not know that the words of the *Salaf* are their opinion and traditions for those who come after them? I used to question Ibn al-Qāsim about the question and he answered it for me. I said to him, "Is this the statement of Mālik?" He said, "That is how I imagine and think." He was scrupulous, not liking to leap into the answer.'

He said, 'The people discussed these questions and Asad kept them from Saḥnūn. Saḥnūn was cautious until they reached him and then Saḥnūn took the *Asadiyya* to Ibn al-Qāsim and read it to him. Ibn al-Qāsim said to him, "There are some things in it which must be changed." He answered about what he doubted and put many things in order because he used to dictate it to Asad from his memory.'

Ibn Ḥārith said, 'Saḥnūn travelled to Ibn al-Qāsim. He had learned *fiqh* according to the science of Mālik. Ibn al-Qāsim showed him these books as one shows a *faqīh* who has understanding. He corrected them with Saḥnūn.'

It is related that when Saḥnūn came to Ibn al-Qāsim, he asked him about Asad. He told him what he had spread of his knowledge in all directions. He was delighted with that. Then he questioned him and Ibn al-Qāsim allowed him in his place. Saḥnūn said to him, 'I want to listen to the book of Asad from you.' He did the *Istikhāra* prayer to Allah and listened to it with him and corrected in it what he doubted of the words of Mālik in it and he answered him in it according to his opinion. He wrote to Asad, 'Read your books against the books of Saḥnūn. I have retracted some of the things which you related from me.'

Asad became angry and said, 'Tell Ibn al-Qāsim: "I followed you, Ibn al-Qāsim. Shall I retract what we agreed upon for what you now retract?"' Asad ceased to listen to him.

He mentioned that one of the companions of Asad came to him when he was weeping. He asked him about it and he told him the story, He said, 'Read my books against his books while I taught him!' He said to him, 'This when you are the one who extolled Ibn al-Qāsim?' He said to him, 'Do not do it. If you had seen him, you would not say this.'

He mentioned that Asad intended to correct it and one of his friends turned him from that. He said to him, 'Will you diminish your worth? You will correct your books against his books while you heard it before he did?' So he abandoned that.

He mentioned that Ibn al-Qāsim heard about that. He said, 'O Allah, do not bless the *Asadiyya*!'

Ash-Shīrāzī said, 'It is dismissed up until today.'

Ash-Shīrāzī said, 'People were content with learning the *fiqh* in the books of Saḥnūn. Saḥnūn meticulously examined them again and he corrected them and structured them in chapters. He set them out and added to them the disagreements of the great companions of Mālik which he chose to mention. After arranging its chapters, he put in *ḥadīth*s and traditions: except for a few scattered books which remained in their original mixed form of oral transmission. These are the books of Saḥnūn: al-*Mudawwana* and *al-Mukhtalaṭa*. They are the basis of the School, and their *riwāya* is preferred over others in the opinion of the Maghribīs. They are the sources from which they compose summaries, on which they write commentaries, and about which they debate and discuss. The *Asadiyya* has been forgotten and is not mentioned now at all. Muḥammad ibn 'Abd al-Ḥakam has a summary of it. Abū Zayd ibn Abī al-Ghamr wrote a summary on it. Al-Barqī also had a summary of it. He is the one who corrected it with Ibn al-Qāsim, and it is the cornerstone of the people of Egypt.'

Aḥmad ibn Khālid said, 'The one who wrote the words of Ibn al-Qāsim (i.e. the *Asadiyya*) was a man from the people of Egypt called al-Aḥdab. Saḥnūn took it and wrote it out and put traditions in it.'

Saḥnūn said, 'You must have the *Mudawwana*. They are the words of a righteous man and his *riwāya*.'

He used to say, 'The *Mudawwana* in knowledge is in the position of the Umm al-Qur'ān in relation to the Qur'an. In the prayer, it dispenses with other than it and what is other than it does not dispense with it. Men pour out their intellects in it and they explain it and clarify it. No one devotes himself to the *Mudawwana* and studies it but that that is recognised in his scrupulousness and asceticism. No one opposes it for something else but that it is known in him. If 'Abd ar-Raḥmān had lived forever, you would have never seen me.'

Muḥammad ibn 'Abd al-Ḥakam said, 'Ibn Wahb came to my father after Ibn al-Qāsim had died. He said to him, "Be kind to Ibn al-Qāsim in his grave and do not relate any of his books," i.e. the *Asadiyya*. My father did not relate any of it except for a question or two by way of discussion.'

Asad later inclined to the books of Abū Ḥanīfa, and he related them. Most of the Kufans listened to them and inclined to them.

When 'Abbās al-Fārisī burned the books of the *Mudawwana* and the other books of the Madinans, Asad flogged him, and a man censured him for that. He said, 'I have saved him from death by flogging him. The governor gave that command because he had burned the books of the people of knowledge which contained the mention of Allah Almighty. I said, "O governor, let me flog him and make him notorious. That is more effective against him." By that, I saved him from execution.'

This 'Abbās was a man of *ḥadīth* who hated the people of *fiqh* and opinion. He attacked Asad and Ibn al-Qāsim. It is said that Ibn al-Qāsim called on Allah to make him notorious in the land, and he complained about that to Asad.

Asad's place in knowledge, excellence and the *Sunna*

Abū al-'Arab said that Asad was trustworthy and was not judged to have any innovation.

Abū Bakr ibn Ḥammād said, 'I said to Saḥnūn, "They say that Asad said that the Qur'an was created." He answered, "By Allah, he did not say that."'

Dāwūd ibn Yaḥyā said, 'I saw Asad reading *tafsīr* and he recited this *āyat*, "*Listen well to what is revealed. I am Allah.*" (20:13-14) Asad said, "Woe to the people of innovations! Their dead are destroyed! They claim that Allah Almighty created words when those created words say, '*I am Allah.*'"'

Yaḥyā ibn Sallām said, 'One day Asad related the *ḥadīth* about the vision of Allah while Sulaymān al-Farrā' the Mu'tazilite was at the back of the assembly. He rejected the vision. Asad heard him and went for him. He grabbed his collar and beard and turned his sandal on him and beat him until he made him bleed. Then he tossed him out of his assembly.'

It is said that while the *tafsīr* of al-Musayyab was read to him about: '*Faces on that day will be radiant, gazing at their Lord*' (75:22-23) while Sulaymān was present and said, 'Is there expectation, Abū 'Abdullah?' Asad seized his collar and a thick sandal in the other hand. He exclaimed, 'Heretic! You will say it first or you will not see it with your eyes!' Sulaymān said, 'Yes, we will see.'

Sulaymān ibn 'Imrān said, 'Asad listened to 12,000 *ḥadīth*s from Hushaym.'

He said, 'I listened to 10,000 *ḥadīth*s from Ibn Abī Zā'ida.'

He said, 'Sometimes I saw Asad hitting his chest, saying, "O my sorrow! If I die, immense knowledge will enter the grave with me."'

He said, 'Because of Asad, knowledge appeared in North Africa.'

Another said, 'Asad taught all the Iraqis in Kairouan. His school was the *Sunna* and he only knew that.'

He said, 'When Asad came to Kairouan, its scholars and notable men listened to him: Saḥnūn ibn Sa'īd and his likes among the Madinans and his companions known for him, like Ma'mar, the Banū Wahb, Sulaymān ibn 'Imrān, the Banu Qādim, Ibn al-Minhāl and all the Kufans. They listened to the books of Abū Ḥanīfa from him.

'When Asad had presented the words of the Iraqīs, the shaykhs of the Madinans said to him, "The second candle has been lit, Abū 'Abdullāh," and so he presented the words of the Madinans.'

Asad said, 'Ibn Ghānim sent to me to ask my advice and I answered him. Then he said after I left, "I do not want to ask advice from anyone in this land except for this young man."'

When Asad came to the door of Ibn Ghānim and knocked on it, it was said, 'Who is it?' He answered, 'Asad the *Faqīh*.' Ibn Ghānim said, 'He has spoken the truth.'

'Imrān ibn Abī Muḥriz said, 'News of the death of Asad reached us and my father thought it noteworthy and stated, "Today knowledge has died."'

Asad said, 'Mālik used to say that if someone builds or plants in land in which there is joint tenancy with people, the partners have compensation for that earth if there remains compensation from it, and then Mālik retracted that and took the position of the people of Iraq: that the land is divided. If the planting is in the portion of the planter, then it belongs to him. If it is in the portion of the other person, he can tell the planter to remove his plants.'

Ziyādat Allāh[1], the amīr of North Africa, asked Asad, Abū Muḥriz al-Kūfī, and Zakariyā' ibn al-Ḥakam for a *fatwā* on the *zindīq*. Abū Muḥriz and Asad said, 'He is asked to repent. If he repents, he is alright. If not, he is killed.'

[1] The Aghlabid amīr of North Africa.

Zakariyā' said, 'The people of knowledge related that if he makes a show of Islam and his heresy is discovered afterwards, then his repentance is not accepted.'

Abū Muḥriz said, 'Give him the sword so that he can kill him!' Zakariyā' said, 'I related this, but I do not follow it.' Abū Muḥriz said, 'Idiot! You provoke this one to kill him while you yourself do not accept it!'

Asad said, 'If he is killed after he repents, then I think that he is a martyr.'

Asad did not think that there was a *ḥadd*-punishment [for slander] on account of direct allusion. He also said that *nabīdh* is unlawful.

A man asked him about the *ḥadīth* from the Prophet ﷺ, 'A man is not a believer until he loves me more than himself, his children, his family, his property and all people.' The man then told him, 'I am afraid I am not like that.'

He said to him, 'Do you think that if the Prophet ﷺ were among us and he was near to being killed that you would ransom him by himself?' He answered, 'Yes.' He said, 'With your family, your children, and your property?' He replied, 'Yes.' He said, 'Then there is no harm.' The man said to him, 'You have relieved me in it, may Allah relieve you!'

ASAD'S APPOINTMENT AS *QĀḌĪ* AND GENERAL

Ziyādat Allāh appointed Asad *qāḍī* in partnership with Abū Muḥriz al-Kinānī (sic. cf. Abū Muḥriz al-Kūfī above) in 203 or 204 AH. They shared the office of *qāḍī*, and relations between them were not pleasant. Asad possessed the most abundant knowledge and *fiqh* of the two, while Abū Muḥriz was the more precise of the two in opinion and the most often correct. Asad continued to be *qāḍī* until he went to Sicily in 212 AH as leader of the army. He was a brave man in addition to his knowledge and *fiqh*. Asad set out out with 10,000 men including nine hundred horsemen.

The reason for the raid on Sicily was that they had a truce with it, and part of the preconditions (of the truce) was that if any of the Muslims came to them and wanted to return, hemust be returned to the Muslims.

Ziyādat Allāh was told that they had captives. The messengers of their king arrived and Ziyādat Allāh gathered the scholars and asked them about the business.

Abū Muḥriz said, 'One must wait until the matter is clear.' Asad said, 'Ask their messengers about that.' Abū Muḥriz said, 'How can their words be accepted against them?'

Asad said, 'The messengers are close to them and through them we can put them in breach (of the treaty). Allah Almighty says, "*Do not become faint-hearted and call for peace when you uppermost.*" (47:35) We are the uppermost.'

The messengers were questioned and they admitted that in their religion they were not allowed to return them. Ziyādat Allāh commanded that they be attacked.

Asad then said to Ziyādat Allāh, 'After being a *qāḍī* and looking into the lawful and unlawful, will you then dismiss me and appoint me as general?' He answered, 'No, but I will appoint you general, which is a greater honour, and I will keep the name of *qāḍī* for you. You are a general-*qāḍī*.'

Asad went to Sicily and conquered much of it. He died while he was besieging Syracuse. He also attacked Sardinia and oversaw its conquest. One of those with him envied him and was routed. That reached the governor. He said to him, 'Such-and-such has reached me. Name for me the one who did that that.' He did not do it.

When Asad left for Sousse in order to go to Sicily from it, the nobles of the men of knowledge went with him and the people escorted him. Ziyādat Allāh commanded that none of his men should do anything except escort him. When he saw the people around him in every direction, the horses whinnying, the drums beating and the banners unfurled, he said, 'There is no god but Allah, alone, with no partner. By Allah, O company of people! Neither my father nor my grandfather has given me command, and none before me has seen the like of this and only the pens have reached what you see. Therefore strive with yourselves in it and apply yourselves to writing down knowledge, and you will obtain this world and the Next by it.'

Sulaymān ibn Sālim related that Asad met the King of Sicily with 150,000 men. The transmitter said, 'I saw Asad and he had a banner in his hand and he was murmuring. He began to recite Yāsīn and then urged the people on. He attacked and they attacked with him. Allah defeated all the Christians. I saw Asad when the blood was flowing down the shaft of the banner until he put it under his arm. He went to withdraw his hand on one of those days and could not do it because of the blood which had congealed under his arm.'

The rest of his reports and his death

'Abd ar-Raḥīm az-Zāhid said, 'When Asad when brought us the books of the people of Madina and those of the people of Iraq, I asked him, "Which of the two views do you command me to follow and to listen to from you?" He replied, "If you desire Allah and the Next World, you must have the words of Mālik. If you desire this world, you must have the words of the people of Iraq."'

Ibn Ḥārith said, 'This man later attacked Asad using this story. He used to say, "The truth in his opinion lay in the school of Mālik while he used to give *fatwā* by something else."'

When 'Imrān ibn Mujāhid conquered Kairouan, he sent to Asad, 'Come out with us.' Asad pretended to be ill and kept to his house.

He said to him, 'If you do not come out with me, I will send someone to you to drag you by your feet.' He told the messenger, 'If you bring me out, I will cry out, "Both the killer and the slain are in the Fire."' When he heard that, he left him alone.

One of them said, 'The amīr sent for Abū Muḥriz and Asad who were the *qāḍīs*. Asad came. Abū Muḥriz was waiting for him with one of the messengers. He asked, "How are you this morning, Abū Muḥriz?" He did not reply to him at all. He went to the amīr. He had Abū Muḥriz sit at his right and Asad at his left. Then he gave Asad the document to read and when he had read, "In the name of Allah, the All-Merciful, Most Merciful,"Abū Muḥriz said to him, "You have made a mistake!"

'Asad said, "Governor, I met him and I greeted him and he did not return the greeting to me. I only read two words and he tells me, 'You have made a mistake!'"

'Ziyādat Allāh looked at him. Abū Muḥriz said, "He did not greet me. If he had greeted me, I would have answered him. He said, 'How are you this morning?' I woke up this morning and was unhappy, so I did not tell him to thereby delight him."

'Then a man came to them and he mentioned to the amīr that he dreamt that: 'Jibrīl descended from the heaven with a light until he stopped in front of you and shook your hand.' (One version has "kissed your hand".) Ziyādat Allāh was delighted by it. He said, "This is justice which Allah will make flow at my hands!"

'Asad said, "The shaykh has lied, amīr." The governor got angry and looked at Abū Muḥriz as if to provoke him by the ill feelings he knew lay between them. Abū Muḥriz said, "Asad spoke the truth and the shaykh has lied. Jibrīl only brings down revelation on a Prophet and the revelation has ceased. This man and his like come to you with the like of this seeking your worldly things, so have fear of Allah." The governor was silent and they both went out. Asad thanked Abū Muḥriz and he retorted, "I did it for Allah, not for you."'

In spite of their mutual estrangement, one of them did not allow what the other did not allow. Asad had no Arabic skill while his companion had eloquent Arabic but few words.

He was asked, 'What is this in which people say about the business of Abū Bakr and 'Alī?' He answered, 'By Allah, the one who deserves to rule after our governor and our *qāḍī* is not hidden from us, so how then could it be hidden from the Companions of Muḥammad ﷺ who deserved command after their Prophet, peace be upon him?'

When Manṣūr[1] overcame Ibn al-Aghlab and approached Kairouan, Asad and Abū Muḥriz, the *qāḍīs*, went out to him. Part of what he said to them was, 'Rebel with us. Do you not know that this is the injustice to the Muslims?'

Abū Muḥriz, who was afraid of him, said, 'Yes, and to the Jews and the Christians.' As for Asad, he said, 'You were his helpers and you both have nearly the same state.'

Asad said, 'When I came from Iraq to Egypt, I went to Ashhab and relied on him. His circle was constricted (due to the great number of people in it), and his knowledge was better than his *dīn*. One day he mentioned Abū Ḥanīfa and belittled him. Then he did the like of that to Mālik. I leapt on him and said, "Ashhab!"

[1] This is the army revolt led by Manṣūr ibn Naṣr at-Tunbudhī against Ziyādat Allāh.

'The students grabbed my clothes and made me sit down and said to me, "What do you want to say to him?" He said, "I say that the like of you and the like of the two of them is like the person who urinates between two oceans. His urine foams and he says, 'This is a third sea.'"'

He added, 'I left him and inclined to Ibn al-Qāsim. He was better for me and more scrupulous than him.'

Asad used to say, 'I am Asad (the Lion) which is the best of beasts. My father was Furāt (the Euphrates) and it is the best of waters. My grandfather was Sinān (spearhead) and it is the best of arms.'

Asad died in 213 AH during the siege of Syracuse during the expedition to Sicily. He was the general of the army and its *qāḍī*. It is said that it was 214 or 217 AH. His grave and mosque are in Sicily.

He was born in 145 AH in Harran. It is also said that it was in 142 or 142 AH.

He arrived from the east in 181 AH.

‘Abdullāh ibn Abī Ḥassān al-Yaḥṣubī

He was one of the tribe of Yaḥṣub. The name of Abū Ḥassān, according to what Abū al-‘Arab and others say, was Yazīd ibn ‘Abd ar-Raḥmān. Ibn Saḥnūn said that name was ‘Abd ar-Raḥmān. It is also said that it was ‘Abd ar-Raḥmān ibn Yazīd.

Abū ‘Alī ibn Abī Sa‘īd said in his book, ‘He was one of the nobles of North Africa by the nobility of his father, his house, his *fiqh* and his *adab*. He lived at Kairouan in the quarter of the Yaḥṣub, and was related to them. His father was from their native Arabs. He had a good performance in the war with the Berbers, and was appointed over al-Arbas.’

Saḥnūn ibn Sa‘īd, Furāt, Sulaymān and Muḥammad ibn Waḍḍāḥ related from him.

Ibn Abī Ḥassān said, ‘When I came to Mālik, I found that he had left and his door was locked. I knocked on the door and a pale slave-girl came out to me and asked, “Are you one of the people of questions or one of the people of needs?”

‘I replied, “I am a stranger who has come seeking.” She said, “This is not your time. Go to the verandah.”

‘I went in. When it was time for him to go out, the door opened (and he described the form of the assembly) and then Mālik came out between that slave-girl and a young man who walked on the earth with pride. Even now I can visualise his beauty and radiance. The hair of his head was bent and curly. When he sat down, he gave his greeting and they returned it. I stood up and greeted him and gave him Ibn Ghānim’s letter. He asked, “Your companion is the *qāḍī*?” I answered, “Yes.” He said, “That is not good for him.”

‘Then the letter was read to him and he said to the people, “This is a letter which has come to us about this man to inform me about his state in his land and his worth. The Prophet, peace be upon him, said, 'When the noble of a people comes to you, honour him.'"

'I stood before him and one of their men made room for me and I sat down. They mentioned knowledge and he said, "Knowledge is only taken from those who are trustworthy in their *dīn*." Then he began to be questioned while I was sitting. Sometimes he said, "Knowledge is vaster than that." He was asked about twenty-five questions while I was seated, and he only answered two of them. He said, "There is no strength nor power except by Allah." I frequented him and he continued to honour me, may Allah have mercy on him.'

He used to give a man three dirhams a day to take a seat for him where he would sit with Mālik. When Ibn Abī Ḥassān came, the man got up for him and he sat down there.

When Ibn Abī Ḥassān came to the assembly of Ibn 'Uyayna, his companions said, 'Bad luck to you!' since Sufyān inclined to him and spoke to him.

Ibn Abī Ḥassān said, 'I heard Mālik said, "The people of intelligence, minds and intellects from the people of the cities are three: those from Madina, then Kufa, and then Kairouan."'

Ibn Wahb said, 'I did not see Mālik incline to anyone more than Ibn Abī Ḥassān.'

His knowledge, excellence and the rest of his reports

Saḥnūn said, 'At the beginning my quest, when a question of *fiqh* was obscure for me, I would go to Ibn Abī Ḥassān. It was as if he had a key in his hand for what was locked.'

A man came to Ibn Wahb and informed him of the death of Ibn Ghānim. Ibn Wahb said, 'We belong to Allah and to Him we return.' He asked, 'Who was appointed after him?' The man replied, 'Abū Muḥriz.' He said, 'I do not know him. Where is Ibn Abī Ḥassān? By Allah, I did not see Mālik incline to anyone more than him.'

Abū 'Alī al-Baṣrī said, "Abdullāh ibn Abī Ḥassān had the greatest extent of *fiqh* in the school of Mālik. He had good clarification, knowledge of the battles and lineages of the Arabs, the transmission of poetry and speaking it. People took the history of North Africa and its wars from him. He related that from his father and he was generous.'

Al-Mālikī said, 'He was eloquent, stalwart in debate, defending the *Sunna*, following the school of Mālik, harsh against the people of innovations, with little awe of kings. He did not fear the censure of any censurer in the Way of Allah.'

Once he came to al-Aghlab when the Ja'farī and al-'Anbarī were debating about the Qur'an. The Ja'farī said, 'This is our Shaykh Abū Muḥammad. He will help me against you.' Ibn Abī Ḥassān said to al-'Anbarī, 'What do you have to do with this? This is a deep sea. You must have such-and-such.' He said, 'If Abū Muḥammad is with him, then this amīr is with me.'

Ibn Abī Ḥassān said, 'When someone comes to you, it is because you are better than the one who is worse than you. If he had been able to go to the one who is better than you, he would have gone to him and not gone to you.'

A man came to Ibn Abī Ḥassān and informed him that his house had been demolished. He asked for his advice in building it and who should build it in his opinion.

Ibn Abī Ḥassān gave him thirty dinars and said, 'Use them to help your building.' One of his children said to him, 'He comes to you to ask your advice and you give to him?' He said, 'I am not a builder. He alluded to what I am known for.'

When the army revolted against Ziyādat Allāh and attacked the houses of Ibn Abī Ḥassān and plundered them and sought for him, he concealed himself and had a bad opinion of them. He said in poetry:

The common army permit ignorant rashness towards
our household, and they split the staff of Islam on every side.
They ravage and revolt in the land through stupidity
while they suppose that Allah will not punish them.
The enmity of hatred of non-Arabs is not unusual
for Nizār and Qaḥṭān of noble lineages,
But they trace their descent from some people to us,
and so their hatred for us is something extraordinary.

When their search for him intensified, Ibn Abī Ḥassān took refuge from the revolting army with those of his people, Yaḥṣub in Sousse. He was related to them by lineage and he sought protection with them and they gave him protection and granted him security.

When Ziyādat Allāh was victorious later in Kairouan, he assembled the scholars and asked them about the state of the army rebelling against him. They informed him about the reward for in pardon and urged him to it. Ibn Abī Ḥassān said, 'Pardon corrupts. "The believer is not bitten from the same stone twice."' It is said that he recited:

> If someone does not do what is seemly,
> there is putting him right by his punishment.

Qāḍī Abū Muḥriz said (and it is said that it was someone else), 'Pardon is closer to *taqwā*." He said to Ibn Abī Ḥassān, "For the sake of your sheep and little mares, you would make the blood of the Muslims lawful?"

Those Kufans, his enemies, found a way to slander him in the army and among the common people through this statement. It was held against him and he fell because of it.

It is said that whoever had heard knowledge from him and written it from went to his books and cut them up at the door of his house. In the morning, there was a lot of that at the door of his house. He apologised for it to those who were fair that he only meant murderers of the army who had devastated the land.

Ibn Abī Ḥassān said, 'I saw the caliph Hārūn when he was running between Ṣafā and Marwa, and he walked in the bottom of the valley and forgot to run. When he passed it, he remembered. I saw him go backwards until he returned to what was before the bottom of the valley. Then he ran in the bottom and caught what he had missed. Those scholars who were present were amazed at that.'

When Ziyādat Allāh repaired the mosque of Kairouan, he said to Ibn Abī Ḥassān, 'The mosque will return to being Muḍar,' because its designer was 'Uqba al-Qurashī and Ziyādat Allāh was a Tamīmī. They were of Muḍar. Hassan ibn an-Nu'mān al-Ghassānī and Yazīd ibn Ḥātim al-Azdī had renovated it before Ziyādat Allāh. Ibn Abī Ḥassān said to him, 'A camel has changed its blankets.'

He once said to him, 'We have obliterated your traces from the mosque.' He said, 'The root is ours, but the branch is yours.'

Ibn Abī Ḥassān said, 'Ziyādat Allāh sent to me when his two

*qāḍī*s, Abū Muḥriz and Asad were arguing about *nabīdh*. Abū Muḥriz allowed it and Asad considered it to be *ḥarām*. He said, "What do you say about strong *nabīdh*?" I said, "You know my bad opinion of it. These are your two *qāḍī*s and they are the two men of *fiqh* of the land debating on it."

'He said, "You yourself must speak." He told the two of them, "Be quiet." I said, "May Allah exalt you! An intellect is equal to a thousand dirhams and then *nabīdh* which is worth one dirham removes it." He said to me, "But then it comes back again." I said, "After showing bad behaviour to the mother and the private parts to the father."'

In one version: '"After vomit in his beard and uncovering his private parts to his family and killing this one and beating that one." He said, "You have spoken the truth."'

This is how Abū 'Alī al-Baṣrī and Muḥammad ibn Ḥārith mentioned the story, although its words are about the same as those of Ibn Ḥārith. I do not know how that us since there is no disagreement between the two of them that intoxicants are *ḥarām*.

Ibn Abī Ḥassān died in 227 AH, although 226 AH is also said.

Ibn Saḥnūn said that he died when he was eighty-seven.

He was born in 140 AH.

Abū 'Uthmān and his brother, Abū Ṭālib, the sons of 'Uthmān al-Ma'āfirī

Known as al-Abzārī according to what some of them said.

Abū al-'Arab and Ibn Ḥārith mentioned Abū Ṭālib, the brother of Abū 'Uthmān and did not name him. They did not call him al-Abzārī.

He mentioned Abū Talib 'Abdulāh ibn 'Uthmān al-Abzārī among those who related from Mālik, although he was another person, and Allah knows best.

Abū al-'Arab said, 'They could have listened to Ibn An'am and Mālik. I suppose that he travelled with Ibn Ghānim.'

Dāwūd ibn Yaḥyā aṣ-Ṣadafī and others related from them both. Abū 'Uthmān was the messenger of Ibn Ghānim to Mālik for his questions. They were men of *taqwā*.

Abū 'Uthmān said, 'I heard Mālik say, "A *qāḍī* must have justice so that he will be protected from the bad opinion of people."'

Ḥātim said, 'I ate with Mālik and saw him eat with three fingers.'

He said, 'I heard Mālik say, "The life of the garment lies in folding it and its fault lies in shortening its sleeves."'

He said, 'When I brought the letter of Ibn Ghānim to Mālik, he said to me, "Give it to Ibn Kināna." Ibn Kināna wrote out the answer. Then he brought it to Mālik and read it to him. If he objected to something, he would correct it.'

Ibn Sha'bān said that Abū 'Uthmān was called Abū Ṭālūt, but no one else mentioned that.

He said, 'The name is Abū Ṭālūt 'Abdullāh.' Another said that his name is his *kunya* and that his actual *kunya* was Abū Muḥammad.

Abū Khārija 'Anbasa ibn Khārija al-Ghāfiqī

He was from the tribe of Ghāfiq. Ibn Sha'bān said that he is also called Abū Khālid.

He listened to Mālik, Sufyān ath-Thawrī, al-Layth. al-Yasa' ibn Ḥamīd, 'Abdullāh ibn Wahb, Rishdīn ibn Sa'd, al-Mughīra ibn 'Abd ar-Raḥmān al-Makhzūmī and Sa'īd ibn 'Īsā. He has oral transmission written down from Mālik like that of Ibn al-Qāsim and Ashhab.

Al-Mālikī said that he was a righteous shaykh. He had knowledge of the different scholars and gave answers. He mostly relied on Mālik. He had the various sciences of *ḥadīth*, *fiqh*, worship, Arabic and other things. His peers in North Africa listened to him: al-Bahlūl ibn Rāshid and others, and those after him like 'Awn ibn Yūsuf, 'Abdullāh ibn Yūnus, Sa'īd ibn Ḥassān al-Qarawī, al-Ja'farī, Abū Sa'īd, al-'Aṭṭār and his sons.

He said, 'Saḥnūn used to respect him and his knew his worth. When he was questioned in his presence, he turned to him. He was older than Saḥnūn. He lived in a fortress in the direction of Sfax.'

Abū al-'Arab said, 'His oral transmission from Sufyān is sound. He is reliable.'

One of them related that he said, 'I came to Sufyān and we found that he had died.'

One of them asked him and he said, 'I listened to Sufyān.'

Abū al-'Arab said, 'I thought that he had met Sufyān in his other journey before this, and Allah knows best. He is a trustworthy and reliable man. His oral transmission from Sufyān is not doubted.'

Aḥmad ibn Bard was asked about Abū Khārija. He said, 'The like of him is called trustworthy. He is a right-acting man. He met Abū Yūsuf but did not take from him. He related from Mālik about someone wearing a turban and not putting it under his chin. He disliked it unless it was short and not excessive.'

Ibn Ḥārith said, 'I heard many people relate wondrous reports from Abū Khārija and describe what did not exist and then will be (i.e. the future), like what is related in Andalusia about Baqī ibn Makhlad. However, the story from Abū Khārija is more detailed and has more wonders.'

Ibn al-Jazzār al-Muṭabbab said in his *Ta'rīf* (and he mentioned the like of what Ibn Ḥārith mentioned): 'One of them said, "He had knowledge of future events." One of them said that it was knowledge from augury of the flight of birds. One of them said from the service of the jinn. One of them claimed that he was a righteous man on whose tongue Allah made the truth flow and so he uttered it.'

The *faqīh* and *qāḍī* Abū al-Faḍl 'Iyāḍ said, 'I am free of any responsibility for these interpretations except for the last one. The sound story will prove it.'

His remarkable reports and proofs and his death

One of them mentioned that he alighted on the road to Sousse and lay down. He then said to his companions, 'Right now two men will come to you to ask about something and you will hear something you dislike. They will have some food with them which you will eat, but which I will not eat.'

There two men came on a mule. They asked about the shaykh and they said to him, 'A man who has a calf dreamt that it went to some leavened bread which he had forbidden it and ate it.' He said that Abū Khārija said to him, 'A mulatto slave will go to his wife while he is absent.'

One of the two men said to the other, 'We forbade him to let him enter, but he did not stop.'

Then they said, 'We have some provisions, so they brought out barley bread, chicken and oil. Those who were present ate and he did not eat from it since he had some wind for which this food would be injurious.'

A man questioned him about a dream that he was ploughing in Ṣafā. Abū Khārija interpreted it and said, 'This is a man who seeks children.'

Abū Khārija used to say, 'O Allah, make me die before the people here who bay like dogs emerge," and he pointed towards the land of the Maghrib.

He built a great mosque which had about twenty immense columns. They asked him, 'Who will raise these columns?' He replied, 'The One who created them.' In the morning the columns were upright and their tops were on them.

Ibn Miskīn said, 'There was a man with us who had a follower. He said to him one day, "I will frighten Abū Khārija." His companion forbade him to do that. He said, "I am going to do it." In the night, Abū Khārija was riding to his house when a phantom met him and then indicated a person to him. Abū Khārija went to him and began to beat him and he fled from him yelling until he vanished into az-Zaytūn. Abū Khārija then left and the follower came to his friend and when he was with him, he told him. He said, "I did tell you not to do it."'

He said, 'Abū Khārija used to pray during the night in a mosque whose people had invited him as a guest. While he was praying, he looked at the corner of the mosque – and he saw later that it was locked – and there was a shaykh who was standing in the prayer. When Abū Khārija greeted him, he drew his sword, brandished it, and went at him saying, "Are you impudent to me?!" There was a flash and he left.'

He used to say, 'The nights and days will not depart until the books of Abū Ḥanīfa will be erased.' It was like that in the time of Saḥnūn.

One of his maxims is that he said: 'There are three signs of *Iḥsān*: restraining wrath, guarding against slander, and veiling faults. There are three signs of gnosis: returning to Allah, total devotion to Allah, and glorifying in Allah. There are three signs of reflection: rapid recollection, applying oneself to consideration, and frequently asking for forgiveness.'

He used to say when he broke the fast, 'Praise be to Allah Who guided me and so I fasted, and praise be to Allah Who provided for me so that I broke the fast. If You punish me, I deserve that. If you forgive me, You are worthy of that.'

He used to say, 'Three are given and envied: useful knowledge, good provision, and accepted action.'

They mentioned that the people were afflicted by seven years of drought. They came to Abū Khārija to ask him to perform the Rain Prayer for them. He said to them, 'Come tomorrow with your women, your children and your animals. Spend the night fasting. In the morning, stand before Him and entreat Him. He will have pity on your state.' They did that. Abū Khārija went out and prayed with them and addressed them and made supplication. Then he sat down for the *Ẓuhr* prayer and the heat was intense, and the children wept and the animals cried out on account of the heat. He prayed *Ẓuhr* with them and spread out his hands and said, "You are our Master. We have only You and none but You. By You, they obtain the high degree and sublime gifts. If it had not been for You, they would not have obtained them. You have vast mercy and You know our states and our ugly actions. We only have You and we do not have other than You. Our hopes are based on You and we kneel in front of You. Our animals are hungry and our land is blackened and dry. Our hearts are fearful and our houses are empty. Your heaven is full and Your treasures are vast, so give us useful water to renew our belief in our hearts. We will not leave the presence of a Noble Generous One until you give us water. Our means to You is Your Prophet whom You made a mercy to us, may Allah bless him and grant him peace.'

Then a wind came up and the heaven poured down abundant rain while Abū Khārija continued to raise his hands, saying, "By this the Noble is known. This is Your action for the one who went to you. By it. You are known and You are described."'

Abū Khārija died in Rabī' al-Akhīr in 210 AH when he was eighty-six years old.

AL-ḤĀRITH IBN ASAD, FROM THE PEOPLE OF QAFṢA

He was godfearing, a man of choice who gave answers. He recited the entire Qur'an every night of Ramaḍān. He learned from Mālik.

Al-Bahlūl ibn Rāshid, 'Abdullāh ibn al-Fāris, Muḥammad ibn Tamīm and others related from him.

Al-Ḥārith said, 'When we wanted to bid farewell to Mālik, Ibn al-Qāsim, Ibn Wahb and myself came to him. Ibn Wahb said, "Advise me." He said, "Be fearful of Allah and investigate the one from whom you transmit." He said to Ibn al-Qāsim, "Be fearful of Allah and spread what you have heard." He said to me, "Be fearful of Allah and you must recite the Qur'an."'

Al-Ḥārith said, 'He did not see me as worthy of knowledge.'

Muḥammad ibn al-Ḥārith said, 'I saw one of the transmissions say that he was asked to give *fatwā* and did not do so, saying, "Mālik did not think me worthy of knowledge."'

Muḥammad ibn Mu'āwiya al-Ḥaḍramī aṭ-Ṭarābulisī

One of the companions of Mālik. He listened to three sections from him and he had other things from al-Layth which Muḥammad ibn Waḍḍāḥ related from him.

Abū al-'Arab at-Tamīmī said, 'He listened to Abū Ma'mar, the *Muwaṭṭā'* from Mālik ibn Anas, al-Layth ibn Sa'd, Ibn Lahi'a, and others. He is famous and reliable. He had age and attainment. He listened to Abū Ma'mar, the companion of Anas ibn Mālik.'

Bakr ibn Ḥammād and Furāt ibn Muḥammad listened to him. Bakr related that Saḥnūn said something about him.

Abū 'Alī ibn al-Baṣrī said, 'He had more knowledge than Muḥammad ibn Rabī'a al-Ḥaḍramī at-Tarābulisī. Ibn Rabī'a was also one of those who related from Mālik, Ibn Lahī'a, Abū Ma'mar, Ibn Abī Ḥāzim and Ibrāhīm ibn Abī Yaḥyā.'

Abū al-'Arab said, 'Muḥammad ibn Mu'āwiya said, "Something of the *Muwaṭṭā'* from the book of prayer remained with me, so I went to Mālik when the people had come in. He askedme, 'Who read to you?' I replied, 'Ḥabīb. I gave him four dirhams and he read twenty-five pages of the book to me. Habib read them to me in a single session. Ḥabīb said to me, "Your dirhams did not miss me, Maghribī!"'"'

In his version of the *Muwaṭṭā'* is the *Collection* of the General Chapter. That is not found with any other of the companions of Mālik. Abū Bakr ibn Muḥammad al-Mālikī mentioned that in the *Kitāb ar-Riyāḍ.*

Zakariyā' ibn Muḥammad ibn al-Ḥakam al-Lakhmī, Abū Yaḥyā

Abū al-'Arab said, 'He was reliable, trustworthy, a man of right action. He was one of the people of knowledge. He listened to Mālik and Ḥaywa ibn Shurayḥ. He used to be asked for *fatwā* at Kairouan along with Asad, Abū Muḥriz, and men of their level. He was among the number of Madinans there.'

He mentioned that he was with a group of scholars with Ziyādat Allāh ibn al-Aghlab. Ziyādat Allāh was brought a bag which contained some women's jewellery and dinars. He gave some of it to those who present and they accepted it with the exception of Zakariyā'. He refused and then left.

When he was appointed, Ziyādat Allāh began to say while he was looking at him, 'By Allah, how excellent you are, Ibn al-Ḥakam!'

Abū al-'Arab also mentioned among the transmitters of Mālik from the people of North Africa: Muḥammad ibn al-Ḥakam al-Lakhmī, and he said that he is a reliable and trustworthy man who died in 206 AH.

And there is Yaḥyā ibn Muḥammad ibn al-Ḥakam al-Lakhmī. Abū'l-'Arab said, 'He is a trustworthy righteous man.'

Ibn Fihr said that he related from Mālik.

Ibn Waḍḍāḥ said, 'I met Yaḥyā ibn Zakariyā' ibn al-Ḥakam in Kairouan when he was an old man.'

FROM THE PEOPLE OF ANDALUSIA

Qar'ūs ibn al-'Abbās ibn Qar'ūs ibn Ḥamīd

It is said: 'Ubayd ibn Manṣūr ibn Muḥammad ibn Yūsuf ath-Thaqafī.

Abū al-Walīd ibn al-Faraḍī said, 'He was one of the people of Córdoba and his *kunya* was Abū al-Faḍl. It is also said that it was Abū Muḥammad. He travelled and listened to Mālik, ath-Thawrī, Ibn Jurayj, al-Layth, Ibn Abī Ḥāzim and others. He was a cultured man of excellence and scrupulousness. He learned legal questions according to the school of Mālik and his companions. He did not have knowledge of *Ḥadīth*. It is said that he listened to the *Muwaṭṭā'* and other questions from Mālik.'

Yaḥyā ibn Yaḥyā said when he mentioned him, 'He was a man from the people of knowledge with much *fiqh*. He met Mālik and took from him.'

Another said, 'None with more manly virtue was seen in Andalusia than Qar'ūs.'

Qāḍī Abū al-Walīd said, 'He was one of those who was suspected in the business of the civil revolt. Allah protected him, i.e. from that which destroyed his friends. Some of that is found in the report of Yaḥyā ibn Muḍar in the first generation.'

Aṣbagh ibn al-Khalīl, Ibn Ḥabīb, and 'Uthmān ibn Ayyūb related from him.

Qar'ūs asked Mālik about the beating with which his father beat people. His father was in charge of the market. He was a righteous man who was harsh against the people of suspicion and he beat them very harshly indeed. Mālik said to him, 'If he did that out of anger for Allah and defence of His forbidden things, I hope that the beating will be light.'

He was one of those suspected of being involved in civil unrest and inciting rebellion against the Sultan.[1] He was driven among those who were driven in iron collars and made to stand before the leather execution mat. A young man repeated the words of the Amīr al-Ḥakam and said to him, 'The like of you from the people of the *dīn* and the trust in knowledge follows the lowly! If your command had been carried out, then the veils would have been rent and private parts allowed until a leader stood to relieve the people.'

He said, 'I seek refuge with Allah from acting or following with a hand or tongue in the like of this. I heard Mālik and ath-Thawri say, "A despotic tyrannical Sultan for seventy years is better than an unrestrained community for an hour of the day."'

Al-Ḥakam said to him, 'You have heard this from both of them?' He said, 'By Allah, I have heard it from them.' So he let him go on his way.

Qa'rūs died in 200 AH.

There are objections to what was mentioned of his *riwāya* from Sufyān and Ibn Jurayj. 'Alī ibn Ḥazm said, 'It is impossible that Qa'rūs related from Ibn Jurayj since Ibn Jurayj died in 150 AH and Qa'rūs died in 220 AH. Qa'rūs did not live long enough for this to be possible. Similarly, Sufyān died in 161 AH.'

[1] Ḥakam I.

Qāḍī Muḥammad ibn Bashīr

The *faqīh* Abū 'Abdullāh ibn Ḥārith said, 'He is Abū 'Abdullāh Muḥammad ibn Sa'īd ibn Bashīr ibn Sharāḥīl (or called Isrāfīl) al-Ma'āfirī. He came from from the army of Beja. He was counted among the Arabs of Egypt. When he was young, he acted as a scribe for Qāḍī al-Muṣ'ab ibn 'Imrān. Then he travelled to the east and met Mālik and sat with him and listened to him. He studied in Egypt as well. Then he went to Andalusia and kept to his estate in Beja until he was summoned to become the *qāḍī* at Córdoba.'

Someone else said that he related the *Muwaṭṭā'* from Mālik.

Aḥmad ibn Khālid said, 'Ibn Bashīr sought knowledge in Córdoba with its shaykhs. He wrote down a lot of it. Then he wrote to the Governor of Beja to ask his protection from an injustice he had endured. Then he withdrew from that and went on *ḥajj*. He fulfilled the obligation and became well known.'

Ibn al-Qūṭiyya said, 'He first acted as a scribe for the governor of his land. Then he disliked that and inclined to knowledge.'

He said that Qāḍī al-Muṣ'ab asked him to act as a scribe for him after he had come from the east.

He related that Mālik used to say, 'Look into these books and do not mix them with others,' meaning the *Muwaṭṭā'*.

Yaḥyā ibn Yaḥyā related a lot from him from Mālik. Part of that is that he asked Mālik about using the milk of the female donkey and he did not see any harm in it.

Praise for him

Yaḥyā ibn Yaḥyā was one of those with the greatest respect for Muḥammad ibn Bashīr and praised him during his life and after his death.

He was asked about wearing the turban. He said, 'It is the dress of the people of the east. They wore them from early times.' It was said to him, 'If you wore it, then the people would follow you.' He said, 'Muḥammad ibn Bashīr wore the silk-wool and he was not followed although Ibn Bashīr was worthy of being followed.'

Ibn al-Qūṭiyya mentioned him and said on him, 'He was the best of the *qāḍī*s in Andalusia and the most excellent and most just of them.'

'Abd al-Malik ibn Ḥabīb said, 'Ibn Bashīr was one of the best Muslims,' and he described his justice and excellence.

He said, 'He used lead us in the *Jumu'a* prayer with a wool-silk hat on.'

Ibn Ḥārith said, 'One of the detailed reports which is without peer due to the extent of the consensus on it is that he was one of the notable *qāḍī*s of guidance, one of those who possessed appositeness, beautiful methods, and well-thought-out opinion, and he was unbending in the truth and supported it. There was no leniency in him for anyone nor sycophancy towards any of the people of the ruler. He only preferred the truth in his judgements. He was very intelligent and also possessed excellent cheerfulness and truthful estimation. He had strong perception.'

His appointment as *qāḍī* and his life

Ibn al-Qūṭiyya said, 'When al-Muṣ'ab ibn 'Imrān died, the amīr al-Ḥakam asked for advice on whom to appoint to it. His ministers, *fuqahā'*, and the men of judgement agreed with him that it should be Muḥammad ibn Bashīr, the scribe of al-Muṣ'ab. His probity and the fact that he alone enjoyed the trust of al-Muṣ'ab were well known. He was appointed *qāḍī* and exceeded al-Muṣ'ab, and was famous for virtue and justice and his traditions remained after him. He remained *qāḍī* until he died. His son Sa'īd was appointed after him.'

Ibn Ḥārith said, 'I saw in one of the books that when Ibn Bashīr took it on, he turned aside on a road to a friend of his who was a man of worship. He stopped with him and spoke to him about his business and his dread that he was being sent for about the office of scribe which he had left.'

His friend said to him, 'I only think that he has sent for you to make you *qāḍī*. The Qāḍī of Córdoba has died.' Ibn Bashīr said to him, 'Since you have said it, what do you think? Advise me and give me some direction.'

The man of worship said to him, 'I will ask you about three things, so give a truthful answer to them. What is your love for eating good food, for wearing soft garments, and riding fine horses?'

Ibn Bashīr answered, 'By Allah, I do not care except for what will repel my hunger, cover my nakedness and carry me.'

He said to him, 'This is one. What is your love for beautiful faces and similar appetites?'

Ibn Bashīr replied, 'By Allah, my self has never looked at this state nor have my thoughts fallen to it.'

He said, 'This is the second. What is your love for praise and lauding, and your dislike of dismissal and your love for authority?'

He said, 'By Allah, I do not care in truth who praises me or blames me. I do not rejoice in authority nor am I adverse to dismissal.' He said to him, 'Accept the office of *qāḍī* and there is no harm for you.'

He mentioned that Ibn Bashīr was twice appointed *qāḍī* in Córdoba. One of his brothers criticised him for being unyielding in the right entailed by judgement and told him, 'I fear that you will be dismissed.'

He used to say, 'I would that he had seen the sorrel mare travelling to road to Mérida.'

It was not very long until an event took place in which Ibn Bashīr's inflexibility was shown and that was the reason for his dismissal. He went to his home town as he wished. It was not very long before the post reached him from the amīr summoning him to Córdoba. On the road, he turned aside to consult a friend who was ascetic and met with him. He told him, 'The Amīr has sent for me and I think that he wants me to be *qāḍī* for a second time. What do you think?'

His friend said to him, 'If you know that you will implement the truth on all parties, and that no censure of a critic will affect you in Allah, then I do not think that you can deny people your good. If you fear that you will not be just, then it is better for you to abandon being *qāḍī*.'

Ibn Bashīr said, 'As for the truth, I do not concern myself with whomever I impose it on if it is apparent to me.' He said to him, 'I do not think that you should deny people your good.'

So he went to Córdoba and was appointed *qāḍī* for the second time.

One of them said, 'The reason for his dismissal was that his authority was removed from some of the elite and he was prevented from judging them. He swore that he would divorce his wife three times, free his slaves and give as *ṣadaqa* what he owned to the poor if he ever then judged between two people. He was dismissed. When the ruler wanted to re-appoint him, he excused himself by those oaths he had made. The ruler insisted and so he set free, divorced his wife and gave *ṣadaqa*. The ruler sent him one of his slave-girls and some property to replace his property and slaves to replace his slaves.'

Abū 'Abd al-Malik ibn 'Abd al-Barr said, 'Muḥammad ibn Bashīr stipulated certain conditions with the amīr, al-Ḥakam, when he was appointed *qāḍī*. There were three guaranteed conditions. He said, "If you abide by them, I will accept. If not, I will not accept. Judgement will be carried out on everyone between you and the guard of the market; if it appears to me that I lack the power, I will tender my resignation and you will discharge me; and my provision will be paid from the booty." He guaranteed all of that for him.'

Ibn Ḥārith said, 'Muḥammad ibn Bashīr, according to what one of the scholars told me, sometimes accepted a witness with him by his scrutiny and insight. Sometimes he relied on the attestation of integrity of the person's private life by reliable people.'

He said, 'He gave judgement in the locked gallery in the southern part of the mosque of Abū 'Uthmān at the beginning of the western suburbs. When he went to judge there, he sat down alone with his pouch in front of him. He began to turn it around with his hand and the litigants would come to him according to his prearranged order. The litigants stood on their feet before him and presented their evidence without shouting, and then he would decide between them.

'His custom was to sit for the litigants from morning until noon. Then he would return to sit after *Ẓuhr* until *'Aṣr*. He only looked at orally heard clear proofs. He wrote down the testimonies and did not listen to that at other than at that moment. No one went aside with him in the assembly of his supervision or his house. He did not read a letter from anyone about a question or a case nor did he visit him.'

Ibn Waḍḍāḥ said, 'When Muḥammad ibn Bashīr was appointed *qāḍī*, he made ten seals which people could use to present (a case) to him. They remained in his pouch until he died. When someone asked him for a seal to present a case, he asked him what he wanted it for. If he was close to Córdoba, he gave it to him, and commanded his scribe to write down his name, his house, and the house of the one who took the seal for it and empowered him to direct the seal to him when his name was near. He warned and threatened him. If he was far away, he respected him according to his distance.'

Yaḥyā ibn Yaḥyā said to Muḥammad ibn Bashīr, 'Circumstances change with people and are not fixed. If the man is considered just with you and you pass judgement according to his testimony with sound investigation, and then a long time passes and he returns to testify with you, then investigate him again and demand that his integrity be proven if he makes you doubt; renew your investigation into him. Act by that and take testimony on that basis and out them on their guard about it.'

In his judgements Ibn Bashīr consulted with 'Abd al-Malik ibn al-Ḥasan Zūnān al-Ghāzī ibn Qays, al-Ḥārith ibn Abī Sa'īd, Ismā'īl ibn al-Bishr at-Tujībī, and Muḥammad ibn Sa'īd as-Sabbā'ī.

Ibn Ḥārith said, 'When they disagreed about something, then he would write to 'Abd ar-Raḥmān ibn al-Qāsim and 'Abdullāh ibn Wahb in Egypt.'

Qāḍī Aslam ibn 'Abd al-'Azīz said that Baqī ibn Makhlad said, 'Muḥammad ibn Bashīr had fine methods in his judgement and subtle paths which no *qāḍī* before him in Andalusia possessed. He can only be compared to those of precedence in the early years of this community. I saw that he only had some scrolls. I found them very succinct, containing the core of the meaning without a lot of excess. There were very few lines different to the discussion which is brought now in our time.'

One of them mentioned that Ibn Samā'a, the master of horses, complained to the ruler that Ibn Bashīr was unjust to him. He said, 'I will put your words to the test immediately. Leave directly and go to him and ask permission to enter. If he gives you permission, your words are true and I will dismiss him. If he does not give you permission except for your case, I will be increased into my insight into him.'

He went out to him. When he asked for permission to see him, the doorman came out to him and said, 'If you have a need, then mention it in the judgement assembly when the Qāḍī sits. As for the Qāḍī, there is no way to meet him.' The ruler learned of that and confirmed him.

Qāsim ibn Hilāl said, 'A man from the people of the desert who was one of his acquaintances testified before Ibn Bashīr. He needed to have his integrity proven. I went to him with Ibn Martanīl and another man. He asked, "What has brought you?" I said, "answered attest to the integrity of this man." He said, "There is no power nor strength except by Allah, the High, the Immense." He opened his judgement with that.'

Qāsim said, 'When I heard him, I fell back and he turned his face towards us and said to us, "By Allah, there is no god but Him. Does he have your approval?" We said to him, "With an oath, may Allah make you thrive?" He said, "By Allah, I will not write a name for him unless you swear that he is like that." We hesitated out of carefulness and left.'

A man he had accompanied during the *ḥajj* testified in his presence. He had a position with him, but he did not accept his testimony. The litigant said to him, 'Inform me why you do not accept, so that I can see if he can be proved to be just (for being a witness).' He said to him. 'He is so-and-so, my friend. Attesting to him just will not help you with me.'

The man heard about and he came to him in his assembly at the heads of the people and asked him about the reason for that. He said to him, 'You and I were joined by upbringing and nurture, seeking knowledge and the path of the *ḥajj*. You know of my inward part what I know of your inward, so tell me the reason before the people so that I know it and admit before the assembly.'

Ibn Bashīr said, 'You have spoken the truth. In all of that, I did not find that you had any injury in your *dīn*. However, we came from the *ḥajj* and alighted in Egypt and began to listen to our shaykhs and reside there. You complained to me about celibacy and looked into buying a servant. You said to me, "I have found a servant whose face is worth such-and-such and she has some skill."

'I told you, "You have no need of her craft. Sell her for goods and leave her. There is no need to add her."

'You disobeyed me and bought her. When I saw that appetite had overcome you in ruining your property by being extravagant on her I feared that the like of that could lead you to the like of this testimony.'

A friend of his called Abū al-Yasā' testified before him and he rejected his testimony. He criticised him for that and said, 'In spite of my love for you and my special connection to you?' He said to him, 'Scrupulousness, Abū al-Yasā'! Scrupulousness, Abū al-Yasā'!' He did not say more than that.

Two men of those who were well thought of testified with him regarding a slave whose master had died. They said that he had freed him and married him to his daughter and left him his property. He gave judgement based on their testimony. It was not long before one of the two witnesses was close to death. He sent for the *qāḍī* saying that he wanted to see him. He went to him. When the witness saw him while he was in his distress, he knelt and began to pull him to him. The *qāḍī* said to him, 'What is wrong with you?' He said, 'I am in the Fire unless you save me from it. The testimony which we testified to in your presence for so-and-so was baseless. Fear Allah and invalidate the judgement.' Muḥammad ibn Bashīr did not do more than place his hands on his knees. Then he got up and said, 'The judgement has been passed and you are for the Fire.' Then he left him.

The *faqīh* and *qāḍī*, Abū al-Fadl 'Iyad, may Allah Almighty have mercy on him, said: 'What Ibn Bashīr did regarding carrying out the judgement was correct. His statement, "You are for the Fire" without saying "If Allah wills" was because he might have intended to be harsh by that towards those like him among the false witnesses. If not, then the will of Allah can lie in pardon for what is greater than this by His immense favour. That He accepts the repentance of his like and wipes out his evil actions by it is promised.'

His clothing

Before he was appointed *qāḍī*, Bashīr had parted his hair and it fell to his earlobes. He wrapped a red cloak around himself in the oldest form. He wore good garments with beautiful quality and he continued his manner of dress when he was *qāḍī*.

Ibn Waḍḍāḥ said, 'Someone who saw Qāḍī Muḥammad ibn Bashīr informed me that he entered the door of General Mosque on Friday wearing a red cloak and with creaking sandals on his feet. He wore his hair parted. Then he stood up and gave the address and prayed in his garment. That is how he sat for judgement between the people. People ignored that out of respect for him. If anyone wanted to obtain anything from him from his *dīn*, he found it harder to obtain than the Pleiades.'

A foreign man came to his assembly for a need that he had. He asked one of those who sat how to go near him and he was directed to him. When he saw him wearing those clothes of his and the trace of the adornment on its edges with dye and the kohl and black on his face, he doubted his business and suspected the one who had guided him. He said, 'People! A foreign man asks you about your *qāḍī* and you have mocked me. I ask you about a *qāḍī* and you show me a piper!'

They silenced him and said, 'We have not lied to you.' He was rebuked from every side. Ibn Bashīr said to him, 'Come and mention your need.' The man did and he found with him what was more than he thought.

Zūnān said, 'I rebuked Muḥammad ibn Bashīr for letting his hair hang down and his wearing silk-wool and red dyed (clothes).' He replied, 'I have a proof for my business. Mālik related to me that Muḥammad ibn al-Munkadir was the master of the reciters and he had locks and that Hishām ibn 'Urwa was the *faqīh* of this land (i.e. Madina) and he wore red dye and that al-Qāsim ibn Muḥammad ibn Abī Bakr aṣ-Ṣiddīq used to wear silk-wool. Why do you censure the one who has a model in those people?'

Muḥammad ibn 'Īsā al-A'shā objected to Qāḍī Muḥammad wearing those garments and always called him, 'The company of ad-Dallāl!' That was the name of a hermaphrodite in Madina. Eventually Ibn Bashīr heard about that. He met him while al-A'shā was in an assembly in which it was possible to speak. Ibn Bashīr inclined to him and said, "Abū 'Abdullāh, evil is something which none is incapable of while good is only obtained by the people of beautiful patience. Whoever imposes praiseworthy discipline on himself should curb what is less than what reached me from you. It is more seemly for you." He was ashamed before him and stopped it after that.

Al-Mabsūṭ reports that Yaḥyā ibn Yaḥyā said, 'You will not find someone with intelligence who clings to what is censured in him. I saw Muḥammad ibn Bashīr wearing what was not known in his land, i.e. the silk-wool. He only wore it for forty days and then he left that since it was thought ugly and not for any other reason.'

Something of his specific judgements which indicate his firmness in the truth, and the rest of his reports

Aḥmad ibn Khālid said, 'The first judgement that Ibn Bashīr implemented was against the Amīr al-Ḥakam about the mill of the bridge at the gate of Córdoba since he considered that the right of the claimant had been established. The Amīr did not have a defence, so he wrote about it and testified against himself. When a long time had passed, he bought it from him with a sound sale. That delighted al-Ḥakam after his disadvantage and he began to say, "May Allah have mercy on Ibn Bashīr! He was excellent in what he did to us in spite of our dislike since we had something ambiguous in our possession, so he made our possession sound for us."'

Ibn Waḍḍāḥ said, 'Ibn Bashīr gave a judgement against the Wazīr, Ibn Fuṭays, about a right which was proved with him, although he learned it by testimony against him. Ibn Fuṭays complained about that to the Amīr and lodged a complaint against him. He sent to Ibn Bashīr about that. He mentioned the complaint of Ibn Fuṭays to him about the judgement carried out against him without him offering a plea, which is his right according to the consensus of the people of knowledge.

'Ibn Bashīr wrote back to him, "Ibn Fuṭays is not one of those who knows those who testified against him because he did not find a way to defame them and he could not avoid their injury. They would have abandoned their testimony as well as those who follow them and so the business of the people would have been lost."'

Ibn Waḍḍāḥ said, 'Sa'īd al-Khayr, the uncle of the Amīr al-Ḥakam, had appointed a trustee who brought a legal action with Muhammad ibn Bashīr in a claim against him. Sa'īd had a document in his hand which contained the testimony of a group of just witnesses. They had all died except for one witness from the people of acceptance along with the testimony of the Amīr al-Ḥakam, his nephew. His uncle needed it in his case when the *qāḍī* accepted the testimony of the other. He set down deadlines for his trustee on the second witness. Sa'īd went to the Amīr and told him that he needed his testimony.

'Al-Ḥakam had respect for his uncle and said, "Uncle, please excuse me from this responsibility. You know that I am not one of the people of testimony in the sight of our judges since we are involved with the temptations of this world so that we are not pleased with it in ourselves. We do not want them to blame us for the like of that in us and we fear that we will be placed in a position of humiliation with this *qāḍī* which we would ransom by our property, so take your litigation wherever the truth takes you. We have that which would injure you and more."

'Sa'īd pressed him in that and decided that he would send his testimony with two *faqīh*s to convey it to the *qāḍī*. They took it to him. He said to them, "I have listened to you both, so stand in right guidance." The guardian of Sa'īd al-Khayr advanced with boldness and confidence. He said, "O Qāḍī, I hand you the testimony of the Amīr on what is said." He took the letter of testimony and looked at it again. Then he said, "This testimony is not effective with me. Bring me another."

'The trustee went to Sa'īd and informed him. He rode immediately to al-Ḥakam and said, "Our power is gone and our might is demeaned! Your Ḥarūrī[1] *qāḍī* dares to reject your testimony! That is what should not be tolerated from him!"

'He went on at length and tried to set the Amīr on Ibn Bashīr while the Amīr kept his head bowed. When he finished speaking, he said to him, "Uncle, this is what we thought would happen. Now is the time for you to leave it. The truth is better for you. The *qāḍī* is certainly sincere for Allah. He did what he had to do and kept to it. If he had not done what he did, Allah would have changed our insight

[1] From a sect of Kharijite schismatics.

into him. May Allah reward him well from us and himself. By Allah, I will not oppose the *qāḍī* afterwards in what he is cautious regarding himself.'"

He mentioned that one of the brothers of Ibn Bashīr censured him in what happened to him regarding that. He said to him, 'Impotent one! Don't you know that there must be pretexts in testimonies? Who would dare to refute the testimony of the Amīr? If I had accepted it and not excluded it for a pretext, I would have diminished the right of the one he testified against.'

It is related that Muḥammad ibn Bashīr had a black slave-girl called Balāgh in the time when he lived in Córdoba. She served him and he enjoyed her when he had the need. When he had slept with her and fulfilled his desire from her, he pushed his hand on her chest and said, 'Balāgh! There is attainment (balāgh) in you for the time being.'

Ibn Ḥārith said, 'One night Amīr al-Ḥakam spent the night with a concubine of his. She missed him in the night and could not find him. Her jealousy was aroused and she went out to follow his tracks. She found him standing under a tree in the garden praying, supplicating with great energy. When he went to his bed, she pressed him for the reason that necessitated that. She thought that something must have happened to him. He said, "That was only because Qāḍī Muḥammad ibn Bashīr has died and I am made fearful by his loss and cannot find anyone to replace him. I put him between me and Allah in the judgements of the people. I relied on him for someone reliable since my self was assured of his justice. I asked Allah Almighty and made supplication to Him with a prayer which demands an answer that He give me good consolation for him and provide me with a replacement for him."'

Ibn Bashīr died in 198 AH.

Al-Ḥakam appointed his son Sa'īd ibn Muḥammad after him. It is also said that it was al-Faraj ibn Kināna. They will be mentioned in their generation if Allah Almighty wills.

Ṭālūt ibn ʿAbd al-Jabbār al-Maʿāfirī

He was one of the people of Córdoba. Abū Bakr ibn al-Qūṭiyya said:

'He was the last to take from Mālik ibn Anas and his likes from the people of knowledge. He was known for right action and virtue. The mosque and well inside the city of Córdoba was ascribed to him. There he lived and was one of those among the notable *fuqahā'* of Córdoba who concealed themselves when the people of Córdoba revolted against their ruler, al-Ḥakam ibn Hishām and he defeated them. He had a famous story which is used as an example of fulfilling the *Dhimma*.

'Ṭālūt hid, fearing for himself, with a Jewish man among his neighbours whom he trusted. He treated him well and he remained with him in the best of states for a year until the intensity of war had died down. The *faqīh* thought he had inconvenienced the Jew. Ṭālūt had an affectionate connection with the *wazīr*, Abū al-Bassām, and he hoped that he would provide a safe conduct for him.

'It grieved the Jew to have him leave him. He gave him good advice and persisted. The *wazīr* went secretly between the two night prayers and appeared to greet him with approval and he asked him where he had been before and he told him. He agreed with his opinion about moving to him and he promised that he would intercede for him. He rode straightaway to the Amīr. He had left someone to guard him. He told the Amīr, "What do you think about a fat calf who has withdrawn into his manger for a year enjoying his food? This Ṭālūt is the head of the hypocrites in my opinion. Allah has given you victory over him." He said, 'Get up and fetch him quickly.'

'He leapt up and sat at the door of his assembly burning with rage against him. It was not long before Ṭālūt came to him. He began to berate him for his wrong actions, saying, "Ṭālūt! Ṭālūt! Praise be to Allah who has let me conquer you! Woe to you! Tell me that if your father or your mother were sitting in my place in this castle, they would have had more kindness and generosity to you than I had for you! Did I ever reject you at all in a need of yours or one for someone else? Did I not visit you many times when you were ill? Did I not share with you in your sorrow over the loss of your wife so that I walked to the funeral in the graveyard of ar-Rabaḍ and I also went with you like to your house? And what about the many other marks of respect which I showed you? So what moved you to what you used in reply to my kind actions? You were not pleased with anything less than stripping me of my power and rushing to shed my blood and injure my honour!"

'Ṭālūt answered him, "I do not find that I have any words at this moment which can save me from your truthfulness. I hated you for Allah alone, so all that you had done did not help you with me at all. They are the portions of your worldly life."

'The Amīr regained his composure and his wrath abated and he was filled with kindness to him. He said, "By Allah, I summoned you present and there is no punishment in the world but that I considered it in order to choose the most atrocious for you. There is a barrier between me and you, so I tell you that that which you hated me for has averted me from you. Go in the security of Allah Almighty. Go wherever you like. Present your needs to me. You will not find me lacking in kindness as long as I remain. I wish that what has happened had not happened."

'Ṭālūt said to him, "You have spoken the truth. If it had not happened, it would have been better for you. There is no averting the command of Allah."

'Ṭālūt continued to be kindly treated by him afterwards until he died very soon after this. Al-Ḥakam was saddened by that and attended his funeral and praised him for his truthfulness.

'After he had granted him security in that assembly, al-Ḥakam asked Ṭālūt, "How did you friend, the *wazīr*, seize you?" He replied, "I let him seize me myself through a trustworthy person because of a connection between me and him so that he might intercede with you on my behalf. Then he did what you saw."

'He asked him, "Where was your refuge before?" and he told him about the Jew.

'Al-Ḥakam said to the *wazīr*, "Shame on you! A man from the enemies of the Dīn preserves this shaykh in his place in the *dīn* and knowledge and puts himself in danger for him and you are the opposite of that although he is one of the best of the people of your religion! You wanted me to increase the evil revenge we have now regretted. Leave me! May Allah disgrace you! Don't show your face to me! Give him his full wage and remove his bed from the house of the office of *wazīr*!" So he fell at the end of the business and his importance departed. He remained in decline and obscurity.'

It was said that his telling him this story and making clear what was between the two men was the reason why the Amīr pardoned Ṭālūt and turned his spite on the *wazīr* who had betrayed him. Allah knows best.

'Abd ar-Raḥmān ibn Mūsā al-Hawwārī, one of the people of Écija (in Seville)

Ibn Ḥārith mentioned that he was appointed *qāḍī* over his land in the time of the amīr, 'Abd ar-Raḥmān ibn al-Ḥakam.

Qāḍī Abū al-Walīd said, 'At the beginning of the caliphate of 'Abd ar-Raḥmān ibn Mu'āwiya, he travelled and met Mālik ibn Anas, Ibn 'Uyayna and those like them. He met al-Aṣma'ī, Abū Zayd, and others among the transmitters of the west. He went to the Arabs and frequented their places. He headed to Andalusia in his journey. He was shipwrecked in terrible weather and lost his books. When he reached Écija, the people came to him on his arrival and to console him for the loss of his books. He said to them, "The outlay is gone and the entry remains." meaning what was in his breast.'

He had good Arabic of a type from the Bedouins and he knew *fiqh*, *tafsīr* and the Qur'anic readings.

He had a book on the *tafsīr* of the Qur'an which I have seen a part of. Muḥammad ibn Aḥmad al-'Utbī and Musayyab ibn Sulaymān al-Istajī related from him. Aṣbagh ibn Khalīl also related from him.

He held the office of *qāḍī* in the reign of al-Ḥakam ibn Hisham after Asbagh ibn Khalīl and his death.

Al-'Utbī said, 'When Abū Mūsā came to Córdoba, neither 'Īsā, Yaḥyā, Sa'īd nor Ḥassān gave *fatwā* until he travelled from there out of respect for him.'

He lived in one of the villages of Móron and then moved to Écija.

‘Abd ar-Raḥmān ibn ‘Ubaydullāh

He was one of the people of Lisbon. Ibn al-Faraḍī and Khālid said that he frequented Córdoba. He listened to Mālik ibn Anas and was honoured by him. More than one person mentioned this.

It is said that he is one of those who related the *Muwaṭṭā’* from him.

‘Abd al-Mālik Zūnān and others related from him.

‘Abd ar-Raḥmān said, ‘One day I was sitting beside Mālik ibn Anas. He looked at Ibn Wahb and said, “Glory be to Allah! What a youth, if it were not for saying too much!”’

Ḥassān and Ḥafṣ, the sons of ‘Abd as-Salām as-Sulamī

He was one of the people of Zaragoza. More than one mentioned their journey to Mālik and their listening to him. Ibn Abī Dulaym said, ‘They related the *Muwaṭṭā’* from him.’

Ibn al-Faraḍī said, ‘They were both excellent. They travelled together to Mālik. Ḥassān was older than Ḥafṣ. He was one of the people of knowledge and the *dīn*. Ḥafṣ had various sciences and was eloquent and clever. His *kunya* was Abū ‘Umar. It is related that he stayed with Mālik for seven years. Mālik brought him near and he fasted uninterruptedly for forty years. Amīr al-Ḥakam summoned him every year to lead the prayer during Ramaḍān.’

SHABṬŪN IBN 'ABDULLĀH AL-ANṢĀRĪ

He was from Toledo. He was appointed *qāḍī* in his city. Abū Sa'īd ibn Mufarraj, Ibn Abī Dulaym and others mentioned him among those who related from Mālik.

Ibn Abī Dulaym mentioned that he listened to the *Muwaṭṭā'* from him. It is said that he heard a lot from him. He listened to him until he died. He died in 212 AH.

Muḥammad ibn Yaḥyā as-Sabā'ī, from the people of Córdoba

He had the *kunya* Abū 'Abdullāh. He was known as Fuṭays ibn Umm Ghāzīya.

He related the *Muwaṭṭā'* from Mālik ibn Anas according to what Ibn Abī Dulaym mentioned, and he listened to known legal questions from him.

Qāsim ibn Hilāl related from him.

Ibn al-Faraḍī said in the book of Aḥmad: 'Muḥammad ibn Sa'īd as-Sabā'ī.' The variant of Ibn Lubāba has: 'Muḥammad ibn Yaḥyā.' I do not know whether they are two men or one man. They disagreed about the name of his father.

It says in the book of Abū Sa'īd al-Miṣrī in one place: 'Muḥammad ibn Yaḥyā as-Sabā'ī of Córdoba. He listened to Mālik ibn Anas.'

He said in another place, 'Muḥammad ibn Sa'īd ibn 'Abdullāh ibn 'Abd ar-Raḥmān ibn Muslim ibn Khaskhās ibn Abī Wa'la as-Sabā'ī of Andalusia of old. He was the *muftī* in his days. They considered him as two men.'

Aḥmad said, 'He was the ancestor of the Sabā'ites in Córdoba.' He said, 'I do not know that he travelled.'

He died in the beginning of the days of Amīr 'Abd ar-Raḥmān ibn al-Ḥakam after 206 AH.

Ibn Ḥārith said that Qāḍī Ibn Bashīr consulted Muḥammad ibn Sa'īd as-Sabā'ī in his judgements.

The Amīr said, 'Perhaps this one is known as Ibn al-Mallūn.' He made a mistake. Ibn al-Mallūn was later than this generation.

Ibn Ḥārith said, 'Muḥammad ibn Sa'īd ibn 'Abdullāh as-Sabā'ī. 'Abd al-Malik mentioned him in his book with Yaḥyā ibn Yaḥyā, 'Īsā ibn Dīnār and his likes, He was one of the people of scrupulousness and good behaviour. He related from Yaḥyā ibn Yaḥyā. He died in about 280 AH.

Dāwūd ibn Ja'far aṣ-Ṣaghīr

He is called Ibn Abī aṣ-Ṣaghīr, a client of the Banu Tamīm. He was a man of Córdoba who listened to Mālik, ad-Darāwardī, Mu'āwiya ibn Ṣāliḥ, Ibn 'Uyayna and Zakariyā' ibn Manẓūr."

Ibn al-Faraḍī said, 'Ibn Wahb and Ibn al-Qāsim related from him, as did Ḥusayn ibn 'Āṣim, al-A'shā, Muṭarrif ibn 'Abd ar-Raḥmān ibn Qays, and Muḥammad ibn Waddāḥ from the Andalusians.'

Ibn Waḍḍāḥ said, 'He related from me and he was appointed Qāḍī of Coimbra.'

Ibn Abī Dulaym said, mentioning him among the Mālikīs, 'He inclined to *Ḥadīth* and it is not mentioned that he had oral transmission from Mālik. Ibn al-Faraḍī mentioned that he listened to Ibn Lubāba. Someone else also mentioned him. It is very well known that he listened to him in Madina.'

Dāwūd said, 'I saw Ibn 'Uyayna doing *ṭawāf* around the House, leaning on a man. He asked him about a *ḥadīth* and he removed his hand from him and spoke a disavowal to him. So I joined him and he leaned on me until he had finished his *ṭawāf*. Then he turned to me and said, "May Allah bless you! 'Alī ibn Abī Ṭālib said, 'The believer is good in help, little in provision.'"'

Muṭarrif ibn Qays said, 'Dāwūd ibn Ja'far was an intelligent, excellent man. About 3000 *ḥadīth*s or more were written from him.'

Ibn Waḍḍāḥ said, 'He was the ancestor of the Banū aṣ-Ṣaghīr with us in Andalusia.'

The youngest generation of the Companions of Mālik

FROM THE PEOPLE OF MADINA

Abū Muṣ'ab Aḥmad ibn Abī Bakr

Abū Bakr's name was al-Qāsim ibn al-Ḥārith ibn Zurāra ibn Muṣ'ab ibn 'Abd ar-Raḥmān ibn 'Awf az-Zuhrī.

He related the *Muwaṭṭā'* and other statements from Mālik and he learned *fiqh* with his companions, al-Mughīra, Ibn Dīnār and others. His book which is a summary on the words of Mālik is famous.

Az-Zubayr ibn Bakkār said, 'He was in charge of the police of 'Ubaydullāh ibn al-Ḥasan in Madina. Then he appointed him *qāḍī*.'

Muṣ'ab ibn 'Abdullāh said, 'He is known by his *kunya*, Abū Muṣ'ab. That he is the *faqīh* of the people of Madina is not rejected.'

Abū Isḥāq ash-Shīrāzī said, 'He was one of the people with the most knowledge among the people of Madina. It is related that he said, "People of Madina! You will continue to be above the people of Iraq as long as I remain alive for you."'

He related from Mālik, al-Mughīra, Ibn Dīnār, Ibrāhīm ibn Sa'd, Ibn Abī Ḥāzim, Ṣāliḥ ibn Qudāma, ad-Darāwardī, al-'Aṭṭāf ibn Khālid, and others.

Al-Bukhārī, Muslim, adh-Dhihlī, Qāḍī Ismā'īl, his brother Ḥammād, the two men of Rayy, Ibn Numayr, Muḥammad ibn Razīn and others related from him. Al-Bukhārī and Muslim transmitted from him in their *Ṣaḥīḥ* volumes.

Ibn Abī Ḥātim said, 'My father and Abū Zur'a related from him. They said that he is truthful.'

Qāḍī Wakī' said in *The Book of the Ṭabaqāt of the Qāḍīs*, 'He was one of the trustworthy people in *ḥadīth*.'

Abū Bakr ibn Abī Khaythama said, 'I went to Makka in 219 AH and I asked my father, "From whom should I write?' He said, 'Do not write from Abū Muṣ'ab, but write from whom you like."'

The Qāḍī said, 'He said that because Abū Muṣ'ab used to incline to opinion while Abū Khaythama was one of the People of *Ḥadīth* and one of those who was averse to that (opinion). That is why he forbade him. However, he is trustworthy. We do not know of anyone who mentioned anything that was not good.'

Ibn Abī Khaythama said, 'Abū Muṣ'ab was one of those who transmitted knowledge. 'Abdullāh ibn al-Ḥassān appointed him Qāḍī of Kufa. Then he mentioned that he was appointed Qāḍī of Madina.'

Ibn Numayr said that he heard Abū Muṣ'ab say that he heard Mālik say, 'The Qur'an is the word of Allah and not created.' Abū Muṣ'ab said, 'Whoever doubts or hesitates about that is a *kāfir*.'

Ḥabīb said that Abū Muṣ'ab said, 'Belief is word and action. It increases and decreases. Whoever says something else is a unbeliever.'

Abū Muṣ'ab said, "Abd al-'Azīz ibn Abī Ḥāzim said to me, "I asked Mālik, 'Who is the best of people after the Messenger of Allah ﷺ?' He replied, 'Abū Bakr and 'Umar.'" Ibn Abī Ḥāzim said, "This is my opinion." Abū Muṣ'ab said, "And my opinion. If I were to have partiality, I would have been partial to my grandfather, 'Abd ar-Raḥmān ibn 'Awf.'"

Al-Bukhārī said that he died in 242 AH in Madina.

Ibn 'Abd al-Barr and others said that it was 241 AH. Ibn al-Jazzār said that it was at the end of it. Ash-Shīrāzī said that he lived to be ninety.

Abū Muḥammad al-Ḥakam

He was from Madina. Ibn Sha'bān mentioned him among the transmitters of Mālik. He is famous for his company with Muḥammad ibn Maslama and 'Abd al-Malik ibn al-Mājishūn.

Qāḍī Ismā'īl, his brother Ḥammād, and Muḥammad ibn al-Ḥakam related from him.

Ya'qūb ibn Ḥamīd ibn Kāsib

He is Abū Yūsuf of Madina who lived in Makka. He related from Mālik, Ibrāhīm ibn Sa'd, ad-Darāwardı, Ibn Abī Ḥāzim, al-Mughīra, Anas ibn 'Iyāḍ and 'Abd al-Mālik ibn al-Mājishūn.

Abū Ḥātim, Abū Zur'a ar-Rāziyān, az-Zubayr ibn Bakkār, and 'Abdullāh ibn Shihāb related from him. Ibn Ma'īn finds him weak for a cause. He said, 'He is reliable in direct transmission but he considered him weak because the Ṭālibites[1] influenced him.'

Abū Dāwūd said, 'I debated with Ibn Ma'īn about his report and those who attacked him and he refrained from it.'

Ibn Waḍḍāḥ said, 'I did not see anyone in the Hijaz with more knowledge of the words of the people of Madina than him.' Saḥnūn said, 'He was a *ḥāfiẓ* master of *Ḥadīth*. He was known as Ibn al-Qāsim. Abū Ḥātim and Abū Zur'a consider him weak.'

Al-Bukhārī said, "He died at the beginning of 241 AH or the end of 240 AH.

[1] Descendants of Ṭālib, the brother of 'Alī. They formed a distinct group of Shi'a, focused on descendants of Ja'far ibn Abī Ṭālib, and led a revolt in Kufa under 'Abdullāh ibn Mu'āwiya from 127 to 130 AH.

Abū ʿAbdullāh Muḥammad ibn Ṣadaqa al-Fadakī

He lived in a part of Madina. Al-Bukhārī said, 'He listened to Mālik and to Muḥammad ibn Yaḥyā ibn Sahl.'

Ibrāhīm ibn al-Mundhir listened to him. He has many questions and *ḥadīth*s reported from Mālik.

Muḥammad ibn Ṣadaqa said, 'Mālik was asked about the man who buys a slave who then has his head cut open to the bone while in his possession so that the blood money is taken for that. He then returns him because of [another] fault and the master asks for the blood money paid for the head wound. He has nothing of that because the head wound did not mar him. If it is an injury which mars him, he is only returned with what is taken.'

Ibn al-Qāsim said, 'It is the same with a penetrating wound and a brain wound.'

ʿĪsā ibn Dīnār said, 'If it mars him, he can choose to return him and what the injury has diminished is not the blood money which he took. If he wishes, he keeps him and takes the price of the fault. If he is not marred, he can either return him and all that he took or keep him, and he has nothing.'

Az-Zubayr ibn Bakkār ibn 'Abdullāh ibn Muṣ'ab

Ibn Thābit ibn 'Abdullāh ibn az-Zubayr ibn al-'Awwām of Madina. He related from Mālik, Abū Ḍamra, his uncle and his father. His *kunya* was Abū 'Abdullāh.

Ibn Abī Khaythama said, 'He was one of the people of knowledge. I heard my uncle, Muṣ'ab ibn 'Abdullāh, tell me more than once in Madina, "Nephew, if any of us obtains proficiency, he will obtain his desire."'

Az-Zubayr was the man of knowledge of Quraysh in his time in *Ḥadīth*, *fiqh*, literature, poetry, reports (history) and lineage. This last subject predominated him. He wrote *The Book of the Summary on the Lineages of Quraysh* and other things.

He was appointed *qāḍī* in Makka and he died there in Dhū al-Ḥijja, 256 AH.

THE MAKKANS COUNTED AMONG THE BAGHDĀDĪS

Hārūn ibn 'Abdullāh az-Zuhrī

Abū Yaḥyā. Al-Muṣ'ab az-Zubayri said, 'He is Hārūn ibn 'Abdullāh ibn Muḥammad ibn Kathīr ibn Ma'n ibn 'Abd ar-Raḥmān ibn 'Awf, and his mother was Sahla bint Ma'n ibn 'Umar ibn Ma'n ibn 'Abd ar-Raḥmān of Makka. He lived in Baghdad.'

Abū Isḥāq ash-Shīrāzī mentioned him in the first generation of the followers. Abū Isḥāq mentioned that he was one of those who related from Mālik and they transmitted *ḥadīth*s and stories from him which bore witness to the fact that he had oral transmission.

Ash-Shīrāzī said, 'He learned *fiqh* with Abū al-Muṣ'ab az-Zubayrī.'

The Qāḍī said, 'He listened to Ibn Wahb and Ibn Abī Ḥāzim. Qāḍī Hārūn has a *riwāya* from al-Mughīra, 'Abd al-Mālik and al-Wāqidī.'

Yaḥyā ibn 'Umar, Yūnus ibn 'Abd al-A'lā, al-Walīd ibn Musāfir, al-'Addās, Abū Ja'far ibn Hārūn al-Aylī, Ja'far ibn Yazid, the Qāḍī Abū al-Mughīra Muḥammad ibn Isḥāq al-Makhzūmī and Muṭarrif ibn Qays related from him.

Ash-Shīrāzī said, 'He knows the most about those who wrote books on the different statements of Mālik.'

Az-Zubayr said in his *Collection*, 'He was one of the *fuqahā'*. He used to undertake to help the people of Madina and he did well.'

Muṭarrif ibn Qays said, 'I listened to him in Makka and stayed with him. He had immense worth. He related from Mālik. Muḥammad ibn 'Abd al-Ḥakam said to me, "I met him and took from him."'

Qāḍī Wakī' said, 'Hārūn az-Zuhrī was one of the *fuqahā'* of the school of the people of Madina among the companions of Mālik and one of the people of extensive literature.'

He and al-Jīzī said, 'He was praiseworthy, honest, and loved in his conduct as *qāḍī*.'

His being appointed *Qāḍī* and his conduct and his inquisition

Al-Muṣ'ab az-Zubayrī said, 'Al-Ma'mūn appointed him Qāḍī of Massisa and then removed him. Then he appointed him Qāḍī of ar-Raqqa and then he removed him. Then he made him Qāḍī of 'Askar al-Mahdī in Baghdad and then removed him. Then he was Qāḍī of Egypt. He remained its *qāḍī* until he was removed at the end of al-Mu'taṣim.

Al-Ḥumaydī said in The Qāḍīs of Egypt, 'After Ibn al-Munkadir, Egypt remained without a *qāḍī* until al-Ma'mūn appointed Hārūn ibn 'Abdullāh az-Zuhrī as *qāḍī*.'

Hārūn said, 'Al-Ma'mūn summoned me and said, "Hārūn, I have appointed you to a land which they called by your name: Egypt."'

Abū 'Umar al-Kindī said in his book on the Qāḍīs of Egypt. 'Hārūn az-Zuhrī came to Egypt from al-Ma'mūn during Ramaḍān in 217 AH. He sat in the General Mosque and there was not any of the business of the *qāḍī* which he did not see to himself and attend to it with the people of Egypt. He investigated the *ḥabūs* and the property of orphans. He devoted himself to their direction himself and took account of them. He beat a man for a state which he saw in him regarding the property of an orphan which he was overseeing and he made him be taken around the city. He brought the property of the absent person and those who did not have heirs to the Treasury and he brought all of that down.'

Al-Mu'taṣim wrote to him to command him to put the *fuqahā'* through the inquisition [about the Qur'an] and he tendered his resignation because of that. Ibn Abī Dāwūd then wrote to [Abū] Bakr al-Aṣamm to command him to impose that on them. He was a leader in that and attacked people in it.

Hārūn used to say, 'Praise be to Allah who excused me from what someone else was tested with.'

He mentioned that the scholars of Egypt received a terrible inquisition in that and that Ibn 'Abd al-Ḥakam the elder was flogged and all the Banū 'Abd al-Ḥakam were flogged and put through the inquisition. Al-Aṣamm also put Abū aṭ-Ṭāhir, Abū Ja'far al-Aylī, Yaḥyā ibn Bukayr, Abū Isḥāq al-Barqī and Abū Rāshid to the test.

He flogged his back with the whip and put him on a donkey with his head towards the tail and took him around the city. He flogged Ibn Kāsib, 'Abdullāh ibn Zayd ibn Ẓabyān, Qābūs ibn Abī Ẓabyān and others.

Some of them replied to him with dissimulation (*taqiyya*). He left those who answered him. Whoever refused him was sent to Ibn Abī Dāwūd in Iraq.

One group fled immediately. One of them was Ibn al-Mawwāz. Others hid. Aṣbagh ibn al-Faraj was one of them. He stayed in his house.

Al-Kindī mentioned that when al-Ma'mūn put the people through the inquisition about the Qur'an, he wrote to the governor of Egypt to arrest Qāḍī Hārūn. He claimed that he had answered him and that he used to only accept the testimony of the one nearest to him. That is dissimulation, and Allah knows best, and obeying what he commanded him.

He indicated that it is the dissimulation of his resignation later and his trial at the hands of this al-Aṣamm and what we will mention later.

Abū 'Amr al-Jīzī said, 'His position bothered Ibn Abī Dāwūd and he removed him from the office of *qāḍī* in Egypt in 226 AH. He did not find a way to dismiss him because al-Mu'taṣim had chosen him. This lasted until it was confirmed to al-Mu'taṣim that he appointed the companions of Ibn al-Munkadir whom al-Mu'taṣim hated, as we mentioned in his reports, and that he made them a retinue. Therefore he dismissed him and appointed Abū Bakr ibn Abī al-Layth al-Aṣamm. He delegated a man to present a case against Hārūn regarding the loss of some money from the Treasury and the fact that Hārūn had given the key of the Treasury to someone who was not reliable. He stated it in great detail and al-Aṣamm demanded that Hārūn be summoned present and debate with him time after time. He degraded him and commanded that he be imprisoned, but the letter of al-Mu'taṣim arrived which removed him from that.

'Allah seized al-Aṣamm quickly thereafter for what he had done to Hārūn and Ziyāda. That was at the hand of al-Ḥārith ibn Miskīn when he was appointed Qāḍī of Egypt. He made al-Aṣamm stand for several days and he flogged him twenty times each day about returning money from the Treasury. Then when [the caliph] al-Mutawakkil came to power after that, he commanded that the beard and hair of al-Aṣamm be shaved and he was to be beaten and taken around Cairo on a donkey. Then he was to be jailed and he and his friends attacked and he should be cursed on the minbar. All of that was carried out.'

Al-Aṣamm was a corrupt Mu'tazilite innovator.

Qāḍī Hārūn died in 228 AH.

His wit and wisdoms in poetry

Qāḍī Wakī' recited in *Ṭabaqāt al-Quḍāt* part of what he said when he left Ibn Abī Dāwūd:

The days of your kindness were not concerned
  with patience in states and other states.
Be patient in them and be patient in what is disliked of them.
  There is acceptance for the one with a hand of kindness.
When he opens the locks of
  many a matter with a locked door,
He constricts the one with an expedient
  by disclosing his device. Man is cunning
Until its keys are received from
  where the mind does not expect.
Seek provision according to the time
  and terms when it will come.
It does not keep you waiting in its moment
  nor can it be hastened before that.
Do not be a slave to desire.
  Perhaps the state will oppose you.
Poverty is better, so strive against wealth
  in which there may be abasement for you.
Money is a blemish for the one who amasses it
  when he does not have favour in it.
A free man is free in the evening
  and poverty does not keep him from that.

Az-Zubayr ibn Bakkār recited by him:

Is yearning anything but a stranger hankering
 while the pact is long when he is near?
I see yearning summoning me to the one I love
 and yearning has a call which is heard and answered.
Allah waters the sides of Madina.
 There a person reaches his beloved.
If the mount takes me too far from them,
 the rapture of the yearning heart remains for them.
At midday – your body is not concerned with one who is haggard
 and the easiest of what I have is to be emaciated.
I said to her, "There is heat in my breast
 which cuts off my breaths and melts me.
When I remember the Hijaz and its people,
 my eye is submerged in overflowing tears."

Abū 'Amr al-Kindī recited by him:

When I suddenly saw the distance from her –
 and it is easy for what is disliked to occur
And all that remains is that an upright one be seen off lame
 and shed a tear of farewell –
Then I glanced and saw her.
 She brought out a finger from beside her cheek.

He mentioned that Hārūn said, 'I recited it to 'Abd al-Malik ibn al-Mājishūn and I ascribed it to a man from the Banu Qays. He said, "It is good, by Allah." I said, "By Allah, I uttered it in my journey to you." He said, "I recognised softness in it when you recited it."'

Qāḍī Wakī' recited an ode by him containing much wisdom and advice. It begins:

Your grey-hair has become well-known in the crossroads
 and I have returned the trusts from youth.
I left off joining with pretty girls,
 and whenever I defied critics in them, I became obedient.
I wore freshness and radiance from youth.
 If only that would return!
Times in which one listened to ardent love and its tale
 in such a way that the hearer inclines to enticement.

So abandon the pretty girls and youth and its memory.
How many a place begins to incline in error!
By Allah, fear and be fearful of your wrong actions with Him
on the Day of Rising and curb yourself.
Do not sleep with a slave by desires
and be followed by virtue and not follow it.
Be a shelter to the tribe in matters when they come
and be a defence for it in (other) matters.
Do not envy its Prophet. Be humble to him.
That is better than you being found humbled at the end.
Facilitate for him what his path demands
so he will lift you by his rising.
When he obtains a portion, then you will have his portion
and you will be separated and gathered in it.
If something arises for you, then endorse it and guard it
from a damage which will be a barrier for you.
Guard it and take it as a sword in readiness
when the cutter meets the hated battle.
Have as much of your friend as you can,
and there is no harm with it when he does not profit you.
Cure enmity from the enemy by encounter
and beware of your enemies near and far.
When he calls you in return in courtesy, then return to him
and let him meet your run with vastness
Excepting envy. That is an enmity which shows pleasure
while it is an effective poison.
Endure it. There is no trick in it. You should know
the descendants and the ascendants.

He also recited:

What does the district have on the day of separation? If they arise
or arrive by the ropes of separation, they are not cut off.
Rather they did not care about a captive in the houses. If they had
cared about him, they would not have done what they did.
When I saw the long-suffering district urging the first fruits,
the rash one rejoiced in separation.

I called out 'Laylā!' but no Laylā replied to me. 'Peace from me!'
  The heart almost bursts.
O Laylā, your family incited me to visit you.
  The house is the same and the gathering in it is gathered.
Now it is better for life after you.
  I will not profit by ease of life after today.
Does the time which has passed return?
  Can grief be averted from the one with the lament?
My little Salmā said, "White hair covers you from age.
  White hair is the least of what does not bring your desire."
O Salmā! If white hair alarms me,
  the palms are skilled in what they carry.
I do not see any wantonness for joy
  and I do not think to fear the vicissitudes of time.
The vicissitudes of time have tested me,
  and I acknowledge the firm spear, however it falls.
Refute the creatures. Desire does not lead me.
  The base one is the one who is guided by desire.
This one and the traitor of the people is a shadow who reviles me,
  as the dog barks for a time and then stops.
I left it opposing me and I thought little of it since I have
  no quenching nor satiety in it.
Nor is my anger put in other than its place nor is their victory,
  since anxiety does not harm me.
I will not be soft to a people, humble to them,
  nor will I repay them with evil if they gather together.
Forbearance for forbearance. If they are rash,
  I am like that in what I bring and what I leave.

FROM THE PEOPLE OF THE EAST

Qutayba ibn Sa'īd

Ibn Jamīl ibn Ṭarīf ibn 'Abdullāh ath-Thaqafī al-Balkhī al-Baghdānī. Baghlan is a village in Khurasan. He was a client of Thaqīf. His *kunya* was Abū Rajā'. He was one of the people of Balkh.

Ṭarīf was the name of his grandfather, the client of al-Ḥajjāj and his baker.

Abū Aḥmad ibn 'Adī and others said that Qutayba was his title and that his name was Yaḥyā.

Ibn Sha'bān said, 'He had many excellent *ḥadīth*s and legal questions from Mālik. He listened to Mālik, al-Layth, Ibn Lahī'a (and he was the last to relate from him), Bakr ibn Muḍar, Ya'qūb al-Iskandarānī, Ḥammād ibn Zayd, Abū 'Awāna, 'Abd al-Wāḥid ibn Ziyād and Ismā'īl ibn Ja'far.'

'Abdullāh ibn az-Zubayr al-Ḥumaydī, Ibn Ḥanbal, Ibn Ma'īn, Abū Khaythama, Abū Bakr ibn Abī Shayba, Ibn Numayr, al-Ḥasan ibn 'Arafa, Sayf ibn Mūsā al-Qaṭṭān, Abū Zur'a, Abū Ḥātim of Rayy, Abū Dāwūd, at-Tirmidhī, an-Nasā'ī, al-Bukhārī and Muslim related from him. They both transmitted a lot from him in the *Ṣaḥīḥ Collection*s.

Ahmad ibn Hanbal praised him.

Yaḥyā said that he is trustworthy and Abū Ḥātim says that he is reliable.

'Abd ar-Raḥmān said, 'I heard my father say, "I was present with Qutayba ibn Sa'īd in Baghdad when Ibn Ḥanbal came and asked him about some *ḥadīth*s and he related them to him. Then Ibn Abī Shayba and Ibn Numayr came in Kufa and they continued to pester him and I pestered him along with them until morning."'

Abū al-Qāsim al-Balkhī mentioned in his treatises that Ḥāfiẓ Ḥamza ibn Muḥammad said, 'Some of the students gathered at door of Qutayba ibn Sa'īd. Some of them asked him to let him hear *ḥadīth*s, and some of them asked him to let him hear *fiqh*. The travellers pestered him. He related much and met some men. He smiled and said:

"The mother of the child asked me for a camel to walk slowly,
and at first it goes slowly, gently. Each of us is tested."'

Qāḍī Wakī' said, 'Qutayba was appointed *qāḍī* in Baghdad. He tried to deputise Bishr al-Marīsī and put him in charge of some of the boxes of the copies of the Qur'an. Bishr said, "I seek refuge with Allah. I am not a delegate." People mobbed him to such an extent that they very nearly killed him.'

Abū Dāwūd said, 'I listened to Qutayba ibn Sa'īd. He was asked about those who hesitate regarding the [non-createdness of the] Qur'an. He said, "Those who hesitate are worse than them," i.e. than the people who state that it is created.'

He mentioned that Isḥāq ibn Rāhawayh wrote to Qutayba once and then again, but he did not answer him. So he wrote to him a third time:

When the brothers missed a meeting,
there is nothing more joyful than the letter.
If a friend writes to his brother,
the right of his letter is the reply.

Abū al-Qāsim al-Balkhī mentioned in his treatises: 'Abū 'Abdullāh Al-Bukhārī said, "Qutayba died at the beginning of Sha'bān in 240 AH when he was ninety-two years old. He was born in Balkh in Rajab, 148 AH."'

FROM THE PEOPLE OF EGYPT

ʿAbdullāh ibn ʿAbd al-Ḥakam ibn Aʿyan

Ibn al-Layth. He was a client of ʿUmayra, a woman among the clients of ʿUthmān ibn ʿAffān. It is also said that he was the client of Nāfiʿ, the client of ʿUthmān ibn ʿAffān. Ibn Shaʿbān said that. His *kunya* was Abū Muḥammad.

He listened to Mālik, al-Layth, Bakr ibn Muḍar, ʿAbd ar-Razzāq, al-Qaʿnabī, Ibn Lahīʿa, Ibn ʿĀliyya, Ismāʿīl ibn Abī ʿAyyāsh, Yaʿqūb ibn ʿAbd ar-Raḥmān az-Zuhrī, al-ʿAṭṭāf ibn Khālid and Ibn ʿUyayna.

Ibn Numayr, Hārūn ibn Isḥāq, his sons, al-Miqdām ibn Dāwūd, Abū Yazīd al-Qarāṭīsī, ar-Rabīʿ ibn Sulaymān ibn Ibn al-Mawwāz, al-ʿAddās, Aḥmad ibn Zukayr, Ibn Ḥabīb, Aḥmad ibn Ṣāliḥ, Muḥammad ibn Muslim and more than one related from him.

Abū ʿUmar ibn ʿAbd al-Barr said, ʻIbn ʿAbd al-Ḥakam was a righteous man, trustworthy, precise in the school of Mālik.'

Al-Kindī said that he was a *faqīh*. Abū Zurʿa ar-Rāzī said that he was truthful and trustworthy.

Muḥammad ibn Muslim said, ʻI wrote from him. He was a shaykh in Egypt.'

Ahmad ibn Ṣāliḥ said the like of that.

Abū Ḥātim ar-Rāzī said that he is truthful.

Aḥmad ibn ʿAbdullāh al-Kūfī said, ʻHe was intelligent, forbearing, and trustworthy. I wrote from him.'

Ash-Shīrāzī said, ʻLeadership went to him in Egypt after Ashhab. He had the best knowledge among the companions of Mālik about his differing statements. Ibn ʿAbd al-Ḥakam listened to the *Muwaṭṭā'* and about three sections from Mālik.'

He related much from Ibn Wahb, Ibn al-Qāsim and Ashhab. He wrote a book in which he summarised what he had heard. Then he made a small summary from that. The Mālikīs of Baghdad relied on these two books among others in their studies. Abū Bakr al-Abharī and other Iraqis and the people of the east wrote commentary on them.

Bishr ibn Bakr said, "I dreamt of Mālik some days after his death. He said to me, 'There is a man in your land who is called Ibn 'Abd al-Ḥakam. Take from him. He is trustworthy.'

Some of his reports, virtues and books

Abū 'Umar al-Kindī said, 'Ibn 'Abd al-Ḥakam was appointed after Ibn al-Munkadir. He refuted the questions of 'Īsā ibn al-Munkadir, the Qāḍī of Egypt. He included among the just witnesses those whom he thought worthy of that, even if they did not have an old testimony. He accepted their testimony. One of the shaykhs among the Egyptians resented that in him. Abū Khalīfa ar-Ra'īnī said to him one day, "This matter is veiled, so unveil it. You include in the testimony those who are not entitled to it."

'Ibn 'Abd al-Ḥakam said to him, "This matter is the *dīn*. I have done what I must do."'

He said, 'The Banū 'Abd al-Ḥakam reached in rank and precedence in Egypt what no one else reached.'

Ibn 'Abd al-Barr said, "Abdullāh was a friend of ash-Shāfi'ī. He stayed with him when he came from Baghdad and he honoured his abode. He went to the utmost to respect him and was with him when he died.'

Ash-Shīrāzī said, 'It is said that he gave ash-Shāfi'ī a thousand dinars and took a thousand for him from one of his friends and a thousand from another two men.'

Ibn 'Abd al-Barr said, "Abdullāh related from ash-Shāfi'ī. He wrote his books from him and his sons, and his son Muhammad clung to him.'

There was conflict and mutual antipathy between 'Abdullāh ibn 'Abd al-Ḥakam and Aṣbagh to the point where each of them began to slander the other. It was said to Ibn 'Abd al-Ḥakam, 'This man obliges you to impose the *ḥadd* punishment on him, so impose the *ḥadd* on him.' He refused and said, 'If he is flogged, we will become a story. It will be said, "So-and-so was given the *ḥadd* punishment on account of so-and-so."'

One of the books of 'Abdullāh ibn 'Abd al-Ḥakam is *Mukhtaṣar al-Kabīr*. It is said that in it he imitated the summary of the books of Ashhab.

There is also *Mukhtaṣar al-Awsaṭ* and *Mukhtaṣar aṣ-Ṣaghīr*.

Mukhtaṣar aṣ-Ṣaghīr is an abridgement of the knowledge of the *Muwaṭṭā'*.

Mukhtaṣar al-Awsaṭ consists of two books. That which is from the *riwāya* of al-Qarāṭīsī adds traditions in it as opposed to that which is from the *riwāya* of Muḥammad, his son, and Sa'īd ibn Ḥassān.

He also wrote: *The Book of Terrors*, *The Book of the Judgement on Building*, *The Book of the Virtues of 'Umar ibn 'Abd al-'Azīz* and *The Book of Ḥajj Rites*.

People paid attention to his *Summaries* as they did not pay attention to any other of the books of the school after the *Muwaṭṭā'* and the *Mudawwana*.

Shaykh Abū Bakr al-Abharī wrote a commentary on *Mukhtaṣar al-Kabīr*.

Al-Ḥaffāf (sic. Khaffaf?) also has a commentary on it.

Abū Ja'far ibn al-Ḥaṣṣāṣ has explanatory notes on about two hundred sections on what he mentioned. I have seen part of it.

Shaykh Abū Bakr al-Abharī also did a commentary on *Mukhtaṣar aṣ-Ṣaghīr*.

Abū Bakr ibn al-Jahm also has a large commentary on it. Muḥammad ibn Abī Zayd summarised it.

The last of those who composed commentary on it from the generation of our shaykhs was a nephew of al-Baṣrī.

Muḥammad ibn 'Abdullāh ibn 'Abd al-Ḥakam has an addition to *Mukhtaṣar aṣ-Ṣaghīr* which opposes ash-Shāfi'ī and Abū Ḥanīfa. In it, he acted in this for Abū 'Abdullāh Muḥammad ibn 'Abd ar-Raḥīm al-Barqī. He added to this the words of Sufyān, Ibn Rāhawayh, al-Awzā'ī, and an-Nakhā'ī. Some of them attributed it to his son, Abū al-Qāsim 'Ubaydullāh ibn Muḥammad al-Barqī.

Abū al-Ḥasan 'Alī ibn Ya'qūb az-Ziyyāt, known as Ibn Ramaḍān, added to this the words of some of the *fuqahā'* whom al-Barqī did not mention. Then, according to what Ibn Ramaḍān mentioned, 'Ubaydullāh ibn 'Umar al-Baghdādī ash-Shāfi'ī, one of the people of

Córdoba, known as 'Ubayd, added the school of Dāwūd, Ibn 'Aliyya, al-Layth and aṭ-Ṭabarī.

Some of them mentioned that the legal questions in the *Mukhtaṣar al-Kabīr* number 18,000. In *al-Awsaṭ* there are four thousand questions. *Mukhtaṣar aṣ-Ṣaghīr* has 1200 questions.

One of them mentioned that the questions in the *Mudawwana* number 36,000.

He also wrote *The Book of Terrors.*

His business with Ibn Ma'īn, his inquisition and his death

Al-Bājī mentioned in his book the report about him with Ibn Ma'īn.[1] I have summarised it. He mentioned that he was a friend of his and he informed him that he would attend his assembly the next day and commanded him to be careful.

Yaḥyā came to him the next day while he was relating *The Book of Terrors* which he had written. He said, 'So-and-so told us,' and he mentioned a number of his shaykhs about what was in his book.

Yaḥyā said to him, 'All of them gave you the *ḥadīth* with all that is in it or did some of them give part of it and others give another part so that you joined your *ḥadīth* together?' His words frightened Ibn 'Abd al-Ḥakam and he was taken aback. He said, 'All of them told it to me.' Yaḥyā got up and said, 'The shaykh lies.'

Abū al-'Arab at-Tamīmī mentioned in *The Book of the Inquisitions* that 'Abdullāh ibn 'Abd al-Ḥakam was questioned regarding the Qur'an at the hands of al-Aṣamm and flogged in the mosque of Cairo with less than thirty strikes in the reign of al-Ma'mūn while Ibn Abī Dāwūd was *qāḍī*.

Abū al-'Arab gives the biography of 'Abdullāh ibn 'Abd al-Ḥakam. He mentioned in the story that the one to whom this was done Ibn 'Abd al-Ḥakam the elder. I believe that it was his son. According to what was mentioned in the reports of Qāḍī az-Zuhrī before, the inquisition of al-Aṣamm took place after 'Abdullāh's death.

Abū 'Umar al-Kindī said, 'Qāḍī 'Īsa ibn al-Munkadir wrote a letter to al-Ma'mūn concerning his brother, al-Mu'taṣim, when he was governor of Egypt. Al-Ma'mūn showed it to al-Mu'taṣim. When

[1] Yaḥyā ibn Ma'īn, the famous *ḥadīth* scholar.

al-Mu'taṣim came to Egypt, he dismissed Ibn al-Munkadir and jailed him until he died in his jail in Baghdad, may Allah Almighty have mercy on him. He jailed 'Abdullāh ibn 'Abd al-Ḥakam since he suspected him about that letter since he was often with Ibn al-Munkadir and had his legal questions. He had indicated to Ibn al-Munkadir that he should not do it, but he did it anyway and disobeyed him.'

'Abdullāh became ill and died on the 21st night of Ramadan in 214 AH when he was sixty.

It is said that he was born in Egypt in 155 AH. It is said that it was 156 AH in the same year that al-Ḥārith ibn Miskīn was born and that 'Abdullāh was two months older than him."

It is also said that it was 150 AH.

Ibn al-Qāsim, Ibn Wahb and Ashhab appointed him trustee (for their wills)

His father, 'Abd al-Ḥakam had the *kunya* of Aū 'Uthmān. He has questions from Mālik on the *mudabbar* and other things.

He died in 191 AH.

As for his sons, they will be mentioned later, Allah Almighty willing.

Yaḥyā ibn 'Abdullāh ibn Bukayr ibn Zakariyā' al-Makhzūmī

He was a client of the tribe of Makhzūm. Al-Kindī said that he was the client of 'Amra, a female client of Umm Ḥajar bint Abi Rabī'a ibn al-Mughīra ibn 'Abdullāh ibn 'Amr ibn Makhzūm.

Ibn Wazir said, 'Three people of Egypt are not known to have a sound *walā'*: Ibn Bukayr, Aṣbagh and Ibn 'Ufayr.'

Al-Kindī said, 'Ibn Bukayr was the leading *faqīh* of the *fuqahā'* in Egypt in his time. Qāḍī al-'Umarī entrusted him and Ashhab with his legal questions.'

He listened to the *Muwaṭṭā'* and other things from Mālik, and he listened to al-Layth ibn Sa'd, al-'Aṭṭāf ibn Khālid, Ibn Lahī'a, Bakr ibn Muḍar, Mufaḍḍal ibn Faḍāla, al-Mughīra ibn 'Abd ar-Raḥmān and Ibn Wahb.

Al-Bukhārī related from him and transmitted from him in his *Ṣaḥīḥ* and Abū Ibrāhīm, az-Zuhrī, Isḥāq ibn Rāhawayh, Aḥmad ibn Ḥanbal, Abū Dāwūd as-Sijistānī, 'Alī ibn 'Umar at-Tamīmī, ar-Ramādī, Abū Zur'a, Yūnus ibn 'Abd al-A'lā and adh-Dhihlī related from him.

Aḥmad ibn 'Abdullāh al-Kūfī said, 'I used to go to Ibn 'Abd al-Ḥakam. Ibn Bukayr passed by him and greeted him, He said, "Our shaykh, Ibn Bukayr, and the man of *ḥadīth* of our land. Excellent praise follows him."'

He mentioned that Yaḥyā ibn Ma'īn said, 'The worst reading is the reading of Ibn Bukayr. Ḥabīb used to allow him two pages in a page.'

This story is false in its root, and Allah knows best, because Mālik, may Allah have mercy on him, and those present with him did not give sound permission like this to them when they memorised the *ḥadīths* of the *Muwaṭṭā'*. One of the companions of Mālik did not like this at all. He said, 'Our reading to Mālik has two pages of the *Muwaṭṭā'* so how can this be sound?'

Al-Bājī said, 'One of the People of *Ḥadīth* spoke on his oral transmission of the *Muwaṭṭā'* and that he heard it in the recitation of Ḥabīb, and that he was firm in al-Layth.'

It is related by means of Baqī ibn Makhlad and others that he heard it from Mālik some ten times and that part of it was in the reading of Mālik.

Abū Aḥmad ibn 'Adī said, 'He is the firmest of people in al-Layth.'

Abū Ḥātim said, 'He wrote down his *ḥadīths* and did not use them as a argument. He understood this business.'

Yaḥyā ibn Bukayr was mentioned to Yaḥyā ibn Ma'īn. He said, 'He is reliable except that his *ḥadīths* from Ibn Wahb are not by good reading by him. An-Nasā'ī considers him weak.'

He was mentioned to Yaḥyā ibn Ma'īn as well. He said, 'No, may Allah bless him. I came to him in his mosque. When he saw me, he prostrated and said, "I did not think that you would come to me."' I think that he did not relate anything but this story from him.

Ibn Bāz mentioned, 'In Egypt, Yaḥyā ibn Bukayr read a book to us which he related from 'Abdulāh ibn Lahī'a from his *ḥadīths*. When he had finished reading it, he said to the people. "Listen to this book. I have heard it from Ibn Lahī'a after he had mixed (it)."'

Some of the people of Andalusia, North Africa and the Maghrib related from him in a group. They included Yaḥyā ibn 'Umar, Furāt ibn Muḥammad and Ibrāhīm ibn Bāz.

He died in Safar, 231 or 232 AH, and he was born in 153 AH.

ʻAbd al-Mālik ibn Maslama ibn Yazīd, a client of the Banū Umayya

His root was from Nubia. He had the *kunya* of Abū Marwān. Abu ʻUmar al-Kindī said that he was a *faqīh* among the companions of Mālik.

He was born in 140 AH and died in 224 AH.

Yūnus ibn Tamīm ibn Yūnus, a client of Zawf ibn Murād, Abū Muʻādh

Al-Kindī said that he was a *faqīh*. Ibn Shaʻbān and Ibn Mufarraj mentioned his *riwāya* from Mālik. He died in 215 AH.

Hānī ibn al-Mutawakkil ibn Isḥāq ibn Ibrāhīm ibn Ḥarmala

He was a client of the Banū Shahāba from Fahm, He lived in Alexandria. A *riwāya* from Mālik is mentioned for him.

Al-Kindī said that he was a *muftī* and a man of the *Sunna*. He died in 241 AH and was born in 138 AH.

Sa'īd ibn al-Ḥakam ibn Muḥammad ibn Abī Maryam al-Jumaḥī

Al-Kindī said that he was a client of Abū Fuṭayma, a client of the Banū Jumaḥ. His *kunya* was Abū Muḥammad. That is how al-Kindī gives his lineage. Al-Bukhārī and Abū Ḥātim said that.

Al-Lālakā'ī related from others: 'Sa'īd ibn Muḥammad ibn al-Hakam.' He related from Mālik, 'Abdullāh ibn al-'Umarī, Ibn 'Uyayna, al-Layth, Ibn Wahb, Sulaymān ibn Bilāl and others.

Ibn Ma'īn, adh-Dhihlī, Abū 'Ubayd, Muḥammad ibn Isḥāq aṣ-Ṣaghānī, al-Bukhārī, Abū Ḥātim and Ya'qūb ibn Sufyān related from him. Al-Bukhārī and Muslim transmitted from him.

It is said that he heard the *Muwaṭṭā'* from Mālik. He has many *ḥadīth*s and other things from him.

Al-Kindī said that he was a *faqīh* from the people of excellence and the *dīn*.

Ibn Ma'īn said that he is trustworthy. Abū Ḥātim said the like of that. Yaḥyā also said that he is one of the trustworthy men.

Aḥmad ibn Ḥanbal was asked, 'From whom should one write in Egypt?' He answered, 'From Ibn Abī Maryam.'

Aḥmad ibn 'Abdullāh al-Kūfī said that he is reliable. Ibn Ayman and al-A'nāqī praised him.

Ibn Waddāḥ mentioned him. He mentioned some of his excellence and his reliability and he exaggerated about him, saying, 'He is the most trustworthy of the trustworthy ones. I wrote only two questions from him in Egypt.'

Ibn Waddāḥ said, 'I heard Ibn Abī Maryam say that his father had two sheets. He wrote his testimony on one of them and his oath on the other.'

One of them said, 'We were with Sa'īd in Egypt. A man came to him to question him about a book he had seen or he asked him to give him *ḥadīth*s and he refused him. Another man asked him and he gave him what he asked for. The first man spoke to him regarding that and he said to him, "This is not from the truth," or words to that effect.'

Ibn Abī Maryam said, 'If you know ash-Shaybānī from as-Saybānī and Abū Ḥamza from Abū Jamra – and both are from Ibn 'Abbās, then we will relate to you and we will select you as we were selected with this.'

Al-Kūfī said, 'He had a long foyer. A man stood up and greeted him. He said, "The peace of Allah is not on you." He did that and acted and the other man thought that he had answered him. I said, "What is this?" He replied, "A foul Qadarī." The another man came and he did the like of that. I asked him about that and he said, "A foul Jahmī, or a foul Rāfiḍite." He was intelligent and I did not see anyone in Egypt with more intellect than him and Ibn 'Abd al-Ḥakam.'

Al-Bukhārī said that he died in 224 AH.

He was born in 144 AH.

‘Abd ar-Raḥmān ibn Abi Ja‘far ad-Dimyāṭī

Abū Isḥāq ibn Sha‘bān said that he related from Mālik and had *isnād* from him.

Ibn Abī Dulaym and Ibn Ḥārith said, ‘He listened to the great companions of Mālik like Ibn Wahb, Ibn al-Qāsim and Ashhab. He has a well-written summary of oral transmissions from them. Yaḥyā ibn ‘Umar and others related from him. These books are known from his name as ad-Dimyāṭiyya.’

Ash-Shīrāzī said, ‘He learned *fiqh* with Ashhab, Ibn Wahb, Ibn al-Qāsim, Muṭarrif, ‘Abd al-Mālik and Ibn Nāfi‘. He related from al-Fuḍayl ibn ‘Iyāḍ.’

Ad-Dimyāṭī said, ‘We came to al-Fuḍayl to listen to him and he did not come out to us. We said to a man who was with us who had a good voice in the Qur’an, “Recite.” He came out to us with the tears flowing onto his beard.’

He said, ‘What is it between you and me that you harm me? Do you seek knowledge? You have left it, by Allah: the Book of Allah.’

Yaḥyā ibn ‘Umar, al-Walīd ibn Mu‘āwiya, ‘Ubayd ibn ‘Abd ar-Raḥmān and others related from him. He died in 226 AH.

‘Abdullāh ibn Muḥammad ibn Isḥāq al-Bayṭārī

His ascription came from the fact that he used to live with Bilal al-Bayṭār, a client of Qays. His *kunya* was Abū Muḥammad.

Abū ‘Umar al-Kindī said, ‘He was a *faqīh* and met Mālik. He died in 231 AH.’

Bilāl ibn Yaḥyā ibn Hārūn al-Aswānī

He was one of the Banū Umayya. Al-Kindī said, ‘He was one of the companions of Mālik.’ He mentioned him among them. He was accepted by the *qāḍī*s of Egypt, but Ibn ‘Ufayr held him in contempt because of what was said about the people of Aswan.

MUḤAMMAD IBN RAMḤ IBN AL-MUHĀJIR IBN AL-MUḤRIZ IBN SALĀM AT-TUJĪBĪ

Abū 'Abdullāh. He was a client of the tribe of Tujīb. It is said that his *kunya* was Abū Bakr. He kept Mālik's company, and he listened to al-Layth, al-Mufaḍḍal and Ibn Lahī'a.

Muslim, 'Alī ibn al-Ḥasan ibn al-Mundhir, Ḥāzim ibn Yaḥyā al-Ḥulwānī, Ibn Waḍḍāḥ, al-Ḥassān ibn Sufyān and Ibn Zabbān related from him. *Riwāya* dominated him and he is trustworthy and reliable.

Al-Kindī said, 'Muslim related a lot from him in his *Ṣaḥīḥ*.'

Ibn al-Jīzī said, 'He was a man of righteousness more reliable than Ibn Zur'a.'

Ibn Zabbān said that he is reliable.

Ibn Waḍḍāḥ said that he is the best shaykh.

Al-Kindī said that he was a *faqīh*.

Ibn Ramḥ said, 'There was some disagreement among us about Mālik and al-Layth (He mentioned some of their disagreement in something which irritated him) to such an extent that they used to form parties. I dreamt of the Prophet ﷺ and I said, "Messenger of Allah! There is a disagreement with us regarding Mālik and al-Layth. What do you think?" He said, "Mālik is the heir of my ancestor."'

Al-Ḥasan ibn 'Alī al-Ashnānī said, 'The speakers say that "my ancestor" means Ibrāhīm the Friend and Prophet, peace be upon him. Others say that it is the *dīn* and still others that it is the *Sunna*.'

Abu 'Umar al-Kindī said in Kitāb al-quḍā: 'Abū Bakr al-Aṣamm was the Qāḍī of Egypt. He ordered its people to stop wearing tall hats. It was the dress of their shaykhs, *fuqahā'* and men of justice (for testimony). He told them, "Do not ape the dress of the *qāḍī*." They did not stop. Once he gathered them in his presence in the mosque and ordered the aides to bare their heads until they submitted to him.

The children were playing with the hats. They did not wear them in his time with the exception of Ibn Ramḥ. He was firm about wearing it and was not opposed.'

He died in Shawwāl, 242 AH. Al-Kindī said in 248 AH. He was born in 152 AH.

FROM THE PEOPLE OF ANDALUSIA

Yaḥyā ibn Yaḥyā al-Laythī

Qāḍī Abū al-Walīd ibn al-Faraḍī said, 'Yaḥyā ibn Yaḥyā ibn Kathīr ibn Wislās ibn Shamāl ibn Manghāyā. His *kunya* was Abū Muḥammad.'

Al-Usaylī said, "His father Yaḥyā had the *kunya* Abū 'Īsā. He was from the tribe of Maṣmūda in Tangier and ruled the Banū Layth. The reason for that is not soundly known.

Ar-Rāzī said in *Kitāb al-Isti'āb*, 'He was from Maṣmūda from Muḍāra, a tribe there.'

Yaḥyā ibn Wislās came with his nephew, Naṣr ibn 'Īsā, among the army of Ṭāriq [ibn Ziyād][1]. Wislās, their ancestor, had become Muslim at the hands of Yazīd ibn 'Āmir al-Laythī. Layth is Kināna. This, and Allah knows best, is the reason they are associated with Layth.

Ar-Rāzī said, 'Then after them, Kathīr ibn Wislās, the grandfather of Yaḥyā arrived. His son Yaḥyā was appointed over Algeria and its non-resident foreigners. Yaḥyā, his son, sought knowledge.'

Abū 'Umar ibn 'Abd al-Barr said, 'Kathīr's *kunya* was Abū 'Īsā. He went to Andalusia and they became known as the Banu Abū 'Īsā.'

The start of his quest for knowledge and his journey

Ar-Rāzī said, 'The reason for the search for knowledge by Yaḥyā ibn Yaḥyā was that he passed by Ziyād[2] while he was speaking to his companions. He inclined to him and sat with him. Ziyād liked that and brought him near one day. He said to him, "My son, if you are resolute to learn, then cut off some of your hair and put your clothes in order (he was wearing servant's clothes)." Yaḥyā did that. Ziyād

[1] Who led the conquest of Spain.

[2] Ziyād ibn 'Abd ar-Raḥmān, known as Shabṭūn.

was happy with him and strove to reach him until his surpassed his students.

'Then after a time, Ziyād said to him, "The men from whom we took knowledge still remain. It is a failure in you to relate from those below them."

'So Yaḥyā left after Ziyād had lent him some money since he had refused his father's money, and he departed. He went on *ḥajj* and listened to Mālik and al-Layth. He met Mālik in 179 AH, the year in which Mālik died. Then he went back to Andalusia and it was only a short time before his father died while still in his position in Algeria. He took what was good from his father's property and then returned and went on *ḥajj* and met the lofty companions of Mālik. Then he returned.'

Ibn Ḥārith mentioned the like of this and said that Yaḥyā made two journeys from Andalusia. He listened to Mālik, al-Layth and Ibn Wahb in the first of the journeys. In the other one, he confined himself to Ibn al-Qāsim and learned *fiqh* with him.

Ibn al-Faraḍī, Abū 'Umar ibn 'Abd al-Barr and others said (adding to one another) that Yaḥyā listened to the *Muwaṭṭā'* of Mālik ibn Anas from Ziyād at the beginning of his intellectual growth. He listened to Yaḥyā ibn Muḍar. Then he travelled when he was twenty-eight and listened to the *Muwaṭṭā'* of Mālik from Mālik, except for *The Book of I'tikāf*, about which he was unsure. He continued to relate it from Ziyād. He listened to Nāfi' ibn Abī Nu'aym al-Qāri', al-Qāsim ibn 'Abdullāh al-'Umarī, Ḥusayn ibn Ḍamīra, and 'Abdullāh ibn Nāfi'. In Makka, he listened to Sufyān ibn 'Uyayna and to al-Layth ibn Sa'd and to the *Muwaṭṭā'* and his *Collection* from 'Abdullāh ibn Wahb in Egypt. He listened to the questions of Ibn al-Qāsim and he took ten books from him and wrote down his oral transmission.

Abū 'Umar said, 'Then he went to Madina to listen to Mālik and found him ill. He stayed in Madina until Mālik died, may Allah have mercy on him, and attended his funeral. Then he returned to Andalusia with much knowledge. After 'Īsā ibn Dīnar, the *fatwā* of Andalusia was based on his opinion and his words. His *riwāya* of the *Muwaṭṭā'* was followed. There are mistakes which are conveyed in the *ḥadīth*s of al-Layth and others. He spoke about them, but did not change them in his book. The transmitters followed him and he told the people about them and they made what was correct clear. As for Ibn Waḍḍāḥ, he corrected it and people related it from him with the corrections. He used to give *fatwā* according the opinion of Mālik. He only left that in some questions which we will mention later.'

Ash-Shīrāzī said, 'Yaḥyā ibn Yaḥyā travelled to Mālik when he was young and learned *fiqh* with the Madinans and the Egyptians among his followers.'

Abū 'Abd al-Malik ibn 'Abd al-Barr said, 'The school of Mālik spread through him and 'Īsā ibn Dīnār. People came to hear the *Muwaṭṭā'* from Yaḥyā. They admired how he wrote it down and they imitated him and followed him.'

Ibn al-Faraḍī said, 'Some men of Andalusia listened to him in his time, and the last to relate from him was his son, 'Ubaydullāh.'

Some of his virtues and reports

Aḥmad ibn Khālid mentioned that none of the people of knowledge in Andalusia since the time Islam entered it was given in precedence, immense worth, and sublime renown that which Yaḥyā ibn Yaḥyā was given. The Amīr, 'Abd ar-Raḥmān ibn al-Ḥakam, respected him as a father is respected and did not reject his words and he sought his advice in all of business and whom he should appoint and dismiss. That is why there were many *qāḍīs* in his time. His knowledge was given preference because of his intellect.

Amīr 'Abd ar-Raḥmān pestered him about appointing him *qāḍī* but he refused him. He entrusted someone to make him sit in the mosque and say to the people, 'This is your Qāḍī.'

He refused to judge. Yaḥyā told him, 'The place I am in is more beneficial and better for you than what you want. When people are wronged by a *qāḍī*, you can have me sit and I will examine his judgements for you. If I am a *qāḍī*, you will be wronged from me as they are wronged from the *qāḍīs*. Who then will they go to to look into my judgements?' They left him alone.

Ibn Lubāba said, 'The *faqīh* of Andalusia was 'Īsā, its man of action was Ibn Ḥabīb and its man of intellect was Yaḥyā ibn Yaḥyā.'

Ash-Shīrāzī said, 'Leadership in Andalusia in knowledge came to him, and Mālik used to admire the demeanour and intellect of Yaḥyā.'

It is related about him that one day he was sitting among the group of the group of the companions of Mālik when someone exclaimed, 'The elephant is here!'

All of Mālik's companions went out to look at it. Mālik said to him, 'Why don't you go out and see it since it does not exist in Andalusia?'

Yaḥyā said to him, '"I came from my land to look at you and learn from your guidance and knowledge and not to look at the elephant.' Mālik liked him and called him a man of intellect.

Abū 'Umar ibn 'Abd al-Barr said, 'Yaḥyā was the Imām of the people of the land, imitated, looked up to, and relied on. He was trustworthy, a man of intellect with good guidance and manner. His manner resembled the manner of Mālik although he did not have insight into *ḥadīth*s.'

Ibrāhīm ibn Bāz said, 'By Allah. There is no god but Him. I have not seen anyone graver than Yaḥyā ibn Yaḥyā at all. I did not see him spit or cough in his assembly nor move from his state. He took on the clothes and manner of Mālik.'

Yaḥyā said, 'When I said farewell to Mālik, I asked him to give me some advice. He said to me, "You must have good counsel for Allah and His Book and the Imams of the Muslims and their common people." Then I went to al-Layth. When it was time for me to leave him, I said the like of that I had said to Mālik to him and he told me the like of what he had said.'

Ibn Ḥārith said, 'Yaḥyā did not think that there should be *qunūt* in the *Ṣubḥ* prayer or any other prayer, following al-Layth. He also disagreed with Mālik about taking the oath with the witness. He did not think that there should be judgement based on it. He also took the position of al-Layth on that. He gave judgement to a trustworthy house when he did not find two arbiters from the people of a couple. He thought that land could be rented for what is produced following the school of al-Layth.'

Abū 'Abd al-Malik ibn 'Abd al-Barr mentioned that Yaḥyā did not think that there were two arbiters and that that was part of what he disliked. He used to come to the *Jumu'a* on foot, wearing a turban.

'Ubaydullāh ibn Yaḥyā related that his father said, 'I was with the chamberlain 'Abd al-Karīm ibn Mughīth in the raid on Narbonne, and my friend Sa'īd ibn Muḥammad ibn Bashīr was with me. He respected us and sent to us and asked for our advice. Sometimes he singled me out to be sent for until I told him, "Do not do it. Perhaps that will annoy my friend."

'One day he sent me a gift of a hundred dinars and the like of it to Sa'īd. I sent it to him and said, "As for myself, I have no need of it. Praise be to Allah, but I will join it to that of my friend because he has need of it."

'When Allah gave victory to the Muslims, we came home. He said to me one day, "Abū Muḥammad, I want to honour you and your friend, so I will give you a position in Andalusia."

'I asked, "How will that be?" He said, "I will give you both a good place of hearing with me."

'I said, "By Allah, you want to abase us, not honour us"

'He said to me, "Abū Muḥammad! Only think the best! What was the opinion of those before you when you went far in honouring them until that was done to them?"

'I said, "May Allah not reward them from themselves or you! By Allah, they have betrayed Allah and His Messenger!" He was ashamed and apologised.'

Aḥmad ibn 'Abd al-Barr mentioned that one of the *qāḍī*s of Córdoba (whom he named) had an excellent school of thought. Yaḥyā ibn Yaḥyā recommended (that he should be appointed.) He obeyed him in Yaḥyā's judgement and did not turn from his opinion even when the *fuqahā'* disagreed with him. It so happened that a case occurred in which Yaḥyā was alone and all of them opposed him. The *qāḍī* deferred judgement in it out of deference to their assembly. Then another case followed it in which he asked Yaḥyā's advice as well. When his letter came to Yaḥyā after his hesitation to implement the first one had envenomed him, he returned it to his messenger and said, 'We will not break his seal nor give him any advice since he hesitated in the judgement of so-and-so in what I indicated to him and he found fault with it.'

When his messenger went to him and informed him what he had

said, he was disturbed by that and rode immediately to Yaḥyā to apologise. He said to him, 'I did not think that this matter would have this effect on you. I will judge for you on my next day Allah willing.' Yaḥyā said to him, 'You will do that in truth?' He said, 'Yes.'

He said to him, 'Now you have truly provoked my wrath. I thought that since your friends opposed me, you had hesitated asking Allah for good through performing the *Istikhāra* prayer and carefully examining the statements. If you go following passion and giving judgement by the pleasure of a weak creature, there is no good in what you bring nor in myself being pleased with it from you. You should resign from that. It will veil you more. If not, I will present the request for your dismissal.' So he got up and asked to resign and was dismissed.

'Ubaydullāh ibn Yaḥyā said, 'My father said to me, "When people came to the Qāḍī of Córdoba, Yaḥyā ibn Muḍar, and saw what was written against him, Sa'īd ibn al-Hassan came to me and said to me, 'What do you think about testifying against him?' I told him, 'Do not do it. Wait and see if you are consulted about the testimony of someone else so that your *fatwā* will be more effective than your testimony.'"'

'Appetite overcame him and he opposed him and testified. The Amīr's letter came to me in which he said, "I have examined the testimonies against so-and-so and I did not see that you had any testimony about him. I have sent to you the letter of the testimonies against him, so examine them and then write to us with your opinion, Allah Almighty willing."'

Yaḥyā replied to him, 'I do not have any knowledge of the reports regarding the man because he did not summon me to his assembly nor did he ask us for advice in his judgements. As regards the testimonies against him, I have examined them. If the like of them had been given in testimony against Mālik and al-Layth, may Allah have mercy on them, they would not have lifted a head afterwards.' So he was immediately dismissed.

Yaḥyā said, 'Al-Layth informed me that he took hold of Rabī'a's stirrup and Rabī'a said to him, "Layth, knowledge serves you."' Yaḥyā said, 'Rabī'a meant that he would attain great knowledge.' Al-Layth did not depart this world until that was seen.

Yaḥyā said, 'I took al-Layth's stirrup and he said to me, "I tell you what Rabī'a said, 'Yaḥyā, knowledge serves you.'"'

Yaḥyā ibn Isḥāq said, 'Yaḥyā ibn Yaḥyā mentioned a *ḥadīth* which he related from Yaḥyā ibn Kathīr. He said, "Knowledge lacks capacity when the body is comfortable."'

He said, 'This *ḥadīth* reached one of the students of knowledge. He remembered it while he was lying on top of his wife before he had had intercourse with her. So he picked up a notebook of knowledge and began to look at it.'

Yaḥyā said, 'I sought this matter on the day I sought it and I only meant myself by it until Allah made ready what He made ready. Then I knew that people needed me. During my time with Ibn al-Qāsim in Egypt, I desired women, so I purchased a slave-girl there. By Allah, I did not see her face for a single day as long as she stayed with me until I sold her since I was preoccupied with Ibn al-Qāsim and his knowledge. Ibn al-Qāsim was the place for that by his worth in scrupulousness and being an Imām.'

He was asked, 'Abū Muḥammad, is the desire for this matter part of what will corrupt the intention?' He answered, 'No, by Allah, the one who does not desire that is not intelligent. Allah Almighty says, "*Make us a good model for the godfearing.*" (25:74)'

Yaḥyā said, 'I came to 'Abd ar-Raḥmān ibn al-Qāsim and he said to me, "From where, Abū Muḥammad?" I answered, "From 'Abdullāh ibn Mālik." He said to me, "Fear Allah. Most of these *ḥadīth*s do not have any action based on them." Then I went to 'Abdullāh ibn Wahb and he said to me, "From where?" I replied, "From Ibn al-Qāsim." He said to me, "Fear Allah, Abū Muḥammad. Most of these questions are opinion."'

Then Yaḥyā returned and said, 'May Allah have mercy on both of them. Both of them were right in what they said. Ibn al-Qāsim forbade me to follow the *ḥadīth*s which do not have any action and he was correct. Ibn Wahb forbade me to let opinion dominate me and use too much of it. He commanded me to follow and he was correct.'

Then Yaḥyā said, 'Following Ibn al-Qasim in his opinion is correct guidance. Following Ibn Wahb in his traditions is guidance.'

Yaḥyā used to compile the questions which Ashhab, Ibn Nāfi'

and others among the companions of Mālik were asked about. He wrote from them and then read them out to Ibn al-Qasim to see what his school was in them. Ibn al-Qāsim began to disagree with them. When Yaḥyā saw that, he folded up his book and put it in his sleeve. Ibn al-Qāsim said to him, 'What's up with you?'

He said, 'Those men have a right just as you have a right. I wrote down their knowledge from them and I did not think to expose them to attack. If this is the case, I have no need of that.' Something similar occurred when he listened to Ziyād, and we mentioned it in his reports.

Amīr 'Abd ar-Raḥmān had intercourse with a slave-girl of his during the day in Ramaḍān. Then he regretted that and sent for Yaḥyā and his companions. He questioned them. Yaḥyā answered immediately and said, 'The Amīr, may Allah honour him, must fast for two consecutive months.'

When Yaḥyā said that, the people fell silent. When they went out, they questioned him, 'Why did you say that specifically to him rather than anything else about the choice in feeding poor people and setting slaves free?' He said, 'If I had opened this door for him, he would have had intercourse every day and then set slaves free. I imposed what is the most difficult on him so that he will not do it again.'

Some of his words, wisdoms, and reports about his keeping himself free of blame, his intellect, and his dress

A man from Quraysh wrote to him to ask about an incident in breaking an oath about which he had some doubts, and he was not content to ask anyone but him. He wrote to him, 'I think that you should be scrupulous in it and not make it easy for people with you so that you become more worthless in their opinion. Peace.'

He said to another person who had asked him about a question of oath-breaking which had occurred in his assembly, 'You should not ask the scholars about all that takes place in your assembly which does not harm your *dīn*. That is better for you. Peace.'

One of the companions of Yaḥyā wanted to go to Ibn al-Qāsim: he wanted to read the questions to him. Yaḥyā thought that was presumptuous and refused him. It was said to him, 'Isn't that good?'

He replied, 'I do not like all that is good in which I disagree with Mālik and Ibn al-Qāsim.' Then ihe was unable to read it to him.

Yaḥyā used to say, 'Help one other to stop embracing each other. The first to start that among us were women, children and eunuchs.'

It was said to Yaḥyā that al-Ḥasan had said, 'If it were not for the fools, this world would not have thrived.' Yaḥyā said, 'But I say, "If it had not been for the forbearing, this world would not have thrived."'

He was told that Sufyān ath-Thawrī had said, 'I only fear the reciters and the *fuqahā'* for myself in what I said.' Ibrāhīm an-Nakhā'ī said that.

Yaḥyā began to seek refuge and said, 'O Allah, do not make us fearful of any of Your creatures!' many times. Then he said, 'A man whom Allah makes fearful of the best of His creation is a bad man.'

Yaḥyā used to say, 'Put timidity between you and people. It is better for establishing your respect.'

A man asked him about a question outside of his assembly and he disliked that. He said, 'When I sit in the assembly of the asker and the answerer, then I will answer you.' It was said to him, 'Why don't you relax in your assembly as you do when you are alone?' He replied, 'If I had done that, there would have been dalliance in front of me. I want to be followed as I followed someone else.'

He wanted to answer a question and asked for help, but did not find help. Then he repeated it and still was not able. A man at his side said to him, 'This inkwell, Abū Muhammad!' He said, 'If it had been, it would have been.' The young man held the notebook to his face and smiled. Yaḥyā looked at him and said, 'If you had sat in your house, it would have been more concealing for you.' He said, 'Whoever wants to act by what he says should be frugal. Whoever does not want that should not be concerned with what he says.'

Yaḥyā used to admire a wise word which the chamberlain 'Abd al-Karīm ibn Mughīth said to him. Once Yaḥyā said to him, 'I want to talk to you about something which makes me feel bashful towards you in severity.' He said to him, 'Abū Muḥammad, every thing conveys diffidence from you in this, so unburden yourself.'

Yaḥyā used to like him and said, 'How excellent forbearance is for man!'

He heard Yaḥyā ibn Yaḥyā speaking on the words of Allah, may He be blessed and exalted! '*Children of Adam! We have sent down clothing to you to conceal your private parts, and fine apparel, but the garment of taqwā – that is best!*' (7:26) He said, 'The garment of *taqwā* is tranquillity and gravity and good behaviour.' Then Yaḥyā withdrew it and added, 'And acting on what is like that.'

He was asked about asceticism in this world and said, 'Whoever is only content with the *ḥalāl* in it is ascetic in it, even if he is devoted to it and eager for it.'

He said, 'When death comes to someone while he is seeking knowledge, there is only one degree between him and the Prophets in the Garden.'

Yaḥyā mentioned the People of the Ramparts (Qur'an: 7) and said, '*We belong to Allah and to Him we return.*' Then he said, 'People who desired an aspect of good and did not obtain it.'

He was asked, 'So is a reward expected for them for their striving in spite of that?' He said, 'There is no hope of reward in opposition to the *Sunna*.'

Some people said to Yaḥyā, 'Abū Muḥammad, if we rely on Allah as He should be relied on, He will bring us provision to our houses as the birds come.' He said, 'By Allah, wild vegetables did not come to 'Īsā, the son of Maryam, while he was sitting down until he went out to the desert to look for them.'

It was said to Yaḥyā, 'Those who passed desired poverty.' He objected to that. He said, 'The one who possesses intelligence should not desire what the Prophet ﷺ sought refuge from.'

Yaḥyā used to wear fine embroidered material, i.e. cotton, which was very expensive, during the *'Īd*s, and when he went to the rulers.

Amīr Muḥammad said, 'One day during my father's lifetime, I rode and met Yaḥyā ibn Yaḥyā. He rode with me. Then he hit my hand and said to me, "This business will come to you, so fear Allah among the slaves of Allah." That advice remained in myself until I came to it and was appointed to command after that.'

The trial of Yaḥyā ibn Yaḥyā

Yaḥyā was one of those suspected of bringing about the rebellion in Córdoba against Amīr al-Ḥakam ibn Hishām. Allah gave al-Ḥakam victory over those who had attacked him and let him take their property. The rest of them went away, and those who fled included 'Īsā ibn Dīnār and Yaḥyā ibn Yaḥyā.

It is mentioned that Yaḥyā left with his brother Fatḥ who was a leader in the cause of the dispute. They disguised themselves at the gate of the Jews of Córdoba intending to flee. The Amīr had warned the people of the gates to kill all of those who passed them whom they suspected. Yaḥyā's brother inclined to the head of the doormen because of some friendship that existed between the two of them. He was confident of him for that reason that he would give him safekeeping and advise him about those who opposed him. His brother Yaḥyā told him not to do that.

When he came near, he uncovered his face and sought his retreat. As soon as his eyes fell upon him, he seized him and commanded that his head be struck off while Yaḥyā was looking on at one side. It increased his alarm and he went to great lengths to disguise himself.

He stayed with some people from Maṣmūda, his people, on his way. They wanted to assassinate him to take what money he had on his stomach. The daughter of one of them warned him about that. When they gathered for *'Ishā'* with him, he got up as if to relieve himself and mounted a mare which he found in the house which was loose and free. He was saved on it. When it seemed to them he had been gone a long time, they went out and found that he had gone. He went until he was safe and stayed at Toledo and returned their mare to them. Its people accepted him and gave him protection.

His protector was known as Abzā. Amīr al-Ḥakam demanded that they surrender him to him. They did not do it and they refused him backed by their own might. The Amīr's letter came to him at last about returning to his land and he gave him a safe-conduct and stated that he would return his goods and money to him. Yaḥyā had written to him about that. He answered him and he returned to Córdoba during the last days of al-Ḥakam. He remained with honour for the rest of his days and the days of his children, and his rank was shown and his excellence and knowledge was famous.

When he went to Córdoba, he had sold all his slaves and wanted to replace them. He was asked about that and said, 'We disliked to have accompany us those who knew the flight and the abasement which came to us.'

His days lasted until he died in the 22nd of Rajab in 234 AH. Ibn al-Faraḍī said that. Ar-Rāzī said, 'In the evening of Wednesday of the 22nd of Dhū al-Ḥijja.' It is said that he died in 233 AH. Ḥāfiẓ Abū 'Umar related that.

He was eighty-two when he died. He left two sons who will be mentioned.

When Yaḥyā died, he gave his trusteeship to Qāḍī Muḥammad ibn Ziyād ibn Rabī', one of this elite, and he is the one who led the prayer over him after his death.

He mentioned that his younger son 'Ubaydullāh preceded him and his elder son Isḥāq advanced when he advanced to pray over him, He said the *takbīr* with the *takbīr* of Ibn Ziyād and gave the *taslīm* when he did.

When Yaḥyā was buried, Ibn Ziyād disapproved of what Isḥāq had done and rebuked him. He said, 'Who put you over this?' Isḥāq said to him, 'Who put you over my father?'

Ibn Ziyād said, 'He commanded that prayer for me. In spite of this, your brother 'Ubaydullāh preceded and he is more right-guided than you in spite of his youth.' At that time 'Ubaydullāh was seventeen. 'By Allah, if it had not been for my care for the person in the grave, I would have disciplined you.'

The praise of Ibn Ziyād on that day for 'Ubaydullāh was the first of the reasons for his leadership.

Yaḥyā ibn Isḥāq ibn Yaḥyā said in the *Kitāb al-Mabsūṭ*, 'My father said to me, "'Abd al-Malik Zūnān and I went to my father Yaḥyā when he was ill and I asked him about his illness. He said to me, "Abū al-Ḥasan, what I am in is lightened for me when I think of the immense thing for which I was created."' Zūnān repeated these words of his and admired them.'

Another time he said to him, 'Abū al-Ḥasan! I wish that I could move away from the Fire, provided that I did not hear the Garden mentioned.'

Yaḥyā ibn Yaḥyā left a famous bequest for the seekers of knowledge.

www.ingramcontent.com/pod-product-compliance
Lightning Source LLC
LaVergne TN
LVHW101612210926
848480LV00008B/11
9781914397509